T0140163

Lecture Notes in Computer Science 12424

More information about this series at http://www.springer.com/series/7409

Constantine Stephanidis ·
Masaaki Kurosu · Helmut Degen ·
Lauren Reinerman-Jones (Eds.)

HCI International 2020 – Late Breaking Papers

Multimodality and Intelligence

22nd HCI International Conference, HCII 2020
Copenhagen, Denmark, July 19–24, 2020
Proceedings

Springer

Editors
Constantine Stephanidis
University of Crete and Foundation
for Research and Technology – Hellas
(FORTH)
Heraklion, Crete, Greece

Helmut Degen
Siemens Corporation
Princeton, NJ, USA

Masaaki Kurosu
The Open University of Japan
Chiba, Japan

Lauren Reinerman-Jones
University of Central Florida
Orlando, FL, USA

ISSN 0302-9743 ISSN 1611-3349 (electronic)
Lecture Notes in Computer Science
ISBN 978-3-030-60116-4 ISBN 978-3-030-60117-1 (eBook)
https://doi.org/10.1007/978-3-030-60117-1

LNCS Sublibrary: SL3 – Information Systems and Applications, incl. Internet/Web, and HCI

Foreword

The 22nd International Conference on Human-Computer Interaction, HCI International 2020 (HCII 2020), was planned to be held at the AC Bella Sky Hotel and Bella Center, Copenhagen, Denmark, during July 19–24, 2020. Due to the COVID-19 pandemic and the resolution of the Danish government not to allow events larger than 500 people to be hosted until September 1, 2020, HCII 2020 had to be held virtually. It incorporated the 21 thematic areas and affiliated conferences listed on the following page.

A total of 6,326 individuals from academia, research institutes, industry, and governmental agencies from 97 countries submitted contributions, and 1,439 papers and 238 posters were included in the volumes of the proceedings published before the conference. Additionally, 333 papers and 144 posters are included in the volumes of the proceedings published after the conference, as "Late Breaking Work" (papers and posters). These contributions address the latest research and development efforts in the field and highlight the human aspects of design and use of computing systems.

The volumes comprising the full set of the HCII 2020 conference proceedings are listed in the following pages and together they broadly cover the entire field of human-computer interaction, addressing major advances in knowledge and effective use of computers in a variety of application areas.

I would like to thank the Program Board Chairs and the members of the Program Boards of all Thematic Areas and Affiliated Conferences for their valuable contributions towards the highest scientific quality and the overall success of the HCI International 2020 conference.

This conference would not have been possible without the continuous and unwavering support and advice of the founder, conference general chair emeritus and conference scientific advisor, Prof. Gavriel Salvendy. For his outstanding efforts, I would like to express my appreciation to the communications chair and editor of HCI International News, Dr. Abbas Moallem.

July 2020   Constantine Stephanidis

HCI International 2020 Thematic Areas and Affiliated Conferences

Thematic Areas:

- HCI 2020: Human-Computer Interaction
- HIMI 2020: Human Interface and the Management of Information

Affiliated Conferences:

- EPCE: 17th International Conference on Engineering Psychology and Cognitive Ergonomics
- UAHCI: 14th International Conference on Universal Access in Human-Computer Interaction
- VAMR: 12th International Conference on Virtual, Augmented and Mixed Reality
- CCD: 12th International Conference on Cross-Cultural Design
- SCSM: 12th International Conference on Social Computing and Social Media
- AC: 14th International Conference on Augmented Cognition
- DHM: 11th International Conference on Digital Human Modeling & Applications in Health, Safety, Ergonomics & Risk Management
- DUXU: 9th International Conference on Design, User Experience and Usability
- DAPI: 8th International Conference on Distributed, Ambient and Pervasive Interactions
- HCIBGO: 7th International Conference on HCI in Business, Government and Organizations
- LCT: 7th International Conference on Learning and Collaboration Technologies
- ITAP: 6th International Conference on Human Aspects of IT for the Aged Population
- HCI-CPT: Second International Conference on HCI for Cybersecurity, Privacy and Trust
- HCI-Games: Second International Conference on HCI in Games
- MobiTAS: Second International Conference on HCI in Mobility, Transport and Automotive Systems
- AIS: Second International Conference on Adaptive Instructional Systems
- C&C: 8th International Conference on Culture and Computing
- MOBILE: First International Conference on Design, Operation and Evaluation of Mobile Communications
- AI-HCI: First International Conference on Artificial Intelligence in HCI

Conference Proceedings – Full List of Volumes

http://2020.hci.international/proceedings

HCI International 2020 (HCII 2020)

The full list with the Program Board Chairs and the members of the Program Boards of all thematic areas and affiliated conferences is available online at:

http://www.hci.international/board-members-2020.php

HCI International 2021

The 23rd International Conference on Human-Computer Interaction, HCI International 2021 (HCII 2021), will be held jointly with the affiliated conferences in Washington DC, USA, at the Washington Hilton Hotel, July 24–29, 2021. It will cover a broad spectrum of themes related to human-computer interaction (HCI), including theoretical issues, methods, tools, processes, and case studies in HCI design, as well as novel interaction techniques, interfaces, and applications. The proceedings will be published by Springer. More information will be available on the conference website: http://2021.hci.international/

General Chair
Prof. Constantine Stephanidis
University of Crete and ICS-FORTH
Heraklion, Crete, Greece
Email: general_chair@hcii2021.org

http://2021.hci.international/

Contents

Multimodal Interaction

Eye Movement Classification Algorithms: Effect of Settings on Related Metrics

Amin G. Alhashim[✉][iD]

The University of Oklahoma, Norman, OK 73069, USA
alhashim@ou.edu
https://about.me/am1ngh

Abstract. The basic building block of any eye tracking research is the eye fixations. These eye fixations depend on more fine data gathered by the eye tracker device, the raw gaze data. There are many algorithms that can be used to transform the raw gaze data into eye fixation. However, these algorithms require one or more thresholds to be set. A knowledge of the most appropriate values for these thresholds is necessary in order for these algorithms to generate the desired output. This paper examines the effect of a set of different settings of the two thresholds required for the identification-dispersion threshold type of algorithms: the dispersion and duration thresholds on the generated eye fixations. Since this work is at its infancy, the goal of this paper is to generate and visualize the result of each setting and leave the choice for the readers to decide on which setting fits their future eye tracking research.

Keywords: Eye tracking · Eye movement classification algorithms · Fixation duration metric

1 Introduction

It is almost impossible to find an eye tracking study that does not utilize the eye fixations in one way or the other. Eye fixations can be used as a standalone metric or as a basis for other metrics such as fixation sequences. (Holmqvist et al. 2015) These eye fixations are a result of a transformation process done on the raw gaze data being produced by the eye tracker devices. There are different categories of algorithms that can be used to do such transformation (Duchowski 2007; Salvucci and Goldberg 2000). The focus of this paper is the identification-dispersion threshold (I-DT) category. This category of algorithms has two thresholds that need to be set: the dispersion threshold and the duration threshold which are explained in Sect. 2.4.2.1 and Sect. 2.4.2.2, respectively.

Salvucci and Goldberg (2000) and Blignaut (2009) suggested a dispersion threshold between 0.5° and 1.0° while Jacob and Karn (2003) decided to fix it to 2.0°. Similarly, Salvucci and Goldberg (2000) and Jacob and Karn (2003) suggested a value between 100 ms and 200 ms for the dispersion threshold while Nyström and Holmqvist (2010) suggested a shorter period between 80 ms and

© Springer Nature Switzerland AG 2020
C. Stephanidis et al. (Eds.): HCII 2020, LNCS 12424, pp. 3–19, 2020.
https://doi.org/10.1007/978-3-030-60117-1_1

150 ms. Table 1 summarizes the different values suggested by different researchers in the literature.

This paper explores the effect of some of suggested values, beside others, for the dispersion and duration thresholds on the resulting eye fixations and scanpath sequences without statistically testing for any significant difference between any of the different settings.

Table 1. Summary of some the suggested values for the dispersion and duration thresholds of the identification-dispersion threshold (I-DT) algorithms in the literature

Reference	Dispersion threshold (°)	Duration threshold (ms)
Salvucci and Goldberg 2000	0.5–1.0	100–200
Jacob and Karn 2003	2.0	100–200
Blascheck et al. 2017	–	200–300
Nyström and Holmqvist 2010	0.5	80–150
Blignaut 2009	0.5–1.0	100–400

To explore the effect of the different settings of the dispersion and duration thresholds on the generated eye fixations by the I-DT algorithms and then on the scanpath strings built based on the eye fixations, the process leading to the final result, the scanpath strings, is explained in details. The process consists of four steps: (1) cleaning the raw gaze data packets generated by the eye tracker device (Sect. 2.4.1), (2) selecting/calculating the threshold values for the I-DT algorithm (Sect. 2.4.2), (3) computing the eye fixations using the I-DT algorithm, and (4) computing the scanpath strings based on the eye fixations (Sect. 2.4.3).

The eye fixations and scanpath strings resulting from the different settings of the dispersion and duration thresholds are reported in Sect. 2.5. The paper ends with a discussion (Sect. 3) and a conclusion (Sect. 4).

2   Methods

2.1   Apparatus

Tobii Pro TX300 (120 Hz) Eye Tracker system with a 24-inch monitor was used to collect the raw gaze data packets. The eye tracker was positioned below the monitor and was not in direct contact with the participant. Different values for the visual angle accuracy were tested for their effect on the eye fixations and the scanpath sequences as described in Sect. 2.4.2.1. The distance from the participant's eyes and the eye tracker device is calculated dynamically and address also in Sect. 2.4.2.1 along with the visual angle accuracy. The different thresholds that have been tested to define the eye fixations are discussed in Sect. 2.4.2.2.

2.2   Participants

One 35-year old male student from the University of Oklahoma took part in the experiment. The participant does not have any visual impairments.

2.3   Procedure

The participant has been asked to read a medial text that contains some difficult words (Fig. 1). This reading task was proceeded by a calibration session for the user vision. The participant has been asked to move away from the eye tracker device once he finished reading the text to avoid recording any unrelated gaze data packets to the experiment.

The most common reason for the vague pain in mother's arm is

the Scapular Dyskinesis or SICK Scapula. The scapulothoracic

muscles are the group of muscles which form the most important

musculoskeletal foundation for the upper quarter of the body.

They are connected to the backbone, scapula (shoulder blade),

and the humerus (arm), together they work in harmony with the

scapulohumeral muscles to provide free movement of the arm.

Fig. 1. The medical paragraph displayed to the participant

The vision of the participant has been calibrated using the Matlab function, *HandleCalibWorkflow*, provided by Tobii Technology Inc. in the Matlab binding API (Tobii Technology Inc. 2015). This script is part of the *RealtimeEyeTrackingSample* example and was used without modification. At the end of the calibration process, a plot for the offset between each eye gaze data and the calibration points is shown (Fig. 2). The participant will be directed to press 'y' on the keyboard if the calibration process is successful or 'n' to repeat the calibration.

After successfully completing the calibration process and pressing 'y' on the keyboard, the text for the reading task was shown immediately and the eye tracker device started recording the raw gaze data packets after pausing for 3 s. The raw gaze data packets can be obtained by calling the *readGazeData* function in the Matlab binding API.

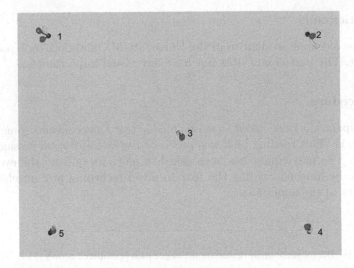

Fig. 2. The offset between each left (shown in red) and right (shown in green) eye gaze data and the calibration points of the participant (shown in blue) (Color figure online)

2.4 Data Analysis

2.4.1 Data Cleaning

Each raw gaze data packet holds 13 pieces of information about each eye. More information about each piece of the raw gaze data can be found in Tobii Analytics SDK Developer Guide available as a PDF file when downloading the Tobii Analytics SDK (Tobii Technology Inc. 2015) or directly via Acuity website (Tobii Technology Inc. 2013). One of the pieces of information in the raw gaze data packet is the **validity code**. This code represents how confident the eye tracker system was when assigning a particular eye gaze data packet to a particular eye. This code ranges from 0 (most confident) to 4 (least confident).

A validity code of 0 assigned to a raw eye data packet captured at a specific point in time for the left and the right eye indicates that the eye tracker is very certain that each of the data packets is associated with the corresponding eye. On the other hand, if the validity code of the raw data packet of one eye is 0 and 4 for the other, the eye tracker detects an eye and it is most probably the eye that has a validity code of 0.

The Data Validity Codes table in the Tobii Analytics SDK Developer Guide summarizes all the possible combinations of the validity codes of the two eyes. The table shows that a validity code of 1 of one eye is only possible with a validity code of 3 or more of the other eye. Also, the only possible combination of a validity code of 2 of one eye is a validity code of 2 of the other eye which means that the eye tracker detected one eye but it is not certain which eye, left or right, this raw gaze data packet represents.

Since we are interested in capturing the gaze of both eyes with high level of certainty, any raw gaze data packet captured at any specific point in time that holds a validly code value that is not 0 for any eye will be discarded. The raw gaze data packets for both eyes, after filtering the invalid packets, will be combined into a single array of 26 columns; 13 identical columns for each eye.

2.4.2 Thresholds Selection

In order for the I-DT algorithm to run, two thresholds must be provided along-side the raw gaze data packets. One of these thresholds is the maximum dispersion (Sect. 2.4.2.1) and the other is the minimum duration (Sect. 2.4.2.2).

2.4.2.1 Dispersion Threshold. The dispersion threshold represents the maximum distance that the ID-T algorithm should tolerate when computing the eye fixations points. This distance has the same measurement unit of the coordinates of the provided gaze data. The value assigned to this threshold depends on the visual error angle that the eye tracker system suffers from. Tobii, in the Product Description of its Tobii Pro TX300 Eye Tracker (Tobii Technology Inc. 2010), reports a visual error angle between 0.4° and 0.6° for different conditions.

This value assigned to the dispersion threshold means if a group of raw gaze points is in close proximity to each other and the maximum distance between any two of them is less than this dispersion threshold value, then these group of raw gaze points is consolidated into a single point called an eye fixation given that they satisfy the minimum duration threshold explained in Sect. 2.4.2.2.

The calculation of the dispersion threshold depends on two factors: the distance of the user from the eye tracker system and the visual error angle of the eye tracker system. The distance of the user from the eye tracker system can be elicited from the raw gaze data packets generated by the eye tracker system as the eye *z-coordinate* value in millimeters (more information can be found in the Tobii Analytics SDK Developer Guide). The average value of these z-coordinates for both eyes constitutes the user's eye distance from the eye tracker system.

The visual error angle reported in the Product Description document of the Tobii TX300 Eye Tracker (Tobii Technology Inc. 2010) is generally between 0.4° and 0.6° depending on the lighting conditions. Visual error angles of 0.4°, 0.5°, and 0.6° were used to calculate the dispersion threshold.

The dispersion threshold (in millimeter) is calculated as follows:

$$dispersionTheshold = eyeDistance * sin(visualErrorAngle)$$

After plugging the eye distance, which is usually 650 mm, and visual error angles to the equation, dispersion thresholds of 4.5 mm, 5.7 mm, and 6.8 mm were obtained. Figure 3 visually illustrate the calculation process.

Tobii provides the 2-dimensional eye gaze positions in what is called Active Display Coordinate System (ADCS). This system encodes the x and y coordinates for the gaze position of both eyes using values between 0 and 1 (see Fig. 4). A value of (0, 0) indicates a gaze position at the top left corner of the active display area which is the monitor in our case. On the other hand, a value of

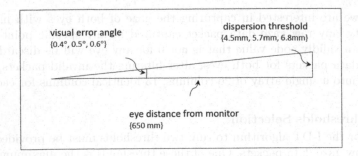

Fig. 3. Dispersion threshold calculations

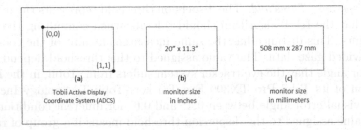

Fig. 4. Different positioning systems

(1, 1) represents a gaze position at the lower right corner of the active display area. For more information about this system, refer to the Tobii Analytics SDK Developer Guide.

Since the dispersion threshold measurement system is different from the measurement system of the eye gaze positions, the eye gaze positions will be converted to the dispersion threshold measurement system which is the millimeter system. To convert from the ADCS system which is the eye gaze positions measurement system, a knowledge of the size of the active display, the monitor, used in the study is necessary. The monitor attached to Tobii TX300 Eye Tracker system measures 508 mm in length and 287 mm in width. The conversion from the ADCS system to the millimeter system is straightforward. The x-coordinates of each eye gaze position needs to be multiplied by the length of the screen which is 508 mm and the y-coordinates needs to be multiplied by the width of the monitor which is 287 mm.

2.4.2.2 Duration Threshold. The duration threshold represents the minimum time (in milliseconds) after which a set of the raw gaze data packets, if they satisfy the maximum dispersion threshold, will be turned into an eye fixation point. The common duration threshold suggested by the literature ranges from 50 to 200 ms (Salvucci and Goldberg 2000; Jacob and Karn 2003; Blascheck et al.2017; Nyström and Holmqvist 2010; Blignaut 2009). Four different duration thresholds, namely, 50, 100, 150, and 200 ms will be examined for their effect on the generated eye fixations by the I-DT algorithm. Along with these common duration threshold values, two more values, 500 and 1000 ms, were investigated.

2.4.3   Finding Scanpath Strings

Finding the scanpath string for each combination of the dispersion and duration thresholds' values goes through two stages. The first stage entails determining the coordinates of the bounding boxes of the each area of interest (AOI) for the sentences (Sect. 2.4.3.1) and words (Sect. 2.4.3.3). The second stage entails implementing a script that computationally decides to which AOI (or AOIs) each of the eye fixations belongs (Sect. 2.4.3.2). An eye fixation will belong to more than one AOI in case the AOIs are interleaving. In the case where no one AOI interleaves with another, each eye fixation will fall into a single AOI.

2.4.3.1 Determining AOI Coordinates of Sentences. The easiest way to determine the coordinates of any AOI is to describe it as a set of rectangles (see Fig. 5). Doing so will ensure smoother implementation of the algorithm that will find the scanpath string. Any rectangular AOI can be described by 2 points. The upper-left corner and the lower-right corner points are used here to describe each AOI. A single AOI could be described by multiple rectangles as in the case of the AOI A and AOI B in Fig. 5.

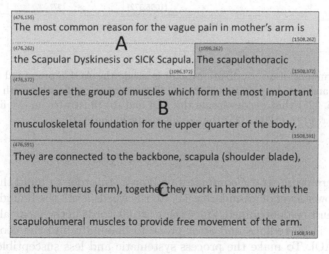

Fig. 5. Representing the AOI of the sentences as a set of rectangles. An AOI can be a combination of multiple rectangles like AOI A which is a combination of two rectangles: the first rectangle has the coordinates (476, 155) and (1508, 262) and the second rectangle has the coordinates (476, 262) and (1096, 372)

2.4.3.2 Finding the Scanpath String of Sentences. After determining the coordinates of the rectangles that specify all the sentences' AOIs, a script will be executed to determine the scanpath string for each set of eye fixations. The *Scanpath Finder* script goes through the eye fixations one by one and determines to which AOI (or AOIs) each eye fixation point belongs. To determine whether an eye fixation point that is represented by (x, y) is within an AOI represented by (x_{ul}, y_{ul}) and (x_{lr}, y_{lr}), the following Boolean value is calculated:

$$d = (x - x_{ul}) \geq 0 \ \wedge \ (x_{lr} - x) \geq 0 \ \wedge \ (y - y_{ul}) \geq 0 \ \wedge \ (y_{lr} - y) \geq 0$$

The value of d is *true* when the eye fixation point is inside the AOI or on its boundary, and it is *false* when the eye fixation point is outside the AOI. Figure 6 illustrates the idea pictorially.

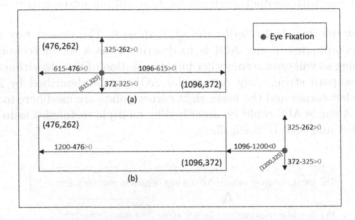

Fig. 6. Determining if an eye fixation point is inside the AOI represented by (x_{ul}, y_{ul}) = (476, 262) and (x_{lr}, y_{lr}) = (1096,372): (a) illustrates an eye fixation with coordinates (x, y) = (615, 325) that resides inside the AOI and (b) illustrates an eye fixation with coordinates (x, y) = (1200, 325) that resides outside the AOI

2.4.3.3 Determining AOI Coordinates of Words. In order to build the scanpath string at a lower level of granularity, i.e., to the words level, the bounding box for each word must be determined. Since there are 69 words in the medical paragraph (Fig. 1), it will be tedious and error-prone to manually find the coordinates of each work AOI. To make the process systematic and less susceptible to errors, the *Words Bounding Box Coordinates Finder* script has been implemented. This Matlab scrip shows the stimuli, which is in our case the medical paragraph, in the same dimensions as it would appear to the participant. In order for the script to generate the coordinates of the AOIs of the words, the user of the script needs first to move the mouse cursor to the right then to the left boundary of the stimuli and click. This step will record the x-coordinates of the left and right boundary of the stimuli that will be used in the subsequent steps to determine the coordinates of the boundary boxes of those AOIs that fall on the left and right edges of the stimuli. Second, the user of the script is required to move the mouse cursor vertically and click on the boundary of each line starting from the upper boundary of the first line and ending with the lower boundary of the last line. This step will record the y-coordinates of the boundary boxes that will be defined in the next step. Now that the left and right boundary of the stimuli as well as the boundary of each row has been captured, the user of the script needs to go over the text and click on the imaginary middle vertical line boundary between each two words.

The imaginary middle vertical line boundary between any two words is shown as a dashed line in Fig. 7. The user of the script needs to hit an Enter/Return after clicking on the boundary between the last two words in each line. When the user of the script reaches the last line and follows that with an Enter/Return click, the script will generate the coordinates of the AOIs with their labels. The labels of these AOIs are based on earlier information provided to the script about the name of each paragraph AOI and the number of words it contains.

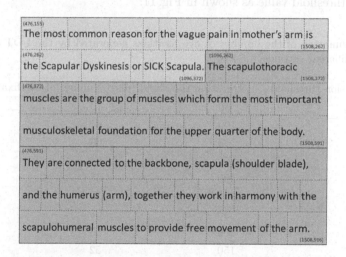

Fig. 7. Illustration of the bounding boxes of the words' AOIs

2.4.3.4 Finding the Scanpath String of Words. Finding the scanpath string of the words follows exactly the same procedure mentioned in Sect. 2.4.3.2. However, the algorithm is provided with the coordinates of the AOIs' bounding boxes of the words instead of the AOI's bounding boxes of the sentences.

2.5   Results

The process of determining the eye fixations from the raw gaze data has been tested on one participant and the result is discussed in Sect. 2.5.1. The scanpath strings based on the sentences level is presented in Section 2.5.2 and based on the words level is presented in Sect. 2.5.3.

2.5.1 Determining the Eye Fixations

The I-DT algorithm has been executed 12 times, using all the possible combinations of the selected values for the dispersion and duration thresholds. A reading task of a short medical paragraph (Fig. 1) that consists of a total of 69 words has been given to one participant to collect the raw gaze data and use in the I-DT algorithm.

Figure 8 shows the eye fixations generated by the I-DT algorithm using the different values for the duration threshold but keeping the dispersion threshold fixed to 0.4°. Similarly, Fig. 9 and Fig. 10 show the eye fixations generated by the I-DT algorithm with the different values of the duration threshold but fixing the dispersion threshold to 0.5° and 0.6°, respectively. Table 2 summarizes the number of eye fixations generated by the I-DT algorithm under the different settings. Generally, the number of eye fixations monotonically decreases as the duration threshold value increases. The number of eye fixations under different values of the duration threshold tends to be less than for those with higher dispersion threshold value as shown in Fig. 11.

Table 2. Summary of the number of eye fixations generated by the I-DT algorithm under the different settings

Dispersion threshold (°)	Duration threshold (ms)	Number of eye fixations
0.4	50	70
	100	67
	150	66
	200	64
	500	38
	1000	12
0.5	50	55
	100	53
	150	52
	200	49
	500	37
	1000	15
0.6	50	43
	100	43
	150	42
	200	39
	500	35
	1000	19

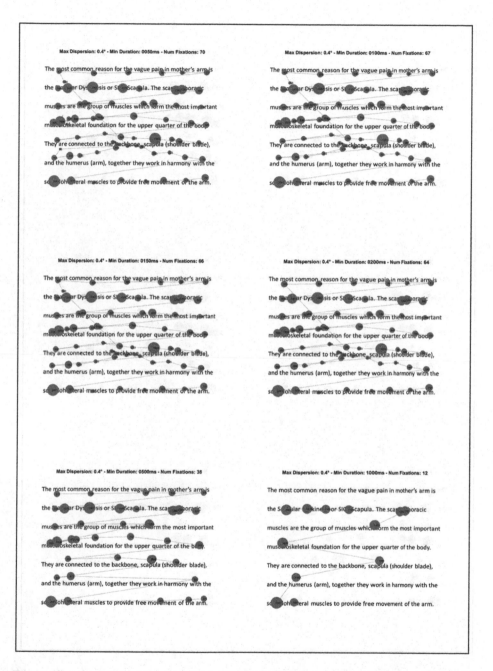

Fig. 8. The eye fixations generated by the I-DT algorithm using a dispersion threshold value of 0.4° and the different duration threshold values

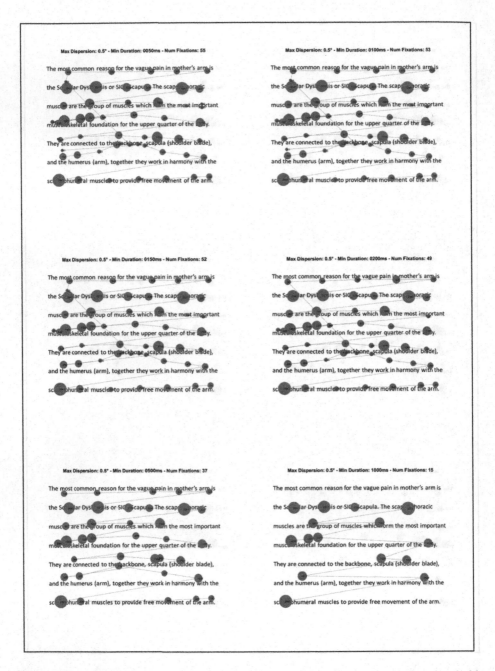

Fig. 9. The eye fixations generated by the I-DT algorithm using a dispersion threshold value of 0.5° and the different duration threshold values

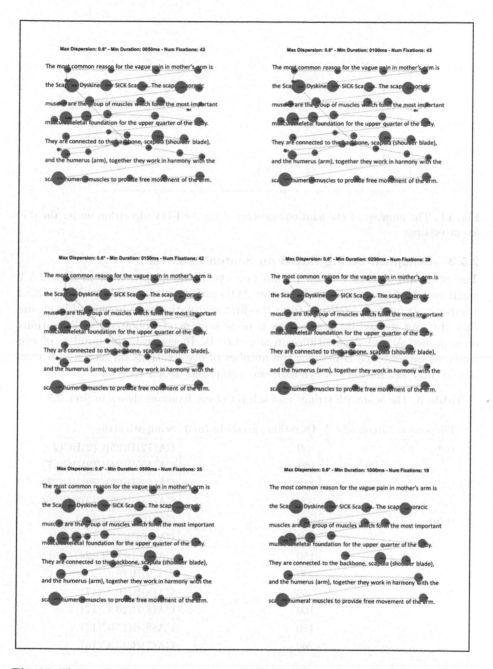

Fig. 10. The eye fixations generated by the I-DT algorithm using a dispersion threshold value of 0.6° and the different duration threshold values

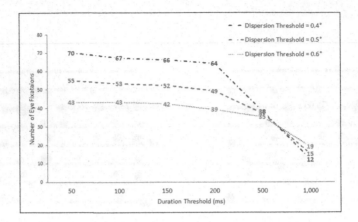

Fig. 11. The number of eye fixations generated by the I-DT algorithm under the different settings

2.5.2 Scanpath String Based on Sentences Level

The scanpath strings obtained from the eye fixations provided in Sect. 2.5.1 when considering the sentences as the AOIs are shown in Table 3. The partial scanpath string $CA(12)B(25)$ from the first scanpath string in the table means that the user started by fixating one time at sentence C followed by 12 fixations on sentence A and 25 fixations on sentence B. In general, the number of eye fixations on sentence B is twice the number of eye fixations on sentence A that has slightly less number of eye fixations compared to sentence C.

Table 3. The scanpath strings for each set of eye fixations shown in Sect. 2.5.1

Dispersion threshold (°)	Duration threshold (ms)	Scanpath string
0.4	50	CA(12)B(25)C(2)BC(29)
	100	CA(12)B(24)C(2)BC(27)
	150	CA(12)B(23)C(2)BC(27)
	200	CA(11)B(23)C(2)BC(26)
0.5	50	CA(10)B(18)C(26)
	100	CA(10)B(17)C(25)
	150	CA(10)B(17)C(24)
	200	CA(9)B(16)C(23)
0.6	50	CA(8)B(16)C(17)
	100	CA(8)B(16)C(17)
	150	CA(8)B(15)C(17)
	200	CA(7)B(14)C(16)

2.5.3 Scanpath String Based on Word Level

The scanpath strings obtained from the eye fixations provided in Sect. 2.5.1 when considering the words as the AOIs are shown in Table 4.

Table 4. The scanpath strings for each set of eye fixations shown in Sect. 2.5.1

Dispersion Threshold (°)	Duration Threshold (ms)	Scanpath String
0.4	50	C06A14A02A03A06A08A10A11A14(2)A15A17A18 B02(3)B03B05B06B05B08B09B10B12B13B14(3) B15B14B15B14(2)B15B09B19B21B22C01C03B15 C06(2)C07C08(2)C09C02C10C12(2)C13C06C05 C06(4)C16C18(2)C19C21(2)C22C24C25C26C27
	100	C06A14A02A03A06A08A10A11A14(2)A15A17A18 B02(3)B03B05B06B05B08B09B10B12B13B14(2) B15B14B15B14(2)B15B09B19B21B22C01C03B15 C06(2)C07C08(2)C09C10C12(2)C13C06C05 C06(3)C16C18(2)C19C21(2)C22C24C25C26C27
	150	C06A14A02A03A06A08A10A11A14(2)A15A17A18 B02(3)B03B05(2)B08B09B10B12B13B14(2)B15 B14B15B14(2)B15B09B19B21B22C01C03B15 C06(2)C07C08(2)C09C10C12(2)C13C06C05 C06(3)C16C18(2)C19C21(2)C22C24C25C26C27
	200	C06A02A03A06A08A10A11A14(2)A15A17A18 B02(3)B03B05(2)B08B09B10B12B13B14(2)B15 B14B15B14(2)B15B09B19B21B22C01C03B15 C06(2)C07C08(2)C09C10C12(2)C13C06C05 C06(2)C16C18(2)C19C21(2)C22C24C25C26C27
	500	A02A03A07A10A11A14(2)A15A17A18B02(3) B03B05B08B10B14(4)B15B09B19B22C03C06 C07(2)C08C11C12C19C21(2)C26C28
	1000	A14A15(2)A17B02(2)B09B14C07C12C21(2)
0.5	50	C06A14A02A04A07A10A11A14A15A17A18B02(2)B03 B06B08B10B12B13(2)B14(3)B15B14B15B08B19B22 C01C02C03C06C07C08C09C02C11C12C13C06(3)C07 C18C19C21(2)C22C24C26C28
	100	C06A14A02A04A07A10A11A14A15A17A18B02(2)B03 B06B08B10B12B13B14(3)B15B14B15B08B19B22C01 C03C06C07C08C09C02C11C12C13C06(3)C07C18C19 C21(2)C22C24C26C28
	150	C06A14A02A04A07A10A11A14A15A17A18B02(2)B03 B06B08B10B12B13B14(3)B15B14B15B08B19B22C01 C03C06C07C08C09C11C12C13C06(3)C07C18C19 C21(2)C22C24C26C28
	200	C06A02A03A06A09A11A14A15A17A18B02(2)B03B06 B08B10B13B14(3)B15B14B15B08B19B22C01C03C06 C07C08C09C11C12C13C06(2)C07C18C19C21(2)C22 C24C26C28
	500	A02A03A07A10A11A14A15A17A18B02(2)B03B06B08 B10B14(3)B15B08B19B22C03C06C07(2)C08C11C12 C06C16C19C21(2)C26C28
	1000	A14A15A17B02B05B09B14(2)B15B22C07 C08C12C19
0.6	50	C06A14A02A04A08A11A14A15A18B02(2)B03(2) B06B09B10B12B13B14(4)B15B18B22C02C06C07 C08C11(2)C12C06(2)C07C18C19C21(2)C24C26
	100	C06A14A02A04A08A11A14A15A18B02(2)B03(2) B06B09B10B12B13B14(4)B15B18B22C02C06C07 C08C11(2)C12C06(2)C07C18C19C21(2)C24C26
	150	C06A14A02A04A08A11A14A15A18B02(2)B03(2) B06B09B10B13B14(4)B15B18B22C02C06C07C08 C11(2)C12C06(2)C07C18C19C21(2)C24C26
	200	C06A02A04A08A11A14A15A18B02(2)B03B06 B09B10B13B14(4)B15B18B22C02C06C07C08 C11C12C06(2)C07C18C19C21(2)C24C26
	500	A02A04A08A11A14A15A18B02(2)B03B06B09 B10B14(2)B15B14B15B18B22C02C06C07C08 C11C12C06C07C18C19C21(2)C24C26
	1000	A14A15A18B02B05B09B10B14(3)B15B22C06 C07C08C11C19C21

3   Discussion and Limitation

The results show that there is a big difference in term of the number of the generated eye fixations under the different settings of the dispersion and duration thresholds of the I-DT algorithm. This difference leads to different scanpath strings under the sentence- and word-level AOIs. Therefore, the conclusion that a researcher may reach based on one setting of the dispersion and duration thresholds could be completely different from the conclusion reached by another researcher who used a different setting of the thresholds. Hence, it is highly recommended that the setting of these two thresholds be reported in the research write-up whenever a conclusion has been based on results obtained directly or indirectly from an I-DT algorithm. This will in turn help in resolving any ambiguity and confusion that can arise from research that starts from the same identical problem but end up with contradicting conclusions.

Given that this work is in progress, it currently has a number of limitations. First, the number of participants, only one, who took place in the experiment is very small which may lead to a non-robust results and conclusions. Second, the raw gaze data on which the eye fixations and fixation scanpaths base had been obtained from a specific eye tracker, Tobii Pro TX300. This eye tracker produces the raw gaze data in a specific format. The developed software system can only run on data that hold the same format produced by Tobii Pro TX300. Third, the work takes into consideration only one classification algorithm, I-DT, and it is unknown if the other classification algorithms will suffer from the same problems. Forth, only the effect on the fixation duration metric has been considered and it is not necessary that the same effect applies on the other eye tracking metrics.

4   Conclusion and Future Work

The identification-dispersion threshold (I-DT) algorithms are tricky in term of the choice that needs to be made to their dispersion and duration thresholds. The paper examined 18 different combinations of the most common values for dispersion and duration thresholds. The eye fixations have been calculated and displayed along with the scanpath strings for each setting of the dispersion and duration thresholds. This paper makes no conclusion on which setting is best for which situation but layout the finding for the reader to make her/his own choice. Therefore, the readers should mindfully choose the values for these thresholds based on the task being analyzed and then report the details of their choice so that other researchers become aware of the context on which the conclusions were made.

In the future, a large number of populations will be recruited to participant in the experiment. The results and the conclusions will then be verified against what is currently presented for any discrepancies. Due to the lack of the availability of other eye tracker devices, the currently developed software system will remain the same except for that the code will be re-written to make more modular. By doing so, the software system will be able to with little modifications to run on different types of eye tracker devices. More eye classification algorithms such as Identification by Velocity Threshold (I-VT) and Identification by Kalman Filter (I-KF) algorithms will be included in the investigation. Also, the effect of the different settings will be investigated on more eye tracking metrics such as number-of-fixation and duration-to-first-fixation metrics.

Acknowledgments. The author would like to thank Dr. Ziho Kang for allowing the use of his Human Factors and Simulation Lab equipment.

References

Blascheck, T., et al.: Visualization of eye tracking data: a taxonomyand survey. In: Computer Graphics Forum 00, 1–25 (2017). https://doi.org/10.1111/cgf.13079

Blignaut, P.: Fixation identification: the optimum threshold for a dispersion algorithm. Attention Percept. Psychophys. **71**(4), 881–895 (2009). https://doi.org/10.3758/APP.71.4.881

Duchowski, A.T.: Eye Tracking Methodology: Theory and Practice, p. 334. Springer, London (2007). https://doi.org/10.1007/978-1-84628-609-4. ISBN: 9781846286087

Holmqvist, K., et al.: Eye Tracking: A Comprehensive Guide to Methods and Measures, p. 560. Oxford University Press, Oxford (2015). ISBN: 9780198738596

Jacob, R.J.K., Karn, K.S.: Eye tracking in human-computer interaction and usability research: ready to deliver the promises. In: Mind's Eye: Cognitive and Applied Aspects of Eye Movement Research, Chapter 4, pp. 573–605 (2003)

Nyström, M., Holmqvist, K.: An adaptive algorithm for fixation, saccade, and glissade detection in eyetracking data. Behav. Res. Methods **42**(1), 188–204 (2010). https://doi.org/10.3758/BRM.42.1.188. ISSN: 1554-351X

Salvucci, D.D., Goldberg, J.H.: Identifying fixations and saccades in eye-tracking protocols. In: Proceedings of the Symposium on Eye Tracking Research & Applications - ETRA 2000, pp. 71–78. ACM Press, New York (2000). https://doi.org/10.1145/355017.355028. ISBN: 1581132808

Tobii Technology Inc., Tobii TX300 Eye Tracker: Product Description (2010). https://www.tobiipro.com/siteassets/tobii-pro/product-descriptions/tobii-pro-tx300-product-description.pdf. Visited 22 June 2017

Tobii Technology Inc.: Tobii Analytics SDK Developer's Guide (2013). http://www.acuity-ets.com/downloads/Tobii%20Analytics%20SDK%20Developers%20Guide.pdf. Visited 22 June 2017

Tobii Technology Inc.: Tobii Pro SDK: Develop Eye Tracking Applications for Research (2015). https://www.tobiipro.com/product-listing/tobii-pro-sdk/%7B%5C#%7DDownload. Visited 22 June 2017

An Antenatal Care Awareness Prototype Chatbot Application Using a User-Centric Design Approach

Mohammed Bahja[1]([✉]), Nour Abuhwaila[2], and Julia Bahja[3]

[1] University of Birmingham, Birmingham, UK
m.bahja@bham.ac.uk
[2] Brunel University London, London, UK
nour.abuhwaila@brunel.ac.uk
[3] King's College London, London, UK
Julia.bahja@kcl.ac.uk

Abstract. The frequency of occurrence of severe infectious diseases, such as SARS-CoV, MERS-CoV, Ebola and COVID-19, has been increasing in recent years, thus putting pressure on the delivery of healthcare services. Pregnant women are some of the most vulnerable patients, as they are more prone to infections and have limited mobility due to their health situation. In addition, preventive measures, such as social distancing and lockdowns have affected their access to healthcare services. Considering these issues, in this study, a prototype chatbot application that can provide antenatal care and support for pregnant women from the comfort of their home is proposed. A user-centric design methodology was adopted, where two midwives, one obstetrician and eleven pregnant women participated in the design and development process by providing regular reviews at various stages of the process. In addition, an online User Experience Questionnaire was employed for collecting the users' experiences after engaging with the protype application for two weeks. The findings reveal that the proposed chatbot application (Alia) is effective in terms of attractiveness, perspicuity, efficiency, stimulation, and novelty. In addition, concerns related to dependability (privacy and security) and supportability were identified. Finally, UEQ scales of pragmatic quality (1.12) and hedonic quality (1.11) related to the chatbot application Alia, reflected good usability, reliability and quality aspects.

Keywords: Pregnancy · Antenatal care · Chatbots · Awareness

1 Introduction

Rapid development of technologies in the healthcare sector has led to the development of innovative delivery of healthcare services being integrated with new technologies for enhancing the patient experience. Virtual assistance for diagnosis, treatment, medication and awareness creation in healthcare are a few of the developments that have been observed in the sector in recent years. Virtual assistants or chatbot technologies have

© Springer Nature Switzerland AG 2020
C. Stephanidis et al. (Eds.): HCII 2020, LNCS 12424, pp. 20–31, 2020.
https://doi.org/10.1007/978-3-030-60117-1_2

become one of the primary foci in the healthcare sector for streamlining and enhancing the various processes by integrating healthcare operations with innovative technologies [1–3]. In light of the COVID-19 pandemic, there has been increasing dependency on virtual assistance and e-awareness tools in the healthcare sector, as the pandemic has led to adoption of various preventive measures, such as closure of transport and limited access to outpatient departments. In addition, higher risk of acquiring the COVID-19 infection in hospitals has presented another major challenge, which has affected the delivery of healthcare services. Increase in the frequency of infectious diseases, such as SARS-CoV, MERS-CoV, Ebola [4] and COVID-19 [5], in the past few months, has demonstrated the urgency of the need long-term preventive measures, such as social distancing, becoming part of a lasting culture [6]. However, patients with acute illness or other conditions, such as dialysis, chronic conditions such as diabetes, respiratory complications, and pregnant women may need to visit hospitals for regular diagnosis and treatment [7, 8]. While patients with critical illnesses have no option but to visit hospitals, remote and regular access to healthcare services is essential during pandemics to reduce the exposure in crowded clinics and hospitals [9].

Global maternal mortality is considerably high, with 2.8 million pregnant women and new-born deaths every year [10]; averaging one death every 11 s. It was elicited that 94% of these deaths occurred in low resource settings, where proper care could not be delivered, and that most of these deaths could have been prevented. These statistics were observed before COVID-19 outbreak, when the access to the healthcare services was considerably more favourable compared to during the pandemic. It was recommended by the World Health Organization that regular counselling by healthcare experts, and a minimum of eight sessions with doctors by pregnant women is a necessary practice to be adopted [11]. In addition, it was found that major complications were accounting for more than 75% of maternal deaths [12], which included severe bleeding (after-birth), infections, high blood pressure during pregnancy (pre-eclampsia and eclampsia), complications from delivery, and unsafe abortion [13]. In addition, poverty, distance to facilities, lack of information, inadequate and poor-quality services as well as cultural beliefs and practices were identified as being salient factors affecting the delivery of care [10]. Furthermore, it was found that more than 90% of all births benefited from informational support and medical care received from a trained midwife, doctor or nurse [14]. Moreover, lack of access to midwives and healthcare professionals can affect pregnant women in receiving timely information.

In light of the COVID-19 outbreak, access to healthcare services has been severely affected due to the rising number of COVID-19 patients and high risk of contamination in hospitals. Delivering effective healthcare services during this pandemic has not always available due to shortage in midwifery staff [7]. Also, physiological changes during pregnancy, especially to the immune system, can increase the severity of viral diseases in pregnant women [15], which has put them at a high risk when accessing healthcare during the pandemic. Hence, service modifications are necessary to allow for the delivery of regular counselling and healthcare support for pregnant women [16].

Considering these issues, including lack of awareness and lack of regular access to healthcare services for pregnant women, remote delivery of healthcare services, such as e-Health and m-Health, have been identified as potential solutions during the COVID-19 outbreak [17]. Focusing on these aspects, in this study, a chatbot-based solution is proposed, through which there can be interaction with pregnant women, increase in their awareness, diagnosis of their condition and assessment of this on a daily basis.

2 Design and Development

For the design and development of the chatbot application prototype, a user-centred design [18–20] was adopted, involving all the stakeholders, including pregnant women, obstetricians, midwives as well as application designers and developers. A User-centred Design (UCD), according to ISO 9241-210 [19–21], involves a series of phases including knowing the users; analysing users' tasks and goals; developing usability requirements; the prototype and design concept; usability testing; and repeating the stages for more features, as shown in Fig. 1.

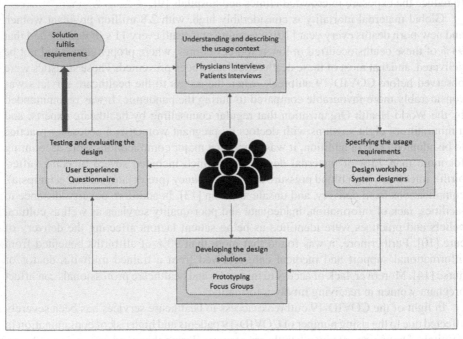

Fig. 1. User-centric design process adopted for the study

As shown in Fig. 1, an iterative/agile development process is adopted, where the results are continuously improved by involving the users and experts in the design and development process. Adopting an iterative process helps in developing a chatbot application, which will meet the user requirements.

The prototypes are tested before the final version is created. A UCD approach has various advantages. It is an efficient and effective design and development process that reduces development costs and the risk of application failure (not meeting the

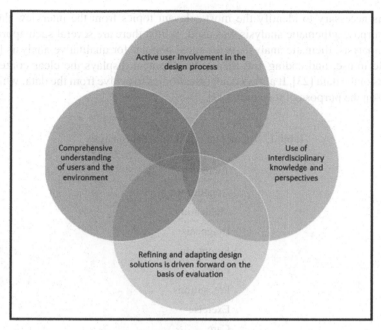

Fig. 2. Underlying principles of UCD

user requirements). Its underlying principles (Fig. 2) reflect a collaborative approach involving all stakeholders.

2.1 Data Collection and Processing

The focus purpose of developing the chatbot application for antenatal care was for creating awareness, diagnosing and assessing patient condition on daily basis. Accordingly, the data was collected from all UK-located stakeholders, including pregnant women, obstetrician and midwives. Pregnant women were recruited from parenting social media group. Participants were contacted by email, in which the purpose of the study was explained and their consent for their participation was requested. After the recruitment of the 11 pregnant women, online open-ended interviews were conducted over Skype with each participant, due to the Covid-19 lockdown restrictions.

The interviews with the pregnant women focused on identifying user-centric aspects, including their technology skills, attitudes, perceptions about using chatbots/virtual assistants for healthcare information and services during pregnancy. Accordingly, the open-ended interviews with the midwives and obstetrician focused on the general care, lifestyle and the precautions needing to be considered during pregnancy. In addition, information relating to different experiences during pregnancy, symptoms and their impact as well as data relating to the answers to the questions raised by the pregnant women participants was collected. The interviews were transcribed and a dataset containing interviews from the midwives, obstetrician and pregnant women was created and processed.

It was necessary to identify the most relevant topics from the interview data and for this purpose a thematic analysis was used. Whilst there are several such approaches for data analysis, thematic analysis is the most popular for qualitative analysis [22]. It is flexible to use, and coding and theme development displays the clear content and semantics of the data [23]. It allows categories/topics to evolve from the data, which can be based on the purpose of the study [22].

Table 1. Themes emerged from data analysis

Topic
Appointments
Medication
Diagnosis
Symptoms
Food
Precautions
Exercise
Care
Treatment

Coding process the interview data, resulted in 18 codes as the outcome. These 18codes were combined to form nine major themes/topics, including appointments, medication, diagnosis, symptoms, food, exercise, precaution, treatment, and care, as shown in Table 1. Two major functionalities of the chatbot were identified accordingly: creating awareness about healthcare for pregnant women, which relates to food, care, precautions, exercise, symptoms, appointments etc.; providing information related to diagnosis process, treatment and care, which relates to healthcare awareness. Then, the common cases and scenarios were identified from the data relating to these topics, using conversational bots created using Amazon Lex (lexical based approach).

2.2 Prototype Design

Amazon Lex was used for designing the chatbot protype model. Pregnancy information provided from the National Health Service (NHS) website pregnancy guide [24] was used along with the data collected from the obstetrician and midwives. Amazon Lex provides the advanced deep learning functionalities of automatic speech recognition (ASR) for converting speech to text, and natural language understanding (NLU) to recognise the intent of the text. The current prototype model uses text to text interaction, with the pregnant women. The chatbot application was embedded with three functionalities (Fig. 3), which are explained in the following sections.

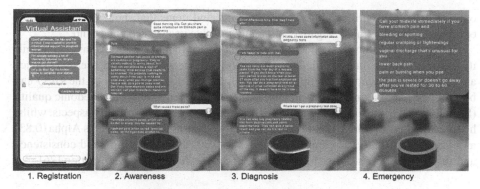

| 1. Registration | 2. Awareness | 3. Diagnosis | 4. Emergency |

Fig. 3. Conversational flows in Chatbot Alia

Registration: The users are greeted by the Chatbot 'Alia', and they are asked to register by clicking the provided link, which will redirect them to a new window, where they need to complete the registration by providing their names along with contact information.

Awareness: One of the primary functions of the proposed chatbot is to create awareness and provide informational support to the pregnant women in relation to various aspects, such as food, exercise, care, precautions etc. An example of information sharing conversation related to stomach pains can be observed in Fig. 3.

Diagnosis: The proposed chatbot also provides information about diagnosis, such as ultrasound scans, pregnancy tests, frequency of tests etc. A conversational flow in relation to the pregnancy tests is presented in Fig. 3, where the chatbot provides information about when, where, and how they can be carried out.

Emergency: The chatbot also provides information in case of emergencies based on the users' input data. For instance, it can be observed from the figure that the chatbot warns the users to contact a midwife in the case of stomach pain associated with other symptoms provided in the conversation.

2.3 Evaluation

The prototype application link was forwarded to the 11 pregnant women participants through email. The users were asked to use the chatbot application for two weeks, after which they were asked to participate in an online user experience survey. The User Experience Questionnaire (UEQ) [25] was used for collecting the participants experiences in using the chatbot application. UEQ has 26 items, which are used for evaluating user experience. The order of the items (i.e. whether the positive term is left or right in an item) is randomised in the questionnaire to minimise answer tendencies. The items are changed to a common order (negative term left; positive term right) and the transformed data are used for all the further calculations. The users answer each item on a scale of seven, reflecting their approval or acceptance towards the factor on the left or right. The distribution of answers can help to find items that show a polarisation of opinions, i.e. where many negative and many positive answers can be found.

UEQ was used for data collection as it can be used to measure both classical usability aspects (attractiveness, efficiency, perspicuity, dependability) and user experience aspects (originality/novelty, stimulation) [26]. In addition, the scales of the UEQ can be grouped into pragmatic (Perspicuity, Efficiency, Dependability) and hedonic quality (Stimulation, Originality). Pragmatic quality refers to task related quality aspects, whilst hedonic quality pertains to non-task related quality aspects. The Cronbach's Alpha (0.83) and Lambda 2 (0.89) values were greater than 0.70, thus indicating good consistency and reliability of the scales. The results are discussed in the following section [26].

3   Results and Discussion

The distribution of the responses over 26 items and their relevant scales are presented in Table 2. Factors, such as ease of use (item 4), speed (item 9), uniqueness/novelty (item 10), attractiveness (item 25) were identified to be effective as they were rated as highly relevant to the chatbot application, Alia, by the majority of the pregnant women users. However, factors such as support received from the application (item 11) and security aspect (item 17), were rated neutral by the majority of the participants. Items related to attractiveness, perspicuity, efficiency, stimulation, and novelty were rated to be most applicable in relation the application, while items pertaining to dependability were mostly rated as average.

Table 2. Distribution of answers on UEQ

S.No.	Item (Left/Right)	1	2	3	4	5	6	7	Scale
1	annoying/enjoyable	1	1	1	2	3	3	0	Attractiveness
2	not understandable/understandable	1	0	1	3	3	2	1	Perspicuity
3	dull/creative	0	1	2	4	2	2	0	Novelty
4	difficult to learn/easy to learn	0	0	0	0	0	2	9	Perspicuity
5	inferior/valuable	0	0	0	1	4	3	3	Stimulation
6	boring/exciting	0	0	1	5	3	2	0	Stimulation
7	not interesting/interesting	0	0	1	2	5	3	0	Stimulation
8	unpredictable/predictable	1	2	4	2	0	1	1	Dependability
9	slow/fast	0	0	0	0	0	2	9	Efficiency
10	conventional/inventive	0	0	0	0	0	2	9	Novelty
11	obstructive/supportive	0	0	1	5	3	2	0	Dependability
12	bad/good	0	0	0	0	3	1	7	Attractiveness
13	complicated/easy	1	1	1	3	3	2	0	Perspicuity
14	unlikable/pleasing	1	0	1	4	3	2	0	Attractiveness

(*continued*)

Table 2. (*continued*)

S.No.	Item (Left/Right)	1	2	3	4	5	6	7	Scale
15	usual/leading edge	0	0	1	4	3	3	0	Novelty
16	unpleasant/pleasant	0	0	1	4	3	3	0	Attractiveness
17	not secure/secure	0	1	1	1	0	2	6	Dependability
18	demotivating/motivating	0	2	2	1	0	2	4	Stimulation
19	does not meet expectations/meets expectations	0	1	1	1	1	1	6	Dependability
20	inefficient/efficient	1	1	0	0	2	7	0	Efficiency
21	confusing/clear	0	2	2	0	0	1	6	Perspicuity
22	impractical/practical	2	0	0	2	5	2	0	Efficiency
23	cluttered/organised	0	2	2	0	0	1	6	Efficiency
24	unattractive/attractive	0	1	0	0	0	1	9	Attractiveness
25	unfriendly/friendly	0	1	0	0	2	4	4	Attractiveness
26	conservative/innovative	0	0	0	3	4	4	0	Novelty

The benchmark graph shown in the Fig. 4 below presents the overall results.

UEQ scales reflect user experience relating to the different factors, with the results being interpreted using the means of these scales. The range of the scales is between −3 (horribly bad) and +3 (extremely good); however, in real applications, in general, only values in a restricted range will be observed [22]. This is due to the calculation of means over a range of different persons with different opinions and answer tendencies (for example the avoidance of extreme answer categories) being extremely unlikely to show values above +2 or below −2. Thus, even a quite good value of +1.5 for a scale looks, from the purely visual standpoint on a scale range of −3 to +3, not as positive as it really is [28, 29]. The UEQ means and variances relating to the various factors are presented in Table 3.

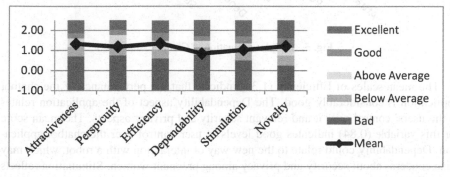

Fig. 4. Benchmark graph

Table 3. UEQ Scale means and variance

Factor	Mean	Variance
Attractiveness	1.318	0.61
Perspicuity	1.182	1.25
Efficiency	1.341	0.68
Dependability	0.841	0.62
Stimulation	1.023	0.48
Novelty	1.205	0.31

It can be observed that all the factors achieved good results, except for dependability. Attractiveness reflects how effective the chatbot application is in gaining the users' attention and engaging them in the application. The mean scale value for attractiveness (1.38) indicates that the application was considered to be attractive by the majority of the users. Perspicuity refers to the clarity and transparency of the application, as a result of which users can make judgements or decisions more effectively. The mean scale value for Perspicuity (1.18) indicates that majority of the users acknowledged the transparency and clarity aspects on the applications. However, the variance of 1.25 relating to this variable indicates that the users' opinions were very spread out from the mean and from one another, as shown in the box plots in Fig. 5.

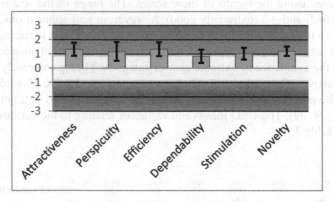

Fig. 5. Boxplot evaluation of Chatbot Alia

The mean scales of Efficiency (1.34) indicate that the performance of the chatbot application is considerably good. The Dependability aspect of the application relates to the users' control over it and relevant security and privacy aspects. The mean score for this variable (0.84) indicates good levels of user control over the chatbot application. Dependability could relate to the new way of interaction with a robot, which may raise concerns about security and privacy among pregnant women. Stimulation reflects how effective the application is in exciting and motivating the users to engage with the chatbot application. The mean scale score (1.02) suggest that the users enjoyed using the application. In addition, the low variance (0.48) indicates that most of the users' opinions were similar and close to the mean scales. Novelty refers to the uniqueness and creativity of the application, which can catch the interest of the users. The mean scale score (1.20) indicates that the application was seen as novel and creative, with the low variance (0.31) reflecting that similar opinions were expressed by the users. In addition, the ratings for pragmatic (1.12) and hedonic quality (1.11) suggest the chatbot was considered to have good usability, reliability and quality.

4 Conclusion

In this study, a chatbot application for providing antenatal care for pregnant women in UK in the areas of informational support, diagnosis and emergencies has been proposed. A user-centric design methodology was adopted for developing the application in order to minimise the risk of application failures and to improve the development process. Chatbot applications have been identified as more effective than other traditional E-learning/support applications, as they provide an effective user-interface and enhance communication in a natural language setting. The findings from this evaluative study revealed that the Chatbot Alia was effective in terms of attractiveness, perspicuity, efficiency, stimulation, and novelty. In addition, concerns relating to dependability (privacy and security), and supportability were identified. That is, it would appear that the dependability factors did not meet the users' expectations, or it may be possible that, as they were new to chatbot applications, they might have concerns regarding privacy and security. However, the overall user experience evaluation revealed that the prototype chatbot application is effective and efficient in providing antenatal care.

This study has both practical and theoretical implications. The user-centric design has been found to be effective when designing the chatbot applications; limiting the frequency of errors and risk of failures in the development process. However, there are a few limitations identified in this study. The number of participants included in the user-centric design process were low, with the lockdown restrictions due to COVID-19 having affected the selection of a larger number of participants. Given the circumstances, online interviews were conducted to collect the data and personal interviews may been more effective in this regard [30, 31]. Future research should be focused on developing chatbot applications with a large sample of participants and focus groups are recommended to enhance the user-centric design process.

References

1. Bahja, M., Lycett, M.: Identifying patient experience from online resources via sentiment analysis and topic modelling. In: IEEE/ACM 3rd International Conference on Big Data Computing, Applications and Technologies, Shanghai, China (2016)
2. Bahja, M., Razaak, M.: Automated analysis of patient experience text mining using a design science research (DSR) approach. In: The Eighth International Conference on Business Intelligence and Technology, Barcelona, Spain (2018)
3. Bahja, M.: Natural language processing applications in business. E-Business, Intech Open (2020). https://doi.org/10.5772/intechopen.92203

4. De Wit, E., van Doremalen, N., Falzarano, D., Munster, V.: SARS and MERS: recent in-sights into emerging coronaviruses. Nat. Rev. Microbiol. **14**(8), 523–534 (2016). https://doi.org/10.1038/nrmicro.2016.81

5. World Health Organization: Coronavirus disease (COVID-2019) situation reports (2020). https://www.who.int/emergencies/diseases/novel-coronavirus-2019/situation-reports/. Accessed 15 June 2020

6. UK Government: Staying alert and safe (social distancing) (2020). https://www.gov.uk/government/publications/staying-alert-and-safe-social-distancing/staying-alert-and-safe-social distancing. Accessed 15 June 2020

7. Royal College of Obstetricians and Gynaecologists: Guidance for provision of midwife-led settings and home birth in the evolving coronavirus (COVID-19) pandemic (2020). https://www.rcog.org.uk/globalassets/documents/guidelines/2020-04-09-guidance-for-provision-of-midwife-led-settings-and-home-birth-in-the-evolving-coronavirus-covid-19-pandemic.pdf. Accessed 15 June 2020

8. Lin, M., Baker, O., Richardson, L., Schuur, J.: Trends in emergency department visits and admission rates among US acute care hospitals. JAMA Intern. Med. **178**(12), 1708 (2018). https://doi.org/10.1001/jamainternmed.2018.4725

9. Smith, A.C., et al.: Telehealth for global emergencies: implications for coronavirus disease 2019 (COVID-19). J. Telemed. Telecare, March (2020). https://doi.org/10.1177/1357633X2 0916567

10. UNICEF: Surviving birth: every 11 seconds, a pregnant woman or newborn dies somewhere around the world. https://www.unicef.org/press-releases/surviving-birth-every-11-seconds-pregnant-woman-or-newborn-dies-somewhere-around. Accessed 12 June 2020

11. WHO: Pregnant women must be able to access the right care at the right time, says WHO. https://www.who.int/news-room/detail/07-11-2016-pregnant-women-must-be-able-to-access-the-right-care-at-the-right-time-says-who. Accessed 12 June 2020

12. Say, L., Chou, D., Gemmill, A., Tunçalp, Ö., Moller, A., Daniels, J., et al.: Global causes of maternal death: a WHO systematic analysis. Lancet Global Health **2**(6), e323–e333 (2014). https://doi.org/10.1016/s2214-109x(14)70227-x

13. WHO: Maternal mortality. https://www.who.int/news-room/fact-sheets/detail/maternal-mortality. Accessed 12 June 2020

14. UN: SDG indicators. https://unstats.un.org/sdgs/indicators/database/. Accessed 12 June 2020

15. Mor, G., Cardenas, I.: The immune system in pregnancy: a unique complexity. Am. J. Reprod. Immunol. **63**(6), 425–433 (2010). https://doi.org/10.1111/j.1600-0897.2010.00836.x

16. Royal College of Obstetricians and Gynaecologists: Coronavirus (COVID-19) Infection in Pregnancy, Information for Healthcare Professionals. https://www.rcog.org.uk/globalassets/documents/guidelines/2020-06-04-coronavirus-covid-19-infection-in-pregnancy.pdf. Accessed 15 June 2020

17. Scott, B., Miller, G., Fonda, S., Yeaw, R., Gaudaen, J., Pavliscsak, H., et al.: Advanced digital health technologies for COVID-19 and future emergencies. Telemed. E-Health (2020). https://doi.org/10.1089/tmj.2020.0140

18. Dirin, A., Nieminen, M.: Assessments of user centered design framework for M-learning application development. In: Zaphiris, P., Ioannou, A. (eds.) LCT 2015. LNCS, vol. 9192, pp. 62–74. Springer, Cham (2015). https://doi.org/10.1007/978-3-319-20609-7_7

19. Bahja, M., Hammad, R., Bahja, M.: User-driven development for UK M-health patient management system. In: Proceedings of the 32 International BCS HCI Conference, Belfast, UK (2018)

20. Bahja, M., Hammad, R., Butt, G.: Importance of chatbot learning in the context of distance education: a user-centric framework for their design & development. In: Proceedings of HCI International 2020 Conference. Lecture Notes in Computer Science (2020)

21. ISO: Ergonomie der Mensch-System-Interaktion – Teil 210: Prozess zur Gestaltung gebrauchstauglicher interaktiver Systeme (ISO 9241-210:2010); Deutsche Fassung EN ISO 9241-210:2010. Beuth Verlag, pp. 1–46 (2011)
22. Nowell, L., Norris, J., White, D., Moules, N.: Thematic analysis. Int. J. Qual. Methods 16(1), 160940691773384 (2017). https://doi.org/10.1177/1609406917733847
23. Javadi, M., Zarea, K.: Understanding thematic analysis and its pitfall. J. Client Care 1(1), (2016). https://doi.org/10.15412/j.jcc.0201010
24. The National Health Services: Your pregnancy and baby guide (2018). https://www.nhs.uk/conditions/pregnancy-and-baby/stomach-pain-abdominal-cramp-pregnant/. Accessed 15 June 2020
25. Schrepp, M., Hinderks, A., Thomaschewski, J.: Construction of a benchmark for the user experience questionnaire (UEQ). Int. J. Interact. Multimed. Artif. Intell. 4(4), 40 (2017). https://doi.org/10.9781/ijimai.2017.445
26. Hinderks, A., Meiners, A., Mayo, F., Thomaschewski, J.: Interpreting the results from the user experience questionnaire (UEQ) using importance-performance analysis (IPA). In: Proceedings of the 15th International Conference on Web Information Systems and Technologies (2019). https://doi.org/10.5220/0008366503880395
27. Bonett, D.B.: Sample size requirements for testing and estimating coefficient alpha. J. Educ. Behav. Stat. 27(4), 335–340 (2002)
28. Schrepp, M.: User Experience Questionnaire Handbook, UEQ (2019). https://doi.org/10.13140/rg.2.1.2815.0245
29. Laugwitz, B., Held, T., Schrepp, M.: Construction and evaluation of a user experience questionnaire. In: Holzinger, A. (ed.) USAB 2008. LNCS, vol. 5298, pp. 63–76. Springer, Heidelberg (2008). https://doi.org/10.1007/978-3-540-89350-9_6
30. Colombotos, J.: Personal versus telephone interviews: effect on responses. Public Health Rep. 84(9), 773–782 (1969). (Washington, D.C.: 1896)
31. Hasley, S.: A comparison of computer-based and personal interviews for the gynecologic history update. Obstet. Gynecol. 85(4), 494–498 (1995). https://doi.org/10.1016/0029-7844(95)00012-g

A User-Centric Framework for Educational Chatbots Design and Development

Mohammed Bahja[1](✉), Rawad Hammad[2], and Gibran Butt[3]

[1] University of Birmingham, Birmingham, UK
M.Bahja@bham.ac.uk
[2] Department of Engineering and Computing, University of East London, London, UK
r.hammad@uel.ac.uk
[3] Academic Unit of Ophthalmology, Inflammation and Ageing, University of Birmingham, Birmingham, UK
G.F.Butt@bham.ac.uk

Abstract. Increasing frequency of epidemics, such as SARS-CoV, MERS-CoV, Ebola, and the recent COVID-19, have affected various sectors, especially education. As a result, emphasis on e-learning and distance learning has been increasing in recent years. The growing numbers of mobile users and access to the internet across the world has created more favorable conditions for adopting distance learning on a wider scale. However, lessons learnt from current experiments have highlighted poor student engagement with learning processes, hence a user-centric approach to design and develop educational chatbots is presented. A User-centric approach enables developers to consider the following: learners' and teachers' technological skills and competencies, attitudes, and perceptions and behaviour; conceptual concerns, such as pedagogical integration on online platforms, assessment procedures, varying learning culture and lifestyles; technical concerns, such as privacy, security, performance, ubiquity; and regulatory concerns, such as policies, frameworks, standards, ethics, roles and responsibilities have been identified in this study. To address these concerns, there is the need for user-centric design and collaborative approaches to the development of distance learning tools. Considering the abovementioned challenges and the growing emphasis on distance learning, we propose chatbot learning as an effective and efficient tool for delivering such learning. In this regard, a user-centric framework for designing chatbot learning applications and a collaborative user-centric design methodology for developing chatbot learning applications is proposed and discussed.

Keywords: Chatbot · E-learning · Engagement · User-centric design framework · Development methodology · Technology-enhanced learning

1 Introduction

Rapid development in the education technology sector has led to innovative pedagogical approaches being integrated with new technologies aimed at enhancing the learning experience. The utilisation of virtual assistance in learning, E-learning and M-learning

© Springer Nature Switzerland AG 2020
C. Stephanidis et al. (Eds.): HCII 2020, LNCS 12424, pp. 32–43, 2020.
https://doi.org/10.1007/978-3-030-60117-1_3

has been increasing exponentially in recent years. Virtual assistants and chatbot technologies have been one of the primary foci in integrating pedagogic approaches with innovative technologies. In the wake of the COVID-19 outbreak and preventive distancing measures, there is now an increasing demand for virtual assistance and E-learning tools in the education sector.

At the peak of the pandemic, most countries closed all their educational institutions to contain the spread of COVID-19, many of which will remain at a reduce capacity for the remainder of the year. According to a recent estimate (7th June 2020), 1.725 billion learners across the world have been affected by the closure of schools and colleges [1]. The pandemic has affected 98.5% of the worldwide student population due to the national and local lockdowns, resulting in the closure of institutions, lack of transport; issues relating to healthcare access etc. [2]. Given the current situation, it is unlikely that educational institutions will open anytime soon. In addition, changes in lifestyles, mobility and travel will have an impact on the future course of access to education. Accordingly, the emphasis on distance learning methods, such as E-learning, chatbot learning, virtual learning has been increasing, as institutions across the globe turn to these platforms to continue [3]. With the increase in the frequency of infectious diseases, such as SARS-CoV, MERS-CoV, Ebola etc. [4] In the past few years, it is crucial that long term strategies in relation to education are developed for ensuring continuity in the learning process, as evidenced recently during the long break due to the COVID-19 pandemic.

This sudden change in the pedagogical approaches, transforming classroom education to virtual and personalised learning, requires a complete updating of the design and development of the distance and E-learning applications. The role of teachers, students, and educational institutions will require major revision and most importantly, the virtual learning applications must cater for the needs of all the stakeholders in education. One of the supporting factors facilitating E-learning is the rapid increase in Internet access across the globe. As of 2019, 4.13 billion worldwide internet users were identified, with 51.98% having mobile internet access and 48.02% able to receive fixed broad band [5]. Given these statistics, widespread implementation of distance and E-learning across the globe can be considered a feasible and sustainable solution, particularly in light of increasing epidemics. However, there exist a number of challenges that must be addressed. Firstly, as the majority of students and teachers are used to traditional classroom teaching practices, both teachers and learners' attitudes, skills and competencies need to be assessed and accordingly, new pedagogic approaches as well as distance and E-learning applications developed [6]. Secondly, issues such as assessment and support that have been mostly undertaken in classrooms will need to be redesigned for virtual environments [6]. Thirdly, the design and contents of distance learning and E-learning applications should be regularly updated in accordance with changes in the curriculum [7]. These applications should be tailored to meet the needs of the users, policies, and underpinning educational pedagogies. In addition, other challenges that are common to information systems, such as security, privacy, reliability, performance, ubiquity etc. that could affect the design and development of distance and E-learning applications require addressing [8].

Chatbots are one potential solution for addressing these issues. They can facilitate real-time user interaction, provide support and assessment features (questions-answers between chatbot and users) as well as being easy to use. Moreover, they can deliver effective performance by integrating NLP (natural language processing), ML (machine learning), AI (artificial intelligence), and DL (deep learning) technologies. Considering these factors, in this paper, a user-centric design framework and user-centric (collaborative) design and development methodology for chatbot learning applications is proposed.

2 Theoretical Background

2.1 Chatbots

Chatbots are machine agents serving as natural language interfaces for data and service providers [9]. They are increasingly being used in a variety sectors, such as commerce, healthcare, and various service industries, for the effective and efficient delivery of information. Whilst chatbot development can be dated back to the 1960s, with ELIZA, the first, being developed at MIT [10], they have become popular in the past few years with the integration of NLP, AI, ML, and DL techniques for enhanced user experience by providing accurate and reliable information. One of the most important applications of chatbots is the delivery of education. Students can interact with chatbots in their natural language as if they are talking to their teachers. They help in obtaining timely assistance or information and accordingly, motivate students in their learning, thereby increasing their productivity [9]. They can be used in ensuring privacy and security, for instance, PriBots, a conventional chatbot provides privacy and security information in a natural setting [9].

Chatbot application in education is in its early stages, and whilst researchers have highlighted their potential benefits, concerns such as technical requirements and the need for a natural language setting, etc. have also been raised, thus making the process of implementation complex [11]. In addition, adopting advance technologies such as supervised learning increases the complexity of chatbot design and necessitates the use of user-centric design approaches. Chatbots have been found to be effective for high school children [12] as learning in high schools is less complex than learning in higher and further education. To maximise the effectiveness of chatbots in learning scenarios, the context of educational processes needs to be considered in chatbot design so e-learner experience can be improved [13]. For instance, students learn differently using diverse learning pedagogies ranging from social learning processes to cognitive ones [14]. This requires effective ML and DL technologies, where the systems are trained under different circumstances, multiple times. However, with the rapid developments in technology, chatbots are increasingly being considered to be pedagogic tools in education, which are expected to gain wider audience and thus, experience increased deployment in the future [15].

2.2 Distance Education and Pedagogy

Distance learning is the process of learning remotely, with more emphasis on independent, self-motivated, and self-regulated learning [16]. The rapid development of

Information and Communication Technologies (ICT) has made distance learning more feasible across the world. As aforementioned, different pedagogical tools have emerged with the use of ICTs, such as E-learning, M-learning, virtual learning, social learning, chatbot learning etc. [17]. All these tools use online platforms for interactions; however, they vary in relation to the design, technical features and the integration of pedagogic approaches, such as collaborative learning, virtual classroom, one-to-one learning etc. All learning approaches that involve the use of online platforms for the purpose of learning can be considered as subsets of distance learning.

The learning process can vary depending on socio-cultural factors, education policies, use of technology, economic factors etc., which means that pedagogical approaches can also differ in different contexts. Hence, whilst it may not be practical to develop an application that fits all [18], it could be possible to develop an application that can be modified according to the needs of its users. User-centric aspects, such as attitudes, behaviour, critical thinking skills, communication skills, using technology as a tool of learning, decision making skills, and problem-solving skills have been identified as having a significant impact on the employability of distance learning approaches [19]. The design of online learning tools significantly affects the learnability, usability, engagement, and experience of the learners [20]. For instance, integrating technology with pedagogy and student culture has been identified to be one of the challenges in developing online learning tools that can effectively engage students. This depends on faculty's ability to integrate ICT into the course design and delivery [21]. The literature supports the notion that enhanced connectivity in mobile learning does not necessarily lead to better online collaboration and networking between students if not underpinned by robust pedagogy [22].

Therefore, it is evident that most of the online learning tools reviewed in previous studies, whilst effective at disseminating information, could not meet the users' requirements. In addition, various problems with respect to the design, such as the integration of technology and pedagogic approaches were identified, which resulted in the development of poor and ineffective online learning applications. Chatbots in this context could be one of the effective solutions, as they facilitate communication in a natural language setting This is unlike other online tools that completely rely on professional language as the medium of communication, which is a one-sided (learning tool to student) and thus, does not allow two-way interaction. Considering these issues, there is a need to collaborate with all stakeholders (learners, teachers, institutions, policy makers, system analysts, designers, developers, and testers) in the design and development of Chatbot learning applications. Accordingly, a user-centric design framework and development methodology are proposed in the following sections.

3 User-Centric Design Framework

Various frameworks for online learning have been proposed in different studies [23–26], which have focused on several theoretical concepts. For instance, the Community of Inquiry Framework [23] was developed for facilitating meaningful learning experiences through three presences: cognitive, social and teaching presence. The framework is focused on the support received by students and teachers in online learning, selection of content and the online learning environment, as the main factors that will determine the experience on online learning platforms. Similar to research on the classroom environment, the online learning environment considers the role of all stakeholders. MOOC (Massive Open Online Courses) reflects the need for thoughtful analysis and investigation of how to use the attributes and resources of ICTs with pedagogic principles and issues related to online learning environment [24, 25]. It includes the components: pedagogical, technological, interface design, evaluation, management, resource support as well as ethical, and institutional factors [25]. However, MOOCs focus extensively on resources, environment, rules and regulations, while little emphasis is given to user-centric aspects, such as the students' and teachers' needs, attitudes and motivation [26]. Nevertheless, emphasis on user-centric factors has been highlighted in a few studies [27–29]. The importance of learners needs along with the resources, support, and pedagogic components in the framework for higher learning have been considered [27]. Similarly, user-centred concerns were identified in a framework for the design and development of chatbot learning [28] and an M-learning framework [29]. It has been contended that User-Centered Design (UCD) [30] involves a series of phases, including knowing the users; analysing users' tasks and goals; developing usability requirements; prototype and design concept; usability testing; and repeating the stages for more features, as shown in Fig. 1.

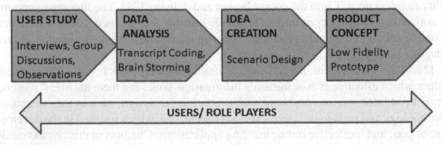

Fig. 1. User-centred design process [30]

As shown above, literature review reveals the little emphasis given to user-centred aspects in designing online learning applications, and more specifically chatbot learning. Hence, a user-centred framework for chatbot design is proposed in this section and shown in Fig. 2. The proposed framework can also be utilised for designing other online learning applications. The framework reflects that the primary focus of the design should be centred around the users and stakeholders of the applications, primarily including learners, teachers and educational institutions. This should be followed by consideration of the conceptual factors, such as pedagogic approaches, which later will need to be integrated with the technical platform. Finally, the appropriate policies and regulations surrounding chatbot learning must be identified and accordingly, the learning applications in this regard can be designed and developed. The layers of the proposed framework are explained as follows:

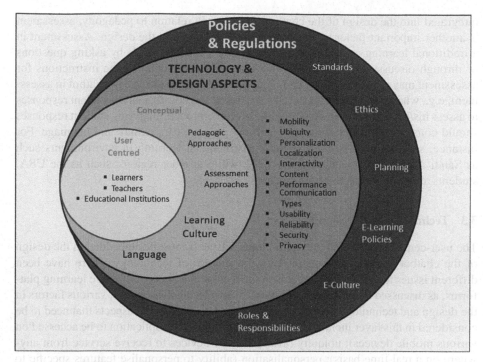

Fig. 2. User-centred framework for designing chatbot learning applications

3.1 User-Centred Factors

The core components of the framework include the primary users/stakeholders associated with the chatbot learning applications. Accordingly, the user-centred factors should focus on assessing the users' needs; attitudes; behavioural aspects, such as motivation (factors that enhance the user's engagement and intention to use) and learnability (factors that enhance the learning process); as well as the roles and responsibilities of learners, teachers, and institutions in an online learning environment. These user-centred aspects should be considered as the basic requirements for the design and development of chatbot learning applications.

3.2 Conceptual Factors

Learning is a process influenced by various factors, such as social, cultural, technological, pedagogical, personal, environmental ones. Hence, the design of chatbot learning applications should considering all the relevant factors of learning. Although, it may not be possible to develop an application that fits for all users [18], by considering and integrating all these conceptual factors, the chatbot design can be adjusted according to the needs of a wider audience. Accordingly, this layer includes the important conceptual factors that can influence the learning process: pedagogic approaches, assessment approaches, learning culture and language. Pedagogic approaches are amongst the most salient factors, as they define the process of learning and instructions, which need to be integrated into the design of the chatbots [27, 28]. In relation to pedagogy, assessment is another important factor which needs to be considered in the design. Assessment in a traditional learning environment in classrooms is usually made by asking questions or through discussions. However, with chatbot learning, defining the instructions for assessment may require complex coding to precisely define the role of chatbot in assessment, e.g., what kind of questions need to be asked and how to analyse student responses to assess his/her level of understanding. As aforementioned, analysing student responses should consider the wider context of learning process, e.g., culture and language. For instance, students may be used to more instructional learning in environments such as Saudi Arabia educational institutes [31], while in other regions, such as the USA, students are more interactive with teachers [32].

3.3 Technology and Design Factors

The user-centric aspects and the socio-cultural aspects must be embedded in the design of the chatbot learning application with the support of technology. There have been different issues identified with regards to the technical aspects of distance learning platforms, as discussed in the previous sections. Considering these issues, various factors in the design and technology layer are identified and proposed. The aspects that need to be considered in this layer include mobility (the ability of the application to be accessed on various mobile devices); ubiquity (availability of devices to receive service from anywhere on a real-time basis); personalisation (ability to personalise features specific to individual users); localisation (according to the learner's culture and needs in a region); interactivity (the interface for communication between the chatbot and learners); content (the content on the application measured with completeness, accuracy and sustainability); performance (speed, efficiency, and effectiveness); communication type (ways of communicating, like messaging, messenger etc.); usability (ease of use, interface, enjoyability, learnability); reliability (how reliable the application is); as well as security and privacy (data protection).

3.4 Policies and Regulations

The outermost layer covers the factors in the wider context, which may include other stakeholders, such as governments and regulatory organisations. It also pertains to the policies and regulations in relation to distance learning along with the appropriate delivery approaches, including chatbot learning. Standards relating to distance learning is one of the important aspects in this context, as most of those being utilised would appear to be the derivatives of the standards for conventional classroom teaching [7], which thus need to be revised and updated. Moreover, ethical implications in relation to teaching, assessment, and various other learning and teaching processes have been raised [33]. To respond to the previously-mentioned points, clear ethical guidelines for distance learning need to be formulated and integrated into the design of chatbot learning applications. Further, other aspects, such as planning [34], E-learning policies [35], E-culture [36], roles and responsibilities [37] must be clearly defined and deployed in the design of chatbot learning applications.

4   User-Centric Design and the Development Methodology

This section presents the application development methodology for chatbot learning as depicted in Fig. 3, which integrates the user-centric design approach specified in the previous section. Unlike stand-alone applications, chatbot learning applications may require frequent updates depending on changes in curriculum, education policies as well as shifts in institutional and learner requirements.

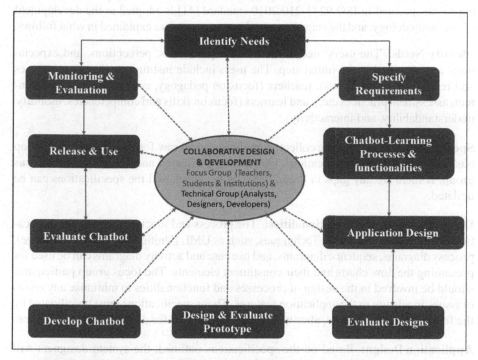

Fig. 3. User-centred methodology for developing chatbot learning applications

A collaborative and iterative development methodology is proposed to minimise the risk of failure. The methodological considerations and process are explained in the following sections.

4.1   Focus Groups

Focus groups should include the actual users of the chatbot learning application. They are considered to be a critical resource for gathering information about the requirements and content for developing the applications [38]. Gathering this data from focus groups can be a complex task, as there is a need to collect different types of information relating to usability and design aspects; content/course/curriculum; pedagogic approaches; assessment aspects etc. Hence, non-statistical methods, such as observations of classroom teaching and assessment approaches, interviews and discussions are recommended to be used in focus group settings [39].

4.2 Collaborative Approach

As explained previously, a collaborative development methodology is considered, where all the users, including teachers, learners and institutions, are actively involved in providing requirements, validating and evaluating these as well as setting the business, design and software specifications [40]. An iterative/agile approach is used in the development methodology, thus acknowledging the need for frequent updates and changes with respect to content, design, pedagogy, and support. Accordingly, the user-centric approach specified in ISO 9241-210:2010 standard [41] is adopted in the development of the methodology, and the stages involved in the process are explained in what follows.

Identify Needs: The users' needs, attitudes, requirements, perceptions, and expectations are identified in the initial step. The users include institutions (focus on policies and regulation requirements); teachers (focus on pedagogy, course structure and content, assessment practices etc.); and learners (focus on skills and competencies, usability, understandability, and interactivity).

Specify Requirements: The collected requirements in raw format are used to develop business requirement specifications, which can be assessed and validated by the focus group. If there are any gaps in these, they can be added, and the specifications can be updated.

Define Processes and Functionalities: The process and functionalities of the application are defined in this stage. Techniques, such as UML (Unified Modelling Language), process diagrams, sequence diagrams, and use case and activity diagrams can be used for presenting the flow charts and their constituent elements. The focus group participants should be involved in the design of processes and functionalities to minimise any errors or issues in relation to the application features. These specifications must be validated by the focus group participants, after which they can be used for designing the application.

Application Design: Based on the specifications outlined, the system designers will design the chatbot learning application. High-level designs related to overall processes and low-level designs related to specific component in each process should be provided.

Evaluate Designs: Both the high-level and low-level designs will be reviewed and validated by the focus group participants, and accordingly, any issues identified will be addressed at this stage.

Design and Evaluate Prototype: A prototype can be considered as the blueprint of actual application. Based on the design specification, a protype application will be developed, which is reviewed and validated by the focus group participants. This consists of protype system testing, where the users identify various issues relating to functions and features, design, content, and any other factors. Accordingly, if any changes or issues are identified by the focus group, they are addressed before proceeding to the next stage.

Develop Chatbot: After protype testing, the actual chatbot learning application will be created by the developers, according to the updated prototype models.

Evaluate Chatbots: Both system testers (system testing) and focus group participants (User Acceptance Testing) are involved in testing the application with both types of testing needing to be passed. Any errors identified at this stage will be addressed and accordingly, the application will be updated.

Release and Use: The chatbot learning application will be ready for use by the learners, teachers, and institutions. Teachers will update the content in the applications, while institutions may structure the curriculum, and other E-policies and students will continue with the learning process.

Monitoring and Evaluation: Any issues arising when using the application in real settings will need to be monitored and accordingly addressed. In the case of curriculum changes, significant course updates or introducing a new pedagogy, which are considered to be major changes; the development process is started again from the first stage of needs identification.

5 Conclusion

Chatbot learning, as discussed in this paper, has the potential to revolutionise online learning, with the integration of advanced technologies, such as NLP, AI, ML, DP etc. However, there are some issues that have been identified in relation to the current online learning tools, which relate to socio-cultural, design, technical, and usability aspects, thus affecting the large-scale implementation of such online learning tools. In addition, whilst the design frameworks for online learning have focused on certain aspects, there has been a lack of research in relation to designing a comprehensive user-centric framework. To address this shortcoming, a user-centric framework for designing chatbot learning applications has been proposed that addresses the limitations and issues identified in literature. In addition, according to the context of learning, there are various stakeholders, processes and regulations that must be considered. Consequently, the system development process is not effective in this context and may result in errors or even failure. To address this, an agile/iterative user-centric methodology has been proposed for developing chatbot learning applications. In addition, the proposed design methodology can also be used for developing other online learning applications. In this context, the authors' future work will be focused on using the proposed user-centric design framework and development methodology for designing a chatbot application for pregnant women to provide antenatal care (awareness, diagnosis, medicine reminder etc.). This will allow for assessment of the applicability of the proposed framework and methodology to a specific medical context, rather than education in general.

References

1. Rodriguez, R.: Time to fix American education with race-for-space resolve. The Harvard Gazette. https://news.harvard.edu/gazette/story/2020/04/the-pandemics-impact-on-edu cation/. Accessed 10 June 2020

2. UNESCO: Education: from disruption to recovery. https://en.unesco.org/covid19/education response. Accessed 10 June 2020
3. UNESCO: Education response to COVID-19 in the Caribbean. https://en.unesco.org/covid19/educationresponse/solutions. Accessed 10 June 2020
4. de Wit, E., van Doremalen, N., Falzarano, D., Munster, V.: SARS and MERS: recent insights into emerging coronaviruses. Nat. Rev. Microbiol. **14**(8), 523–534 (2016). https://doi.org/10.1038/nrmicro.2016.81
5. Statista, Mobile internet usage worldwide - statistics & facts. https://www.statista.com/topics/779/mobile-internet/. Accessed 10 June 2020
6. Raftree, L., Martin, N.: What's Holding Back Mobile Phones for Education?. Stanford Social Innovation Review (2013)
7. Sharples, M.: The design of personal mobile technologies for lifelong learning. Comput. Educ. **34**(3–4), 177–193 (2013)
8. Ken, M.: Low-key m-learning: a realistic introduction of m-learning to developing countries. In: Conference on Understanding, Learning in the Mobile Age, Budapest, Hungary (2016). https://doi.org/10.13140/rg.2.1.1032.4962
9. Brandtzaeg, P.B., Følstad, A.: Why people use chatbots. In: Kompatsiaris, I., et al. (eds.) INSCI 2017. LNCS, vol. 10673, pp. 377–392. Springer, Cham (2017). https://doi.org/10.1007/978-3-319-70284-1_30
10. Bahja, M.: Natural language processing applications in business. In: E-Business, Intech Open (2020). https://doi.org/10.5772/intechopen.92203
11. Winkler, R., Söllner, M.: Unleashing the potential of chatbots in education: a state-of-the-art analysis. In: Academy of Management Annual Meeting (AOM) - Chicago, USA (2018)
12. Benotti, L., Martínez, M., Schapachnik, F.: Engaging high school students using chatbots. In: Proceedings of the 2014 Conference on Innovation & Technology in Computer Science Education - Iticse (2014). https://doi.org/10.1145/2591708.2591728
13. Hammad, R., Odeh, M., Khan, Z.: eLEM: a novel e-learner experience model. Int. Arab J. Inf. Technol. **14**(4A), 586–597 (2017)
14. Hammad, R., Odeh, M., Khan, Z.: Towards a generalised e-learning business process model. In BUSTECH 2017, the Seventh International Conference on Business Intelligence and Technology (2017)
15. Cunningham-Nelson, S., Boles, W., Trouton, L., Margerison, E.: A review of Chatbots in education: practical steps forward. In: AAEE - Annual Conference of Australasian Association for Engineering Education (2019)
16. Simpson, O.: Supporting Students in Online Open and Distance Learning. Routledge, New York (2018)
17. Zhang, S., Liu, Q., Chen, W., Wang, Q., Huang, Z.: Interactive networks and social knowledge construction behavioral patterns in primary school teachers' online collaborative learning activities. Comput. Educ. **104**, 1–17 (2017). https://doi.org/10.1016/j.compedu.2016.10.011
18. Keengwe, J., Bhargava, M.: Mobile learning and integration of mobile technologies in education. Educ. Inf. Technol. **19**(4), 737–746 (2013). https://doi.org/10.1007/s10639-013-9250-3
19. Al-Emran, M., Elsherif, H., Shaalan, K.: Investigating attitudes towards the use of mobile learning in higher education. Comput. Hum. Behav. **56**, 93–102 (2016)
20. Yousafzai, A., Chang, V., Gani, A., Noor, R.: Multimedia augmented m-learning: issues, trends and open challenges. Int. J. Inf. Manage. **36**(5), 784–792 (2016)
21. Zaborova, E.N., Glazkova, I.G., Markova, T.L.: Distance learning: students' perspective. Sotsiologicheskie issledovaniya [Sociological Studies] **2**, 131–139 (2017)
22. Kearney, M., Burden, K., Rai, T.: Investigating teachers' adoption of signature mobile pedagogies. Comput. Educ. **80**, 48–57 (2015)

23. Fiock, H.S.: Designing a community of inquiry in online courses. Int. Rev. Res. Open Distrib. Learn. **21**(1), 135–153 (2020)
24. Kaplan, A.M., Haenlein, M.: Higher education and the digital revolution: about MOOCs, SPOCs, social media, and the Cookie Monster. Bus. Horiz. **59**(4), 441–450 (2016). https://doi.org/10.1016/j.bushor.2016.03.008
25. Doyle, R.: E-Learning Framework for Massive Open Online Courses (MOOCs). http://asianvu.com/bk/framework/?page_id=171. Accessed 11 June 2020
26. Ruipérez-Valiente, J., Muñoz-Merino, P., Leony, D., Delgado Kloos, C.: ALAS-KA: a learning analytics extension for better understanding the learning process in the Khan Academy platform. Comput. Hum. Behav. **47**, 139–148 (2015). https://doi.org/10.1016/j.chb.2014.07.002
27. Parker, J.: An authentic online community of learning framework for higher education: development process, Semantic Scholar (2016)
28. Bahja, M., Hammad, R., Hassouna, M.: Talk2Learn: a framework for chatbot learning. In: Scheffel, M., Broisin, J., Pammer-Schindler, V., Ioannou, A., Schneider, J. (eds.) EC-TEL 2019. LNCS, vol. 11722, pp. 582–586. Springer, Cham (2019). https://doi.org/10.1007/978-3-030-29736-7_44
29. Bahja, M., Hammad, R.: A user-centric design and pedagogical-based approach for mobile learning. In: Proceedings of the Tenth International Conference on Mobile, Hybrid and Online Learning, IARIA, Rome, Italy, pp. 100–105 (2018). ISBN 978-1-61208-619-4
30. Dirin, A., Nieminen, M.: Assessments of user centered design framework for M-learning application development. In: Zaphiris, P., Ioannou, A. (eds.) LCT 2015. LNCS, vol. 9192, pp. 62–74. Springer, Cham (2015). https://doi.org/10.1007/978-3-319-20609-7_7
31. Hamouda, A.: An exploration of causes of Saudi students' reluctance to participate in the English language classroom. Int. J. Engl. Lang. Educ. **1**(1), 17–34 (2013)
32. Howard, T.C.: Telling their side of the story: African-American students' perceptions of culturally relevant teaching. Urban Rev. **33**, 131–149 (2001). https://doi.org/10.1023/A:1010393224120
33. Kelly, A.E., Seppa, M.: Changing policies concerning student privacy and ethics in online education. Int. J. Inf. Educ. Technol. **6**(8), 652–655 (2016)
34. Ma, K., Liu, L., Sukhatme, G.: Informative planning and online learning with sparse Gaussian processes. In: IEEE International Conference on Robotics and Automation (ICRA) (2017). https://doi.org/10.1109/icra.2017.7989494
35. Welle-Strand, A., Thune, T.: E-learning policies, practices and challenges in two Norwegian organizations. Eval. Program Plan. **26**(2), 185–192 (2003). https://doi.org/10.1016/s0149-7189(03)00006-5
36. Shipunova, O.D., Berezovskaya, I.P., Murekyo, L.M., Evseev, V.V., Evseeva, L.I.: Personal intellectual potential in the e-culture conditions. Education **39**(40), 15 (2018)
37. Hung, M.: Teacher readiness for online learning: scale development and teacher perceptions. Comput. Educ. **94**, 120–133 (2016). https://doi.org/10.1016/j.compedu.2015.11.012
38. Krueger, R., Casey, M.: Focus Groups. Sage, London (2014)
39. Richey, R.C., Klein, J.D.: Design and development research. In: Spector, J.M., Merrill, M.D., Elen, J., Bishop, M.J. (eds.) Handbook of Research on Educational Communications and Technology, pp. 141–150. Springer, New York (2014). https://doi.org/10.1007/978-1-4614-3185-5_12
40. Eason, K.: User-centred design: for users or by users? Ergonomics **38**(8), 1667–1673 (1995)
41. International Organization for Standardization: ISO 9241-210:2010 - Ergonomics of human-system interaction – Part 210: Human-centred design for interactive systems, Iso.org (2010). https://www.iso.org/standard/52075.html. Accessed 11 June 2020

CollegeBot: A Conversational AI Approach to Help Students Navigate College

Mohinish Daswani, Kavina Desai, Mili Patel, Reeya Vani,
and Magdalini Eirinaki(✉)

Computer Engineering Department, San Jose State University,
San Jose, CA 95192, USA
{mohinishmaheshkumar.daswani,kavina.desai,mili.patel,reeya.vani,
magdalini.eirinaki}@sjsu.edu

Abstract. In an organization as big as a university that has many distinct departments and administrative bodies, it becomes almost impossible to easily obtain information online or by other means. Assistance over the phone or in-person is often limited to office hours and the information online is scattered through numerous (often nested) web pages, often independently administered and maintained by each sub-division. In this work, we present CollegeBot, a conversational AI agent that uses natural language processing and machine learning to assist visitors of a university's web site in easily locating information related to their queries. We discuss how we create the knowledge base by collecting and appropriately preprocessing information that is used to train the conversational agent for answering domain-specific questions. We have evaluated two different algorithms for training the conversational model for the chatbot, namely a semantic similarity model and a deep learning one leveraging Sequence-to-Sequence learning model. The proposed system is able to capture the user's intent and switch context appropriately. It also leverages the open source AIML chatbot ALICE to answer any generic (non domain-specific) questions. We present a proof-of-concept prototype for San Jose State University, to demonstrate how such an approach can be easily adopted by other academic institutions as well.

Keywords: Chatbot · Conversational AI · Natural language processing · Deep learning · Sequence-to-Sequence · AIML · Semantic sentence similarity.

1 Introduction

Conventional methods of communication with companies and other organizations like email, call centers, or automated voice response system, are often time-consuming, slow, and tedious. These communication methods might be restricted to certain working days or a certain number of hours per day. To address these

© Springer Nature Switzerland AG 2020
C. Stephanidis et al. (Eds.): HCII 2020, LNCS 12424, pp. 44–63, 2020.
https://doi.org/10.1007/978-3-030-60117-1_4

issues, companies and businesses have started to adopt automated systems like chatbots, voice assistants, and other conversational AI. Chatbots are software programs that can converse with humans and provide answers to their questions. About 67% of the clients utilized conversational AI for client assistance in the business a year ago [11]. The simplest form of chatbots that is employed by many companies are keyword-based and return predefined answers to a set of generic questions. Some more advanced ones include answers to domain-specific questions pertaining to particular tasks in the company. However, we rarely see such chatbots be used by universities and other academic institutions.

In an organization as big as a university that has many distinct departments and administrative bodies, it becomes almost impossible to easily obtain information online or by other means. Assistance over the phone or in person is often limited to office hours and the information online is scattered through numerous (often nested) web pages, independently administered and maintained by each sub-division. In this work, we present CollegeBot, a conversational AI agent that uses natural language processing (NLP) and machine learning (ML) to assist visitors of a university's web site in easily locating information related to their queries. Our approach caters to a necessity for domain engineering as it includes end-to-end implementation from data retrieval using a web crawler, to data preprocessing and real-time response generation to the end user's queries.

We considered and evaluated two different algorithms for training the conversational model for the chatbot. The RNN-based Sequence-to-Sequence (seq2seq) model is one of the state-of-the-art models used in the literature for AI chatbot systems [15]. The second model we evaluated is a semantic similarity model that follows a more traditional NLP approach. We evaluate the two approaches based on the computational efficiency in terms of time, and the correctness of the answers produced by them using the *BLEU* Score method. The proposed system is also able to capture the user's intent and switch context appropriately in a fast and efficient manner. In addition to the trained model used to respond to domain-specific questions, our prototype also uses ALICE bot, an open-sourced implementation of pre-coded AIML files to carry out informal conversation, usually used in the beginning of a chat.

In the rest of this paper, we discuss the technical design, preliminary experimental evaluation, and proof-of-concept prototype implementation of College-Bot. We provide a brief review of related work in Sect. 2 and discuss the system architecture in Sect. 3. We then explain how we created the system's knowledge base in Sect. 4 and discuss in detail the design and evaluation of the training algorithms in Sect. 5. Finally, we present some technical details of our prototype in Sect. 6 and conclude in Sect. 7.

2   Related Work

We can distinguish between two kinds of chatbots, one which is based on a set of rules and principles to be followed for a particular query, and another that is based on artificial intelligence (AI) systems that iteratively get smarter and more efficient. Two of the most popular open-sourced chatbots are ELIZA and ALICE. ALICE (Artificial Linguistic Internet Computer Entity) is one of the most popular and award-winning chatbots that primarily focuses on natural language understanding and pattern matching [2]. The famous pattern matching algorithm of ALICE is a simple depth-first search technique used to find the longest matching sequence and then generate an appropriate response based on the pattern matched. The underlying data structure that ALICE is built upon is AIML. AIML stands for Artificial Intelligence Markup Language and is an extension of the traditional XML (Extensible Markup Language). AIML was designed by the Alicebot open source community to empower individuals to include pattern information into chatbots [1]. In ALICE the core design of the chatbot engine and language knowledge model [2] are isolated. This offers us the chance to effortlessly introduce a newly designed language model on the top of the base system. On the contrary, ELIZA is built using more complicated rules and directions, that requires coming up with input transformation functions, output transformation functions, and complex keyword patterns that show input and output [2].

There exist several domain-specific chatbots. For instance, MamaBot is a conversational AI system built to help pregnant women, mother, children, and their families [13]. The authors outline three main aspects of building a chatbot architecture: intent identification and classification, entity recognition, and response generation. They use the open-source Microsoft Bot Framework which internally uses LUIS (Language Understanding Intelligent Service) as its cognitive service. Another example is the bank chatbot introduced in [4]. The authors discuss the process of applying NLP on the user input, using ML classification algorithm to identify the class it belongs to, and then finally applying cosine similarity between the input query and the questions of that same identified class.

Among the few chatbots related to college inquiries is UNIBOT [7]. The authors introduce a new algorithm for finding the relevant answer from the knowledge database. The database consists of a row that has all the questions and more than one row is allocated for the answers, as it is presumed that one question might map to multiple answers. The user input is fetc.hed, stopwords are removed, the keywords are extracted, and then it searches in the database using either pattern matching or comparing SQL regex. In [3] the authors leverage the implementation of ALICE chatbot as a domain-specific chatbot that can act as an information system for undergraduate students. They present three chatbots that have different knowledge repositories: BaseBot, the most basic implementation containing the AIML files, UFaqBot(Dom_eng), a domain engineered system designed with knowledge repository, and UFaqBot(rep), a hybrid system which is an amalgamation of basic dialog conversation and domain knowledge. This setup is very similar to our proposed system, that leverages ALICE for generic questions, includes a domain-specific chatbot engine, and switches between the two as needed. However our approach in the domain-specific chatbot differs from our CollegeBot.

As we are dealing with a domain-specific conversational AI system, a user will be asking the chatbot specific questions about a particular topic. Thus, entity extraction and context identification NLP techniques are also very important. Additionally, as input comes in free-form text, there can be more than one ways to pose the same question. The chatbot system should recognize such similarities. Depending on the query representation method, this can be done employing vector similarity metrics such as cosine similarity, which is what we use in our semantic similarity engine, or ontology-based metrics like Wu-Palmer similarity and path similarity, used in [5].

Neural networks have been recently introduced for dialogue generation in conversational AI agents. As described in [14], the Sequence-to-Sequence (seq2seq) model depends on the recurrent neural network (RNN) that takes in the input sentence one token at a time and in a similar way predicts the output sequence one token at a time. At the time of training the model, the correct output sequence is fed into the model, so that backpropagation can be performed to make the learning more accurate. Long sequences can be problematic for deep neural networks on the grounds that they necessitate the dimensionality of the input and output to be fixed. In [12] the authors talk about the Long Short-Term Memory (LSTM) approach that can tackle the basic seq2seq problems. The approach is to utilize one layer of LSTM to read the input sequence, compute a fixed-size vector representation of that input sequence, and use the other LSTM to extricate the output sequence from that vector representation. The approach most similar to ours is discussed in [8]. This paper discusses the design of a web assistant where the ML module is based on the RNN wherein the seq2seq model is fed the input sequence as multiple tokens and it further gives a proper arrangement of tokens as the output sequence.

There is a lot of research and studies conducted on chatbots, however, various challenges have also been identified in developing one. We researched these challenges to find a way to address them while developing our applications. Challenges include limited amount of training data, context modeling and context switching, emotion recognition, natural language processing, language specialization, speaker-listener specific modeling, and many more. A general rule for ML systems is that the more the training data, the better the model is. Chatbots, especially those relying on deep learning, need lots of training data for the machine to learn the chatting pattern and to create a model to correctly maintain a conversation about a topic. Moreover, a common challenge in NLP is learning and understanding the syntax. There can be multiple ways a question or statement be made. For example, "What's the weather?" can be asked as "Could you check the weather?" [9]. We explore how different approaches in designing the chatbot engine address the aforementioned issues.

3   System Architecture

Figure 1 shows the system architecture of CollegeBot. Chatbots need a *knowledge base* to generate appropriate responses to the user's queries. To gather data for our knowledge base we have used a web crawler. The data relating to the university is spread across several web pages and needs to be aggregated, filtered, grouped, and indexed. For our system prototype we collected most of the data from FAQs pages posted on various SJSU web pages for various topics such as admissions, international student and scholar services, courses offered, majors, and so on. The process is described in Sect. 4. However this selection could be expanded to cover more pages within a University.

The data is next fed to the *Preprocessor* module. In this module, we employ NLP techniques to bring the data in appropriate format for input to the *Training* module. This module is employed both in the back-end but also in the front-end part of our architecture, used to preprocess the questions of the end user prior to submitting it to the chatbot engine. The *Preprocessor* module, along with the *Training* and the *Engine* modules consist the core part of CollegeBot. They rely on NLP and ML to be able to decode a user's question and retrieve the most appropriate answers. We considered and evaluated two different algorithms for training the conversational model for the chatbot, namely a semantic similarity model and a seq2seq-based model, which we discuss in detail in Sect. 5.

In the front-end, the system checks whether the question is domain-specific or not. The system sends the domain-specific questions to the *Preprocessor* and subsequently the chatbot *Engine* module. The *Engine* then checks whether there exists a context for the sentence. If a context is found then it identifies the most similar question to the user query and returns the corresponding answer as the response. If the context is not found then it will check for the new context, append it, find the most similar question and return the corresponding answer as the response. The back-end then takes the response from the *Engine* and sends it to the front-end where it is displayed to the user, as shown in Fig. 2. Non domain-specific questions are handled by the *ALICE AIML* server. We discuss the technical details of the core modules of the CollegeBot prototype in more detail in Sect. 6.

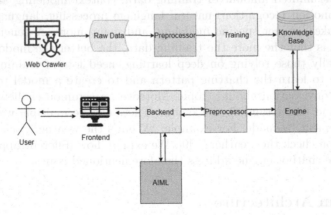

Fig. 1. CollegeBot system architecture

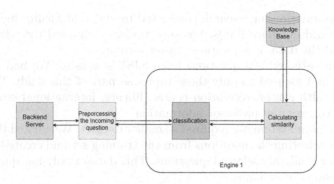

Fig. 2. Semantic sentence similarity Engine

4   Knowledge Base Creation

4.1   Data Collection

For creating the knowledge base for our proof-of-concept prototype we used the San Jose State University (SJSU) website[1]. We collected most of the data from the FAQs posted on the SJSU website for various topics such as admissions, international student and scholar services, courses offered, majors, and so on using a web crawler. We designed the web crawler to start from a particular page and collect all the links present on that page. It then filters the list to return the links which point to the SJSU website. The crawler then visits those pages, parses each page, and creates a list of python dictionaries containing questions, answers, relevant URLs, and the context/category of the question. It identifies all the questions and answers using regex for pattern matching. It also identifies any hyperlinks present in the answers and also adds them to the python dictionary. As shown in Fig. 3 the answer contains the hyperlink "Registrar" which points to the URL for the SJSU office of the registrar. The web crawler identifies this URL in the answer and adds it to the dictionary of FAQs. The crawler also captures the context for which the FAQs are posted and also adds it to the python dictionary. When the web crawler starts parsing a new page for FAQs it takes the title of the page as the context for all the FAQs present in that page. In the example of Fig. 3 the context is "GAPE" (Graduate Admissions and Program Evaluations) which was taken from the title of that page. An example of the python dictionary created for each FAQs is also shown in Fig. 3. This dictionary is then added to the python list which is then stored in a comma-separated file once the entire page is parsed. This process is repeated again for the next link.

During the process, the web crawler can encounter some pages where it is not able to parse the data. We made a list of all those links and changed the regex for identifying FAQs for those links. Additionally, some of the topics such

---

[1] http://www.sjsu.edu.

as faculty information, or research conducted by different faculty members and departments did not have FAQs. For such topics, we visited the SJSU website and collected the data in a question-answer format.

In all, we gathered 923 questions from SJSU's website. We had shortlisted some topics and focused on only those topics as part of this study. We covered topics like health center, recreation center, library, international students cell, admissions, courses and professor information.

For testing our system, we required a smaller dataset. We created this dataset by randomly selecting the questions from the training set and created variations of a few other randomly selected questions. This dataset only has questions and expected answers as columns.

Q. Can I take undergraduate classes as a graduate student?
A. Yes, graduate students may take undergraduate classes. However, lower division (freshman and sophomore) courses numbered 1-99 cannot be used for graduate degree credit and are not included in the GPA computation. For additional assistance and inquires about registration in undergraduate classes, please visit the _Registrar_.

Regex for identifying question: Q\.(.*?)
Regex for identifying answer:
(.*?)
Regex for identifying links in answer: <a\s+(?:[^>]*?\s+)?href="([^"]*")

Dictionary created:
{'question': 'Can I take undergraduate classes as a graduate student?', 'answer': 'Yes, graduate students may take undergraduate classes. However, lower division (freshman and sophomore) courses numbered 1-99 cannot be used for graduate degree credit and are not included in the GPA computation. For additional assistance and inquires about registration in undergraduate classes, please visit the Registrar.', 'link': 'https://www.sjsu.edu/registrar/', 'context': 'gape'}

Fig. 3. Example for converting text to python dictionary using regex for pattern matching

5 Training Algorithms

For training our model, we considered two options, a purely NLP-based one, and a deep learning one. We discuss both, as well as the preprocessing steps applicable to each one in detail here.

5.1 Semantic Similarity Model

If we break down the logic of a chatbot in simple terms, it comes down to recognizing if a similar kind of question exists in our data repository or not. However, there can be more than one ways of posing a question as shown in Fig. 4. While humans can easily understand which sentences mean the same thing and which sentences are totally different, this is not as straightforward for a conversational agent like a chatbot. However, the system should recognize such similar input queries and generate the appropriate response for that. As shown in Fig. 4, the two queries "What is the last date to enroll?" and "When is the

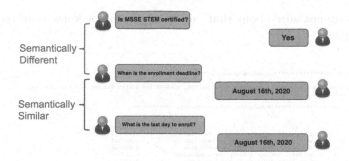

Fig. 4. Semantic similarity example

enrollment deadline?" have the same meaning (and there might be even more ways of posing the same question).

When employing this model, the system finds semantic sentence similarity. To do this, all questions in the knowledge base need to be first preprocessed, through stemming and lemmatization. We also created a dictionary for storing all the synonyms and we replaced all the similar words with the standard abbreviations across the whole dataset (e.g. words like "United States", "United States of America", "America", "USA" will be replaced by a common synonym "US" everywhere in the sentence). As we are dealing with a domain-specific conversational AI system, a user will be asking specific questions about a particular topic. Thus, entity extraction and context identification NLP techniques are also important.

In order to identify relevant questions in the knowledge base, even when not phrased identically by the end user, we calculate a similarity score between the (preprocessed) user query and the queries stored in the knowledge base. The similarity is calculated using word vectors with the help of the word2vec algorithm. This algorithm employs multi-layered neural network structure, which is modelled to form linguistic contexts of words. The algorithm takes as input a text corpus and gives a vector space as the output. There is a unique vector assigned in the space for each different word in the corpus. Thus the comparison is essentially done between these word vectors by calculating their cosine similarity and then a score between 0 to 1 is returned as the similarity score for comparison between two sentences.

Therefore, for each incoming query, the system sorts all questions in the knowledge base in descending order of similarity. A threshold for the similarity score is preset and if the highest similarity score from the matched question is greater than the decided threshold, then the corresponding answer to that question is returned to the end user. An example of the top-10 relevant questions to a user query is shown in Fig. 5. It can be observed that the incoming question was identified as almost 90% similar to the first question in the list. On the other hand, if there is no proper match between the incoming question and any of the questions from the dataset, we set a fallback mechanism and a generic response such as "I am not sure about that" or "Sorry, I do not know that" is returned as the response.

```
***************************** Incoming question *****************************

 I had enrolled in an upper division course at other CSU, however the course did not turn out that well, so what form
 should I use

***************************** Similarity *****************************

                                         Questions  Similarity score
0  I took an upper division GE course at another CSU, but...   0.895677
1  Can I take a course from my technology major (MIS, CMP...   0.864332
2  I have already published a master's thesis, a PhD diss...   0.856760
3          As a ChAD student, how can I apply for graduation?  0.853763
4  I completed all of my lower division GE and I have pas...   0.830573
5  I took an American Institutions (US 1, US 2, US3) cour...   0.824764
6  I tried to enroll in a class, but the enrollment (regi...   0.821910
7  I tried to enroll in a class, but the enrollment (regi...   0.821910
8  I tried to enroll in a class, but the enrollment (regi...   0.821910
9  Do I need to sign up for utilities, or internet service?   0.819263
```

Fig. 5. Implementation of semantic sentence similarity

Although this approach yields high accuracy, it is inefficient in terms of time taken to generate the response, as the system needs to preprocess and calculate, in real-time, the similarity between the user query and all questions in the system's knowledge base. Additionally, such approach does not take into consideration the context, i.e. previous questions the user might have asked. Humans can interpret the context easily and the conversations never break. However, sometimes when a user is interacting with an AI chatbot, they may not explicitly mention the context in every question, and thus the bot may not give an appropriate, context-specific response. This results in either a wrong answer or the bot saying that it doesn't know the answer, even though the bot was trained to have the answer for that specific question as well. See for example the questions in Fig. 6. The user first asks about Open University and the response by the bot is accurate. The user follows up asking about the application deadline (implying this applies to Open University admissions), but the bot cannot interpret that. So, it returns the answer for which it found the maximum similarity for the question resulting in a contextually wrong answer.

To overcome this problem, we categorized the knowledge base into a few specific categories or contexts, such as Open University, GAPE (Graduate Admissions & Program Evaluations), MSSE (Master of Science in Software Engineering), ISSS (International Student & Scholar Services), and so on. Whenever a

Question (User)	Response (*CollegeBot*)
What is an Open University?	"Open University," or "Continuing Education" at SJSU allows individuals that are not registered in a degree program to take university courses. There are a number of restrictions.
What is the application deadline?	University Graduate admission deadlines are listed at http://www.sjsu.edu/gape/prospective_students/deadlines/

Fig. 6. Sequence of questions and responses without context

question is asked, the query is preprocessed reducing every noun in the question to a specific word from the dictionary and saving it in the user's browser environment. When a question follows without a context, the bot assumes that the user is referring to the previous context and the saved context is appended to the query. Once the context is identified, the similarity score is calculated only for the questions pertaining to this context, thus reducing the time to return the accurate response as well. This results in context-specific answers, as shown in Fig. 7. We observe that the response returned by the bot for the same question about the application deadline is now pertaining to Open University.

Question (User)	Response (*CollegeBot*)
What is the Open University?	"Open University," or "Continuing Education" at SJSU allows individuals that are not registered in a degree program to take university courses. There are a number of restrictions.
What is the application deadline?	Please see the registration website for Open University: https://www.sjsu.edu/openuniversity/registration/

Fig. 7. Sequence of questions and responses with context

One shortcoming of this methodology is that it plainly depends on the similarity score calculated between the sentences. This algorithm used word vectors to find the similarity between sentences but it would not be able to link different synonyms. For example "What is the deadline" and "What is the last date" includes two different ways implying the word deadline, however these words would have different representations in the form of word vectors. Thus the similarity score between these kind of sentences would not be very high.

5.2   Seq2seq Model

In this model, we leverage deep neural networks (DNNs) by employing the seq2seq algorithm. DNNs [12] are strong models which can achieve incredible performance on learning difficult and complex tasks such as speech recognition or object detection. However such networks can be only be applied to use cases or problems with input parameters and target variables encoded in a fixed dimensionality. However this does not apply in cases when the text sequence length is unknown at the beginning. Answering free-form user questions falls under this category, as the questions (and answers) are modelled as a sequence of words of variable length. Our approach incorporates a multi-layered LSTM (Long Short-Term Memory), a modified version of Recurrent Neural Network (RNN), that maps the given input sequence to a vector or matrix with a fixed dimension. The next step of the LSTM decodes back the input sequence from the vector or matrix and produces the output.

As a part of preparing the data file to be fed to the algorithm, we manually append a delimiter between the question and the answer so that the algorithm can distinguish between those two and store them as a vector pair. Also, the algorithm takes care of removing unnecessary special characters and symbols. We first pre-process the data by tokenizing the sentences and converting the words into numbers that uniquely identify them. These tokens are stored into a vocabulary so that we can convert them back to words. After processing the data, the algorithm converts the question and answer pair into word vectors and then performs the encoding and decoding on those vectors. An example is shown in Fig. 8.

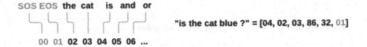

SOS EOS the cat is and or

"is the cat blue ?" = [04, 02, 03, 86, 32, 01]

00 01 02 03 04 05 06 ...

Fig. 8. Tokenizing a sentence [10]

The tokenized number form of the sentences is sent as a batch to the encoders. The batch is of a fixed size and the length of the sentences in each batch is also fixed. To maintain the size of sentences, padding is added. The sentences are also padded with a token at the beginning to identify the start of the sentence and a token is appended at the end of the sentence to identify the end of the token. An example of this is shown in Fig. 9.

The matrix or tensor thus formed is transposed to be sent to the RNN. The encoder takes the input from the tensor till an end of the sentence is encountered and a vector representation called context vector is the output. The tokens which are semantically closer are grouped together in the n-dimensional point which are passed into the next layer, bi-directional Gated Recurrent Unit (GRU). GRU is essentially a modified and updated version of a traditional LSTM approach which proves to be computationally less costly than LSTM. The GRU then generates a new tensor by reading the input tokens in forward order in the first layer of GRU and in reverse order in the second layer.

The information is passed from the encoder to the decoder in the form of a context vector. Certain words in the input sequence are of greater importance than the other words and thus more attention needs to be given to them. For

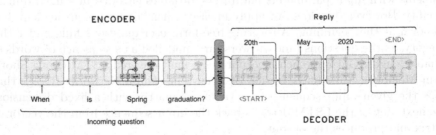

Fig. 9. Example of the encoder decoder architecture

that purpose, we use the Luong Attention layer mechanism. A weighted sum of all the encoder outputs is calculated and then that computed context vector is used in calculating the hidden state of the decoder. Thus, the output of the decoder depends on three things: decoder output from previous step, the hidden vector of the decoder, and the context vector computed from the attention layer.

The next step is to train the model. This step consists of setting the right value of the hyper-parameters such as number of iterations, teacher forcing rate, learning rate and so on. The training time depends on the size of the data and the number of epochs. After the training process is completed, the model reads the user input, evaluates it and finds the relevant answer with the help of the model trained earlier. Thus, this approach gives a faster reply on the fly, but it takes a very long time for the model to train.

Due to limited input data, the model does not converge quickly during training. One way to ensure better convergence is to provide the expected answer to the decoder instead of using the decoder's predicted value. This mechanism is called "Teacher forcing". Another shortcoming we encountered during the implementation of this model is that it fails when a word outside the vocabulary is given. When a question contains an unrecognized word, it does not generate an answer. The model should ignore the unrecognized word and try to find an answer. This shortcoming is due to the limited size of the data and can be overcome with a rich training dataset.

5.3   Evaluation

We evaluated the two training models in terms of their response time and accuracy. For testing response time, we provided the same queries to both the models to calculate the time it takes for them to return an output. Half of the test queries were identical to some included in the training data (i.e. the knowledge base) and the other half were rephrased questions. We also wanted to evaluate the accuracy of the model as a function of the number of the correct answers predicted for the input queries. We selected a subset of queries to evaluate the models' accuracy. Half of the queries were rephrased questions, while the other half included only a few keywords. We discuss our results and findings in what follows.

We used *BLEU* (Bilingual Evaluation Understudy) score to evaluate the accuracy of responses for both the models. *BLEU* score is a metric to compare the similarity between a generated statement to a reference statement. The score metric ranges from 0.0 to 1.0 where 0 means no similarity and 1 means perfect match. It is defined as follows [6]:

$$BLEU = BP * exp(\sum_{n=1}^{N} w_n \log p_n)$$

$$BP = \begin{cases} 1 & \text{if } c > r \\ e^{(1-r/c)} & \text{if } c \leq r \end{cases} \qquad (1) \\ (2)$$

where c denotes the candidate sentence length and r the reference length. In essence, the score takes a weighted geometric mean of the logs of n-gram precisions up to some length (usually 4), adding a penalty for too-short predictions.

We used "sentence_bleu" from Python's NLTK library[2] to measure the correctness of the answer generated by both the models. We wrote a script to measure the *BLEU* score of the test data with various threshold values to determine the correctness of the model. *BLEU* Score gives us results between 0 and 1. Additionally we are measuring the time taken by both the models to respond to a user query. Thus, the average time taken by the semantic similarity model was 2.03 s and that for the seq2seq model was 0.41 s. However, the training time for the seq2seq model was considerably higher (and, in some setups with a larger input dataset, the system would not converge even after thousands of iterations).

Semantic Similarity Model. We measured the accuracy of the semantic similarity model by using the true positive values and the size of the dataset. Our preliminary findings after implementing the Semantic Similarity approach was that the loss of context in the conversations breaks the dialogue or renders the responses meaningless. Moreover without having a category to search for, the model has to look for answers in the entire dataset, which increased the complexity of the solution and time to return an answer. Also, we noticed that nouns in a question can have multiple synonyms which the users can use. And if these are not mapped to the dataset then the responses would be inaccurate.

To overcome all these limitations, we devised a few steps of preprocessing. We created a dictionary for the most common nouns in the datasets and added all the synonyms the users might use. As part of the preprocessing step, when the user query comes the model, the preprocessor will replace all the nouns in the question with dedicated nouns in the dataset as mapped by the dictionaries. We added the categories for each question in the dataset and similarly saved the context of the incoming query in the user's environment to keep the model context-aware in the conversation. The bot would now search for the responses in that specific category the user is referring to. This drastically reduced the computation time for the model. So, we concluded that more the categories we divide the dataset into, the faster the processing becomes. As shown in Fig. 10, the accuracy of the model was persistently over 90% for various sizes of input query size.

Seq2seq-Based Model. The answer generated by the algorithm is termed as actual answer and the correct answer is termed as expected answer. We measure the *BLEU* score of these two and if the score is above the threshold value, we increase the number of true positive answers. We measure the score for each pair of the expected and actual answers over the test data set. We finally calculate the number of correct answers based on our threshold and find the accuracy percentage using the total test data set size and the true positive answer values.

---

[2] https://www.nltk.org/_modules/nltk/translate/bleu_score.html.

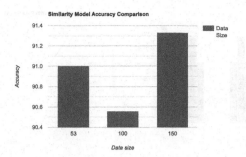

Fig. 10. Semantic similarity: performance in various sized data sets

To find the balance between the number of iterations and the data size where the model would converge, we trained various models of same data size and varying number of iterations. We gathered results for the test data for threshold values of 0.7, 0.75 and 0.8 for the seq2seq model, for various numbers of queries. We also measured the decrease in loss using "maskedNLLLoss" while increasing the number of iterations to see how the dataset is modeled to work with the algorithm. The results, for various test data sizes and number of iterations are shown in Figs. 11, 12, 13, 14, 15 and 16. We observe that the optimal hyperparameters vary depending on the dataset size, but we can achieve 80% or higher *BLEU* score accuracy for the optimal parameters for each dataset.

We observed that, since the seq2seq model generates its vocabulary from the training dataset, it is unable to recognize the word that is outside of its vocabulary. So, one limitation of seq2seq model is that it will not provide an answer when a word outside of its vocabulary is used to ask a question. If we are limiting the vocabulary by limiting the dataset, then the chances of the model not recognizing a new word increases by default due to the nature of the algorithm. Thus, to extract the best possible result of seq2seq model, we need to train the model for appropriate number of epochs and feed in with a large enough dataset such that the vocabulary of the model can be formed properly. On the other hand, a larger corpus of training questions requires a larger number of iterations to converge and increases the computational complexity of the model.

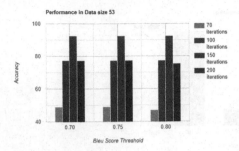

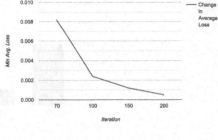

Fig. 11. Seq2Seq: performance in dataset of size 53

Fig. 12. Seq2Seq: average Loss with Data size 53

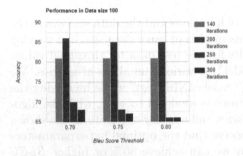

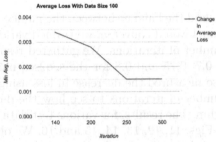

Fig. 13. Seq2Seq: performance in dataset of size 100

Fig. 14. Seq2Seq: average Loss with data size 100

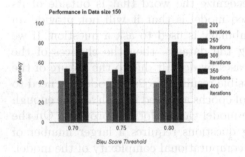

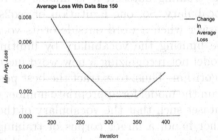

Fig. 15. Seq2Seq: performance in dataset of size 150

Fig. 16. Seq2Seq: average Loss with data size 150

6 CollegeBot Prototype

Figure 1 shows the system architecture of the CollegeBot prototype. After experimenting with both training models, we decided to implement the semantic similarity model in our proof-of-concept prototype. We have created a distributed architecture using React.js as frontend server, Java server for AIML, and Python Flask servers in the backend. The Python Flask servers in the backend are responsible only for minor tasks, thus creating a micro-service architecture.

Figure 17 explains the flow of this system. The frontend takes the user input and sends it to the Python Flask *server1* where it checks whether the question is a domain-specific question. If it is a domain-specific question it sends the question to Python *server2* for query processing. This server preprocesses the input question with techniques such as lemmatization and stemming and sends the response back to *server1*. The *server1* then sends the received string to the semantic similarity engine on *server3*. The engine then checks whether there exists a context for the sentence. If a context is found then it finds the most similar question to the user input and returns the corresponding answer as the response. If the context is not found then it will check for the new context, append it, find the most similar question and return the corresponding answer as the response. The backend then takes the response from the engine and sends it to the frontend where it is displayed to the users. If the question was not domain-specific then the server sends the question to the AIML server that sends a response back to *server1*, that forwards the response to the frontend. A snapshot of the UI of the CollegeBot prototype is shown in Fig. 18.

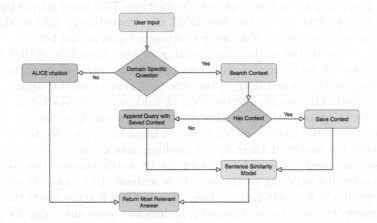

Fig. 17. CollegeBot Q&A process flow

6.1 AIML Engine

We have integrated the open-sourced ALICE chatbot [1] as part of our system prototype, to handle generic, non-domain-specific questions. ALICE has in-built coded AIML files which have generic patterns and templates to serve basic user questions such as "Hi", "How are you", "What time is it", and so on. ALICE maintains the data in the AIML (Artificial Intelligence Markup Language) format which is an extension of the traditional XML format. This format has been implemented by many other chatbots as well because it very convenient to maintain the data in such kind of templates and patterns. AIML is built of data objects known as the AIML objects which portrays the behavior of intelligent systems. It comprises of several units/tags which are termed as topics and categories in the AIML terminology. A category can be understood as an event which comprises of patterns, that are specific user inputs, and templates, which are the corresponding answers to those patterns.

Program AB is a readily available implementation of the Alicebot. We have used the basic Java implementation of Program AB.[3] After building Program AB as a Maven project, we can chat with the system. There are multiple AIML files already present in the program which lets the system answer all the generic questions. Whenever a new input query comes, a pattern matching algorithm is applied across all the AIML files present and the pattern that has the highest match is identified and its corresponding answer is send out as the response.

We should note at this point that we also ran some tests after developing our own AIML files. We used another open-source platform for testing the manually written AIML files. A lot of wildcard characters can be used to yield better results. Also, AIML tags such as srai help in writing the same question in different ways and we can point all those questions to one answer. This way we can capture different types of ways a user can pose a question. This open source platform provides a convenient way to test the AIML files immediately after writing and it gives a nice experience as if we were chatting with an actual bot.

However, one of the major shortcomings of this approach is that it is a very basic way of retrieving answers and there is no scope of performing any preprocesing on the stored data. Thus, the performance of this approach can be very limited. The use of different kind of wildcards and AIML tags are not sufficient for building a proper intelligent chatbot system. Also, the text written in pattern tag should exactly match with the incoming query. So, the incoming query would not match if there is any spelling mistake made by the user or if the user has used completely different set of words to pose that question. AIML expects the ordering of the text in a sentence to be exactly similar to the text written in the pattern tag. Thus, this method is quite restrictive about how it expects the text to be. Moreover, it does not leave any scope for proper preprocessing step before passing the query as an input. For all these reasons, we decided to go with the semantic similarity engine to handle domain-specific questions.

6.2   Semantic Similarity Engine

The incoming query is passed as an input to the system to perform general preprocessing on it, as discussed in detail in Sect. 5.1. Using the custom-made dictionary of synonyms, the system checks and replaces all query words with their corresponding synonym abbreviations. The sentence is then stemmed using a Porter Stemmer[4] before being sent to the semantic similarity chatbot engine.

---

[3] https://code.google.com/archive/p/program-ab/downloads.
[4] https://www.nltk.org/api/nltk.stem.html#module-nltk.stem.porter.

The engine, depicted in Fig. 2, is the part where we are finding the semantic sentence similarity between the sentences. We used Python's spacy library[5] which uses word2vec to create word vectors and calculate the similarity score (using cosine similarity). We compute a similarity score between the incoming query and all the questions present in the data repository. As mentioned in Sect. 5.1, as soon as the query hits the similarity model, the algorithm tries to identify a context. If it does not already have a context, then it finds a context and associates it with that question. If there already is a context associated, then the model proceeds to retrieve the most similar question classified under that context from the knowledge base, and returns the respective answer. If the model was not able to find a question from the database having the similarity score above the threshold, then that existing context is disassociated from the incoming query. Further, the incoming query, now having no context, is compared for similarity for all the questions in the database and the most generic answer is written. For subsequent questions, the model already knows what context the user is referring to so the search is narrowed down and the performance is improved.

Fig. 18. SJSU CollegeBot UI

7   Conclusions

In this work we present CollegeBot, a conversational chatbot that employs information retrieval, natural language processing, and machine learning, to assist students in navigating the website of a university. We compare and evaluate two training models, and conclude for a small-sized dataset the semantic similarity model outperforms the seq2seq model in terms of accuracy. The seq2seq model is faster than the semantic similarity model, however it does not converge

---

[5] https://spacy.io/usage/vectors-similarity.

fast for a small-sized dataset and needs an appropriate number of iterations to train the model properly. In such cases, where the training dataset is relatively small, the semantic similarity model is a better choice. We also introduce the notion of context. CollegeBot can maintain context in a user session and retrieve the appropriate answers to subsequent, semantically-related questions. We also present our proof-of-concept prototype of CollegeBot for San Jose State University, demonstrating how such an approach could easily be implemented for other academic institutions and beyond. As part of our future work, we plan to explore leveraging libraries like Wordnet to automatically map nouns to their synonyms existing in our knowledge base. This will let the model map new incoming words to the questions in the datasets and return accurate results. Similarly, we plan to explore how additional similarity metrics, like Wu-Palmer, could be leveraged to improve the accuracy of the system.

References

1. Abushawar, B., Atwell, E.: ALICE Chatbot: Trials and Outputs: Computación y Sistemas **19**(4) (2005). https://doi.org/10.13053/cys-19-4-2326
2. Bani, B., Singh, A.: College enquiry chatbot using A.L.I.C.E. Int. J. New Technol. Res. (IJNTR) **3**(1), 64–65 (2017)
3. Ghose, S., Barua, J.: Toward the implementation of a topic specific dialogue based natural language chatbot as an undergraduate advisor. In: International Conference on Informatics. Electronics and Vision (ICIEV), pp. 1–5. IEEE, Dhaka (2013)
4. Kulkarni, C., Bhavsar, A., Pingale, S., Kumbhar, S.: BANK CHAT BOT - an intelligent assistant system using NLP and machine learning. Int. Res. J. Eng. Technol. **4**(5) (2017)
5. Lalwani, T., Bhalotia, S., Pal, A., Bisen, S., Rathod, V.: Implementation of a chat bot system using AI and NLP. Int. J. Innov. Res. Comput. Sci. Technol. (IJIRCST) **6**, 26–30 (2018). https://doi.org/10.21276/ijircst.2018.6.3.2
6. Papineni, K., Roukos, S., Ward, T., Zhu, W.: BLEU: a method for automatic evaluation of machine translation. In: Proceedings of the 40th Annual Meeting on Association for Computational Linguistics (ACL 2002), pp. 311–318 (2002). https://doi.org/10.3115/1073083.1073135
7. Patel, N., Parikh, D., Patel, D., Patel, R.:AI and web based human-like interactive university chatbot (UNIBOT). In: 3rd International conference on Electronics, Communication and Aerospace Technology (ICECA), pp. 148–150, India (2019)
8. Prajwal, S., Mamatha, G., Ravi, P., Manoj, D., Joisa, S.: Universal semantic web assistant based on sequence to sequence model and natural language understanding. In: 9th International Conference on Advances in Computing and Communication (ICACC), pp. 110–115 (2019). https://doi.org/10.1109/ICACC48162.2019.8986173
9. Rahman, A., Mamun, A., Islam, A.: Programming challenges of chatbot: current and future prospective. In: 2017 IEEE Region 10 Humanitarian Technology Conference (R10-HTC), pp. 75–78, Dhaka, December 2017
10. Sandeep, S.: End to end chatbot using sequence to sequence architecture (2019). https://medium.com/swlh/end-to-end-chatbot-using-sequence-to-sequence-architecture-e24d137f9c78. Accessed 10 June 2019

11. Shukairy, A.: Chatbots in customer service - statistics and trends [infographic] (n.d.). www.invespcro.com/blog/chatbots-customer-service/#:~:text=The %20use%20of%20chatbots%20in,a%20human%20agent%20by%202020. Accessed 12 June 2020

12. Sutskever, I., Vinyals, O., Le, Q.: Sequence to sequence learning with neural networks. In: NIPS, pp. 3104–3112. Curran Associates Inc. (2014)

13. Vaira, L., Bochicchio, M., Conte, M., Casaluci, F., Melpignano, A.: MamaBot: a system based on ML and NLP for supporting Women and Families during Pregnancy. In: Desai, B. (eds.) 22nd International Database Engineering Applications Symposium (IDEAS 2018), pp. 273–277. ACM (2018). https://doi.org/10.1145/3216122.3216173

14. Vinyals, O., Le, Q.: A neural conversational model. In: Proceedings of the 31st International Conference of Machine Learning, France (2015)

15. Zhang, Y., Xu, T., Dai, Y.: Research on chatbots for open domain: using BiLTSM and sequence to sequence. In: Proceedings of the 2019 International Conference on Artificial Intelligence and Computer Science, pp. 145–149 (2020). https://doi.org/10.1145/3349341.3349393

User Expectations of Social Robots in Different Applications: An Online User Study

Xiao Dou[1]($\boxtimes$), Chih-Fu Wu[2], Xi Wang[3], and Jin Niu[2]

[1] The Graduate Institute of Design Science, Tatung University, Taipei, Taiwan
douxiao0808@outlook.com
[2] Department of Industry Design, Tatung University, Taipei, Taiwan
[3] City College of Dongguan University of Technology, Dongguan, China

Abstract. Social robots are expected to engage in various occupational roles in people's daily lives. In this study, online questionnaires were used to measure user expectations of social robots in different applications in terms of sociability and competence. One-way analysis of variance and hierarchical cluster analysis results indicated that users have different expectations of robots depending on the application. Robots for education and healthcare are expected to exhibit extremely high sociability and competence. By contrast, robots performing security tasks are expected to be more competent and less sociable, and the opposite is expected of robots for companionship and entertainment. The results of this study can help establish future social robot design guidelines for different applications.

Keywords: Social robot · User expectation · Robot application · User acceptance

1 Introduction

The rapid development of artificial intelligence and sensing technology has galvanized the swift development of robotics. Social robots are increasingly present in the service sector [1, 2], in education [3, 4] and as companions [5, 6] and are likely to be engaged in various occupational roles in people's daily lives [7, 8]. The common goal of human–robot interaction (HRI) study is to achieve intuitive, safe, and natural interactions and improve user acceptance of social robots [9–12]. Users' prior expectations regarding a robot could influence their evaluations of that robot [13]. User expectations are antecedents of user acceptance and satisfaction [13, 14]. For example, robots used for companionship may be expected to exhibit relatively high social skills [13]. If their design fails to meet user expectations, it will lead to lower acceptance. Knowledge regarding user expectations of social robot applications has not kept pace with the rapidly evolving field of robotics. To improve user acceptance of robots, user expectations of robots in different applications should be investigated [15].

Although studies have explored the diverse possibilities of social robot applications [2, 16, 17], no classification system, based on user expectations, exists for these applications. Such a system can improve understanding regarding the occupational roles

© Springer Nature Switzerland AG 2020
C. Stephanidis et al. (Eds.): HCII 2020, LNCS 12424, pp. 64–72, 2020.
https://doi.org/10.1007/978-3-030-60117-1_5

of robots and serve as a reference for robot design. This study investigated and compared user expectations of different social robot applications. A classification system was developed that can divide robots' applications based on sociability and competence evaluations of the robot. This can help predict the functional as well as socially relevant aspects of social robots before realistic applications.

2 Literature Review

The International Federation of Robotics [2, 18] reported approximately 67 service robot applications, which include companionship and use in education, agriculture, and the military. These applications encompass almost all possible robot applications for the foreseeable future and cover all service robot appearances, humanoid or nonhumanoid. Lohse et al. [19] conducted a study on the relationship between different social robots' appearance and their application categories, and proposed 13 categories and 27 associated tasks. However, these categories lack appropriate definitions, and some tasks overlap (e.g., health care and caregiver; pet and toy). In another study, Lohse et al. [20] provided definitions for each application category, and they also divided future robot applications into private, public, and both environments.

Hegel et al. [16] proposed a classification system consisting of four dimensions: 1) private versus public, 2) intensity of interaction, 3) complexity of interaction model, and 4) functional versus human-like appearance. Savela et al. [17] conducted a systematic review on the social acceptance of robots in different occupational fields, and they divided the robots' applications into nine categories. However, applications in the same category are still fairly different. For example, the category "social and health care" includes housework and education applications, which clearly are very different in terms of task and user expectation. Li et al. [21] also reported various robot applications and investigated the relationship between these applications and robot appearance. However, no comprehensive comparison of robot applications from a user-centered perspective has been conducted. This results in a lack of clear definitions of different social robots' applications and in users regarding these tasks as similar. Our research was conducted primarily using the definitions of various robot applications outlined in Lohse et al. [20] (Table 1).

The Computers are Social Actors paradigm [22] suggests that people tend to automatically perform social categorization of social robots and treat them as social entities [15, 23, 24]. Compared with industrial robots, there should be a greater focus on the evaluation of social robots' functional and social aspects [16]. The effort of improving public acceptance should be limited not only to optimizing the social robot itself but also the relationship between its target users and the application environment [25].

Standard measurement tools such as Godspeed scales [26] and Robot of Social Attribution Scale [15, 27] mainly evaluate basic robot properties, and currently no standard tools can measure user expectation of robot applications. Warmth and competence are two universal dimension of social cognition in interpersonal interaction [28, 29]. Powers and Kiesler [30] investigated the effects of appearance and voice frequency on the attribution of sociability and competence to a robot. Dou et al. [31] observed both social and competence evaluation when people interact with social robots. Therefore, in this study, we will use sociability and competence to measure user expectations.

3 Method

3.1 Selection of Target Social Robot Applications

Compared with mechanical robots, humanoid robots may be expected to exhibit superior social skills due to their appearance, in addition to excellent performance of functions [20]. The application of such robots in numerous contexts (e.g., education or companionship) is considered promising [8, 16, 17]. In this study, we selected eight applications that are common in research or have been used commercially. These are presented in Table 1 Seven social robot applications and definitions.

Table 1. Seven social robot applications and definitions

Application	Definition
Service	Service robot is either a receptionist, a sales robot, or a robot used for representation
Healthcare	Robots used for therapy (e.g. autism therapy) and as support for sick or old people
Companion	Companionship consists of all robots that keep company
Security	Security applications include robots used for surveillance, military tasks, exploration, tasks that are dangerous for humans (e.g. minesweeping), and for protection
Education	Robots that teach certain tasks or abilities. The robots in this case are supplements to real teachers especially when learning languages
Personal assistant	Personal assistant or Interface describes robots used as butlers, organizers or interfaces
Entertainment	Entertainment robots is to entertain their users and to be a pastime
Public assistant	Public assistants are guides (museum), information terminals or translators

3.2 Questionnaire and Measurement

This study collected data through online questionnaires. Considering that robot appearance strongly affects user expectations, this study used text to describe the application and tasks of the robot. A corresponding questionnaire was used for each selected social robot application, and each questionnaire consisted of three sections. The first section contained the introduction of the application (e.g., robots used in education) based on the definitions of Hegel et al. [19]. The second section presented a task-oriented conversation script between a human and robot, which was simulated and formulated through expert discussion. The third section consisted of user expectation evaluation.

Numerous studies have observed sociability and competence evaluation during HRI [29–32]. Therefore, user expectation of social robots' applications was measured using these two evaluation items (sociability and competence) on a 7-point Likert scale, with 1 denoting "extremely low" and 7 denoting "extremely high". Participants were asked to what degree they wanted the robot to be competent or social in a particular application. A sample questionnaire is presented in Table 2. Questionnaire Participants were asked to rate their expectation of the social robot's application immediately after reading the explanation and conversation script on each of the seven questionnaires.

Table 2. Questionnaire

	Questionnaire	Examples
Section 1	Introduction of the application	Service robot in a shop can provide product and inventory information, inquiry inventory, and so on
Section 2	Conversation script	C = Customer, R = Robot C: Hello R: Hello, how may I assist you? C: I want to buy a washing machine R: Sure, what type of washing machine would you like? C: What are the differences between a frequency conversion washing machine and a fixed frequency washing machine? R: The advantage of a frequency conversion washing machine is that it adjusts the rotation speed of the electrical motor through voltage fluctuation during the washing and spin cycles. This improves energy efficiency and quietness. Moreover, a frequency conversion washing machine can select the appropriate water flow rate, washing time, spin speed, and spin time depending on the weight and material of the clothes washed. By contrast, a fixed frequency washing machine is easier to use and learn C: Thank you! I will think about it R: OK, thank you for coming!
Section 3	User expectation evaluation	To what extent do you want the robot to be sociable or competent in this application? 7-point Likert scale

3.3 Participants

A total of 36 participants completed the questionnaire. After the exclusion of incomplete questionnaires, 31 valid questionnaires were received (9 men, 22 women; age range 18–42 years). The questionnaires were distributed online, and most participants were students from Tatung University and City College of Dongguan University of Technology.

4   Results and Discussion

4.1   User Expectations Regarding Sociability and Competence in Robots

One-way analysis of variance was used to analyze user expectations of social robot applications based on sociability and competence evaluations. A significant difference was observed between users' sociability [F (7, 247) = 8.706, p < 0.001] and competence [F (7, 247) = 24.707, p < 0.001] expectations depending on the occupation of the robot.

Sociability. A significant difference was observed in the sociability evaluations for robots used in security compared with those used in the service industry, health care, education, entertainment, as companions, and as personal assistant (Table 3 Mean and standard deviation of sociability and competence in robot applications). Users expected less sociability from robots performing security tasks than tasks related to service and health care. No significant difference was observed between security [mean (M) = 3.42, standard deviation (SD) = 1.12] and public assistant (M = 4.65, SD = 1.38) applications (Fig. 1).

Table 3. Mean and standard deviation of sociability and competence in robot applications

Robot application	Sociability	Competence
Service	5.23 (0.88)	4.77 (1.61)
Healthcare	5.16 (1.32)	5.94 (1.69)
Companion	5.19 (1.62)	3.10 (1.62)
Security	3.42 (1.12)	6.45 (1.12)
Education	5.19 (1.32)	5.71 (1.32)
Personal assistant	5.03 (1.68)	4.9 (1.68)
Entertainment	5.77 (1.61)	2.50 (1.61)
Public assistant	4.65 (1.38)	4.87 (1.38)

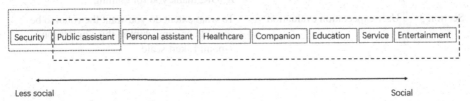

| Security | Public assistant | Personal assistant | Healthcare | Companion | Education | Service | Entertainment |

Less social   Social

Fig. 1. User expectation of sociability in social robots in different applications

Competence. Users expected social robots used in security (M = 6.45, SD = 1.12), healthcare, and education tasks to be significantly more competent than in other tasks. Robot used in entertainment (M = 2.5, SD = 1.61) and companion robots (M = 3.1,

SD = 1.62) received significantly lower ratings for competency expectation than robots used in the service sector (M = 4.77, SD = 1.61), as public assistants (M = 4.87, SD = 1.38) and as personal assistants (M = 4.9, SD = 1.68; Fig. 2 User expectation of competence in social robots in different applications).

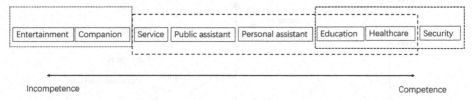

Incompetence   Competence

Fig. 2. User expectation of competence in social robots in different applications

4.2 Hierarchical Cluster Results of User Expectations

Hierarchical cluster analysis, used to compile the sociability and competence evaluations, resulted in four groups: group 1 (healthcare and education), group 2 (service, personal assistant, and public assistant), group 3 (companion and entertainment), and group 4 (security; Fig. 3 Coordinate system of user expectations of social robots in different applications).

To present the results more intuitively, a coordinate system was established on the basis of the means of each application. In this coordinate system, the midpoint was (3.5, 3.5); thus, user expectations were divided into four quadrants. User expectation in the first quadrant was defined by high competence (HC) and low sociability (LS); users expect the robot to exhibit excellent task performance and tolerate LS. The only application in this quadrant was security robots. This result is consistent with studies conducted by Tay et al. [24] and Dou et al. [33]. They claimed that gender stereotypes can influence user acceptance. Security is perceived to be a male-dominated industry. Moreover, in stereotypically male-dominated jobs the emphasis is on competence rather than sociability [15, 34].

Most of the applications (e.g., service, education, and health care) were located in the second quadrant, in which users expect robots to exhibit both high sociability (HS) and HC. Hierarchical cluster analysis identified two groups in the second quadrant. Social robots used in healthcare and education are expected to exhibit extremely high sociability and HC in task performance. However, robots used as public assistants, personal assistants, and in the service sector can exhibit slightly lower competence levels but should be more sociable.

Entertainment and companionship robots were located in the fourth quadrant, which is defined by HS and low competence (LC). This suggests that users expect these robots to be more sociable and may be willing to tolerate lower task performance. Chang et al. [5] reported that users prefer robots with a high-pitched female voice for companionship tasks. A high-pitched female voice is believed to be more warm and kind than a male voice [35] because of female-related social stereotypes. This may explain the placement of entertainment and companionship tasks in this quadrant.

No robot application was located in the third quadrant, in which LS and LC levels are expected. This indicates that users generally have high expectations for the application of social robots.

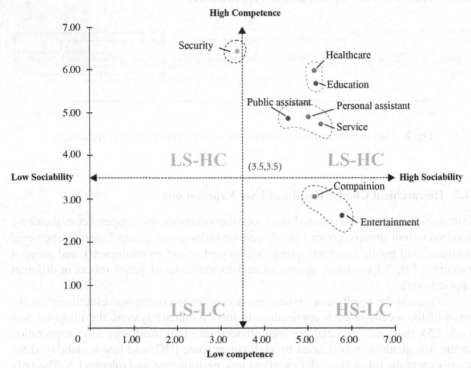

Fig. 3. Coordinate system of user expectations of social robots in different applications

4.3 Limitation and Further Research

Although this study revealed some useful findings, it has limitations. First, a particular type of social robot can be applied in various scenarios and perform more than one task. For instance, service robots can be used in restaurant ordering or as shopping receptionists. This study only used the typical task according to the definition provided by Losen et al. [20]. Therefore, this is a preliminary exploratory study, and users' expectations of other application tasks can be discussed further on the basis of the current study results.

Second, text is used to simulate the HRI in different applications; therefore, the content of the script may affect user perception of the corresponding application tasks and potentially affect their expectations. Moreover, social robots could be used for short- and long-term interaction studies in the future to explore how user expectations change.

5   Conclusion

In this study, user expectations for different social robot applications were investigated using two evaluation items: sociability and competence. User expectations affect the acceptance of robots for various applications. Analysis revealed that users have different expectations for robots to be used in various occupational fields. Social robots for education and health care are expected to have extremely high sociability and competence. By contrast, robots performing security tasks are expected to be more competent but less sociable, whereas users have the opposite expectation of robots for companionship and entertainment.

References

1. Bertacchini, F., Bilotta, E., Pantano, P.: Shopping with a robotic companion. Comput. Hum. Behav. **77**, 382–395 (2017)
2. IFR: Introduction into Service Robots, 4 (2012)
3. Broadbent, E., et al.: How could companion robots be useful in rural schools? Int. J. Social Robot. **10**(3), 295–307 (2018)
4. Kennedy, J., Baxter, P., Senft, E., Belpaeme, T: Social robot tutoring for child second language learning. In: 2016 11th ACM/IEEE International Conference on Human-Robot Interaction (HRI), pp. 231–238 (2016)
5. Chang, R.C.S., Lu, H.P., Yang, P.: Stereotypes or golden rules? Exploring likable voice traits of social robots as active aging companions for tech-savvy baby boomers in Taiwan. Comput. Hum. Behav. **84**, 194–210 (2018)
6. De Graaf, M.M., Allouch, S.B., Klamer, T.: Sharing a life with Harvey: exploring the acceptance of and relationship-building with a social robot. Comput. Hum. Behav. **43**, 1–14 (2015)
7. Savela, N., Turja, T., Oksanen, A.: Social acceptance of robots in different occupational fields: a systematic literature review. Int. J. Social Robot. **10**(4), 493–502 (2017). https://doi.org/10.1007/s12369-017-0452-5
8. Fong, T., Nourbakhsh, I., Dautenhahn, K.: A survey of socially interactive robots. Robot. Auton. Syst. **42**(3–4), 143–166 (2003)
9. Martínez-Miranda, J., Pérez-Espinosa, H., Espinosa-Curiel, I., Avila-George, H., Rodríguez-Jacobo, J.: Age-based differences in preferences and affective reactions towards a robot's personality during interaction. Comput. Hum. Behav. **84**, 245–257 (2018)
10. Hirano, T., et al.: How do communication cues change impressions of human–robot touch interaction? Int. J. Social Robot. **10**(1), 21–31 (2018)
11. Stanton, C.J., Stevens, Catherine J.: Don't stare at me: the impact of a humanoid robot's gaze upon trust during a cooperative human–robot visual task. Int. J. Social Robot. **9**(5), 745–753 (2017). https://doi.org/10.1007/s12369-017-0422-y
12. Beck, A., et al.: Interpretation of emotional body language displayed by a humanoid robot: a case study with children. Int. J. Social Robot. **5**(3), 325–334 (2013). https://doi.org/10.1007/s12369-013-0193-z
13. de Graaf, M.M.A., Allouch, S.B.: The influence of prior expectations of a robot's lifelikeness on users' intentions to treat a zoomorphic robot as a companion. Int. J. Social Robot. **9**(1), 17–32 (2016). https://doi.org/10.1007/s12369-016-0340-4
14. Hsieh, C.-C., Kuo, P.-L., Yang, S.-C., Lin, S.-H.: Assessing blog-user satisfaction using the expectation and disconfirmation approach. Comput. Hum. Behav. **26**(6), 1434–1444 (2010)
15. Stroessner, S.J., Benitez, J.: The social perception of humanoid and non-humanoid robots: effects of gendered and machinelike features. Int. J. Social Robot. **11**(2), 305–315 (2018). https://doi.org/10.1007/s12369-018-0502-7

16. Hegel, F., Lohse, M., Swadzba, A., Wachsmuth, S., Rohlfing, K., Wrede, B.: Classes of applications for social robots: a user study. In: RO-MAN 2007-The 16th IEEE International Symposium on Robot and Human Interactive Communication, Jeju, Korea, pp. 938–943. IEEE (2007)
17. Savela, N., Turja, T., Oksanen, A.: Social acceptance of robots in different occupational fields: a systematic literature review. Int. J. Social Robot. **10**(4), 493–502 (2018). https://doi.org/10.1007/s12369-017-0452-5
18. IFR: World robotics service robots. In: International Federation of Robotics (2018)
19. Lohse, M., Hegel, F., Swadzba, A., Rohlfing, K., Wachsmuth, S., Wrede, B.: What can I do for you? Appearance and application of robots. In: Proceedings of AISB, pp. 121–126 (2007)
20. Lohse, M., Hegel, F., Wrede, B.: Domestic applications for social robots - an online survey on the influence of appearance and capabilities. J. Phys. Agents **2**, 21–32 (2008)
21. Rau, P.L.P., Li, Y., Li, D.: A cross-cultural study: effect of robot appearance and task. Int. J. Social Robot. **2**(2), 175–186 (2010). https://doi.org/10.1007/s12369-010-0056-9
22. Nass, C., Steuer, J., Tauber, E.R.: Computers are social actors. In: Conference Companion on Human Factors in Computing Systems - CHI 1994 (1994)
23. Cheng, Y.W., Sun, P.C., Chen, N.S.: The essential applications of educational robot: requirement analysis from the perspectives of experts, researchers and instructors. Comput. Educ. **126**, 399–416 (2018)
24. Tay, B., Jung, Y., Park, T.: When stereotypes meet robots: the double-edge sword of robot gender and personality in human-robot interaction. Comput. Hum. Behav. **38**, 75–84 (2014)
25. Stephanidis, C., et al.: Seven HCI grand challenges. Int. J. Hum. Comput. Interact. **35**(14), 1229–1269 (2019)
26. Bartneck, C., Kulić, D., Croft, E., Zoghbi, S.: Measurement instruments for the anthropomorphism, animacy, likeability, perceived intelligence, and perceived safety of robots. Int. J. Social Robot. **1**(1), 71–81 (2009). https://doi.org/10.1007/s12369-008-0001-3
27. Carpinella, C.M., Wyman, A.B., Perez, M.A., Stroessner, S.J.: The robotic social attributes scale (RoSAS). In: Proceedings of the 2017 ACM/IEEE International Conference on Human-Robot Interaction - HRI 2017, pp. 254–262 (2017)
28. Fiske, S.T., Cuddy, A.J.C., Glick, P.: Universal dimensions of social cognition: warmth and competence. Trends Cogn. Sci. **11**, 77–83 (2007)
29. Oliveira, R., Arriaga, P., Correia, F., Paiva, A.: Making robot's attitudes predictable: a stereotype content model for human-robot interaction in groups. In: Paper Presented at the Workshop Explainable Robotic Systems, Chicago, IL, USA (2018)
30. Powers, A., Kiesler, S.: The advisor robot: tracing people's mental model from a robot's physical attributes. In: Proceedings of the 1st ACM SIGCHI/SIGART Conference on Human-Robot Interaction, pp. 218–225. ACM (2006)
31. Dou, X., Wu, C.-F., Lin, K.-C., Gan, S., Tseng, T.-M.: Effects of different types of social robot voices on affective evaluations in different application fields. Int. J. Social Robot. (2020). https://doi.org/10.1007/s12369-020-00654-9
32. Hwang, J., Park, T., Hwang, W.: The effects of overall robot shape on the emotions invoked in users and the perceived personalities of robot. Appl. Ergon. **44**(3), 459–471 (2013)
33. Dou, X., Wu, C.-F., Lin, K.-C., Tseng, T.-M.: The effects of robot voice and gesture types on the perceived robot personalities. In: Kurosu, M. (ed.) HCII 2019. LNCS, vol. 11566, pp. 299–309. Springer, Cham (2019). https://doi.org/10.1007/978-3-030-22646-6_21
34. Cuddy, A.J., Fiske, S.T., Glick, P.: Warmth and competence as universal dimensions of social perception: the stereotype content model and the BIAS map. Adv. Exp. Soc. Psychol. **40**, 61–149 (2008)
35. Mullennix, J.W., Stern, S.E., Wilson, S.J., Dyson, C.L.: Social perception of male and female computer synthesized speech. Comput. Hum. Behav. **19**, 407–424 (2003)

Creating Emotional Attachment with Assistive Wearables

Neda Fayazi[✉] and Lois Frankel

Carleton University, Ottawa, Canada
neda.fayazi@carleton.ca

Abstract. Wearable technology plays a significant role in improving the quality of life for people, especially individuals who deal with the issue of aging and disability. Despite the advantages, there are some barriers that cause these users to reject or abandon their wearable devices. In the design of these devices, the literature suggests that little attention has been given to the psychological and social needs of the users. However, some researchers are exploring various strategies to design inclusive wearables and minimize the stigma associated with assistive wearables. This paper provides a literature review of the current approaches and frameworks related to wearable technology, with a qualitative focus on the discourse about the design of emotionally engaging and meaningful products. It suggests that there is an opportunity in the area of assistive technology to design inclusive wearables that not only alleviate the stigma attached to the devices, but also lead to the creation of long-term product attachment.

Keywords: Wearable technology · Assistive wearables · Product abandonment · Emotional attachment

1 Introduction

The use of wearable technologies enhances the quality of life for many people especially the elderly and people with disabilities, impairments, and chronic diseases. However, it is common knowledge that design innovations in this area are often driven more by technology advances rather than sensitivity to human needs, capabilities, and values.

Researchers in the area of wearable computing are concerned about how little attention has been given to the relationship between technology and the human body in terms of emotional engagement and wearability (Kettley 2007; Wallace 2007; Wright et al. 2008; McCann 2009; Bush 2015; Møller and Kettley 2017). From a technical and user-oriented perspective, functionality, comfort, and ease of use have gained much attention, while the deeper emotional, sensory, and social influences on people's relationships with these artifacts have been neglected (McCarthy et al. 2006). This negligence results in a significant challenge in people's experiences with wearable technologies. People have a low degree of attachment towards the devices and because of this tend to stop using them after a short period of time (Fortmann et al. 2015; Bush 2015).

This issue warrants more attention specifically for the elderly, who could benefit from using wearable assistive technologies. This not only includes seniors who require

© Springer Nature Switzerland AG 2020
C. Stephanidis et al. (Eds.): HCII 2020, LNCS 12424, pp. 73–88, 2020.
https://doi.org/10.1007/978-3-030-60117-1_6

special care, but the whole senior population as their social, physical, and cognitive abilities decline over time. With aging, seniors might turn into 'stigmatized people' who experience a low level of social acceptance (Goffman 1986). They may attempt to constantly adapt their social identities through assistive technologies (e.g. hearing aids, canes, wheelchairs, etc.) already identified as "stigma symbols" (Goffman 1986). For seniors, using wearable technologies designed for them can even diminish their self-confidence as it is a sign of aging. Based on different studies, seniors and disabled persons who require assistive technologies might abandon them due to stigmatization and the perception of being disabled which relates to the issues of identity (Brickfield 1984; Hocking 1999). The stigma around using these products is often connected to their appearance which causes a negative impact on the identity and self-esteem of the individuals (Skogsrød 2014). Therefore, individuals do not feel emotionally or personally attached to their devices, even though they might require their use for doing daily tasks.

Overemphasis on the function and technological aspect of devices more often misdirects the producers from paying attention to the ergonomics, emotional, and social impacts of wearing digital devices. This disconnect can be clearly seen in the field of medical devices. Medical devices are often not aesthetically appealing, and often the data feedback may not be easily understood and read by the wearer (McCann 2009). As mentioned by McCann (2009), designers should take into consideration both the human physiology of older wearers as well as the psychological 'feel good factor'. Negligence of these requirements results in products that people are not willing to interact with for a long time.

This issue reveals the importance of developing a strong user-product attachment when it comes to designing assistive wearables. Through providing an overview of the literature, this paper begins to generate conceptual suggestions for creating long-term product attachment with assistive technologies that may benefit a range of populations, especially seniors and people with disabilities. This paper provides contributions by developing a framework that combines models and theories for creating a user-wearable technology attachment and proposing this framework as a creative method in the design of assistive wearables.

2 Related Work

2.1 Assistive Wearables

Technology as an extension has been interwoven into our everyday life in a pervasive and ubiquitous way. The human body can be extended physically through different technologies including prosthetics, handheld, wearable, implanted, and clothing (Uğur 2013). The International Electrotechnical Committee classifies digital technologies based on the degree of intimacy of the device to the human body: (1) near-body electronics, (2) on-body electronics, (3) in-body electronics, and (4) electronic textiles (European Commission 2016). As mentioned by Silina and Haddadi (2015), it is very important to define the terminologies for body-focused wearables correctly to reduce misunderstandings among multidisciplinary researchers. If we combine the classifications explained above, we have the prostheses and implants in 'in-body electronics', handheld in 'near-body electronics', wearable in 'on-body electronics', and clothing in 'electronic textiles'.

Steve Mann (2013), known as the father of wearable computing and wearable augmented reality (AR), defines wearable computing as a miniature body-borne computer and sensory device which can be worn under, over, or inside clothing. Thus, based on Mann's (2013) definition, wearable technology not only refers to the on-body electronics but also includes electronic textiles and smart clothing. Wearables can sense the wearer(s) and/or the environment around them, be worn on or attached to the human body for easy interaction and allow the body to freely and independently move, while they are connected to a technological system in real time (Chatterjee et al. 2016; Uğur 2013; European Commission 2016).

Wearable technology has different applications in communication, health and wellness, sports, medicine, entertainment, industrial, police, and military (Chatterjee et al. 2016; Frankel 2007; Carpi and De Rossi 2005; Helmer et al. 2008). Wearables can be classified into four main categories based on their target function which include: assistive, workplace, consumer product and healthcare (Chatterjee et al. 2016). Consumer product technologies enable users to easily achieve everyday tasks or goals. Workplace technologies support users' performance, efficiency, and safety in the workplace. Healthcare technologies enable the evaluation and monitoring of vital signs, diet, physical activity, and general well-being of the patients (Sun et al. 2014). Assistive technologies augment users' capabilities given specific physical limitations such as visual, auditory, or any other physical impairments (Chatterjee et al. 2016). Therefore, digital body-worn artifacts can be classified in different categories as shown in Fig. 1. Figure 1 shows where 'assistive wearables' can be situated in this classification.

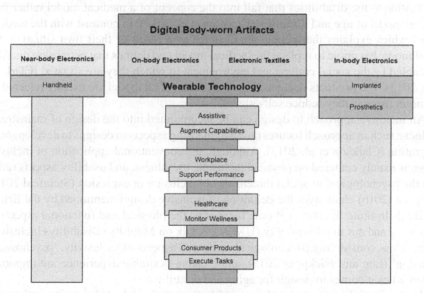

Fig. 1. Classification of digital body-worn artifacts – author's interpretation

2.2　Abandonment of Assistive Wearables

Current literature identifies the importance of considering people's social and psychological needs in addition to their physical needs when designing wearable technologies (Bush 2015; Bush and ten Hompel 2017; Kettley 2007; McCarthy et al. 2006; Møller 2018; Møller and Kettley 2007; Uğur 2013; Wallace 2007; Wright et al. 2008). Neglecting these considerations results in users experiencing a low level of attachment towards their devices as well as a tendency to abandon them (Bush 2015; Fortmann et al. 2015). Different factors that contribute to the acceptance or rejection of wearable devices include: appearance, wearability, degree of compatibility with personal human values and capabilities, stigmatizing features, cost, compatibility, reliability, usefulness (utility & usability), degree of trust and safety, privacy, mobility, social influence, age and gender, as well as culture and the user's technical experience (Buenaflor and Kim 2013; Kettley 2007; Møller and Kettley 2017; Nielsen 1994; Silina and Haddadi 2015).

Among these factors, feelings of stigma and social isolation have a huge impact on the adoption of assistive technologies by the users. Different studies investigate the relationship between stigma in assistive products and product abandonment (Hocking 1999; Pape et al. 2002, Phillips and Zhao 1993 cited in Jacobson 2014). Using wearable assistive technology in public can have sociocultural impacts such as societal stigma, judgment, and social isolation causing users to hide or abandon their devices (Profita 2016; Vaes et al. 2012). The perspective towards designing exclusive products and services that is centered exclusively on age and disability brings up some issues since it relates age and disability with both deficiency and incapability. This approach pays a lot of attention to the disabilities that fall into the concept of a medical model rather than a social model of age and disability (Clarkson et al. 2013). In contrast with the medical model which explains that people are disabled as a result of their own situation, the social model has come to replace the medical model and defines that people are disabled or enabled by the social context and environment in which they are situated (Clarkson et al. 2013). The products designed based on the medical model are usually rejected by the target users as they reduce self-esteem.

An inclusive approach to design can be incorporated into the design of mainstream products; such an approach focuses on destigmatising aspects of designs to develop social integration (Clarkson et al. 2013). Although, the conventional application of inclusive design is mainly centered on physical inclusion, usefulness, and usability aspects rather than the psychological or social dimensions of inclusion or exclusion (Steinfeld 2013). Nickpour (2016) challenges the definition of inclusive design mentioned by the British Standards Institute in 2005 as it only focuses on the physical and functional aspects of inclusivity and not the desirability (UXPA UK talk on Mobility+Disability+Inclusivity 2016). Thus, considering psychological and social aspects of inclusivity, 'psychosocial inclusion' (Lim and Nickpour 2015), and creating desirable experience are important factors when it comes to design for aging and disability.

The user might not accept the use of an assistive product due to its appearance which is socially segregating than integrating (Jacobson 2014). It is possible to bring together aesthetic and function and create mainstream products rather than exclusive products such as disability aids and equipment (Cassim 2015; Benktzon 1993 cited in Clarkson et al. 2013). Attractive products make the product look trendy, stylish, and desirable which can minimize the stigma gradually (Skogsrød 2014). However, a product's attractiveness is not only affected by its appearance but also the way it functions and what it communicates about its user is an important factor (Crilly et al. 2004 cited in Jacobson 2014).

From the research perspective creating socially acceptable, expressible, and fashionable AT is limited, however from the practical aspect, it has started to gain more attention (Profita 2017). A noticeable example of an assistive product that has transformed into a fashion accessory over centuries is eyewear (Pullin 2009; Bush and ten Hompel 2017). The combination of aesthetics and marketing in the design of eyeglasses has shifted the opinion of the public from 'visually impaired' to 'fashionable' (Skogsrød 2014).

Various factors can be taken into consideration when designing assistive technology (AT) to minimize the stigma and increase the social acceptability of these products. These factors include: concealing AT behind the accessory and jewellery, cultural background, size of the device (tiny and small devices are more effective in preventing stigma), familiarity of the look (use of a product among a large population minimizes the perception of disability), location on the body (products being worn on the wrist, arm, hand, or clothes are not stigmatizing), status of the wearer (perceived power or status of the user impacts the perception of disability), presenting the user as active and in command, personalization and customization (Valamanesh 2014). Personalization of assistive products which refers to the customization of a product by considering users' identity-related preferences is a great way of managing stigma (Jacobson 2014). Decorative casts, wheelchairs, eye patches, and crutches are examples of expressive AT that includes the personal decoration of the device (Profita 2017). The conceptual framework by Vaes et al. (2012) proposes the strategy of 'reshaping the meaning of the product' to deal with the product related stigma. Such reshaping can be achieved through de-identification (hiding the stigmatizing features, e.g. skin-colored and translucent hearing aids), identification (self-expression, e.g. wearing the hearing aid like a piece of jewellery/earlobe piercing), meaningful interaction with other products (completing with widely accepted products, e.g. hearing aid combined with glasses), and advances in material and technology.

The importance of trans-disciplinary collaboration can be viewed in reshaping the meaning of assistive products. Heiss et al. (2016) focus on this collaboration between experts from the disciplines of design, craft, and technology to develop a medical wearable device (Smart Heart cardiac monitoring necklace) with a non-medical appearance.

2.3 User-Wearable Technology Attachment

Product Attachment. John Bowlby (1979), known as the father of attachment theory, explains 'attachment' as an affectional bond between individuals. Applying this terminology in the realm of product design, the attachment is a positive emotional connection between a possessor and a product. Product attachment is defined as the degree and strength of the emotional connection an individual experiences with an object (Schultz et al. 1989; Schifferstein et al. 2004). As mentioned by Schultz et al. (1989), attachment directly relates to the basic self-development processes extending over the full product life cycle. It often involves current and past self-definitional experiences and memories and is relevant to the usage phase of consumption. Although product-related memories usually form as the owner starts using the objects and creating narratives and stories around the piece, there seems to be an opportunity for designers to take part in boosting product attachment (Mugge et al. 2008).

There is a relationship between product attachment and emotion. Strong product attachment usually brings about positive emotions in individuals. On the other hand, products that do not create this experience of attachment often do not trigger any emotions or result in negative emotions such as dislike, regret, boredom, etc. (Mugge et al. 2008; Savaş 2004; Schultz et al. 1989). The only exception is the emotion of sadness (e.g. sadness and love can be simultaneously experienced in response to a jewellery piece that is a reminder of the loss of someone special in life) (Mugge et al. 2008).

In the design of products, it is important to understand how to create positive emotional responses to the products that are not short-term and last longer. Different design researchers have introduced various emotion-focused frameworks to illustrate positive product experience and enhance the subjective well-being of people through design (Desmet and Pohlmeyer 2013; Jordan 2000; Norman 2004).

Long-lasting product attachment happens when the user feels the product is 'irreplaceable'. At this level, the product embraces meaning beyond the functional, and this meaning is deeply attached to the product in a way which is inseparable (Mugge et al. 2005). Grayson and Shulman (2000) define 'irreplaceable possession' as the object that the owner refuses to replace with an exact copy of it as the alternative object doesn't reveal the same meaning to the person. Schifferstein et al. (2004) suggest that in order to form consumer-product attachment, designers should create associations between the product and person, places or events (memories), or design a product that stimulates enjoyment (sensory and aesthetic pleasure). Based on the findings of various studies, a product can become 'irreplaceable' though four determinants: (1) pleasure, (2) memories, (3) self-expression, and (4) group affiliation (Mugge et al. 2005, 2008, 2009).

Mugge et al's (2007) conceptual model of product attachment explores the relationships between product attachment, satisfaction, pleasure (as a result of a product's utility and appearance), and memories. Based on their model, the product's utility has both direct and indirect (via the mediator of pleasure) effects on satisfaction (Fig. 2) as well as indirect effects (via the mediator of pleasure) on product attachment (Fig. 3). They posit that since an average performing product performs according to expectations, it can contribute to the user's product satisfaction, but it is unlikely to create product attachment. The product's appearance also indirectly affects product satisfaction and attachment through the mediator of pleasure (Figs. 2 and 3). Therefore, in contrast with product satisfaction, product attachment directly associates with memories, sense of past, and product's symbolic meaning. As shown in Fig. 3, types of pleasure that lead to product attachment are the ones that carry the user's memories and symbolic meanings associated with that product. Memories associated with the product have a significant impact on the formation of user-product attachment (Schifferstein et al. 2004).

Therefore, to achieve a long-term relationship with a product, we need to design meaningful products which bring about eudaimonic happiness. In particular, taking a hedonic design approach satisfies a user's pleasure and comfort needs, whereas a eudaimonic satisfies a user's needs for purpose and self-realization (Desmet and Nijhuis 2013). Figure 4 is based on the framework by Desmet and Nijhuis (2013), and demonstrates that

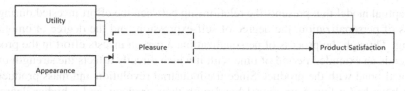

Fig. 2. Formation of product satisfaction. Based on the model by Mugge et al. (2007)

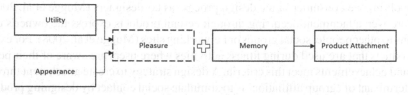

Fig. 3. Formation of product attachment. Based on the model by Mugge et al. (2007)

designing pleasurable products and activities leads to hedonic happiness while designing meaningful products and activities leads to eudaimonic happiness.

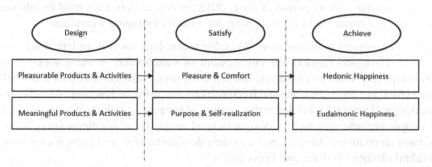

Fig. 4. Pleasurable vs. Meaningful products and activities. Based on the framework by Desmet and Nijhuis (2013)

Based on Ryff's (1989) model of psychological well-being, Casais et al. (2016) identified six happiness-related ways in which products can be symbolically meaningful: 1) positive relations with others (the meaning of belongingness), 2) personal growth (meaning of self-development), 3) purpose in life (meaning of motivation), 4) environmental mastery (development of skills that contribute to environmental mastery), 5) autonomy (meaning of being independent and autonomous) and 6) self-acceptance (meaning of identity).

Another determinant of product attachment is self-expression (Mugge et al. 2008). The product expresses the personal identity of the owner; and therefore, it embraces special meaning to her/him (Mugge et al. 2008). Based on the research by Mugge et al. (2008), product personalization is a design strategy to create emotional bonding with products through the determinant self-expression. Mugge et al. (2009) developed a conceptual model that presents the relationship between the effort invested during the process of personalization, the degree of self-expression, and the degree of emotional bonding. Through the process of personalization, a person invests effort in the product and spends an extended period of time with it which directly affects the strength of the emotional bond with the product. Since the industrial revolution and mass production, people have had a lower emotional bond with their products and a higher degree of consumption levels (Savaş 2004). To solve this issue, companies have tried to implement product personalization in different ways such as offering mass-customization services and involving the consumer in the design process as co-designers (Mugge et al. 2009).

Moreover, attachment occurring through certain products express the owner's connections to other people, social groups or networking sites (Mugge et al. 2008). For example, products that are used during fitness activities where users are aware of their peers' goals and achievements meet this criteria. A design strategy to create attachment through the determinant of 'group affiliation' is to stimulate social contact by designing products that can be shared with other members of the group. This determinant has been defined by other design researchers as 'socio-pleasure' (Jordan 2000), 'relationship-focus interaction' (Desmet and Roeser 2015), 'positive relations with others' and 'belongingness' (Casais et al. 2016).

Attachment with Wearable Technology. To minimize the issue of abandoning wearable devices after a short period of time, different researchers have tried to introduce approaches and frameworks for designing emotionally engaging wearables.

Multidisciplinary Collaboration: Wearable technology itself is an interdisciplinary area of research and requires the engagement of stakeholders working together in a multidisciplinary team of engineers, fashion designers, industrial designers, and other experts (McCann 2016; McCann and Bryson 2009). Focusing on function and technology in the design of wearables has led to the creation of gadgets. In order to design a wearable that people become attached to, designers need to design non-gadgets (jewellery) as they have an enduring lifespan, non-transferable significance, and present elements of individual identity (Wallace and Press 2003).

Multidisciplinary collaboration between wearable technology makers and fashion designers can benefit all the disciplines involved and specifically help to focus on both the digital and physical layers at the same time when designing digital body-focused artifacts. Collaboration between these disciplines may result in the creation of new terminologies at the intersection of fashion and wearable technology. The terms include digital jewellery, interactive jewellery, smart jewellery, computational jewellery, tech jewellery, therapeutic jewellery, medical jewelelry, smart clothing, etc. The interpretation of the terms may differ by practitioners across various disciplines. The term 'Interactive jewellery' has emerged from the intersection of jewellery and wearable technology (Versteeg et al. 2016). Similar to 'interactive jewellery', 'digital jewellery' is defined as a jewellery piece that contains electronic components (Koulidou 2018). Digital jewellery can create the experience of product attachment in three ways: personal use (using an object for a period of time), symbolism (creating a sense of familiarity and attaching people to another place, person, event, or memories), and digital function of the piece (Wallace and Press 2003). Thus, personal attachment with the piece will be achieved based on function as well as personal significance which may lead to long-term and meaningful attachment with the object. Koulidou (2018) proposed a framework for digital jewellery to show how craft practices and digital technologies can create poetic and emotionally rich interactions. The outside layer of this framework is the *materiality and form* which represents the maker's sensitivity in working with materials and the narrative of the piece in the form of digital jewellery. The second layer represents the *poetic qualities of the interaction* with digital jewellery. This layer is related to the function of the object and the interaction of the wearer with the piece. The third layer represents the personal anchor point which is the *personal and intimate engagement* with the piece. This layer differentiates digital jewellery from other wearable technologies. This is where a meaningful relationship can take place between the wearer and the piece and supports one's sense of self (Koulidou 2018). Therefore, combining contemporary craft and jewellery with digital technologies is considered to be a creative methodology for designing digital jewellery and new practices in interaction design (Kettley 2012; Koulidou 2018; Wallace and Press 2003). This approach has the potential for creating meaningful designs (Kettley 2012).

Biopsychosocial Approach to the Design of Wearables. In the design of wearable technologies, it is significant to consider multiple aspects of the human body: physical, psychological, and social (Uğur 2013). Bush and ten Hompel (2007) discuss current approaches to the design of medical wearables that are dependent on a biomedical approach, noting it cannot address the biopsychosocial needs of the wearer and results in poor attachment towards these intimate objects. They proposed a biopsychological approach to the design of wearables and identified eight design factors that influence wearability: Fit and Function, Style and Aesthetics, Materials and Making, Emotional Engagement and Meaning. They emphasize that designing an object which is 'meaningful' for the wearer can increase its wearability. By considering these factors, wearable medical devices can change their meanings over time, similar to how eyeglasses transformed from medical aids into fashion and style accessories over centuries (Bush and ten Hompel 2017; Pullin 2009).

The biopsychological approach to the design of wearables is person-centric rather than body-centric and focuses more on the issues of importance to the wearer than the body itself (Bush and ten Hompel 2017). To succeed in the design of wearables, we should be required to apply a user centered design (UCD) approach which focuses on end-users' needs and limitations at all stages within the design process and throughout the development lifecycle (Venere and Matteo 2014). The application of 'co-design' and 'empathic' approaches in the design process help to include the wearer's needs and desires (Bush and ten Hompel 2017). In the co-design process, users act as co-designers and participate in idea generation and the design development process (Sanders and Stappers 2008). To develop more inclusive and creative designs, users–who are usually 'design excluded'– should be involved in the early stages of developing design ideas as 'design partners' (Goodacre and Cassim 2010; Lee and Cassim 2009).

Møller and Kettley (2017) apply such an empathic design approach in the design of future wearable health technologies and discuss their 'accessory approach' as a means of understanding the wearer's preferences and designing personalized and customized wearables. The accessory approach is a design framework which involves a wearer's physical, psychological, and social needs (Møller 2018; Møller and Kettley 2017).

Møller and Kettley (2017) borrow Cunningham's framework of narrative contemporary jewellery and show how the accessory can act as a platform to support the relationship between maker, wearer, and viewer. Cunningham's model (2008) expands the definition of narrative jewellery and places it within a wider framework. It holds that the role of jewellery is in creating a dialogue and relationship between maker, wearer, and viewer. Jewellery has the potential to stimulate memories for the maker, wearer, and viewer. It embraces the maker, wearer, and viewer's experiences, histories, meanings, and interpretations. Møller and Kettley (2017) expand on Cunningham's maker–wearer–viewer model (showing three social actors involved in the narrative) to dissolve the roles and identities between these three actors. As discussed previously, multidisciplinary collaboration is significant in designing future wearable technology (Kettley et al. 2015; McCann 2016; McCann and Bryson 2009; Silina and Haddadi 2015). However, we can say that this collaboration is not limited to the disciplines involved in the making process; it includes wearers and viewers as actors and co-designers in the development of wearable technologies.

3 Discussion

To design meaningful products, researchers focus on collaboration among different disciplines in the design of wearable technology devices (Kettley 2012; Kettley et al. 2015; Koulidou 2018; McCann 2016; McCann and Bryson 2009; Silina and Haddadi 2015; Versteeg et al. 2016; Wallace and Press 2003). This integration of art, design, and technology can lead to the creation of new areas and terminologies in the field of wearable technology. These new areas take human needs, emotions, capabilities, and values into consideration.

In Fig. 5, we illustrate how overlapping the physical and digital layers can bring about new opportunities in the design of wearable technologies. 'Fashionable technology' as an intersection of art, design, and technology is a term introduced by Seymour in 2008. It is defined as "designed garments, accessories, or jewellery that combine aesthetics and style with functional technology" (Seymour 2008, p. 12). The term 'Interactive jewellery' has emerged from the intersection of jewellery and wearable technology (Versteeg et al. 2016). Based on the examples of digital jewellery/interactive jewellery in the literature, this term has been usually referred to as the intersection of jewellery and consumer wearables. 'Therapeutic jewellery' is defined as the application of contemporary jewellery in medical devices (Bush and ten Hompel 2017).

There have been developments in the area of consumer wearables but little attention seems to have been paid to assistive wearables. Similar to the transition of eyeglasses from a medical assistive technology to a fashion accessory (Pullin 2009), there is potential for more integration of jewellery with assistive technology in other areas such as hearing aids, etc. Pullin (2009) emphasized the importance of this integration as it challenges the association of assistive technology with disability. As shown in Fig. 5, there are opportunities for the intersection of jewellery with assistive technologies and even workplace wearables. This integration could lead to the creation of an interdisciplinary area and new terminology as a subcategory of fashionable technology.

Focusing on the area of medical and assistive technologies, an inclusive approach to the design of products often focuses more on the usability and functional aspects and

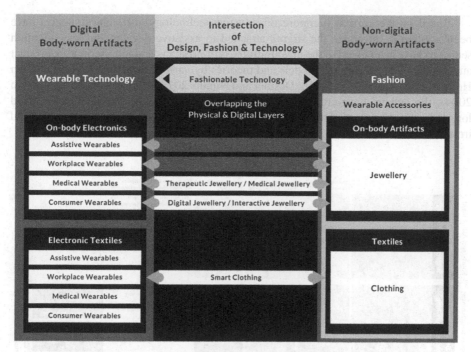

Fig. 5. Intersection of the physical and digital layers - author's interpretation

ignores user-product interaction in terms of desirability (Nickpour 2016) and meaningfulness. Medical and assistive devices are often designed based on the medical model of disability and ageing and ignore the social model (Bush and ten Hompel 2017; Clarkson et al. 2013). This seems to lead to the design of stigmatizing products which ignore the social integration of the target group. Stigma or embarrassment often happens when wearing an assistive product that looks more like a medical device than a mainstream fashion product (Skogsrød 2014).

As mentioned earlier, contemporary researchers attempt to alleviate the stigma attached to these devices by considering various factors in the design of assistive technologies. These strategies include concealment of the stigmatizing features, expression of the status of the wearer, familiar and fashionable styles and combinations with widely accepted products, advances in material and technology, size of the device, cultural background, location on the body, and personalization (Jacobson 2014; Vaes et al. 2012; Valamanesh 2014). Skogsrød (2014) notes that, 'mainstream aesthetics' in the design of assistive products can particularly help to minimize stigma. This relationship between aesthetics and stigma is significant in the design of assistive products. If the appearance supports the users' feeling of being 'more disabled', it will influence them emotionally and lead to product abandonment (Skogsrød 2014). In addition, personalizing the product's appearance helps the user to change the product in a way that expresses his/her identity and brings about feelings of joy, pride, and a sense of belonging instead of stigma and shame (Vaes 2012).

Based on the current literature on assistive technology, different strategies have been applied to minimize the stigma attached to assistive devices, but less attention seems to have been given to the meaningfulness of products and long-term user-product attachment. Considering the models and theories by various researchers (Bush and ten Hompel 2017; Casais et al. 2016; Desmet and Nijhuis 2013; Mugge et al. 2008; Norman 2004), the authors have created a framework (Fig. 6) to show the potential to build long-term emotional attachment with assistive wearables by designing meaningful and irreplaceable wearables.

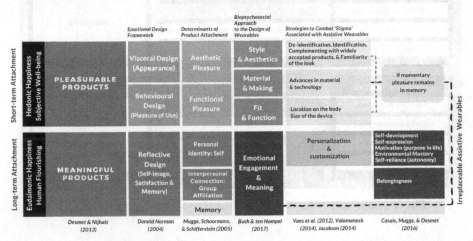

Fig. 6. Long-term emotional attachment with assistive wearables – proposed framework by authors

The top row shows that pleasurable wearables can lead to hedonic happiness and short-term attachment with the product. To create pleasurable wearables, designers should take aesthetics and functional factors into consideration. Bush and ten Hompel (2017) refer to the layers of style and aesthetics, material and making, and fit and function in the design of wearables. In the bottom row, Desmet and Nijhuis (2013) mention that creating meaningful products can lead to eudaimonic happiness. Therefore, designing meaningful wearables should create eudaimonic happiness and long-term attachment. Norman (2004) introduced 'reflective design' as one of the three levels of design related to the self-image and memories the object carries. Bush and ten Hompel's (2017) biopsychological approach also emphasizes the role of emotional engagement and meaning in the design of wearables. To create long-term attachment, Mugge et al. (2008) suggest designing products that express the owner's personal identity and connection to other people and social groups as well as stimulating product-related memories. Casais et al. (2016) identify six ways to design symbolically meaningful products: positive relations with others (the meaning of belongingness), personal growth (meaning of self-development), purpose in life (meaning of motivation), environmental mastery (development of skills that contribute to environmental mastery), autonomy (meaning of being independent and autonomous) and self-acceptance (meaning of identity).

Based on this proposed framework (Fig. 6), there is an opportunity in the area of assistive technology to design inclusive wearables that not only alleviate the stigma attached to these devices but also lead to long-term product attachment. In the future, it is important to explore the role of personalization, customization (features like colors, size, kinetic motion, etc.), and features in products that represent aspects of self (self-development, self-expression, motivation in life, environmental mastery, and autonomy) in creating meaningful and desirable assistive wearables. Other factors for investigation include how wearables can support belongingness, networking with support groups of peers, and family integration. Future research could also explore how wearables are able to provide emotional support in response to behaviour changes, sadness, etc. The role of positive memories associated with products can also be investigated in the design of irreplaceable assistive wearables.

4 Conclusion

Abandonment of wearable technology is one of the current issues across a wide range of target groups, specifically people who deal with aging and disability, and require the use of these devices on a daily basis. This paper provides an overview of reasons for the abandonment of assistive wearables in the current literature. It presents them as complex issues that involve psychological and social perceptions related to the needs of specific user groups. It points out that there seems to be an absence in the design of meaningful devices for improving the quality of people's lives.

This paper brings different strategies for the design of inclusive wearables together. It attempts to associate the diverse approaches, terms, and factors that may be helpful in reducing the stigma attached to adopting assistive wearables in everyday life across researchers and across disciplines. Through a survey of the literature and initial synthesis of these perspectives and the opportunities they indicate; this paper hopes to open the door for future directions that could influence the design of emotionally engaging and meaningful wearables that would lead to long-term product attachment.

References

Bush, P.: The craft of wearable wellbeing. In: Proceedings of the Third European Conference on Design4Health 2015, Sheffield, UK, Sheffield Hallam University (2015)

Bush, P., ten Hompel, S.: An integrated craft and design approach for wearable orthoses. Des. Health 1(1), 86–104 (2017)

Bowlby, J.: The Making and Breaking of Affectional Bonds. Tavistock Publications, London (1979)

Brickfield, C.F.: Attitudes and perceptions of older people toward technology. In: Robinson, K., Livingston, J., Birren, J.E., Regnier, V.A., Small, A.M., Sterns, H.L. (eds.) Aging and Technological Advances, pp. 31–38. Springer, New York (1984)

BSI TBSI: Design management systems. Managing inclusive design. Guide BS 7000-6:2005 (2005)

Buenaflor, C., Kim, H.: Six human factors to acceptability of wearable computers. Int. J. Multimed. Ubiquitous Eng. 8(3), 103–113 (2013)

Carpi, F., De Rossi, D.: Electroactive polymer-based devices for e-textiles in biomedicine. IEEE Trans. Inform. Technol. Biomed. 9(3), 295–318 (2005)

Casais, M., et al.: Using symbolic meaning as a means to design for happiness: the development of a card set for designers. In: Proceedings of the 50th Anniversary Conference on Design Research Society. (DRS 2016), Brighton, UK, June 2016

Casais, M., et al.: Symbolic meaning attribution as a means to design for happiness. In: Proceedings of the Tenth International Conference on Design and Emotion - Celebration and Contemplation 2015 (2016)

Cassim, J.: Issues and techniques in the inclusive design of apparel for the active ageing population. In: McCann, J., Bryson, D. (eds.) Textile-Led Design for the Active Ageing Population, pp. 283–305. Woodhead Publishing, Cambridge (2015)

Chatterjee, A., Aceves, A., Dungca, R., Flores, H., Giddens, K.: Classification of wearable computing: a survey of electronic assistive technology and future design. In: 2016 Second International Conference on Research in Computational Intelligence and Communication Networks (ICRCICN), pp. 22–27. IEEE, September 2016

Clarkson, P.J., Coleman, R., Keates, S., Lebbon, C.: Inclusive Design: Design for the Whole Population. Springer Science and Business Media, London (2013). https://doi.org/10.1007/978-1-4471-0001-0

Cunningham, J.: Contemporary European Narrative Jewellery: the prevalent themes, paradigms and the cognitive interaction between maker, wearer and viewer observed through the process, production and exhibition of narrative jewellery (Doctoral dissertation, University of Glasgow) (2008)

Desmet, P., Pohlmeyer, A.E.: Positive design: an introduction to design for subjective well-being. Int. J. Des. 7(3), 5–19 (2013).

Desmet, P., Nijhuis, J.: Four opportunities to design for well-being. Inspirational poster. Delft Institute of Positive Design, Delft (2013)

Desmet, Pieter M.A., Roeser, S.: Emotions in design for values. In: van den Hoven, J., Vermaas, Pieter E., van de Poel, I. (eds.) Handbook of Ethics, Values, and Technological Design, pp. 203–219. Springer, Dordrecht (2015). https://doi.org/10.1007/978-94-007-6970-0_6

European Commission: Smart Wearables: Reflection and orientation paper, Brussels (2016). http://ec.europa.eu/newsroom/document.cfm?doc_id=40542

Fortmann, J., Heuten, W., Boll, S.: User requirements for digital jewellery. In: Proceedings of the 2015 British HCI Conference, pp. 119–125. ACM, July 2015

Frankel, L.: Connecting virtual and visceral: an introduction to the evolution of wearable computers for industrial designers. In: Proceedings of the National Conference, Congress and Education Symposium, Industrial Designers Society of America and the International Council of Societies of Industrial Design. (CONNECTIONS 07), pp. 17–20. San Francisco (2007)

Goodacre, L., Cassim, J.: Footwear Design Challenge Workshop: Report to Arthritis Research UK of the Footwear Design Challenge Workshop. University of Central Lancashire (2010)

Goffman, E.: Stigma: Notes on the Management of Spoiled Identity. Simon and Schuster, New York (1986)

Grayson, K., Shulman, D.: Indexicality and the verification function of irreplaceable possessions: a semiotic analysis. J. Consum. Res. 27(1), 17–30 (2000)

Helmer, R.J., Mestrovic, M.A., Farrow, D., Lucas, S., Spratford, W.: Smart textiles: position and motion sensing for sport, entertainment and rehabilitation. In: Advances in Science and Technology, vol. 60, pp. 144–153. Trans Tech Publications (2008)

Heiss, L., Beckett, P., Carr-Bottomley, A.: Redesigning the trans-disciplinary: working across design, craft and technological boundaries to deliver an integrated wearable for cardiac monitoring. In: Proceedings of the 2016 ACM Conference on Designing Interactive Systems, pp. 691–699. ACM, June 2016

Hocking, C.: Function or feelings: factors in abandonment of assistive devices. Technol. Disabil. **11**(1,2), 3–11 (1999)

Jordan, P.W.: Designing Pleasurable Products: an Introduction to the New Human Factors. Taylor and Francis, New York (2000)

Jacobson: Personalised Assistive Products: Managing Stigma and Expressing the Self (Doctoral Dissertation, Aalto University School of Arts, Design and Architecture) (2014)

Kettley, S.: Crafting the wearable computer: design process and user experience (Doctoral dissertation, Edinburgh Napier University) (2007)

Kettley, S.: The foundations of craft: a suggested protocol for introducing craft to other disciplines. Craft Res. **3**(1), 33–51 (2012)

Kettley, S., Walker, S., Townsend, K.: Evidencing embodied participatory design. In: Proceedings of Critical Alternatives Conference, 17–21 August, Aarhus, Denmark (2015)

Koulidou, N.: Why should jewellers care about the digital? J. Jewellery Res. **17**, 17–33 (2018)

Lee, Y., Cassim, J.: How the inclusive design process enables social inclusion. In: International Association of Societies of Design Research (IASDR), pp. 1–10 (2009)

Lim, Y., Nickpour, F.: Inclusive design; from physical to psychosocial – a literature analysis toward a definition of psychosocial dimensions in design. In: DS 80-9 Proceedings of the 20th International Conference on Engineering. Design (ICED 15), vol. 9, pp. 27–30 (2015)

Mann, S.: Wearable computing. In: the Encyclopedia of Human-Computer Interaction. 2nd edition, By the Interaction Design Foundation, 7 February 2019 (2013)

McCarthy, J., Wright, P., Wallace, J., Dearden, A.: The experience of enchantment in human–computer interaction. Pers. Ubiquit. Comput. **10**(6), 369–378 (2006)

McCann, J., Bryson, D. (eds.): Smart clothes and wearable technology. Elsevier, Amsterdam (2009)

McCann, J.: Smart clothing for ageing population. In: McCann, J., Bryson, D. (eds.) Smart Clothes and Wearable Technology. Elsevier, Amsterdam (2009)

McCann, J.: Sportswear design for the active ageing. Fashion Practice **8**(2), 234–256 (2016)

Møller, T., Kettley, S.: Wearable health technology design: a humanist accessory approach. Int. J. Des. **11**(3), 35–49 (2017)

Møller, T.: Presenting the accessory approach: a start-up's journey towards designing an engaging fall detection device. In: Proceedings of the 2018 CHI Conference on Human Factors in Computing Systems, p. 559. ACM, April 2018

Mugge, R., Schoormans, J.P., Schifferstein, H.N.: Design strategies to postpone consumers' product replacement: the value of a strong person-product relationship. Des. J. **8**(2), 38–48 (2005)

Mugge, R., Schifferstein, H., Schoormans, J.: Product attachment and satisfaction: the effects of pleasure and memories. ACR Eur. Adv. **8**, 325–331(2007)

Mugge, R., Schoormans, J.P., Schifferstein, H.N.: Product attachment: design strategies to stimulate the emotional bonding to products. In: Schifferstein, N.H., Hekkert, P. (eds.) Product Experience, pp. 425–440. Elsevier (2008)

Mugge, R., Schoormans, J.P., Schifferstein, H.N.: Emotional bonding with personalised products. J. Eng. Des. **20**(5), 467–476 (2009)

Nickpour, F.: Mobility+Disability+Inclusivity: Supporting an independent automotive experience, 2016 UXPA event, UK (2016). https://www.youtube.com/watch?v=RxsfQKl20kk

Nielsen, J.: Usability Engineering. Morgan Kaufman Publishers, San Francisco (1993)

Norman, D.: Emotional design, Why We Love or Hate Everyday Things. Basic Civitas Books, New York (2004)

Profita, H.P.: Designing Wearable Assistive Computing Devices to Support Social Acceptability and Personal Expression (Doctoral dissertation) (2017)

Profita, H.P.: Designing wearable computing technology for acceptability and accessibility. ACM SIGACCESS Accessibility Comput. **114**, 44–48 (2016)

Pullin, G.: Design Meets Disability. MIT Press, Cambridge, Mass (2009)

Sanders, E.B.N., Stappers, P.J.: Co-creation and the new landscapes of design. Co-design **4**(1), 5–18 (2008)

Schifferstein, H.N., Mugge, R., Hekkert, P.: Designing Consumer-Product Attachment. In: McDonagh, D., Hekkert, P., Van Erp, J., Gyi, D. (eds.) Design and Emotion: The Experience of Everyday Things, pp. 327–331. Taylor and Francis, London (2004)

Savaş, ö.: A perspective on the person-product relationship: attachment and detachment. In: McDonagh, D., Hekkert, P., Van Erp, J., Gyi, D. (eds.) Design and Emotion: The Experience of Everyday Things, pp. 316–320. Taylor and Francis, London (2004)

Seymour, S.: Fashionable technology: The Intersection of Design, Fashion, Science, and Technology. Springer, New York (2008). https://doi.org/10.1007/978-3-211-74500-7

Schultz, S.E., Kleine, R.E., Kernan, J.B.: These are a few of my favorite things: toward an explication of attachment as a consumer behavior construct. Adv. Consum. Res. **16**(1), 359–366 (1989)

Silina, Y., Haddadi, H.: New directions in jewelry: a close look at emerging trends and developments in jewelry-like wearable devices. In: Proceedings of the 2015 ACM International Symposium on Wearable Computers, pp. 49–56. ACM, September 2015

Skogsrød, I.: Empathy and Aesthetics: Combating Stigma in the Design of Assistive Products. Artikkelsamling PD9-Institutt for Produktdesign, NTNU, Spring/autumn (2014)

Steinfeld, E.: Creating an inclusive environment. Trend Spotting at UD 2012 Oslo. Trends in Universal Design (2013)

Sun, M., et al.: eButton: a wearable computer for health monitoring and personal assistance. In: Proceedings of the 51st Annual Design Automation Conference, pp. 1–6. ACM (2014)

Uğur, S.: Wearing Embodied Emotions: A Practice-Based Design Research on Wearable Technology. Springer, Milan, Italy (2013). https://doi.org/10.1007/978-88-470-5247-5

Vaes, K.R.V., Stappers, P.J., Standaert, A., Desager, K.: Contending stigma in product design: using insights from social psychology as a stepping stone for design strategies. In: Out of Control; Proceedings of the 8th International Conference on Design and Emotion, London, Great Britain, 11–14 September 2012, Central Saint Martins College of Arts and Design (2012)

Valamanesh, R.: Important factors in the design of assistive technology to avoid the stigmatization of users. Arizona State University (2014)

Venere, F., Matteo, I.: When human body meets technology: the designer approach to wearable devices. In: 5th STS Italia Conference, pp. 989–1004. ITA (2014)

Versteeg, M., van den Hoven, E., Hummels, C.: Interactive jewellery: a design exploration. In Proceedings of the TEI 2016: Tenth International Conference on Tangible, Embedded, and Embodied Interaction, pp. 44–52. ACM, February 2016

Wallace, J.: Emotionally charged: a practice-centred enquiry of digital jewellery and personal emotional significance (Doctoral dissertation, Sheffield Hallam University) (2007)

Wallace, J., Press, M.: Craft knowledge for the digital age. In: Proceedings of the 6th Asian Design Conference, October 2003

Wright, P., Wallace, J., McCarthy, J.: Aesthetics and experience-centered design. ACM Trans. Comput.-Hum. Interact. (TOCHI) **15**(4), 18 (2008)

AuDimo: A Musical Companion Robot to Switching Audio Tracks by Recognizing the Users Engagement

W. K. N. Hansika[✉], Lakindu Yasassri Nanayakkara, Adhisha Gammanpila, and Ravindra de Silva

Robotics and Intelligent Systems Laboratory, Department of Computer Science, University of Sri Jayewardenepura, Nugegoda, Sri Lanka
kushan989@gmail.com

Abstract. Music has become an integral part that enriches human lives. It serves as a method of entertainment in social gatherings. Consequently Different playlists of music are played to energize, uplift, and comfort listeners in social gatherings. If most in that group of people don't like the songs playing energy in between them can be lost. In this study, a musical companion robot was developed to interact with the audience through its rhythmic behaviors and through the song selections done by the robot based on the moods of the audience using Neural Networks and emotion recognition through facial recognition. The study demonstrated high levels of user acceptance based on the feedback received from a sample set of 15 volunteers within the age range of 21–25 years. Though The robot's interaction through its rhythmic behaviors was a success, the song selection algorithm was below the level of acceptance at the startup of the robot. However, as the data demonstrates, the robot was able to accomplish the task of enhancing the audience through its appearance and behaviors.

Keywords: Social robotics · Human computer interactions · Music analysis

1 Introduction

Music is a universal language [4] and has become a part of each human's life in such a way that they listen to different types of music based on numerous aspects. As for instance based on the situation, the emotions and moods and even based on time of the day. This is also applicable for both individuals and for a group of people. However when it comes to listening to music with a group of people there is a considerably high possibility that the music played is not preferred to certain people based on their mood at that time. As a result the overall experience for certain humans will be less enthusiastic.

Therefore the objective of this study was to develop a musical companion robot with an intelligent system that classifies and plays songs based on the moods of the audience.

© Springer Nature Switzerland AG 2020
C. Stephanidis et al. (Eds.): HCII 2020, LNCS 12424, pp. 89–106, 2020.
https://doi.org/10.1007/978-3-030-60117-1_7

1.1 Motivation

Organization of Music Collection. To find the relevant information efficiently, playlists and music collections have to be arranged in the best way possible. The search process is ideally focused upon a wide range of properties. The categorization, access, and ordering of files can be achieved in a more natural, straightforward manner by correctly assigning properties to the material. Books in physical library for example. They been arranged on keywords (comparable with tags), genre or era. Organizing digital music files will be done in the same way, i.e. natural and effective for people. Digital files can be quickly rearranged into other classes or categories compared to the grouping of material in a library; for example, files categorized by genre criteria can be rearranged according to another category, based on artist or year. The indexes can be constructed in case of need. This can be done by choosing various criteria, such as filenames, primary metadata, or tags. A daunting problem is finding a secure, straightforward and hierarchical organization with access to a the amount of data and files (in this case music tracks). While browsing or digging through an individual music listener's huge database of songs, new tools are necessary to fulfill the user's file management level requirements. By using new tools for classification and retrieval, music listeners will see the related output from those tools that fulfill their requests.

Enhance Group Engagement. In an occasion where a set of humans listens to track or songs like a picnic or a family party, if a person within the group isn't interested in the music which is playing at the moment, that particular character unearths it very difficult to revel in himself and it can be identified via his behavior [6]. In a situation like above, there ought to be a character to study the behaviors and reactions of the listener's and decide whether they're enjoying the tune or not. If they may be no longer taking part in, the person that controls the song needs to change the music to a different song from a different tempo, different mood or a different genre to ensure that everyone inside the institution is taking part in the music and no longer feeling bored. Furthermore, that character ought to be accountable to beautify the engagement of the audience and to maintain the target audience alive every time. However, the cognitive workload of picking up a track from a huge series of music prevents the person who controls tune to enjoy the moment.

1.2 Objective

The main objective of this study was to develop a musical companion robot with an intelligent system that classifies songs input by the user and switching tracks by observing the behaviors of the audience.

2   Background and Related Work

2.1   Social Robotics

Unlike robots that have become common sights in factories and warehouses that have restricted human contact, social robots [10] are built to communicate with us. Social (or sociable) robots are built to interact with people in a normal, interactive way often to produce positive results in a variety of applications, such as education, safety, quality of life, entertainment, communication, and tasks that require collaborative teamwork. A quite challenging task is the long-term goal of creating social robots which are capable and effective partners for people. They will need to communicate with people using both verbal and nonverbal cues, obviously. They will need a wide range of social-cognitive abilities and other mind theories to understand human actions and be intuitively understood by humans. Advances in artificial intelligence made that possible. There are suggestions that social robots' emotional intelligence would allow them to make a real difference in the lives of vulnerable people in society.

2.2   Human-Robot Interaction (HRI)

When social robotics is increasingly cross-disciplinary beyond engineering and computer science, and ultimately draws on human-computer interaction knowledge and resources, the term Human-Robot Interaction [7] gradually substitutes for the word "social robotics". HRI as a crossdisciplinary area lies between robotics, AI, cognitive science, psychology (developmental), design of interactions, biology and especially ethology. As part of the field it would be beneficial to have studies in pedagogy, sociology, philosophy and science and technology. HRI discusses the human perception of robot systems, user-friendliness, design issues (anthropomorphic, zoomorphic or practical robots) and ethical considerations.

2.3   Human Moods and Emotions

Human beings are continuously being exposed to emotions and moods. A mood is a kind of internal subjective state in a person's mind, which can hold for hours or days. The American psychologist Robert E. Thayer (1982) has done research on moods and the behavior of humans regarding moods [13]. The mood is a relatively long-lasting, affective or emotional state, according to the findings of his study. Unlike an emotion, its course takes place over a longer period of time and there is no direct effect of individual events or triggers in shifting a mood. Where feelings, such as fear or surprise can change for a short time, often due to a specific cause or occurrence, moods appear to last longer. Siemer (2005) states that moods, in contrary to emotions, are not being directed at a specific object [11]. When one has the sadness feeling, one is usually depressed about a specific state of affairs, such as an irrevocable personal loss. In contrast, if one is in a sad mood, one is not sad about anything specific, but sad "about nothing (in particular)". In addition, Robbins & Judge (2008) state that emotions are intense feelings that are directed at someone or something, whereas moods are feelings that tend to be less intense than emotions and lack a contextual stimulus. Both emotions and Moods are elements of affect: a broad range of emotions that people experience. To order to distinguish the use of moods in this study instead of feelings, we believe that emotion is a part of mood. In a mood, which is a global sentiment, multiple emotions may occur. We are looking at the music tracks in this study. Songs have an overlaying feeling in the form of a mood, with several feelings that can shift over the duration of the music.

2.4   Thayer's Arousal-Valence Emotion Plane

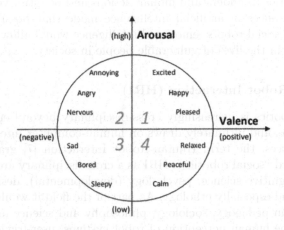

Fig. 1. Thayer's arousal-valence Emotion Plane

As can be seen in Fig. 1, Thayer's arousal-valence emotion plane [13] displays several moods in the four different classes. These moods may have a negative valence (the aspect of tension), such as the "sad" or "angry" mood, or a positive valence expressing moods like "relaxed" or "happy". Linked to the energy aspect, the arousal factor on the y-axis distinguishes the different moods from the calm and quiet activity at the bottom to the extreme and strong mood at the top.

2.5   Robotic Music Companions

Travis is a robotic smartphone speaker dock and music listening companion. Travis is a musical entertainment robot computationally controlled by an Android smartphone, and serves both as an amplified speaker dock, and a socially expressive robot. It has rhythm-based music search capability. Travis [3] is designed to enhance a human's music listening experience by providing social presence and audience companionship, as well as by embodying the music played on the device as a performance. The Keepon robot [12] is another example of some other related work dealt with rhythmic human-robot interplay (HRI). Keepon is a small creature-like robot whose movement is controlled by using a rhythm-based software system. This system had considered dance as a form of social interaction to explore the properties and importance of rhythmic movement in general social interaction.

3   Methodology

3.1   Hardware Design

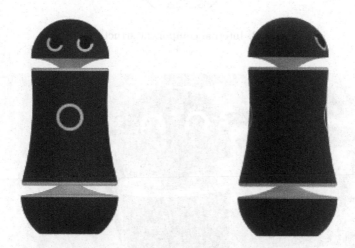

Fig. 2. Final design of AudiMO (front & side view)

Minimalist Design. The major task we had to overcome was design this as a semi-humanoid appearance. A typical humanoid robot may contain legs, hands and also other parts of a human body. For accomplish the design phase we were followed Minimalist Design Principles. Figure 2 shows the finalised design.

In its most stripped-down definition, minimalism is about designers expressing only the most essential and necessary elements of a product or subject by getting rid of any excessive and, therefore, unnecessary components and features. This principal is widely using when designing social robots.

Internal Structure. Figure 3 shows the internal component structure if the robot while the Fig. 4 shows the final built design of the robot. Motors are denoted in black color. We can divide the structure into the main 3 components. Head, Body, and Base.

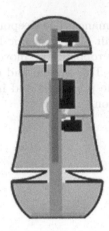

Fig. 3. Internal component structure

Fig. 4. Final built outlook of the robot.

3.2   Software Framework

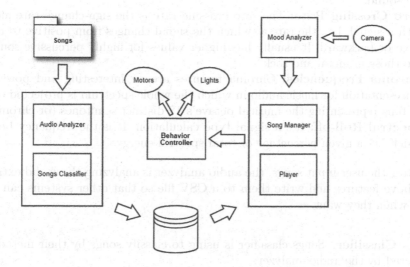

Fig. 5. System architecture

This system has 2 components as shown in Fig. 5. A C# desktop application and a Python Server. Python Server contains the Audio Analyzer and the Songs Classifier. Song Manager and the Behavior Controller contains in the C# application. These 2 components communicate using HTTP. All the data are store in a local database. So that both components can access it when it wants.

Audio Analyzer. To classify songs we need to extract meaningful features from audio clips. We can extract those features from online resources or by analyzing locally. Because this is a portable system its best for doing it locally. For analyzing audio signals a python package called LIBROSA [2] is used in this study.

LIBROSA is a Python module to analyze audio signals in general but geared more towards music. It includes the nuts and bolts to build a MIR(Music information retrieval) system. There are many features that we can extract from an audio clip. For this study, we have chosen 5 features. Mel-Frequency Cepstral Coefficients, Spectral Centroid, Zero Crossing Rate, Chroma Frequencies, Spectral Roll-off.

1. **Mel-Frequency Cepstral Coefficients:** A signal's Mel frequency cepstral coefficients (MFCCs) are a small set of features (usually about 10–20) that define the overall shape of a spectral envelope in a concise manner. It models human voice characteristics.

2. **Spectral Centroid:** It indicates where the "center of mass" for a sound is located and is calculated as the weighted mean of the frequencies present in the sound.
3. **Zero Crossing Rate:** The zero crossing rate is the sign-change rate along with a signal, i.e., the rate at which the signal changes from positive to negative or backward. It usually has higher values for highly percussive sounds like those in metal and rock.
4. **Chroma Frequencies:** Chroma features are an interesting and powerful representation for music audio in which the whole spectrum is projected onto 12 bins representing the musical octave's 12 distinct semitones (or chroma).
5. **Spectral Roll-off:** It's a signal type calculation. It is the frequency below which lies a given percentage of total spectral energy.

After the user input songs, the audio analyzer is analyzing those and extract the above features and write them to a CSV file so that other systems can use them when they want.

Songs Classifier. Songs classifier is using to classify songs by their metadata extracted by the audio analyzer.

Machine Learning. The aim of this part of the system is the automatic assignment genre tags for music, based on metadata extracted by the audio analyzer. In this word, "automatic" means users don't want to classify songs themselves: using some machine learning techniques this part of the system will do for them. We used a NN(Neural Network) for implement the classifier in this study.

1. **Data Set**
   For this study, I used the famous GITZAN dataset [1]. This dataset contains 1000 sound clips belongs to 10 different genres, namely blues, classical, country, disco, hip hop, jazz, reggae, rock, metal, and pop. Each genre consists of 100 sound clips and each audio track 30 s long.
   All the features extracted by audio analyzer then appended into a .csv file so that classification algorithms can be used [8].
2. **Preprocessing the data**
   Pre-processing refers to the transformations applied to our data before feeding it to the algorithm. Data Preprocessing is a technique that is used to convert the raw data into a clean data set. In other words, whenever the data is gathered from different sources it is collected in raw format which is not feasible for the analysis. The aspect is that data set should be formatted in such a way that more than one Machine Learning and Deep Learning algorithms are executed in one data set, and best out of them is chosen.
   For this data set, we used Standardize preprocessing technique to rescale values and Label encoding to encode categorical values.

Mood Analyzer. Mood analyzer is used to determine whether the audience likes the currently playing song and are they engaging with that song. So basically this is about a group of people rather than an individual. For that task, we have to track multiple faces in real-time. AFFDEX SDK is used for this study to overcome that challenge.

Tool for Facial Expressions. AFFDEX SDK [9] is a cross-platform real-time facial expression recognition toolkit that can automatically code the expressions of multiple people simultaneously. This has four major components as shown in Fig. 6.

1. **Face and facial landmark detection**
   Landmark detection can identify 34 landmarks from each facial bounding box.
2. **Face texture feature extraction**
3. **Facial action classification**
   Histogram of Oriented Gradient (HOG) features are extracted from the image region of interest defined by the facial landmark points. It's using Support Vector Machine(SVM) Classifier trained on 10 000s of manually coded facial images.
4. **Emotion expression modelling**
   The emotions expressions are combinations of facial actions. Eg: Anger, Disgust, Fear, Joy, Sadness, Surprise and Contempt

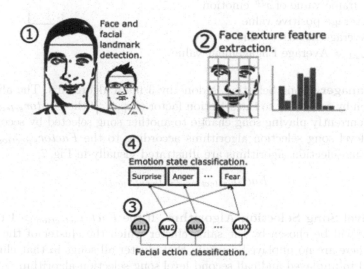

Fig. 6. The flow of the process

This is capable of identifying 20 expressions and 7 emotions. And also can determine gender and whether the person is wearing glasses. Using all the emotions and expressions will reduce accuracy. So that we selected a sample from them which suitable this study most such as Joy, Surprise, Disgust, Sadness, Nose Wrinkle and Smile.

All the emotions, expressions values vary from 0 to 100 except Valance. It varies from −100 to 100. Valance is a measure of the positive or negative nature of the recorded persons experience.

Mood Summarising Algorithm. Mainly we focused on negativity and the positivity of the audience. So all the emotions selected divided into two categories according to Thayers arousal-valence emotion plane. (This is briefed in Sub Sect. 2.4). System store first 10 frames (initial value) values and summarize it and send summarized values to Song Manager.

Following parameters were calculated for each songs. (Equation 1, 2 & 3)

$$C_{pos} = (\sum_{i=1}^{T}(e_{joy,i} + e_{surprise,i} + e_{smile,i} + e_{valance,i}))/4 * T \qquad (1)$$

$$C_{neg} = (\sum_{i=1}^{T}(e_{sad,i} + e_{disgust,i} + e_{nose_wrinkle,i} + e_{sad,i}))/4 * T \qquad (2)$$

$$C_{engagement} = (\sum_{i=1}^{T}(e_{engagement,i}))/T \qquad (3)$$

T = Total time frames
$e_{x,i} = i^{th}$ frame value of xth emotion
C_{pos} = Average positive value
C_{neg} = Average negative value
$C_{engagement}$ = Average Engagement value

Song Manager. Song Selection is done by 3 main algorithms. The algorithm was chosen by according to the selection factor (Eq. 4). If the $Factor_{selection} < 1$ then the currently playing song change to another song selected by second level or third level song selection algorithms according to the $Factor_{selection}$ value. All the song selection algorithms are illustrated visually in Fig. 7

$$Factor_{selection} = (c_{pos}/c_{neg}) \qquad (4)$$

First Level Song Selection Algorithm. If the $Factor_{selection} > 1$ then the next song will be chosen by the same cluster which the cluster of the current song. If there are no unplayed songs in that cluster all songs in that cluster are initialized to unplayed and call second level song selection algorithm.

Second Level Song Selection Algorithm. If the $Factor_{selection}$ between 1 and 0.5 that means the Current overall mood percentage is negative but not that much high. The next song will be played in a similar genre of the previous song.

Third Level Song Selection Algorithm. If the $Factor_{selection} < 0.5$ that means current overall mood percentage is negative but high. Then the next song will be played in dis-similar genre of the previous song.

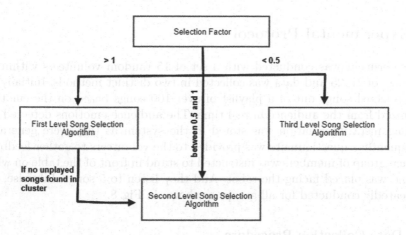

Fig. 7. Levels of song classification algorithm

Behaviours Controller. This study main objective is to build a music companion robot. To overcome that objective we added some rhythmic behaviors to enhance the engagement of the audience. We used song BPM to decide the behavior pattern. The behavior controller mainly consists of 3 parts. Motors, Actuators, and Lights.

Controlling Motors. Movements of the robot and the speed of those movements totally depended according to the BPM that analyses by audio analyzer. Dynamixel SDK for C# was used for controlling servo motors through the application that was developed. In every beat of the song, the speed of the motors (Rounds per Minute) and the goal position of each motor were changed to make rhythmic moves.

Controlling Actuator. Since the MightyZAP linear actuators did not have SDK available, the actuator datasheet was analyzed to communicate with the actuator. Communication between the actuator and the controlling PC was carried out via the controller USB2Dyanmixel. In the controlling method, the data packets which should be sent to the actuator, including headers, checksum and so on, were constructed according to its data sheet. The constructed data packets were sent through serial communication to the USB2Dyanmixel controller to achieve the desired actuator functionality.

Controlling Lights. Real-time audio analysis to control the lights according to the music should be done. To this end the Open Frameworks toolkit sound module was used. The parameters identified from the Open Frameworks toolkit were sent as a serial signal to the Arduino micro controller.

4   Experimental Protocol

The experiment was conducted with a set of 15 random volunteers within the age range of 21–25 and data was collected in two distinct methods. Initially the robot selected songs out of a playlist of over 100 songs based on the emotions recognized from the audience in real time. The audience emotions detected and the song meta information was stored in the system as they were generated. Subsequently a questionnaire was provided to the volunteers to gather feedback.

Each group of members was instructed to stand in front of the table on which Audimo was placed facing the robot. And they listen to 5 songs. Likewise, this is repeatedly conducted for all groups as shown in Fig. 8.

4.1   Data Collection Procedure

Mainly data was collected using two different methods. During the experiment phase audience mood changes through out the song and song changes made by the system stored in the system. And also user feedback was gathered using a questionnaire.

Data Collected by the System

- Emotion values of the audience captured throughout every time frame of each song.
- Summary mood values of each song stored along with the output of the song changing system to evaluate the success of the song changing algorithm.

Questionnaire. The user feedback was gathered by a questionnaire with 17 questions divided into 3 sections. In the first sections gathered personal details like age, gender, and their musical preferences. And the second section was instructed to fill during the experiments to gather their moods for specific songs and song changes done by the system. And also the Synchronisation of robot rhythmic behaviors to different type songs. The last section used the measure of the Appearance of the robot, Change of Listening experience and to get Suggestions for Improvements.

Fig. 8. Experimental setup with the volunteers

5   Results

A survey was conducted with a set of 15 volunteers within the age range of 21–25 years and three parameters were measured. Namely the overall experience in generation of music by the robot, the transition of songs from one to another and the robot design.

5.1   Songs Classifier Accuracy

Statistically measure the model accuracy. We use a Confusion Matrix [5] to evaluate the performance of the model of genre prediction.

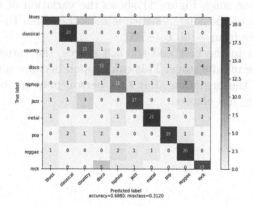

Fig. 9. Confusion matrix

The Fig. 9 shows the trained classifier performance in the form of a confusion matrix. Columns show the actual while rows show predicted genres. For example country column with value 2 shows that 2 country genre tracks were predicted as a pop genre. All correctly identified tracks are lay in the main diagonal of the matrix. We can derive some important performance measures using a confusion matrix.

Figure 10 demonstrates the gathered precision information directly via the experiment.

	precision	recall	f1-score
0	0.810	0.680	0.739
1	0.800	0.800	0.800
2	0.652	0.600	0.625
3	0.625	0.600	0.612
4	0.647	0.440	0.524
5	0.630	0.680	0.654
6	0.875	0.840	0.857
7	0.826	0.760	0.792
8	0.571	0.800	0.667
9	0.548	0.680	0.607
accuracy			0.688
macro avg	0.698	0.688	0.688
weighted avg	0.698	0.688	0.688

Fig. 10. Precision, recall, F1 and accuracy of the model

5.2   Data Captured from the System

The song will be tracked at the beginning and when half of the song has elapsed and at the end of the song. Figure 11 shows the variation of valence over each frame in each stage of the song. Valence is not other than the recorded person experience. It ranges from −100 to +100.

We can see that in the first and the last stages, the variation of valence is high rather than the middle stage. This can happen because sometimes a person may like a song at the beginning, but that person may get boring when more than half of the song has elapsed.

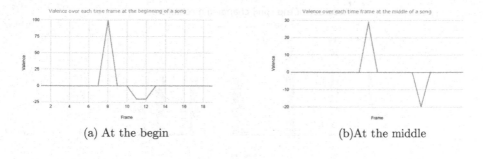

(a) At the begin   (b)At the middle

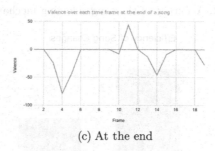

(c) At the end

Fig. 11. Valence in different stages over each time frame of a song

5.3   Survey Summary

As per the results shown in Fig. 12 for the Accuracy of Song changing mechanism, 60% of the volunteers were satisfied, 26.7% were not satisfied and 13.3% resulted in neutral response.

Similarly as Fig. 13 depicts, 68% of the volunteers responded with positive feedback for the transition of songs while 32% shared negative responses.

On the other hand, design of the robot was measured under two criteria.

Firstly based on the first impression. As per the results shown in Fig. 14 for the first impression, 25% resulted in very positive, 37.5% positive, 6.3% not impressive and 31.3% as neutral.

As the second criteria, overall design was measured. As per the results shown in Fig. 15 50% resulted as impressive, 25% good and 25% with neutral feedback. No negative feedback was received.

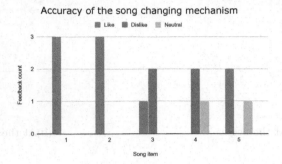

Fig. 12. Accuracy of the song changing mechanism

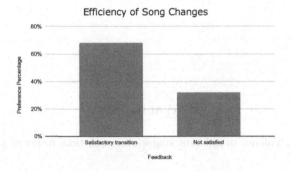

Fig. 13. Efficiency of song changes

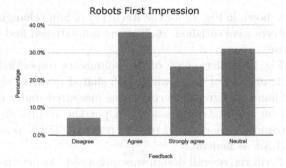

Fig. 14. Robots first impression

6   Discussion

When analyzing mood detection accuracy, we can see that AFFDEX SDK identified positive emotions and expressions accurately rather than negative ones. Among the user feedback, there are comments provided for wrong identification of emotions by the robot. In the first session the system tracks audience behaviors only at the beginning of the song. Most of the participants suggested that

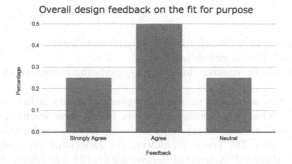

Fig. 15. Overall design feedback on the fit for purpose

it should be done at the middle and end of the song as well. So after making the required changes to the algorithm in the second session it produced better results relative to the first session. When we capture behaviors from the audience the AFFDEX SDK has the capability to detect each person's face separately and detect emotion values separately. But it can't track emotions separately from each person. Hence we couldn't analyze the mood of each person separately in this study. Another aspect that we saw when a person doesn't like a song is their mood is not enough for recognizing it. As a result there are some people when they don't like something they don't express it in their faces. Hence, gesture recognition should be used for the behavior identification process. The rhythmic behaviors of the robot are not always synchronous with the rhythm of the song. Because we cannot set the BPM of the song each time frame as the speed of the motors. There is always a delay when communicating over serial.

7   Conclusion

The music companion robot was able to attract audience attention through its design and synchronous behaviours. According to the participants' subjective experience, their moods have been enhanced primarily by the music companion robot appearance. Because of the audio analyzer users can add songs locally and also the rhythmic behaviors of the robot im- proved. The system wasn't able to capture audience behaviors in the initial stage. But after doing amendments to the algorithm it accomplished that task better than the previous stage.

References

1. Data sets. http://marsyas.info/downloads/datasets.html
2. Librosa. https://librosa.github.io/librosa/
3. Travis/Shimi robotic speaker dock. http://guyhoffman.com/travis-shimi-robotic-speaker-dock/
4. Blogger, G.: Why music is a universal language, January 2016
5. Brownlee, J.: What is a confusion matrix in machine learning, January 2020. https://machinelearningmastery.com/confusion-matrix-machine-learning/
6. Keltner, D., Sauter, D., Tracy, J., Cowen, A.: Emotional expression: advances in basic emotion theory. J. Nonverbal Behav. **43**(2), 133–160 (2019). https://doi.org/10.1007/s10919-019-00293-3
7. Kerstin, D.: Mutual gaze: implications for human-robot interaction. Front. Comput. Neurosci. **5** (2011). https://doi.org/10.3389/conf.fncom.2011.52.00024
8. Li, T., Tzanetakis, G.: Factors in automatic musical genre classification of audio signals. In: 2003 IEEE Workshop on Applications of Signal Processing to Audio and Acoustics (IEEE Cat. No. 03TH8684). https://doi.org/10.1109/aspaa.2003.1285840
9. Mcduff, D., Mahmoud, A., Mavadati, M., Amr, M., Turcot, J., Kaliouby, R.E.: AFFDEX SDK. In: Proceedings of the 2016 CHI Conference Extended Abstracts on Human Factors in Computing Systems - CHI EA 16 (2016). https://doi.org/10.1145/2851581.2890247
10. Rouse, M.: What is social robot? - definition from whatis.com, May 2019. https://searchenterpriseai.techtarget.com/definition/social-robot
11. Siemer, M.: Mood-congruent cognitions constitute mood experience. Emotion (Washington, D.C.) **5**, 296–308 (2005). https://doi.org/10.1037/1528-3542.5.3.296
12. Spectrum, I.: Keepon, May 2018. https://robots.ieee.org/robots/keepon/
13. Thayer, R.E.: The Biopsychology of Mood and Arousal. Oxford University Press (1990)

Transmission of Rubbing Sensation with Wearable Stick-Slip Display and Force Sensor

Honoka Haramo, Vibol Yem[✉], and Yasushi Ikei

Tokyo Metropolitan University, Tokyo, Japan
{haramo,yem,ikei}@vr.sd.tmu.ac.jp

Abstract. This paper introduces a system of tactile transmission on the tip of index finger and reports the effect of skin deformation force and vibration on the friction sensation of the material. There are two sides for the system: tactile-sender and tactile-receiver. We used a force sensor to measure the dynamic friction of a material at the tactile sender side. Due to the amplitude of stick-slip vibration is very small and impossible to measure by the current force sensor, we attempted to investigate the effect of a sinewave form vibration that we processed by a computer software. A wearable stick-slip display with a cylindrical shape contactor was developed for the tactile-receiver side. Contactor is directly attached to a shaft of a DC motor. It was confirmed that, the DC motor can provide high fidelity vibration sensation, therefore, the contactor can present both skin deformation and stick-slip vibration. Experiment's result showed that, the intensity of friction sensation of the participants did not proportional to the friction measured by a force senor. We considered that it was because the friction coefficient of the material attached to the end of the force sensor was different to that of human skin. Moreover, the result showed that, participants adjusted the strength of skin deformation stimulated by the tactile device stronger to perceive more similar to the rubbing sensation of a real material that has higher stickiness perception. We also confirmed that higher frequency of vibration affected the perception of slippery.

Keywords: Tactile transmission · Tactile communication · Stick-slip display · Tactile sender · Tactile receiver · Tele-presence

1 Introduction

Telepresence or telexistence is one technology in the field of virtual reality, which enables a person to sense that he or she is being in a remote area without directly going to that place [1]. This technology is useful to increase the quality of tele-operation or tele-communication. To realize such a technology, audio and visual transmission system with high quality have been largely developed. Currently, transmission of the sensation of touch or rubbing an object's surface is also actively studied for a local user to explore the property of the remote materials. However, there are still challenges for the tactile transmission with realistic sensation of touch due to the small range of tactile feeling that reproduced by a tactile display.

© Springer Nature Switzerland AG 2020
C. Stephanidis et al. (Eds.): HCII 2020, LNCS 12424, pp. 107–116, 2020.
https://doi.org/10.1007/978-3-030-60117-1_8

To reproduce a sensation of rubbing or touching a material, various wearable tactile devices have been largely developed. Vibration is popularly used for reproducing material texture sensation [2–4]. Most of these devices are small and lightweight. However, though vibration was found that it affects the friction sensation, it is still difficult to control stick-slip sensation in wide range to increase the realistic sensation of rubbing a material. Other studies have developed skin deformation devices to provide reaction force to the finger pad [5–7]. However, these devices are suitable for stretching the skin only but all of these cannot be used to provide slip sensation continuously because of the limitation of the contactor's movement. Our study aimed to reproduce stick-slip sensation of various materials with a cylindrical contactor that can be rotated and provide stick-slip sensation continuously. We designed this stick-slip display that allows the contactor to rotate and slip on the skin continuously. Our device also can provide wide range frequency of vibration sensation by the DC motor that actuated with alternative current input [8]. We considered that, the friction sensation can be controlled by changing the strength of skin deformation, frequency and amplitude of stick-slip vibration.

In this study, we developed a system of tactile transmission on a fingertip in which we used a wearable stick-slip display to present rubbing sensation and a force sensor to measure friction force of a material during rubbing its surface. Our system is lightweight and simple in mechanism. This paper reports the characteristics of our system and the effect of skin deformation and vibration on the sensation of friction (i.e. stickiness and slippery). The result of our experiment showed that, the intensity of friction sensation of the participants did not proportional to friction measured by the force senor. The result also showed that, participants adjusted the strength of skin deformation stimulated by tactile device stronger to perceive more similar to the rubbing sensation of a real material that stimulates higher stickiness perception. We also confirmed that higher frequency vibration affected the perception of slippery.

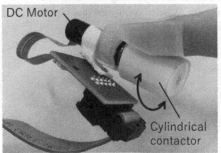
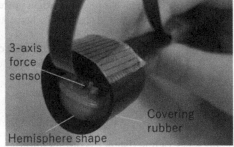

Fig. 1. Wearable stick-slip display (left) and 3-axis force sensor (right).

2 System

2.1 Force Sensor for Material Surface Measurement

A force sensor (μDynPick, WACOH) was used to measure the frictional force of the material. A hemisphere imitating the shape of a human finger pad was attached to this sensor. The hemisphere was made with a 3D printer and covered with a rubber that mimics the friction of a human finger pad. Also, by attaching a 3D printed handle, the sensor can be moved on the surface of the material (Fig. 1(right)).

2.2 Wearable Stick-Slip Display

This wearable device consists of a DC motor, a cylindrical contactor, and parts to be worn on a finger. These parts were made by a PLA − 3D printer with a stacking pitch of 0.1 mm. The contactor can rotate with stick-slip movement on the skin. A silicone tube was attached to the surface of the contactor to increase the friction (Fig. 1(left)). The mounting parts can be changed in size from small to large according to the size of the finger, and they can be easily attached and detached on the fingertip. In addition, this device is as light as 20 g and has a simple mechanism, so it does not hinder finger movement.

The sense of stick-slip depends on the coefficient of kinetic friction between the finger skin and the surface of the material. Many conventional devices could not continuously control the stick-slip sensation due to the restriction of the contact movement. The design of this study enabled the contact to present a continuous sliding sensation. In addition, skin deformation, slipperiness and vibration can be presented simultaneously by the driving method of DC motor.

2.3 Relationship Between a Kinetic Friction Force of a Material and a Tangential Force to Stimulate the Skin

Figure 2 shows the relationship between kinetic friction force of a material measured by the force sensor and the tangential force stimulating the skin. Tangential force F_s to deform the skin of finger pad was calculated with the following equation:

$$F_s = (F_n \times K_p \times K_s)/r \tag{1}$$

where, F_n is a kinetic friction force of a material, K_p and K_s are proportional coefficients. r is the radius of cylindrical shaped contactor. K_p is a constant value that can be adjusted from 0.0 to 1.0 to perceive the sensation by stick-slip display most similar to friction of the real material. K_s is the value that depends on the motor controller. To estimate the value of K_s, we evaluated our motor controller as shown in Fig. 3. K_p was fixed to 1.0. In this evaluation, F_n was set in six values of 0.2, 0.4, 0.6, 0.8, 1.0 and 1.2 [N].

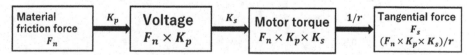

Fig. 2. Schematics of the relationship between friction force and shear force.

Figure 4 showed the graph of the relationship between F_s and F_n while K_p was fixed at 1.0. The result indicated that K_s was approximately 6.0. Therefore, Eq. (1) can be

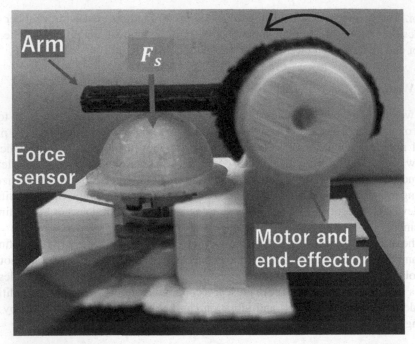

Fig. 3. Overview of evaluation apparatus to estimate the relationship between F_s and F_n while K_p was fixed at 1.0.

optimal for each material with the following equation:

$$F_{s\_m} = 6.0 \times K_{p\_m} \times F_{n\_m}/r \left(0.0 \leq K_{p\_m} \leq 1.0\right) \tag{2}$$

where m represents number of each material at the tactile sender side. F_{s_m} is estimated force to stimulate the skin.

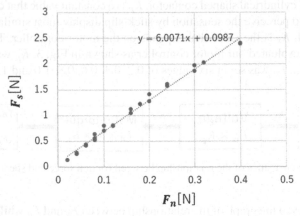

Fig. 4. Estimation result of the relationship between F_s and F_n while K_p was fixed at 1.0.

3 User Study

3.1 Purpose

First, we aimed to observe whether the perception of slipperiness of the material is proportional to friction force measured by the force sensor or not. Then, we investigated the relationship between the slipperiness of the material and the proportional coefficient K_{p_m} that adjusted by each participant to change stimulation force F_s according to their perception of friction sensation. Last, we investigated the relationship between the slipperiness of the material and the vibration frequency of contactor.

3.2 Participants and Design

There were sixteen university students, thirteen males and three females from 20 to 24 year of age participated this user study.

- Order of friction coefficient and slippery perception of the materials

    In order to investigate the characteristics of the sensor, the dynamic friction force between the sensor and the material surface was measured. In addition, in order to investigate how the slipperiness perception of the material, participants were asked to rub each material and to order the slipperiness of the material.

- Relationship between slipperiness sensation of material and stimulation force presented to finger pad

    Participants rubbed the real material with their fingers and compared it with the stimulus of the contactor. They adjusted the proportional coefficient K_{p_m} of each material from 0 to 1 in increments of 0.01. When they found a proper value of K_{p_m}, the dynamic friction force that measured by the sensor while rubbing was recorded.

- Relationship between the slipperiness perception of the material and the magnitude of the selected vibration frequency

    First, K_{p_m} was kept constant at 0 (no skin deformation), and participants were asked to adjust the vibration amplitude of four types of frequencies of 30, 100, 300, 500 [Hz] until they could perceive the vibration. Next, K_{p_m} was set to a value that they previously adjusted for a material to allow them to sense both skin deformation and vibration. While the correspondent material was rubbed with the sensor, they were asked to select a proper frequency of five types of 0, 30, 100, 300, 500 [Hz]. 0 [Hz] represented that they preferred only skin deformation F_{s_m} without additional vibration.

3.3 Procedure

Four types of materials, Teflon, wooden surface, chloroprene rubber, and silicone rubber, were used for comparison (Fig. 5 (left)). Participants the contactor to the index finger of right hand, and were instructed to move the finger in the same direction of the rubbing (Fig. 5 (right)). They used their index finger of left hand to rub the real material for the comparison of rubbing sensation between the stimulations of real material and contactor.

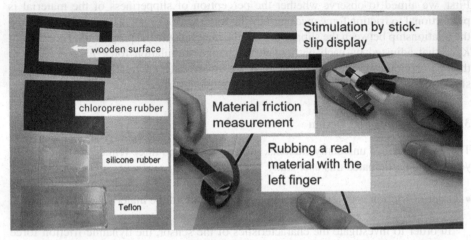

Fig. 5. Materials (left) and overview experiment (right).

4   Result

• Order of friction coefficient and slippery sensation of each material

Table 1 shows the average value of the friction coefficient of each material that measured by the force sensor. The frictional force increased in the order of Teflon, chloroprene rubber, wooden surface, and silicon rubber. Table 2 shows the ranking of slippery perception of the material. The ranking of slipperiness was as follows: 87.5% of the participants ranked first on wooden surfaces, 81.25% for Teflon as second, 68.75% for chloroprene rubber as third, and 75% for silicone rubber as fourth. Therefore, many subjects answered that they felt slippery in the order of wooden surface, Teflon, chloroprene rubber or silicone rubber. It was found that the friction coefficient measured by the material surface measurement sensor was different from the friction coefficient felt by participants.

Table 1. Friction force of each material measured by sensor

Wooden surface	Teflon	Chloroprene rubber	Silicon rubber
0.95	0.82	0.83	1.04

Table 2. Percentage ranking of slipperiness order of the materials

Order	Wooden surface	Teflon	Chloroprene rubber	Silicon rubber
1st	87.5	12.5	0	0
2nd	12.5	81.25	6.25	0
3rd	0	6.25	68.75	25
4th	0	0	25	75

- Relationship between slipperiness sensation of material and stimulation force presented to finger pad

Figure 6 shows the average value of the adjusted proportional coefficient K_{p_m} for the material slipperiness order of each participant. It indicated that K_{p_m} increased as the coefficient of friction perceived by participants increased. One-way repeated measures analysis of variance showed the main effect (F $(3,45) = 10.59$, $p < 0.01$). Multiple comparisons result with Bonferroni test showed the significant difference between 1st and 3rd, 1st and 4th, 2nd and 4th ($p < 0.01$ for each), 2nd and 3rd ($p < 0.05$).

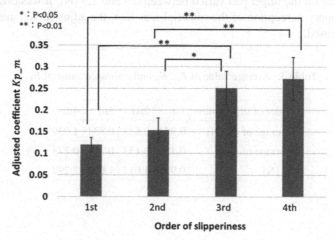

Fig. 6. Average value of adjusted K_{p_m}

- Relationship between the slipperiness perception of the material and the magnitude of the selected vibration frequency

Figure 7 shows the average value of the selected frequency for each order of slippery perception of each participant. It indicated that the selected frequency was smaller for a material that they felt more slippery. One-way repeated measures analysis of variance showed the main effect of $p < 0.05$, but no significant difference in multiple comparisons.

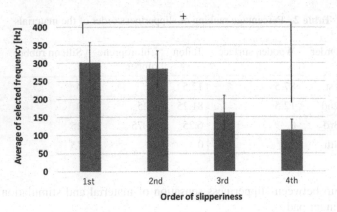

Fig. 7. Average value of selected frequency.

- Estimation of tangential force on finger tap

Tangential force F_s on the finger pad by the contactor is the proportional to the kinetic friction force F_n of the material measured by the sensor. Table 3 shows the average value of F_n, K_p and F_s for each slippery order of the materials. It showed that the adjusted tangential force on the finger pad varied between 0.9 and 2.3 [N]. It was observed that, when the slippery perception of the material was less, the adjusted K_p and tangential force F_s increased.

Table 3. Average value of F_n, K_p and estimated value of F_s

Order of slipperiness	1st	2nd	3rd	4th
Average of F_n [N]	0.954	0.823	0.834	1.039
Average of K_p	0.12	0.153	0.251	0.273
F_s [N]	0.925	1.017	1.693	2.292

5   Discussion

- Order of friction coefficient and slippery sensation of each material

Result of experiment showed that, the order of the frictional force measured by the force sensor and the slipperiness perceived by participants did not correspond. It is considered that, the friction coefficient for each material differs between the surface of the force sensor and the finger pad of a human. Therefore, it is required to investigate the material of the sensor surface that its friction coefficient closed to that of a human finger pad. Though, frictional force measured by the sensor is not proportional to the slipperiness perceived by humans, friction force presented by contactor can be adjusted by changing the value of K_p.

In future work, we aimed to combine with other sensors, such as microphone or accelerometer and investigate the relationship between sensor dimension and rubbing sensation dimension.

- Relationship between slipperiness sensation of material and stimulation force presented to finger pad

The results show that the higher the slipperiness perceived by participants, the higher the proportional coefficient K_p. The reason is that the material that perceived less slippery has a stronger tangential force on the skin of the finger pad when rubbing the real material, and it required to adjust the value of K_p higher.

One-way repeated measures analysis of variance showed significant differences between the slippery orders of 1st and 3rd, 4th and 2nd, 3rd and 4th, but it was not for the orders of 1st and 2nd, 3rd and 4th. It is considered that the difference in slipperiness between the 2nd and 3rd was larger than the difference in slipperiness between the 1st and 2nd or the 3rd and 4th. Therefore, most participants chose wooden surface or Teflon for the 1st and 2nd, and chose chloroprene rubber or silicone rubber for the 3rd and 4th order of slipperiness.

- Relationship between the slipperiness perception of the material and the magnitude of the selected vibration frequency

The average value of the selected frequency increased when the material was perceived slipper. However, no significant difference was found in multiple comparison test. This might be due to that, 500 [Hz] vibration was too smooth, which some participants felt it similar to the condition of 0 [Hz] that there was no vibration. Therefore, although the vibrations of these two frequencies are similar in perception, but the frequency is greatly different, thus the variation was large. Therefore, it is considered that the magnitude of the vibration frequency is not proportional to the sense of slipperiness. In this experiment, the frequency was not adjusted freely, but was selected from five types of vibration. Therefore, depending on the participants and the material, some respondents answered that none of the frequencies matched the actual rubbing sensation. However, they could select one frequency that they felt the closest.

- Estimation of tangential force stimulated on finger pad

Table 1, 2 and 3 showed that, the slipperiness perceived by participants was not proportional to the friction force of materials that measured by the sensor. Therefore, F_s was not proportional to F_n (Table 3). However, participants could adjust coefficient K_{p_m} to perceive tangential force F_s that stimulated by contactor proportional to the friction force that they perceived during rubbing the real material. Therefore, though the maximum of friction that measured by the sensor was about 1.0 [N] but they actually perceived the friction force about 2.29 [N].

6 Conclusion

We developed a tactile transmission system that enables user to transmit a rubbing sensation from sender side to receiver side with a force sensor and a wearable stick-slip display. Contactor is a cylindrical shape that actuated by a DC motor and can present both skin deformation and stick-slip vibration sensation. The result of a user study indicated that, the intensity of friction sensation of the participants did not proportional to friction measured by the force senor. Participants adjusted the strength of skin deformation stimulated by tactile device stronger to perceive more similar to the rubbing sensation of a real material that stimulates higher stickiness perception. It was also confirmed that higher frequency of vibration affected the perception of slippery.

Acknowledgement. This research was supported by JSPS KAKENHI Grant Number JP19K20325 and KEISYA KAKNHI.

References

1. Tachi, S.: Telexistence: enabling humans to be virtually ubiquitous. IEEE Comput. Graph. Appl. **36**(1), 8–14 (2016)
2. Konyo, M., Yamada, H., Okamoto, S., Tadokoro, S.: Alternative display of friction represented by tactile stimulation without tangential force. In: Ferre, M. (ed.) EuroHaptics 2008. LNCS, vol. 5024, pp. 619–629. Springer, Heidelberg (2008). https://doi.org/10.1007/978-3-540-69057-3_79
3. Poupyrev, I., Maruyama, S., Rekimoto, J.: Ambient touch: designing tactile interfaces for handheld devices. In: Proc. ACM UIST, pp. 51–60 (2002)
4. Culbertson, H., Romano, J., Castillo, P., Mintz, M., Kuchenbecker, K.J.: Refined methods for creating realistic haptic virtual textures from tool-mediated contact acceleration data. In: Departmental Papers (MEAM), p. 284 (2012)
5. Minamizawa, K., et al.: Gravity grabber: wearable haptic display to present virtual mass sensation. In: Proc. ACM SIGGRAPH Etech (2007)
6. Leonardis, D., et al.: A wearable fingertip haptic device with 3 DoF asymmetric 3-RSR kinematics. In: Proc. IEEE World Haptics Conf., pp. 388–393 (2015)
7. Tsetserukou, D., et al.: LinkTouch: a wearable haptic device with five-bar linkage mecha-nism for presentation of two-DOF force feedback at the fingerpad. In: Proc. IEEE Haptics Symp., pp. 307–312 (2014)
8. Yem, V., Kajimo, H.: Wearable tactile device using mechanical and electrical stimulation for fingertip interaction with virtual world. In: Proc. IEEE Virtual Reality (VR), pp. 99–104 (2017)

Reading Aloud in Human-Computer Interaction: How Spatial Distribution of Digital Text Units at an Interactive Tabletop Contributes to the Participants' Shared Understanding

Svenja Heuser[✉], Béatrice Arend, and Patrick Sunnen

University of Luxembourg, Porte des Sciences 11, 4366 Esch-sur-Alzette, Luxembourg
{svenja.heuser,beatrice.arend,patrick.sunnen}@uni.lu

Abstract. This paper is concerned with how the spatial distribution of written informings in a serious game activity at an interactive tabletop (ITT) induces participants to read aloud interactionally relevant information to each other in the process of co-constructing a shared understanding.

Engaging in an unfamiliar game activity, the participants are all equally dependent on written informings from the interface that serve as a game manual and provide crucial information for jointly achieving the game task(s). When it comes to making use of these written informings, we find the participants to read them aloud, making them accountable within the group.

Our findings from multimodal video analysis of two reading-aloud cases suggest that the written informing's directionality and distribution (here, either designed as 'distributed' or 'shared' among the interface) regulate the participants' access to information. And that participants who cannot visually access the information they are interested in reading (aloud) co-organize fine-grained joint successive actions build on and actualized by read-aloud utterances. These joint actions allow them to align their orientation and share their understanding of game activity-relevant content.

Keywords: Reading aloud · Interactive tabletop · Collaboration · Conversation analysis · Interface design

1 Introduction

This paper addresses how participants mutually co-construct a shared understanding [1, 2] of an unfamiliar collaborative game activity they are engaging in (Fig. 1). The focus is on how they rely on written informings [see e.g., 3] displayed on the interface. These informings, mediated by an interactive tabletop (ITT, see Fig. 2) [4, 5], are designed to serve as a kind of game manual, to offer guidance and to provide the participants with crucial information for a gradual and joint familiarization with the ITT-activity. The collaborative activity is new to the participants and designed in a way that they all have to rely on these informings in order to jointly achieve several game task(s).

© The Author(s) 2020
C. Stephanidis et al. (Eds.): HCII 2020, LNCS 12424, pp. 117–134, 2020.
https://doi.org/10.1007/978-3-030-60117-1_9

Fig. 1. Three participants (For the purpose of data protection, we edited the figures) engaging in 'Orbitia', each positioned at a referent control station. Together, they form a space mining crew, utilizing their control stations to steer a mining rover across the interface, collect essential minerals while avoiding damages and being economical with the resources provided.

Throughout our video corpus[1], participants recurrently read aloud, allowing them to jointly and publicly share newly introduced information that is provided by the ITT-system. In order for this new information to become part of a shared and intertwined understanding among the participants, it is related to what was already made sense of by then. In this process, it must be assessed and agreed upon to then form the basis of the group's joint next actions [2]. The way how participants use these read-aloud actions, as one way to share information and contribute to the group's co-construction of a shared understanding, is also 'influenced' by the design of the written informings on the ITT-interface (the spatial distribution and directionality of written informings, see Sect. 2). We shall see that the directionality of the digital text units regulates the participants' access to information. The same applies to the ratio of proximity and distance between both, the written informing on the interface (that is to be read aloud) and the participant (who aims to read it aloud).

In particular, by analyzing video data of multiparty game interaction at the ITT, we will show how participants use these written informings from the interface for producing reading-aloud accounts that facilitate shared understanding of the game activity in situ.

Relying on a multimodal conversation analytic approach [7, 8], we will present two cases of participants' reading alouds, one from a designated 'shared' written informing (information designed to be equally accessible to each participant) and one from designated 'distributed' written informings (information designed to provide privileged access to a particular player role by compartmentalizing it, see Sect. 2). At the end, we

---

[1] The above-mentioned video recordings are derived from the 'ORBIT' project (acronym for 'Overcoming Breakdowns in Teams with Interactive Tabletops') [6]. The research conducted especially on 'reading aloud' is part of the first author's dissertation project.

will point to some practical design implications that become relevant with regard to our analysis.

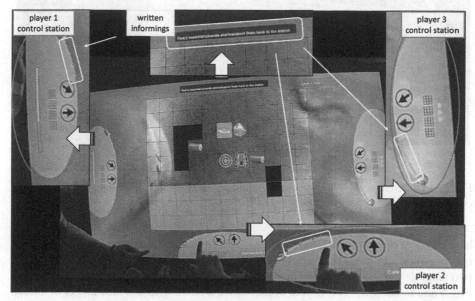

Fig. 2. Game world 'Orbitia', showing a planetary surface with three player 'control stations' (orange) (equipped with e.g., each two steering controls to maneuver the rover), a central grid and written informings (yellow). (Color figure online)

2 Interface Design

In the multiparty interaction at our ITT interface Orbitia, participants read aloud written informings mediated by the interface. In the here discussed excerpts, participants are all equally dependent on related information in order to jointly achieve the game task(s). As mentioned above, the written informings on the interface (each mostly about one to three sentences long) provide crucial information, serving as a game manual and offering guidance throughout the activity.

Looking more closely at research on text material being vocalized in participants' reading-aloud actions in game activity contexts, studies show that these so-called in-game texts [3] provide valuable resources for the players' joint goal orientation within the game activity [9]. It can also be found that the way they are located, formulated [10] (and translated [11]) influences the degree of supportiveness for the activity and the way the participants turn towards these written informings and similar activity-relevant information [12].

By design, the written informings displayed on the interface are either designed as 'distributed' or 'shared' among the participants (Fig. 3). *Shared informings* can be found in the large rectangular space of the interface that is represented as the planet's surface:

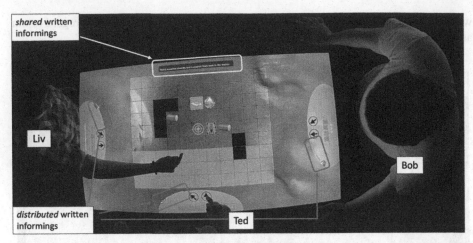

Fig. 3. In different areas of the interface, Orbitia provides written informings as 'shared' (e.g., on top, yellow) resp. 'distributed' (e.g., in each control station, orange). (Color figure online)

here either at the 'top' of the interface, visualized in a text box (see Fig. 3, e.g., 'Find two minerals and transport them back to the station.'), or others, related to the ITT's two tangible widgets[2], displayed in a corona around the handle (e.g., 'drone' widget, see Fig. 4 and footnote 3: 'This is your drone. Move it on the grid and the number of hidden items will be displayed. Press the button to see them (4 attempts). This information will be sent to your control stations.'). *Distributed informings* can be found in the personal control stations of each player's position at the ITT. They are either permanently visible (e.g., as control station's labels, see Fig. 2, e.g., 'Mining Control Station') or visualized by the participants' activation. Besides the above-mentioned permanent written informings, all other informings need to be activated (respectively requested) by touching the referent digital buttons.

Next to the above-mentioned considerations concerning the distribution of written informings, also the mere size and shape of the tabletop interface and the designated participant positioning at the three sides (see Fig. 1 and 3) do come with certain restrictions in terms of directionality and visibility of the written informings when it comes to reading – or even more critical – reading aloud. Therefore, the directionality of graphic structures such as written informings must be carefully considered in the design process. The design approach of the above-shown interface was to provide for the shared written informings to be as directionless as possible, so that all participants had more or less equal visual accessibility for reading them. However, the more tilted (the closer to a

---

[2] In this paper, we will only focus on one of the two tangible widgets: the 'drone' tangible. As soon as the other tangible widget ('info' tangible) is inserted on the ITT, the interface system offers touchable 'info' icons at specific points across the interface (for requesting the related written informings). The 'info' tangible is also needed (on the table) for the other tangible widget ('drone' tangible) to display its attached written informing. In the subsequent version of Orbitia (described in [13]) we removed the info-widget and replaced it with distributed touch info-buttons.

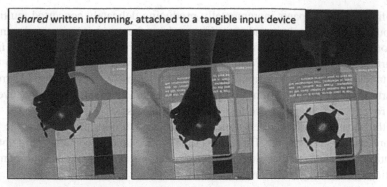

shared written informing, attached to a tangible input device

Fig. 4. The drone widget with a 'shared' text box attached. The latter is activated resp. visualized by the tangible's insertion onto the ITT surface.

180-degree rotation), the harder respectively the more strenuous it is to read them[3]. In contrast, distributed written informings (locally allocated according to each player's role in the game activity) should not be too easily accessible for other players in order for the informational asymmetry to induce collaborative exchange within the group [13]. Therefore, distributed informings face the respective individual player (and reader, see Fig. 3), shared informings however are either positioned on top of the interface (Fig. 3) or are attached to the mobile tangible widgets that can be positioned as required for a more convenient joint access (Fig. 4).

3 Reading Aloud

We consider reading aloud as a participants' practice of verbalizing resp. reading (parts of) written informings from the interface in a hearable voice, and by that, making this information mutually accessible within the group.

So far, the research on reading aloud in general is mainly conducted within a linguistic or a pedagogical framework and based on controlled speech data. E.g., these studies investigate recordings of instructed speakers reading aloud specific passages of a text repeatedly [14, 15] or audio recordings from telephone conversations [16]. In fact, only a few studies more closely deal with naturally occurring interactional phenomena in reading practices in general, and even less with read-aloud-speech in particular. All in all, the reading-aloud practice has only been investigated by a few scientists from a conversation analytic perspective. Swerts & Geluykens [17] have examined speakers' prosodic performances in reading-aloud utterances, functioning as markers of information units, informing recipients about discourse boundaries. Koole [18] found that in classroom contexts reading aloud is often used by the student to localize a problematic passage in a written text that might have not yet been understood correctly.

---

[3] In a following version, the attached box with the written informing itself rotates with the rotation of the tangible widget. This is expected to facilitate the visual accessibility to the text from all sites of the interface.

We find our participants incrementally producing delicately concerted multimodal read-aloud accounts for their understanding on how the game activity works and how they should proceed. In this process, they couple informational entities, they find on the interface (e.g., a written informing: 'Here is [...] your mining rover. Tap on the arrows to steer it.'), with corresponding touchable icons (e.g., two steering arrows at each participant's control station) and possible referent functions (e.g., maneuvering a mining rover across the grid to collect essential minerals).

So, the participants make their noticing of the written informings accessible for the other participants' assessment. The agreed upon understanding remains valid until new information is introduced that alters this understanding, building the basis for any joint next actions in this very situational context.

4 Inducing Shared Understanding

In order for the participants to collaboratively engage in the game activity, they need to interdependently and reciprocally develop and maintain a shared understanding of what the activity's goal is and of what they need to do as a group to achieve that common goal.

In particular, it is a continuously and 'jointly building up [of] a reciprocal understanding of each other's resources' [2: p. 3] that ideally results in a shared understanding among the group members [19]. Therefore, participants need to jointly figure out 'how they are going to work together, [...] with whom they are working' [20: p. 35], and, especially in a human-computer interaction context, 'how they should use [the] technology' [20: p. 35]. In this light, participants of our game activity need to make use and sense of multiple resources, create a joint focus, work interdependently, exchange ideas and information, and by that co-construct shared understanding of the game's task(s) and goal(s) [see 19].

More specifically, we aimed on creating an environment where the participants need to exchange on the resources provided. For that purpose, Orbitia provides three player roles (each player being in charge of either 'damage', 'mining' or 'energy' control, see Sect. 6.1, Fig. 5) with specific functions and responsibilities for the participants to take (over) within the game scenario. Additionally, multiple essential resources like written informings are made accessible in different ways. They are designed to be either as equally 'shared' as possible, or locally 'distributed' among the participants across the interface according to their roles in the game [13]. The above-mentioned design implementations create an asymmetry of knowledge among the participants that aims at inducing collaboration within the group. In the effort of understanding the rules and goals of the joint game activity, the participants need to articulate, piece together, discuss and evaluate on this complementary information. Exactly these processes can provide them with deeper and mutual insights into their roles as resources, and at the same time contribute to co-constructing, adjusting and maintaining a shared understanding.

Our focus of analysis is on "how knowledge is invoked and deployed as part of societal member's practical concerns" [1: p. 76]. In that sense, we observe (and understand) shared understanding as a mutual interactional accomplishment which dynamics depend on the fine-grained and constant reciprocal displaying of one's own and the monitoring of the other's understanding of the situation. It is an accomplishment that has to be jointly checked upon to be maintained over time.

5 Method and Data

The interface system was designed in the context of an interdisciplinary research project 'ORBIT' [6], bringing together researchers from social and computer sciences. Several user studies were conducted so far. The video corpus shows each three participants engaging in the game activity Orbitia in the lab facilities of a research institution. The analysis in this paper considers two read-aloud cases from one participant group. So far, the video recordings of three participant groups (95 min.) have been scrutinized for the phenomenon in question here.

By relying on a conversation analytic approach [7, 21] in its multimodal under-standing [8, 22], we shall examine the fine-tuned coordination of the interactional exchange between the participants' group and the ITT, and in more detail, one particular interactional practice for achieving shared understanding, which is reading aloud.

CA includes examining interactional phenomena, detecting procedures that consti-tute human social interaction working on case analysis and investigating the phenomenon across a corpus. Furthermore, CA informed analysis focuses on the participant's observ-able actions captured in video recordings. This research approach works on the analytical reconstruction of the participants' perspective and orientation to the specific context, here of human-computer interaction in situ.

Here, we can show how three participants jointly discover and mutually co-construct a shared understanding of game relevant features and challenges by reading aloud written informings. We find that co-constructing and maintaining shared understanding of both, previous and next actions, builds upon and is part of complex interactional processes. Making one's own understanding accountable and monitoring respectively assessing the other's responses is essential to achieving shared understanding. Here, reading aloud written informings from the ITT is a common way of how participants make text informa-tion from the interface accountable and include it into the ongoing interaction. The two cases presented in this paper will show how participants come to a shared understanding, gradually co-organizing their inter-exchange of information by reading aloud.

6 Case Analyses

We present two cases and point out, how reading aloud written informings from parts of the interface that may not be equally visually accessible for every participant is inter-actionally realized. In particular, the first case will show how the participants' reading aloud in the process of coming to a mutually shared understanding of their respective player positions and roles in the game activity is co-organized when coping with des-ignated *distributed* written informings (see case I). Whereas the second case will show how their reading aloud, working on a mutual understanding of the digital interface structure and its respective tangible drone widget is co-organized when coping with a designated *shared* written informing (case II).

Additionally, it will be outlined how the written informings' distribution and directionality contribute to co-constructing shared understanding in the sequential unfolding of the game activity.

6.1 Case I: Coping with 'Distributed' Written Informings

Right at the beginning of their engagement with the game activity, the participants begin to explore the digital surface (icons, texts and buttons) they find on the interface's grid and at each player's control stations (Fig. 5). To make sense of the semiotic resources at hand, the participants share and discuss their findings.

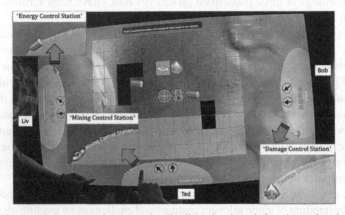

Fig. 5. ITT from top view, zooming in on the distributed written informings of each participants' control station (orange boxes). (Color figure online)

In Orbitia, each control station marks a position at the ITT and at the same time provides for a position and role for the player in the game activity. For that purpose, the stations are visually demarcated from the rest of the interface and labeled with the respective role allocation: 'Energy Control Station', 'Mining Control Station' and 'Damage Control Station' (Fig. 5).

In the following sequence[4] Liv is focused on the possible steering functions. Each player is provided with two complementary steering directions in her/his control station, enabling them to jointly maneuver a rover over the planet's surface.

---

[4] The transcript lines indicate the participant and the interactional resource that is transcribed: ver = verbal conduct, ges = gestural conduct, pos = the participants' physical conduct in term of positioning movements. Additionally, the italics marked with an asterisk show the references between transcript lines and figures.

Transcript 1

```
001 Liv-ver  YOU go (-) UP (.) wa yeah (.)
    Bob-head             *tilting head                    *fig. 6a)
002 Liv-ver  UP (.) UP-
003          (0.7)
004 Ted-ver  [oke: -]
005 Bob-ver  [damage] control STATion-
006 Liv-ver  you cannot go UP,
007 Ted-ver  mining control STATion-
    Ted-ges     *pointing @his station's informing        *fig. 6b)
008          (1.2)
009 Ted-ver  SO:-
010          (1.1)
011 Liv-ver  basically its ME, (.)
012          who could conTROL it?
013 Ted-ver  you have- (.)
014          [ENergy control- ]
    Ted-pos     *bending to side of P3                     *fig. 6c)
015 Bob-ver  [you have ENergy-] (.)
016          I have DAMage control- (.)
017          and he has MIN[ing-]
    Ted-ges           *pointing @Ted's station's informing  *fig. 6d)
018 Ted-ver           [yea-]
019          and we have THIS:-
020          (--) ah- (.) OBjects,
```

Liv, engaged into the steering functions, is instructing Ted ('you go up', transcript 1, l. 1) in terms of using the directional arrows in front of him, verbalizing and (gesturally) demonstrating her understanding of 'up' (see Fig. 6a, l. 1). His 'up' is her 'left', showing her already undertaken change of perspectives within her steering instruction elicited by the interface's design (in particular, by the above-mentioned distribution of steering resources). The instructed Ted presses both arrows without receiving visual feedback from the interface and as a response produces a stretched 'oke' (l. 4). Meanwhile Bob tilts his head, aligning with Ted's perspective onto the ITT interface next to him (l. 1, Fig. 6a), then returning to his upright home position at the table, visually orienting down onto his control station and reading aloud its label ('damage control station', l. 5) which overlaps with Ted's current turn. Liv responds with a question referring to Ted's steering attempt ('you cannot go up', l. 6) with a high rising intonation at the end and does not address Bob's (read aloud) account on his written station's label.

Now Ted reads aloud his control station's label ('mining control station', l. 7) and simultaneously performs a pointing gesture onto the latter (Fig. 6b). With the vocalization of the second word he orients slightly to Liv's control station to his left (Fig. 6c), then to Bob's station to his right. In the course of about two seconds after Ted's read-aloud utterance, Liv visually orients to Ted's station, then to Bob's and then to her own. And so, do the others. Within the first and the second reading aloud utterance, each participant

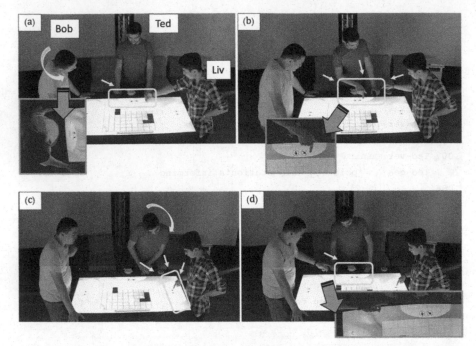

Fig. 6. a-d. ITT-areas made relevant by specific deployment of bodily resources (e.g., finger pointing, bending over torso) for achieving joint visual orientation onto the relevant area on the interface (yellow borders and arrows). (Color figure online)

visually orients at least once to each other participant's control station, readjusting their heads and gazes for the purpose of getting (better) visual access, before orienting down again to their own control stations right in front of them.

Thereafter Ted expands his previous read-aloud turn (l. 7) with a stressed and stretched pivotal marker ('so', l. 9) [see e.g., 24 or 25]. When no one jumps in offering relevant information, Liv makes an account for her understanding of the way (at least) the steering is handled ('it's me who could control it', l. 11–12). She does that with intonation rising high at the ends of both sentences, prosodically realizing a question for clarification. Thereby she keeps on following her exploratory interest of how the steering is conducted, while at the same time responding to the read-aloud accounts of Bob and Ted. As the other two utter respectively share that they are in charge of each 'damage' and 'minerals', she states her understanding of being responsible for the steering 'control' (l. 11–12), and that the two others cannot assist her with that.

After Liv states her understanding of her role in this game activity, Bob and Ted both orient towards her panel: Bob on the opposite side making himself taller, Ted on the connected side leaning down and to her station (Fig. 6c). He first utters 'you have' (l. 13) and then pauses while bending over to Liv's panel even more, tilting his head so that he can more easily access respectively read what is written on the top of her control station. This direct response to Liv's question raised is followed by a pause, giving Ted time to fully bend over (Fig. 6c) and produce the reading (aloud) of the two words ('energy control', l. 14). Ted's response is designed for Liv to inform her about his understanding of what she is responsible of ('you have energy control', l. 13–14). He is, on the one hand, responding to her question raised if her task in this game and player configuration was to control the steering all by herself ('it's me who could control it', l. 11–12), and, on the other hand, providing her with the information about what her personal station's label is actually saying. His account is a paraphrasing utterance, incorporating a read-aloud information into the syntax of his utterance (first part: Ted's own speech material, adjusted to address liv: 'you have', and second part: a read-aloud utterance from Liv's control station: 'energy control'). Within the pause of Ted's above-described utterance, Bob initiates an utterance himself, overlapping with Ted's read-aloud part (l. 14). In particular, not only the realization of both utterances slightly overlaps, but also their content is partly congruent: Bob and Ted both utter 'you have energy' (l. 13–15).

Bob verbalizes (1) 'you have energy' (l. 15), looking onto Liv's side, (2) 'I have damage control' (l. 16), looking down onto his panel, (3) 'and he has mining' (l. 17), orienting slightly to his left towards Ted's panel. The last part is accompanied by a deictic gesture into the direction of Ted's station, reaching its gestural peak with the uttering of 'he' (referred to Ted, l. 17, Fig. 6d). Each of these three clauses is constituted of a) the personal pronoun of the player that is referred to (from Bob's personal perspective, designed for Liv's understanding): 'you' refers to Liv, 'I' refers to himself, 'he' to Ted. Then b) the grammatically referent verb form of possession and c) the one noun of each station's label that differentiates the three control stations from one another ('energy' for Liv, 'damage' for himself and 'mining' for Ted). He can extract that from the previous reading and reading aloud actions and incorporates it into a consecutive and precise enumeration.

For the purpose of making his very own understanding accountable and trying to make the others understand, Bob is occupying his own and each of the other participants' perspectives, positions and roles at the ITT. He sums up what the other stations are saying (and meaning) in relation to each other, working on a coupled understanding on how the relations of positions, functions, tasks and responsibilities are intertwined among the participants and across the interface.

Also, Ted's and Liv's visual orientation follows Bob's enumeration of station labels, directing their visual orientation to the addressed stations, one after the other. Bob's expanded summary of the station's labels (that Ted initiated with his read aloud) is responded to with Ted's positive assessment ('yea', l. 18). Ted then extends this utterance, enumerating and grabbing the two tangible widgets they have been provided with, introducing further unfamiliar things ('this objects', l. 19–20) for the group to jointly make sense of. No matter what, they proceed with initiating joint next actions, and among others, discussing about the location of the rover (which is to be steered jointly across the interface).

Findings Case I: In order for the group to jointly figure out how to proceed with relevant next actions, the participants systematically access and share information from three distributed written informings from each participants' control station that are all informationally coherent but not congruent. With the help of read-aloud accounts (sharing the specific information and its location, making it accountable for everyone to both see and hear), the participants build the basis for the group's involvement with and exchange

about the new verbally introduced information. Bob makes accountable that he under-
stands himself and Ted already being 'on the same page' and that they now both make
the effort of also getting Liv on board to finally reach some shared understanding. Their
subsequent synoptic utterances (performed by two participants, Ted and Bob, l. 13–17),
precisely designed for its recipients, root on the information recently introduced by the
participant's read alouds (l. 5 and 7) and are therefore mutually dependent.

6.2   Case II: Coping with a 'Shared' Written Informing

After coming to the shared understanding of each participant's allocated role in the game
activity (see case I), they now commence inspecting and manipulating the two tangible
widgets ('info' and 'drone' tangible). After the participants inserted one widget ('info')
onto the ITT surface, they are now inserting the second widget ('drone', see Fig. 7a). Once
the tabletop system detects the widget in proximity of the surface a highlighted corona
is visualized around the handle together with a text (see Sect. 2, Fig. 4 and Sect. 6.2,
Fig. 7a–b) that is designed to be used as a shared written informing for all participants
to access equally: 'This is your drone. Move it on the grid and the number of hidden
items will be displayed. Press the button to see them (4 attempts). This information will
be sent to your control stations.' (see Fig. 7a and b)

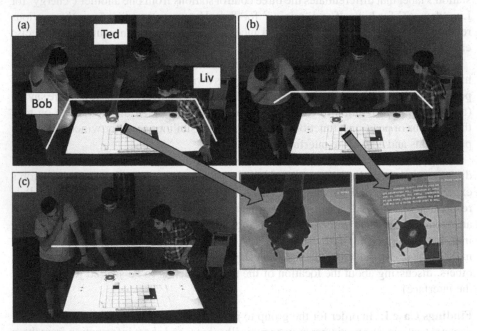

Fig. 7. a–c. Participants' physical (re-)positioning movements alongside the ITT (yellow lines)
after insertion of the drone tangible that activates the written informing (orange boxes). (Color
figure online)

In the following sequence[5] the visualization of a shared written informing elicits the participants' alignment of orientation onto the text unit and its reading aloud.

Transcript 2

```
001 Liv-ver  so what is THAT-
002          (1.7)
003 Ted-ges  *grabbing and inserting of tangible*
    Liv-pos       *bending over to tangible              *fig. 7a)
004          (2.1)
005 ITT      *corona with text appears
006          (1.2)
007 All-pos  *(re)positioning to long ITT-side (Ted) -->      *fig. 7b-c)
008 Ted-ver  this is your DRO:ne- (-) move it [on   xxx  xxx-]
    All-pos                   --*(all aligned)                *fig. 7c)
009 Bob-ver                              [move it on the] grid and
010          the number be displayed- (-)
011 Liv-ver  [(xxx xxx ) button (inaudible --------------------)]  ⎤ over-
012 Bob-ver  [press the button to see them (0.3) four attempts-]  ⎦ lap
013 Liv-ver  [(inaudible --------------------------)FOUR attempts-] ⎤ over-
014 Bob-ver  [this information (xxx) sent to your control stations-].⎦ lap
015 Ted-ver                                        [oke-]
016 Bob-ver  SO::
017          (1.1)
018 Liv-ver  so we don't know basically what is HERE (.) right,
```

Showing her interest in the exploration of the above-described drone tangible, Liv orients to it, (first verbally: 'so what is that', transcript 2, l. 1), making it accountable and interactionally relevant for the others' next actions, as we shall see in the following. Ted then grabs the drone-widget from the side of the table and moves it over the interface in front of him (l. 3), while Liv bends over the tabletop to cover a maximum distance to get clear sight (then physically: l. 3, Fig. 7a). The written informing appears (l. 5). It is directed towards Ted so that he can easily get visual access, while the other two have a more lateral view (see Fig. 7a).

Bob, who's sight onto the written informing is blocked by Ted's arm, bends down strongly (Fig. 7b) until Ted retracts his arm, steps back slightly and makes space for the other two participants (Bob, Liv) to initiate (re)positioning movements towards the long side of the table (Ted's side; see Fig. 7a–c, l. 7). Before they are all aligned in one row (Fig. 7c), Ted, who is already in visual proximity of the text initiates a read-aloud utterance (l. 8, see also Fig. 8). He starts with the text's first sentence and his first contribution in the process of building a shared understanding. When Bob finds his place alongside Ted, he sets in reading aloud (l. 9, Fig. 8) with the beginning of the second sentence of both, the written informing and Ted's reading-aloud utterance. His

---

[5] The transcript lines also indicate the ITT's conduct: ITT = visual feedback of the interface system. In addition, the 'x's' mark inaudible verbal conduct of one to two syllables. Longer inaudible parts of utterances are simply marked 'inaudible'.

accountable sharing of information overlaps with Ted's read-aloud utterance (l. 8 and 9). Ted as a response cancels his reading aloud in the middle of the second sentence. So, only a few syllables after Bob starts to speak simultaneously. Only shortly after Liv's arrival at the long side of the table (Fig. 7c) and Ted's turn-termination, Liv initiates a read-aloud utterance herself (l. 11, see also Fig. 8). She sets in with both, the third sentence of the written informing and Bob's utterance. The latter however is overlapping with Bob's current read aloud. The two of them simultaneously come to the completion of their reading aloud of (parts of) the rest of the written informing (l. 13 and 14, Fig. 8). Both, Bob's and Liv's read alouds are syntactically elliptic and not completely congruent to the written informing's text. Liv's read aloud is in addition not vocalized clearly for most parts, prosodically designed in a low-voiced and by tendency mumbled manner (which would make it hard for the recipients to utilize her utterance as an informing account). Nevertheless, the other participants treat it as accounts of engagement. Ted anticipates and treats the completion of the joint read-aloud action of the other two participants and assesses the new information input with a pivotal marker 'oke' (l. 15). Liv thereafter sums up her understanding of where the drone tangible (they just manipulated and read about) should be deployed (enabling them to see 'what is here', l. 18). They then (not transcribed here) will commence to explore the interface together on the basis of their only just discovered and shared information, and of course their understanding.

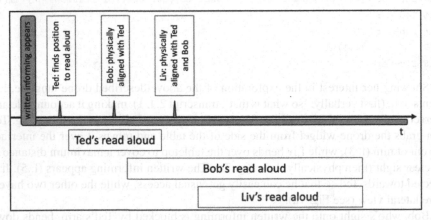

Fig. 8. Scheme of the sequential unfolding of participants' actions: (re) positioning movements in relation to the production of read aloud utterances and their overlaps.

As described above, the participants co-organize their reading-aloud utterances in a fluent taking over and smooth blending in, producing a successive chaining of actions that facilitates one joint read-aloud action. In fact, they all perceive not only the other's joint bodily orientation onto the same text entity, but also the(ir) referent joint verbal read-aloud action. There seems to be no necessity of reading it (aloud) again, even though their utterances (themselves, and even more so jointly) might not have been perfectly acoustically perceivable to one another, word for word. Nevertheless, they mutually display their joint engagement regarding the relevance of the read-aloud written informings as well as their joint alignment regarding the practice to interactionally handle written informings. The participants' accomplishment of the above-described joint read-aloud action is directly followed by positive assessment and by the inclusion of the introduced information into the organization of joint next actions.

Findings Case II: In order to visually access the shared written informing in the tangible's corona simultaneously, the participants undertake interactional work by physically (re)positioning their bodies at the ITT interface and verbally orchestrating a continuous and jointly (at least) hearable reading-aloud action. By doing so, they all equally and simultaneously make their engagement into the current activity interactionally accountable. Here, participants prosodically and temporally couple the text and its reading-aloud in some rhythmic drive, where group members 'jump in' at the right spot at the right time (instead of starting new at the text's beginning) to maintain the progressing multi-layered interplay of the joint read-aloud action in the process of developing shared understanding.

7 Conclusion

Due to the interface's design that presets the location (and accessibility) of written informings, in the process of exploring the 'distributed' written informings in their control stations (case I), Bob and Ted both share their understanding of each participants' different position and role by reading (them) aloud. To also include Liv into this process, they successively produce a complex series of utterances, sharing and aligning all participants' perspectives and referent roles, made accessible through their reading aloud of the relevant written informings. The latter are each directed to the referent stations' player position, enabling direct visual access for the one participant at that very station while at the same time restricting but not hindering the visual access from other stations' positions at the ITT. Due to this specific three-parted spatial distribution, the participants solve the interactional challenge of information (in)accessibility by taking each other's perspectives and publicly sharing their accumulated understanding(s) of it.

Coping with the 'shared' written informing (case II), the participants reciprocally (both physically and verbally) adjust their joint actions in a different way. Here, the properties of the shared written informing (designed to be as equally accessible as possible for all participants), in particular the text's position (in arm's reach of the participant who operates the tangible widget) and directionality (in optimal angle for the latter to read) elicits them to all align their bodies and perspectives at this participant's side of the table and to jointly access all relevant information. Co-organizing a shared turn [see 26, 27] they manage to utilize the specific structures provided by the interface to temporarily align their perspectives and synchronize their actions. As a result, they can all jointly proceed with broadening, deepening and aligning their understanding of the situation on the basis of the new information. The way they jointly co-produce this read-aloud action, they assure that it was fully reciprocally accountable and equally perceivable, because each participant has both read it (aloud) and witnessed each of the other's to have read it (at least partly) aloud.

Both cases presented in this paper show the participants' fine-grained co-organization of joint successive actions when dealing with the interactional challenge of accessing relevant information on an interface, actualized and constructed by read-aloud utterances. These read-aloud's serve as a vehicle for the participants' mutually displaying and monitoring of the individual's as well as the other's understanding in the process of co-constructing a shared understanding within the group. Furthermore, the spatial distribution of text across the horizontal interface facilitates the participants' interactional effort for accomplishing an alignment of their multimodal resources and orientations. So, the participants jointly reach a shared understanding of game activity-specific content.

Based on the above-described observations on how participants in our game activity Orbitia cope with (the reading aloud of) differently distributed written informings on the interface we could see that these informings and their spatial distribution induce collaborative exchange among the participants.

Slightly different to our expectations (the designated *shared* written informings to be rather equally accessible for the participants, and the designated *distributed* written informings to provide rather privileged access for particular participants), the written informings, designed as *shared* and co-equally accessible (see case II) likewise required the group's joint adjustment actions for the purpose of reading them aloud (although of course in a different way). In a next iteration of the interface system, this designated 'shared' text attached to the drone tangible was fixed to the latter in a way that by participants' rotation of the tangible the text would rotate as well. It would be interesting for future analyses to investigate on how e.g., this design adjustment now facilitates the participants to access the drone's written informing and share it within the group.

Acknowledgements. We thank the Luxembourg National Research Fund (FNR) for funding the ORBIT project (Overcoming Breakdowns in Teams with Interactive Tabletops) under the CORE scheme and our project colleagues Valérie Maquil and Hoorieh Afkari from the Luxembourgish Institute of Science and Technology (LIST). We also thank the participants.

References

1. Arnseth, H.C., Ludvigsen, S., Wasson, B., Mørch, A.: Collaboration and problem solving in distributed collaborative learning. In: Dillenbourg, P., et al. (eds.) European Perspectives on Computer-Supported Collaborative Learning: Proceedings of Euro-CSCL 2001, pp. 75–82 (2001)
2. Arend, B., Heuser, S., Maquil, V., Afkari, H., Sunnen, P.: Being a space mining crew: how participants jointly discover their complementary resources while engaging into a serious game at an interactive tabletop (ITT). In: Gadille, M., Caraguel, V. (eds.) Building the New Millenium Skills for Project Management in Higher Education: How Virtual Worlds Can Help Teachers And Students?, EDULEARN20, 12th Annual International Conference on Education and New Learning Technologies (2020)
3. Evans, J.: Translating board games: multimodality and play. J. Specialised Transl. **20**, 15–32 (2013)
4. Antle, A., Wise, A.: Getting down to details: using theories of cognition and learning to inform tangible user interface design. Interact. Comput. **25**(1), 1–20 (2013)
5. Anastasiou, D., Maquil, V., Ras, E., Fal, M.: Design implications for a user study on a tangible tabletop. In: Proceedings of the 15th International Conference on Interaction Design and Children, pp. 499–505. ACM, New York (2016)

6. Sunnen, P., Arend, B., Maquil, V.: ORBIT - overcoming breakdowns in teams with interactive tabletops. In: Kay, J., Luckin, R. (eds.), Rethinking Learning in the Digital Age: Making the Learning Sciences Count, 13th International Conference of the Learning Sciences (ICLS) 2018, London, UK, pp. 1459–1460 (2018)
7. Psathas, G.: Conversation Analysis: The Study of Talk-in-Interaction, vol. 35. Sage Publications, Thousand Oaks (1994)
8. Mondada, L.: The organization of concurrent courses of action in surgical demonstrations. In: Streeck, J., et al. (eds.). Embodied Interaction. Language and Body in the Material World, pp. 207–226. Cambridge University Press, Cambridge (2011)
9. Thorne, S.L., Fischer, I., Lu, X.: The semiotic ecology and linguistic complexity of an online game world. ReCALL 24(3), 279–301 (2012)
10. Mason, J.: Video games as technical communication ecology. Techn. Commun. Q. 22(3), 219–236 (2013)
11. Šiaučiūnė, V., Liubinienė, V.: Video game localization: the analysis of in-game texts. Stud. Lang. 19, 46–55 (2011)
12. Woodruff, A., Szymanski, M.H., Aoki, P.M., Hurst, A.: The conversational role of electronic guidebooks. In: Abowd, G.D., Brumitt, B., Shafer, S. (eds.) Ubicomp 2001: Ubiquitous Computing, UbiComp 2001, vol. 2201, pp. 187–208. Springer, Heidelberg (2001). https://doi.org/10.1007/3-540-45427-6_16
13. Sunnen, P., Arend, B., Heuser, S., Afkari, H., Maquil, V.: Developing an interactive tabletop mediated activity to induce collaboration by implementing design considerations based on cooperative learning principles. In: Stephanidis, C., Antona, M. (eds.) 22nd HCI International Conference 2020. Denmark, Springer, Copenhagen (2020). https://doi.org/10.1007/978-3-030-50729-9_45
14. Thorsen, N.: Intonation and text in Standard Danish. Ann. Rep. Inst. Copenhagen 18, 185–242 (1984)
15. Lass, N.J., Lutz, D.R.: The consistency of temporal speech characteristics in a repetitive oral reading task. Lang. Speech 18(3), 227–235 (1975)
16. Local, J., Walker, G.: How phonetic features project more talk. J. Int. Phonetic Assoc. 42(3), 255–280 (2012)
17. Swerts, M., Geluykens, R.: Prosody as a marker of information flow in spoken discourse. Lang. Speech 37(1), 21–43 (1994)
18. Koole, T.: Teacher evaluations. Evaluating Cogn. Competences Interact. 225, 43 (2012)
19. Roschelle, J., Teasley, S.D.: The construction of shared knowledge in collaborative problem solving. In: O'Malley, C. (ed.) Computer Supported Collaborative Learning, NATO ASI Series, vol. 128, pp. 69–97. Springer, Berlin (1995). https://doi.org/10.1007/978-3-642-850 98-1_5
20. Mulder, I., Swaak, J., Kessels, J.: Assessing group learning and shared understanding in technology-mediated interaction. J. Educ. Technol. Soc. 5(1), 35–47 (2002)
21. Schegloff, E., Jefferson, G., Sacks, H.: A simplest systematics for the organization of turn-taking for conversation. Language 50(4), 696–735 (1974)
22. Deppermann, A.: Multimodal interaction from a conversation analytic perspective. J. Pragmat. 46(1), 1–7 (2013)
23. Selting, M., Auer, P., Barth-Weingarten, P., et al.: A system for transcribing talk-in-interaction: GAT 2, translated and adapted for English by Couper-Kuhlen, E., Barth-Weingarten, P. (eds.) Gesprächsforschung - Online-Zeitschrift zur verbalen Interaktion 12, pp. 1–51 (2011)
24. Szczepek Reed, B., Reed, D., Haddon, E.: NOW or NOT NOW: Coordinating restarts in the pursuit of learnables in vocal master classes. Res. Lang. Soc. Interact. 46(1), 22–46 (2013)
25. Proske, N.: Zur Funktion und Klassifikation gesprächsorganisatorischer Imperative. In: Diskursmarker im Deutschen Reflexionen und Analysen, pp. 73–101. Verlag für Gesprächsforschung, Göttingen (2017)

26. Lerner, G. H.: Turn-sharing. In: The Language of Turn and Sequence, pp. 225–256. Oxford University Press, New York (2002)
27. Pfänder, S., Couper-Kuhlen, E.: Turn-sharing revisited: an exploration of simultaneous speech in interactions between couples. J. Pragmat. **147**, 22–48 (2019)

Speech Recognition Approach
for Motion-Enhanced Display
in ARM-COMS System

Teruaki Ito[✉], Takashi Oyama, and Tomio Watanabe

Faculty of Computer Science and System Engineering, Okayama Prefectural University,
111 Kuboki, Soja, Okayama 719-1197, Japan
tito@ss.oka-pu.ac.jp

Abstract. This research proposes an idea of motion-enhanced display that utilizes the display itself as the communication media which mimics the motion of
human head to enhance presence in remote communication. The idea has been
implemented as an augmented tele-presence system called ARM-COMS (ARm-
supported eMbodied COm-munication Monitor System). Basically, ARM-COMS
detects the orientation of a subject face by the face-detection tool based on an
image processing technique, and mimics the head motion of a remote partner in
an effective manner. In addition to that, ARM-COMS makes appropriate reactions when a communication partner speaks even without any significant motion
in video communication by using audio signal during talk.

This paper covers two topics. The first one is a new design of the ARM-
COMS robotic arm, with the configuration of six-axis servo motors to enable
further smooth motion. In addition to the hardware configuration, the software
configuration is also presented based on the ROS framework.

The second topic is a camera stabilizer-based experimental configuration. This
study worked on a feasibility study of experimental configuration of ARM-COMS.
If it works feasible, the approach could be applied to the redesigned ARM-COMS
robotic arm system.

Keywords: Embodied communication · Augmented tele-presence robotic arm ·
Motion-enhanced display · Audio interaction · Speech recognition

1 Introduction

A various types of video communication tool are now freely available to many people.
However, these tools address the two types of critical issues, which are the lack of tele-
presence feeling and the lack of relationship feeling in remote video communication as
opposed to a face-to-face communication.

Several ideas of robot-based remote communication systems have been proposed
as one of the solutions to the former issue; these robots include physical telepresence
robots. Remote communication can be basically supported by the primitive functions of

© Springer Nature Switzerland AG 2020
C. Stephanidis et al. (Eds.): HCII 2020, LNCS 12424, pp. 135–144, 2020.
https://doi.org/10.1007/978-3-030-60117-1_10

physical tele-presence robots, such as a face image display of the operator, as well as tele-operation function such as remote-drivability to move around, or tele-manipulation.

The second issue in the lack of relationship-type feeling in remote video communication is another big challenge. Recently, an idea of robotic arm-type systems draws researchers' attention. For example, Kubi, which is a non-mobile arm type robot, allows the remote user to "look around" during video communication by way of commanding Kubi where to aim the tablet with an intuitive remote control over the net. Furthermore, an idea of enhanced motion display has also been reported to show its feasibility over the conventional display. However, the usage of the human body movement of a remote person as a non-verbal message is still an open issue.

This research proposes an idea of motion-enhanced display that utilizes the display itself as the communication media which mimics the motion of human head to enhance presence in remote communication. The idea has been implemented as an augmented tele-presence system called ARM-COMS (ARm-supported eMbodied COmmunication Monitor System). In order to mimic the head motion using the display, ARM-COMS detects the orientation of a face by face-detection tool based on an image processing technique. However, ARM-COMS does not make appropriate reactions if a communication partner speaks without head motion in video communication, which has been often recognized during communication experiments. In order to solve these problems, this study proposes a voice signal usage in local interaction so that ARM-COMS makes an appropriate action even when the remote partner does not make any head motion.

First, this paper overviews ARM-COMS, including its basic concept, basic functions, and experimental results conducted so far. This paper covers two topics. The first one is a new design of the ARM-COMS robotic arm, with the configuration of six-axis servo motors to enable further smooth motion. In addition to the hardware configuration, the software configuration is also presented based on the ROS framework.

The second topic is a camera stabilizer-based experimental configuration. This study worked on a feasibility study of experimental configuration of ARM-COMS. If it works feasible, the approach could be applied to the redesigned ARM-COMS robotic arm system. Considering the results from these topics, this paper addresses the direction of the research.

2 System Reconfiguration of ARM-COMS(ARm-Supported eMbodied COmmunication monitor System)

2.1 Basic Concept of ARM-COMS and Its Typical Configuration

ARM-COMS (ARm-supported eMbodied COmmunication Monitor System) is basically composed of a tablet device, such as smart phone or tablet PC, and a desktop type of robotic arm. The function of the tablet works as a typical ICT (Information and Communication Technology) device, whereas the robotic arm serves as a manipulator of the tablet, of which position and movements are autonomously controlled based on the interaction of a user who communicates with remote person through ACM-COMS. The interaction is initiated by speech signal and head motion of the partner.

Figure 1 shows the system configuration overview of ARM-COMS for the experiment in this study. Face detection procedure of a prototype of ARM-COMS is based on the algorithm of FaceNet, which includes image processing library OpenCV 3.1.0, machine learning library dlib 18.18, and face detection tool OpenFace which were installed on a control PC with Ubuntu 14.04. More detailed description was reported in the reference paper.

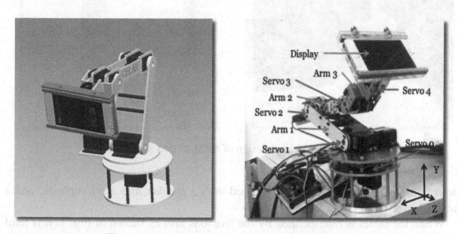

Fig. 1. Basic system configuration of ARM-COMS

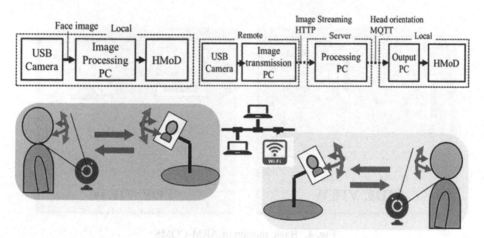

Fig. 2. Basic system configuration for ARM-COMS experiments

2.2 New Design of ARM-COMS Robotic Manipulator

ARM-COMS was initially designed as a combination of table PC with a five axis robotic arm system as shown in Fig. 1. Considering the restriction of this robotic arm, a new design of robotic arm system was studied and implemented as shown in Fig. 3. The manipulator of the robotic arm is composed of six sets of servo motors with a motor

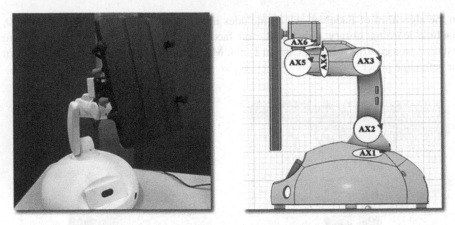

Fig. 3. Updated design of ARM-COMS system

controller, single board computer equipped with a speaker and a microphone, and a camera as shown in Fig. 3.

When the tablet is manipulated by the five axis arm as shown in Fig. 1, it is hard to keep the tablet face at the user all the time. This new designed robotic arm makes it possible to keep the tablet face to the user in any position of the tablet as shown in Fig. 4.

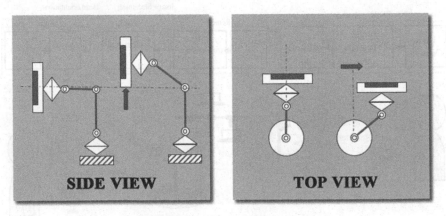

Fig. 4. Basic motion of ARM-COMS

2.3 Reconfiguration of ARM-COMS Data Transmission

ARM-COMS was originally configured based on MQTT communication, which is based on the combination of publisher, MQTT server, and subscriber. Publisher defines each message as a topic and delivers it to the MQTT broker, and then is transferred to the subscriber, which is illustrated in Fig. 5. The subscriber selects a message based on its topic and receives only the message which matches the selected topic. Each message is specified as three types of QoS (Quality of Service). QoS0 is not guaranteed to be delivered. QoS1 is to be sent at least one time, which is quick to be delivered if it works fine but its delivery would be without guarantee. QoS2 is guaranteed to be delivered.

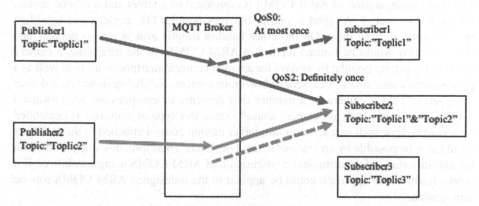

Fig. 5. MQTT-based data transmission

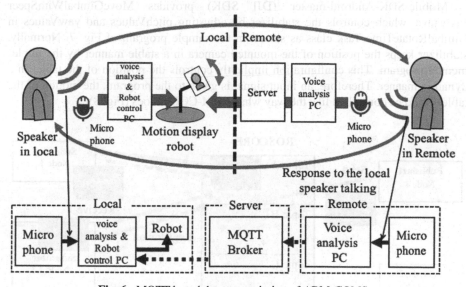

Fig. 6. MQTT-based data transmission of ARM-COMS

The communication process of the renovated system was also reconfigured was based on ROS, or Robot Operating System. ROS provides libraries and tools to help in creating ARM-COMS applications, which is more functional and flexible than the MQTT configuration in Fig. 6.

3 Experimental Configuration of ARM-COMS System

3.1 Feasibility Study of Stabilizer for ARM-COMS Component

The basic configuration of ARM-COMS is composed of a tablet and a robotic arm as mentioned in Sect. 2. A tablet is one of the very popular ITC devices and is widely used in general these days. On the other hand, a robotic arm is not so popular and its availability would be limited for use in ARM-COMS. In the meantime, a camera stabilizer is getting popular these days for amateur camera/smartphone users as well as a professional cameraman. A camera stabilizer, or camera–stabilizing mount, is a device designed to hold a camera in a manner that prevents or compensates for unwanted camera movement, such as "camera shake". Since this type of stabilizer is controlled by a manipulator such as a servo motor, tablet motion control attached to the stabilizer would also be possible by an external control program. Therefore, this study worked on a feasibility study of experimental configuration of ARM-COMS using a stabilizer. If it works feasible, the approach could be applied to the redesigned ARM-COMS robotic arm system.

A three-axis stabilizer (DJI Osmo Mobile 2) was selected to control the behavior of a tablet as shown in Fig. 2.

Mobile-SDK-Android-master (DJI SDK) provides MoveGimbalWithSpeer View.java, which controls the stabilizer by adjusting pitchValues and yawValues in GimbalRotateTimerTask class as shown in the sample program of Fig. 7. Normally, stabilizer keeps the position of the mounted camera in a stable manner by the implemented program. This configuration implicitly controls the position of the tablet in a dynamic manner. Therefore, an input signal is given to the program, the motion of the tablet could be controlled like the way what ARM-COMS does (Fig. 8).

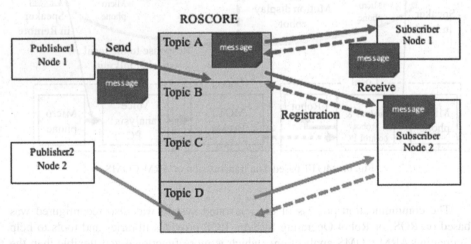

Fig. 7. ROS-based data communication process

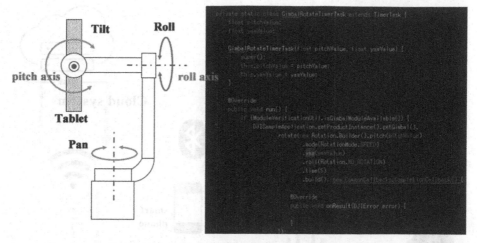

Fig. 8. An example of stabilizer control program

3.2 Stabilizer-Based ARM-COMS

Since the motion control of tablet using the stabilizer was confirmed in the preliminary experiment, experimental stabilizer-based system configuration was implemented as shown in Fig. 9. The components of this configuration were a tablet (a smartphone in this case), a stabilizer, a microphone, and PC. The stabilizer was connected to control PC via Bluetooth. However, the control program was implemented in the control PC, an Android smartphone was connected to the PC via USB cable and the program was transmitted through the stabilizer through Bluetooth of the smartphone.

Speech recognition through USB microphone: Android Speech recognizer was used to recognize the speech of a subject person. As a result, the spoken message was recognized/recorded as a text message, which was transmitted to the PC. Four types of Japanese keyword, or up, down, right, and left were reserved for target word in the program.

3.3 Experimental Results

Experiments: A subject was asked to speak a sentence including one of the keywords. If a keyword was detected, a specific action dedicated to each keyword was taken. For example, if a subject says "Look down", the keyword "down" is recognized and down-motion was initiated as shown in Fig. 10. Expected action was recognized by a simple speech sentence.

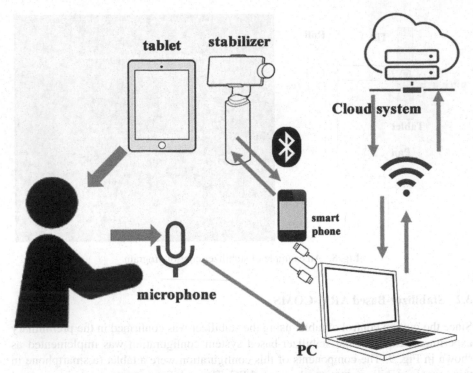

Fig. 9. Speech-based processing to control stabilizer

Fig. 10. Smartphone interface to control a stabilizer

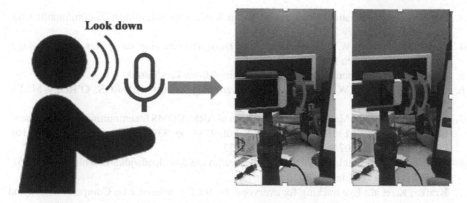

Fig. 11. Speech-based motion

4 Concluding Remarks

ARM-COMS detects the orientation of a subject face by the face-detection tool based on an image processing technique, and mimics the head motion of a remote partner in an effective manager. In addition to that, ARM-COMS makes appropriate reactions when a communication partner speaks even without any significant motion in video communication. However, smooth motion was still in question to be solved for an effective use of ARM-COMS.

In this paper, a new design of the ARM-COMS robotic arm was reported and its outline was described. The configuration of the robot with six-axis servo motors was presented. In addition to the hardware configuration, the software configuration based on the ROS framework was presented.

Another trial with a camera stabilizer was also presented to show the feasibility of the new approach for ARM-COMS. As opposed to the normal usage of camera stabilizer, dynamic control of tablet experiment showed the feasibility of this approach. Feasibility study of this kind of approach is under consideration to apply to the new design of ARM-COMS robotic arm system.

Acknowledgement. This work was partly supported by JSPS KAKENHI Grant Numbers JP19K12082 and Original Research Grant 2019 of Okayama Prefectural University. The author would like to acknowledge Risa Tanaka and all members of Kansei Information Engineering Labs at Okayama Prefectural University for their cooperation to conduct the experiments.

References

1. Android Studio. https://developer.android.com/studio/index.html?hl=ja. Accessed 28 February 2020
2. Bertrand, C., Bourdeau, L.: Research interviews by Skype: a new datacollection method. In: Esteves, J. (Ed.), Proceedings from the 9th European Conferenceon Re-search Methods, pp. 70–79. Spain: IE Business School (2010)

3. DJI (Da-Jiang Innovations Science and Technology). https://developer.dji.com/mobile-sdk/. Accessed 24 February 2020
4. Ekman, P., Friesen, W.V.: The repertoire or nonverbal behavior: categories, origins, usage, and coding. Semiotica **1**, 49–98 (1969)
5. FASTRK. http://polhemus.com/motion-tracking/all-trackers/fastrak
6. Gerkey, B., Smart, W., Quigley, M.: Programming Robots with ROS. O'Reilly Media, Sebastopol (2015)
7. Ito, T., Watanabe, T.: Motion control algorithm of ARM-COMS for entrainment enhancement. In: Yamamoto, S. (ed.) HIMI 2016. LNCS, vol. 9734, pp. 339–346. Springer, Cham (2016). https://doi.org/10.1007/978-3-319-40349-6_32
8. JDK. http://www.oracle.com/technetwork/java/javase/downloads/jdk8-downloads-2133151.html. Accessed 28 February 2020
9. Krafka, K., et al.: Eye tracking for everyone. In: IEEE Conference on Computer Vision and Pat-tern Recognition (CVPR) (2016)
10. Lee, A., Kawahara, T.: Recent development of open-source speech recognition engine julius. Asia-Pacific Signal and Information Processing Association Annual Summit and Conference (APSIPA ASC) (2009)
11. Light, R.: Mosquitto: server and client implementation of the MQTT protocol. J. Open Source Softw. **2**(13), 265 (2017). https://doi.org/10.21105/joss
12. Mehrabian, A., Williams, M.: Nonverbal concomitants of perceived and intended persuasiveness. J. Pers. Soc. Psychol. **13**(1), 37–58 (1969). https://doi.org/10.1037/h0027993
13. Stephen, J.: Understanding body language: birdwhistell's theory of kinesics. Corp. Commun. Int. J. ((2000). https://doi.org/10.1108/13563280010377518)
14. Schoff, F., Kalenichenko, D., Philbin, J.: FaceNet: a unified embedding for face recognition and clustering. IEEE Conf. CVPR **2015**, 815–823 (2015)
15. Society 5.0. https://www.japan.go.jp/abenomics/_userdata/abenomics/pdf/society_5.0.pdf. Accessed 28 February 2020
16. Watanabe, T.: Human-Entrained Embodied Interaction and Communication Technology, pp. 161–177. Emotional Engineering, Springer (2011)
17. Watanabe, T.: InterRobot: speech-driven embodied interaction robot. J. Robot. Soc. Jap. **26**(6), 692–695 (2006)
18. W3C Specification. https://wicg.github.io/speech-api/. Accessed 24 February 2020
19. Web Speech API. https://developer.mozilla.org/en-US/docs/Web/API/Web_Speech_API. Accessed 24 February 2020

Individual's Neutral Emotional Expression Tracking for Physical Exercise Monitoring

Salik Ram Khanal[1]([✉]), Jaime Sampaio[1,3], João Barroso[1,2], and Vitor Filipe[1,2]

[1] Universidade de Trás-os-Montes e Alto Douro, Vila Real, Portugal
{salik,jbarroso}@utad.pt
[2] Institute for Systems and Computer Engineering, Technology and Science, INESC TEC, Porto, Portugal
[3] Research Center in Sports Sciences, Health Sciences and Human Development, CIDESD, Vila Real, Portugal

Abstract. Facial expression analysis is a widespread technology applied in various research areas, including sports science. In the last few decades, facial expression analysis has become a key technology for monitoring physical exercise. In this paper, a deep neural network is proposed to recognize seven basic emotions and their corresponding probability values (scores). The score of the neutral emotion was tracked throughout the exercise and related with heart rate and power generation by a stationary bicycle. It was found that in a certain power range, a participant changes his/her expression drastically. Twelve university students participated in the sub-maximal physical exercise in stationary bicycles. A facial video, heart rate, and power generation were recorded throughout the exercise. All the experiments, including the facial expression analysis, were carried out offline. The score of the neutral emotion and its derivative was plotted against maxHR% and maxPower%. The threshold point was determined by calculating the local minima, with the threshold power for all the participants being within 80% to 90% of its maximum value. From the results, it is concluded that the facial expression was different from one individual to another, but it was more consistant with power generation. The threshold point can be a useful cue for various purposes, such as: physiological parameter prediction and automatic load control in the exercise equipment, such as treadmill and stationary bicycle.

Keywords: Physical exercise intensity · Emotion analysis · Deep learning · Facial expression

1 Introduction

Physical exercise is a key determinant of health status; therefore, organizations worldwide recommend its incorporation as part of one's daily routine. Adequate physical fitness relates to reduced risks of developing physical and mental disease [1, 2] and improvements in life span [3]. Exercise testing and prescription are fundamental to optimize the dose-response relationship of physical exercise and, therefore, successfully

© Springer Nature Switzerland AG 2020
C. Stephanidis et al. (Eds.): HCII 2020, LNCS 12424, pp. 145–155, 2020.
https://doi.org/10.1007/978-3-030-60117-1_11

cope with hypokinetic-related diseases [4]. Thus, guidelines highlight the need of monitoring the main exercise variables, such as frequency, mode, duration, and intensity, so that it is possible to reach adequate levels of physical activity. This process is particularly improved with the help of technology.

Several technological advances have brought a variety of monitoring techniques to the sports sciences field, making physical exercise more intuitive and effective. The primary purpose of exercise monitoring is to measure psychophysiological changes caused by physical exercise, which assists in self/automatic controlling of the effort or load. In the case of self-controlled exercise, the exercise load can be monitored with respect to heart rate changes, where the target heart rate is pre-defined [5]. Another purpose is to collect information not only about the heart rate, but also body temperature and blood pressure, before, during, and after exercise. Therefore, most of the exercise monitoring systems consist of a tool to measure physiological changes, but they are not limited to that. Exercise can also be monitored without measuring these parameters.

In self-assessment methods for physical exercise monitoring, one of the noticeable limitations is that inexperienced individuals are often unable to pace themselves. For this reason, objective assessments as direct physiological measurements are preferred. Recent trends in exercise monitoring rely on objective assessments, whether it is contact-sensors or non-contact techniques [6]. However, although the objective methods might overcome some limitations compared to subjective methods, there are still some significant limitations associated with the measurement of physiological parameters in terms of accuracy. Usually, the prediction of physiological parameters is based on the average sample of subjects, which is inefficient for predicting the performance of an individual [7].

The results of the latest studies involving facial expression analysis in sports science reveals that facial expressions analysis can also be one of the candidate methods to be used as a tool for monitoring physical exercise [8, 9]. When a person gets tired, their facial expression changes. Using various supervised classification methods, emotion can be detected with a probability value for each emotion. It is hypothesized that continuous tracking of facial expression based on Ekman's emotions [10] might have a correlation with the intensity of the exercise, which could be a useful cue for exercise monitoring.

Despite the changes in facial expressions regarding the intensity of the physical exercise, it is a well-known fact that the change from a neutral emotion caused by the intensity of the exercise and its relationship to psychophysiological parameters has bever been examined. Various studies in the literature analyse the facial expression during exercise and they have found significant changes in the individual's expression [8, 9], which is a useful cue for exercise monitoring. In this study, we present a different approach of facial expression analysis for exercise monitoring, using a confidence value of neutral emotion. However, the analysis is only about the expression, not the emotion. The emotional state may not change during physical exercise, while the facial expression changes. In this paper, we track the individual's neutral emotion throughout the physical exercise, while being statistically analyzed with the heart rate.

2 Related Works

The human face conveys information of feelings and intentions caused by either their physical or mental state. Pain, tiredness, and illness due to exertion are reflected by facial expressions [9, 11], therefore, the analysis of facial expressions might be an interesting cue to monitor exercise intensity level. Most of the previous studies focus on locating facial landmarks and their correlation to psychophysiological parameters to analyze facial expression [8, 12, 13].

Khanal [9, 11] explored various methods of automatic classification of exercise intensities using computer vision techniques while performing sub-maximal incremental exercises in a cycle ergometer. The facial expression was analyzed by extracting 68 facial feature points. The intensity was classified into two, three, and four classes using kNN, a Support Vector Machine (SVM), a discriminant analyses, and also a Convolutional Neural Network (CNN). The classification accuracy increased to 99% in two classes of classification and to 96% in four classes of classification. The results showed that facial expression is a good method to identify exercise intensity levels.

A different way of using facial expressions to analyze physical effort was presented by Uchida [8]. The facial images were analyzed at different levels of resistance training. The authors evaluated the changes in facial expression changes using Facial Action Coding System (FACS) and the facial muscle activity using surface electromyography. The association of these parameters was low, though statistically significant.

Miles [12] also presented an analysis of the reliability in tracking data from facial features across incremental exercise on a cycle ergometer. The results differed according to the part of the face being analyzed, but a higher reliability was found for the lower part of the face. A non-linear relationship between facial movements and power output were also determined. The power output, heart rate, RPE, blood lactate, positive and negative effects in the corresponding exercise intensity were satisfied in the two blood lactate thresholds and a maximum probability MAP a posteriori. These results show the potential in using the tracking of facial features as a non-invasive way of obtaining psychophysiological measures to access exercise intensity.

Still regarding the use of facial features to evaluate levels of exertion, mouth and eyes are particularly interesting parts that express information concerning muscle actions. Thus, there is a variety of facial expressions and emotions heavily controlled by the eyes and mouth. Therefore, tracking the movement of these facial regions could be a key idea to analyze exercise intensity [14]. Recently, the eye-blink rate and open-close rate of the mouth were tracked using the Viola and Jones algorithm for image processing [15] during sub-maximal exercise in a cycle ergometer [14]. The eye-blinking rate was correctly identified with 96% of accuracy. Additionally, the higher the exercise intensity, the higher the eye and mouth movement.

3 Methodology

3.1 Data Collection

Facial images were collected in a normalized laboratory setting (SportTech Lab from the University of Trás-OS-Montes and Alto Douro) with twelve subjects familiarized with cycloergometer protocols. The subjects underwent a submaximal cycling exercise (Wattbike cycle ergometer, Wattbike Ltd, Nottingham, UK). They started pedaling at 50 W and the intensity was increased by 50 W every 2-min (approximate cadence of 70 rev.min − 1). The heart rate data were collected at 1 Hz using the Polar T31 transmitter monitor (Polar Electro, Kempele, Finland) and the power output was calculated by measuring the chain tension over a load cell sampled at 100 Hz (Wattbike cycle ergometer, Wattbike Ltd, Nottingham, UK). A stationary camera at 90° angle between the face and the camera was adjusted to capture the facial video (see Fig. 1).

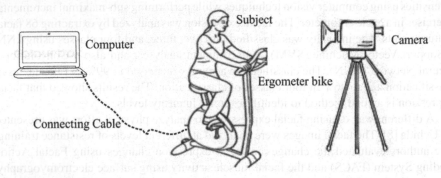

Fig. 1. Illustration of data collection during physical exercise on a stationary bicycle.

All the participants were required to complete the consent form before stating the exercise. Each participant carried out 5 min of warm up exercises with the load of 50 W and 2 min rest before collecting video data and other physiological parameters. The detailed information about the subjects is shown in following Table 1.

3.2 Experiments

In this paper, we present a non-contact method based on computer vision to analyze the neutral emotional expression from the subject's face during a sub-maximal physical exercise carried out in a stationary bicycle. The primary purpose of the study is to find out how neutral emotion changes with physical exercise intensity, heart rate, and power. The heart rate was synchronously recorded with the video using a contact sensor device during the exercise. All the experiments were carried out individually. The detail block diagram of the methodology is shown in Fig. 2.

The recorded video was processed off-line to track the neutral emotion score using a facial expression analysis. Although the frame rate of recorded video was 25 Hz, the frames extracted for emotion recognition from the video were re-sampled to 1 Hz.

Pre-processing. To overcome the problem of blurring due to motion effect, the Wiener–Hunt deconvolution algorithm was applied [16]. The blur is detected by calculating variance of pixels. After de-blurring, the Gaussian filtering was applied in each frame for noise reduction.

ROI Selection. The Viola and Jones [15] face detection algorithm was applied to detect the participant's face. The detected face was resized to 48 × 48 pixels.

Table 1. Physiological data about the subjects participating in the data acquisition protocol.

Subject ID	Gender	Age (years)	Weight (KG)	Height (cm)	Initial HR* (bpm)	Final HR* (bpm)	Duration (mm:ss)
Subject1	Male	22	64.2	172	93	191	9:30
Subject2	Male	33	66.9	177	70	180	16:00
Subject3	Female	19	64.2	177	87	191	9:05
Subject4	Male	36	83.2	182	91	191	15:00
Subject5	Female	24	66.6	170	97	184	9:20
Subject6	Female	29	47	157	114	193	8:00
Subject7	Male	33	83	186	101	180	16:00
Subject8	Male	22	90.7	195	101	201	12:00
Subject9	Male	24	87.3	194	115	188	11:00
Subject10	Male	25	86.1	190	90	190	8:00
Subject11	Female	26	55	155	87	179	11:05
Subject12	Male	22	75.8	182	98	195	14:00

* The initial heart rate was recorded in the beginning of the exercise (after 5 min of warm up exercise) and the Final HR was recorded at the end of the exercise.

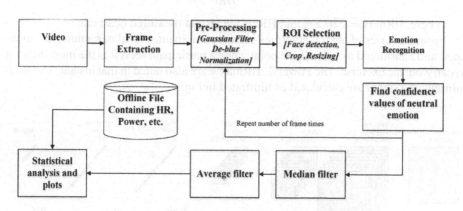

Fig. 2. Block diagram of proposed method.

Emotion Detection. The seven basic facial expressions defined by Ekman were recognized by a Convolutional Neural network (CNN), giving probability values (scores) for each emotion frame-by-frame (one frame per second) from the facial video collected during the physical exercise. However, only score values of neutral emotion were analyzed throughout the video. The CNN architecture was designed and then trained, tested, and validated with a FER2013 dataset [17].

CNN architecture. A CNN architecture based on ConvNet was designed with three hidden layers and two fully connected layers, as shown in Fig. 3. Each block of layer consists Convolutional Layer, Pooling Layer, and Fully-Connected Layer. These layers were stacked to form a full ConvNet architecture.

Input Layer [48 × 48]: holds the raw pixel values of 2D the image of the faces. The first part of each layer consists of a convolutional layer (Conv2d) which can have spatial batch normalization, Maxpooling (Poll size = (2, 2)), dropout (0.25) and ReLU activation. Each layer consists of these five tasks. After 3 convolutional layers, the network is led to two fully connected layers that always have Affine operation and ReLU activation.

We implemented this architecture in the well-known python library Keras. The experiments were carried out in Google Colab GPU. The model was trained and validated with FER2013 [17]. dataset. After validation, facial emotions with individual scores were detected for each sequential image frame.

Filters. Before analyzing and plotting, the score series of neutral emotion was smoothed using a median and moving average filter. A one dimensional signal of neutral emotion scores was formed, where each index of array is taken from a frame.

Statistical analysis and plots. The pattern of neutral emotions score was plotted against time. We also plotted it against HRmax% and Powermax% applied. The HRmax% is calculated as expression

$$HRmax\% = \frac{HRmax}{HRi} \times 100\% \tag{1}$$

Where, HRmax = 220-age and HRi is the instant measured heart rate.

From the series of neutral emotions of each participant, a local minimum was calculated and considered as a threshold point when a participant feels it is the most difficult to carry out the exercise. The Power%, HRmax% are also noted in that instant. The local minima of a signal are calculated as illustrated in Fig. 4.

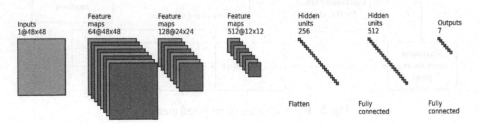

Fig. 3. Proposed CNN architecture consisting of three hidden layers and two fully connected layers.

4   Results

The score of neutral emotions throughout the exercise was plotted against various parameters. First, the neutral emotions' score values and its first derivative against time was

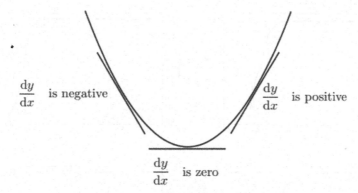

Fig. 4. Local minima of a signal. A local minimum is a point where the first derivative is zero.

plotted to illustrate the pattern and thresold point. Four randomly selected participants plots are shown in Fig. 5. The time duration was not equal for all the participants because the load, duration of exercise, and speed depend on individual's psychophiological parameters. The primary purpose of the study was to find out a point in a signal (score vs time) where the participants change expression unusually. This can be carried out using first derivate of the signal representing confidence values of neutral emotion. If the signal is more smooth, it is difficult to visualize the peak, in this situation, derivate of signal can help. Mathmatically, the inflection point is a point in a curve where local maximum or minimum and the curvature is zero. As illustrated in Fig. 5, the threshold point is calculated for all the participants and find out the maxHR% and power generation in that instant. The blue signal in the plot represents original signal representing neutral emotion index and pink signal represents the first derivative of it. As illustrated in figure, the pink signal shows the deviation of signal more sharply.

The same signal illustrated in Fig. 5 is also plotted against the power generated during physical exercise (see Fig. 6) as a scatter plot. The same participants were choosen to plot scatter plot as Fig. 5. The primary aim of this research was to find out a time point when a person starts fluctuating their facial expression drastically. For all the users, a threshold point (threshold time, HR, and Power) from where neutral emotion drastically changes was calculated. From this figure, we can find out the threshold point in terms of power instead of time, because the maximum duration is quite dependent on psychophiological feature of individual.

The power and neutral emotion was also plotted to know the threshold value of power dissipation when a subject starts fluctuating their neutral emotion. The duration was measured in seconds. The threshold time point, threshold power point, total duration, maximum power dissipation or power at the end of the exercise is presented in Table 2. The threshold point was calculated mathematically using a local minimum value of the first derivative of the neutral emotion series. A very interesting result is that all the participants start changes in their neutral expression when the maxPower% is in between 80%–90%.

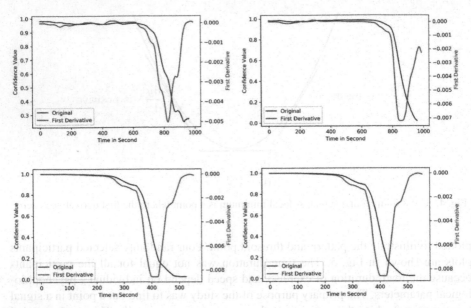

Fig. 5. Probability value of neutral emotion and its first derivate plot with respect to time, from four randomly selected participants.

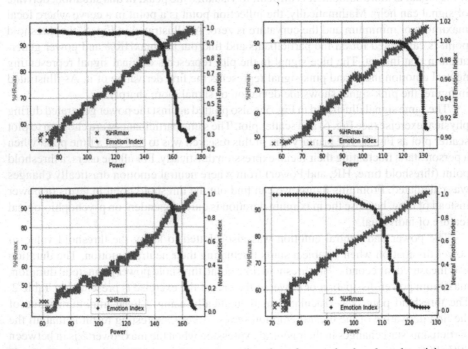

Fig. 6. Scatter plot of %HRmax and neutral emotion, from four randomly selected participants.

Table 2. Calculating the threshold points from the facial expression for all the subjects.

Subject ID	Duration (Min)	Max Power units	Threshold Power units	Threshold time units	MaxPower %
Subject1	16	180	150	13.33	83
Subject2	12	150	120	10.88	80
Subject3	7	120	80	4.11	66
Subject4	9	130	110	7.08	84
Subject5	15	150	130	10.41	86
Subject6	9	140	120	9.00	85
Subject7	16	170	155	13.75	91
Subject8	12	140	120	8.33	85
Subject9	6	225	175	3.33	77
Subject10	5	200	180	4.5	90
Subject11	7	115	105	5.4	91
Subject12	9	130	110	6.66	84

5 Discussion

Despite many state-of-art studies focusing on emotion analysis in sports science, facial expression changes with respect to neutral emotion has never been examined. Exercise monitoring using a multimodal approach is a common and accurate approach in exercise monitoring to predict exercise intensity from physiological parameters, facial expression, rate of perceived exertion (RPE) etc. Most of the studies focused on physiological parameters to predict exercise intensity [18–20]. Due to widespread applications of facial expression analysis applied in various fields, it was hypothesized that facial expression is one of the important features related to exercise intensity. Though many studies have presented the effect of exercise intensity or fatigue in detecting facial emotion, finding a close association with physiological parameters and other psychological parameters, exercise intensity or fatigue from the facial expression was never tested.

The use of physiological parameters such as heart rate, heart rate variability and body temperature to predict emotions is becoming a reliable approach [21–24], but the use of facial emotions/facial expressions to predict these parameters is never done in the literature. In the present study, neutral emotional expressions were used to analyze the intensity of the physical exercise and found an interesting pattern of neutral emotional expression changes during physical exercise. The neutral emotion score was plotted against time, HRmax, and power. Among all, power is the parameter most associated to changes in facial expression.

Miles [12] illustrated the reliability of the measurement of exercise intensity by using a facial feature points analysis. The results showed reliable measures of exercise intensity based on facial feature point movements with respect to the exercise intensity. Authors have statistically illustrated this reliability though its correlation to exercise intensity was never measured. The results presented in our study are similar to the hypothesis presented in the study by Miles.

The limitations of this study are the following: (1) The number of subjects is only twelve and they are also not equally distributed according to gender; therefore, the results might not be generalized. (2) We only consider neutral expression scores; the results might be better if more parameters are considered. (3) Each participant performed only a single trial;therefore, the result can not be generalized.

6 Conclusion and Future Work

From the results obtained, it is concluded that neutral emotion deviates during physical exercise and it is a very important cue for analyzing physical exercise, but it is quite an individual one. The important fact from the study is that each participant has a point from where they start changing their expression sharply, which might represent very important information about the sub-maximal exercise, as well as have some relationship between other physiological factors. The major limitation of this study is the limited number of subjects and the fact that each subject carried out just a single experiment. This work can be extended with more and diverse types of participants, in addition to having participants perform the experiment more than once.

Acknowledgements. This work was supported by Portuguese FCT – Foundation for Science and Technology - project UID0445/2020.

References

1. Reed, J.L., Pipe, A.L.: Practical approaches to prescribing physical activity and monitoring exercise intensity. Can. J. Cardiol. **32**(4), 514–522 (2016)
2. Schuch, F.B., et al.: Exercise as a treatment for depression: a meta-analysis adjusting for publication bias, pp. 1879–1379 Electronic (2016)
3. Das, P., Horton, R.: Rethinking our approach to physical activity. Lancet (London, England) **380**(9838), 189–190 (2012)
4. Bayles, M.P., Swank, A.M.: ACSM's exercise testing and prescription. American College of Sports, Medicine (2018)
5. Hunt, K.J., Fankhauser, S.E.: Heart rate control during treadmill exercise using input-sensitivity shaping for disturbance rejection of very-low-frequency heart rate variability. Biomed. Sign. Process. Control **30**, 31–42 (2016)
6. Xie, K., et al.: Non-contact heart rate monitoring for intensive exercise based on singular spectrum analysis. In: 2019 IEEE Conference on Multimedia Information Processing and Retrieval (MIPR) (2019)
7. Aboagye, E., et al.: Individual preferences for physical exercise as secondary prevention for non-specific low back pain: a discrete choice experiment. PLoS ONE **12**(12), e0187709–e0187709 (2017)
8. Uchida, M.C., et al.: Identification of muscle fatigue by tracking facial expressions. PLoS ONE **13**(12), e0208834 (2018)
9. Khanal, S.R., et al.: Classification of physical exercise intensity by using facial expression analysis. In: 2018 Second International Conference on Computing Methodologies and Communication (ICCMC) (2018). https://doi.org/10.1109/ICCMC.2018.8488080

10. Ekman, P.: Basic emotions. Handb. Cogn. Emot. **98**(45–60), 16 (1999)
11. Khanal, S.R., Sampaio, J., Barroso, J., Filipe, V.: Classification of physical exercise intensity based on facial expression using deep neural network. In: Antona, M., Stephanidis, C. (eds.) HCII 2019. LNCS, vol. 11573, pp. 455–467. Springer, Cham (2019). https://doi.org/10.1007/978-3-030-23563-5_36
12. Miles, K.H., et al.: Facial feature tracking: a psychophysiological measure to assess exercise intensity? 1466–447X Electronic
13. Khanal, S., et al.: Using emotion recognition in intelligent interface design for elderly care. In: Trends and Advances in Information Systems and Technologies. Cham: Springer International Publishing (2018). https://doi.org/10.1007/978-3-319-77712-2_23
14. Khanal, S.R., et al.: Physical exercise intensity monitoring through eye-blink and mouth's shape analysis. In: 2018 2nd International Conference on Technology and Innovation in Sports, Health and Wellbeing (TISHW) (2018). https://doi.org/10.1109/TISHW.2018.855 9556
15. Viola, P., Jones, M.: Rapid object detection using a boosted cascade of simple features. In: Proceedings of the 2001 IEEE Computer Society Conference on Computer Vision and Pattern Recognition. CVPR 2001 (2001)
16. Orieux, F., Giovannelli, J.F., Rodet, T.: Bayesian estimation of regularization and point spread function parameters for Wiener-Hunt deconvolution. J. Opt. Soc. Am. **27**(7), 1593–1607 (2010)
17. Goodfellow, I.J., et al.: Challenges in representation learning: a report on three machine learning contests. In: International Conference on Neural Information Processing. Springer (2013)
18. Jonsdottir, J., et al.: Intensive multimodal training to improve gait resistance, mobility, balance and cognitive function in persons with multiple sclerosis: a pilot randomized controlled trial. Front. Neurol. **9**, 800 (2018)
19. Chowdhury, A.K., et al.: Prediction of relative physical activity intensity using multimodal sensing of physiological data. Sens. (Basel, Switzerland) **19**(20), 4509 (2019)
20. Vieluf, S., et al.: Exercise-induced changes of multimodal interactions within the autonomic nervous network. Front. Physiol. **10**, 240 (2019)
21. Jang, E.H., et al.: Analysis of physiological signals for recognition of boredom, pain, and surprise emotions. J. Physiol. Anthropol. **34**(1), 25–25 (2015)
22. Hwang, R.J., et al.: Physical activity and neural correlates of sad facial expressions in premenstrual syndrome. J. Gynecol. Obstet. **6**(3), 56–66 (2018)
23. Critchley, H.D., et al.: Activity in the human brain predicting differential heart rate responses to emotional facial expressions. NeuroImage **24**(3), 751–762 (2005)
24. Pezzulo, G., et al.: Increased heart rate after exercise facilitates the processing of fearful but not disgusted faces. Sci. Rep. **8**(1), 398 (2018)

Exploring Pointer Assisted Reading (PAR): Using Mouse Movements to Analyze Web Users' Reading Behaviors and Patterns

Ilan Kirsh[1]([✉]) [iD] and Mike Joy[2] [iD]

[1] The Academic College of Tel Aviv-Yaffo, Tel Aviv, Israel
kirsh@mta.ac.il
[2] University of Warwick, Coventry, UK
M.S.Joy@warwick.ac.uk

Abstract. This paper explores Pointer Assisted Reading (PAR), a reading behavior consisting of moving the mouse cursor (also known as the pointer) along sentences to mark the reading position, similarly to finger-pointing when reading a book. The study shows that PAR is an uncommon reading technique and examines methods to extract and visualize the PAR activity of web users. An analysis shows that PAR data of real users reveal reading properties, such as speed, and reading patterns, such as skipping and rereading. Eye-tracking is usually used to analyze user reading behaviors. This paper advocates for considering PAR-tracking as a feasible alternative to eye-tracking on websites, as tracking the eye gaze of ordinary web users is usually impractical. PAR data might help in spotting quality issues in the textual content of a website, such as unclear text or content that might not interest the website users, based on analyzing reading properties and patterns (e.g. reading speed, skipping, and rereading). Accordingly, PAR-tracking may have various practical applications in a wide range of fields, and particularly in educational technology, e-learning, and web analytics.

Keywords: Mouse pointer · Mouse cursor · Eye-tracking · Website · Web pages · Reading · Human-computer interaction · Educational technology · E-learning · Distance learning · Web analytics · Document · Text · Sentence · Word

1 Introduction

Reading habits and behaviors vary from person to person. This paper explores the behavior of reading text online with the aid of a mouse. Moving the cursor (also known as the pointer) of a pointing device (e.g. a mouse or a touchpad) to point at sentences and words while reading can be referred to as Pointer Assisted Reading (PAR) [16].

© Springer Nature Switzerland AG 2020
C. Stephanidis et al. (Eds.): HCII 2020, LNCS 12424, pp. 156–173, 2020.
https://doi.org/10.1007/978-3-030-60117-1_12

Previous studies have already shown proximity between the mouse cursor position and the user's eye gaze on the screen during mouse activity (as discussed in Sect. 2). Based on this knowledge, we can consider mouse cursor movements along lines of text in the direction of reading (left to right in English) as representing eye gaze movements, and accordingly, reflecting the reading of these lines of text.

The primary purpose of this study is to explore and examine PAR activity and to investigate and illustrate reading behaviors that are reflected in PAR data, such as changing reading speed, sentence skipping, and word rereading. This study paves the way to exciting, new research directions and practical applications.

This paper is organized as follows. Section 2 presents related work. Section 3 introduces the implementation of tracking and visualizing mouse movements, which was used in this research to collect, manage, and present relevant data. Section 4 shows that PAR is uncommon, proposes methods for "mining" PAR activity from mouse movement data, and presents experimental results that demonstrate the effectiveness of these methods. Section 5 presents and analyzes examples of PAR sessions of real users. Section 6 discusses the results. Lastly, Sect. 7 concludes this paper and suggests possible further work.

2 Related Work

User attention data are essential in many applications, including in educational technology, online learning, e-commerce, news websites, online advertising, and web analytics, as well as in studying reading habits and behaviors.

Eye and gaze tracking data have been used for estimating user attention in many applications and studies, including, for example, to assess the mental workload that a user interface places on users and to identify usability issues [13], to measure levels of attention to advertising [22], to guarantee user attention on application permission authorization [15], to measure mobile web user interest [23], and to evaluate the effect of social information on user enjoyment of online videos [25].

User attention data are particularly important in analyzing reading behaviors. Eye-tracking has been used in many studies on reading in recent years, including to distinguish between reading and skimming [2], to explore second language vocabulary acquisition while reading [27], to examine the effect of location-driven logo placement on attention and memory [11], to assess the effects of listening to music while reading [34], to explore the reading development of elementary school children over time [31], to identify reading disabilities and dyslexia [1], and to compare first-language reading to second-language reading [7].

Although eye-tracking technology is powerful and accurate, it has significant availability and scalability limitations. Technically, integrating eye-tracking into web pages is possible [8], but it is impractical for most websites, as eye-tracking normally requires special equipment on the client-side to capture accurate data, it requires user collaboration, and it can raise privacy concerns, as it makes use of cameras. A common solution is to use the alternative client-side user actions, such as page scrolling, mouse movements, and clicks, as implicit indicators of user attention [5,18,33]. Tracking user actions in modern browsers can be achieved by embedding special client-side JavaScript code in web pages. At least 15 commercial web analytics services track user mouse activity [17].

By collecting data on the client-side, the evaluation of user attention at any point in time can be easily reduced from the entire web page to the viewport, which is the visible part of the page. This has been used recently to investigate general reading patterns of online articles [6,30], including, for example, backtracking (scrolling back in the browser). The viewport is large, particularly when websites are accessed from desktop and laptop computers, so it can provide only a very general indication of the attention position.

The position of the mouse cursor can indicate the position of user attention more precisely [12]. When a user moves or clicks the mouse, the position of the mouse cursor is relatively close to the position of the eye gaze on the screen [4,28]. Mouse-tracking information, as an indication of user attention, has been studied in various contexts, including in web search [10,12,26,28], e-commerce [29], web marketing [32], performing tasks [24], and online surveys [3].

Collective user attention on a web page, based on mouse activity, can be visualized by heatmaps [17,20,21]. Such heatmaps are used in many commercial web analytics services [17].

Recent studies show that in the context of textual web pages, horizontal mouse movements in the direction of reading (left to right in English) are more frequent than mouse movements in other directions [16,19] and that those mouse movements are indeed related to reading activity [16].

Jarodzka and Brand-Gruwel [14] proposed to separate eye-tracking research on reading behaviors and patterns into three levels:

- Level 1: Reading sentences and single words;
- Level 2: Reading and comprehending a complete text;
- Level 3: Reading and processing several text documents.

Interestingly, while implicit client-side indicators are widely used as a replacement for eye-tracking in many applications, including in analysis of reading behaviors at levels 2 and 3 (a whole text and multiple documents, respectively), to the best of our knowledge, client-side indicators, including mouse movements, have never been used to analyze reading behaviors at level 1, i.e. sentences and words, which is what this paper does.

3   Mouse Cursor Tracking and Visualization

This study examined PAR activity of users on the ObjectDB developer guide pages.[1] A special PAR Server was implemented in order to track, store, report, and visualize mouse movements. Figure 1 shows the architecture that was used.

To track mouse movements, a reference to a *Tracking Script* was embedded in all the web pages. As a result, every page request from the website returned a revised version of the page that triggered an additional request to load the Tracking Script from the PAR Server. The Tracking Script (implemented in JavaScript) tracked the user's mouse move events and reported them back to the *Collector* component in the PAR Server. The Collector stored the data anonymized in a dedicated database, adhering to industry standards of data anonymization and user privacy preservation.

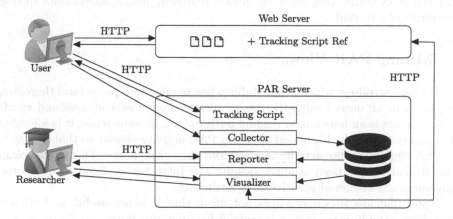

Fig. 1. Architecture of the PAR Server

Mouse movement data were available for research through two components in the PAR server. The *Reporter* component was used to retrieve mouse movement data, including cumulative statistics, via queries. The *Visualizer* component was used to visualize individual page views by displaying mouse movements on web pages. Figure 2 demonstrates the implemented visualization with a sample PAR activity of a real user.

Mouse movements to the right are displayed as solid green lines. Mouse movements to the left are displayed as dashed red lines. Different colors and styles for different directions are very helpful in inferring the mouse movement directions and the reading progression from a still picture. In addition, one direction represents mainly reading activity (the right direction for LTR languages such as English), and the other direction represents mainly progressing to the next line of text (the left direction for English), so distinct colors and styles help in identifying reading patterns.

---

[1] https://www.objectdb.com/java/jpa.

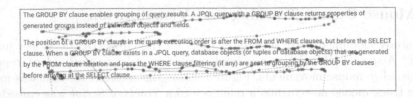

Fig. 2. Visualization of mouse movements for PAR activity analysis (Color figure online)

The circles on both the green and red lines represent the positions of the mouse cursor in reported mouse events. Mouse events are tracked at a rate of one event per one-tenth of a second (i.e. 10 events per second), so the green and red lines connecting adjacent circles represent mouse movements during one-tenth of a second.

4   Mining PAR Views

Unlike page scrolling, which is inevitable when reading web pages (and therefore, employed by all users), using the mouse cursor to point at sentences and words while reading is an uncommon reading pattern [16]. In some sense, it is a hidden phenomenon, and the likelihood of seeing PAR activity similar to that in Fig. 2, by exploring the mouse activity in a random page view, is low. This may explain why it had hardly been studied, despite the intensive work on using mouse movement data as an alternative to eye-tracking.

Note, that low prevalence does not mean that it is not useful, as feedback data from sample users is also beneficial for analytics purposes. However, low frequency means that to examine PAR, we need a method for mining potential PAR views in a web usage dataset, i.e. filtering page views with a high probability of PAR activity.

The dataset that was used in this study consists of 389,424 page views of the 69 web pages of the ObjectDB developer guide. Data were collected from desktop users for a period of several months (ending in March 2020). Mobile users have been excluded as they normally do not use a mouse. We refer to these page views as collection 1. Two filters have been applied on collection 1 in a row, generating collection 2 and collection 3, which are much smaller but have higher probabilities to include PAR activity.

The first filter is trivial. PAR activity requires moving the mouse. Therefore, PAR is more likely in page views where the users moved the mouse longer. Figure 3 shows the distribution of the page views in collection 1 by the total time of mouse movements in seconds. By focusing on page views that include at least 64 seconds of mouse movements, which we refer to as collection 2, we significantly increase the probability of observing PAR activity.

Naturally, we cannot cover every PAR session by ignoring 98.5% of collection 1, but our goal is modest, we prioritize precision over recall and can toler-

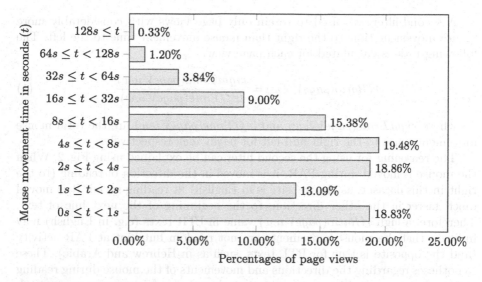

Fig. 3. Distribution of page views in collection 1 by mouse movement time

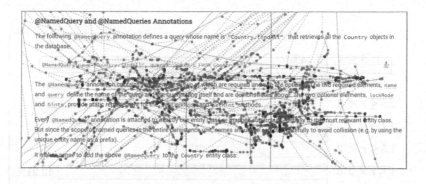

Fig. 4. Scattered mouse activity

ate a high false-negative rate as the objective is to find sample PAR sessions to investigate.

Collection 2 still has page views with no PAR activity, because frequent and long mouse movements are not necessarily related to PAR, as shown in Fig. 4.

On a side note, several similar examples of scattered mouse movements have been observed in collection 2. It is possible that the user fidgeted with the mouse while reading. It might also correlate with obsessive-compulsive disorders, but that is a matter for separate studies.

A second filter was used to retain only page views with considerably more mouse movement time to the right than mouse movement time to the left. The following ratio is calculated for each page view:

$$rlRatio(pageView) = \frac{rightTime(pageView)}{leftTime(pageView)} \qquad (1)$$

where $rightTime(pageView)$ and $leftTime(pageView)$ are the total mouse movement times to the right and left for $pageView$, respectively.

The reasoning for using the second filter can be explained using Fig. 2. When the mouse is moved during PAR, it is moved in the direction of reading (to the right in this dataset, as the website is in English) at reading speed. It is moved much faster in the other direction, to the beginning of the next line of text. Therefore, a high $rlRatio(pageView)$ value in LTR texts (e.g. in English) may indicate that the mouse movements are not random but hint at PAR activity (and the opposite is true for RTL texts, such as in Hebrew and Arabic). These hypotheses regarding the directions and movements of the mouse during reading activity are supported by a recent statistical analysis of mouse movements [16]. Figure 5 shows the distribution of the page views in collection 2 by $rlRatio$ values.

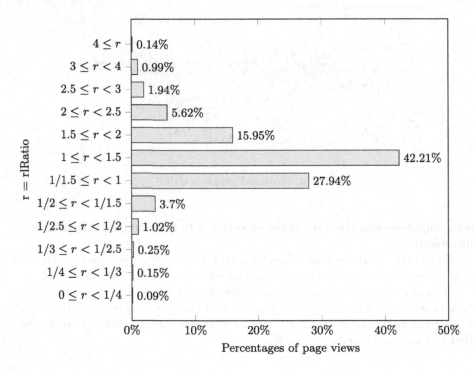

Fig. 5. Distribution of page views in Collection 2 by $rlRatio$

Note that the distribution of page views in Fig. 5 is not exactly symmetric around $rlRatio = 1$. As expected, $rlRatio \geq 1$ is significantly more frequent than $rlRatio < 1$ in this population of page views, which relative to collection 1, is richer with PAR activity.

To minimize false-positive errors (at the cost of a higher false-negative rate) and to improve the quality of the remaining page views (with respect to their PAR activity potential), this new filter was applied as a second-tier on top of the first filter, i.e. on collection 2. The result, collection 3, retains only page views in collection 2 with $rlRatio(pageView) \geq 3$, which is a small fraction of collection 1 (the complete dataset).

A computer program selected 40 random sample page views from each of the three collections and combined them into one set of 120 untagged sample page views. An examiner (an undergraduate student of International Business and Languages) was asked to count the number of text lines in each page view that appear to have been read with moving the mouse cursor as a pointer, i.e. hinting at PAR activity. Table 1 and Fig. 6 show the results. In Fig. 6, the 40 sample page views of each collection are in descending order of the number of identified PAR lines.

Table 1. Collections & Results

	Collection 1	Collection 2	Collection 3
Filter	None	$move\ time \geq 64$ s	$move\ time \geq 64$ s and $rlRatio \geq 3$
Collection size (views)	389,424	6,971	79
Sample size (views)	40	40	40
Views with PAR activity	8	36	40
% Views with PAR activity	20%	90%	100%
Identified PAR lines	16	217	481
Identified PAR lines/view	0.4	5.4	12.0

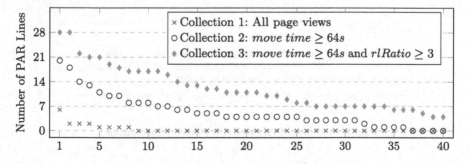

Fig. 6. Identified PAR lines in 120 page views

The sample page views from collection 1 had very little PAR activity (only 16 lines in total for 8 page views, where the other 32 page views had no identified PAR activity at all). This shows that PAR is indeed uncommon and that obtaining page views with PAR requires deliberate "mining". As expected, PAR activity was more frequent in collection 2, and even more so in collection 3.

5   Exploring PAR Using Examples

Mining page views with a high probability of PAR activity, as discussed in Sect. 4, combined with visualizing mouse cursor movements on pages, as described in Sect. 3, paves the way for exploring PAR by examining real examples.

Note that we can assume that the mouse movements visualized in these examples represent eye gaze movements (and accordingly, reading patterns) and that the positions of the mouse cursor reflect eye gaze positions. As discussed in Sect. 2, previous studies have already shown significant proximity between the mouse cursor position and the eye gaze position on a screen when a user moves the mouse.

The primary concern regarding the feasibility of using PAR data is that relevant mouse-tracking data may not be available, because as discussed previously, PAR is not a common reading technique. This section shows that the page views in collection 3 contain mouse-tracking data that are similar to eye-tracking data, and therefore, PAR-tracking data might replace eye-tracking data of web users, which are usually unavailable. Accordingly, the feasibility concern is reduced to whether the amount of PAR-tracking data that can be obtained is sufficient for practical applications. This is discussed in Sect. 6.

Figure 7 shows a typical PAR activity. Green, which represents movements from left to right, is more dominant than red, which represents movements in the opposite direction (from right to left). Lines between two adjacent circles represent mouse movements during one-tenth of a second. The green circles are much closer together than the red circles because right mouse movements are mostly carried out at reading speed, whereas left movements to the beginning of the next lines of text tend to be much faster [16].

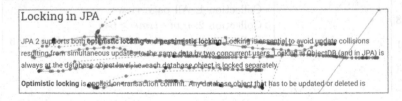

Fig. 7. A typical PAR activity (Color figure online)

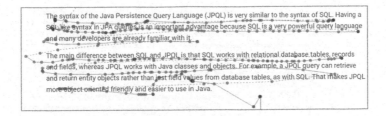

Fig. 8. Cutting corners at the end of text lines (Color figure online)

Most of the mouse cursor movements are shorter than the full-text width, because of a "cutting corners" effect, as shown, for example, in Fig. 7. Even users that use PAR extensively use shortcuts where possible, and apparently, moving the mouse to the very first and last characters of the text lines is not essential for benefiting from PAR. Some users cut corners on both the left and right sides of the text lines, as demonstrated in Fig. 7, while others move the mouse over the first word in text lines but occasionally skip the last word, as demonstrated in Fig. 8.

This is a drawback of PAR-tracking data compared to eye-tracking data, as eye-tracking provides accurate data also at the edges of text lines. To overcome this issue, the missing information regarding reading the start and the end of text lines has to be completed through other means. For example, further work could explore the possibility of extrapolating the missing information using the user's average reading speed.

The vertical position of the mouse cursor relative to the text lines varies. Sometimes it is above the text, sometimes below the text, and sometimes on the text. Changes in the vertical position of the mouse cursor during reading activity are probably due to the difficulty of tracing perfectly straight lines with manual movements.

In browsers, a mouse cursor placed on text usually shows as a thin vertical bar, and therefore, does not normally hide the characters in the text (unlike the green and red lines in the visualization that occasionally hide the text). Consequently, moving the cursor over the text, as seen in Fig. 7, does not necessarily disrupt reading.

The position of the mouse cursor relative to the text seems to reflect personal preferences. Figure 9 shows a PAR activity with the cursor position mainly below the text lines. At first glance, it may be challenging to figure out whether the user traces text lines from above or below. The division of the text into paragraphs is helpful in that regard, as usually the last line of a paragraph is shorter than the full-text width, so we can expect it to be matched with a relatively shorter green movement line.

Sometimes, however, as shown in Fig. 10, the mouse movement lines are vaguer, and their total count does not match the total number of text lines in the paragraph. In these cases, it is difficult to match mouse cursor movements

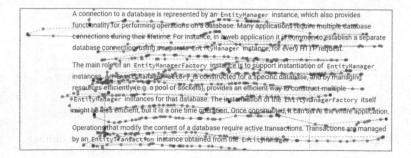

Fig. 9. Pointer below text: matching by text lines lengths

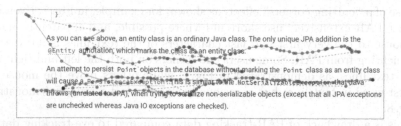

Fig. 10. Vague PAR: no clear way to match mouse cursor movements with text (Color figure online)

with text lines, and therefore, such mouse movement data may be less useful as PAR data.

When it is possible to match mouse movements with text words, it may provide valuable knowledge about the specific page view. When accumulated across distinct page views (of the same web page) of different users, it may also provide information about the page content.

An analysis of Fig. 11 gives several interesting insights. Firstly, we can find out which parts of the text have been read by the user and which parts have

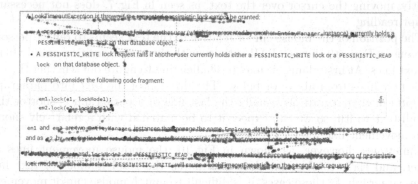

Fig. 11. Skipping, repeating, and reading speed (Color figure online)

been skipped. In a page view with heavy PAR use, a jump such as the one from the word "lock" on the third line to the code fragment below, usually indicates that some lines of text have not been read. Although it is possible for a PAR user to occasionally read lines of text without moving the mouse, checking the timestamps of the mouse events before and after that jump (which are not shown in Fig. 11) confirms that, indeed, these text lines have been skipped by the user.

Secondly, we can see which parts of the text have been read more than once. Most of the first text line in Fig. 11 is covered by two distinct green lines, indicating that it has been reread.

Thirdly, the reading speed is revealed. The density of green circles on Lock-TimeoutException (on the first text line in Fig. 11), PESSIMISTIC_READ, and PESSIMISTIC_WRITE (on the last two text lines) is lower than the average density of green circles in this figure. Apparently, less time is needed to read these long technical strings (relative to their widths in pixels) compared to ordinary text words that require reading alongside thinking and comprehending. This demonstrates the dynamic nature of reading speed. Changes in reading speed are shown in most of the examples in this section. These might be valuable in spotting text complexity and unclarity.

Figure 12 shows an interesting attempt by a user to cut corners and read the last line quickly, but then, possibly because of difficulties in understanding the text at a glance, the user backtracks and reads that line again from the beginning.

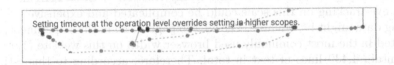

Fig. 12. Cutting corners and then rereading from the beginning (Color figure online)

Figure 13 shows another example of backtracking and rereading. A careful examination of this PAR activity (focusing on the green lines and circles) reveals that the first text line was read once, the second line, the third line, and the beginning of the fourth line were read twice, and the last sentence was read once. This visualization represents the reading activity of a single user. If this pattern repeats in the PAR activity of other users, it may indicate that these sentences are not sufficiently clear.

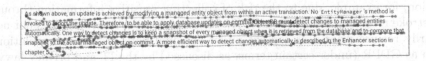

Fig. 13. Rereading lines of text (Color figure online)

Figure 14 shows another example of varying reading speed. The end of the sentence is read much slower than the beginning of the sentence. If this pattern repeats in the PAR activity of other users it may indicate that the end of the sentence is complex and may require simplification.

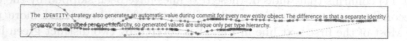

The IDENTITY strategy also generates an automatic value during commit for every new entity object. The difference is that a separate identity generator is managed per type hierarchy, so generated values are unique only per type hierarchy.

Fig. 14. Varying reading speed (Color figure online)

6 Discussion

The experiment discussed in Sect. 4 shows that PAR is not a common reading behavior. Based on the number of manually identified PAR lines in a sample of page views, as shown in Table 1, the frequency in the complete dataset (collection 1) is only 0.4 PAR lines per page view. This is a very rough estimate because of the small size of the sample (and we also expect to have different frequencies on different websites), but it shows that PAR activity is uncommon.

According to this estimate, there are over 155,000 PAR lines in this dataset, i.e. the examples in Sect. 5 cover only a tiny fraction of these PAR lines. Collecting eye-tracking on this scale could be complicated and expensive, so PAR-tracking data might be valuable. The 69 web pages used in this experiment, when presented in the most commonly used browser width on this website (1,920 pixels) contain 4,430 lines of text in total. Therefore, according to this estimate, each text line has on average about 35 PAR lines. The more frequently read lines (which are probably more important when considering how to improve the website content) may have much more PAR data in this dataset.

PAR-tracking might be a useful alternative to eye-tracking when eye-tracking data are unavailable. Particularly, eye-tracking may be impractical on public websites, as it requires active user collaboration, special equipment (to achieve high accuracy), and it may raise privacy concerns among users, as it makes use of cameras. On the other hand, PAR data can be collected in all modern browsers using embedded client-side JavaScript code.

Mouse movement tracking and recording is a core element of "session recording", which is a common practice in modern web analytics [17]. Session recording raises interesting questions in the context of user privacy and personal data protection, for example, due to the risk of collecting sensitive information through keystroke recording unintentionally [9]. However, session recording does not necessarily require prior user consent under personal data protection regulations, such as GDPR (under certain terms, as discussed by the IT and privacy lawyer

Arnoud Engelfriet [9]). If the data collected is completely anonymized, which is a standard practice in web analytics, then it is no longer considered personal data (e.g. by GDPR). Therefore, PAR-tracking can be used on almost any website, as long as data protection standards are preserved, and it could be useful if there are enough users and sufficient traffic.

This study has not used eye-tracking to confirm that the mouse movements that appear to be related to PAR activity indeed match the user's eye gaze while reading. As PAR activity is uncommon, such an experiment would require collecting eye-tracking data for a large number of users, in order to capture the natural PAR activity of the small percentage of users that use PAR. However, the significant proximity of the cursor position to the user's eye-gaze on a screen, when the user moves the mouse, has already been shown in previous studies, as discussed in Sect. 2. Based on this knowledge we can assume that mouse cursor movements along lines of text in the direction of reading (left to right in English) correlate with eye gaze movements in the same direction, and therefore, this reflects reading.

As shown in Sect. 5, the start and the end of text lines are often not covered by mouse movements, because of the "cutting corners" effect. This is a drawback of PAR data compared to eye-tracking data, and further work could look at practical solutions to complete the missing data by other means, for example, based on the user's average reading speed.

PAR-tracking data might be valuable in educational technology, e-learning, and web analytics, as it can show what users read, which parts of the text they skip, which sentences slow their reading speed down, which paragraphs they reread, etc., as demonstrated in Sect. 5. This information might help in spotting issues and obstacles in texts and in improving the overall quality of text content.

PAR-tracking may also be useful in research on reading, which is often performed using eye-tracking. Eliminating the availability and scalability constraints posed by eye-tracking and using PAR-tracking instead may open new doors. For example, international, worldwide research on reading behaviors and patterns on standard websites may become more feasible.

Because of the low prevalence of PAR, we cannot expect to analyze the behavior of every individual user. However, the applications mentioned above do not require data for every user. Data from a sample of users that use PAR might be sufficient in these applications, similar to the way that feedback from sample users is usually sufficient in surveys.

7   Conclusions and Further Work

This paper examines methods to extract and visualize PAR activity and demonstrates and analyzes sample PAR activity of real web users. The potential of PAR data in various applications, as well as the challenges, are discussed.

Further work could seek to develop PAR recognition methods to identify PAR more accurately, matching mouse movements to words in the text. PAR recognition ability might enable replacing eye-tracking with PAR-tracking in many applications, as discussed in this paper. PAR recognition could also help in exploring PAR further, e.g. in calculating the frequency of PAR more precisely and in learning about PAR users, which is essential if we want to treat PAR-tracking data as an accurate representation of the entire website audience.

References

1. Asvestopoulou, T., Manousaki, V., Psistakis, A., Andreadakis, V., Aslanides, I., Papadopouli, M.: DysLexML: screening tool for dyslexia using machine learning, pp. 1–6. ArXiv abs/1903.06274, March 2019
2. Biedert, R., Hees, J., Dengel, A., Buscher, G.: A robust realtime reading-skimming classifier. In: Proceedings of the Symposium on Eye Tracking Research and Applications, ETRA 2012, pp 123–130. Association for Computing Machinery, New York (2012). https://doi.org/10.1145/2168556.2168575
3. Cepeda, C., et al.: Mouse tracking measures and movement patterns with application for online surveys. In: Holzinger, A., Kieseberg, P., Tjoa, A.M., Weippl, E. (eds.) CD-MAKE 2018. LNCS, vol. 11015, pp. 28–42. Springer, Cham (2018). https://doi.org/10.1007/978-3-319-99740-7_3
4. Chen, M.C., Anderson, J.R., Sohn, M.H.: What can a mouse cursor tell us more? correlation of eye/mouse movements on web browsing. In: CHI 2001 Extended Abstracts on Human Factors in Computing Systems, CHI EA 2001, pp. 281–282. Association for Computing Machinery, New York (2001)
5. Claypool, M., Le, P., Wased, M., Brown, D.: Implicit interest indicators. In: Proceedings of the 6th International Conference on Intelligent User Interfaces, IUI 2001, pp. 33–40. Association for Computing Machinery, New York (2001). https://doi.org/10.1145/359784.359836
6. Conlen, M., Kale, A., Heer, J.: Capture & analysis of active reading behaviors for interactive articles on the web. Comput. Graph. Forum **38**(3), 687–698 (2019). https://onlinelibrary.wiley.com/doi/abs/10.1111/cgf.13720https://doi.org/10.1111/cgf.13720
7. Dirix, N., Vander Beken, H., De Bruyne, E., Brysbaert, M., Duyck, W.: Reading text when studying in a second language: an eye-tracking study. Read. Res. Q. (2019). https://doi.org/10.1002/rrq.277
8. Eraslan, S., Yesilada, Y., Harper, S.: "The best of both worlds!": integration of web page and eye tracking data driven approaches for automatic AOI detection. ACM Trans. Web **14**(1), 1–31 (2020)
9. Gilliam Haije, E.: Are session recording tools a risk to internet privacy (2018). https://mopinion.com/are-session-recording-tools-a-risk-to-internet-privacy/
10. Guo, Q., Agichtein, E.: Exploring mouse movements for inferring query intent. In: Proceedings of the 31st Annual International ACM SIGIR Conference on Research and Development in Information Retrieval, SIGIR 2008, pp. 707–708. Association for Computing Machinery, New York (2008). https://doi.org/10.1145/1390334.1390462

11. Hernandez, M., Wang, Y., Sheng, H., Kalliny, M., Minor, M.: Escaping the corner of death? an eye-tracking study of reading direction influence on attention and memory. J. Consum. Mark. **34**, 1–10 (2017). https://doi.org/10.1108/JCM-02-2016-1710

12. Huang, J., White, R., Buscher, G.: User see, user point: gaze and cursor alignment in web search. In: Proceedings of the SIGCHI Conference on Human Factors in Computing Systems, CHI 2012, pp. 1341–1350. Association for Computing Machinery, New York (2012)

13. Iqbal, S., Bailey, B.: Using eye gaze patterns to identify user tasks. In: The Grace Hopper Celebration of Women in Computing, vol. 04, January 2004

14. Jarodzka, H., Brand-Gruwel, S.: Tracking the reading eye: towards a model of real-world reading. J. Comput. Assist. Learn. **33**(3), 193–201 (2017). https://onlinelibrary.wiley.com/doi/abs/10.1111/jcal.12189. https://doi.org/10.1111/jcal.12189

15. Javed, Y., Shehab, M.: Look before you authorize: Using eye-tracking to enforce user attention towards application permissions. Proc. Priv. Enhancing Technol. **2017**(2), 23–37 (2017). https://content.sciendo.com/view/journals/popets/2017/2/article-p23.xml

16. Kirsh, I.: Directions and speeds of mouse movements on a website and reading patterns: a web usage mining case study. In: Proceedings of the 10th International Conference on Web Intelligence, Mining and Semantics (WIMS 2020), Biarritz, France, pp. 129–138. Association for Computing Machinery, New York, June 2020. https://doi.org/10.1145/3405962.3405982

17. Kirsh, I., Joy, M.: A different web analytics perspective through copy to clipboard heatmaps. In: Bielikova, M., Mikkonen, T., Pautasso, C. (eds.) ICWE 2020. LNCS, vol. 12128, pp. 543–546. Springer, Cham (2020). https://doi.org/10.1007/978-3-030-50578-3_41

18. Kirsh, I., Joy, M.: Splitting the web analytics atom: from page metrics and KPIs to sub-page metrics and KPIs. In: Proceedings of the 10th International Conference on Web Intelligence, Mining and Semantics (WIMS 2020), Biarritz, France, pp. 33–43. Association for Computing Machinery, New York, June 2020. https://doi.org/10.1145/3405962.3405984

19. Kirsh, I., Joy, M., Kirsh, Y.: Horizontal mouse movements (HMMs) on web pages as indicators of user interest. In: Proceedings of the 22nd HCI International Conference (HCII 2020), Communications in Computer and Information Science. Springer, Cham, July 2020

20. Lamberti, F., Paravati, G., Gatteschi, V., Cannavò, A.: Supporting web analytics by aggregating user interaction data from heterogeneous devices using viewport-DOM-based heat maps. IEEE Trans. Industr. Inf. **13**, 1989–1999 (2017)

21. Lamberti, F., Paravati, G.: VDHM: viewport-DOM based heat maps as a tool for visually aggregating web users' interaction data from mobile and heterogeneous devices. In: Proceedings of the 2015 IEEE International Conference on Mobile Services, MS 2015, USA, pp. 33–40. IEEE Computer Society (2015)

22. Lee, J., Ahn, J.H.: Attention to banner ads and their effectiveness: an eye-tracking approach. Int. J. Electron. Commer. **17**(1), 119–137 (2012). https://doi.org/10.2753/JEC1086-4415170105

23. Li, Y., Xu, P., Lagun, D., Navalpakkam, V.: Towards measuring and inferring user interest from gaze. In: Proceedings of the 26th International Conference on World Wide Web Companion, WWW 2017 Companion, International World Wide Web Conferences Steering Committee, Republic and Canton of Geneva, CHE, pp. 525–533 (2017). https://doi.org/10.1145/3041021.3054182

24. Milisavljevic, A., Hamard, K., Petermann, C., Gosselin, B., Doré-Mazars, K., Mancas, M.: Eye and mouse coordination during task: from behaviour to prediction. In: International Conference on Human Computer Interaction Theory and Applications, Setúbal, Portugal, pp. 86–93. SciTePress, January 2018. https://doi.org/10.5220/0006618800860093

25. Müller, A.M., Baumgartner, S.E., Kühne, R., Peter, J.: The effects of social information on the enjoyment of online videos: an eye tracking study on the role of attention. Media Psychol., 1–22 (2019). https://doi.org/10.1080/15213269.2019.1679647

26. Navalpakkam, V., Jentzsch, L., Sayres, R., Ravi, S., Ahmed, A., Smola, A.: Measurement and modeling of eye-mouse behavior in the presence of nonlinear page layouts. In: Proceedings of the 22nd International Conference on World Wide Web, WWW 2013, New York, NY, US, pp. 953–964. Association for Computing Machinery (2013). https://doi.org/10.1145/2488388.2488471

27. Pellicer-Sánchez, A.: Incidental vocabulary acquisition from and while reading: an eye-tracking study. Stud. Second Lang. Acquisition **36**(1), 97–130 (2015)

28. Rodden, K., Fu, X.: Exploring how mouse movements relate to eye movements on web search results pages. In: Proceedings of ACM SIGIR 2007 Workshop on Web Information Seeking and Interaction, pp. 29–32. Association for Computing Machinery, New York (2007). http://research.microsoft.com/~ryenw/proceedings/WISI2007.pdf

29. Schneider, J., Weinmann, M., vom Brocke, J., Schneider, C.: Identifying preferences through mouse cursor movements - preliminary evidence. In: Proceedings of the 25th European Conference on Information Systems (ECIS), Guimarães, Portugal, pp. 2546–2556. Research-in-Progress Papers (2017)

30. Smadja, U., Grusky, M., Artzi, Y., Naaman, M.: Understanding reader backtracking behavior in online news articles. In: The World Wide Web Conference, pp. 3237–3243. WWW 2019. Association for Computing Machinery, New York (2019). https://doi.org/10.1145/3308558.3313571

31. Strindberg, A.: Eye movements during reading and reading assessment in Swedish school children: a new window on reading difficulties. In: Proceedings of the 11th ACM Symposium on Eye Tracking Research & Applications, ETRA 2019. Association for Computing Machinery, New York (2019). https://doi.org/10.1145/3314111.3322878

32. Tzafilkou, K., Protogeros, N., Yakinthos, C.: Mouse tracking for web marketing: enhancing user experience in web application software by measuring self-efficacy and hesitation levels. Int. J. Strateg. Innov. Mark. **01** (2014). https://doi.org/10.15556/IJSIM.01.04.005

33. Zahoor, S., Bedekar, M., Kosamkar, P.K.: User implicit interest indicators learned from the browser on the client side. In: Proceedings of the 2014 International Conference on Information and Communication Technology for Competitive Strategies, ICTCS 2014. Association for Computing Machinery, New York (2014)
34. Zhang, H., Miller, K., Cleveland, R., Cortina, K.: How listening to music affects reading: evidence from eye tracking. J. Exp. Psychol. Learn. Mem. Cogn. 44 (2018). https://doi.org/10.1037/xlm0000544

The Effects of Robot Appearances, Voice Types, and Emotions on Emotion Perception Accuracy and Subjective Perception on Robots

Sangjin Ko, Xiaozhen Liu, Jake Mamros, Emily Lawson, Haley Swaim, Chengkai Yao, and Myounghoon Jeon[✉]

Department of Industrial and Systems Engineering, Mind Music Machine Lab, Virginia Tech, Blacksburg, VA, USA
{sangjinko,xliu26,jakem17,emily03,haley1,yaock,
myounghoonjeon}@vt.edu

Abstract. In human-robot interaction, natural and intuitive communication between robot and human is one of the most important research topics. Emotion plays a crucial role to make natural and social interactions. Research has focused more on robots' appearances and facial emotional expressions, but little research has investigated robots' voices and their mixed effects with robot types and different emotions for users to perceive robots' emotional states. In this study, anthropomorphic and zoomorphic robots, four different voice types, and seven different emotional voices were used as mixed factors to discuss how these influence users' perception on robots' emotional expression and other characteristics. Sixteen participants were asked to read fairy tales to robots and determine robots' emotional states when the robots verbally responded. Overall, the anthropomorphic robot (Nao) was preferred over the zoomorphic robot (Pleo), but this appearance did not influence emotion recognition accuracy or other robot characteristics. Participants showed lower accuracy in recognizing negative emotions with high arousal: anger, fear, and disgust. TTS was rated lower than other human voices in all robot characteristics, such as warmth, honesty, trustworthiness, and naturalness. Implications and design directions are discussed with the results.

Keywords: Human-robot interaction · Emotion recognition · Robot appearance · Robot voice

1 Introduction

Research on social robots has sharply increased. To design social robots, it is important to consider key variables to influence robots' sociability, trust, and acceptance. Previous studies in human-robot social interaction discovered that users expect natural and intuitive communication with robots [1–3]. Emotion is a critical component to enable this natural and intuitive communication. To express emotions effectively and accurately, robots can utilize many different sensory cues. However, research has focused more on facial expressions [4] and a comprehensive study on the correlation between different

C. Stephanidis et al. (Eds.): HCII 2020, LNCS 12424, pp. 174–193, 2020.
https://doi.org/10.1007/978-3-030-60117-1_13

factors and emotion perception is still rudimentary. In this paper, an exploratory experiment was conducted to study users' perception on robots' emotional states with mixed factors, including robot appearances, voice types, and emotions. Participants were asked to read fairy tales to robots and determine robots' emotional states when the robots made a comment.

1.1 Related Work

Companion Robots and Natural Communication

The prospect of introducing companion robots into an individual's daily life has received a significant focus from those working and conducting research in the field of Human-Robot Interaction. The development and integration of effective robot companions hold a tremendous degree of promise, given the potential for robots to assist people or even perform tasks that exceed their capabilities.

Previous studies have indicated broad support for the concept of companions, with participants viewing a robot's roles as an assistant, machine, or servant to conform to their expectations of the robot's function [1]. A much greater support and confidence was expressed for robots to be charged with performing household tasks as opposed to tasks dealing with children or animals [1]. A robot companion's ability to communicate is as significant as establishing the social context under which such a companion should operate. Humanlike communication is a desired trait [1]. Studies have similarly shown that the natural language interface of a robot receives more attention in comparison to its functionality, suggesting that the communicative behavior may be a more critical component of the system [3]. Proposed criteria by which to evaluate communicative behavior includes the ability of a robot to detect communication partners and pay attention to them, as well as its comprehension of speech, gestures, and its surrounding environment so as to understand an assigned task [3]. Such criteria revolve around maximizing the social aptness of robot companions so that they may interact and carry out tasks in a natural way.

Expressing one's own emotions and reading others' emotions is also critical for facilitating this natural interaction. To express emotions effectively and accurately, a number of verbal (e.g., voice style, accent, gender, and affective prosody) and nonverbal (e.g., appearance, facial expression, gesture, and movement) cues can be used.

In the current study, we explored the scenario where our participants served as a storyteller and our robots were emotionally empathized with them and responded to the story. We specifically considered the robots' ability to convey emotions, which is a critical part of human-like communication.

Form Factor of Robots

In the design of robots, there are two typical forms of design; one is anthropo-morphic, and the other is zoomorphic [5]. Each one has its unique characteristics and deals with different tasks. In studies on robots' form factor (or appearance) and users' perception, anthropomorphic and zoomorphic robots were preferred over machine-like ones or imaginary creatures [7–9]. Anthropomorphic and zoomorphic robots may have different working scenarios. The more a robot's appearance is human-like shaped, the more intelligent people think it is [10]. Also, during the interaction with humans, anthropomorphic robots may be more able to convey emotional expressions more effectively because their appearance is similar to humans [5]. However, the influence of facial expression of anthropomorphic robots on users' perceptions are sometimes controversial, maybe due to the Uncanny Valley [6]. In other words, a robot's suitability to being like a human or an animal is highly dependent on what kind of task it has and what intelligence level it wants users to perceive. Preference to an anthropomorphic or zoomorphic robot is influenced by many complex factors. In our work, we investigated the effects of voice types on each robot, by applying both qualitative and quantitative measures, examining user perception from broader perspectives.

Robots' Emotion Expression

In terms of emotional expression, emotional vocal expressions can effectively influence the behavior of perceivers [11]. Research explains a robot's emotion expression process in relation to communication theory: 1) a robot's internal state drives expressions, 2) specific robot behaviors are related to specific user reactions, and 3) the situation is an important driver of emotion expressions [12]. Emotion perception is an important source of information about the theory of mind and emotions can be perceived from facial expressions, voices, and whole-body movements [13]. As mentioned, emotion expression and emotion perception play a critical role in human-robot interaction and are widely studied in a range of disciplines. However, previous studies have been dominated by robots' facial emotions and other modalities such as vocal and tactile processes have been less frequently considered [14, 15]. The present study focused more on auditory stimuli by including various emotive voices, representing seven different emotions and investigated the differences in users' emotion perception.

1.2   Research Questions

From this background, we tried to attain a deeper understanding of the effects of robots' appearances, voices, and emotion types on users' perception about robots and their emotions. More specifically, we were interested in the following research questions:

• How can robot appearances, voices, emotion types, and their interactions influence people's perception of robots' emotional states?
• How can robot appearances and voices, and their interactions influence people's perception of robots' characteristics?
• How can robot appearances and voices, and their interactions influence people's preference on robots?

To answer these research questions, we conducted a preliminary empirical experiment in which young adults (college students) interacted with two robots (human-like and animal-like) using four different voices (regular human, characterized human-like, characterized animal-like, text-to-speech) and seven emotions (six basic emotions + anticipation). We collected our participants' emotion recognition accuracy and other subjective perception on robots.

2 Method

2.1 Participants

Sixteen university students participated in the study (Age: M = 23.5, SD = 3.97). Six participants identified themselves as male and the other ten participants identified as female. Participants were ethnically diverse (3 Asians, 2 Hispanic, 9 Caucasians, 1 Middle easterners, and 1 Africans). Participants participated in the experiment for at most 2 h and participants were compensated with $20 ($10 per hour). All participants agreed to participate after reviewing the consent form approved by the VT IRB.

2.2 Robotic Systems and Stimuli

Two robots, NAO and Pleo, having different appearances and features were employed in the experiment (Fig. 1). We used these two robots, which represent an anthropomorphic robot and zoomorphic robot each, to contrast the effects that robotic appearance has on people's emotion perception. NAO is a small-size anthropomorphic robot (Height: 22.6 inch, Length: 10.8 inch, Width 12.2 inch) having similarity to human and Pleo is a zoomorphic robot (Height: 8 inch Length: 15 inch, Width 4 inch) which looks like a little dinosaur. Both robots played recorded auditory feedback, which were emotive utterances, to participants following the storylines. Two different stories ("The three little pigs" and "The boy who cried wolf") were used in this experiment.

Fig. 1. Pictures of robots (NAO, Pleo)

Four voice types were created for seven emotional expressions. We first categorized different voice types as a synthesized voice (text-to-speech or TTS voice) and a recorded human voice. The human voices were provided by two female native speakers in our research group and all the voices were speaking American English with American accents. Next, the recorded human voice was subdivided into three categories that included a regular voice and a characterized voice for each robot (i.e., characterized NAO voice and characterized Pleo voice). The characterized voices for NAO and Pleo were designed to exaggerate emotional expressions with the robots' characters while the female speakers envisioned the characteristics of robots from their appearances.

The TTS voices were generated using text-to-speech [16] engines. Microsoft's female voice and the iOS female voice were used, which were provided by default with the respective operating systems. These TTS voices included no emotional information beyond the words themselves.

Seven different emotions were presented throughout each story including Ekman's six basic emotions. The six basic emotions (anger, disgust, fear, happiness, sadness, and surprise) were chosen for their prevalence in psychology. In addition to them, the seventh emotion, anticipation, was chosen for its similarity to fear and surprise [17]. Its inclusion allows us the opportunity to see if participants can discern an emotion that is not traditionally regarded as a basic emotion and to gauge confusion between emotions with subtle differences. The seven emotions were fit into both stories ("The three little pigs" and "The boy who cried wolf") as depicted in Table 1.

Table 1. Dialogues in stories for presenting different emotions

Presented emotions	Robots' utterance in a story	
	The boy who cried wolf	The three little pigs
Anger	That's not nice!	They shouldn't tease him like that
Anticipation	This should be good.	I wonder what's going to happen!
Disgust	Gross!	He can't want to EAT them!
Fear	He's going to eat the sheep!	Oh no!
Happiness	That sounds nice!	Good!
Sadness	All his sheep are gone	He destroyed their homes
Surprise	Why didn't they help?	Woah, that's fast!

2.3 Design and Procedure

A 2 (robots) × 4 (voice types) × 7 (emotions) within-subject design was applied. Therefore, 8 different combinations of robots and voice types were provided to each participant with all 7 emotions. The presented order and the number of each combination were counterbalanced such that 1) each combination was almost equally presented about 20 times across participants in total and 2) levels of each treatment were presented at least once to each participant. Therefore, each participant interacted with all 8 conditions of robots and voice types and all 7 presented emotions. The 8 conditions were separated into two sessions to help participants recall and compare four different conditions. In each condition, the participant was instructed to read the script in front of a robot and listen to the emotional comment from the robot at various points in the story. The whole procedure including each step and the experiment environment are depicted in Figs. 2, 3 and 4 below.

The participants were asked to fill out several questionnaires after listening to each comment generated from the robot, after finishing reading each full story, and after experiencing four conditions. Specifically, after each response to seven emotions, each condition, and each session, the surveys were conducted for measuring the accuracy of emotion recognition and robot characteristics (Warmth, Honesty, Trustworthiness), naturalness (Natural, Human-like, Robot-like) and preferences (Likability, Attractiveness) of presented emotions. The questionnaire consisted of open questions, seven-point Likert scales (1: Lowest, 7: Highest), and single-choice questions. (Table 2).

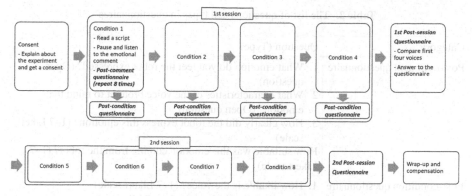

Fig. 2. The flow diagram of the procedure

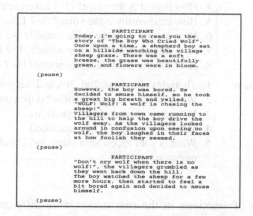

Fig. 3. An example of part story the participant read (The Boy Who Cried Wolf)

Fig. 4. Experimental setting

Table 2. The list of questions and types in questionnaires

Category	Question (Type)
Post-comment questionnaire	1. What emotion do you feel the robot expressed? (Open question) 2. What characteristics of the voice brought to mind that emotion? (Open question) 3. How clearly did the robot express this emotion? (1–7 Likert scale) How suitable was this emotion coming from the robot? (1–7 Likert scale)
Post-condition questionnaire	1. How likable is the voice? (1–7 Likert scale) 2. How attractive is the voice? (1–7 Likert scale) 3. How warm is the voice? (1–7 Likert scale) 4. How honest is the voice? (1–7 Likert scale) 5. How trustworthy is the voice? (1–7 Likert scale) 6. How natural does the voice sound? (1–7 Likert scale) 7. How human does the voice sound? (1–7 Likert scale) 8. How robotic does the voice sound? (1–7 Likert scale)
Post-session questionnaire	1. Thoughts about 1st, 2nd, 3rd, and 4th voices (Open question) 2. Which story was your favorite? (Open question) 3. What is your sex? (Open question) 4. What is your age? (Open question) 5. What is your race and/or ethnicity? (Multiple-choice, Open question)

Presented orders of emotions in the two stories were different, but the order in each story was fixed to maintain the storylines. To generalize the results, we employed two different stories having the same 7 emotions presented and two different voice groups having the same characteristics but recorded by different female speakers and two different female text-to-speech (TTS) engines. The examples of the presented order are depicted in Table 3. To validate the equivalence in accuracy, clarity, suitability, and preference of the two stories and two voice groups, the results were analyzed as below (Table 4), showing similar results in all categories.

3   Results

3.1   Data Collection

The answers to open questions regarding emotions were interpreted by two examiners. Each examiner categorized all the answers into seven pre-defined emotions or marked as 'indistinguishable' if the answers do not fall into any categories. Two examiners worked independently, and the inter-rater reliability test showed that 87.8% (787/896) of the results were consistent with the high coefficient value of Cronbach Alpha using variance (=0.96). If interpretations from examiners were different, a third examiner reviewed the answers and decided which emotion the answer fell into.

Table 3. Examples of the presented order

PID	Start	Trial 1	Trial 2	Trial 3	Trial 4	Trial 5	Trial 6	Trial 7	Trial 8
1	Robot	NAO	Pleo	NAO	Pleo	NAO	Pleo	NAO	Pleo
	Voice type	Regular	Characterized NAO	TTS	Characterized Pleo	TTS	Regular	Characterized Pleo	Characterized NAO
	Story*	Pigs	Wolf	Pigs	Wolf	Pigs	Wolf	Pigs	Wolf
	Voice group	Group A	Group A	Group A	Group A	Group B	Group B	Group B	Group B
2	Robot	Pleo	NAO	Pleo	NAO	Pleo	NAO	Pleo	NAO
	Voice type	Characterized NAO	Characterized Pleo	Regular	TTS	Regular	Characterized NAO	TTS	Characterized Pleo
	Story*	Pigs	Wolf	Pigs	Wolf	Pigs	Wolf	Pigs	Wolf
	Voice group	Group B	Group B	Group B	Group B	Group A	Group A	Group A	Group A

*Pigs: The three little pigs, Wolf: The boy who cried wolf

Table 4. Accuracy, clarity, suitability, and preference over stories and voice groups

		Accuracy	Clarity	Suitability	Preference
Story	The boy who cried wolf	51.2%	4.96	4.93	4.35
	The three little pigs	59.3%	5.27	5.24	4.66
Voice group	Group A	57.6%	5.11	5.17	4.66
	Group B	53.1%	5.12	5.01	4.37

3.2   Emotion Perception: Accuracy, Clarity, Suitability, and Features

First, the accuracy of emotion perception, defined as the proportion of correct emotion answers, was analyzed. Figure 5 and Table 5 show the inferential statistics of accuracy across presented emotions, voice types, and robots. Regarding presented emotions, anger, disgust, and fear showed significantly lower accuracies (below chance level) than other emotions. Therefore, we removed these three emotions from further accuracy analyses. Results were analyzed with the aligned rank transform (ART) [43] for nonparametric factorial analyses since there are 3 factors (Robots, Voice Types, and Emotions) and dependent variable (1: correct, 0: wrong) is not normally distributed. The ART allowed analyzing the aligned-ranked data with a 2 (Robots) × 4 (Voice Types) × 4 (Emotions) repeated measures analysis of variance (ANOVA) and testing all main effects and interaction effects.

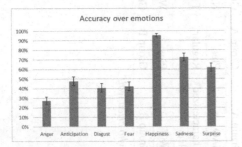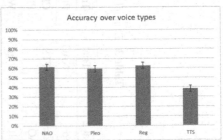

Fig. 5. Accuracy of perceiving emotions over emotions and voice types

For accuracy, there was no significant difference between Nao ($M = 57.1\%$, SD correct $= 0.5\%$) and Pleo ($M = 53.6\%$, SD correct $= 0.5\%$). The result revealed a statistically significant difference across voice types. However, there was significant interaction effect between emotions and voice types. For the multiple comparisons among voice types, paired-samples t-tests were conducted. All pairwise comparisons in this comparison applied a Bonferroni adjustment to control for Type-I error, which meant that we used more conservative alpha levels (critical alpha level $= .0083$ (0.05/6)). Participants showed significantly lower accuracy in a TTS voice than all other three voice types.

Table 5. Statistics for emotion perception (accuracy, clarity, suitability)

Measures	Conditions		Statistics
Accuracy (%)	Main effect for voice types		$F(3, 839) = 16.08, p < .0001$
	Interaction between voice types and emotions		$F(18, 839) = 3.39, p < .0001$
	Characterized NAO $M = 0.61$, SD $= 0.48$	TTS $M = 0.38$, SD $= 0.48$	$t(839) = 90.65$, $p < .0001$
	Characterized Pleo $M = 0.59$, SD $= 0.49$		$t(839) = 80.69$, $p < .0001$
	Regular $M = 0.62$, SD $= 0.48$		$t(839) = 97.33$, $p < .0001$
Clarity	Main effect for robots		$F(1, 838) = 4.9321, p = .0266$
	NAO $M = 5.22$, SD $= 1.77$	Pleo $M = 5.00$, SD $= 1.78$	$t(838) = 2.22$, $p = .0266$
	Main effect for voice types		$F(3, 838) = 99.40$, $p < .0001$
	Characterized NAO $M = 5.75$, SD $= 1.21$	TTS $M = 3.58$, SD $= 2.13$	$t(838) = 14.91$, $p < .0001$
	Characterized Pleo $M = 5.55$, SD $= 1.36$		$t(838) = 13.56$, $p < .0001$
	Regular $M = 5.56$, SD $= 1.31$		$t(838) = 13.65$, $p < .0001$
	Main effect for emotions		$F(6, 838) = 3.90$, $p = .0007$
	Disgust $M = 4.78$, SD $= 1.89$	Surprise $M = 5.54$, SD $= 1.70$	$t(838) = 3.91$, $p = .0001$
	Happiness $M = 4.89$, SD $= 1.70$		$t(838) = 3.35$, $p < .0008$

Table 6 shows how participants misclassified emotions.

Second, clarity and suitability of perceived emotions over robots, voice types, and presented emotions were analyzed as shown in Fig. 6. Clarity and suitability were rated using a 1 to 7 Likert-scale (1: Lowest, 7: Highest). Again, only answers that correctly recognized emotions were considered. Overall, there were differences found in clarity over emotions and voice types. For robots, there were no significant differences found in both clarity and suitability categories. Results were analyzed with a 2 (Robot) $\times$ 4 (Voice Type) $\times$ 7 (Emotions) repeated measures analysis of variance (ANOVA). The result revealed a statistically significant difference in clarity ratings over robots, voice types, and presented emotions. Nao showed significantly higher clarity rating than

Table 6. The confusion matrix between presented and perceived emotions

Perceived		Presented						
		Anger	Anticipation	Disgust	Fear	Happiness	Sadness	Surprise
Anger	Count	35	0	12	0	0	0	2
	Col %	27.3%	0.0%	9.4%	0.0%	0.0%	0.0%	1.6%
Anticipation	Count	0	61	3	0	5	0	8
	Col %	0.0%	47.7%	2.3%	0.0%	3.9%	0.0%	6.3%
Disgust	Count	2	0	52	0	0	0	0
	Col %	1.6%	0.0%	40.6%	0.0%	0.0%	0.0%	0.0%
Fear	Count	2	1	15	54	0	0	5
	Col %	1.6%	0.8%	11.7%	42.2%	0.0%	0.0%	3.9%
Happiness	Count	0	46	1	1	96	0	0
	Col %	0.0%	35.9%	0.8%	0.8%	75.0%	0.0%	0.0%
Sadness	Count	51	0	5	18	0	93	0
	Col %	39.8%	0.0%	3.9%	14.1%	0.0%	72.7%	0.0%
Surprise	Count	0	4	4	18	1	2	79
	Col %	0.0%	3.1%	3.1%	14.1%	0.8%	1.6%	61.7%
Indistinguishable	Count	38	16	36	37	26	33	34
	Col %	29.7%	12.5%	28.1%	28.9%	20.3%	25.8%	26.6%

Pleo. For the multiple comparisons among voice types, paired-samples t-tests were conducted and the result is shown in Table 5. TTS showed significantly lower clarity rating than the other three voice types. For the multiple comparisons among seven emotions, paired-samples t-tests were conducted. All pairwise comparisons in this item applied a Bonferroni adjustment to control for Type-I error, with an alpha levels = .0023 (0.05/21). Surprise showed significantly higher clarity rating than disgust and happiness. For suitability ratings, the result revealed that TTS showed significantly lower score than the other three voice types. No other differences were found.

Finally, the features by which to perceive emotions were analyzed with the results as shown in Table 7. The answers were collected from an open question ("What characteristics of the voice brought to mind that emotion?") and the number of occurrences of words was counted. Each participant was allowed to provide multiple answers for each comment. Most of the emotions were perceived from tone by 40.9%, pitch by 15.6%, and context by 12.4%.

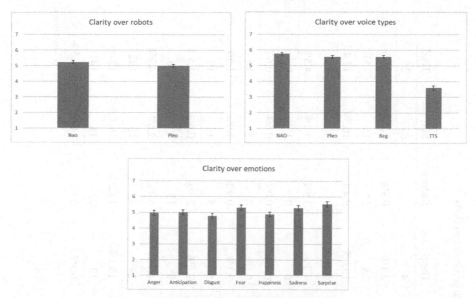

Fig. 6. The rating scores of clarity over robots, voice types, and emotions

3.3 Characteristics: Warmth, Honesty, and Trustworthiness

Figure 7 and Table 8 show the rating scores in trustworthiness over voice types and robots. Results were analyzed with a 2 (Robot) × 4 (Voice Type) repeated measures analysis of variance (ANOVA). For robots, there were no significant differences found in three categories. The result revealed a statistically significant difference in trustworthiness among voice types. There was no interaction effect between robots and voice types. For the multiple comparisons among voice types, paired-samples t-tests were conducted. Warmth and Honesty showed the exactly same pattern as trustworthiness (i.e., no other differences except for voice types with TTS being significantly lower).

3.4 Naturalness: Natural, Human-like, and Robot-like

Figure 8 and Table 9 show the rating scores in "robot-like" over voice types. Results were analyzed with a 2 (Robot) × 4 (Voice Type) repeated measures analysis of variance (ANOVA). For robots, there were no significant differences found in all three categories. The result revealed a statistically significant difference in the rating scores in "robot-like" among voice types. There was no interaction effect between robots and voice types. For the multiple comparisons among voice types, paired-samples t-tests were conducted. Participants showed significantly higher rating scores for TTS than all other three voice types. In addition, characterized Pleo showed significantly higher robot-likeness rating than regular voice. Natural and Human-like showed the exactly opposite pattern as Robot-like (i.e., TTS was significantly lower than others).

Table 7. The result of surveys on features that used to perceive emotions

Feature		Anger	Anticipation	Disgust	Fear	Happiness	Sadness	Surprise	Total
Contents	Count*	1	1	1	2	4	1	8	25
	Col %**	1.3%	1.0%	1.3%	1.9%	2.1%	0.4%	5.2%	2.0%
Context	Count	14	20	19	11	25	22	16	153
	Col %	18.7%	20.0%	23.8%	10.4%	13.0%	9.4%	10.3%	12.4%
Familiarity	Count	0	4	2	10	9	9	5	56
	Col %	0.0%	4.0%	2.5%	9.4%	4.7%	3.8%	3.2%	4.5%
Indistinguishable	Count	0	0	0	1	0	0	1	8
	Col %	0.0%	0.0%	0.0%	0.9%	0.0%	0.0%	0.6%	0.6%
Length	Count	0	0	2	1	6	2	3	19
	Col %	0.0%	0.0%	2.5%	0.9%	3.1%	0.9%	1.9%	1.5%
Loudness	Count	1	0	0	2	5	5	1	19
	Col %	1.3%	0.0%	0.0%	1.9%	2.6%	2.1%	0.6%	1.5%
Mood	Count	6	6	3	2	9	15	4	58
	Col %	8.0%	6.0%	3.8%	1.9%	4.7%	6.4%	2.6%	4.7%
Pitch	Count	14	10	8	22	29	45	25	192
	Col %	18.7%	10.0%	10.0%	20.8%	15.1%	19.2%	16.1%	15.6%
Pronunciation	Count	13	17	12	16	12	23	18	141
	Col %	17.3%	17.0%	15.0%	15.1%	6.3%	9.8%	11.6%	11.5%

(continued)

Table 7. *(continued)*

Feature		Anger	Anticipation	Disgust	Fear	Happiness	Sadness	Surprise	Total
Speed	Count	2	2	2	5	9	13	9	57
	Col %	2.7%	2.0%	2.5%	4.7%	4.7%	5.6%	5.8%	4.6%
Tone	Count	25	40	31	34	84	99	65	503
	Col %	33.3%	40.0%	38.8%	32.1%	43.8%	42.3%	41.9%	40.9%
Total	Count	75	100	80	106	192	234	155	1231
	Col %	100.00%	100.00%	100.00%	100.00%	100.00%	100.00%	100.00%	100.00%

* The total number of answers

** The proportion of the count in each column

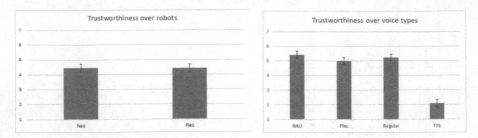

Fig. 7. The rating scores of trustworthiness over voice types

Table 8. Statistics for characteristics (trustworthiness)

Measures	Conditions		Statistics
Trustworthiness	Main effect for voice types		$F(3, 112.1) = 45.54$, $p < .0001$
	Characterized NAO $M = 5.40, SD = 1.49$	TTS $M = 2.09$, $SD = 1.37$	$t(112.1) = 10.07$, $p < .0001$
	Characterized Pleo $M = 5.00, SD = 1.39$		$t(112.1) = 8.83$, $p < .0001$
	Regular $M = 5.21, SD = 1.21$		$t(112.1) = 9.56$, $p < .0001$

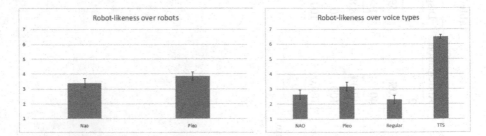

Fig. 8. The rating scores of robot-like over voice types

3.5 Preferences: Likability and Attractiveness

Figures 9, 10 and Table 10 showed the rating scores in "likability" and "attractiveness" over robots and voice types. Results were analyzed with a 2 (Robot) × 4 (Voice Type) repeated measures analysis of variance (ANOVA). For "likability", participants showed significantly higher rating scores for characterized Nao than characterized Pleo. The result also revealed a statistically significant difference in the rating scores over voice types. There was no interaction effect between robots and voice types. For the multiple comparisons among voice types, paired-samples t-tests were conducted. Participants showed significantly lower rating scores for TTS than all other three voice types. For "attractiveness", the result revealed a statistically significant difference in the rating

Table 9. Statistics for naturalness (natural, human-like, robot-like)

Measures	Conditions		Statistics
Robot-like	Main effect for voice types		$F(3, 98.7) = 55.07$, $p < .0001$
	Characterized Nao $M = 2.63, SD = 1.69$	TTS $M = 6.50$, $SD = 0.68$	$t(104.1) = 10.73$, $p < .0001$
	Characterized Pleo $M = 3.16, SD = 1.62$		$t(104.0) = 9.24$, $p < .0001$
	Regular $M = 2.30, SD = 1.48$		$t(90.9) = 10.87$, $p < .0001$
	Characterized Pleo $M = 3.16, SD = 1.62$	Regular $M = 2.30$, $SD = 1.48$	$t(90.9) = 2.38$, $p = .0195$

scores over voice types. For the multiple comparisons among voice types, paired-samples t-tests were conducted. Participants showed significantly lower rating scores for TTS than all other three voice types. Also, participants showed significantly lower rating scores for characterized Pleo than either characterized NAO or regular voice.

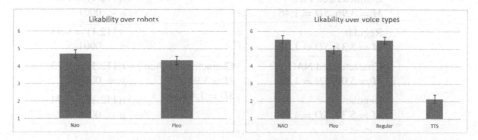

Fig. 9. The rating scores of likability over robots and voice types

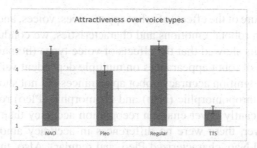

Fig. 10. The rating scores of attractiveness over voice types

Table 10. Statistics for naturalness (likability, attractiveness)

Measures	Conditions		Statistics
Likability	Main effect for robots		$F(3, 112.1) = 6.33$, $p = .0146$
	NAO $M = 4.69$, SD $= 1.85$	Pleo $M = 4.33$, $SD = 1.87$	$t(112.1) = 2.52$, $p = .0146$
	Main effect for voice types		$F(3, 112.1) = 40.32$, $p < .0001$
	Characterized NAO $M = 5.53, SD = 1.24$	TTS $M = 2.12$, $SD = 1.36$	$t(112.1) = 9.32$, $p < .0001$
	Characterized Pleo $M = 4.93, SD = 1.21$		$t(112.1) = 7.78$, $p < .0001$
	Regular $M = 5.48, SD = 1.09$		$t(112.1) = 9.56$, $p < .0001$
Attractiveness	Main effect for voice types		$F(3, 112.1) = 35.43$, $p < .0001$
	Characterized NAO $M = 5.00, SD = 1.48$	TTS $M = 1.87$, $SD = 1.09$	$t(112.1) = 8.36$, $p < .0001$
	Characterized Pleo $M = 3.96, SD = 1.46$		$t(112.1) = 5.66$, $p < .0001$
	Regular $M = 5.31, SD = 1.28$		$t(112.1) = 9.39$, $p < .0001$
	Characterized NAO $M = 5.00, SD = 1.48$	Characterized Pleo $M = 3.96$, $SD = 1.46$	$t(112.1) = 2.72$, $p = .0085$
	Regular $M = 5.31, SD = 1.28$		$t(112.1) = 3.74$, $p < .0004$

4   Discussion

To get a holistic picture of the effects of robot appearances, voices, and emotions types on users' perception on robots' emotions and characteristics, we conducted a preliminary study. Overall, results showed that the effects of voice types (human vs. TTS) seem to be larger than those of robot appearances on multiple dependent variables.

For emotion recognition accuracy, robot appearances did not show a significant difference between anthropomorphic (Nao) and zoomorphic (Pleo) robots. As expected, TTS showed significantly lower emotion recognition accuracy than other three human voice types. However, there were no differences in accuracy among the three voice types (characterized Nao, characterized Pleo, and regular). Also, there were no differences among the three human voice types for clarity and suitability. Taken together, this might imply the potential for using characterized voice for different purposes where appropriate (e.g., for children) without degrading emotion recognition accuracy, as long as it is a human voice. However, the result shows that the emotion recognition accuracy significantly varies depending on the expressed emotions. As shown in Fig. 5, happiness, sadness and surprise showed relatively higher accuracy than anger, disgust, and fear. Anticipation was placed in between. This might happen because happiness, sadness, and surprise are more common emotional states the participants can expect from the fairy tales. Anger, disgust, and fear are all negative-high arousal emotions. The participants might not expect these types of high strength, negative emotions from the fairy tales. However, the relationship between accuracy and each emotion shown in the present study is not in line with the results of the previous study [e.g., 18]. The difference might stem from different experimental settings (e.g., emotional words, prosody, context given by fairy tales, etc.). Thus, more iterative research is required to unpack the underlying mechanisms. For the misclassified emotions, valence showed a big impact. Based on the confusion matrix, anger (negative) was mostly misclassified as sadness (negative) (39.8%) and anticipation (positive) was mostly misclassified as happiness (positive) (35.9%). Based on the participants' self-report, most of the emotions were perceived from tone by 40.9%, pitch by 15.6%, and context by 12.4%, which shows that affective prosody is more critical than the content itself.

For robot characteristics, there was no statistically significant difference between the two robots, but there were differences between all human voices and TTS. We can cautiously infer that people did not perceive any differences among the regular, characterized Nao and characterized Pleo in terms of warmth, honesty, and trustworthiness.

Similarly, for naturalness, there was no statistically significant difference between the two robots even though participants consistently showed a tendency to perceive higher natural ($M = 4.39$, $SD = 2.18$ vs. $M = 3.88$, $SD = 1.93$), higher human-like ($M = 4.73$, $SD = 2.07$ vs. $M = 4.2$ $SD = 1.9$), and lower robot-like ($M = 3.42$, $SD = 2.22$ vs. $M = 3.87$, $SD = 2.16$) from Nao, compared to Pleo. As expected, there were significant differences in these ratings between all human voices and TTS.

Finally, participants liked Nao significantly more than Pleo from the two robot types. They gave the highest rating to characterized Nao voice, followed by Regular, characterized Pleo, and TTS, even though only TTS was significantly different from other voice types. Participants also gave higher attractiveness rating to Nao ($M = 4.25$, $SD = 1.96$) than Pleo ($M = 3.83$, $SD = 1.82$), which did not reach the statistical significance level due to large variance. All three human voices were significantly more attractive than TTS. Also, both characterized Nao and regular voice were significantly more attractive than TTS. Again, this shows the potential for use of the characterized voice, at least, for anthropomorphic robots.

This exploratory study can provide practical guidelines for the voice design of various robots and further research studies. People seemed to generally perceive higher preference for an anthropomorphic robot compared a zoomorphic robot, which is in line with literature [8]. However, using either characterized or regular human voice did influence neither people's emotion recognition nor their perception about robot characteristics, such as warmth, honesty, and trustworthiness, as well as naturalness. Therefore, this study supports using human voice as a medium to express robots' emotions with a different voice design choice, depending on users, goal, and context.

5   Limitations and Future Work

The results of this experiment have been limited by several factors. First, only female voice was used in this study. Depending on the gender of the voice, the results might be different. Second, the sample size was small and not sufficient to draw a firm conclusion. Due to the COVID-19, the experiment was not run as much as planned. In future work, more participants with diversity should be recruited to generalize the results. Another limitation includes that the questionnaire for emotion recognition was an open-ended, which caused considerable confusion and lower accuracy rate. In future work, a questionnaire with more specific emotion options can be provided with additional open-ended input. Finally, the different speaker systems of different robots might also have influenced on the result (e.g., clarity) and should be addressed in the next study.

References

1. Dautenhahn, K., Woods, S., Kaouri, C., Walters, M.L., Koay, K.L., Werry, I.: What is a robot companion-friend, assistant or butler? In: Proceedings of the International Conference on Intelligent Robots and Systems 2005, IEEE/RSJ, pp. 1192–1197 (2005)
2. Vu, C., Cross, M., Bickmore, T., Gruber, A., Campbell, L.: U.S. Patent No. 8,935,006. In: U.S. Patent and Trademark Office, Washington, DC (2015)
3. Wrede, B., et al.: Research issues for designing robot companions: BIRON as a case study (2004)
4. Schirmer, A., Adolphs, R.: Emotion perception from face, voice, and touch: comparisons and convergence. Trends Cogn. Sci. 21(3), 216–228 (2017)
5. Lohse, M., Hegel, F., Swadzba, A., Rohlfing, K., Wachsmuth, S., Wrede, B.: What can I do for you? Appearance and application of robots. Proc. AISB 7, 121–126 (2007)
6. Seyama, I., Nagayama, S.: The uncanny valley: effect of realism on the impression of artificial human faces. Teleoperators Virtual Environ. 16(4), 337–351 (2007)
7. Li, D., Rau, P., Li, Y.: A cross-cultural study: effect of robot appearance and task. Int. J. Soc. Robot. 2(2), 175–186 (2010)
8. Hosseini, F., Hilliger, S., Barnes, J., Jeon, M., Park, H., Howard, M.: Love at first sight: mere exposure to robot appearance leaves impressions similar to interactions with physical robots. In: Proceedings of the 26th IEEE International Symposium on Robot and Human Interactive Communication (RO-MAN), pp. 615–620. IEEE (2017)
9. Barnes, J., FakhrHosseini, M., Jeon, M., Park, H., Howard, A.: The influence of robot design on acceptance of social robots. In: Proceedings of the 14th International Conference on Ubiquitous Robots and Ambient Intelligence (URAI), pp. 51–55. IEEE (2017)
10. Hegel, F., Krach, S., Kircher, T., Wrede, B., Sagerer, G.: Understanding social robots: a user study on anthropomorphism. In: Proceedings of the 17th IEEE International Symposium on Robot and Human Interactive Communication, Roman, pp. 574–579. IEEE (2008)
11. Bachorowski, J., Owren, M.: Sounds of emotion: production and perception of affect-related vocal acoustics. Ann. New York Acad. Sci. 1000(1), 244–265 (2003)
12. Fischer, K., Jung, M., Jensen, L.: Emotion expression in HRI – when and why. In: Proceedings of the 14th ACM/IEEE International Conference on Human-Robot Interaction (HRI) (2019)
13. Frith, D., Frith, U.: The neural basis of mentalizing. Neuron 50(4), 531–534 (2006)
14. Calvo, A., D'Mello, S.: Affect detection: an interdisciplinary review of models, methods, and their applications. IEEE Trans. Affect. Comput. 1(1), 18–37 (2010)

15. Schirmer, A., Adolphs, R.: Emotion perception from face, voice, and touch: Comparisons and convergence. Trends Cogn. Sci **21**(3), 216–228 (2017)
16. Williams, G., Watts, N., MacLeod, C., Mathews, A.: Cognitive Psychology and Emotional Disorders. John Wiley & Sons, Oxford (1988)
17. Barnes, J., Richie, E., Lin, Q., Jeon, M., Park, H.: Emotive voice acceptance in human-robot interaction. In: Proceedings of the 24th International Conference on Auditory Display (2018)
18. Jeon, Myounghoon, Rayan, Infantdani A.: The effect of physical embodiment of an animal robot on affective prosody recognition. In: Jacko, Julie A. (ed.) HCI 2011. LNCS, vol. 6762, pp. 523–532. Springer, Heidelberg (2011). https://doi.org/10.1007/978-3-642-21605-3_57

Development for Tablet-Based Perimeter Using Temporal Characteristics of Saccadic Durations

Naoki Maeshiba[✉], Kentaro Kotani, Satoshi Suzuki, and Takafumi Asao

Department of Mechanical Engineering, Kansai University, Suita, Japan
{k238630,kotani,ssuzuki,asao}@kansai-u.ac.jp

Abstract. Visual field examination is essential for the early detection of glaucoma. The purpose of this study was to construct a visual field inspection system using a tablet terminal for early detection of glaucoma. In this study, the presentation time of numbers used for visual recognition was optimized to construct a visual field inspection system using a tablet terminal. The optimization was based on human optical characteristics. That is, experiments clarified the relationship between the viewing angle and the presentation time of numbers, and the optimal presentation time at the presentation position of each target was obtained. Next, to evaluate the effectiveness of the optimized system, a visual field test was performed using a tablet-type perimeter to incorporate the system, and the accuracy of Marriott blind spot detection was obtained as a substitute index for the visual field abnormality. As a result of the evaluation experiment, the detection rate of Marriott blind spots was 66.7%. In this paper, we discuss the detection rate of Marriott blind spots and individual differences. In conclusion, it was shown that the accuracy of visual field measurement was improved by using the perimeter that incorporates the proposed system.

Keywords: Glaucoma · Perimeter · Saccade

1 Introduction

Glaucoma is the leading cause of blindness in Japan, with 1 in 20 Japanese over 40 years old having glaucoma [1]. Glaucoma is a disease in which the visual field is narrowed due to optic nerve damage. Since the prevalence increases with age, the number of glaucoma patients increases as the elderly population increases [2]. In general, there are almost no subjective symptoms in the early stage of glaucoma, and the symptoms may have considerably progressed when it is noticed that vision loss or visual field loss occurs. The current mainstream treatment method for glaucoma is to prevent the progression by prescription of eye drops to reduce the elevated intraocular pressure. However, in the current medical treatment, it is essential to detect the disease early because it is not possible to recover the lost visual acuity or restore the visual field [3]. Therefore, a device that can adequately determine the presence or absence of glaucoma development is needed.

Devices such as Goldmann perimeter and Humphrey perimeter have been introduced as typical ones in the clinical field. These perimeters are medical devices for diagnosing

© Springer Nature Switzerland AG 2020
C. Stephanidis et al. (Eds.): HCII 2020, LNCS 12424, pp. 194–208, 2020.
https://doi.org/10.1007/978-3-030-60117-1_14

the progress of visual field defects and do not function as consumer devices that promote early subjective symptoms. Furthermore, these perimeters are required to continue to fixate one point for 10 to 20 min for the examination of one eye due to the measurement principle peculiar to the perimeter. As a result, the patient's concentration decreases during the test, and it is challenging to keep their eyes on from the fixation point, which increases the burden on the patient [4]. Also, it has been reported that in preschool children and the elderly, the test procedure is often difficult to understand, and the test results are not reliable [5]. Furthermore, these perimeters have a mechanism in which the patient operates the button based upon the subjective judgment of the patient. There may be a substantial delay in time, which causes the problem that the reliability of the test results becomes low [5]. Another problem with the current mainstream perimeters is that they are installed only in large hospitals with ophthalmology because they are relatively large-scale devices. Therefore, there is a problem that glaucoma patients with no subjective symptoms do not have the opportunity to undergo the examination. We have solved these problems and developed a small visual field inspection system using a tablet terminal that can easily measure the visual field for early detection. Tablet terminals can be carried at a low cost. They can be used in situations such as homes, waiting rooms at clinics as well as remote locations [6], thus increasing the number of opportunities for visual field examination.

In the proposed system, we developed a Superimposed fixation pattern to solve the difficulty of keeping the patient gazing at the fixation point. The superimposed fixation pattern [4] works effectively because there is the principle of the visual field, defining that the visual field around the target is constant if the optical axis captures the target. Using this principle, it is possible to extract the visual field area only by moving the line of sight naturally. This natural behavior-based technique eliminates the need to gaze at one point for a long time, shortens the examination time, and reduces the burden on the patient.

Furthermore, we decided to introduce the voice recognition function to automatically evaluate whether or not the user correctly recognized the target, instead of users' subjective evaluation. Previously, we proposed a system for objective visual judgment by determining whether the numbers presented after the target presentation could be read out correctly. If the numbers were read out correctly, it was determined that eye movements were performed appropriately. The size of the target was the same as the target used in a conventional perimeter. However, the numbers presented after the target had to be displayed relatively large so that the patient could read without stress. Then, even though the target itself was not visible due to the visual field abnormality, the number presented right after the target disappeared may be perceivable due to its large size. As a result, eye movement occurs after perceiving a number, and vocal data is recorded by chance. When such an unexpected eye movement occurs, the area that should be judged to be abnormal visual field may be misdiagnosed as "area without visual field abnormality." We analyzed the temporal factors related to the target and number presentation that caused this misdiagnosis. As a result, this problem would be solved by optimizing the target presentation time and the number presentation time, respectively. The time required for eye movement is related to the distance between the fixation point and the target, as well as the distance between the eye and the display. In this study, the viewing angle is used as an index to express the distance from the fixation point to the target position.

In this study, we conducted an experiment to optimize the presentation time of numbers used in the developed visual field measurement system and clarified the relationship between the presentation time of numbers and the viewing angle of a person. This experiment and its results are summarized as Experiment 1. Furthermore, we improved the tablet-type visual field inspection system that introduced the optimum presentation time determined in Experiment 1. The evaluation experiment of this system and its results are summarized as Experiment 2.

2   Proposed System for Optimizing Presentation Time of Targets and Numbers for Voice Recognition

We developed a tablet-based perimeter for screening diseases such as glaucoma. This system consists of a tablet terminal with a visual field inspection app, a stand for fixing the tablet terminal, and a visual field drawing PC. MATLAB is used to generate the visual field from the inspection results. For the tablet terminal, Apple's iPad 6th Generation Wi-Fi (MR7G2J/A) was used.

Application for the perimeter was developed by based on Swift. The application works for the following steps:

1. When the app is started, a fixed viewpoint is presented on the tablet display as shown in Fig. 1. The patient gazes at the fixation point.
2. After a certain time, target 1 (T1) is presented in the predetermined visual field. The patient maintains his/her gaze at the fixation point and moves the gaze from the fixation point to the target when the presented T1 is perceived.
3. After the saccade is generated toward the location that T1 was presented, the target changes to the number, which is defined as target 2 (T2), shown in Fig. 1. The patient then reads out the number displayed at that position. Speech recognition system equipped on the tablet stores the value read by the patient.
4. T2 changes to a new fixation point and the patient repeats a series of procedures.

If the patient cannot see T1, the fixation point being focused disappears, and a new fixation point is presented at the same time. The system records the target that the patient could not perceive as suspected that potential visual field defect in the corresponding area might exist in the area of T2 vicinity.

The system covers a total of 54 locations of the whole visual field to be tested and it takes about five minutes for completing to test all locations for each eye. After completing the session, this system judges the visual field loss state by comparing the patient's answers stored by the voice recognition function with the presented numerical values and constructs the entire visual field image.

The coordinate position for the visual field examination used in this system was the same as that defined by the "center 24-2" used in Humphrey's perimeter, a visual field diagnostic device routinely used in ophthalmic practice. In this system, inspection positions were covered to draw the visual field within a viewing angle range of $\pm 30°$.

The fixation point was drawn as a red circle, and T1 was drawn as a black circle. One out of five single-digit numbers from 0 to 4 was shown as the T2 display. The size of the fixation point and the target T1 was the same as Goldman type-III (diameter: viewing angle 0.45°) used in Humphrey perimeter, and the number shown at T2 area was appeared at the center of the square. To make it easier for patients to read the numbers on the display, T2 is displayed at a viewing angle of 1.5° which is larger than the target T1. The time from duration between when the fixation point was presented and when T1 was presented was randomly determined from 2.5 s, 3.0 s, and 3.5 s. Also, DT1, which was the presentation time of T1, was randomly selected from 1.5 s, 2.0 s, and 2.5 s. This randomization was to prevent the generation of eye movements at the same tempo unintentionally by making the variable onset time of the target.

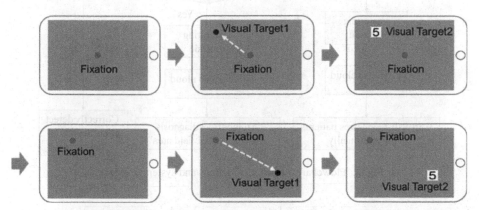

Fig. 1. Relationship between screen transition and subject's reaction when using visual field analyzer application developed in this study.

3   Experiment 1

3.1   Objective of the Experiment

In the proposed system, it was judged that T1 could be visually recognized if T2 was read out correctly, and then it was evaluated as a "normal visual field area." On the contrary, if it was judged that T1 could not be visually recognized even though T2 was correctly read out, it was evaluated as a "abnormal visual field area". In other words, the judgment of the visual field defect of this system depended on the logic that T2 is read out only when the patient can see T1. However, since T2 was presented with a larger size than T1 so that the appearance of numbers can be detected without saccadic eye movement. In this case, T1 was not visible, so it had to be judged as a "abnormal visual field area" (Fig. 2). In other words, if the patient could not see T1 and changed to T2 and then saw T2 and performed a saccade, the target presentation time DT2 had to be set so that T2 could not be perceived, described as shown in Fig. 3, case 1. On the other hand, when the viewing angle was large, it seemed that the time required for saccade has become longer, and when DT2 was too short, T1 was visible, but T2 cannot be recognized (Fig. 3, case 2). Therefore, in order to introduce the target presentation time considering these viewing angles and saccadic duration, the purpose of this experiment was to find the optimum DT2 for each viewing angle.

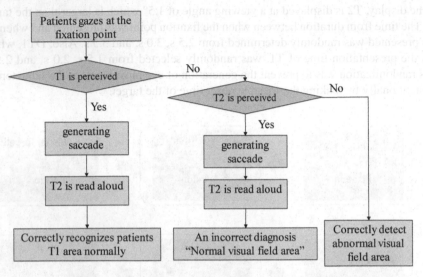

Fig. 2. Flowchart for patients' actions and system response

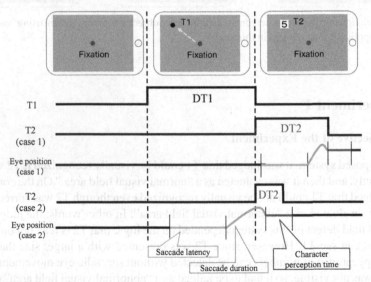

Fig. 3. Time chart of the proposed system. Eye position at the top indicates the case when T1 was recognized and eye position at the bottom shows the case when T1 was not recognized and T2 was recognized.

3.2 Participants

The participants were six healthy university students (21 to 22 years old). Both eyes were measured, and each eye was measured in order. The vision correction status of the participants was as follows: 1 person with eyeglasses, two persons without vision correction, and three persons with contact lenses.

3.3 Experimental Apparatus

The experiment consisted of a PC (Dell Inspiron 3470) for image presentation and a monitor (24 inch). The size of the monitor was 50 cm × 26 cm, and the monitor was placed 480 mm away from the participants. Generation and presentation of the target stimulus used in the experiment and time management were performed by a program created in Unity. The experimenter confirmed the recording of the speech data of the participants.

3.4 Experimental Condition and Data Analysis

The fixation point and T2 (visual stimulus composed of numbers) were presented on the monitor. The fixation point always existed in the center, and T2 was shown on the circumference centered on the fixation point. The size of T2 was presented at a viewing angle of 1.5°. The T2 showed on the monitor and responses made by participants were recorded on the PC with assistance with experimenter in chronological order. '

The independent variables were 1) viewing angle (degrees) and 2) presentation time DT2 (seconds). The viewing angle was the geometric angle from the fixation point to the location of presentation stimulus T2 (Refer to Fig. 4). Since the maximum viewing angle of the proposed system described in Sect. 2 was set to 30°, the viewing angle level was set to 6 patterns in 5° increments in the range of 5 to 30°.

The presentation time DT2 was set as the duration of T2. Focusing on human visual characteristics, the levels of DT2 were 6 levels of 0.4 s, 0.3 s, 0.25 s, 0.2 s, 0.15 s, and 0.1 s. This experimental model has three possible visual characteristics: saccade latency, saccade duration, and character perception time (Fig. 3). The time from the recognition of the target to the start of the saccade (latency) is generally said to be about 200 ms in a normal person without knowing the location of the target in advance [7]. The duration required for gaging movement with a viewing angle of 10° is about 110 ms [8]. Besides, the time required to recognize a number is about 100 ms [9] for a single digit. Therefore, the time needed to perceive a number after saccade generated by visually identifying T2 with peripheral vision is about 410 mseconds. In other words, T2 can be visually recognized in about 410 ms by a healthy person, and the problem of misdiagnosis shown in Fig. 2 occurs, thus we decided to consider DT2 as 0.4 s or less. On the other hand, it is necessary to set DT2 longer than 0.1 s because it takes about 0.1 s to recognize a single-digit number [9]. In the proposed system, T2 can be identified if DT2 is set to 0.1 s. However, if DT2 is 0.1 s at all target positions, problems such as case 2 shown in Fig. 3 are expected to occur. Therefore, it is necessary to give DT2 a time margin at the target position where the viewing angle is large. All in all, DT2 is set in the range of 0.1 s to 0.4 s, and the optimum value of DT2 was obtained from this range by experiments.

As a dependent variable, we defined accidentally identified rate as the rate of the correct verbal response of the numbers presented on the monitor among participants without taking proper steps. If DT2 becomes small, the time margin for recognizing the number decreases, thus the accidentally identified rate decreases. Also, the viewing angle affects the saccade distance. Since the time required for saccade increases as the saccade distance increases, the viewing angle is also an essential factor for setting DT2. Consequently, it was decided to experimentally verify the optimum value of DT2 using the viewing angle and the accidentally identified rate.

The viewing angle was presented four times for each level of DT2, and DT2 was evaluated at six levels, that is, 24 trials were performed per participant.

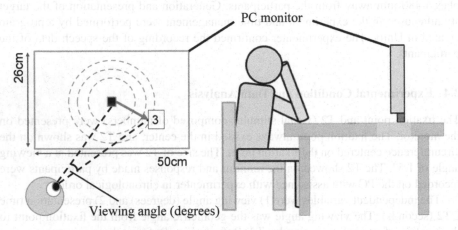

Fig. 4. Experimental condition

3.5 Experimental Procedure

The experimental procedure was as follows.

1. Participants were informed about inspection procedures 2) to 6). Participants were instructed (1) not to move their line of sight to anything other than the fixation point and the presented number, (2) not to move the position of the head or body, and (3) not to speak words other than the numbers.
2. The participants adjusted the position of their heads and took the posture of hiding their eyes opposite to the examination eye, with their hands and placing their elbows at the table. The experiment started from the right eye. Participants instructed to gaze at the fixation point displayed in the center.
3. First, a practice trial was conducted under the condition that DT2 was set to 0.5 s. The practice trial encouraged participants to understand the examination method. The results of the practice trials were not recorded.
4. After the practice trial, the experiment started.

5. Participants perform saccades when the numbers presented can be seen by peripheral vision, and read out the numbers when they are visible. If the participant could not see the number, he voiced it. After that, the viewpoint was returned to the central fixation point, and the next number was presented.
6. The experimenter recorded the numbers read out by the participants (or the answer that they could not see).

3.6 Results

Figure 5 shows the relationship between the presentation time DT2 for each viewing angle, and the average accidentally identified rate of the left and right eyes of all participants. Accidentally identified rates at 6 levels of DT2 = 0.1 s to 0.4 s are plotted. The purpose of Experiment 1 was to determine DT2 to minimize the risk of the misdiagnosis shown in Fig. 2. Based on this result, we conclude that it is appropriate to select DT2 with an accidentally identified rate of 0%.

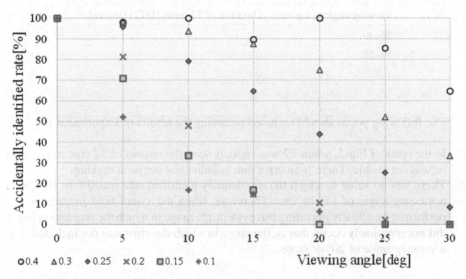

Fig. 5. Relationship between viewing angles and accidentally identified rate

In consideration of case 2, the largest value in the range of DT2 discussed in Fig. 2 was selected. According to Fig. 5, DT2 was in the range of 0.1 s to 0.2 s when the viewing angle was 30°, and the accidentally identified rate was 0%. Similarly, at a viewing angle of 25°, only 0.1 s to 0.15 s and at a viewing angle of 20° were 0.15 s. Therefore, DT2 at a viewing angle of 30° was set to 0.2 s, and DT2 at a viewing angle of 25° and a viewing angle of 20° was set to 0.15 s.

As a result of the experiment, there was no DT2 with an accidentally identified rate of 0% in the viewing angle range of 15° or less. Therefore, the optimum value of DT2 was discussed in the previous study. According to Obama et al. [10], the visual system was capable of recognizing characters presented within a radius of about 10° with the fixation point at that time as the center when the saccade was not programmed. In other words, T2 presented within 10° can be recognized unless the presentation time was set to 0.1 s or less (the time required for character recognition [9]). However, when DT2 was set to less than 0.1 s, it was considered that T2 could not be recognized even if T1 was generally recognized during the examination; thus, it was not suitable as a visual recognition condition. Therefore, it was necessary to set DT2 to a value exceeding 0.1 s. Therefore, the minimum value of DT2 was set to 0.1 s within the viewing angle of 10°. Finally, for 15°, DT2 has almost the same accidentally identified rate in the time range from 0.1 s to 0.2 s; thus, we examined which time should be appropriate. According to Fukuda [11], the appearance of letters in peripheral vision varies depending on the presented retinal region. Among them, 6.5° to 16° is defined as the far fovea. With this definition as a reference, DT2 = 0.1 s was set for a viewing angle of 15°, similar to 10° (Table 1).

Table 1. Relationship between viewing angles and the duration of T2 onset (DT2)

Viewing angles (degrees)	Duration of T2 onset (DT2) (seconds)
26–30	0.2
17–25	0.15
1–16	0.1

The following points should be noted regarding the results of Experiment 1.

1. In the result of Fig. 5, when T2 was vaguely seen, the answer of T2 contained guess or was not visible. There is an error due to individual decision making.
2. There was no value at which the accidentally identified rate was 0% in DT2 with a viewing angle of 15° or less. Therefore, when the visual field inspection was performed by actually operating this system, the range in which the problem in Fig. 2 did not completely occur, that is, the range in which the error was not included, was a viewing angle of 20° or more.

4 Experiment 2

4.1 Objective

We developed a tablet-type visual field inspection system that introduced the presentation time DT2 determined in Experiment 1. In Experiment 2, the effectiveness of the improved visual field inspection system was verified. In this experiment, healthy university students were recruited as experiment participants. In general, visual field inspection detects visual field abnormalities, and healthy people often do not have visual field abnormalities. Therefore, we decided to evaluate whether the Marriott blind spot, which is a physiological blind spot in humans, can be accurately detected. If the Marriott blind spot can be detected properly, it can be suggested that the inspection system detected the abnormal field of view, and the system's effectiveness can be shown [12].

4.2 Participants

The participants were eight healthy university students (21 to 22 years old). Only the right eyes were evaluated. The participants' vision correction status was as follows: 4 persons with eyeglasses, two persons without vision correction, and two persons with contact lenses.

4.3 Experimental Condition

Number of targets was presented to the Marriott blind spot was three times in one examination. The viewing distance from the tablet device was 320 mm. Figure 6 shows the experimental environment. An eye patch was attached to the unexamined eye. Participants were seated in a position where the right eye was in the center of the tablet. Since the face may move during the examination, we used a system that suspends the test when the position of the face changes to an area where the Marriott blind spot can be seen and prompts the re-correction of the face position. The developed system was designed to stop when the viewing distance between the front and rear is 275.9 mm to 380.9, and the left and right are over $320 \tan 2.5°$ (radius 13.97 mm). In Experiment 2, we evaluated the target presentation scheme, thus, decided not to use the voice recognition function, but to record the numbers spoken by the participants manually.

Since the Marriott blind spot's position may slightly vary from person to person, we measured the visual distance at which the information about the Marriott blind spot was not visually obtained for each subject. The target was presented at the center of the tablet terminal and the Marriott blind spot, and the viewing distance was measured. The Marriott blind spot is assumed to be a circle with a center (horizontal 15°, vertical 3°) and a diameter of 5°. Lmin is the minimum visual distance at which the target at the blind spot is invisible, while Lmax is the maximum distance. (See Fig. 7)

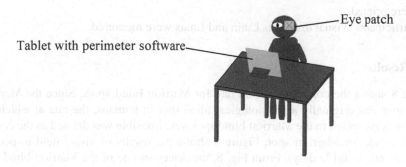

Tablet with perimeter software

Eye patch

Fig. 6. Experimental condition

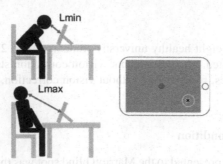

Fig. 7. Viewing distance measurement

4.4 Experimental Procedure

The inspection procedure was as follows.

1. Participants received an explanation about inspection procedures 2) to 6). Participants were instructed (1) not to move their line of sight to anything other than the fixation point and the presented number, (2) not to move the position of the head or body, and (3) not to speak words other than the numbers.
2. Participants put the eye patch on their left eye and took a comfortable posture.
3. The position was adjusted so that the distance from the eye to the tablet surface was 320 mm.
4. The application was started, and the practice trial started. The practice trial encouraged participants to understand the examination method.
5. After the practice trial, the visual distance of 320 mm was measured again, and the primary inspection (target: 54 points) was performed.
6. The visual recognition results were shared with the PC, and the inspection results were printed.
7. Participants' visual distances Lmin and Lmax were measured.

4.5 Results

Figure 8 shows the correct detection rate for Marriott blind spots. Since the Marriott blind spot was originally a physiological blind spot in humans, the rate at which the test points presented to the Marriott blind spot were invisible was defined as the correct detection rate for Marriott spot. Figure 9 shows the results of visual field inspection (Participants A and D only). From Fig. 8, the detection rate of the Marriott blind spot position for all participants was 66.7%. Figure 10 shows the measured Lmin and Lmax for each participant. According to Fig. 10, it was found that the values of Lmax and Lmin and the difference between the maximum and minimum viewing distances (Lmax – Lmin) differ for each individual.

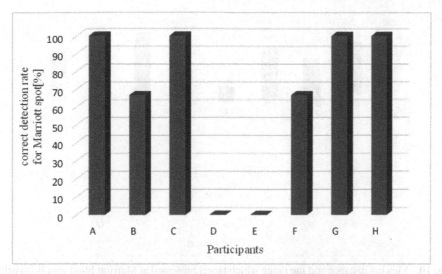

Fig. 8. Correct detection rate for Marriott blind spots

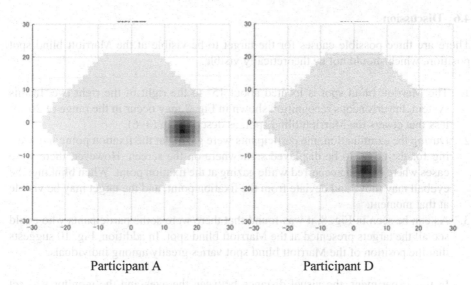

Participant A   Participant D

Fig. 9. Results of visual field examination (Participant A and D)

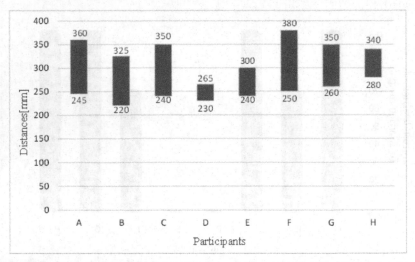

Fig. 10. Viewing distance and the range which target presented at Marriott blind spot is invisible for each participant

4.6 Discussion

There are three possible causes for the target to be visible at the Marriott blind spot position, which should not be theoretically visible.

1. The Marriott blind spot is located about 15° to the right of the right eye. In this system, the erroneous recognition shown in Fig. 2 may occur in the range of 20° or less that covers the Marriott blind spot, as described in (3–6).
2. During the examination, the participants were gazing at the fixation point and waiting for the target to be displayed somewhere on the screen. However, there were cases where blinking occurred while gazing at the fixation point. When blinking, the eyeball may move and deviate from the fixation point, and the target may be visible at that moment.
3. As can be seen in Fig. 8, it was found that there were some participants who could see all the targets presented at the Marriott blind spot. In addition, Fig. 10 suggests that the position of the Marriott blind spot varies greatly among individuals.

In this experiment, the visual distance between the eyes and the monitor was set to 320 mm. As shown in Fig. 10, in the case of participants D and E, the distance of 320 mm is outside the range of the Marriott blind spot, that is, the distance is visible even if the target is presented at the position of the Marriott blind spot. The results of the experiment confirm that participants D and E set the viewing distance at which the information presented at the blind spot was visible. For eliminating the variation between individuals, the detection rate was recalculated using the data of 6 people, excluding the data of these 2 participants and was 88.9%. In the study by Kobayashi et al. [13], 81.6% of the central positions of the Marriott blind spots were measured by visual field measurement using a Goldmann perimeter, which suggests that the present system was also appropriate.

5 Conclusion

In this study, we developed a visual field inspection system for the early detection of glaucoma. This system presents numbers in a size that is easy to visually recognize after the target offset so that the objective visual judgment can be performed. In this paper, the target presentation time DT2 was optimized based on the physiological characteristics of human saccades. Experiment 1 was performed to obtain the quantitative information necessary for optimization. For 6 participants, we obtained the accidentally identified rate when the viewing angle DT2 corresponding to the viewing distance moving in the saccade and the presentation time DT2 were changed. Based on the results of Experiment 1 and previous studies, the optimum presentation time DT2 for each viewing angle was DT2 = 0.1 s for viewing angles 1 to 16°, DT2 = 0.15 s for viewing angles 17 to 25°, and DT2 for viewing angles 26 to 30° = 0.2 s.

Furthermore, in Experiment 2, we conducted visual field inspection using the developed visual field inspection system and focused on the detection rate of Marriott blind spots, and examined the effectiveness of the system. As a result, the detection rate of Marriott blind spots was 66.7%.

There were three possible reasons why the target presented on the Marriott blind spot, which should not be perceived originally, was accidentally visible. First, there was an accidental saccade that cannot be covered by just optimizing the presentation time of the two types of targets, and second, there was a case in which the participants may have looked away from the fixation point. And, finally, it was inferred that there were cases where the individual differences in the position and shape of the Marriott blind spot could not be covered in this study. Therefore, we asked each participant to maintain the invisible state of the target presented at the theoretical Marriott blind spot position and observe the maximum and minimum values of the visual distance in that state. Then, it was found that the size and range of the viewing distance differed significantly among the participants. In particular, it was found that there was a participant who could see the target even if the target was presented at the theoretical position of the Marriott blind spot with the visual distance of 320 mm set as the experimental condition. The detection rate of Marriott blind spots was 88.9% when those participants were excluded.

In conclusion, the effectiveness of the proposed visual field inspection system was demonstrated. Although some participants could accidentally see the targets presented to the Marriott blind spot, it was thought that this was primarily due to individual differences among the participants. However, note that the visual field inspection practically did not aim at the detection of blind spots. The visual recognition of blind spots in this report did not lead to the conclusion that the visual field inspection system was unreliable. On the other hand, the existence of the gap between the Marriott blind spot positions among individuals suggested the necessity of system improvement in the future. It was considered that grasping the position and shape of the Marriott blind spot for each individual was a point to be solved for the generalization of the proposed system.

References

1. Saito, Y.: Saikin no Ryokunaisyou Chiryo. [Recent glaucoma medical treatment]. Showa Univ. J. Med. Sci. **76**(4), 414–420 (2016). (in Japanese)
2. Nakazawa, T.: New field of glaucoma through effective inspection. Jpn. Assoc. Certified Orthoptists **47**, 7–13 (2018). (in Japanese)
3. Nishiyama, H., Hiraishi, H., Iwase, A., Mizoguchi, F.: Design of glaucoma diagnosis system by data mining. In: The 20th Annual Conference of the Japanese Society for Artificial Intelligence (2006). (in Japanese)
4. Kotani, K., et al.: Visual field screening system by using overlapped fixation patterns. IEEJ Trans. Electron. Inf. Syst. **131**(9), 1577–1586 (2011). (in Japanese)
5. Suga, M., Tabata, Y., Nagata, S., Minato, K.: Development of a quantitative perimeter screening system for infants on an immersive VR display. Inst. Electron. Inf. Commun. Eng. (IECE) **88**(9), 1971–1978 (2005). (in Japanese)
6. Vingrys, A.J., Healey, J.K., Liew, S., et al.: Validation of a tablet as a tangent perimeter. Transl. Vis. Sci. Tech. **5**(4), 3 (2016)
7. Honda, H.: Gankyu Undo to Kukan Teii [Eye movement and spatial localization] (Kazama Shobo, 1994), 9–10, 14. (in Japanese)
8. Fukushima, M.: Clinical application of saccadic reaction time. Jpn. Assoc. Certified Orthoptists **15**, 110–120 (1987). (in Japanese)
9. Fukuda, T.: Picture and vision (IV) -letter perception-. J. Soc. Photogr. Imaging Jpn. **48**(1), 29–36 (1985). (in Japanese)
10. Kohama, T., Hatano, T., Tsuyoshi, S., Yoshida, T.: An analysis of eye movements on character recognition. Inst. Image Inf. Telev. Eng. **18**(32), 9–16 (1994). (in Japanese)
11. Fukuda, T.: The functional difference between central vision and peripheral vision in pattern perception. J. Inst. TV Engrs. of Japan. **32**(6), 492–498 (1978). (in Japanese)
12. Inakagata, S., et al.: Objective pupillographic perimetry using a flat panel display. Jpn. Soc. Med. Biol. Eng. **43**(1), 179–183 (2005). (in Japanese)
13. Kobayashi, A., Fukai, S.: The current training provided for students in orthoptics on the quantitative kinetic goldmann perimetry. Jpn. Orthoptic J. **38**, 321–328 (2009). (in Japanese)

Automatic Page-Turner for Pianists with Wearable Motion Detector

Seyed Ali Mirazimzadeh$^{(\boxtimes)}$ and Victoria McArthur

Carleton University, Ottawa, ON K1S5B6, Canada
{ali.mirazimzadeh,victoria.mcarthur}@carleton.ca

Abstract. This study describes a novel combination of wearable devices and digital music notation system to support hands-free page turning during music performances. Our proposed system follows the pianist's hands and traces the movements of both wrists in three-axes and sends data to the central computer via a WIFI connection. We used the MIDI format as a standard digital notation system in our study which contains more than 128 notes in 10 octaves. Each piece of music includes a series of smaller and equal sections called measures. Using the MIDI numbering format, the median value of all notes in each measure is available. By comparing the normalized median values and data from the wearables with cross-correlation and dynamic time warping techniques, we can sync these two series, predict the current playing measure, and turn the page at the correct time. The motivation and structure of this study are for pianists; however, this project has the potential to customized for other instruments.

Keywords: Wearable device · Automatic page-turning · Hands motion detection

1 Introduction

Page-Turning is the necessary process in reading books or other types of documents and requires at least one hand to complete. Numerous limitations can disrupt this process, including physical issues such as neurological disorders, spinal cord injuries, amyotrophic lateral sclerosis (ALS), or other disabilities that involve motor function or upper limb dysfunction [1]. In different situations, this process can be challenging if both hands are required for accomplishing a task during page-turning. For example, musicians often need both hands to play a music piece, and turning pages can cause a short delay in their performance. In piano concerts, pianists may play from memory, or utilize a page terner who sits close to them during the performance and turns the page at the correct time. These solutions might reduce delay or distraction caused my page-turning during live performances, however, these solutions introduce risk due to human factors. Another concern is the physical structure of sheet music, which, if bound may not stay open to the correct page easily, or if unsecured on the music stand could easily fall or be dropped during performance. Many academic disciplines have addressed this limitation and suggested automatic hands-free page-turning mechanisms as an assistive technology [2, 3].

© Springer Nature Switzerland AG 2020
C. Stephanidis et al. (Eds.): HCII 2020, LNCS 12424, pp. 209–218, 2020.
https://doi.org/10.1007/978-3-030-60117-1_15

Among different solutions, we have selected a minimal and lightweight smart electronic kit, the NGIMU [14] kit, which is described in Sect. 3.1 of this paper. Utilizing 2 kits (one per hand), we are able to simulate and track the pianist's hand movements to understand which notes are currently being played and turn the music score pages automatically. Our motivation is to eliminate additional human factors in the task of page-turning during musical performance.

2   Related Work

Previous studies within this area of research mostly focused on video and image processing techniques to detect the positions of the pianist's hands or fingers. Various elements have been considered, including the determination of skin colour, the shape of the hands, light and shadows generated when pressing piano keys by comparing video frame data [4], painting finger nails with different colours [5], and recognizing the light lumens and area between fingers for tracking their actions with using depth camera [6] (see Fig. 1. Four different pictures of previous studies that used various techniques in automatic hand tracking and page-turning systems. (A) shows the result of tracking pianist's skin colour, shape of hands, light, and shadows).

Machnacz [7] invented the first mechanical page-turner in 1972. However, the concept of today's portable page-turners was created by Carr and Lucero [8] in 1992. Carr and Lucer's device was designed to be installed on the music stand and had two separate foot pedals used by the pianist for switching pages. Almost all modern page-turner devices [9, 10] inherited the pedal system, and only mechanical parts are replaced with digital gadgets like tablets or touch screen displays. The size and ubiquity of tablets made them an obvious alternative to paper-based music sheets [11]. The piano has three foot pedals for adjusting tones and sustaining notes. As such, there has been some concern that adding two additional pedals for turning pages could confuse the pianist. Other musicians who may perform while standing (e.g., solo clarinetist), may find it difficult to use their feet to turn the page while performing [11].

As an alternative to pedals, researchers have conducted several studies investigating the tracking body gestures to facilitate hands-free page turning. Head movements and gestures were observed in a study [12] using computer vision. The system detected the initial face position at the start of the performance and traced any movement (right or left) with a facial landmarks tracking algorithm. In another study [11], researchers used Google Glass as a wearable device to detect the head motion and recognized winking as a trigger for turning the digital music score. The eye-gazing tracking system was the core method of another study [13] for making an automatic page-turner for musicians.

Almost all of the aforementioned studies used several types of equipment to support video, audio, and face tracking that require highly controlled variables (e.g., controlling the light of the scene or precisely regulating the distance of components in relation to the performer), making them inappropriate for use during live performances. In this study, we were motiviated to identify and test a lightweight wearable solution and fault-tolerant hardware and software package capable of addressing these limitations while supporting musicians during live performances.

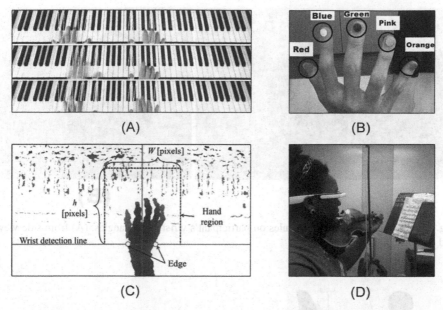

Fig. 1. Four different pictures of previous studies that used various techniques in automatic hand tracking and page-turning systems. (A) shows the result of tracking pianist's skin colour, shape of hands, light, and shadows. (B) indicates a study that participants used different paint on their fingers nails to facilitate the tracing of their fingers in video processing. (C) shows the result of tracking light lumens in a video frame for determining space between the pianist's fingers. (D) shows the study that used Google Glasses for detecting facial gestures.

3   Project Description

3.1   Hardware

In order to capture and track the pianist's hand movements, we used the NGIMU [14] kit, which has an embedded inertial measurement unit (IMU) module. This kit has a 3-axis gyroscope, accelerometer, magnetometer, and on-board attitude and heading reference system (AHRS) sensor, which provides a drift-free measurement of orientation relative to the Earth. This package can also transmit its sensor's data in real-time via WIFI connection and is also covered by plastic housing with a body strap that allows us to fix the device securely on the pianist's wrists (see Fig. 2. Showing the NGIMU modules on participant's wrist in two angles. (A) from side view, and (B) from top). For processing data, we used a laptop with Intel Core i9 CPU, 16gb of RAM, and Windows 10 operating system. For presenting data (music scores), we used Microsoft's surface pro 4. All devices are connected to a single WIFI router (see Fig. 3. Schematic diagram of our proposed system shows its components and connections between the elements).

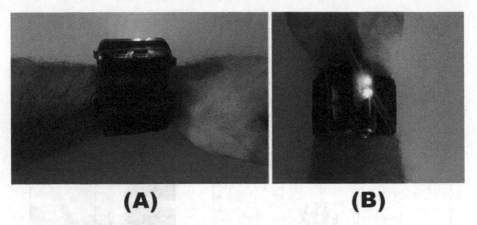

(A)   **(B)**

Fig. 2. Showing the NGIMU modules on participant's wrist in two angles. (A) from side view, and (B) from top view.

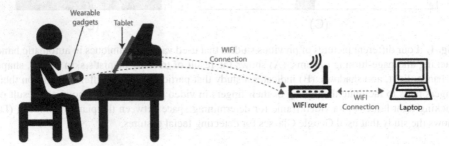

Fig. 3. Schematic diagram of our proposed system shows its components and connections between the elements.

3.2 Software

We chose Python as the primary programming language for this study due to its strong open-source community and full compatibility with our wearable device. We also selected musical instrument digital interface (MIDI) as a standard format for digitalizing music scores. MIDI is a global communication protocol for storing and transmitting digital music information [15]. MIDI acts as a unified language for digital music equipment like synthesizers, controllers, and computers to aid their communication. Unlike the analogue system that transfers sound signals, MIDI transfers the event data, which contains note pitch, note velocity after-touch, knob movement, etc. The event data does not include any sound. Therefore, a MIDI sequencer is required to transfer that data into sound. The MIDI protocol also covers more than 10 octaves with 127 notes from note 0 (C,8.175 Hz) to note 127 (G,12.543 kHz), which supports all notes of the modern-day piano. We divided the software part into three main subsections: i) receiving the gadgets data, ii) reading and computer the digital music score, and iii) syncing previous steps and showing the result on the tablet's screen.

4 Study Design

4.1 Preparation

For this study, we have selected five piano pieces from both classical and modern styles with low speed (tempo less than 90 beats per second) and digitalized them with MuseScore3 [16] software. In the next step, we exported them into MIDI format. Our wearable devices (left and right hand) only detect wrist movements, so we were not able to track finger movement to determine which keys were pressed. To resolve this limitation, we changed the unit of measurement from notes to measures. In music notation, a vertical line (bar-line) splits a piece into smaller and equal sections, which are called measures (see Fig. 4. Showing the boundaries of four measures of piano).

Fig. 4. Showing the boundaries of four measures of piano sheet music.

The maximum possible range of keys that can be played on a piano by one hand at a time varies from musician to musician, and is achieved by stretching the hand to press keys with the thumb and little finger simultaneously (often used to play octaves with the same hand). In this case, the position of the wrist will be in the middle. Therefore, we can assume that the median value of notes based on MIDI numbering format in each measure can be aligned to the pianists' wrist position in three axes (see Fig. 5. Showing the number of each note in MIDI format and the calculation of the median values of notes for each measure). In other cases where there is a distance between notes in one measure (the notes are in different octaves) and more hand movements are required to perform them, the system automatically divides the measurements again.

The combination of all median values was the reference for our calculations in this study (see Fig. 6).

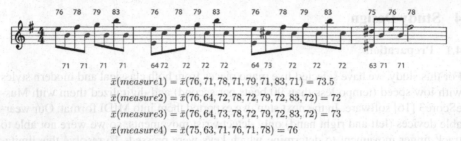

$$\bar{x}(measure1) = \bar{x}(76, 71, 78, 71, 79, 71, 83, 71) = 73.5$$
$$\bar{x}(measure2) = \bar{x}(76, 64, 72, 78, 72, 79, 72, 83, 72) = 72$$
$$\bar{x}(measure3) = \bar{x}(76, 64, 73, 78, 72, 79, 72, 83, 72) = 73$$
$$\bar{x}(measure4) = \bar{x}(75, 63, 71, 76, 71, 78) = 76$$

Fig. 5. Showing the number of each note in MIDI format and the calculation of the median values of notes for each measure.

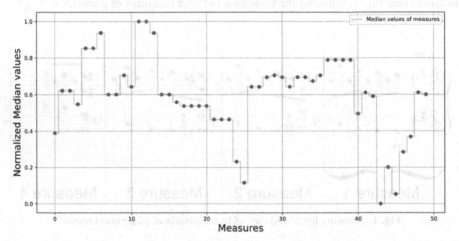

Fig. 6. Showing the median values of 50 measures. All median numbers are normalized.

4.2 Receiving and Computing Data

As mentioned above, we used IMU modules with a 3-axis accelerometer, gyroscope, and magnetometer to monitor the pianist's wrist movement. All sensors transmit data in 50 Hz via the WIFI connection to the central computer. In general, if a function gives us the position of the object as a function of time, the first derivative gives its velocity, and the second derivative provides its acceleration. Therefore, by double integrating the value of the accelerometer sensor, we can calculate the displacement of our object in three axes. The calculation of position is relative and depends on the previous measurements, so any noise or non-valid data can affect the position estimation dramatically. Academic papers have addressed this problem as the generic limitations of IMUs and suggested to use other devices like GPS to correct the misalignments in intervals [17].

The output of tracking wrist movements in three axes gives us three data series. To align those series with series generated made by the MIDI engine, we used Cross-Correlation and Dynamic time warping methods. Cross-correlation is a mathematical algorithm which is mostly used in signal processing for measuring the similarities of two series as a function of a time-lag applied to one of them. Dynamic time warping is another approach to find the optimal global alignment between two sequences by comparing series with a distance matrix instead of calculating the Euclidean distance (Figs. 7 and 8).

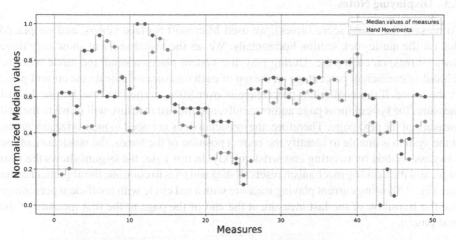

Fig. 7. Showing two series of pianist's right-hand movement and median values of notes for 50 measures

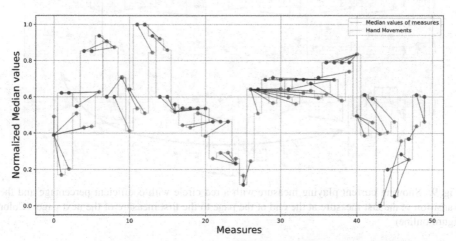

Fig. 8. Dynamic Time Warping method applied to the right hand's movement (x-axis) series and median values of notes for 50 measures. Showing the optimum alignment of nodes between the two sequences.

To resolve the motion detection problem, we set the MIDI series as a reference and sent the future expectation movements to reduce noise during the movement calculation. In this method, in the first phase, we get the reliability coefficient after cross-correlation and dynamic time warping algorithms. For all amounts over 90%, the system sent the expectation movement of the next three measures to IMU's movement calculation function for adjusting and discarding noise (see Fig. 10. Full flowchart of our proposed automatic page-turning).

4.3 Displaying Notes

To present the visual score (notes), we used Microsoft Surface tablets, and we placed that on the music rack section horizontally. We set the visual score to show only three rows (staves) on each page. During play, the system places a small red circle with the reliability coefficient percentage on the top of each measure to indicate the current place in the score. If the coefficient percentage is over 90% on the last row, before the last measure, the system turns page automatically, and the last measure will move to the first measure of the next page. Therefore, the musician does not need to memorize any notes. If the system is unable to identify the correct position of the hands, the musician can use a bypass method by twisting one wrist quickly. In this case, the system shows the next page, and the tracking mechanism resets all data and tries to continue the alignment again (see Fig. 9 Showing current playing measure with a red circle with coefficient percentage and the transition of the last measure at the end of the page to the first measure of the next page.).

Fig. 9. Showing current playing measure with a red circle with coefficient percentage and the transition of the last measure at the end of the page to the first measure of the next page. (Color figure online)

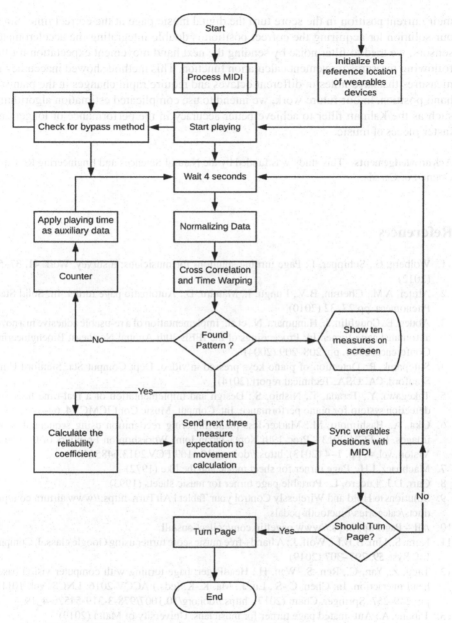

Fig. 10. Full flowchart of our proposed automatic page-turning system.

5 Conclusion

In this study, we present a novel approach to hands-free page turning for musicians using wearable technology. The device maps the pianist's hand movements during their performance in three axes and aligns them with digitalized music notes in MIDI to locate their current position in the score turn the digital music page at the correct time. Since our solution for acquiring the correct position is double integrating the accelerometer sensors, we tried to filter noise by sending the next hand movement expectation for the following measures movement calculation function. This method showed inaccuracy in measures that have notes in different octaves and require rapid changes in the pianist's hand position. In our future work, we intend to use complicated estimation algorithms, such as the Kalman filter to achieve better accuracy in the performance of longer and faster pieces of music.

Acknowledgements. This study was funded by the Natural Sciences and Engineering Research Council of Canada.

References

1. Wolberg, G., Schipper, I.: Page turning solutions for musicians: a survey. Work **41**, 37–52 (2012)
2. Aluței, A.M., Chetran, B.V., Lungu, I., Mândru, D.: Automatic page turner. In: Solid State Phenomena, pp 27–32 (2010)
3. Abueg, E., Coughlin, J., Hanumara, N., et al.: Implementation of a re-usable adhesive in a novel automated page-turner. In: Proceedings of the IEEE 30th Annual Northeast Bioengineering Conference, 2004, pp. 208–209 (2004)
4. Suteparuk, P.: Detection of piano keys pressed in video. Dept Comput Sci, Stanford Univ, Stanford, CA, USA, Technical report (2014)
5. Takegawa, Y., Terada, T., Nishio, S.: Design and implementation of a real-time fingering detection system for piano performance. Int. Comput. Music Conf ICMC **74**, 67–74 (2006)
6. Oka, A., Hashimoto, M.: Marker-less piano fingering recognition using sequential depth images. In: FCV 2013 - Proc 19th Korea-Japan Joint Workshop on Frontiers of Computer Vision, vol. 4, pp. 1–4 (2013). https://doi.org/10.1109/FCV.2013.6485443
7. Machnacz, J.H.: Page turner for sheet music and the like (1972)
8. Carr, D.J., Lucero, L.: Portable page turner for music sheets (1993)
9. Solutions to Hold and Wirelessly Control your Tablet I AirTurn. https://www.airturn.com/pro ducts/categories/bluetooth-pedals
10. All – PageFlip. https://www.pageflip.com/collections/all
11. Kora, S., Lim, B.B.L., Wolf, J.: A hands-free music score turner using Google glass. J. Comput. Inf. Syst. **59**, 297–307 (2019)
12. Tang, Z., Yan, C., Ren, S., Wan, H.: HeadPager: page turning with computer vision based head interaction. In: Chen, C.-S., Lu, J., Ma, K.-K. (eds.) ACCV 2016. LNCS, vol. 10118, pp. 249–257. Springer, Cham (2017). https://doi.org/10.1007/978-3-319-54526-4_19
13. Tabone, A.: Automated page turner for musicians. University of Malta (2019)
14. NGIMU – x-io Technologies. https://x-io.co.uk/ngimu/
15. McKay, C.: Automatic Genre Classification of MIDI Recordings. McGill University, Canada (2004)
16. Free music composition and notation softwareIMuseScore
17. Caron, F., Duflos, E., Pomorski, D., Vanheeghe, P.: GPS/IMU data fusion using multisensor Kalman filtering: introduction of contextual aspects. Inf. fusion **7**, 221–230 (2006)

A Sociable Robotic Platform to Make Career Advices for Undergraduates

W. K. Malithi Mithsara[1](✉), Udaka A. Manawadu[2](✉),
and P. Ravindra S. De Silva[1](✉)

[1] Robotics and Intelligent Systems Laboratory, Department of Computer Science,
University of Sri Jayewardenepura, Nugegoda, Sri Lanka
malithi@sci.sjp.ac.lk, ravi@sjp.ac.lk
[2] Robot Engineering Laboratory, Graduate School of Computer Science
and Engineering, University of Aizu, Aizuwakamatsu, Japan
m5232115@u-aizu.ac.jp

Abstract. Most of the undergraduates couldn't figure out a proper direction for their future careers since advising depends on the person and students show aversion in revealing their information to other humans. This research focused on creating a social robotic platform to interact with undergraduates in the field of computer science to realize possible career paths, as recent researches show social companion robots tend to form a stronger bond, which helps the addressee to share their information easily. The robot was created as a tabletop robot employing minimalistic design with a friendly view attached with speech synthesis for communicating purposes. Data was collected from 202 persons, who followed a degree in computer science. Data contains their experience, qualifications, and skills. Thereafter an artificial neural network was created using supervised learning to predict the career path with 95% performance accuracy. The experiment was performed by engaging 15 students from the final year who are a doing degree in computer science and they were asked to provide feedback on the interactions with the robot. The gathered responses highlighted robot animacy, interaction, technology and usefulness. Therefore, from the results it can be concluded that a majority of the students accepted the robot, interacted without hesitation and had friendly conversations with the robot where they valued the generated output from the robot.

Keywords: Human-robot interaction · Companion robot · Artificial neural network

1 Introduction

With respect to the dynamic nature of the information technology (IT) and computing field, numerous related studies concluded that the future graduates have not adequately prepared during their university degree, for the job opportunities lying ahead [19]. At present, the computing and IT fields are rapidly

© Springer Nature Switzerland AG 2020
C. Stephanidis et al. (Eds.): HCII 2020, LNCS 12424, pp. 219–230, 2020.
https://doi.org/10.1007/978-3-030-60117-1_16

changing with great alterations in industry and business patterns. This is poses a huge challenge for fresh graduates to gain the required technical skills that would allow them to perform well in their jobs [18]. Proper guidance should be given to a fresh graduate as the first job may decide the whole career of a person [14].

Advice from the universities and families may cause wrong career choices [11]. The given advice were either not useful or put the student in a difficult situation as the advices were generic and the skills of students are different from each other. In recent years, companion robots have shown great promise in the field of robotics, namely the robots that are specifically designed and programmed to produce physical and verbal communications and in some methods maintain emotional interaction with human beings [5]. In the last few years, robotic companions presented some assuring results in communication and problem-solving in day-to-day activities of humans [2]. There has been growing interest in developing animated agents for learning environments. Several types of researches have stated that companion robots have had a positive effect on the student environment [3]. Due to the aforementioned reasons it was decided to build a Sociable Robotic Platform to make career advices for undergraduates.

Various studies that discuss the use of companion and career prediction methods. Odahara et al. [12] proposed the concept of addressivity and hearership in their robot "Talking Ally". In here, the robot identifies an addressee's eye-gaze behaviors that give state of hearership and then produce the utterances. There has to be smooth communication between human and robot using bodily interaction. The robot has the potential to manipulate turn-initial, modality, and entrust behaviors to increase the liveliness of conversations, which are facilitated by maintaining the hearer's engagement in the conversation and shifting the direction of the conversation. The results of the study show that in order to persuade the addressee the resources of the hearer were significant in generating or adjusting to the structure of utterances. Addressivity and hearership is a major concept to build the companion. Therefore, addressivity and hearership concepts and additionally verbal communication were considered for building the companion robot. Liu et al. [10] developed a fortune teller that predicts the career path. The objective of the research was to predict the future career stages of a given user and model their career path. As for employees, they can get information about their current career job position using linked data and then predict their next job-hopping, as well as the whole picture of their own career paths. For an example they take a software engineer and define it to compose four stages, namely software developer, senior software developer, manager and chief executive officer (CEO). They analyzed each stage of job position and built the mathematical model and used that to predict the career path. This is one of the researches done for deciding career path in computer field. Factors used in the above mentioned research was used to examine and build the career prediction model. Jibo is the first social companion robot designed for the home that looks, listens and learns and recognizes people, and accurately deliver messages to the right people at the right time and place [8]. Face detection, voice recognition and minimalistic and friendly design of Jibo was considered to create this model of companion robot. Rane et al. [15] studied about Jibo by considering design and technologies, natural language processing and artificial intelligence. They concluded that Jibo is managing the interaction by natural conversation and touch screen with animation making the design simpler. Subahi et al. [18] proposed a research, for career path prediction based on measuring and analyzing the student's performance in higher education. In this study, they investigated a new artificial neural network (ANN) approach for career path prediction (CPP) based on analyzing computer science's body of knowledge (BoK) in degree programs. An initial design was created, for validating purposes, of a single-layer ANN is introduced, trained, tested and applied to real-world graduate records to classy them into groups or most appropriate career path for each. From this research, an artificial neural network (ANN) for future career prediction was utilized for the current research.

By using all of the concepts behind the above research studies, a robotic companion is introduced that interacts with the undergraduate who is doing a degree in computer science and guiding for their future career based on their experience, academic qualifications, and skills. Primarily major four job roles are considered such as, software engineer, quality assurance engineer, business analyst in the IT industry, and the academic field. The reason for selecting a small domain is to trial and get the results and the team wishes to apply this to other fields as well. When deciding these career paths need identifying the factors affecting the selection of a career path. Therefore, a large amount of past data was collected which include results obtained from computer-related subjects, grade point average (GPA), programming language knowledge, extracurricular activities, etc. from the IT professionals on current employees in the above mentioned fields. After identifying the relationships among the collected data and a machine learning model was created to make decisions about the career paths.

2   Design and Methodology

2.1   Design of the Robot

It is important to be aware of the robot design by considering the environment, sensing, and intelligence of the robot [6]. Firstly, it after considering the domain of students that will be tested and decided that robot doesn't have to walk for continued conversation since the conversation should give a real-time experience of an interview. Therefore, a tabletop robot was constructed using a 3D printing face with a mobile phone holder and the body was made by using plastic material and the whole design is minimalistic [6]. The Intel RealSense [9] camera was placed to track the user's eye behaviors in real-time. Figure 1 shows the initial design sketch of the robot.

The robot is integrated with a microphone and a speaker which can detect the human, their voice and give responses. The robot changes its face direction according to the human eye gaze behaviors using a servo motor. The eye behaviors (neural, listening, and talking) of the robot was developed using mobile

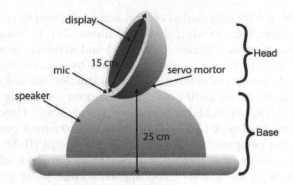

Fig. 1. The design and measurements of the tabletop robot that has employed minimalistic design concepts. Mobile phone screen is used as the display and in the base of the robot a minicomputer is placed.

applications which are Android studio and Firebase and the animation was created by Unity. Robots operates in the neural mode in order to start the conversation. Listening and talking modes change according to the conversation between the robot and the student. Figure 2 shows the three animations that was considered. The animation was created with glasses to portray a matured look as it will increase the engagement between the user and the robot in this research [16].

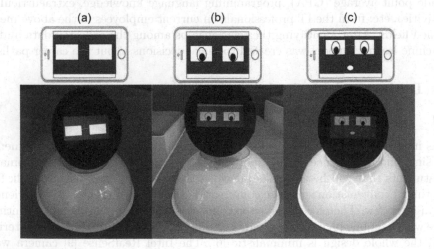

Fig. 2. How the robot's animation of facial behaviors change according to the situations. (a) In idol situations (b) In listening mode (c) In talking mode

2.2   Processing Architecture

Figure 3 shows the overall processing architecture of the robot. The robot's conversation is built using tflearn in tesorflow. Also, at the end of the conversation, the robot will give the most suitable career path for the human by using its artificial neural network. Google text-to-speech (GTTS) system was used to implement the speech synthesis of the robot.

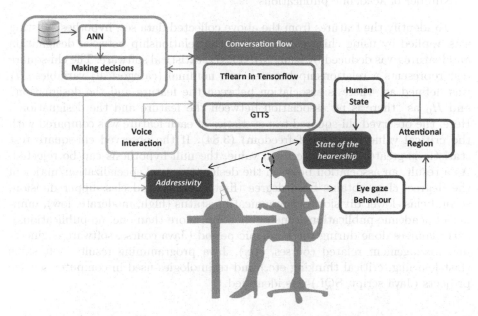

Fig. 3. How the robot's conversation is built according to human voice and behaviors.

Figure 3 depicts the outline of the complete process flow; following subtopics further discuss different aspects showed in this figure.

Dataset. In order to predict the career, it is required to build a dataset; So, a questionnaire was prepared to collect the data from past students who are currently pursuing career paths both in academics and in the relevant industry in the field of computer science. The target job roles are software engineer, business analyst and quality assurance engineer which are the most favorable paths for a computer science graduate. A structured questionnaire was provided to 202 past students and data was collected from them in order to create the model. The questionnaire was created using some of the following employability characteristics.

– Current designation
– Specialization/Major of the degree

- Class obtained in the bachelor's degree
- Extra courses done during academic period
- Results of the core computer science subjects obtained from the bachelor's. degree
- Tools and technologies used in computer science projects
- Skills (fast learning, critical thinking, presentation skills, public speaking, etc.)
- Number of academic publications

To identify the features from the above collected data set, hypothesis testing was applied by using chi-square test and the relationship between designation and features was deduced by using MINITAB statistical software. The chi-square test represents a relationship between two nominal (categorical) variables. H_1 was defined as "there is association between the feature and the designation" and H_0 as "there is no association between the feature and the designation". Here, the observed chi-squared test statistics of each feature was compared with the critical value (degrees of freedom) (3.84). If the observed chi-square test statistic is greater than the critical value, the null hypothesis can be rejected. As a result, an association between the designation and specialization/major of the degree, class obtains from degree (first class, second class-upper division, second class-lower division), communication status (high, moderate, low), number of academic publications (one publication, more than one, no publications), extra courses done during the academic period (Java course, software engineering, management related courses, etc.), Java programming results, soft skills (fast learning, critical thinking etc.) and technologies used in computer science projects (Java script, SQL) was identified.

Building the Artificial Neural Network. Supervised learning algorithm was used to predict the career path since the responses are known. All supervised learning techniques are a form of classification or regression. The responses are subjected to multiclass classification in order to predict the job role as software engineer, business analyst, and quality assurance engineer in the IT industry or the academic field. ANN was applied for the predication in this research. The ANN modeling and evaluations are performed using free cloud service called Google Colab, which is provides popular libraries such as Tensorflow and Keras. Deep learning applications can be developed by using it [7]. Since the degree type has three categories, special degree (specialized in one subjects), general (3 year degree that study 3 subjects for entire period) and honored degree, machine learning algorithm may be able to understand and harness this relationship and then the degree type is encoded using one-hot algorithm. Other variables, class, communication status, Java programming results and number of publications are weighted categories, so they were coded into 1–2 and 1–4. Finally, soft skills and technologies were coded as zero and one according to their answer. The modeled ANN has 15 input features which are identified statistically as given above and two hidden layers, where each hidden layer consists of 15 neurons that provide the best outcome throughout some simulations with different hidden layer with neuron settings (Fig. 4). The second layer with 15 neurons is fed into a four-output neuron that carries the decision of the variables, which provides the prediction of the career path. The rectified linear activation (relu) function is a piecewise linear default activation function for many types of neural networks because a model that uses it is easier to train and often attains greater performance and that will output the input directly if it is positive, otherwise, it will output zero [4]. Output layer used, "softmax" activation function. Because, the "softmax" function provides the probability distribution of the events over "n" different events. Data samples of 202 were divided to 0.8 for training and 0.2 for testing. In the training and learning phase, "adam" optimization algorithm is used to determine the optimal weights that are provided to the next input layer. The model was trained with 1000 epoch. Overall, the artificial neural network model has reached a best prediction accuracy of 95%, through the limitations. The visualization graph of ANN is given below.

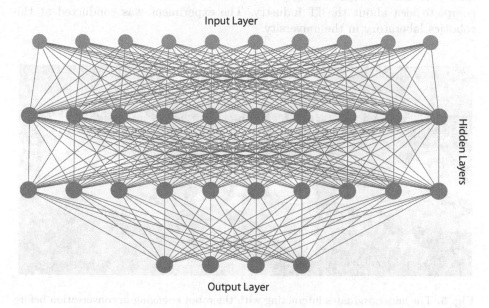

Fig. 4. Visualization of the Artificial Neural Network. The input layer is shown in green, the hidden layers are in blue and the four output layers are shown in red. (Color figure online)

Conversation Model. Conversation between the robot and human was constructed using tflearn model in tensorflow. Tflearn is a modular and transparent deep learning library built in the tensorflow environment [1]. JSON file with tags, patterns and responses were created. The "tags" are the number of questions and "pattern" represents the student conversation and "responses" depict the robot conversation. Patterns in the dataset are extracted into list of words using nltk.tokenize package. Tokenization is the process by which a big amount of text is divided into smaller parts called tokens and it is imported from the NLTK (natural language tool kit) library [13]. Then stemming the words reduces the vocabulary [17]. Word stemming can be demonstrated in an example as follows; if a word is written as "special" then the stem is "spec". The tflearn model has four layers and input layer consists of a word list which is encoded using one hot encoding and three fully connected layers with 8 neurons. Output layer consists of the 12 no neurons for "tags" and the activation function is "softmax". Afterwards, the dataset of JSON file is trained using a neural network to take a sentence of words and classify into tags in a file.

2.3   Experimental Protocol

As in Fig. 5 the experiment was performed by engaging 15 Students from the final year who are doing a degree in computer science in the university. Because, final year students are seeking jobs and most of the students do not have a complete idea about the IT industry. The experiment was conducted at the robotics laboratory in the university.

Fig. 5. The undergraduates interacting with the robot engaging in conversation before evaluating its performance.

After the experiment, the student is given a structured questionnaire with 10 questions to provide feedback on areas such as animacy, interaction, technology and usefulness of robot with on a three-point Likert scale with the response anchors; 0) Not at all (1) Somewhat (2) Average (3) For the most part (4) Completely. The questionnaire was divided into three categories and each question was coded as given below (Table 1).

Table 1. The three facets of social bonding evaluated through the parameters addressed in the questionnaire.

Factors	Code	Questions
Animacy	Q1	Did you Understand what the robot was doing?
	Q2	Did you accept the robot?
	Q3	Are face behaviors of robot giving you a friendly or compatible look?
Interaction and Conversation	Q4	How much where you interested in the robot?
	Q5	Did you find the conversation between the robot and you to be useful?
Technology and Usefulness	Q6	Was the robot's appearance useful?
	Q7	Did you find the conversation between the robot and you to be useful?
	Q8	Did you think the robot ask enough questions to predict your career?
	Q9	Did the robot predict your dream job?
	Q10	Did you change your target after the conversation with the robot?

3   Results and Discussion

Figure 6 displays the average mean opinion score (MOS) values where the horizontal axis shows the social bonding three factors combined with their related questions.

The mean opinion score (MOS) is the all the individual scores' arithmetic mean that ranges from 0 (not at all) to 4 (completely) where a value that is equal to 2 is average [20]. As in the Fig. 6, students have given different answers and cumulatively the results show that the majority understood the questions, the conversation was carried out smoothly and the students accepted and found the robot interesting. Most of the students accepted the facial behaviors (neural, listen, talking) and whole appearance of the robot and therefore it can be said it has a friendly view. Through the results observed in MOS it can be concluded that every student had a useful conversation with the robot.

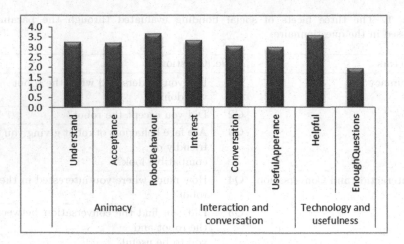

Fig. 6. Depicted the average mean opinion score (MOS) of the students based on the questionnaire (Q1 to Q8). Answers of Q9 and Q10 were not collected in a Likert scale.

The students were asked to write down their target career before the experiment. At the end of the conversation the robot gave a career path prediction for the student. The robot was able to predict the careers 8 students wrote before the experiment accurately. As for the other 7 students that the robot gave different career predictions, they informed they will give it further thought and will consider the given prediction. This was something supplementary to the research that took notice. Compared to other countries, Sri Lanka is still in the beginning stage of embracing robotics, therefore this type of interaction and technology is something atypical to Sri Lankans. Due to this reason, they may take time to accept the decisions given by a robot.

3.1   Real Time Interaction Results

We employed a simple method to track the addressee attention region, which is a main reference for generating the robot's speech interactions and animation. The robot (RealSense camera) collected the data of eye gaze behaviors at every 60 frames as a segmentation point [12]. Parallel to the robot, The virtual plane is constructed in parallel to the robot, as shown in Fig. 7. Middle of the frame has high score as in the Fig. 6, so it can be concluded that, most of the time the robot and the student had continuous interaction during the conversation.

Fig. 7. Three attention-regions were defined for the virtual-plane for the analysis of continuous interaction.

4   Conclusion

The aim of this study was to construct a career guiding companion robot for the undergraduate students in the university. It was built using minimalistic design and it has friendly facial behaviors (neural, listen, talking). The robot was trying to make face-to-face interactions with the student by managing its motor skills. In the testing period, a questionnaire was prepared highlighting the factors of animacy, interaction and technology, and collected feedback about the robot from 15 students in the university. Initially, the target career of each student was recorded. Throughout the testing time, students were actively interacted with the robot. From the 15 tested students the robot was able to predict the job of 8 students. The gathered responses highlighted robot animacy, interaction, technology and usefulness. Therefore, it can be concluded that a majority of the students accepted the robot, interacted without hesitation and had friendly conversations with the robot where they valued the generated output from the robot. By the results of the questionnaire, it can concluded that most of the students accepted and understood the robot and they had useful conversations with the robot.

5   Future Work

This study did not test the correctness of the student answers. Therefore, the authors wish to add another validation question set to get the correctness of the student answers. This may be considered a further validation of the robot as well. The research should be broadened by testing with more students and students from other regions not limiting to Sri Lanka. Because that will give more accurate test results. The authors will focus to improve the robot's prediction by increasing the number of the questions in the final questionnaire given, to enhance the database to a level that it can predict a plethora of career opportunities to undergraduates of different disciplines.

References

1. Abadi, M., et al.: Tensorflow: a system for large-scale machine learning. In: 12th USENIX Symposium on Operating Systems Design and Implementation (OSDI 2016), pp. 265–283 (2016)
2. Belpaeme, T., Kennedy, J., Ramachandran, A., Scassellati, B., Tanaka, F.: Social robots for education: a review. Sci. Robot. **3**(21), eaat5954 (2018)
3. Broadbent, E., et al.: How could companion robots be useful in rural schools? Int. J. Soc. Robot. **10**(3), 295–307 (2018)
4. Brownlee, J.: A gentle introduction to the rectified linear unit (ReLU). Machine Learning Mastery (2019). https://machinelearningmastery.com/rectified-linear-activation-function-fordeep-learning-neural-networks
5. Dautenhahn, K.: Socially intelligent robots: dimensions of human-robot interaction. Philos. Trans. Roy. Soc. B Biol. Sci. **362**(1480), 679–704 (2007)
6. Glas, D., Satake, S., Kanda, T., Hagita, N.: An interaction design framework for social robots. In: Robotics: Science and Systems. vol. 7, p. 89 (2012)
7. Google colab. https://colab.research.google.com/
8. Hodson, H.: The first family robot (2014)
9. Intel realsense technology. https://www.intel.com/content/www/us/en/architecture-and-technology/realsense-overview.html
10. Liu, Y., Zhang, L., Nie, L., Yan, Y., Rosenblum, D.S.: Fortune teller: predicting your career path. In: Thirtieth AAAI Conference on Artificial Intelligence (2016)
11. Moote, J., Archer, L.: Failing to deliver? exploring the current status of career education provision in England. Res. Pap. Educ. **33**(2), 187–215 (2018)
12. Ohshima, N., Ohyama, Y., Odahara, Y., De Silva, P.R.S., Okada, M.: Talking-ally: the influence of robot utterance generation mechanism on hearer behaviors. Int. J. Social Robot. **7**(1), 51–62 (2015)
13. Perkins, J.: Python Text Processing with NLTK 2.0 Cookbook. Packt Publishing Ltd., Birmingham (2010)
14. Pollard, E., et al.: Understanding employers' graduate recruitment and selection practices: main report (2015)
15. Rane, P., Mhatre, V., Kurup, L.: Study of a home robot: Jibo. Int. J. Eng. Res. Technol. **3**(10), 490–493 (2014)
16. Setapen, A.A.M.: Creating robotic characters for long-term interaction. Ph.D. thesis, Massachusetts Institute of Technology (2012)
17. Stemming and lemmatization. https://nlp.stanford.edu/IR-book/html/htmledition/stemming-and-lemmatization-1.html
18. Subahi, A.F.: Data collection for career path prediction based on analysing body of knowledge of computer science degrees. JSW **13**(10), 533–546 (2018)
19. New world of work: are universities preparing students for future careers? https://www.timeshighereducation.com/hub/pa-consulting/p/new-world-work-are-universities-preparing-students-future-careers. Accessed 20 August 2019
20. Youssef, K., Yamagiwa, K., Silva, R., Okada, M.: ROBOMO: towards an accompanying mobile robot. In: Beetz, M., Johnston, B., Williams, M.-A. (eds.) ICSR 2014. LNCS (LNAI), vol. 8755, pp. 196–205. Springer, Cham (2014). https://doi.org/10.1007/978-3-319-11973-1_20

Development and Evaluation of a Pen Type Thermal Sensation Presentation Device for SPIDAR-Tablet

Kaede Nohara[1]([✉]), Yasuna Kubo[1], Makoto Sato[2], Takehiko Yamaguchi[3], and Tetsuya Harada[1]

[1] Tokyo University of Science, 6-3-1 Niijuku, Katsushika-Ku, Tokyo, Japan
`nohara.kaede.hrlb@gmail.com`
[2] Tokyo Institute of Technology, 4259 Nagatsuta-Cho, Midori-Ku, Yokohama, Kanagawa, Japan
[3] Suwa University of Science, 5000-1 Toyohira, Chino-City, Nagano, Japan

Abstract. It is thought that anyone can get high learning effect anywhere by VR learning with tablet device. In this study, we focused on the field of thermodynamics having difficulties in understanding the basic logical structure for high school students. The purpose is to assist understanding of thermodynamic principles by simulating and visualizing the invisible phenomena with VR. We developed a system for controlling the temperature of a pen type thermal sensation presentation device and implemented it on SPIDAR-tablet using iPad. And we constructed an experimental simulation content of thermodynamics with a piston and a cylinder. It presents the pressure and the temperature of the gas in the cylinder as the force and the thermal sensation respectively. Then, we conducted an experiment to investigate the effects of presenting the sensations on adiabatic change simulation of thermodynamics. Many participants felt easier to imagine the principle of it when presenting both the force and the thermal sensation than when presenting only the force sensation. Therefore, it is considered that the understanding of the principle was improved by presenting the thermal sense. However, there were many opinions that they could not feel the enough change in the force.

Keywords: VR learning system · Force sense feedback · Thermal sense feedback

1 Introduction

1.1 Background and Purpose

In recent years, educational methods using information and communication technologies such as personal computers, tablet device and the Internet have become widespread. Furthermore, learning support systems using VR have been developed. By using VR, it is expected that it will become possible to experience phenomena that cannot be realized originally, that high learning effects will be obtained in VR space, and that learners will be able to participate independently. Therefore, we thought that anyone could get high

C. Stephanidis et al. (Eds.): HCII 2020, LNCS 12424, pp. 231–240, 2020.
https://doi.org/10.1007/978-3-030-60117-1_17

learning effects everywhere by incorporating VR technology using tablet device into the learning. In this study, we developed a learning support system for thermodynamics, where it is difficult to understand the basic logical structure. The purpose is to develop a tablet device with visual, force and thermal sensations and to assist understanding of thermodynamic principles by presenting invisible phenomena using the device.

1.2 Outline of Research

We developed and implemented a pen type thermal sensation presentation device on SPIDAR-tablet [1] using iPad [2]. We developed a novel tablet device with function that can present the force and the thermal sensation simultaneously and evaluated it using thermodynamics learning system originally developed.

2 Proposed Device

2.1 SPIDAR-Tablet

SPIDAR-tablet is a haptic device that can present force sense to user's fingertip during touch panel operation of a tablet device. Four strings are connected to a ring, and the tensions of the strings are controlled by motors attached to the corners on the tablet device. The force can be presented on the finger via the ring. In this paper, we employed the SPIDAR-tablet for iPad shown in Fig. 1.

Fig. 1. SPIDAR-tablet for iPad

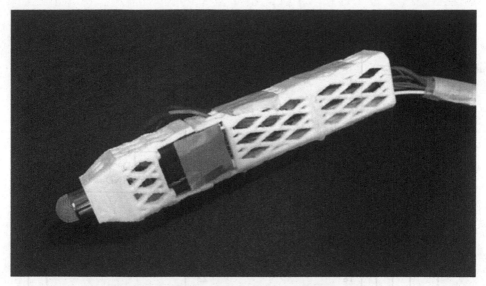

Fig. 2. Pen-type thermal sensation presentation device

2.2 Pen-Type Thermal Sensation Presentation Device

As the device for adding the thermal sensation on the SPIDAR-tablet, we developed a pen-type thermal sensation presentation device shown in Fig. 2. This device has a heat sink with fan inside a frame made by a 3D printer and has four small Peltier elements with copper plates on the grip to enable presenting thermal sensations at two fingertips.

2.3 Temperature Control Circuit

We constructed a control circuit to control the temperature of the pen-type thermal sensation presentation device. Figure 3 shows the circuit diagram. The CPU is PIC24FJ64GB004 (Microchip Technology Inc.) and the motor driver is BD6212HFP (ROHM Co., Ltd.) for controlling the Peltier elements.

Software Configuration. Figure 4 shows the system configuration of the temperature control. The target temperature is set according the simulation on the tablet device. And the target temperature is sent to CPU by BLE communication. The CPU compares the target temperature with the temperature of the Peltier element and determines the PWM duty ratio by PID control.

2.4 Evaluation of Temperature Presentation

Copper plates are placed on Peltier elements and the temperature is transmitted from Peltier elements to copper plates, and when the user holds the pen at the copper plates, the temperature is presented. There is a temperature sensor between Peltier elements and copper plates. We used PWM control to control the temperature, and its duty ratio was

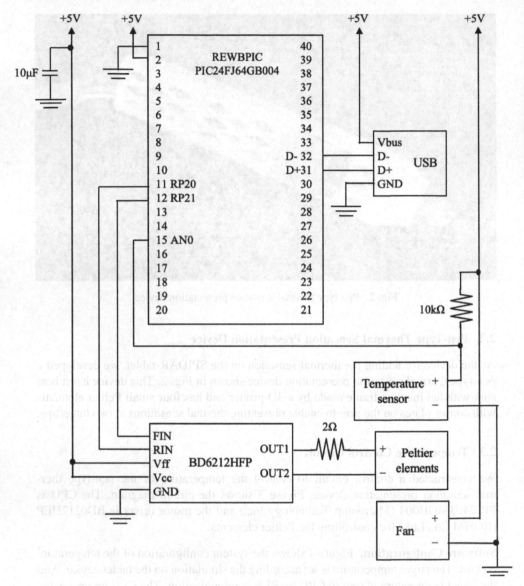

Fig. 3. Temperature control circuit diagram

determined by PID control. Figure 5 shows the measurement results of the temperature sensor when the temperature of Peltier elements was set to change from 24 °C to 40 °C. By optimizing the PID coefficient, we shortened the response time and reduced the ripple at around 40 °C.

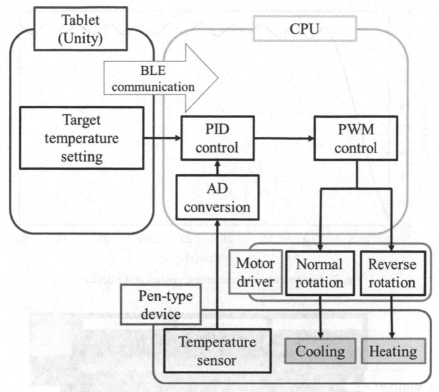

Fig. 4. Temperature control system configuration diagram

3 Evaluation Experiment

3.1 Developed Application

In this research, we realized a thermodynamic experiment using a piston and a cylinder in a virtual space using a SPIDAR tablet with a pen-type thermal sensation presentation device. We developed virtual space using Unity 3D [2] which is one of the developing environments for 3D programs. Figure 6 shows an example of the developed virtual space.

In this application, the devices present the pressure and the temperature of the gas in the cylinder as the force and the thermal sensation respectively, and the movement and temperature change of particles inside present visually. When the learner moves the piston by touch operation, the velocity of the particles and the indicate value of the thermometer change according to the selected one of four state changes of the thermodynamics.

3.2 Experimental Method

We conducted an experiment to investigate the effects of presenting the thermal sensation on adiabatic change simulation of thermodynamics. In this experiment, the number of

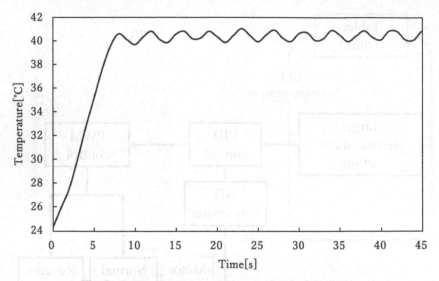

Fig. 5. Temperature response characteristics of the device

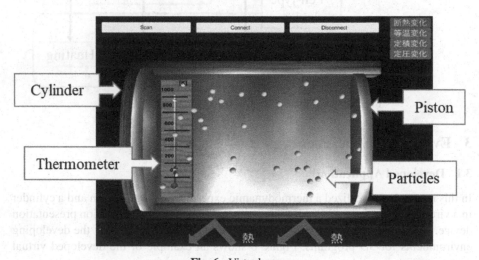

Fig. 6. Virtual space

participants was 20. Figure 7 shows the visual presentation of the tablet device, and Fig. 8 shows the experimental environment. First, we lectured the principle of the adiabatic change used in the experimental simulation to the participants. Next, we explained the experimental procedure as follows. The position 1 in Fig. 7 is the initial position of the piston, the position 2 is the start position for the operation, and the position 3 is the maximum compressed position. The participants operated according to the following instructions from (1) to (6).

(1) Touch the piston located at the position 1 with the pen and wait for a signal (until the temperature stabilizes at 33 °C).
(2) Move the piston to the position 2 and wait 10 s.
(3) Move the piston to the position 3 for 10 s.
(4) Move the piston to the position 2 from 3 for 10 s.
(5) Wait 10 s at the position 2.
(6) Move the piston to the position 1 and wait for a signal (until the temperature stabilizes at 33 °C)

Preliminary Operation Task for Training (Task 1). The participants were allowed to move the piston freely for 30 s. During this task, only the pressure of the gas in the cylinder was presented as the force sensation.

Operation task with the force and thermal sensation (Task 2). The research participants operated according to the instructions (1)–(6). During this task, the pressure and the temperature of the gas in the cylinder as the force and the thermal sensation respectively.

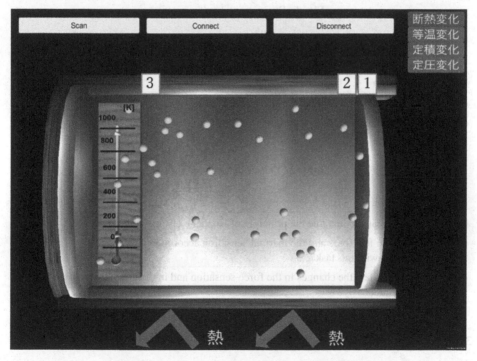

Fig. 7. The visual presentation of the tablet device

Questionnaires. Afterwards, they were asked to answer the questionnaires and state their opinions on this task. Table 1 shows the questionnaires for Task 1, Table 2 shows the questionnaires for Task 2, and Table 3 shows the options for the questionnaires.

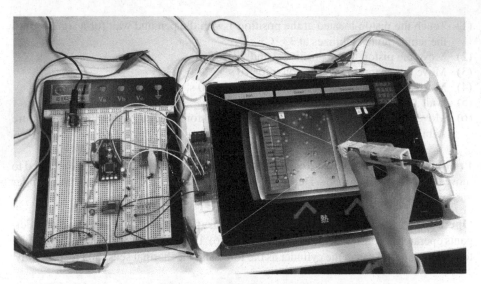

Fig. 8. Experimental environment

Table 1. Questionnaires for Task 1

Number	Question
(1)	Was it easy to imagine the principle of adiabatic change with this task?
(2)	Did you feel the force according to the principle of adiabatic change with this task?

Table 2. Questionnaires for Task 2

Number	Question
(1)	Was it easy to imagine the principle of adiabatic change with this task?
(2)	Did you feel force and the thermal sensation according to the principle of adiabatic change with this task?
(3)	Did you feel the changes in the force sensation and in the thermal sensation simultaneously?

3.3   Experimental Results and Discussions

Table 4 shows the average score of the questionnaire. Table 5 shows specific opinions. It is difficult to evaluate the difference between two tasks due to the difference of the experimental condition, however, in question (1) and (2) in Table 4, all scores were above 3 and the score of Task 2 was higher than that of Task 1 in question (1). This system has been shown to be effective in imagining the principle of adiabatic change, and that the presentation of thermal sensations is more effective. Next, in question (3) in Table 4, the score was 3.85, which was lower than the other scores. This is probably

Table 3. Options for the questionnaires

Score	Answer contents
1	Strongly disagree
2	Disagree
3	Neither agree nor disagree
4	Agree
5	Strongly agree

because the force feeling was smaller than the thermal feeling, as the opinion 1 and 2 in Table 5. It seems that it is necessary to change the motors to more powerful ones. Also, from Table 5, it can be seen that many participants found the learning content fun and interesting. This is thought to lead to an improvement in learning motivation.

Table 4. Average score

Question number	Average score	
	Task 1	Task 2
(1)	4.30	4.80
(2)	4.05	4.45
(3)	–	3.85

Table 5. Specific opinions

Number	Answer
1	The research participant focused on changing the thermal sensations, and had difficulty feeling the force sensation
2	The force sensation was small
3	The research participant found it fun and interesting as learning content

4 Conclusions and Future Work

In this research, we developed a temperature control system for a pen-type thermal sensation presentation device and added it to SPIDAR-tablet for iOS. And we developed a device that can present simultaneously the force and the thermal sensations. Also, we evaluated this system using thermodynamic learning content originally developed. As a result, the presentation of both the force sensation and the thermal sensation helps learners to understand the principles of thermodynamics. However, many participants felt that it was difficult to feel changes in the force and thermal sensation simultaneously and they could not feel the enough change in the force. It is considered that the intensity of the force sensation was too small. Therefore, it seems that it is necessary to change the motors to more powerful ones. In addition, we plan to design and construct a small circuit board and implement on the frame. Also, we aim at developing new applications for this system.

Acknowledgments. We would like to thank all the research participants. This work was supported by JSPS KAKENHI Grant Number JP17H01782.

References

1. Tasaka, Y., Yamada, K., Kubo, Y., Saeki, M., Yamamoto, S., Yamaguchi, T., Sato, M., Harada, T.: Development of frame for SPIDAR tablet on windows and evaluation of system-presented geographical information. In: Yamamoto, S., Mori, H. (eds.) HIMI 2018. LNCS, vol. 10904, pp. 358–368. Springer, Cham (2018). https://doi.org/10.1007/978-3-319-92043-6_30
2. Apple Inc. https://www.apple.com/ipad/. Accessed 12 June 2020
3. Unity Technologies. https://unity.com. Accessed 12 June 2020

CountMarks: Multi-finger Marking Menus for Mobile Interaction with Head-Mounted Displays

Jordan Pollock[1] and Robert J. Teather[2](✉)

[1] School of Computer Science, Carleton University, Ottawa, ON, Canada
[2] School of Information Technology, Carleton University, Ottawa, ON, Canada
rob.teather@carleton.ca

Abstract. We designed, implemented, and evaluated CountMarks, a novel menu that extends marking menus with multi-touch input on a secondary touchscreen, for use with smart glasses and head-mounted displays. We experimentally compared CountMarks to marking menus. Results indicate that CountMarks offers faster selection and better search accuracy, but slightly worse selection accuracy. A second experiment compared standing vs. walking while using CountMarks, and handheld vs. on-leg interaction. Results indicate that CountMarks can be used effectively with a handheld device while both standing and walking. We present an example application employing CountMarks in a mock Netflix UI, to demonstrate how the technique can be applied in existing applications.

Keywords: Mobile VR · Smart glasses · Marking menus · Multi-touch

1 Introduction

Low-cost self-contained head-mounted displays (HMDs) are now a reality and are advancing to more closely resemble everyday eyewear. Smart glasses give the user supplementary information while performing a task; the user need not move their head to look away from their main task. Because such workflows typically engage the hands, the user generally does not have access to direct touch interaction with virtual elements and data. Current methods for interacting with HMDs include handheld devices ("wands") like those with the Oculus Rift or HTC Vive, or combinations of speech and gestures, like with the HoloLens. These can be impractical: speech recognition is inappropriate for public use [29] and in air gestures (including wands) are prone to arm fatigue [12] and gesture recognition problems [8]. Handheld devices introduce mapping problems and cumbersome interaction [28].

Interaction techniques should be designed in consideration of the environment in which they will be used. Smart glasses may exacerbate the problems associated with distracted device usage[1] as they provide ever-present, information-rich displays. Consequently, interaction with such devices should be designed considering everyday usage

---

[1] For examples, see, e.g., https://www.nhtsa.gov/risky-driving/distracted-driving or https://news.osu.edu/distracted-walking-injuries-soar-for-pedestrians-on-phones/.

© Springer Nature Switzerland AG 2020
C. Stephanidis et al. (Eds.): HCII 2020, LNCS 12424, pp. 241–260, 2020.
https://doi.org/10.1007/978-3-030-60117-1_18

scenarios, such as usage while sitting, standing, or walking [22]. Ideally, the technology should be unobtrusive [34], be socially acceptable, and performant. To satisfy these requirements we first developed CountMarks, a multi-touch marking menu for selection with mobile HMDs (see Fig. 1).

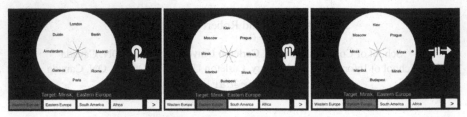

Fig. 1. From left to right showing a) a user places a finger on the screen to open the first menu. b) Placing two fingers on the screen to open the 2nd menu. c) Swiping right with two fingers to select the target.

CountMarks extends marking menus [18] (see Fig. 2), with multi-touch swipe gestures on touch devices (e.g., smartphones), providing more menu items in fewer submenu layers than marking menus. Our approach combines marking menus with Count Menus [1] (Fig. 2b), which count the fingers used on one hand to select a specified linear menu. The finger count on the other hand then determines which item is selected from the open menu. CountMarks combines these two strategies, employing marking menu gestures with finger count. We envision using CountMarks with HMDs, smart glasses, or external displays (e.g., TVs). CountMarks uses the number of fingers touching the screen during swipe to determine which of up to four options is selected. We use a mode changing double tap to provide additional menu options.

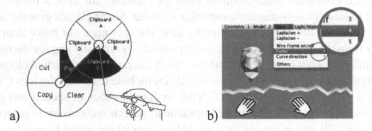

Fig. 2. a) Marking menu (via Kurtenbach, 1993 [18]); b) Count menu (Bailly et al. 2012 [1])

We discuss the design of CountMarks, and then present two user studies. The first study compares two CountMarks variants to classic marking menus and demonstrates the effectiveness of our approach. The second study evaluates one CountMarks variant in standing and walking use cases. We then present an example CountMarks implementation on an existing interface. Finally, we discuss strengths and weaknesses of using CountMarks and suggest future work to improve its design.

To our knowledge, our experiments are the first evaluations of marking menu interaction in mobile use cases and with input at the leg, despite previous research on marking menus designed for smartphone use [40].

2 Related Work

2.1 Marking Menus and Count Menus

Marking menus [18] (see Fig. 2a) are swipe-gesture based menus that are quicker and more accurate than typical linear menu selection [2]. Modern marking menus show that multiple individual strokes improve selection speed and accuracy [37]. The primary limitation of marking menus is that they only support up to 8 items per menu and two levels of depth to retain 90% selection accuracy [17]. In general, broad menus (i.e., menus with more items in a single menu level) perform better than deep menus (i.e., menus requiring drilling down into a hierarchy, increasing the number of selections required to select an item) because users tend to get lost in deep menu hierarchies [14]. As a result, variations of marking menus have been created to increase breadth: the flower menu [3] which uses curved instead of linear strokes, and the zone and polygon menus [38] which let users make different selections based on where their swipe gesture begins. These variations demonstrate that greater breadth can increase selection speed and/or accuracy.

Marking menus help transition users from novice to expert [18]. Novices search the menu hierarchy to find the desired target. In contrast, experienced users may already know how to find or access a target item and may use gesture shortcuts to select it. Much like other shortcuts, these gestures must first be learned by the user. Due to the effort required to learn them, Expert shortcuts are rarely used [19], even by experienced users who know about shortcuts [7].

Lepinski et al. [20] first explored multi-touch input for marking menus as a way to increase menu breadth. By holding different combinations of fingers (chords) to a touch surface different menus popup which the user can swipe on to make selections on a large touch surface. While most chords were difficult to perform, a simple subset were shown to offer faster selections than traditional marking menus.

Finger Count menus [1] (Fig. 2b) let the user select menus and items according to the number of fingers used in a gesture, regardless of which fingers are used. This technique uses two hands: one hand to select one of 5 menus and the other hand to select one of 5 items from that menu. Count Menus were found to be simple to use and easy to learn [4] and twice as fast as 3D, in-air marking menus [24] while maintaining similar accuracy [16].

2.2 Interaction Techniques for HMDs and Smart Glasses

In-air gestures are an obvious choice for interacting with HMDs because they offer the freedom to interact with all of the space in front of the user at any time. However, gestures can be obtrusive, attention-grabbing and often unnatural or dissimilar to normal gestures which can make them potentially embarrassing to use in public settings [15, 23, 26].

Additionally, in-air gestures have the well-known problem of "gorilla arm syndrome" where gesture can yield excessive arm fatigue [12].

Researchers have sought to leverage the "anywhere, anytime" nature of gestural interaction while avoiding these limitations. One approach involves mounting depth trackers to the shoulders [10] or hips [21] to turn normal surfaces into touch surfaces, or to support subtle in-air gestures without raising the arm. These touch recognition techniques provide tactile feedback, improving gesture recognition accuracy and precision [6]. Other researchers have considered using touch on the body itself as an input source, for example, using the user's skin [11, 30, 31]. Skin supports a large number of gestures such as grab, pull, press, scratch shear, squeeze, and twist [31].

The palm is a logical choice for on-skin touch interaction [31]. Previous work has shown that multi-stroke palm gestures can be detected with 90% accuracy [30] but requires bulky accessories. While other research explored interactions on other body parts such as the ear [32, 39], there is little research on the leg as an input surface, despite previous work showing that 9% of gestures produced in gesture elicitation [31] were performed on the leg (vs. 51% on the hand, 12% on a ring, and 10% between fingers). Some researchers have looked at areas such as belts [9] and pockets [23, 25]. Smart textiles (e.g., a finger sleeve providing bend and pressure input) offer accuracy greater than 80% while walking, running and driving [35]. All these areas provide possible interaction surfaces for the implementation of CountMarks.

3 Design and Implementation of CountMarks

CountMarks extends marking menus [18] by detecting how many fingers are placed on a secondary touchscreen. This allows up to 4 times the number of selections possible in each swipe direction. This leverages the benefits of both marking menus (speed, accuracy, and scale-invariant) and Count Menus (simple, intuitive, and the ability to "short-cut" parts of the menu) [4]. CountMarks supports the well-known "recognition over recall" principle better than marking menus: previous work [14] found that marking menu navigation can be difficult as users can get lost in the hierarchy. In contrast, broader menus, like CountMarks, offer better recognition [27].

Marking menus typically hold up to 8 menu items in a single menu level [18], or 64 items over two levels. In contrast, CountMarks can fit 32 items in a single menu level (four fingers, eight directions) and 1024 items over two menu levels. For a larger number of items, we added the ability to change modes via a double tap on the screen with one finger, to access another set of menus or items.

We designed CountMarks with smart glasses in mind, due to the challenges faced by their public and mobile nature. We describe these design considerations next.

3.1 Social Acceptability

Because of the public nature of smart glasses, we designed CountMarks to comply with Hsieh et al.'s [13] recommendations for social acceptably:

1. Isolate sensing technology from the glasses,
2. Use relative pointing for adapting to various postures,
3. Design small movements for subtle interaction,
4. Aim for intuitive gestures,
5. Enhance tangibility.

CountMarks is more subtle than in-air gestures as it uses small touch gestures on a peripheral surface. Noting the poor precision of in-air interaction due to the absence of tactile feedback [8], we employ CountMarks on a smartphone touch screen. This leverages hardware users already own, rather than requiring an additional device. Future implementations could instead use smart textiles, or skin-based input [11] providing users precise haptic feedback, while allowing them to perform gestures wherever is most comfortable. We predict this may be on the hand or the upper leg.

Like marking menus, CountMarks allows swipe gestures anywhere on the touch surface. This facilitates eyes-free interaction, as the user does not need to see the surface; the user simple swipes in the desired direction with the appropriate number of fingers. We now discuss two CountMarks variants, *MenuCount* and *ItemCount*.

3.2 CountMarks Variant #1: MenuCount

MenuCount presents different menus based on how many fingers touch the screen. Holding fingers on the screen opens and preview each menu. Changing the number of fingers changes which menu is displayed on the primary display (e.g., HMD). MenuCount is seen in Fig. 3 (left), where the user has activated the "Animals" menu by touching two fingers to the screen. The user swipes in the direction of the desired item with the same number of fingers used to open the menu. Finally, the arrow to the right of the menus indicates that a double tap mode change is available, and toggle 4 more menus.

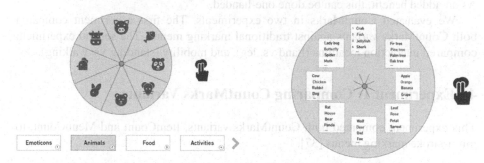

Fig. 3. (Left) *MenuCount Variant*: The user presses two fingers to the touch surface; this opens the 2nd menu. A two-finger swipe up would select the "pig" icon. (Right) *ItemCount Variant*: The user presses two fingers to the touch surface; this highlights all the 2nd options in each sub-menu. A two-finger swipe up would select "fish" from the top menu.

3.3 CountMarks Variant #2: ItemCount

ItemCount presents a single large radial menu containing up to eight linear sub-menus in each of (up to) eight directions. See Fig. 3 (right). Each linear menu can display four items at once. Items are selected by touching the screen with the required number of fingers and swiping in the direction of that item's menu. When touching the screen, all selectable menu items corresponding to the finger count are highlight. For example, a single finger touching the screen highlights all top menu items, two fingers highlights all the second items, etc. Similar to MenuCount, a double-tap toggles another four menu items in each menu. With ItemCount, this is presented as ellipses at the bottom of each linear sub-menu, as seen in Fig. 3 (right).

3.4 Interaction Location

We designed both CountMarks variants to work on the human body because it is comfortable and easy for people to interact with [28]. Body-based input provides tactile feedback and leverages proprioception, allowing precise and well-coordinated interactions. Since reliable detection of on-body input is an on-going engineering challenge [11, 33, 36], we instead implemented our prototypes using a smartphone as a proof of concept. We considered two main interaction locations: the palm and leg.

Palm interaction is likely the most intuitive on-body input location since people naturally perform interactions on their palm [31]. Conveniently for the purpose of our study, it is also the most natural place to interact with a smartphone. We note potential limits of palm-based input: it necessitates the use of both hands for interaction, and is potentially fatiguing as users must hold out both hands. Thus, we also consider the upper leg as a less obvious, but potentially ergonomic and efficient location for interaction. With interaction occurring on the leg the user can rest their arms at their side, as they naturally do while standing, and perform interactions where their hand meets their leg. As an added benefit, this can be done one-handed.

We evaluated CountMarks in two experiments. The first experiment compared both CountMarks variants against traditional marking menus. The second experiment compared interaction locations (hand vs. leg), and mobility (standing vs. walking).

4 Experiment 1: Comparing CountMarks Variants

This experiment compared both CountMarks variants, ItemCount and MenuCount, to multi-stroke marking menus [37].

4.1 Participants

We recruited 18 participants (mean age of 25.95 years, SD = 6.2, all right-handed, 10 female). Participants were recruited via posters on campus and social media.

4.2 Apparatus

We used a Samsung Galaxy S8 smartphone (running Android 8.0) as the touch input device. The smartphone was secured to the desk 10 in. from the participant. A 23.5-in. BenQ 1920 × 1080p computer monitor was positioned 19 in. away from the participant (Fig. 4), connected to a PC with an Intel Core i7-7700K 4.20 GHz CPU and 32 GB of RAM running 64-bit Windows 10.

Fig. 4. Apparatus showing the position of the display and smartphone.

We developed a Unity Android application (Fig. 5) that controlled a desktop Unity app. Touch input detected by the smartphone was sent to the desktop app via Unity Remoting. The desktop monitor displayed the menus, rather than the smartphone screen which was used exclusively for input.

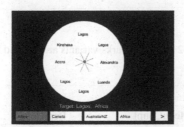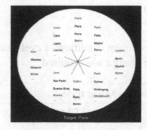

Fig. 5. Both CountMarks variants in their level 3, 8 × 8 configurations (left) MenuCount and (right) ItemCount.

The software presented a series of menus and menu items, with a target item listed at the bottom of the screen. Participants selected items from the menus via swiping gestures on the phone, as described earlier. The visual layout of each menu changed according to the menu style (see Fig. 5). The number of root menus and the number of items per menu changed according to difficulty level.

The software recorded time, and both correct and erroneous selections per trial. Execution time and number of fingers were recorded per selection.

4.3 Procedure

Participants were briefed on arrival, then provided informed consent. We then explained the task, which was based on Bailly et al. [5]. The task required selecting each instance of a specified target city name from all menus, organized by titles of countries and continents (Fig. 5). The menus were randomized so half of them included the target. Similarly, the menu items (cities) were randomized and in each target menu, the target item appeared as half of the menu items plus or minus one. This unpredictability ensured that participants could not count targets in each menu but would have to search for the targets to confirm none were left.

After a target item was correctly selected it disappeared from the menu leaving a blank space (or dashed lines for ItemCount). Trials started and ended when the participant double tapped the smartphone screen with two or more fingers. The first two trials of each block were practice trials. When participants believed they had found all target instances, they double tapped with two fingers to end the trial. Participants were instructed to complete each trial as quickly but accurately as possible.

Participants performed the task on 3 difficulty levels using each menu style: Menu-Count, ItemCount and Marking Menu. They received a 3-min practice period each time they started a new menu style. Difficulty level was based on the number of menus, items per menu, and whether a mode change double-tap was required.

4.4 Design

Our experiment employed a 3 × 3 within-subjects design. The independent variables were menu style (ItemCount, MenuCount and Marking Menu) and difficulty level (levels 1, 2 and 3). Menu style was counterbalanced according to a Latin square. For each menu style, participants progressed through 3 levels of difficulty. See Table 1 for a summary of the conditions.

Table 1. Experiment conditions. Levels 1 and 2 of CountMarks variants are ordered by whether or not a mode change was required.

Difficulty Level	Menu style								
	Marking Menu			MenuCount			ItemCount		
	1	2	3	1	2	3	1	2	3
Menu items	4 × 8	8 × 4	8 × 8	4 × 8	8 × 4	8 × 8	8 × 4	4 × 8	8 × 8
Mode change	No	Yes	Yes	No	Yes	Yes	No	Yes	Yes

There were 7 trials with each difficulty level. Each trial consisted of 7 (for difficulty levels 1 and 2) or 15 (for level 3) individual target selections. In total, each participant performed 49 target selections for difficulty levels 1 and 2, and 105 target selections for difficulty level 3, for a total of 203 individual target selections for each menu style, or 609 selections total. Over all 18 participants, our analysis is based on 10962 target menu selections over 1134 trials. The experiment took about 1 h for each participant.

Dependent variables included *total selection time, selection accuracy*, and *search accuracy*. Total selection time is the average time (in seconds) per selection. We further sub-divided total selection time into execution time and reaction time. Execution time is measured as the time from touching the screen to releasing the finger from the screen, i.e., how long it takes to perform a selection gesture. Reaction time is total selection time minus execution time, i.e., the time required for participants to understand the stimulus and touch the screen. Selection accuracy (%) is the number of correct selections divided by the total number of selections. Finally, since participants could end trials without selecting all targets, search accuracy is the number of correct selections divided by the total number of targets presented.

4.5 Results

Total Selection Time. Total selection time is seen in Fig. 6 separated by reaction and execution time. We found significant main effects for both menu style ($F_{2,34} = 25.03$, $p < .001$) and difficulty level ($F_{2,34} = 62.49$, $p < .001$) on selection time.

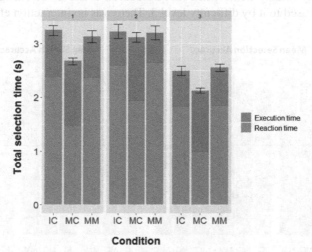

Fig. 6. Total selection time for each menu style (IC = ItemCount, MC = MenuCount, MM = Marking Menu) by difficulty level. Error bars show $\pm 1SD$.

Post-hoc testing with the Tukey-Kramer test revealed that MenuCount offers faster selections (2.64 s) than both ItemCount (3.00 s) and Marking Menu (2.97 s). This supports our hypothesis that the increased breadth of CountMarks offers faster selection time over menus with two depths.

Post-hoc testing with the Tukey-Kramer revealed that difficulty level 3 offered faster selection (2.39 s) than levels 2 (3.18 s) and 1 (3.02 s). We believe this is likely due to always presenting difficulty levels in the same order; it corresponds to participants improving with practice. The added difficulty of introducing the mode change did not seem to offset gains from learning effects.

Selection Accuracy. Selection accuracy by menu style is seen in Fig. 7 (left). ANOVA revealed a significant main effect of menu style on selection accuracy ($F_{2,34} = 14.26$, $p <$

.001). A Tukey Kramer posthoc revealed that Marking Menu was more accurate (97.91%) than MenuCount (95.00%) which was more accurate than ItemCount (88.44%). We believe this is due to the added complexity of extra fingers needed to perform selections with the two CountMarks variants; more fingers increases the opportunity for errors.

Search Accuracy. Search accuracy by menu style is seen in Fig. 7 (right). There was a significant main effect for menu style on search accuracy ($F_{2,34} = 100.98, p < .001$). A post-hoc Tukey-Kramer test showed that MenuCount (97.43%) and ItemCount (96.45%) had significantly better search accuracy than Marking Menu (92.16%).

This supports our hypothesis that CountMarks can improve search accuracy by increasing menu breadth. We also found a significant main effect for difficulty level on search accuracy ($F_{2,34} = 3.73, p < .05$). A Tukey-Kramer posthoc shows level 2 was significantly less accurate than levels 1 or 3. This was likely due to participants having difficulty finding items when first introduced to the mode-change double-tap, then becoming used to it by difficulty level 3. There was no interaction effect found.

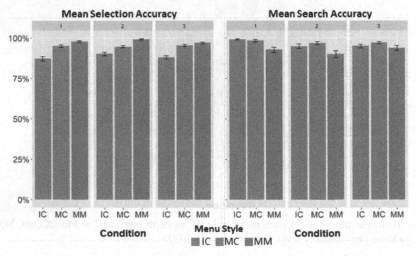

Fig. 7. Mean selection and search accuracy by condition. Error bars show ±1*SD*.

4.6 Discussion

Overall, the MenuCount variant outperformed Marking Menus in selection speed and search accuracy. Marking Menus offered better selection accuracy. These results align with Lepinski et al.'s study [20] comparing multitouch marking menus to multi-stroke marking menus. They report that by increasing menu breadth with multi-finger chording gestures, their multi-touch marking menu could decrease selection speed.

Of the two CountMarks variants, MenuCount was faster and offered better selection accuracy than ItemCount. ItemCount's low selection accuracy may be due to two factors: item location did not always perfectly match its selection direction and participants may have been confused how many fingers to select with due to blank spaces left by previously selected items. Alternatively, participants may have been confused by how many fingers were required for selection as evidenced by ItemCount showing over twice as many errors from selecting items that had already been selected compared to MenuCount. This suggests an alternative design, where remaining items (not yet selected) could move up in the linear menu to take the place of selected ones.

The two CountMarks variants also had quite different execution and reaction times. ItemCount required more search (i.e., reaction) time for targets, while MenuCount had a longer execution time, but the overall shortest total selection time. This suggests that breaking the search component up into smaller, more easily accessible and reversible components (menus can be quickly previewed by placing a number of fingers down and releasing them) selection time improved. However, ItemCount offered better search accuracy than MenuCount. We believe this reflects the ability for participants to see more items at once and determine whether any targets remain.

The differences between difficulty levels 1 and 2 were minimal. These two levels showed either 4 menus with 8 items each or 8 menus with 4 items each. Level 2 also required a double tap gesture to access the other set of items or menus. The double tap is likely why MenuCount took longer in level 2. ItemCount was not significantly different across the two difficulty levels, suggesting its difficulty level 2 layout (4 menus $\times$ 8 items + double tap) was quicker to search than having all 32 items displayed at once across 8 menus in level 1. This suggests that breadth offers better efficiency to a point, at which point semantic groupings offer better efficiency, despite additional menu depth. Difficulty level 3 outperformed the rest likely due to practice effects and the larger number of targets and selections without breaks in between.

5 Experiment 2: CountMarks Use Scenarios

We evaluated MenuCount in more realistic use cases (standing vs. walking) using a head-mounted display.

5.1 Participants

We recruited 20 participants (mean age of 24.6 years, $SD = 4.3$, all right handed, 12 female). Nine participants reported often texting while walking. Six participated in Experiment 1. Participants were recruited via posters and social media.

5.2 Apparatus

We used the same Samsung Galaxy S8 smartphone as the touch input device. We used a Microsoft HoloLens HMD, to more realistically simulate smart-glasses usage scenarios. The software was built in Unity and used Unity's built-in networking tools, UNet, to take input from the Android app to the same desktop computer as Experiment 1. The computer display was wirelessly mirrored to the HoloLens via the HoloLens Remoting app.

Depending on the condition, the smartphone was either held in the participant's non-dominant hand or mounted on the upper part of the leg in a comfortably reachable position for the dominant hand. Participants walked on a Tempo Fitness 610T treadmill. Figure 8 depicts the hardware setup. The software recorded reaction time, execution time, and selection and search accuracies, as in Experiment 1.

Fig. 8. A participant walking while using CountMarks on a leg-mounted smartphone.

5.3   Procedure

Upon arrival, participants were briefed and provided informed consent prior to starting. They were then given a demonstration of how to properly wear the HoloLens to see the full display. We began the experiment by identifying which way participants thought was "up" when swiping on their leg. This was non-obvious because "up" depends on the participant's frame of reference, and could mean up relative to the participant, the forward direction they were facing, or the direction their hand is pointing at the time of interaction. Participants were shown an image of an arrow pointing to the top of the monitor and asked to perform a swipe gesture on the leg-mounted smartphone to determine the "up" direction. While we recorded it, it was not used to determine the swipe direction during the study, which instead used a consistent swipe direction for all participants (towards the knee, based on pilot testing).

Participants then completed a demographic questionnaire before receiving instructions on how to use CountMarks to complete the Novice Task. They were given 3 min to practice CountMarks with an unrecorded trial. After practice, we found a comfortable treadmill walking speed for each participant. We asked participants to walk on the treadmill at a speed of 2.0 mph while wearing the HoloLens. Participants could increase or decrease the speed by up to 0.5 mph (the smallest increment on the treadmill). No participant chose to go higher than 2.0 mph, but 12 participants chose to go slower. In walking conditions, the treadmill was activated at the chosen speed. In standing conditions, participants stood on the deactivated treadmill.

The experiment task was identical to that used in Experiment 1. Participants performed 4 trials per condition.

5.4 Design

The experiment employed a 2 × 2 within-subjects design, with the following independent variables and levels:

- Device position (hand, leg)
- User stance (standing, walking)

The order of device position and user stance conditions were counterbalanced via a Latin square.

The dependent variables included *selection time* (further sub-divided into *reaction time, execution time*), *selection accuracy,* and *search accuracy.* All were calculated as described in Experiment 1.

In total, 20 participants were tested across 2 user stances with 2 device positions. In each condition, participants completed 4 trials of 15 selections each, for a total of 20 participants × 2 user stances × 2 device positions × 15 selections per trial * 4 trials = 4800 selections across 320 trials. The experiment took about 30 min to complete.

5.5 Results

Due to a software error the final trial of some of the first 5 participants was not recorded. Of the remaining 4800 recorded selections, we filtered selections faster than 0.001 s reaction or execution times, and those with longer than 10 s reaction or execution, leaving 4397 selections. These times were either too fast or slow to be intentional and were thus software or hardware errors.

Selection Time. Analysis of variance revealed a significant main effect of device position on selection time (F1,19 = 26.82, p < .001). Holding the device in the hand offered faster selection time (2.00 s) than interacting with the device on the leg (2.41 s). This may suggest that the leg is an unfamiliar place for interaction. Analysis of variance revealed a significant main effect of user stance on selection time (F1,19 = 6.94, p < .01). Participants had faster selection times while standing (2.09 s) than when walking (2.30 s). The interaction effect between device position and user stance was also significant (F3,57 = 6.15, p < .05). When walking, selection time was much higher on the leg than the hand. In contrast, device position had little impact when the user was standing. Total selection times for each condition are seen in Fig. 9.

Selection and Search Accuracy. Analysis of variance revealed a significant main effect of device position on accuracy ($F_{1,19} = 76.89, p < .001$). Selections with the device in the hand were more accurate (95.56%) than selections with the leg-mounted device (84.50%). As before, this is likely because the leg is an unfamiliar interaction location. See Fig. 10 (left). The main effect of user stance on selection accuracy was also significant ($F_{1,19} = 51.44, p < 0.001$). Participants were more accurate while standing (94.53%) than while walking (85.71%). The device position/user stance interaction effect was significant ($F_{3,57} = 33.69, p < .001$) This is seen Fig. 10; walking was substantially worse with leg-mounted conditions, than hand-held. This is likely due to the added impact of the device moving on the leg during walking.

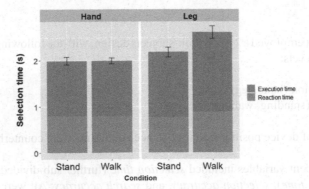

Fig. 9. Selection times broken down by condition. Error bars show $\pm 1SD$.

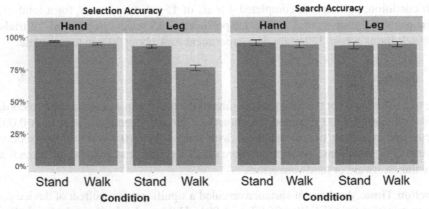

Fig. 10. (Left) Selection accuracy broken down by condition. (Right) Search accuracy by condition. Error bars show $\pm 1SD$ for mean trial accuracy.

Search Accuracy. There were no significant effects for user stance or device positioning on search accuracy. See Fig. 10 (right). Search accuracy was slightly lower in this experiment (93.55%) than in level 3 of the first experiment (97.13%).

5.6 Discussion

The goal of this experiment was to assess realistic use cases of CountMarks by testing different device positions (the hands vs the leg) with different user stances (standing and walking). For both selection time and accuracy, the combination of leg-mounted device and walking was significantly worse than other conditions. Search accuracy was consistent across all conditions. This makes sense; unlike Experiment 1, which compared different visual menu layouts, we only used a single variant of CountMarks (MenuCount) in this experiment. Clearly, the menu layout impacts search accuracy, while the style of interaction with the menu (and other external factors like grip and mounting of the device) influence selection speed and accuracy.

As described earlier, we asked participants to define the "up" swipe direction on their leg at the onset of the experiment. As expected, results were mixed; 40% of participants said they would swipe from back to front, 30% would swipe towards their feet and 30% would swipe towards their head. Future work could further explore how this preconceived orientation of swipe gesture affects performance. The inconsistency of participants' default "up" swipe direction when perform on the leg suggests that a calibration setting may be beneficial to CountMarks. This confusion may contribute to the lower accuracy of leg interactions. Future implementations could allow users to choose their desired swipe orientation to improve accuracy further.

6 Overall Discussion

While Experiment 1 validated the efficiency of CountMarks, Experiment 2 explored interactions using CountMarks in mobile settings at different device positions. Selection speed and accuracy was comparable for corresponding conditions in both experiments (e.g., the Experiment 2 hand-held position vs. the difficulty level 3 in Experiment 1). Search accuracy was the only measure notably different between the two experiments. This is likely due to the higher variance seen in Experiment 2; the standing hand-held condition offered a comparable 95.10% search accuracy vs. 97.17% in Experiment 1. Such gestures would also work in practical contexts, unlike the desk-mounted touchscreen used in our first experiment.

6.1 CountMarks Compared to Other Techniques

Table 1 shows selection times for CountMarks compared to several other reported studies on marking menus.

Table 2 A comparison of performance for different marking menu styles using 8 × 8 menus. Note that while the methodologies are not identical for each evaluation, they correspond to the same or similar tasks. *Polygon uses 12 × 12. **CountMarks in the standing, handheld condition. *** MenuCount variant at difficulty level 3.

Name of technique	Selection type	Selection time	Selection accuracy
Kurtenbach marking menu [15]	Expert	~2.3 s	80%
Multi-stroke marking menu [37]	Expert	~2.3 s	93%
Polygon menu* [38]	Expert	~2.0 s	95%
Multi-touch marking menu [20]	Novice	2.37 s	93.60%
Multi-touch marking menu [20]	Expert	0.81 s	85.10%
CountMarks (Exp. 2) **	Novice	1.99 s	96.50%
CountMarks (Exp. 1) ***	Novice	2.64 s	97.40%

Selecting targets required two search components: the first to choose a menu, and the second to find the target in the menu. While selecting a menu relies on visual search to find the correct menu, subsequent menu selections may not require the initial menu search when selecting multiple targets in the same menu. Such selections may be performed like *expert* selections that do not require search.

We include comparable conditions from both Experiment 1 and 2 data. These are the MenuCount + difficulty level 3 condition (Experiment 1) and standing with the phone in the hand condition (Experiment 2). Notably, despite requiring search, the Experiment 2 condition was faster than, or at least comparable to expert selection (i.e., without search) with most other marking menus while offering better accuracy. On average (2.315 s), CountMarks is comparable to other techniques, but the higher performance seen in Experiment 2 suggests great potential of the technique.

According to Kurtenbach [15] acceptable accuracy depends on the consequence of errors, and the difficulty in reversing them. Compared to other marking menus (Table 2), ideal accuracy should be around 95%, but these studies only tested selection while sitting at a desktop computer with a stationary input device. It is unclear what an acceptable error rate is for mobile interactions. As seen in Table 2, CountMarks outperformed other marking menu variants in terms of selection accuracy.

6.2 User Stance and Device Position

We evaluated marking menu selections in two previously unexamined domains: standing vs. walking, and with the input device handheld vs. leg-mounted. We were surprised that walking did not affect selection speed during the hand-held condition and increased selection speed by only 0.41 s during the unfamiliar leg condition. This suggests that users can use CountMarks almost as quickly while moving as when standing still. Since we intended CountMarks to be used with a mobile HMD, this is an important finding.

Compared to standing, walking slightly reduced selection accuracy by around 2% when the device was handheld. While standing, leg-mounted selection had accuracy of 92.5% which is still comparable to other marking menu techniques (Table 2). Leg-mounted accuracy dropped considerably to 75.9% when walking. Since past marking menus have not been tested in walking/standing scenarios, it is unclear if our results are typical for such conditions.

Compared to Experiment 1, we anticipated lower accuracy for the Experiment 2 Leg/Walking conditions due to device location being on the body part used for motion. This motion causes the plane of the interaction surface to be constantly changing. As the leg moves while walking, the touch surface shifts its orientation with the leg such that the horizontal axis of the phone is not the same at all times. Therefore, swipe directions may need to be relative to the orientation of the device in motion. Eight participants specifically mentioned the difficulty of coordinating hand and leg movements when making selections. Despite this difficulty, we were surprised with how accurate user were able to perform Leg/Walking gestures. We propose that future work investigate adjusting the user's swipe direction based on the input device's change in orientation while walking. We hypothesize that by fixing issues of orientation during leg movement and calibrating for users' preconceived notion of "up" that the leg may become a viable option for mobile marking menu interactions.

7 Example Application

Despite their reported efficiency [5], marking menus are rarely used in commercial products. We argue that CountMarks opens up the design space for designers to implement marking menus into modern applications. To demonstrate that CountMarks is flexible enough for use in existing applications, we developed a Netflix mockup using Count-Marks (Fig. 11). Netflix was chosen to demonstrate selection from a large number of menu items, it is not intended as a mobile use scenario.

Fig. 11. A demo Netflix application where the user has 3 fingers held down to select the middle row of movies. Swipe directions to specify a desired movie are indicated by yellow arrows on the currently indicated row.

The user can scroll vertically by sliding one finger on the screen. Touching two or more fingers on the screen activates CountMarks to select from different movie genres. Touching two fingers activates the top row, three fingers activate the middle, and four fingers activate the bottom row. Upon activating a row in this fashion, the row becomes highlighted, and arrows appear in the corner of the movie images, corresponding to the swipe direction required to select that movie. Swiping left or right with the desired number of fingers will horizontally scroll the specified row. Finally, a double tap toggles the selection mode to focus on the top bar of items where the user can select settings and other options.

While the Netflix app has content neatly organized into rows and columns, future work is needed to investigate how CountMarks can generalize to other less structured user interfaces to make selections. Websites and many other applications have undergone major redesigns over the last decade to accommodate small screen mobile devices. It is unclear how interfaces will change for smart glasses.

8 Conclusions

In this paper, we demonstrate how we designed, implemented and evaluated a novel multi-touch marking menu technique designed for mobile interactions with HMDs. This work was inspired by previous research on Count Menus, marking menus, and on-body interaction, to create an interaction technique that is designed to be fast, accurate, ergonomic and appropriate for use in a public setting. We conducted two experiments to evaluate CountMarks. The first experiment compared two variations of CountMarks to existing marking menus. CountMarks overcomes the limited breadth of traditional marking menus by allowing 32 items in a single depth and up to 64 items with a mode shifting double tap. Our findings show that the MenuCount variation of CountMarks offers quicker selection and improved search accuracy than multi-stroke marking menus at the cost of a minor decrease in selection accuracy.

In the second experiment, participants used the MenuCount variant with a Microsoft HoloLens while standing and walking and with the phone held in the hand and attached to the leg. Walking slightly reduced selection time but did cause a significant decrease in accuracy when the input device was at the leg. Leg interactions in general were slower and more prone to errors than handheld interactions. Overall, we show that Novice selection using CountMarks outperforms even Expert selection from most other marking menu variations. Future work should explore expert selection with CountMarks as well as the ergonomic and social acceptability of CountMarks when performed at different device positions.

Altogether we contribute an improved marking menu style of selection using multiple fingers. We provide empirical evidence into the strengths and weakness of performing these interactions while in mobile settings and with different device input locations. Expanding upon well-established marking menus, we believe CountMarks is a viable alternative for mobile interaction with HMDs that would otherwise use in-air gestures, voice or joystick-based controls.

References

1. Bailly, G.: Finger-count & radial-stroke shortcuts: two techniques for augmenting linear menus on multi-touch surfaces. In: Hand, pp. 1–4 (2010)
2. Bailly, G., Lecolinet, E., Nigay, L.: Visual menu techniques. ACM Comput. Surv. 49(4), 1–41 (2016)
3. Bailly, G., Lecolinet, E., Nigay, L.: Flower menus. In: Proceedings of the Working Conference on Advanced Visual Interfaces – AVI 2008, p. 15 (2008)
4. Bailly, G., Müller, J., Lecolinet, E.: Design and evaluation of finger-count interaction: combining multitouch gestures and menus. Int. J. Hum. Comput. Stud. 70(10), 673–689 (2012)
5. Bailly, G., Lecolinet, E., Nigay, L.: Wave menus: improving the novice mode of hierarchical marking menus. In: Baranauskas, C., Palanque, P., Abascal, J., Barbosa, S.D.J. (eds.) INTER-ACT 2007. LNCS, vol. 4662, pp. 475–488. Springer, Heidelberg (2007). https://doi.org/10.1007/978-3-540-74796-3_45
6. Cao, C.G.L., Zhou, M., Jones, D.B., Schwaitzberg, S.D.: Can surgeons think and operate with haptics at the same time? J. Gastrointest. Surg. 11(11), 1564–1569 (2007). https://doi.org/10.1007/s11605-007-0279-8

7. Carroll, J.M., Rosson, M.B.: Paradox of the active user. In: Carroll, J.M. (ed.) Interfacing Thought: Cognitive Aspects of Human-Computer Interaction, pp. 80–111. MIT Press, Cambridge (1987)

8. Cockburn, A., Quinn, P., Gutwin, C., Ramos, G., Looser, J.: Air pointing: design and evaluation of spatial target acquisition with and without visual feedback. Int. J. Hum. Comput. Stud. **69**(6), 401–414 (2011)

9. Dobbelstein, D., Hock, P., Rukzio, E.: Belt: an unobtrusive touch input device for head-worn displays. In: Proceedings of the ACM CHI 2015 Conference on Human Factors in Computing Systems, vol. 1, pp. 2135–2138 (2015)

10. Harrison, C., Benko, H., Wilson, A.D.: OmniTouch. In: Proceedings of the 24th Annual ACM Symposium on User Interface Software and Technology – UIST 2011, p. 441 (2011)

11. Harrison, C., Tan, D., Morris, D.: Skinput. In: Proceedings of the 28th International Conference on Human Factors in Computing Systems – CHI 2010, p. 453 (2010)

12. Hincapié-Ramos, J.D., Guo, X., Moghadasian, P., Irani, P.: Consumed endurance. In: Proceedings of the 32nd Annual ACM Conference on Human Factors in Computing Systems – CHI 2014, February, pp. 1063–1072 (2014)

13. Hsieh, Y.-T., Jylhä, A., Orso, V., Gamberini, L., Jacucci, G.: Designing a willing-to-use-in-public hand gestural interaction technique for smart glasses. In: Proceedings of the 2016 CHI Conference on Human Factors in Computing Systems – CHI 2016, pp. 4203–4215 (2016)

14. Kiger, J.I.: The depth/breadth trade-off in the design of menu-driven user interfaces. Int. J. Man Mach. Stud. **20**(2), 201–213 (1984)

15. Koelle, M., Kranz, M., Andreas, M.: Don't look at me that way! – understanding user attitudes towards data glasses usage. In: MobileHCI 2015 Proceedings of the 17th International Conference on Human-Computer Interaction with Mobile Devices and Service, pp. 362–372 (2015)

16. Kulshreshth, A., LaViola, J.J.: Exploring the usefulness of finger-based 3D gesture menu selection. In: Proceedings of the 32nd Annual ACM Conference on Human Factors in Computing Systems – CHI 2014, pp. 1093–1102 (2014)

17. Kurtenbach, G., Buxton, W.: The limits of expert performance using hierarchic marking menus. In: Proceedings of the SIGCHI Conference on Human Factors in Computing Systems – CHI 1993, pp. 482–487 (1993)

18. Kurtenbach, G.: The design and evaluation of marking menus. University of Toronto, Toronto (1993)

19. Lane, D.M., Napier, H.A., Peres, S.C., Sandor, A.: Hidden costs of graphical user interfaces: failure to make the transition from menus and icon toolbars to keyboard shortcuts. Int. J. Hum. Comput. Interact. **18**(2), 133–144 (2005)

20. Lepinski, G.J., Grossman, T., Fitzmaurice, G.: The design and evaluation of multitouch marking menus. In: Proceedings of the 28th International Conference on Human Factors in Computing Systems – CHI 2010, p. 2233 (2010)

21. Liu, M., Nancel, M., Vogel, D.: Gunslinger: Subtle Arms-down Mid-air Interaction, pp. 63–71 (2015)

22. Lucero, A., Vetek, A.: NotifEye. In: Proceedings of the 11th Conference on Advances in Computer Entertainment Technology – ACE 2014, pp. 1–10 (2014)

23. Pielot, M., Hesselmann, T., Heuten, W., Kazakova, A., Boll, S.: PocketMenu: non-visual menus for touch screen devices. In: Proceedings of the International Conference on Human Computer Interaction with Mobile Devices and Services (MobileHCI 2013), pp. 327–330 (2012)

24. Ren, G., O'Neill, E.: 3D Marking menu selection with freehand gestures. In: IEEE Symposium on 3D User Interfaces 2012, 3DUI 2012 - Proceedings, pp. 61–68 (2012)

25. Saponas, T.S., Harrison, C., Benko, H.: PocketTouch. In: Proceedings of the 24th Annual ACM Symposium on User Interface Software and Technology – UIST 2011, Figure 1, p. 303 (2011)
26. Serrano, M., Ens, B.M., Irani, P.P.: Exploring the use of hand-to-face input for interacting with head-worn displays. In: Proceedings of the SIGCHI Conference on Human Factors in Computing Systems, pp. 3181–3190 (2014)
27. Shneiderman, B.: Direct manipulation: a step beyond programming languages (excerpt). In: Readings in Human-Computer Interaction: A Multidisciplinary Approach, pp. 461–467 (1987)
28. Teather, R.J., Stuerzlinger, W.: Pointing at 3D target projections with one-eyed and stereo cursors. In: Proceedings of the SIGCHI Conference on Human Factors in Computing Systems, pp. 159–168 (2013)
29. Tung, Y.-C., et al.: User-defined game input for smart glasses in public space. In: Proceedings of the 33rd Annual ACM Conference on Human Factors in Computing Systems – CHI 2015, pp. 3327–3336 (2015)
30. Wang, C.-Y., et al.: PalmGesture: using palms as gesture interfaces for eyes-free input. In: Proceedings of the 17th International Conference on Human-Computer Interaction with Mobile Devices and Services, pp. 217–226 (2015)
31. Weigel, M., Mehta, V., Steimle, J.: More than touch: understanding how people use skin as an input surface for mobile computing. In: Proceedings of the 32nd Annual ACM Conference on Human Factors in Computing Systems – CHI 2014, pp. 179–188 (2014)
32. Weigel, M., Lu, T., Bailly, G., Oulasvirta, A., Majidi, C., Steimle, J.: iSkin: flexible, stretchable and visually customizable on-body touch sensors for mobile computing. In: Proceedings of the 33rd Annual ACM Conference on Human Factors in Computing Systems – CHI 2015, pp. 2991–3000 (2015)
33. Weigel, M., Nittala, A.S., Olwal, A., Steimle, J.: SkinMarks: enabling interactions on body landmarks using conformal skin electronics. In: Proceedings of the 2017 CHI Conference on Human Factors in Computing Systems – CHI 2017, pp. 3095–3105 (2017)
34. Weiser, M.: The computer for 21st century. Sci. Am. Ubicomp Pap. **265**(3), 8 (1991)
35. Yoon, S.H., Huo, K., Ramani, K.: Wearable textile input device with multimodal sensing for eyes-free mobile interaction during daily activities. Pervasive Mob. Comput. **33**, 17–31 (2016)
36. Zhang, Y., Zhou, J., Laput, G., Harrison, C.: SkinTrack: using the body as an electrical waveguide for continuous finger tracking on the skin. In: Proceedings of the 2016 CHI Conference on Human Factors in Computing Systems – CHI 2016, pp. 1491–1503 (2016)
37. Zhao, S., Balakrishnan, R.: Simple vs. compound mark hierarchical marking menus. In: Proceedings of the 17th Annual ACM Symposium on User Interface Software and Technology – UIST 2004, vol. 6, no. 2, p. 33 (2004)
38. Zhao, S., Agrawala, M., Hinckley, K.: Zone and polygon menus: using relative position to increase the breadth of multi-stroke marking menus. In: Proceedings of the SIGCHI Conference on Human Factors in Computing Systems, pp. 1077–1086 (2006)
39. Zhao, S., Dragicevic, P., Chignell, M., Balakrishnan, R., Baudisch, P.: earPod: eyes-free menu selection using touch input and reactive audio feedback. In: Proceedings of the SIGCHI Conference on Human Factors in Computing Systems, p. 1395 (2007)
40. Zheng, J., Bi, X., Li, K., Li, Y., Zhai, S.: M3 gesture menu. In: Proceedings of the 2018 CHI Conference on Human Factors in Computing System – CHI 2018, pp. 1–14 (2018)

Single-Actuator Simultaneous Haptic Rendering for Multiple Vital Signs

Juliette Regimbal[ID], Nusaiba Radi[ID], Antoine Weill–Duflos[ID],
and Jeremy R. Cooperstock[✉][ID]

Department of Electrical and Computer Engineering and Centre for Interdisciplinary
Research in Music, Media and Technology, McGill University, Montreal, Canada
{juliette,antoinew,jer}@cim.mcgill.ca

Abstract. Haptic displays have been investigated as a possible way to
reduce the effects of alarm fatigue in clinical environments. Previous displays have employed multiple vibrotactile actuators, using the spatial
dimension to aid in conveying information of a number of vital signs.
However, inspired by prior work investigating multidimensional tactons,
we wished to examine the effectiveness of a single actuator to communicate information regarding multiple vital signs simultaneously. The
results of our evaluation suggest that this is not only feasible, but that
with a carefully designed encoding strategy, we may be able obtain perception performance comparable to that achievable with multi-actuator
displays.

Keywords: Single actuator · Haptic chord · Simultaneous signals

1 Introduction

The World Health Organization recommends noise be limited in hospital environments to avoid increasing stress in patients [2]. Recommended values are often
exceeded by large margins in real-world operating rooms (OR) and intensive care
units (ICU) [7,16]. These high noise levels not only exacerbate the stress levels
of hospital clinicians, but can negatively impact patient recovery by reducing
their quality of sleep [18].

A significant proportion of this noise comes from medical alarms, which
exhibit high error rates. This exacerbates "alarm fatigue", in which medical
professionals become desensitized to the alarms, and tend to ignore or silence
them [6,17], with detrimental effects on patient outcomes, including death.

Although it would not address the problem of false positives, a haptic display
for patient alarms would transfer stimulus from the overloaded audio channel
to the less used haptic channel, and further allow for personalized delivery of
alarm information only to those clinicians for whom it is relevant. Moreover,
the addition of haptic signaling to a pre-existing auditory display was found to
reduce the perceived workload of responding to the display, without decreasing

© Springer Nature Switzerland AG 2020
C. Stephanidis et al. (Eds.): HCII 2020, LNCS 12424, pp. 261–270, 2020.
https://doi.org/10.1007/978-3-030-60117-1_19

participant performance [5]. These factors could significantly alleviate noise in the OR and ICU, thereby helping to reduce alarm fatigue.

Previous research has explored haptic displays for use in medical alarms. These have primarily used multiple vibrotactile actuators, or "tactors", distributed across the body, employing spatial and temporal location to encode information [9,14,15]. To date, the presentation of multiple vibrotactile features for this purpose has been largely sequential: one or more tactors are actuated in series in order to convey information to the wearer regarding one or more vital signs [13], which may be overly demanding of the wearer's short-term memory.

Earlier examples of haptic rendering for vital sign levels also tended to use multiple tactors. Notably, Ferris and Sarter employed an apparatus consisting of eighteen tactors. Their comparison of a discrete tactile alarm condition against different designs of a continuous tactile display for monitoring multiple vital signs found that the former was preferred by participants, but the continuous monitoring displays resulted in superior performance in terms of response time, diagnostic accuracy, and physiological management scores [9]. If similar benefits could be obtained with reduced hardware requirements, this would offer a more energy- and space-efficient solution that would likely face fewer hurdles to adoption.

We were thus motivated to tackle the challenge of designing a vibrotactile encoding strategy that could efficiently convey information regarding multiple vital signs, in parallel. This requires the use of multiple vibrotactile features to encode separate, simultaneous messages. In practice these features may conflict with each other in unexpected ways, resulting in an effect known as "tactile clutter" [8], which decreases the intelligibility of the information conveyed. To be usable in a medical environment, a display must also be understandable when the user's attention is focused on another task rather than on the display itself.

This paper introduces a method of encoding the levels of three vital signs—heart rate, blood pressure, and peripheral oxygen saturation (SpO_2)—each of which can take on one of three different states—normal, high, and low—using a single vibrotactile actuator. Our approach differs from previous work, which also conveyed through a single actuator information regarding three parameters, each of which may take on multiple values [4]. First, similar to the behavior of present-day auditory patient monitors, we render a haptic representation of patient vital signs in both alarm states and "normal" (i.e., non-alarm) states, and second, we display these vitals continuously. Of central importance to the success of this approach is the design of an effective encoding strategy, described in the following section.

2   Display Design

The vital signs are encoded into a multidimensional haptic icon or "tacton" [3], composed of a series of vibrations rendered by a tactor attached to the wrist. Each vital sign is represented by a different feature of the tacton.

2.1 Beats, Tempo, and Chords

Our vibrotactile encoding employs a train of four-beat measures, with the tempo (number of beat per minute) varying based on the parameters described in Sect. 2.2. A second parameter available to us is the number of beats of each measure in which a vibration is rendered, and the third parameter relates to frequencies of vibration. Human vibrotactile perception is sensitive to a smaller range of frequencies than audition [11]. A person's ability to haptically discriminate between frequencies separated by intervals of 20 Hz decreases at frequencies greater than 60 Hz [10]. As such, frequency is generally a poor feature for information encoding, especially while other features of the signal may vary simultaneously. An alternative to a single frequency is to present two frequencies simultaneously as a chord, consisting of the base frequency, f, and the chordal frequency, f_c. The difference between the two frequencies, expressed as the number of equally tempered semitones separating them, results in a sense of consonance or dissonance [20]. Dissonance is perceived by the user as the sense of roughness in the rendered waveform.

The degree of overall consonance tends to increase with the base frequency, attaining a maximum as f_c reaches $2f$, i.e., 12 semitones or a full octave, and decreases to a minimum for chordal frequencies slightly offset from the base frequency [20]. A difference of zero semitones (rendering a single frequency) is by definition in perfect consonance with itself.

2.2 Mapping

In designing the display, care was taken to make changes to each feature sufficiently distinct so as to facilitate their disambiguation. For example, a user should not mistake a change in a haptic chord with a change in tempo. The encodings used for our vibrotactile display are summarized in Table 1.

Table 1. Each vital sign is related to the modified feature of the pulse train and the value of that feature at the different vital sign levels.

Vital sign	Feature modified	Level		
		Low	Normal	High
Heart rate	Tempo	80 bpm	160 bpm	320 bpm
Blood pressure	Pulses per measure	1 pulse	2 pulses	3 pulses
SpO$_2$	Chord	80 Hz and 25.2 Hz	80 Hz	80 Hz and 190.2 Hz

Blood pressure is expressed as the number of beats per measure in which a vibration is rendered, which we refer to as "pulses": one pulse for low blood pressure, two pulses for normal, and three pulses for high. The remaining beat(s) of the measure are silent to delimit the different groupings.

The most obvious mapping is that of expressing the heart rate as the tempo at which the beats are rendered. For the purposes of our experiment, we selected heart rates of 40, 80, and 160 heartbeats per minute as low, normal, and high heart rate values, respectively. However, we doubled these rates to obtain the corresponding tempi of 80, 160, and 320 beats per minute (bpm). Thus, for the case of a normal heart rate and normal blood pressure, the pulse train consists of measures in which pulses are rendered for two out of the four beats, at a rate of 160 bpm. This feels equivalent to an actual heart rate of 80 bpm, illustrated in Fig. 1 (upper), whereas for a high heart rate and high blood pressure, we have 320 bpm of which pulses are rendered three beats out of every four, as seen in Fig. 1 (lower).

This mapping was chosen since different levels of the vital signs are represented discretely, making it difficult to confuse them. Furthermore, since a new rendering occurs every few seconds, independently of the previous values, the user is not required to focus continuously on the number of pulses.

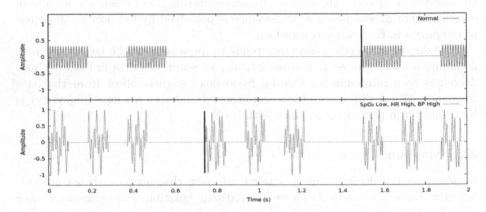

Fig. 1. Examples of haptic waveforms representing the vital signs. The upper waveform occurs when all vital signs are normal. Two pulses occupy the first two beats of each measure. The lower waveform occurs when SpO2 is low, heart rate is high, and blood pressure is high (although such a combined alarm event was not allowed in our experiment). This waveform is represented by a dissonant chord at increased tempo, three beats per measure. The first measure starts at 0s for both waveforms and lasts until the black bar. (Color figure online)

We opted to use the haptic chord for SpO$_2$ level, since this vital sign is typically represented by hospital monitors using auditory tone pitch [12]. A single frequency (0 semitones) was chosen to represent a normal level of SpO$_2$. Through trial and error, chordal frequency offsets of −8 and +3 semitones were found to be significantly dissonant to be distinguishable from the single frequency and perceived sufficiently distinctly to express the two abnormal levels (high and low). To further distinguish the resulting chords, the respective chordal frequencies, f_c, associated with high and low SpO$_2$ were then offset by ±12 semitones (one octave), resulting in chordal frequency offsets of −20 semitones

(25.2 Hz) for low SpO_2 and +15 semitones (190.2 Hz) for high SpO_2. A base frequency of 80 Hz was selected through multiple rounds of pilot testing.

To reduce the risk of desensitization to the semi-continuous haptic stimuli, amplitude was maintained at 40% of maximum, except for abnormal levels of SpO_2 or blood pressure, when it was increased to 100%. Through pilot testing, we determined that abnormal heart rate states could still be easily discriminated at the reduced amplitude.

3 Evaluation Methodology

A portable implementation of the display described in Sect. 2 was developed and used to evaluate participants' response accuracy and response time to events in which one of the vital signs changed to an abnormal level.

3.1 Apparatus

The encoding method described above was implemented as a set of Pure Data patches, which take inputs for the values of the three vital signs. An Android application, running on a Xiaomi Mi Pad 4 tablet, generates vital signs in accordance with the procedure described in Sect. 3.3, and renders the encoded vitals using libpd. This application also collects user responses and runs a simultaneous distractor task.

The apparatus, illustrated in Fig. 2, consists of a Haptuator Original (Tactile Labs, Montreal) [19] vibrotactile actuator, driven using one audio channel from the Android tablet, and amplified by a SURE Electronics class-D audio amplifier, while the second channel provides audio input to a pair of headphones.

Fig. 2. The Xiaomi Mi Pad 4 audio is split with one channel sent to the headphones and the other to a SURE Electronics audio amplifier connected to the Haptuator Original.

3.2   Participants

Participants were recruited under approval of the McGill Research Ethics Board, file number 388-0217. A total of fourteen participants performed the experiment, and were compensated 10CAD for their time.

3.3   Procedure

Participants first had the Haptuator strapped to the top of one wrist. The experiment consisted of a calibration phase, training phase, a practice test, and a full test. The headphones were worn during the practice and full tests.

Calibration. During the calibration phase, the overall amplitude of the pulses was adjusted by the participants so that they could be easily felt but were not too strong. Participants were allowed to return to calibration during the training phase as they were exposed to the actual encoding.

Training. All the vital signs began rendered in normal states. Participants were then introduced to the abnormal states one at a time, in a set order of blood pressure, heart rate, and SpO_2. For the purposes of our experiment, only a single vital sign was allowed to enter an abnormal state at any particular time. Participants were then allowed to manually control the states of each vital sign and indicate when they are ready to continue.

Practice. At this point, the distractor task was introduced. The names of colors were spoken at a rate of one per second, played through headphones with pink noise overlaid. Participants listened to this audio stream and tapped a button labelled "blue" whenever the word "blue" was heard.

The practice test proceeded through five different abnormal states. The times between abnormal states were generated using a Poisson distribution with $\lambda = 20\,\text{s}$. The specific abnormal states rendered were selected with a discrete uniform distribution. Participants were instructed to consider the distractor task as their primary activity. They were also informed that when a vital sign enters an abnormal state, a correct answer will result in the vital sign returning to normal, as if a clinician had corrected the problem causing the abnormal value. If participants did not respond correctly to an abnormal state within 30 s, the vital sign would return to normal on its own. Participants were allowed to ask questions during this test.

A metric was imposed before testing began that participants must respond correctly to four of the five different states, within two trials, to proceed to the next test. This performance metric ensured a reasonably short training time, and was designed to exclude participants who were either having difficulty learning the encoding or were otherwise non-compliant. In this case, which occurred for only one of the fourteen recruited participants, that participant's data were excluded from the results.

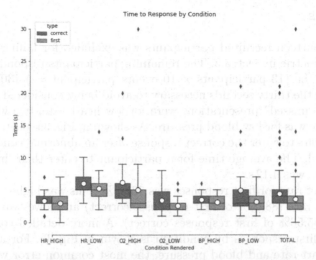

(a) Comparison of time for participants to respond to a rendered event, as well as the time to respond *correctly* to the event.

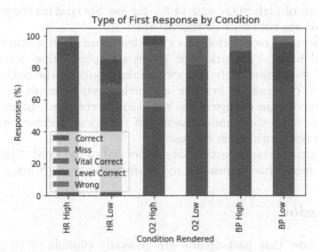

(b) Types of first responses to rendered events. "Vital Correct" and "Level Correct" refer respectively to a participant answering the correct vital sign but not the level and the right level but not the vital sign.

Fig. 3. Response times and first response types by rendered event.

Full Test. The full test proceeded in the same manner as the practice with some adjustments. Participants were not allowed to ask questions, and the number of abnormal states was increased to ten, with $\lambda = 90\,s$ for the Poisson distribution. Participants still had to respond to the distractor task as before.

4 Results

One of the fourteen recruited participants was excluded for failing to pass the practice test metric in Sect. 3.3. The remaining participants responded correctly to 95.38% of the (13 participants × 10 events/participant =) 130 events presented within the thirty seconds necessary to avoid being considered as a "miss". Three of the "missed" presentations were for low heart rate, two were for high SpO_2, and one was for low blood pressure. As shown in Fig. 3a, participants took on average 4.96 s to enter the correct response after an abnormal condition began to be rendered. The average time for a participant to enter their first response, correct or not, was 4.12 s.

The correct rate for first responses was 73.85%. This was highest in response to high heart rate (88.00% of first responses correct) and lowest in response to high SpO_2 (55.56% of first responses correct). A more detailed comparison of the types of first responses by condition is shown in Fig. 3b. For alarm events related to heart rate and blood pressure, the most common error was incorrect recognition of the associated vital sign, for example confusing high heart rate with high blood pressure. However this was not the case for SpO_2, for which the most common error was in interpretation of the level, which occurred in 33.3% of the instances of high SpO_2 and 14.3% for low SpO_2. This suggests that the selected chords are not easily distinguishable.

Clearly, incorrect recognition of a vital sign alarm event would be unacceptable in a real hospital scenario, but it bears emphasis that detection of the "event" itself was impressively high, with misses only on the SpO_2 high event, which occurred one time. In practice, a clinician would consult a patient monitor upon perceiving the change of the vital sign, as conveyed through the haptic mechanism, to verify their understanding of the actual patient condition, as is the case at present with audio alarms.

For the distractor task, participants responded to the word "blue" in 83.08% of cases. The mean time to respond to the distractor was 920 ms.

5 Conclusion

The results show that participants are generally capable of (i) perceiving a change from a normal to an abnormal state and (ii) quickly identifying the abnormal state. First response accuracy rates and first response times are comparable to those achieved with a three-actuator apparatus, worn on the leg, in a different experiment conducted by our group [1]. Based on more recent pilot data, we believe that the relatively poor disambiguation of the dissonant chords rendered may be resolved with different values of the chordal frequencies. Once such tuning of the various encoding parameters has been carried out, an important test for future work would be to compare these displays under the same conditions. This would offer a clearer understanding of the tradeoffs between the single-actuator display and more complicated hardware, in the context of vibrotactile displays for medical purposes. It bears emphasis that the device, consisting of a single vibrotactile actuator, strapped to the wearer's arm, is highly mobile, and therefore, suitable for testing in a realistic hospital use-case scenario. Additionally, the portable nature of the apparatus allows for future work to employ more realistic settings.

Acknowledgment. We would like to thank Joseph J. Schlesinger and Parisa Alirezaee for their time and advice throughout this project.

References

1. Alirezaee, P., Weill-Duflos, A., Schlesinger, J., Cooperstock, J.R.: Exploring the effectiveness of haptic alarm displays for critical care environments. In: Haptics Symposium. IEEE, Washington, D.C., March 2020
2. Berglund, B., Lindvall, T., Schwela, D.H.: Guidelines for Community Noise. Whurr, London (1999)
3. Brewster, S., Brown, L.M.: Tactons: structured tactile messages for non-visual information display. In: Proceedings of the Fifth Conference on Australasian User Interface, vol. 28, pp. 15–23. AUIC 2004, Australian Computer Society Inc, AUS (2004)
4. Brown, L.M., Brewster, S.A., Purchase, H.C.: Multidimensional Tactons for non-visual information presentation in mobile devices. In: Proceedings of the 8th Conference on Human-computer Interaction with Mobile Devices and Services. Mobile-HCI 2006, Helsinki, Finland, pp. 231–238. ACM, New York (2006). https://doi.org/10.1145/1152215.1152265
5. Burdick, K.J., et al.: Using multisensory haptic integration to improve monitoring in the intensive care unit. Auditory Percept. Cogn. **2**(4), 1–19 (2020). https://doi.org/10.1080/25742442.2020.1773194
6. Cvach, M.: Monitor alarm fatigue: an integrative review. Biomed. Instrum.Technol. **46**(4), 268–277 (2012). https://doi.org/10.2345/0899-8205-46.4.268
7. Darbyshire, J.L., Young, J.D.: An investigation of sound levels on intensive care units with reference to the WHO guidelines. Crit. Care **17**(5), R187 (2013). https://doi.org/10.1186/cc12870
8. Erp, V., Jan, B., Veltman, J., van Veen, H., Oving, A.: Tactile torso display as countermeasure to reduce night vision goggles induced drift. Technical report, Human Factors Research Institute, Soesterberg, Netherlands (2003)
9. Ferris, T.K., Sarter, N.: Continuously informing Vibrotactile displays in support of attention management and multitasking in Anesthesiology. Hum. Factors **53**(6), 600–611 (2011). https://doi.org/10.1177/0018720811425043
10. Formby, C., Morgan, L.N., Forrest, T.G., Raney, J.J.: The role of frequency selectivity in measures of auditory and vibrotactile temporal resolution. J. Acoust. Soc. Am. **91**(1), 293–305 (1992). https://doi.org/10.1121/1.402772
11. Franzén, O., Nordmark, J.: Vibrotactile frequency discrimination. Percept. Psychophys. **17**(5), 480–484 (1975). https://doi.org/10.3758/BF03203298
12. Goldman, J.M., Robertson, F.A.: Pulse-OX Tone Conveys Vital Information. APSF Stresses Use of Audible Monitor Alarms, p. 20 (2004)
13. Gomes, K.M., Reeves, S.T., Riggs, S.L.: The evaluation of tactile parameters and display prototype to support physiological monitoring and multitasking for anesthesia providers in the operating room. IEEE Trans. Haptics, p. 1 (2019). https://doi.org/10.1109/TOH.2019.2960017

14. Katzman, N., Gellert, M., Schlesinger, J.J., Oron-Gilad, T., Cooperstock, J.R., Bitan, Y.: Evaluation of tactile cues for simulated patients' status under high and low workload. In: International Meeting. Human Factors and Ergonomics Society (HFES), October 2019. https://doi.org/10.1177/1071181319631285

15. Ng, J., Man, J.: Vibro-monitor: a vibrotactile display for physiological data monitoring. In: Human Interface Technologies Conference (2004)

16. Otenio, M.H., Cremer, E., Claro, E.M.T.: Noise level in a 222 bed hospital in the 18th health region - PR. Revista Brasileira de Otorrinolaringologia **73**(2), 245–250 (2007). https://doi.org/10.1590/S0034-72992007000200016

17. Sendelbach, S., Funk, M.: Alarm fatigue. AACN Adv. Crit. Care **24**(4), 378–386 (2013). https://doi.org/10.4037/NCI.0b013e3182a903f9

18. Xie, H., Kang, J., Mills, G.H.: Clinical review: the impact of noise on patients' sleep and the effectiveness of noise reduction strategies in intensive care units. Crit. Care **13**(2), 208 (2009). https://doi.org/10.1186/cc7154

19. Yao, H.Y., Hayward, V.: Design and analysis of a recoil-type vibrotactile transducer. J. Acoust. Soc. Am. **128**(2), 619–627 (2010). https://doi.org/10.1121/1.3458852

20. Yoo, Y., Hwang, I., Choi, S.: Consonance of Vibrotactile chords. IEEE Trans. Haptics **7**(1), 3–13 (2014). https://doi.org/10.1109/TOH.2013.57

Development of an Interface that Expresses Twinkling Eyes by Superimposing Human Shadows on Pupils

Yoshihiro Sejima[1](✉), Makiko Nishida[2], and Tomio Watanabe[3]

[1] Faculty of Informatics, Kansai University, 2-1-1 Ryozenji-cho,
Takatsuki-shi, Osaka 569-1095, Japan
sejima@kansai-u.ac.jp
[2] Faculty of Design, Okayama Prefectural University, 111 Kuboki, Soja-shi, Okayama, Japan
[3] Faculty of Computer Science and Systems Engineering,
Okayama Prefectural University, 111 Kuboki, Soja-shi, Okayama, Japan

Abstract. Human eyes are related to own affects and emotions, and seem to twinkle when human has positive affects and emotions such as a strong interest and eagerness. Human is subconsciously attracted to the twinkling eyes. In this study, aiming at the development of a novel communication interface that attracts human, we focused on the reflected glare on the surface of eyeballs and proposed an expression method that superimposes human shadows on pupils. We conducted an impression experiment to evaluate the proposed method and demonstrated that the method was effective for attracting human. Based on the result, we developed an advanced interface that expresses twinkling eyes for attracting human. The developed interface generates a pseudo reflected glare by superimposing human shadow on each pupil as a pseudo-self-image.

Keywords: Non-verbal communication · Affective expression · Attractiveness · Reflected glare

1 Introduction

As the saying goes "The eyes say more than the mouth," human affects and emotions are reflected in the eyes [1]. Human estimates talker's affects and emotions during embodied interaction and communication based on impressions including eyes. For example, human often likens positive/negative impressions that can be read from facial expressions to their eye's appearance, such as "Eyes are laughing." Among them, when human has strong positive affects and emotions such as a strong interest, eagerness or higher motivation, his/her eyes seem to twinkle [2]. Human is subconsciously attracted to the twinkling eyes. Therefore, it is expected to develop a novel interface that attracts human subconsciously by reproducing the twinkling eyes and applying it to human interaction and communication.

In this study, aiming at the development of a novel interface that attracts human, we focused on the reflected glare on the surface of eyeballs and proposed an expression

© Springer Nature Switzerland AG 2020
C. Stephanidis et al. (Eds.): HCII 2020, LNCS 12424, pp. 271–279, 2020.
https://doi.org/10.1007/978-3-030-60117-1_20

method that superimposes human shadows on pupils. In addition, we confirmed that the proposed method was effective for attracting human by the sensory evaluation. Based on the result, we developed an interface that expresses twinkling eyes. The developed interface generates a pseudo reflected glare by superimposing human shadow on each pupil as a pseudo-self-image.

2 Expression Method of Twinkling Eyes

2.1 Concept

In this study, we focused on a "reflected glare" on the eyeball surface as an optical characteristic based on a natural environment. For example, a metal material having a high reflectance causes reflected glare due to the specular reflection. In addition, humans unintentionally estimate the specular reflectivity, the texture and the gloss of the material [3]. Therefore, it is expected that an impression that high reflection is caused on the eyeball surface can be generated by expressing the surrounding reflection on eyes. Specially, we focused on human shadows as a reflected glare in the surroundings reflection. The human shadow has a function that increases the presence of user in the space [4] and a function that enhances the self-reference [5]. Furthermore, human can easily notice the shadow as oneself by removing the noise such as the background. Therefore, we proposed an expression method that superimposes the human shadow on the pupils as the reflected glare.

Figure 1 shows the concept of the proposed method. In this method, the human shadow was superimposed on the pupils as the reflected glare on the eyeball surface. The superimposed human shadow can express the degree of reflection by changing its shade. Furthermore, not only superimposing the human shadow but also enlarging the pupil can create an illusion that is interested in the talker. The expression method leads to attract human and enhance the human interaction and communication.

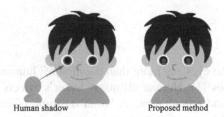

Human shadow   Proposed method

Fig. 1. Concept of the expression of twinkling eyes.

2.2 Expression Method of Twinkling Eyes

The proposed method is an imitation for a reflection on the eyeball surface. Since human eyeball has a spherical shape, it is effective to express the human shadow on a curved surface instead of superimposing the human shadow on a plane. Therefore, in this method, a distortion to the curved surface in the eyeballs is expressed by enlarging only the upper body of the human shadow (Fig. 2). Figure 3 shows example images applying the proposed method. The left image is the original image, and the right image is the superimposed image using the Photoshop. It can be confirmed from the enlarged image in which human shadow is reflected in eyes.

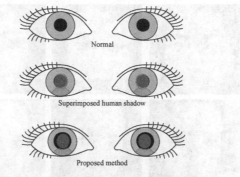

Normal

Superimposed human shadow

Proposed method

Fig. 2. Expression method of twinkling eyes.

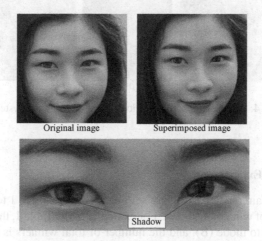

Original image   Superimposed image

Shadow

Fig. 3. Example of the expression method.

2.3 Impression Experiment

An impression experiment using stimulus images was performed in order to confirm the effect of superimposing human shadow. In this experiment, the three modes were compared: "(A) Original" without processing, "(B) Dilated pupil" in which the pupillary area is enlarged at 1.5 times based on the previous research [6], and "(C) Proposed method" in which the human shadow is superimposed on pupils.

In this experiment, two types of female stimulus images and one type of male (Fig. 4). Stimulus images were presented side by side using a 12.1-inch monitor (1600 × 900 pixels). The participants were instructed to perform a paired comparison of modes. In the paired comparison experiment, based on their preferences, they selected the better mode in terms of attractiveness. The presentation of each mode was random for each participant in consideration of the order effect. The participants were 12 females and 15 males.

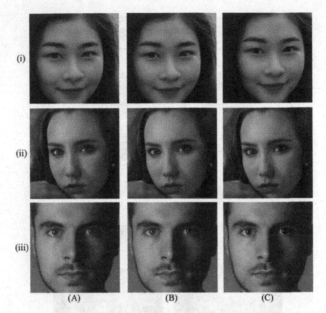

Fig. 4. Example of a communication scene using the system.

2.4   Result of the Experiment

The results of the paired comparison are summarized from Table 1 to Table 3. In these tables, the number of winners is shown. For example, in the Table 1, the number of mode (A)'s winner is ten to mode (B), and the number of total winners is nineteen. In order to evaluate these results quantitatively, we introduced the Bradley-Terry model given in the Eq. (1) and the Eq. (2) [7]. The calculated results of the evaluation from Table 1 to Table 3 are shown from Fig. 5 to Fig. 7.

$$p_{ij} = \frac{\pi_i}{\pi_i + \pi_j} \tag{1}$$

$$\sum_i \pi_i = const.(= 100) \tag{2}$$

π_i : Intensity of i

p_{ij} : probability of judgement that i is better than j

Table 1. Result of paired comparison for the stimulus images (i).

	(A)	(B)	(C)	Total
(A)		10	9	19
(B)	17		12	29
(C)	18	15		33

Table 2. Result of paired comparison for the stimulus images (ii).

	(A)	(B)	(C)	Total
(A)		9	9	18
(B)	18		10	28
(C)	18	17		35

Table 3. Result of paired comparison for the stimulus images (iii).

	(A)	(B)	(C)	Total
(A)		7	18	25
(B)	20		20	40
(C)	9	7		16

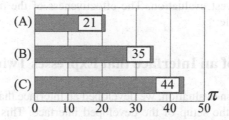

Fig. 5. Comparison of π based on the Bradley-Terry model for the stimulus images (i).

In the Fig. 5, the consistency of mode matching was confirmed by performing a goodness of fit test ($x^2(1, 0.05) = 3.84 > x_0^2 = 0.00$) and a likelihood ratio test ($x^2(1, 0.05) = 3.84 > x_0^2 = 0.00$). In the Fig. 6, the consistency of mode matching was confirmed by performing a goodness of fit test ($x^2(1, 0.05) = 3.84 > x_0^2 = 0.57$) and a likelihood ratio test ($x^2(1, 0.05) = 3.84 > x_0^2 = 0.57$). In the Fig. 7, the consistency of mode matching was confirmed by performing a goodness of fit test ($x^2(1, 0.05) = 3.84 > x_0^2 = 0.87$) and a likelihood ratio test ($x^2(1, 0.05) = 3.84 > x_0^2 = 0.87$).

From the Fig. 5 and 6, the same evaluation tendency is shown for the female. In particular, the mode (C) that is the proposed method was higher evaluated than the

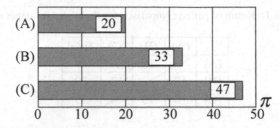

Fig. 6. Comparison of π based on the Bradley-Terry model for the stimulus images (ii).

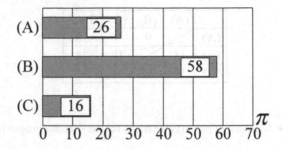

Fig. 7. Comparison of π based on the Bradley-Terry model for the stimulus images (iii).

mode (B) that is effective to attract human as the previous method. This is because the superimposition of human shadows increases the connection to the self rather than the dilated pupil that increases the attractiveness. On the other hand, in the male stimulus image of Fig. 7, the mode (B) was evaluated most highly, and the proposed method mode (C) was the lowest evaluation. The effectiveness of the proposed method was demonstrated for female.

3 Development of an Interface that Expresses Twinkling Eyes

Based on the impression evaluation, we developed an interface that expresses twinkling eyes. Figure 8 shows the setup of the developed interface. This interface consists of a desktop PC with Microsoft Windows 10 (CPU: Corei5 2.70 GHz, Memory: 8 GB, Graphics: NVIDIA Geforce GT 730), non-contact motion tracking device (Microsoft Kinect Windows V2), hemispherical displays (Gakken WORLDEYE), and an image distributor (SANWA SUPPLY VGA-HDSP2K). In order to represent a pupil response with the hemispherical display, the 3D CG model for the pupil response was introduced. This 3D CG model consists of a pupil and an iris (Fig. 9). The color of the iris was chosen to be blue because it is an easily distinguishable color to recognize the pupil response such as the dilation and contraction. The smooth pupil response was realized by generating the forward and back movement of the 3D CG model which plays the role of the pupil on the Z-axis at 5.2 mm/frame so that pupil response would not create a feeling of strangeness. The frame rate at which the 3D CG model was represented was 30 fps, using Microsoft DirectX 9.0 SDK (June 2010).

When a participant approaches the interface, the pupil enlarges or contracts according to the distance between the participant and the interface as if the interface is interested in the participant. In addition, the shadow of the participant is superimposed on the 3D space as a texture and changes according to the distance in real time. This blurry human area looks like self-shadow which is reflected by the lighting. The blurry image is superimposed on the 3D space as a texture to coincide with the center of the image and the pupillary axis of 3D model. By this CG method, the reflected image generates based on the correspondence relationship between the position of participant and the position of interface. An example of communication scene using the developed interface is shown in Fig. 10. The developed interface looks like vivid and twinkling by superimposing on the shadow. In addition, enlarging pupils create an atmosphere of interest to the participants.

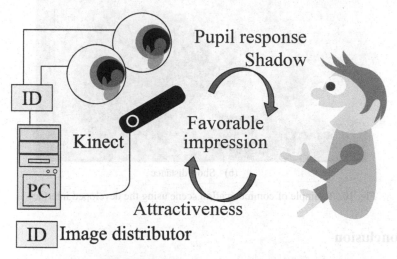

Fig. 8. Setup of the developed interface.

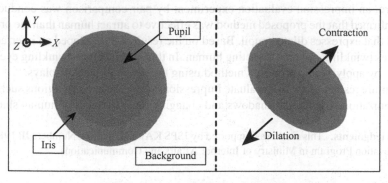

Fig. 9. 3D CG model of pupil and iris.

(a)   Long distance

(b)   Short distance

Fig. 10. Example of communication scene using the developed interface.

4   Conclusion

In this paper, we focused on "reflected glare" on the surface of the eyeball and proposed an expression method that superimposes a human shadow as a pseudo self-image. Furthermore, an impression evaluation experiment by pair comparison was conducted. It was confirmed that the proposed method was effective to attract human than the previous method that expresses dilated pupil. Based on the result, we developed an interface that expresses twinkling eyes for attracting human. In this interface, the twinkling eyes were realized by applying the proposed method using the hemispherical displays.

In future research, we will evaluate impressions under various conditions such as the synchronization with human shadows and changing the brightness of human shadows.

Acknowledgments. This work was supported by JSPS KAKENHI Grant Numbers JP 19K12890 and Innovation Program in Ministry of Internal Affairs and Communications.

References

1. Hess, E.H.: The role of pupil size in communication. Sci. Am. **233**(5), 116–119 (1975)

2. ROHTO Pharmaceutical Co.,Ltd: Women's brightness (brightness) tends to decrease with age. https://www.rohto.co.jp/news/release/2018/0412_01/ Reference date: November 19, 2019 in Japanese

3. Yamamoto, H.: Perception of surface color and texture. J. Text. Mach. Soc. Jpn. **64**(8), 477–483 (2011)

4. Kyoho, R., Yamamoto, K., Kuramoto, I., Tsujino, Y.: Impression of the shadow-based representation of existence probability. IPSJ SIG Tech. Rep. **2011**(9), 1–8 (2011)

5. Sejima, Y., Ishii, Y., Watanabe, T.: An embodied communication system with avatar-shadow's color expressions based on an interaction-activated communication model in voice communication. Trans. JSME **85**(873), 1–10 (2019)

6. Sejima, Y., Egawa, S., Sato, Y., Watanabe, T.: A pupil response system using hemispherical displays for enhancing affective conveyance. J. Adv. Mech. Des. Syst. Manuf. **13**(2), 1–9 (2019)

7. Luce, R.D.: Individual Choice Behavior: A Theoretical Analysis. J. Wiley, New York (1959)

MUCOR: A Multiparty Conversation Based Robotic Interface to Evaluate Job Applicants

H. A. S. D. Senaratna[1($\boxtimes$)], Udaka A. Manawadu[2], W.K.N. Hansika[1],
S. W. A. M. D. Samarasinghe[1], and P. Ravindra S. De Silva[1]

[1] Robotics and Intelligent Systems Laboratory, Department of Computer Science,
University of Sri Jayewardenepura, Nugegoda, Sri Lanka
sajinisenaratna@gmail.com, kushan989@gmail.com
maheshd95@gmail.com, ravi@sjp.ac.lk
[2] Robot Engineering Laboratory, Graduate School of Computer Science
and Engineering, University of Aizu, Aizuwakamatsu, Japan
m5232115@u-aizu.ac.jp

Abstract. "MUCOR" is a robotic interface made up of three small-sized, table-top robots that go through Linkedin profiles of job applicants and discuss the applicants' information. Robots categorize applicants into ordered levels based on their competencies mentioned. Robots built following minimalist design concepts consist of a cylindrical head and a body that occupy less space. A score is calculated for each candidate and categorized into levels by a model built including Agglomerative Clustering and Gaussian Mixture Model. The model itself identifies the number of levels into which the applicants can be categorized, through the iterations. MUCOR is built for job recruiters who spend more time to find background information about applicants prior to an interview. Conversation among robots and the user creates a Passive Social Interface in which the user does not involve in the conversation, but gain knowledge by listening. The recruiter only has to input the LinkedIn IDs into a mobile application and listen to the conversation among robots. MUCOR was experimented with professional recruiters and their feedback highlighted that the synchronization of speech with the robot's body movements has a fair impact on the user experience about the robot behavior.

Keywords: Human-robot interaction · Multiparty conversation · Passive Social Interface · Role switching · Clustering

1 Introduction

Recruitment is an important part of Human Resource Management (HRM), as it is used to acquire one of the company's most important capital, the intellectual capital [1]. Recruiting the correct person is a key contributor to the success of an

© Springer Nature Switzerland AG 2020
C. Stephanidis et al. (Eds.): HCII 2020, LNCS 12424, pp. 280–293, 2020.
https://doi.org/10.1007/978-3-030-60117-1_21

organisation. It is a direct reflection of the legitimacy and professionalism of a business. The process of recruitment can be expensive and time-consuming. An organization's need is to find the best, spending the least amount of resources. An effective recruitment process should reduce the time involved in searching, screening & interviewing. It would streamline these procedures and make the search more efficient for viable candidates. Therefore, it is mandatory to have an effective recruitment process to attract the right kind of staff who are ideal fits for the needs of the business. To identify the right candidates, recruiters do a background study before recruiting them. This consumes more time when done manually.

Deshpande et al. has proposed a system for resume analysis which saves time spent by recruiters to go through resume and select the best candidate [2]. Using the proposed system the recruiter should input the resumes to get them analysed. The take-up of social media in the society, has naturally led some companies to consider its use as a recruitment tool [1]. As per the findings of a survey conducted by Robert Walters Group which is a specialist professional recruitment group, among job seekers, a LinkedIn profile is perceived as the most important of social media channels, with 85% of survey respondents holding membership of this site [3]. Facebook and Twitter were cited as the second (74%) and third (39%) most popular options [3]. Through social media, recruiters can screen through the candidate's personal life, views, interests, goals as well as their employment history and skills. This also consumes more time since the recruiter need to manually go through each of the profiles. If there is someone who would summarize the profiles and do a comparison for the recruiter it will be more time saving and convenient. But the companies are not willing to spend their resources in such an activity.

As solutions for the above concern, currently some of the organizations have started using innovative products. LinkedIn Recruiter is one such platform [4]. Recruiters can search and call upon potential candidates for interviews via LinkedIn recruiter. Khosla et al. developed a communication robot for conducting job interviews and measuring emotional and cultural fitness of a candidate for a sales job [5]. Matilda is also another social robot that had been developed to shortlist job applicants and interview them for sales positions [6]. Matilda determine whether the interviewee is emotionally fit and culturally compatible for a sales position using her ability to 'read' and respond to human emotions, such as facial cues, voice and touch [7].

Another robot named Vera has been developed to find, call and interview an applicant [8]. Vera has been made to function based on a detailed job description of what the role entails, the skills needed and a script of interview questions provided by the recruiter [9]. Vera can interact with humans naturally, recognizing their emotions [10]. Tengai is also another social robot which is built to avoid the interview results being bias to judges' personal opinion about the interviewee on factors such as outer appearance [11]. Moubayed et al. highlight the importance of having a three dimensional display of faces in the context of face-to-face human-robot interactions [12]. Tengai robot head was designed as a three dimensional head to which an animated computer model is projected.

Almost all of the existing solutions can schedule and conduct interviews for applicants. Some of them are built targeting only a specific job role or an industry. The existing solutions contribute by saving time spent on manual scheduling of interviews. But, the time a recruiter need to spend on gaining background knowledge about the candidates is not yet saved. The existing systems and solutions are only capable of finding candidates who would match the requirements of the company but they does not compare and find the best candidate. Currently available robots judge the candidates only by considering the answers provided and/or their facial expressions and gestures [6]. Also, candidates are not assessed based on their social media presence which is checked by most of the recruiters today. At present most of the companies look into additional information about the candidates' attitudes rather than knowledge. Thus, the recruiters look for convenient and time saving ways to understand the candidates more and filter the best. At the same time, the interviewers' decision is influenced by most of the external and personal factors. A study conducted by researchers at Israel's Ben-Gurion University with the participation of eight judges for ten months, found that parole approvals dipped sharply as the day wore on. After meal breaks, the rate of approval shot back up to its original levels [6]. Similarly this can happen at job interviews too leading to incorrect or bias recruitment decisions. As a solution for this we suggest a robotic interface that can go through the LinkedIn profiles of applicants, analyse the gathered data and discuss about the applicants in an informative manner. Since the robot has no emotional or physical effects on the decisions, the results will not be bias. Also, the recruiter only need to listen to the conversation among the robots to get an idea about the candidates prior to an interview which makes his work more convenient.

The robotic interface was built with three small sized robots with a structure which is designed following minimalist design concepts. It was decided to have three robots instead of one robot reciting the information, so that the recruiter can understand more about the content by listening to the conversation [13]. As found by M. Zarkowski the robots adhering to human-like turn-taking conversations, reduce conversational errors and enhance the communicative performance by 29% compared to an ordinary conversation [14]. Thus we have used multiparty communication among robots so as to improve the communicative performance of the robots resulting a better user experience. Also we selected three robots over two, so that the switching of roles among the robots will make the conversation more interesting to the listener and the flow of the conversation will not be boring.

2   Design of MUCOR

2.1   Hardware Design

When designing the shape of a single robot of MUCOR, one of the major concerns was to make the structure minimal so that the outer appearance of the robots will not interrupt the user listening to the conversation. The whole robotic interface actually occupy three times the space occupied by a single robot. Thus, designing a robot occupying less space was also an important factor to consider. As seen in Fig. 1, a robot is designed with two parts, upper part (Head) and lower part (Base). Both upper and lower parts are cylindrical in shape with no other elements attached. All three robots are given the same shape with same dimensions, also to make the user concentrate more on the conversation without getting distracted.

Fig. 1. A single robot of MUCOR designed following minimalist design concepts. A simple cylindrical shape was given to the robot with no other parts attached. (Color figure online)

Since the robots are to be used by recruiters, mostly at an office environment, MUCOR was designed such that the three robots can be kept on a table occupying less space. The robots of MUCOR are not locomotive. Thus, the robots do not move from one place to another by itself. Each robot move its head up and rotate partially when it's his turn to talk. The whole interface consisting of three robots was made such that it is light in weight and can be easily carried from one place to another.

As seen in Fig. 1, an LED light band was attached to each of the robots to make it easier for the user to identify which robot is in which state of the conversation. Further, when light band is Green in color then that robot is in listening state. When one of the robots gets its turn to talk, the light band will change its color to Blue. Although it was decided as Blue for the speaker, the colors were switched as Green for the speaker and Blue for the others during the experiment for a better user experience, considering concepts of color psychology.

During the conversation among the robots, the role of each robot changes among Speaker, Addressee and Side-participant. As the three robots are engaged in the conversation, the head of each robot will slide up and rotate partially when its role changes to "Speaker". Interior of the robot includes the structure required to move the head up and partially rotate as seen in Fig. 2.

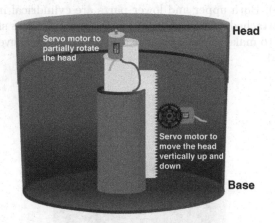

Fig. 2. Internal structure of a robot. Includes the mechanism to lift the head up and rotate.

The base of the robot was designed with a hollow axis in the center, along which the head was slid up as seen in Fig. 2. The mechanism is functioned by a movable rod, a 3D printed cogged bar (rack) which is fixed on the wall of movable rod and a 3D printed cogwheel. The cogwheel was rotated by attaching it to the shaft of a servo motor which is fixed on the inner wall of the base. At the top of the movable rod, another servo motor is fixed whose shaft is attached to the head of the robot. Thus when the shaft of the second motor is rotated, the head of the robot rotates. Also the Arduino boards required to program each robot and the RGB LED stripes are placed inside the robot. The LED stripes were fixed to the roof of the head from inside, such that the light from the LEDs fall onto the surface where the robots are kept as seen on Fig. 1.

2.2 Software Design

In this study the robots' conversation is supposed to be based on the information they collect by going through the LinkedIn profiles of the candidates. Since we could not get permission from LinkedIn Cooperation to access LinkedIn profile information via an Application Programming Interfaces (API), we created a database with fields that match with the fields in a standard LinkedIn Profile. Out of all available fields, what fields to include were decided by studying the interview questions and marking schemes followed by interviewers of recognized Information Technology based organizations. As per the recruiters, each of the fields has its own weight on the total mark a candidate will score. Thus, each of the fields were assigned with a weight which was used when calculating a score

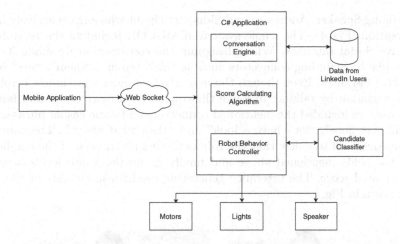

Fig. 3. System architecture of MUCOR.

for each of the candidates. With the consent of the job seekers, information was extracted from their LinkedIn profiles for the selected fields. The database was created on MySQL Workbench and fed to the conversation engine and score generating algorithm, whenever a user calls a data entry by the LinkedIn ID, inputting via the mobile application.

When two people are in a one-to-one conversation both of them should make an effort to engage in the conversation either as a listener or as a speaker. It is the same for a robot and a human who are in a one-to-one conversation. For a robot to carry on the conversation with a human, human should respond to the robot. The human might have to speak, move or show some hand gesture or facial expression to continue the conversation. The robot should also wait for the other person's response to continue with the conversation or any activity he is intended to perform next. Thus, a successful one-to-one conversation need more effort from both parties [15]. Exerting an effort sometimes might be a burden to the user. A busy user who need to get the work done by the robot but do not have enough time to respond and actively engage in a conversation would prefer a better solution where the work get done even without waiting for his response.

In this study we have developed a conversation where there are three roles for the participants. Unlike in a one-to-one conversation where there's only the speaker and the listener, here we have the role of Bystander additionally. A Bystander does not need to speak or actively engage in the conversation. Bystander will listen to the conversation that takes place among the robots. Thus, the social interface that is built in this study is a Passive Social Interface. In a Passive Social Interface the user does not need to participate in the conversation but can gain information without exerting an effort unlike in an Interactive Social Interface where the user has to play the role of a speaker too [15]. For the user (recruiter) of this study, the three robots of MUCOR separately is an Interactive Social Interface because as seen in Fig. 3 the three robots change its roles among Speaker, Addressee and Side-participant who engage actively in the conversation (Fig. 4). The whole system of MUCOR including the recruiter, is a Passive Social Interface. When designing the conversation we made it more human-like by including connectors such as "ah", "emm", "ehem", "err" in the respective instances. Even though the user is a bystander who do not involve in the conversation by talking, to make the conversation more closer and familiar to the user we included the mentioned connectors and some casual phrases such as "hii...over here", "let's have a look" and "then what about". The conversation was designed to a flow that the robots discuss about each of the candidates under the fields mentioned above and finally group them into levels based on the generated score. The utterance generating mechanism consists of the main parts shown in Fig. 5.

Fig. 4. Switching of roles (Addressee, Speaker and Side-participant) among the robots during a conversation

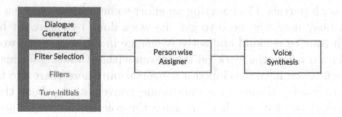

Fig. 5. Utterance generating mechanism of MUCOR

3   Methodology and Experimental Protocol

Studying the data gathered from recruiters of well known IT companies in Sri Lanka, a weight was defined for each of the fields (criteria) mentioned in Table 1.

Based on the predefined weights, a score is calculated for each of the candidates by the Score Calculating Algorithm. A score is calculated for each of the fields and the final score of a candidate is the weighted average of the field wise scores. If n is the number of fields, the total score of a candidate is calculated as shown in Eq. (1).

Total Score of a Candidate

$$= \sum_{i=1}^{n} Score \; for \; the \; i^{th} \; field \times Weight \; of \; the \; i^{th} \; field \quad (1)$$

Table 1. Score calculation for a single candidate based on weights as per Eq. 1

Field	Calculations		
	Score	Weight	Total
Working experience	12	20%	2.4
Bachelors degree	15	15%	2.25
Masters completed	18	10%	1.8
Other academics	12	5%	0.6
Certifications	12	5%	0.6
Publications	0	10%	0
Volunteering experience	14	15%	2.1
Technical skills	13	20%	2.6
Total	**96**	**100%**	**12.35**

The score calculated for each of the candidates are fed to the Clustering Algorithm to group the candidates into levels. In this study we grouped the candidates using an unsupervised clustering algorithm, which is Gaussian Mixture Model (GMM).

We researched on nature of the results when using Gaussian Mixture Model alone to cluster the generated scores. GMM groups the data points that lie in a single distribution to a single cluster. Gaussian Mixture Models are probabilistic models where the probability of a data point belonging to each of the defined distributions is considered. The probability density function of GMM is stated as,

$$f(x|\mu, \sigma^2) = \frac{1}{\sqrt{2\pi\sigma^2}} \times e^{-\frac{(x-\mu)^2}{2\sigma^2}} \quad (2)$$

where x is the input data point, μ is the mean of the distribution and σ is the variance. Mean and the variance of the Gaussian distributions are calculated using Expectation Maximization Algorithm.

When GMM was directly applied to a sample of 30 candidate scores generated from 30 profiles, it resulted in clusters which could not be distinctly

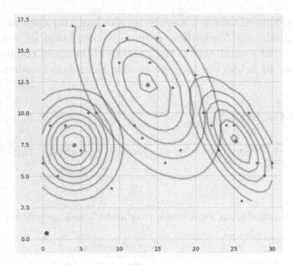

Fig. 6. Overlapped clusters when Agglomerative Clustering was not applied before applying Gaussian Mixture Model.

identified. The clusters were overlapped as seen in Fig. 6. Thus, we introduced Agglomerative clustering to the process before applying GMM to the data set. Agglomerative clustering is a Hierarchical clustering method which initiates its bottom-up approach by considering each data point as a single cluster. In this study we have used Ward linkage which merges clusters such that it generates the smallest increase in cluster's variance. When Agglomerative clustering was applied first and GMM was applied second, it resulted distinct clusters with minimum overlaps as seen in Fig. 7.

To conduct the experiment on MUCOR, initially data of 30 candidates were fed to the database. From the 30 candidates 5 candidates were picked upon their availability to participate at the experiment. The experiment was conducted at an office premises with the participation of 10 recruiters in different designations of the IT industry. The robots were set up in a quite room so that the recruiter is not disturbed by any external interference. The three robots were placed on a table in front of the recruiter who was seated.

Before MUCOR was introduced to the recruiter, he/she is given Curriculum Vitae (CV) of 5 candidates which includes the LinkedIn identity of each of them. The recruiter is asked to follow the normal workflow he/she follows before interviewing a particular candidate. Thus, some of the recruiters read the CV and called the candidate for the interview while some of the recruiters did a background search on LinkedIn. Then, before the candidate was called upon to the interview, recruiter is asked to use MUCOR. The experiment was conducted separately for all the recruiters. One of the sessions is seen in Fig. 8.

While the experimental interviews were conducted, the changes in the user behavior when using MUCOR were observed from a distance. At the very

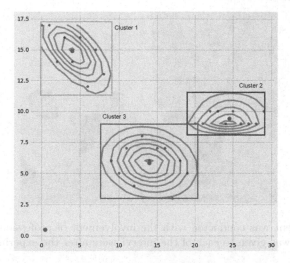

Fig. 7. Distinct clusters when Agglomerative Clustering was applied before applying Gaussian Mixture Model. Cluster 1 is formed with the separation of candidates who got highest scores from the score generating algorithm. Similarly Cluster 2 and Cluster 3 follows in decreasing order of scores.

beginning the recruiters meet MUCOR, their facial expressions showed an excitement towards the experience. Almost all the recruiters who participated in the experiment were listening to MUCOR with great intent throughout.

After the recruiter conduct the interview, he/she is given a questionnaire to provide feedback on areas such as effectiveness, accuracy and user experience of MUCOR. The questions about user experience were segregated into four main sections as follows.

- User journey
- Effect of the design of robots on the experience
- Synchronization of robot behaviors
- Listening experience.

The first set of questions in the questionnaire were focused on user's feedback about the robots' appearance and the first impression about the robots. The responses were gathered to observe whether the user prefer the minimalist design and whether the design helped the user to concentrate on the conversation. Under the subsection Procedure, user's feedback on the flow of events he had to go through until finish listening to the conversation, were gathered. This covers his experience of entering the LinkedIn identities via a mobile application too. Next set of questions were based on how synchronized the robots' movements were with the conversation. This checked whether the user noticed the color changes in the lights which were synchronized with the switching of roles during the conversation. Experience as a Listener section covered user's feedback on the used dialogue style, wording and the flow of the conversation.

Fig. 8. Experiment was conducted with the involvement of professional interviewers. A questionnaire was given to each of the interviewers after the experiment.

The second part of the questionnaire is targeted on user's feedback about the efficiency of the robotic system in summarizing the content to a conversation, calculating scores and grouping them into levels. This section also covers the user's feedback on the accuracy of the grouping.

4   Results

As per the results obtained from the survey, all users have either agreed or strongly agreed on all the three facts; that the first impression was good, robots' size matched its purpose and behavior and that the minimalist design concepts followed had helped him concentrate more on the conversation without being distracted by the outer appearance of the robots.

As seen in Fig. 9, almost all the users who have given a higher rating for the movements in the robot body synchronized with its speech has also rated the behavior of the robots higher. Thus the robot body synchronization with speech has an impact on user's experience on the behavior of the robots.

Also the category wise breakdown and clustering of candidates into levels were rated high. This implies that the clustering algorithm used has given fair enough results leading to a good user feedback. Areas covered in the conversation received somewhat of a moderate rating. As observed in Fig. 10 all recruiters who have given a lower rate for the efficiency of the evaluation of candidates has also given a 2 or 3 rate for the areas covered. This concludes that the areas that were covered in the conversation should be revised to a more summarized structure that will evaluate the candidate faster.

Overall, the feedback resulted that the time and effort of recruiters which was earlier spent for searching for candidate's background information before an interview, is saved with MUCOR.

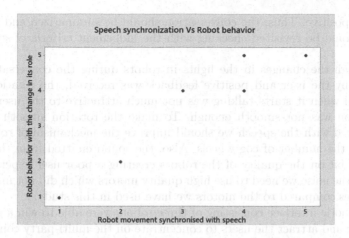

Fig. 9. Feedback on robot movement synchronization with speech compared with the feedback on the robot behavior with change in roles.

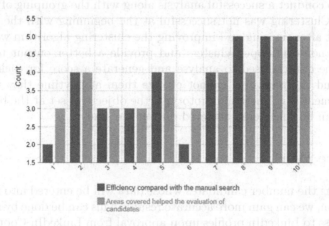

Fig. 10. Feedback on efficiency of evaluation compared with the feedback on areas covered.

5   Discussion and Conclusion

Although this study was planned to connect the application to actual LinkedIn profiles to retrieve candidate information, there was no response from LinkedIn Cooperation on the permission. Thus, we had to move forward with a database created from scratch such that the data fields were same as the fields in a LinkedIn profile. We should have overcome this limitation if we were able to gain permission from LinkedIn Cooperation to access actual LinkedIn profiles.

When the experiment was conducted, although overall results were positive, the feedback on the efficiency of MUCOR or in other words the time taken to complete the full conversation delivering the most important information, was not much positive. Thus, the conversation should be summarized and the fields of data should be revisited checking with the judgement criteria of some more recruiters.

Although the changes in the lights in robots during the conversation were identified by the user and positive feedback was received, the rotation of the robot head when it starts talking was not much attractive to the user because the rotation was not smooth enough. To make the rotation smooth and well synchronized with the speech we should improve the mechanism of rotation by increasing the number of cog wheels. Also, the sound emitted from the motors disturbs a bit on the quality of the robots creating a poor user experience. To overcome the noise we need to use high quality motors which did not match with the finances compared to the motors we have used in this study.

The robotic interface consisting of three robots were able to win a good first impression and attract the users to concentrate on the multi-party conversation through its minimalist design and synchronous behaviors. As per the subjective responses of the recruiters who participated in the experiment, the robots were able to conduct a successful analysis along with the grouping of candidates into levels. Clustering was not successful at the beginning with the overlapped clusters, but after revising and improving the clustering algorithm we were able to generate non-overlapped clusters and provide a better output to the user. Although the criteria used to analyse and generate a score for each candidate was fixed and the recruiters cannot change them at anytime they want, since the development is a functional prototype, the objectives set at the beginning of the study can be considered achieved during the study.

6 Future Work

By increasing the number candidates whose data will be entered into the clustering algorithm, we can gain more accurate results. This can be done by implementing the access to LinkedIn profiles upon approval from LinkedIn Cooperation, so that we can access many accounts to get data. As of now the judging criteria and weights assigned to each of the fields are fixed and should be changed from code level. Developing the solution further so that the recruiter can define his own judging criteria and weights for the fields through a graphical user interface can be added to the system in future. With this development the system becomes open for recruiters from any industry.

Personalizing the three robots into three areas or targeting three recruiters, to be used by a panel of interviewers at the same time, also can be considered as an improvement that can be done in the future. The robotic interface currently does not take in any response from user's end. If the robots are developed to capture user responses via hand gestures, facial expressions, voice and eye movements then the system will be more attractive to users and also will be able to keep the attention of the user to the conversation throughout.

References

1. Oksanen, R.: New technology-based recruitment methods, May 2018. Tampub.uta.fi
2. Deshpande, A., Deshpande, D., Khatri, D., Das, P., Mentor, F., Khedkar, S.: Proposed system for resume analytics. Int. J. Eng. Res. Technol. (IJERT) 5(11), 468–471 (2016)
3. Using social media in the recruitment process, Robertwalters.co.nz, 01 Jan 2019. https://www.robertwalters.co.nz/hiring/hiring-advice/using-social-media-in-the-recruitment-process.html
4. The Industry-Standard Recruiting Tool — LinkedIn Talent Solutions, Linkedin.com, 01 Jan 2000. https://business.linkedin.com/talent-solutions/recruiter. Accessed 18 Feb 2019
5. Khosla, R., Chu, M.-T., Yamada, K.G., Kuneida, K., Oga, S.: Innovative embodiment of job interview in emotionally aware communication robot. In: The 2011 International Joint Conference on Neural Networks (2011)
6. Tarling, S.: Robots muscle in on the job interview, Financial Times, 17 Nov 2016. https://www.ft.com/content/b71f0afa-9c36-11e6-8324-be63473ce146
7. Matilda the robot can read emotions, Latrobe.edu.au (2011). https://www.latrobe.edu.au/news/articles/2011/article/matilda-the-robot-can-read-emotions. Accessed 09 Feb 2020
8. International Journal of Social Robotics - Springer, Springer.com (2019). https://link.springer.com/journal/12369
9. Umoh, R.: Meet the robot that's hiring humans for some of the world's biggest corporations, CNBC, 20 Apr 2018. https://www.cnbc.com/2018/04/20/this-robot-hires-humans-for-some-major-corporations.html. Accessed 18 Feb 2019
10. Robot Vera, Robotvera.com, 01 Jan 2000
11. Welcome to Tengai - the World's First Unbiased Interview Robot, Tengai Unbiased (2019). https://www.tengai-unbiased.com/. Accessed 09 Feb 2020
12. Al Moubayed, S., Beskow, J., Skantze, G., Granström, B.: Furhat: a back-projected human-like robot head for multiparty human-machine interaction. In: Esposito, A., Esposito, A.M., Vinciarelli, A., Hoffmann, R., Müller, V.C. (eds.) Cognitive Behavioural Systems. LNCS, vol. 7403, pp. 114–130. Springer, Heidelberg (2012). https://doi.org/10.1007/978-3-642-34584-5_9
13. Karatas, N., Yoshikawa, S., De Silva, P.R.S., Okada, M.: NAMIDA: multiparty conversation based driving agents in futuristic vehicle. In: Kurosu, M. (ed.) HCI 2015. LNCS, vol. 9171, pp. 198–207. Springer, Cham (2015). https://doi.org/10.1007/978-3-319-21006-3_20
14. Zarkowski, M.: Multi-party turn-taking in repeated human-robot interactions: an interdisciplinary evaluation. Int. J. Social Robot. 11, 693–707 (2019). https://doi.org/10.1007/s12369-019-00603-1
15. Yoshiike, Y., De Silva, P.R.S., Okada, M.: MAWARI: a social interface to reduce the workload of the conversation. In: Mutlu, B., Bartneck, C., Ham, J., Evers, V., Kanda, T. (eds.) ICSR 2011. LNCS (LNAI), vol. 7072, pp. 11–20. Springer, Heidelberg (2011). https://doi.org/10.1007/978-3-642-25504-5_2

Usability Evaluation of Smartphone Keyboard Design from an Approach of Structural Equation Model

Yincheng Wang[1], Junyu Huo[2], Yuqi Huang[1], Ke Wang[1], Di Wu[3], and Jibo He[1(✉)]

[1] Tsinghua University, Beijing 100084, China
{wang-yc18,huangyq17,ke-wang17}@mails.tsinghua.edu.cn,
hejibo666@mail.tsinghua.edu.cn
[2] Tongji University, Shanghai 201804, China
huojun_yu@163.com
[3] Beijing Normal University, Beijing 100048, China
little_woody@163.com

Abstract. Keyboard input is the mainstream input method on smartphones, and the keyboard design plays an important role in input experience. Previous studies mainly measured descriptive variables through inputting phrases to evaluate the usability of keyboard design. However, the development of screen technology brings about more precise and attributional data that could in-depth explore and assess the details of keyboard design. This study adopted a single factor (Phone screen size: Small, 5-in. vs. Large, 6.5-in.) within-subject design through inputting English character pairs to build up the usability evaluation structural equation model. Traditional measurements and new attributional measurements, including Point Pressure, Point Interval Response Time, and Point Duration, were taken as modeling indicators. The results showed that Word Per Minute was not fitted to evaluate keyboard designs with other indicators in both screen sizes, and new attributional measurements could replace this indicator. For the large-screen smartphone, the well-fitted model consists of three factors, including Input Speed (Point Duration and Point Interval Response Time), Objective Experience (Point Pressure and Word Error Rate), and Subjective Feedback. For the small-screen smartphone, the well-fitted model consists of two factors, including Efficiency (Point Interval Response Time, Word Error Rate, and Point Duration) and Subjective Feedback. These findings provide an effective approach to evaluate the usability of keyboard design for future studies, thus enlightening the keyboard optimization method.

Keywords: Keyboard design · Usability evaluation · Structural equation model · Smartphone

1 Introduction

1.1 Importance of Keyboard Design

Keyboard input has always played an essential role in human-computer interaction and is considered as the mainstream input method on smartphones [1, 2]. For instance, the

© Springer Nature Switzerland AG 2020
C. Stephanidis et al. (Eds.): HCII 2020, LNCS 12424, pp. 294–304, 2020.
https://doi.org/10.1007/978-3-030-60117-1_22

daily average users (DAUs) of Sogou mobile keyboard had reached 480 million in the first quarter of 2020 [3]. However, the keyboard design influence input efficiency and comfort [4], and the enlargement of the phone screen has led to poor input experience with various discomfort of fingers, e.g., hand diseases, thumb osteoarthritis, and carpal tunnel syndrome [6–9]. They have to repeatedly change their holding posture and typing posture when they are inputting on the keyboard of the large-screen smartphone, e.g., touching the key P by only using the left hand. Compared with two-handed usage, one-handed usage suffers from more severe discomfort and input inefficiency [10, 11].

The usability of keyboard design could be reflected as input experience of users, including input speed, simple to use, input efficiency [5], and input comfort. Therefore, variable keyboard designs have been proposed to optimize the usability of keyboards on smartphones, e.g., Microsoft WordFlow Keyboard [3], the size-adjustable function of the Sogou mobile keyboard, IJQWERTY [12], and Quasi-QWERTY [13].

1.2 Keyboard Design Evaluation Method

Previous studies mainly adopted input tasks on smartphones to test the effect of the proposed keyboard design. Input tasks on smartphones refer to that participants are recruited to input characters, words, or phrases under different experimental conditions. The input materials were mainly extracted from the phrase library proposed by Mackenzie and Soukoreff [14]. The measurements consisted of two factors, including input performance and subjective experience. First, the input performance could be evaluated by Word Per Minute and Word Error Rate. Second, the subjective experience was evaluated by Subjective Workload, Perceived Usability, Perceived Exertion and Pain, Perceived Performance and Preference, and Intent to Use [1]. Although the inputting task and mentioned measurements were widely used, they were descriptive indicators. They could not in-depth explore the keyboard design with a few specific suggestions that could be proposed for the keyboard design optimization.

With the boom of screen technology, more precise and new attributional user data could be collected to evaluate the usability of keyboard design, and different types of smartphones have different performance. This study developed Point Pressure, Point Interval Response Time, and Point Duration as additional modeling indicators. However, whether previous or additional indicators could form a systematic model and its validity remained unknown.

A keyboard performance evaluation experiment was conducted to test the effect of mentioned indicators and built up a new comprehensive evaluation model, i.e., the structural equation model which could test the hypotheses among observed and latent variables [15, 16], to enlighten the keyboard design and evaluation method [6].

2 Method

2.1 Participants

Thirty-four right-handed participants (17 females; aged from 17 to 32, $M = 22.41$ years, $SD = 2.70$ years) were recruited from Tsinghua University. Half of them were experienced with the QWERTY keyboard, and the others were experienced with the T9 keyboard for at least three months. All of them had normal or corrected to normal vision without the color blindness, color weakness, or physical hand disability, and were familiar with the basic mobile phone operation. All participants were asked only to use their right hand to finish the inputting task.

2.2 Materials

Participants were asked to finish the experiment on Huawei Changxiang 6S (5-in. screen, 294 ppi, 1280 × 720 px, 138 g weight, phone size of 143.5 × 69.9 × 7.6 mm) and Honor 8X (6.5-in. screen, 397 ppi, 2340 × 1080 px, 175 g weight, phone size of 160.4 × 76.6 × 7.8 mm) by inputting pairs of 26 English characters on our self-developed traditional QWERTY keyboard software (Fig. 1). On the keyboard software, the width-height ratio of each letter key was around 0.7, and the software could record and calculate all the general typing events on the phone screen, e.g., Word Error Rate and Point Duration.

Twenty-six English letters were randomly paired to form 26 × 26 = 676 pairs, which were randomly divided into eight groups (four groups for each condition), i.e., 338 pairs for each condition. Pairs instead of words were used in this study to precisely record the input data between two characters.

Fig. 1. The interface of the traditional QWERTY keyboard software. The width-height ratio of each letter key was around 0.7, and that of functional keys (Delete, Space, and Enter) was around 1.4. The height of all keys was the same. The function of Delete and Space was forbidden, and participants could only type the letter key and click the Enter key to finish each trial.

2.3 Procedure

The experimental process of this study was as follows. First, the experimenter informed the participant about the content of the experimental task and let them sign informed consent under the voluntary principle. Second, the experimenter collected the basic information of the participant. Third, the participant was asked to wash their hands and enter into the practice part before the experiment officially began. They needed to finish 50 randomly selected pairs in 150 ms, and the error rate should be less than 20%. Qualified participants then proceeded to the main trials, and they should input each pair as quickly as possible while ensuring accuracy. Fourth, the order of the eight groups of pairs was random, and the participant would randomly complete all questionnaires and scales when each group was finished. After finishing the input task, the participant filled in the total feedback.

2.4 Experiment Design

A single factor within-subject experiment design was adopted in this study. The independent variable was phone size (Small, 5-in. vs. Large, 6.5-in.). Twelve indicators were collected, including Word Per Minute, Word Error Rate, Point Interval Response Time, Point Duration, Point Pressure, Subjective Workload (NASA-TLX; Six facets), Perceived Exertion and Pain (Borg CR10), Intent to Use, Perceived Usability (System Usability Scale), and Perceived Performance and Preference (consisting of three indicators, i.e., Perceived Accuracy, Perceived Speed, and Preference).

Word Per Minute. Word Per Minute referred to the number of words (i.e., pairs in this study) that the participant correctly inputted per minute. The higher the value, the faster the input speed.

Word Error Rate. The pair was considered as an error as long as the participant inputted the wrong character. Word Error Rate referred to the rate of errors in each group of pairs, i.e., the number of errors divided by the number of total pairs in each group. The higher the value, the lower the input accuracy.

Point Interval Response Time. Point Interval Response Time referred to the reaction time or transition time between two touchpoints of each correctly inputted pair, i.e., the start time of the second character minus the departure time of the first character. The higher the value, the worse the typing performance.

Point Duration. Point Duration referred to the dwell time of each correct touchpoint, i.e., the departure time minus the start time of each touchpoint. The higher the value, the longer the time the finger stayed in a posture, which reflected the reaction of participants and affected the finger fatigue.

Point Pressure. Point Pressure referred to the pressure value of each correct touchpoint pressed by fingers on the screen. In reality, most mobile phones do not adopt the real pressure-sensitive screen. Therefore, for them, the collected pressure value is the size of the capacitive object on the touchscreen. In some smartphones, the collected pressure value is ranged from 0 to 1, while in the others, that will be automatically calibrated and do not have the "ceiling effect" in a reasonable range [17].

Subjective Workload. Subjective Workload referred to the workload subjectively perceived by participants, and it was measured by the NASA-TLX 21-point scale which had 6 facets, including Mental, Physical, Time, Performance, Effort, and Frustration. The higher the score, the higher the workload [18].

Perceived Exertion and Pain. Perceived Exertion and Pain was measured by the Borg CR10 Scale which the score was ranged from 0 to 10. The higher the score, the more pain the interface imposed on the users [19].

Intent to Use. Intent to use referred to the likelihood that the participant would intend to use the object, and it was measured by a 10-point scale. The higher the score, the higher the likelihood [20].

Perceived Usability. Perceived Usability referred to the usability of the object perceived by the participant, and it was measured by the System Usability Scale (SUS), which was an industry-standard 10-item and 5-point questionnaire. The responses of each participant would be calculated as a single score ranged from 0–100. The high score indicated that the participant thought that the object had high usability [21].

Perceived Performance and Preference. Perceived Performance consisted of Perceived Speed and Perceived Accuracy, i.e., the input performance subjectively perceived by the participant. The preference referred to how much the participant preferred the object. Perceived Speed, Perceived Accuracy, and Preference were measured by the 50-point scale, and the high score indicated that the participant felt that his input performance was satisfactory and preferred the object [20].

2.5 Data Analysis

We used Amos version 17.0 to build up the model. The value of Point Pressure on 6S was limited and ranged from 0 to 1, while that on 8X was automatically calibrated by touch-screen and unlimited. They represented two kinds of smartphones, and only the value of Point Pressure on 8X was used in this study. For a well-fitted model, $p > .05$, the value of GFI, AGFI, and NFI > 0.90, while the value of RMR and RMSEA < 0.08 [22].

3   Results

Based on the data collected by the self-developed keyboard software, questionnaires, and scales, this study constructs six models (Figs. 2, 3, 4, 5, 6, and 7) to explore whether the 12 indicators could be used to evaluate the usability of keyboard design. Indicators are divided into different factors based on their meanings and definitions.

Models 1, 2, and 3 are for the large-screen smartphone, while Models 4, 5, and 6 are built up for the small-screen smartphone. Subjective Feedback consists of all the data collected by questionnaires and scales, including Subjective Workload with six facets, Perceived Performance and Preference (Perceived Speed, Perceived Accuracy, and Preference), Perceived Usability, Intent to Use, and Perceived Exertion and Pain.

Table 1 shows the results of modeling and the fit indices.

Model 1 consists of Word Per Minute, Word Error Rate, and Subjective Feedback (Fig. 2). Using these three factors to evaluate the usability of keyboard design is the common method highly adopted by researchers and designers. However, the fit indices indicate that Model 1 is not well-fitted (GFI, AGFI, and NFI < 0.9 while RMR and RMSEA > 0.08).

Table 1. Data analysis of different models.

	χ^2	df	p	GFI	AGFI	NFI	RMR	RMSEA
Large screen – Model 1	2.476	78	.530	.565	.414	.324	142.530	.218
Large screen – Model 2	2.285	113	.341	.913	.864	.753	.063	.245
Large screen – Model 3	**2.285**	**113**	**.394**	**.945**	**.901**	**.916**	**.057**	**.062**
Small screen – Model 4	1.485	78	.004	.675	.562	.394	60.485	.125
Small screen – Model 5	3.152	100	.374	.810	.847	.911	.081	.112
Small screen – Model 6	**2.446**	**100**	**.263**	**.991**	**.905**	**.963**	**.054**	**.022**

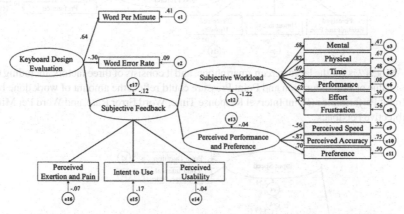

Fig. 2. Model 1 is for the large-screen smartphone, and it consists of three factors, including Word Per Minute, Word Error Rate, and Subjective Feedback.

Model 2 consists of all the indicators involved in Model 1 and adopts the new indicators, including Point Duration, Point Pressure, and Point Interval Response Time (Fig. 3). Three factors are used to evaluate the usability of keyboard design in Model 2, i.e., Comfort, Input Performance, and Subjective Feedback. For the Comfort, the value of Point Duration and Point Pressure could reflect the amount of work done by fingers and finger fatigue. For the Input Performance, Word Per Minute and Point Interval Response Time represent the typing speed, while the Word Error Rate shows the input accuracy. However, the fit indices indicate that Model 2 is not well-fitted (AGFI and NFI < 0.9 while RMSEA > 0.08).

Model 3 consists of Input Speed, Objective Experience, and Subjective Feedback (Fig. 4). Word Per Minute is deleted, and it is replaced by Point Duration and Point Interval Response Time because these two indicators reflect the Input Speed and the whole process of inputting a pair. For the Objective Experience, Point Pressure reflects the physical fatigue and comfort about objective touching events while Word Error Rate reflects the objective input accuracy. The fit indices indicate that Model 3 is well-fitted (GFI, AGFI, and NFI > 0.9 while RMR and RMSEA < 0.08).

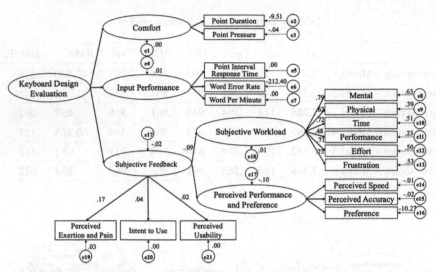

Fig. 3. Model 2 is for the large-screen smartphone, and it consists of three factors, including Comfort (the value of Point Duration and Point Pressure could reflect the amount of work done by fingers), Input Performance (Point Interval Response Time, Word Error Rate, and Word Per Minute), and Subjective Feedback.

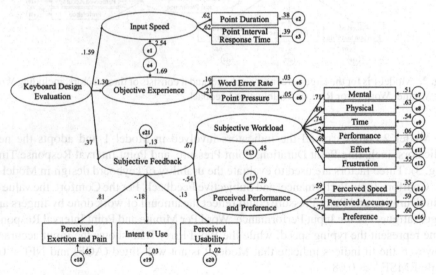

Fig. 4. Model 3 is for the large-screen smartphone, and it consists of three factors, including Input Speed, Objective Experience, and Subjective Feedback.

Model 4 is for the small-screen smartphone, and its structure is the same as Model 1 (Fig. 5). The fit indices indicate that Model 4 is not well-fitted (GFI, AGFI, and NFI < 0.9 while RMR and RMSEA > 0.08).

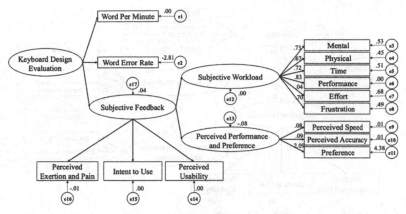

Fig. 5. Model 4 is for the small-screen smartphone, and it consists of three factors, including Word Per Minute, Word Error Rate, and Subjective Feedback.

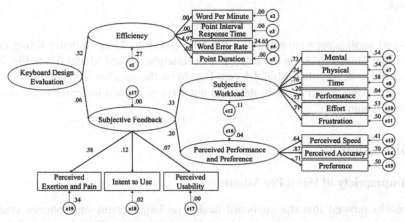

Fig. 6. Model 5 is for the small-screen smartphone, and it consists of two factors, including Efficiency (Word Per Minute, Point Interval Response Time, Word Error Rate, and Point Duration) and Subjective Feedback.

Based on Model 4, Model 5 added Point Interval Response Time and Point Duration, which constitute the Efficiency along with Word Per Minute and Word Error Rate (Fig. 6). However, the fit indices indicate that Model 5 is not well-fitted (GFI and AGFI < 0.9 while RMR and RMSEA > 0.08).

Being identical to Model 3, Model 6 deletes Word Per Minute, and it only consists of two factors, i.e., Efficiency and Subjective Feedback. Efficiency is composed of Point Interval Response Time, Point Duration, and Word Error Rate (Fig. 7). The fit indices indicate that Model 6 is well-fitted (GFI, AGFI, and NFI > 0.9 while RMR and RMSEA < 0.08).

The results indicate that Model 1 and Model 4 (see Fig. 2 and Fig. 5), which consist of all existing indicators that have been commonly adopted, are not suitable for both

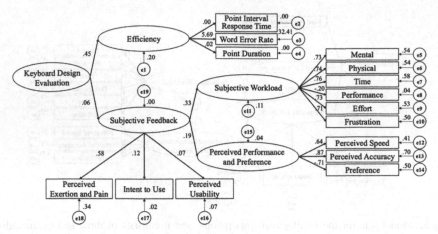

Fig. 7. Model 6 is for the small-screen smartphone, and it consists of two factors, including Efficiency (Point Interval Response Time, Word Error Rate, and Point Duration) and Subjective Feedback.

large- and small-screen smartphones. Model 3 (see Fig. 4) has a better fitting degree than Model 2 (see Fig. 3) on the large-screen smartphone, and Model 6 (see Fig. 7) has a better fitting degree than Model 5 (see Fig. 6) on the small-screen smartphone. This result reveals that Word Per Minute could not serve as a good indicator to measure the keyboard design.

4 Discussion

4.1 Impropriety of Word Per Minute

The results showed that the keyboard design on large-screen smartphones could be evaluated better from three factors: Input Speed, Objective Experience, and Subjective Feedback, including eleven indicators (Model 3, see Fig. 4), i.e., Word Error Rate, Point Interval Response Time, Point Duration, Point Pressure, Subjective Workload, Perceived Exertion and Pain, Intent to Use, Perceived Usability, Perceived Performance and Preference (Perceived Accuracy, Perceived Speed, and Preference). The keyboard design on small-screen smartphones could be evaluated better from two factors: Efficiency and Subjective Feedback, including ten indicators (Model 6, see Fig. 7), i.e., Word Error Rate, Point Interval Response Time, Point Duration, Subjective Workload, Perceived Exertion and Pain, Intent to Use, Perceived Usability, Perceived Performance and Preference (Perceived Accuracy, Perceived Speed, and Preference).

The findings indicated that Point Duration, Point Interval Response Time, and Point Pressure could well fit the evaluation model by replacing Word Per Minute. Word Per Minute is a descriptive indicator and ignored the cognitive variables, confounding factors, and the precise response time between every two characters of one word. Therefore, it is only a rough indicator reflecting speed, which could not directly attribute to input performance or keyboard design.

4.2 Limitation and Future Study

Although several indicators are attributional, these models also could not absolutely explain the disadvantage and advantage of the keyboard design [16]. Compared with the phrases proposed by Mackenzie and Soukoreff [14], character pairs adopted by this study as input materials might lack ecological validity, though they were used to in-depth explore the transition and input performance between two touchpoints. In addition, the sample size could be expanded in the future to further verify the results.

With the development of technology, the usability evaluation of keyboard design on smartphones should be more precise and inspirational. The structural equation model in this study only explored which indicators were well-fitted to evaluate the usability of keyboard design, while whether there are other possible relations (e.g., mediating and moderating effects) among the indicators remain unknown and could be studied in the future. Based on the above, future research could build up a predictive model for the evaluation of keyboard design which could predict all subjective and objective dimensions of user experience through the inputting data that are automatically collected by the keyboard software. It has a high application value for the input method editor company.

These findings provide an effective basic approach and structure to evaluate the usability of keyboard design for future studies and enlighten the keyboard optimization method to researchers and designers with more precise suggestions.

Acknowledgements. This research is supported by Tsinghua University Initiative Scientific Research Program (Ergonomic design of curved keyboard on smart devices).

References

1. Lee, S., Zhai, S.: The performance of touch screen soft buttons. In: SIGCHI Conference on Human Factors in Computing Systems on Proceedings, Boston, pp. 309–318. ACM (2009)
2. Smith, B.A., Bi, X., Zhai, S.: Optimizing touchscreen keyboards for gesture typing. In: 33rd Annual ACM Conference on Human Factors in Computing Systems on Proceedings, pp. 3365–3374, ACM, New York (2015)
3. Sougou Inc. https://corp.sogou.com/newscontent?id=291. Accessed 14 June 2020
4. Zhai, S., Kristensson, P.O.: The word-gesture keyboard: reimagining keyboard interaction. Commun. ACM 55(9), 47–52 (2012)
5. Microsoft Garage. https://www.microsoft.com/en-us/garage/profiles/word-flow-keyboard/. Accessed 14 June 2020
6. Chachris, E.A., Sirinya, V., Lucy, R.: Musculoskeletal disorder and pain associated with smartphone use: a systematic review of biomechanical evidence. J. Hong Kong Physiother. J. 38(2), 77–90 (2018)
7. Chang, J., Choi, B., Tjolleng, A., Jung, K.: Effects of button position on a soft keyboard: muscle activity, touch time, and discomfort in two-thumb text entry. Appl. Ergon. 60, 282–292 (2017)
8. Gehrmann, S.V., Tang, J., Li, Z.M., Goitz, R.J., Windolf, J., Kaufmann, R.A.: Motion deficit of the thumb in CMC joint arthritis. J. Hand Surg. 35(9), 1449–1453 (2010)
9. Kim, G., Ahn, C.S., Jeon, H.W., Lee, C.R.: Effects of the use of smartphones on pain and muscle fatigue in the upper extremity. J. Phys. Ther. Sci. 24(12), 1255–1258 (2012)

10. Girouard, A., Lo, J., Riyadh, M., Daliri, F., Eady, A.K., Pasquero, J.: One-handed bend interactions with deformable smartphones. In: 33rd Annual ACM Conference on Human Factors in Computing Systems on Proceedings, Seoul, pp. 1509–1518. ACM (2015)

11. Lee, M., Hong, Y., Lee, S., Won, J., Yang, J., Park, S.: The effects of smartphone use on upper extremity muscle activity and pain threshold. J. Phys. Ther. Sci. **27**(6), 1743–1745 (2015)

12. Bi, X., Zhai, S.: IJQwerty: what difference does one key change make? Gesture typing keyboard optimization bounded by one key position change from Qwerty. In: 2016 CHI Conference on Human Factors in Computing Systems on Proceedings, San Jose, pp. 49–58. ACM (2016)

13. Bi, X., Smith, B.A., Zhai, S.: Quasi-qwerty soft keyboard optimization. In: SIGCHI Conference on Human Factors in Computing Systems on Proceedings, Atlanta, pp. 283–286. ACM (2010)

14. MacKenzie, I.S., Soukoreff, R.W.: Phrase sets for evaluating text entry techniques. In: CHI 2003 Extended Abstracts on Human Factors in Computing Systems, pp. 754–755. ACM, New York (2003)

15. Bollen, K.A., Long, J.S.: Testing Structural Equation Models, 1st edn. SAGE Publications, Newbury Park (1993)

16. Kline, R.B.: Principles and Practice of Structural Equation Modeling, 4th edn. Guilford Press, New York (2015)

17. Android Developer. https://developer.android.com/reference/android/view/MotionEvent.html#getPressure%28%29. Accessed 14 June 2020

18. Hart, S.G., Staveland, L.E.: Development of NASA-TLX (task load index): results of empirical and theoretical research. In: Hancock, P.A., Meshkati, N. (eds.) Human Mental Workload, pp. 139–183. North-Holland, Oxford

19. Borg, G.: Principles in scaling pain and the Borg CR Scales®. Psychologica **37**, 35–47 (2004)

20. Turner, C.J., Chaparro, B.S., He, J.: Text input on a smartwatch qwerty keyboard: tap vs. trace. Int. J. Hum. Comput. Interact. **33**(2), 143–150 (2017)

21. Brooke, J.: SUS: a retrospective. J. Usability Stud. **8**(2), 29–40 (2013)

22. Wen, Z., Hou, J., Herbert, M.: Structural equation model testing: cutoff criteria for goodness of fit indices and Chi-square test. Acta Psychologica Sinica **36**(2), 186–194 (2004)

Understanding Voice Search Behavior: Review and Synthesis of Research

Zhaopeng Xing[1]([envelope]), Xiaojun Yuan[2], Dan Wu[3], Yeman Huang[3], and Javed Mostafa[1]

[1] University of North Carolina at Chapel Hill, Chapel Hill, NC 27599, USA
zhaopeng@live.unc.edu
[2] University at Albany - State University of New York, Albany, NY 12203, USA
[3] Wuhan University, Wuhan, Hubei, China

Abstract. This article reviews the recent user-oriented studies on voice search interaction and aims to understand how users perform and perceive voice search. With a systematic data collection and screening process, twenty-seven publications were included. We found that the current studies sampled predominantly young and well-educated population. Four topics of interest in voice search were identified, i.e., query characteristics, query strategy, spoken conversational search, user's perception. The result reveals the influences of voice-based modality on users' search behavior and perceptions and the review concludes with potential directions of research on voice search interaction.

Keywords: Voice search · Spoken conversational search · Search behaviour · User-oriented study · Literature review

1 Introduction

With remarkable progress made in automatic speech recognition and natural language understanding, recent years we have witnessed growing interests in voice-based natural language interface, especially in assisting search tasks [1]. These natural language search interfaces allow command-like or spoken conversational search by incorporating voice modality into the query-response search paradigm, such as Google voice search [2], spoken question-answering [3, 4]. This voice-enabled interaction improves users' access to information in the "on the go" and hands-off scenarios (e.g., driving, cooking). It also potentially benefits those who have difficulties, such as the elderly and the blind, in fine-grained control operations and in complex navigation and browsing on graphical interfaces [5–8].

Voice search has become a new research direction in the interactive information retrieval community [9, 10]. Growing research interest has emerged in understanding *how the voice-based modality influences users' information search behavior and perceptions*. Studies that focus on this question are usually user-oriented experiments, with a purpose of informing interface design, implementation and rigorous evaluation of voice search systems (e.g., [11–14]). These studies have presented rich evidence and approached this question from various perspectives. In order to present an integrated

© Springer Nature Switzerland AG 2020
C. Stephanidis et al. (Eds.): HCII 2020, LNCS 12424, pp. 305–320, 2020.
https://doi.org/10.1007/978-3-030-60117-1_23

picture of voice search interaction and meet research interests, this survey synthesizes findings in voice search studies and aims to 1) uncover critical research topics; 2) systematically elucidate voice search behavior and perceptions; 3) identify potential research directions in voice search interaction.

2 Background

The research in voice search interaction lies at the intersection of interactive search behavior, voice modality, and conversational search.

2.1 User-Oriented Study on Search Behavior

Information search has long been studied as a crucial part of work tasks for decades, It is a process where an information seeker acquire information via an information retrieval system to fill existing knowledge gap [15–18]. A main thread of the studies are user-oriented experiments which examined users' search interaction at behavioral and perceptual level [15, 19, 20]. These studies generally focus a specific aspect of the search process (e.g., query behavior, result examination, perceived difficulties, engagement, cognitive load) and examine search interaction under effects of particular conditions (e.g., interaction modality) [19, 21]. In this review, we focus on the studies conducted in controlled settings (e.g., lab experiment) where user's behavior and experience can be captured and interpreted within a certain context [20, 22].

2.2 Spoken and Written Communication

The differences between spoken and written language have been widely evidenced by early studies in both socio-linguistics and human-computer interaction domain. For example, the spoken language 1) tends to be less restricted in linguistic structure and more expressive in information delivery [23]; 2) requires speakers' less effort to generate utterance but can impose additional burdens on the hearer's memory loads due to its linear and sequential format [24, 25]; 3) tends to come with paralinguistic cues which refer to the communication signals other than language (e.g., vocal signals, facial expression) and complement the perception of verbal message for hearers [26, 27].

In search scenarios, the differences have been characterized with regard to information needs and query topics in several large-scale query log analysis studies [2, 28–30]. The voice search is more likely to involve entertainment topics as food, drink, recipes, movies, shopping, travel, local business or to be used for multimedia information search, such as video and music. The voice search, for privacy concerns, is rarely used for sensitive topics, such as health, adult, social network, and personal lifestyle.

2.3 Conversation Search Frameworks

That the search process can be seen as an interactive dialogue is not a new concept. [31] and [32] empirically investigated the information transfer process between a librarian intermediary and patron. This process was interpreted as a question negotiation process where the patron stated the problems as information needs and the librarian performed search by translating the needs into queries that fitted the IR system [15]. [33] realized information seeking strategies proposed by [34] in a form of interactive dialogue, by adopting the "COnversational Roles" communication model [35, 36].

Recent studies have proposed several theoretical frameworks to model the conversational search interaction. [37] characterized the properties of a conversational search agent: 1) allow and assist users to reveal their intents and information needs; 2) reveal itself to users what it can and cannot do; 3) allow both sides to involve and be able to initiate the conversation; 4) maintain context of the dialogue; 5) retrieve and rationalize result set. [38] conceptualized the possible actions of a conversational agent in assisting search: 1) Inquiry: elicit and clarify users' information need/preference by asking questions; 2) Reveal: disclose the founded information; 3) Traverse: navigate search results; 3) Suggest: make suggestions; 4) Explain: explain the results and the rationale of a particular course of action. This study also identified decision-making points of an conversational agent should consider during the search. [39] conceptualized the conversational search interaction based on empirical conversation dataset. It characterized the conversational search process and proposed a model that introduced a discourse perspective to the interpretation of the spoken conversational search interaction.

3 Related Studies

There have emerged several studies regarding the voice search. [40] presented an overview of voice search architecture and revealed technical challenges in design and implementation. [41] discussed the practical challenges of implementing voice search systems and propose a voice search system in South Africa language. [42] discussed potential research opportunities of voice search studies for children, by reviewing the research in children's search behavior and their perceptions of technologies for question answering. [43] reviewed the studies that focused on the user experience with voice-based interfaces and examined evaluation methods. However, none of these studies focused on the question mentioned in the introduction section. This study fills this gap and, to our knowledge, it is the first review about users' voice search behavior and perceptions.

4 Methods

4.1 Data Search Strategy

A systematic search strategy was employed with 34 terms regarding voice interaction (e.g., "voice interface," "spoken interface," "conversational interface") and 22 regarding search interaction (e.g., "information search," "search behavior," "mobile search," "web search"), combined with "and". The search terms were validated by a librarian and a domain expert in information retrieval. The publications were retrieved from four electronic databases: Scopus, Web of Science, Association for Computing Machinery Digital Library, and PubMed. The data were collected in July 2019 and updated in May 2020. The records were then imported to Covidence[1] for data deduplication and following the

---

[1] www.covidence.org.

screening. We observed a growth of research interests in healthcare conversational interaction for both consumers [44, 45] and professionals [46]. PubMed was thus included to explore the studies conducted within a healthcare context. In addition, we examined the reference list of the records in the full-text screening process for potentially relevant publications.

4.2 Inclusion and Exclusion Criteria

The following criteria were created to screen the collected publications: 1) A study should explicitly express interests in understanding users' search behavior and perceptions of voice search interactions, rather than in assessing goodness of a system (e.g., speech recognition error rate, retrieval precision, and recall); 2) human participants should be involved in search tasks that prompted them to elicit search behavior on a real, simulated system or human intermediary.

A publication was excluded if 1) it reported no empirical findings; 2) it focused on search interaction by more than two parties, such as collaborative search [47, 48]; 3) focused on multimedia search (i.e., the retrieval of audio and video collection).

4.3 Data Screening

Two reviewers independently reviewed abstracts and full-texts based on the predefined criteria. Disagreements were resolved in discussion with an adjudicator. The reference of each included record was examined to maximize the specificity. Additional relevant studies were identified and added to the inclusion pool. Cohen's kappa score was calculated at the screening stage to assess the agreement between two reviewers. During the screening, we found that some studies were conducted based on the same user experiment but reported findings from different aspects. We included these related studies for a comprehensive coverage. We also found some studies that reported preliminary findings of an experiment and a full-scale study that provided more details followed. We only included the full-scale studies in this case.

5 Results

The systematic data collection and screening resulted in 27 publications and 21 unique studies[2], as shown in Fig. 1. Two reviewers reached an agreement at a substantial level (Cohen's k = 0.71; agreement = 86.36%). Five publications were identified through a review of reference citations from the primary publications set (N = 48) and three publications were identified in the data update.

The majority of the publications were published in the past 5 years (see Table 1). The study sample size ranges from 10 to 544 participants. Fifteen studies collected participants' age information and only one focused on the population over 65. Fourteen

---

[2] Some of the publications were based on the same experiment but reported different aspects of the findings. In this review, a "study" refers to an experiment and a "publication" refers to a retrieved publication.

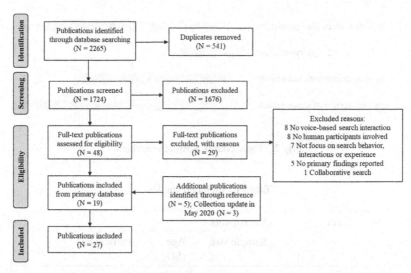

Fig. 1. Prisma diagram

studies reported subject recruitment source and twelve of them recruited the participants from universities or companies (see Table 1). There were no health-related studies found in this study.

The included publications investigated the voice search interaction and perceptions from one or more than one of the following topics (see Fig. 2):

- *Voice query characteristics.* The studies characterized voice queries in comparison with text queries in terms of structural and linguistic features, such as the query length, count, duration, linguistic characteristics, vocabulary use.
- *Query strategy.* The studies examined the query formulation and reformulation tactics used in voice search. This included the adaptive query strategies in response to Automatic Speech Recognition (ASR) errors.
- *Spoken conversational search.* In addition to the query-response paradigm, a conversation search paradigm has been increasingly studied. The studies characterized spoken dialogue acts performed by a seeker (i.e., participants) and an agent (i.e., a simulated system or human intermediary) in information search tasks and explored communication strategies used by the agent (e.g., information inquiry, result presentation, conversational style). The information inquiry (i.e., actively elicit users' needs and refining queries by asking clarification questions) and result presentation (i.e., present search results in audio) in this review have the same definitions as the "Reveal" and "Inquiry" action in [38]. The paralinguistic communication was discussed with respect to the effects of non-verbal cues and conversational style patterns over a search dialogue.
- *User's perception.* Users' perceptions were investigated in terms of preferences, perceived challenges and expectations.

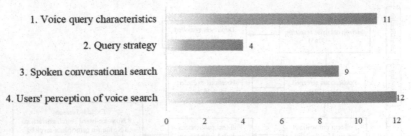

Fig. 2. Topic counts across the studies

Table 1. Included studies

Studies	Year	Participants			Topic
		Sample size	Age (SD)	Participants	
Bigot et al. [25]	2004	48	26 (4.60)	France Telecom employees or trainees	1, 4
Du & Crestani [49]	2005	10	NR	NR	1
Crestani & Du [50]	2006	12	NR	NR	1, 4
Bigot, Rouet, et al. [51]	2007	18	20–27	NR	1, 4
Bigot, Terrier, et al. [52]	2007	48	22–35	NR	1
Bigot et al. [53]	2010	48	30 (9.26)	NR	1
Jiang et al. [11]; Jeng et al. [54]	2013; 2016	20	23.7 (4.72)	University students	1, 2, 4
Trippas et al. [55]	2015	36	NR	NR	3
Kiseleva et al. [56]	2016	60	25.53 (5.42)	University students and full-time employees	3, 4
Begany et al. [57], Yuan & Sa [58]	2016; 2017	44	28.4 (10.2)	University students	1, 4
Kang et al. [59]	2017	544	NR	Online crowdsourcing	1, 2

(*continued*)

Table 1. (*continued*)

Studies	Year	Participants			Topic
		Sample size	Age (SD)	Participants	
Thomas et al.[60, 61], McDuff et al. [62]	2017; 2018	44	25–64	Customers from Microsoft's in-house support services	3
Trippas et al. [14, 39, 63]	2017; 2018; 2020	26	30 (11)	73% are university students; 19% are employed;	3
Arguello et al. [12]	2018	307	NR	Online crowdsourcing	1, 2, 4
Dubiel et al. [64]	2018	22	28.67 (9.9)	University students	3, 4
Kiesel et al. [65]	2018	14	29.2 (8)	University students/staff	3
Ziman & Walsh [66]	2018	15	80.7 (5.9)	NR	4
Kiesel et al. [67]	2019	12	32 (8.4)	University students/staff	3, 4
Sa & Yuan [13]	2019	32	22.3 (15.1)	University students	1, 2, 4
Dubiel et al. [68]	2020	24	NR	University students	3
Kiesel et at. [69]	2020	518*	18–64	Subjects recruited in a university	3, 4

* This study consists of two stages where 500 participants were surveyed and another 18 participants were requested to complete search tasks with a simulated system. NR = Not Reported.

5.1 Voice Query Characteristics

Compared with text queries, voice queries were longer on average in both words and characters and had a longer duration [12, 49–51, 58, 59]. The participants tended to issue more queries in speech than in text in a search task [25, 52, 53, 58]. However, Bigot et al.[25, 53] found that the participants issued shorter queries in semi-structured dialogue with a simulated spoken dialogue system where the responses were predefined.

In addition, the voice queries were linguistically natural and descriptive. They contained higher proportion of the linguistic parts which also presented in human's natural language [13, 58, 59], such as indicative words (e.g., "wh-," "how"), non-noun parts (e.g., verb, preposition), deeper parser structure, full-sentence and noun-phrase structure and frequent use of conversational requests, e.g., "show me," "do not search," "look at."

[49, 50] compared voice and text queries characteristics in English versus Mandarin. They found that voice queries were longer and contained more stopwords and contents in both languages, but that the Mandarin voice queries took a longer duration. The voice query characteristics can also be varied in terms of interaction targets, where participants tended to issue lengthier and more natural queries to human than to real system [12].

5.2 Query Strategy

Voice queries were commonly formulated with subjective criteria and judgments. For example, search criteria can be related to information complexity (e.g., "simple," "easy to understand") and preferences (e.g., "not the healthy side") [12]. [59] reported the same observations in movie search tasks. The participants expressed needs with unstructured and ambiguous information attributes (e.g., "movies with open endings or plot twists), personal emotional experience (e.g., "sad movie"), movie quality (e.g., "interesting characters, clever plot") or the resemblance to other movies (e.g., "something like Pulp Fiction").

The commonly used tactics to modify a voice query included query generalization, specification, term reordering and substitution [11, 13]. The phonetic strategies (e.g., stressing and repeating the partial or entire query) were also used to correct the queries [11, 54], especially in response to ASR errors, which were not observed in text search. The participants attempted to refine a particular part of a query in voice search [13, 59], which was simple in text queries but challenging by spoken language. Specifically, they used three main approaches: 1) use commands or specification operations to specify changes, e.g., "change T to NT," "add/put/insert/remove/delete/no/eliminate NT (after T/before T) (i.e., T stands for a term to be replaced and NT is a new term); 2) add the criteria without making any reference to antecedent queries, assuming system's memory capability; 3) replace a particular part of a query and retain the rest.

5.3 Spoken Conversational Search

Spoken Conversational Acts. [14, 39, 63] described conversational search interaction with a two-level model, i.e., task and discourse, where the search task interaction is based on the discourse interaction (see Table 2). Both of the seeker and agent took responsibilities, as described in the table, for completing search tasks and maintaining dialogue. This study acknowledged the increasingly complex and collaborative relationship between a seeker and an agent, compared with traditional text search. For example, the requests were issued in a wider variety of forms (e.g., query babbling, instructions) in addition to query-like requests and each request can convey multiple dialogue intents. The agent was expected to proactively contribute to search progress, such as making suggestions and determining which results to report. The seeker was also found to request the agent to make decisions in some cases.

Information Inquiry. The seekers demonstrated a different dialogue behavior pattern with the information inquiries by an agent (i.e., more dyads, shorter utterance, a higher proportion of polite and positive utterances) [64, 68]. [65, 67] found that the seekers appreciated the clarification questions asked by the system to help them ambiguate

Table 2. Schema model [39]

Seeker	Discourse Level	Agent
*	**Discourse management:** check if the other understands messages.	*
*	**Visibility of system status:** seeker requests feedback about the current interaction.	*
*	**Grounding:** seeker coordinates the shared information or a common ground for communication.	
*	**Navigation:** seeker navigates search results by instructing the agent.	
	Task Level	
*	**Information request:** request information (i.e., forming, suggesting, refining, confirming, repeating, spelling, or embellishing information requests).	*
	Result presentation: agent presents the results.	
*	**Search assistant:** assistance is requested by seeker or provided by the agent.	*
*	**Search progression:** seeker provides feedback on search progress.	

requests. The seekers also reported particular preferences how a clarification question should be provided, such as providing three alternative interpretations and having a positive tone (e.g., "you probably mean...?").

Results Presentation. The form of audio results presentation can influence the search process. The audio result presentation in general results in longer reception time (i.e., listening), poor task performance, higher mental workload, more request repetitions and lower user satisfaction [51, 55]. More specifically, the audio form changed the way a seeker examined a result, i.e., the latest audio results were favored, rather than the first several results [55]. The way result contents are organized also matters. [68] compared the effects of a list- and summary-based result presentation, respectively, and found that the latter form led to a more successful search outcome. [55] compared the truncated and full-length summary presentations in audio. The truncated results were favored when a single facet query was issued, because of its easiness to recall the response, but vice versa when a multi-faceted query was issued. The result was also found to be presented by the agents as an integration of a search engine result page (SERP) and a particular website content in spoken search dialogue [14], which was thought suitable for the audio-only result presentation. When the SERP was visually available, the answer box and images, which are two common forms of results in Google voice search, were proved to improve seekers' search experience [56].

Paralinguistic Communication. The non-verbal cues by an agent was found to influence seekers' search experience. [62] found that a seeker's negative impression of the communication was associated with the loss of the visual expressiveness of the agent's non-verbal cues. [61] investigated the conversational style patterns in spoken search dialogue (i.e. a tendency to be interpersonal or independent in a dialogue [70]). The style was measured by a set of non-verbal speech features, including the use of personal pronouns, rate of speech, pause/turn-taking, expressive phonology, overlap and restatement). This study found that a seeker attempted to align the conversational style to the agent's over the course of a dialogue, in order to reduce cognitive efforts. However, no best conversational style existed between seekers and agents [61].

5.4 User's Perception

Mixed perceptions were reported in the included studies. Compared with text search, the voice search was thought to be more natural [50], fun to use, innovative and convenient to issue queries [57], especially for those with troubles in typing [66]. The voice search was favored in specific situations, such as in hands-off scenarios (e.g., driving, walking) and when a query contained hard-to-spell vocabularies, but not in public or noisy scenarios [54]. In addition to factual search, they also expected the voice search to assist them with accessing reliable opinions and arguments for decision making and convincing others [69]. Similarly, the participants also preferred to search arguments or opinions by voice query at home either with a friend or alone, rather than in the presence of strangers.

The challenges were mostly associated with voice query formulations and ASR errors. The participants were unsatisfied with the voice search for the onerousness in modifying queries [13] and also for frequent ASR errors [11, 51, 54, 56, 59]. These challenges further resulted in unexpected useless search results and repeated but unnecessary queries. The lack of confidence and familiarities with voice search coincides with such challenges. Participants were concerned about a system's incapability of understanding queries or finding useful information [12] and showed lower confidence in voice search systems [69]. Participants expected to have text input as an alternative to efficiently generate queries [50, 57, 58] and to address the ASR errors [54]. In addition, the older adults encountered greater challenges than their younger counterpart [66]. They were more likely to be interrupted by the system, which led to more errors when having difficulties in verbalizing queries. Their preference for text input seems more intense because of its higher familiarity and easier access to query suggestions [66].

6 Discussion

We reviewed 27 publications (i.e., 21 studies) and systematically synthesized the topics and findings. Most of the included studies are published in recent five years which may indicates that voice search is still in its early stage and draws increasing attention.

A sample bias can be apparently observed towards the young and well-educated population. This overlooked user cohorts that can potentially benefit from using voice search. For example, the users with visual impairments [5] and advanced age [71, 72] have been found to experience greater challenges on searching, navigating, and examining information on the graphical search engine. Future studies should give attention to these cohorts and explore the impact of voice search on their interaction pattern.

It is also obvious that the voice modality brings in the influences on search behavior in terms of query characteristics, query strategies, and perceptions. It also introduced the influential factors that do not exist in text search, such as ASR errors and paralinguistic communication. The participants report the lack of experience and confidence but generally acknowledge the advantages of voice search and have expectations of how voice search should function.

The spoken conversational search can be seen as an advanced extension of voice search paradigm which incorporates human-like language and dialogue strategies into search interaction and enables a more collaborative and proactive search pattern than traditional web search [39]. This pattern transition is reflected in a system's the interactive dialogue acts, its increasing decision-making space to perform search and communication functions, and its potential influences of the paralinguistic cues.

The voice search, along with spoken conversational search, has received intensive research interest and some research agendas have been recently proposed [9, 73]. Based on the findings in this review, we highlight the following research topics which are insufficiently investigated and potentially critical for improving voice search experience.

- *Multimodal input for search tasks.* A multimodal input modality allows users to flexibly switch between modalities to take control of search process (e.g., correct ASR errors and partially modify the queries). In addition, it can provide multiple channels to interpret users' intentions. People express needs not only explicitly through query but also implicitly through connotations. For example, "- How about this website?" (Agent) "- It's interesting" (User), where the user may indicate a lack of interest in the results. This interpretation requires an integration from multiple input streams in addition to word sequence, such as the facial expression. Future studies are needed to understand how to fuse such multimodal input signals to interpret user's explicit and implicit intents in voice search.
- *Proper participation of spoken conversational search system.* As the user-system interaction becomes more collaborative and interdependent in spoken conversational search, the system is expected to communicate in a naturalistic way that advances users' intention and fulfill information needs, without dominating the interaction or overwhelming users with results. This requires systems to utilize the proper communication strategies aligned with social norms in assisting search tasks [74]. Some efforts have recently been seen to incorporate social communication into the understanding of voice search (e.g., reveal the understanding of user's requests and elicit user's needs by asking clarification questions [37, 38]), but further empirical studies are still needed to understand how to enable a system to be socially naturalistic and proper in search tasks.
- *Argumentation and sentiment in voice search.* As observed in the voice queries and the users' expectations, participants tended to express opinions and judgments, and inquire arguments and evidence using voice search. This tendency induces some interesting research questions. For example, the users' assessors to the relevance and quality of a result may no longer be restricted to its content and source but also include how logical, persuasive and contributive the result is to the resolution of information needs [75]. How to retrieve or construct arguments and present evidence based on such subjective criteria can be challenging. Another unsolved question can be the interpretation of users' sentiment in voice search. As the availability of paralinguistic cues and flexible expressions, the query becomes affective and involves one's sentiments. To better

understand such affective signals will potentially contribute to the decoding of users' opinions and perceptions of the information relevance and quality.

- *Privacy concerns.* One of the main concerns about voice-based interfaces is privacy issue. The use of such modality is sensitive to public surroundings and information of private nature [76, 77]. This is also the case in search tasks, especially in some privacy-sensitive cases, such as health information access [78]. Due to the natural form of the conversational search and the system's proactive engagement, users may disclose information more than it is needed without awareness. It thus critical to avoid improper prompts to users and able to alert users to the potential leakage of private information. In addition, future studies should also examine users' perceptions of privacy concerns under voice search context, which is insufficiently discussed in the included studies.

This review should be interpreted with its limitations. Given the scope of this review, this review does not include the studies that address the design and evaluation of voice search systems. These studies may also, to some extent, provide observations regarding voice search behavior and perceptions. Future studies can expand the scope to this type of studies. In addition, it is challenging to synthesize the findings in a consistent manner due to the limited number of studies and the variability of the methods applied in these studies. Some studies reported quantitative findings while some were qualitative and narrative, which results in weak comparability. It is also possible that some behavior measurements were not captured or insufficiently reported in these studies. These limitations call for future works that involve a broader scope and more rigorous synthesis and analysis approaches.

7   Conclusion

We review and synthesize the findings of the current research in voice search to understand users' search interaction and perceptions. Four topics of interest were identified, including query characteristics, query strategy, spoken conversational search, user's perception. As an emerging research topic in IR, the voice search still has many more questions than answers in users' behavior. We expect the voice search to be able to benefit a wider variety of users and involve in everyday search task in a more capable and error-free manner. Future studies can contribute to the understanding of voice search regarding the multimodal input, proper involvement of a spoken conversational search agent, argumentation and sentiment, and privacy concerns.

Acknowledgments. The authors would like to appreciate the support from the librarians at Health Science Library at the University of North Carolina at Chapel Hill. This study is partially supported by the Carolina Health Informatics Program and the Laboratory of Applied Informatics Research at the University of North Carolina at Chapel Hill. The authors also thank the reviewers for thoughtful and thorough review.

References

1. Hearst, M.A.: Search User Interfaces. Cambridge University Press, New York (2009)

2. Schalkwyk, J., et al.: Your word is my command: google search by voice: a case study. In: Neustein, A. (ed.) Advances in Speech Recognition, pp. 61–90. Springer, Boston (2010). https://doi.org/10.1007/978-1-4419-5951-5_4s
3. Wilcock, G.: WikiTalk: a spoken Wikipedia-based open-domain knowledge access system. In: Proceedings of the Workshop on Question Answering for Complex Domains. p. 57 (2010)
4. Lee, C.-H., Wang, S.-M., Chang, H.-C., Lee, H.-Y.: ODSQA: open-domain spoken question answering dataset. In: 2018 IEEE Spoken Language Technology Workshop (SLT), pp. 949–956. IEEE (2018)
5. Sahib, N.G., Tombros, A., Stockman, T.: A comparative analysis of the information-seeking behavior of visually impaired and sighted searchers. J. Am. Soc. Inf. Sci. 63, 377–391 (2012)
6. Smith, A.L., Chaparro, B.S.: Smartphone text input method performance, usability, and preference with younger and older adults. Hum. Factors 57, 1015–1028 (2015)
7. Vtyurina, A., Fourney, A., Morris, M.R., Findlater, L., White, R.W.: Bridging screen readers and voice assistants for enhanced eyes-free web search. In: Liu, L., White, R. (eds.) The World Wide Web Conference on – WWW 2019, pp. 3590–3594. ACM Press, New York (2019)
8. Oard, D.W.: Query by babbling: a research agenda. In: Proceedings of the First Workshop on Information and Knowledge Management for Developing Region - IKM4DR 2012, p. 17. ACM Press, New York (2012)
9. Trippas, J.R., Thomas, P., Spina, D., Joho, H.: Third International Workshop on Conversational Approaches to Information Retrieval (CAIR 2020): Full-Day Workshop at CHIIR 2020. Proceedings of the 2020 Conference on Human Information Interaction and Retrieval, pp. 492–494. ACM, New York (2020)
10. Culpepper, J.S., Diaz, F., Smucker, M.D.: Research frontiers in information retrieval. SIGIR Forum. 52, 34–90 (2018)
11. Jiang, J., Jeng, W., He, D.: How do users respond to voice input errors? Lexical and phonetic query reformulation in voice search. In: Proceedings of the 36th International ACM SIGIR Conference on Research and Development in Information Retrieval – SIGIR 2013, p. 143. ACM Press, New York (2013)
12. Arguello, J., Choi, B., Capra, R.: Factors influencing users' information requests. ACM Trans. Inf. Syst. 36, 1–37 (2018)
13. Sa, N., Jenny Yuan, X.: Examining users' partial query modification patterns in voice search. J. Assoc. Inf. Sci. Technol. 71(3), 251–263 (2019)
14. Trippas, J.R., Spina, D., Cavedon, L., Joho, H., Sanderson, M.: Informing the design of spoken conversational search: perspective paper. In: Proceedings of the 2018 Conference on Human Information Interaction & Retrieval, CHIIR 2018, pp. 32–41. ACM Press, New York (2018)
15. Ingwersen, P., Järvelin, K.: The turn: Integration of information seeking and retrieval in context. Springer, Dordrecht (2005). https://doi.org/10.1007/1-4020-3851-8
16. Ruthven, I., Kelly, D. (eds.): Interactive Information Seeking, Behaviour and Retrieval. Facet (2011)
17. Vakkari, P.: Task-based information searching. Ann. Rev. Info. Sci. Tech. 37, 413–464 (2005)
18. Belkin, N.J., Oddy, R.N., Brooks, H.M.: Ask for information retrieval: part i. background and theory. J. Doc. 38, 61–71 (1982)
19. Kelly, D.: Methods for evaluating interactive information retrieval systems with users. FNT Inf. Retrieval 3, 1–224 (2009)
20. White, R.W.: Interactions with Search Systems. Cambridge University Press, Cambridge (2016)
21. Liu, J., Shah, C.: Interactive IR User Study Design, Evaluation, and Reporting. Synthesis Lectures on Information Concepts, Retrieval, and Services, vol. 11, p. i–75 (2019)
22. Grimes, C., Tang, D., Russell, D.: Query logs alone are not enough. In: Presented at the WWW 2007 Workshop on Query Log Analysis: Social and Technological Changes (2007)

23. Akinnaso, F.N.: On the differences between spoken and written language. Lang. Speech **25**, 97–125 (1982)

24. Zoltan-Ford, E.: How to get people to say and type what computers can understand. Int. J. Man Mach. Stud. **34**, 527–547 (1991)

25. Bigot, L.L., Jamet, E., Rouet, J.-F.: Searching information with a natural language dialogue system: a comparison of spoken vs written modalities. Appl. Ergon. **35**, 557–564 (2004)

26. Roberts, C., Street, B.: Spoken and written language. In: Coulmas, F. (ed.) The Handbook of Sociolinguistics, pp. 168–186. Blackwell Publishing Ltd, Oxford (2017)

27. Jurafsky, D., Ranganath, R., McFarland, D.: Extracting social meaning. In: Association for Computational Linguistics (2009)

28. Guy, I.: The characteristics of voice search: comparing spoken with typed-in mobile web search queries. ACM Trans. Inf. Syst. **36**, 1–28 (2018)

29. Yi, J., Maghoul, F.: Mobile search pattern evolution: the trend and the impact of voice queries. In: Proceedings of the 20th International Conference Companion on World Wide Web – WWW 2011, p. 165. ACM Press, New York (2011)

30. Kamvar, M., Beeferman, D.: Say what? Why users choose to speak their web queries. In: INTERSPEECH 2010. isca-speech.org (2010)

31. Ingwersen, P.: Search procedures in the library—analysed from the cognitive point of view. J. Doc. **38**, 165–191 (1982)

32. Belkin, N.J.: Cognitive models and information transfer. Soc. Sci. Inf. Stud. **4**, 111–129 (1984)

33. Belkin, N.J., Cool, C., Stein, A., Thiel, U.: Cases, scripts, and information-seeking strategies: on the design of interactive information retrieval systems. Expert Syst. Appl. **9**, 379–395 (1995)

34. Belkin, N.J., Marchetti, P., Cool, C.: BRAQUE: design of an interface to support user interaction in information retrieval. Inf. Process. Manage. **29**, 325–344 (1993)

35. Stein, A., Thiel, U.: A conversational model of multimodal interaction. In: Proceedings of the 11th National Conference on Artificial Intelligence (AAAI 1993), pp. 283–288. AAAI Press/The MIT Press, Menlo Park (1993)

36. Sitter, S., Stein, A.: Modeling the illocutionary aspects of information-seeking dialogues. Inf. Process. Manage. **28**, 165–180 (1992)

37. Radlinski, F., Craswell, N.: A theoretical framework for conversational search. In: Proceedings of the 2017 Conference on Conference Human Information Interaction and Retrieval – CHIIR 2017, pp. 117–126. ACM Press, New York (2017)

38. Azzopardi, L., Dubiel, M., Halvey, M., Dalton, J.: Conceptualizing agent-human interactions during the conversational search process (2018)

39. Trippas, J.R., Spina, D., Thomas, P., Sanderson, M., Joho, H., Cavedon, L.: Towards a model for spoken conversational search. Inf. Process. Manage. **57**, 102162 (2020)

40. Wang, Y.-Y., Yu, D., Ju, Y.-C., Acero, A.: An introduction to voice search. IEEE Signal Process. Mag. **25**, 28–38 (2008)

41. Barnard, E., Schalkwyk, J., Heerden, C.V., Moreno, P.J.: Voice search for development (2010)

42. Lovato, S.B., Piper, A.M.: Young children and voice search: what we know from human-computer interaction research. Front. Psychol. **10**, 8 (2019)

43. Kocaballi, A.B., Laranjo, L., Coiera, E.: Understanding and measuring user experience in conversational interfaces. Interact. Comput. **31**, 192–207 (2019)

44. Laranjo, L., et al.: Conversational agents in healthcare: a systematic review. J. Am. Med. Inform. Assoc. **25**, 1248–1258 (2018)

45. Vaidyam, A.N., Wisniewski, H., Halamka, J.D., Kashavan, M.S., Torous, J.B.: Chatbots and conversational agents in mental health: a review of the psychiatric landscape. Can. J. Psychiatry (2019). https://doi.org/10.1177/0706743719828977

46. Kumah-Crystal, Y.A., Pirtle, C.J., Whyte, H.M., Goode, E.S., Anders, S.H., Lehmann, C.U.: Electronic health record interactions through voice: a review. Appl. Clin. Inf. **9**, 541–552 (2018)
47. Shah, C., González-Ibáñez, R.: Evaluating the synergic effect of collaboration in information seeking. In: Proceedings of the 34th International ACM SIGIR Conference on Research and Development in Information – SIGIR 2011, p. 913. ACM Press, New York (2011)
48. Avula, S., Arguello, J., Capra, R., Dodson, J., Huang, Y., Radlinski, F.: Embedding search into a conversational platform to support collaborative search. In: Proceedings of the 2019 Conference on Human Information Interaction and Retrieval, CHIIR 2019, pp. 15–23. ACM Press, New York (2019)
49. Du, H., Crestani, F.: Spoken versus written queries for mobile information access: an experiment on Mandarin Chinese. In: Su, K.-Y., Tsujii, J., Lee, J.-H., Kwong, O.Y. (eds.) IJCNLP 2004. LNCS (LNAI), vol. 3248, pp. 745–754. Springer, Heidelberg (2005). https://doi.org/10.1007/978-3-540-30211-7_79
50. Crestani, F., Du, H.: Written versus spoken queries: a qualitative and quantitative comparative analysis. J. Am. Soc. Inf. Sci. **57**, 881–890 (2006)
51. Bigot, L.L., Rouet, J.-F., Jamet, E.: Effects of speech- and text-based interaction modes in natural language human-computer dialogue. Hum Fact. **49**, 1045–1053 (2007)
52. Bigot, L.L., Terrier, P., Amiel, V., Poulain, G., Jamet, E., Rouet, J.-F.: Effect of modality on collaboration with a dialogue system. Int. J. Hum Comput Stud. **65**, 983–991 (2007)
53. Bigot, L.L., Terrier, P., Jamet, E., Botherel, V., Rouet, J.-F.: Does textual feedback hinder spoken interaction in natural language? Ergonomics **53**, 43–55 (2010)
54. Jeng, W., Jiang, J., He, D.: Users' perceived difficulties and corresponding reformulation strategies in Google voice search. J. Libr. Inf. Stud. **14**, 25–39 (2016)
55. Trippas, J.R., Spina, D., Sanderson, M., Cavedon, L.: Results presentation methods for a spoken conversational search system. In: Proceedings of the First International Workshop on Novel Web Search Interfaces and Systems – NWSearch 2015, pp. 13–15. ACM Press, New York (2015)
56. Kiseleva, J., et al.: Understanding user satisfaction with intelligent assistants. In: Proceedings of the 2016 ACM on Conference on Human Information Interaction and Retrieval – CHIIR 2016, pp. 121–130. ACM Press, New York (2016)
57. Begany, G.M., Sa, N., Yuan, X.: Factors affecting user perception of a spoken language vs. textual search interface: a content analysis. Interact. Comput. **28**(2), 170–180 (2016)
58. Yuan, X.J., Sa, N.: User query behaviour in different task types in a spoken language vs. textual interface: a Wizard of Oz experiment. In: ISIC, the Information Behaviour Conference, Zadar, Croatia, 20–23 September 2016 (2017). Part 2. Information Research, 22(1), paper isic1615. IRinformationrearch
59. Kang, J., Condiff, K., Chang, S., Konstan, J.A., Terveen, L., Harper, F.M.: Understanding how people use natural language to ask for recommendations. In: Proceedings of the Eleventh ACM Conference on Recommender Systems - RecSys 2017, pp. 229–237. ACM Press, New York (2017)
60. Thomas, P., McDuff, D., Czerwinski, M., Craswell, N.: MISC: a data set of information-seeking conversations. Presented at the August 2017
61. Thomas, P., Czerwinski, M., McDuff, D., Craswell, N., Mark, G.: Style and alignment in information-seeking conversation. In: Proceedings of the 2018 Conference on Human Information Interaction&Retrieval, CHIIR 2018, pp. 42–51. ACM Press, New York (2018)
62. McDuff, D., Thomas, P., Czerwinski, M., Craswell, N.: Multimodal analysis of vocal collaborative search: a public corpus and results. In: Proceedings of the 19th ACM International Conference on Multimodal Interaction, ICMI 2017, pp. 456–463. ACM Press, New York (2017)

63. Trippas, J.R., Spina, D., Cavedon, L., Sanderson, M.: How do people interact in conversational speech-only search tasks: a preliminary analysis. In: Proceedings of the 2017 Conference on Conference Human Information Interaction and Retrieval – CHIIR 2017, pp. 325–328. ACM Press, New York (2017)

64. Dubiel, M., Halvey, M., Azzopardi, L.: Investigating how conversational search agents affect user's behaviour, performance and search experience. In: ACM SIGIR CAIR Workshop (CAIR 2018), New York, NY, USA. strathprints.strath.ac.uk (2018)

65. Kiesel, J., Bahrami, A., Stein, B., Anand, A., Hagen, M.: Toward voice query clarification. In: The 41st International ACM SIGIR Conference on Research & Development in Information Retrieval, SIGIR 2018, pp. 1257–1260. ACM Press, New York (2018)

66. Ziman, R., Walsh, G.: Factors affecting seniors' perceptions of voice-enabled user interfaces. In: Extended Abstracts of the 2018 CHI Conference on Human Factors in Computing Systems, CHI 2018, pp. 1–6. ACM Press, New York (2018)

67. Kiesel, J., Bahrami, A., Stein, B., Anand, A., Hagen, M.: Clarifying false memories in voice-based search. In: Proceedings of the 2019 Conference on Human Information Interaction and Retrieval, CHIIR 2019, pp. 331–335. ACM Press, New York (2019)

68. Dubiel, M., Halvey, M., Azzopardi, L., Anderson, D., Daronnat, S.: Conversational strategies: impact on search performance in a goal-oriented task. In: Proceedings of the 2020 Conference on Human Information Interaction and Retrieval. ACM, New York (2020)

69. Kiesel, J., Lang, K., Wachsmuth, H., Hornecker, E., Stein, B.: Investigating expectations for voice-based and conversational argument search on the web. In: Proceedings of the 2020 Conference on Human Information Interaction and Retrieval, pp. 53–62. ACM, New York (2020)

70. Tannen, D.: Conversational Style: Analyzing Talk Among Friends. Oxford University Press, Oxford (2005)

71. Sanchiz, M., Chin, J., Chevalier, A., Fu, W.T., Amadieu, F., He, J.: Searching for information on the web: impact of cognitive aging, prior domain knowledge and complexity of the search problems. Inf. Process. Manage. 53, 281–294 (2017)

72. Dommes, A., Chevalier, A., Lia, S.: The role of cognitive flexibility and vocabulary abilities of younger and older users in searching for information on the web. Appl. Cogn. Psychol. 25, 717–726 (2011)

73. André, E., et al.: Conversational search. In: Dagstuhl Seminar 19461, vol. 9, pp. 34–83 (2020)

74. Thomas, P., Czerwinski, M., McDuff, D., Craswell, N.: Theories of conversation for conversational IR. In: Presented at the SIGIR 3th International Workshop on Conversational Approaches to Information Retrieval (CAIR 2020), March 2020

75. Wachsmuth, H., Stein, B., Ajjour, Y.: "PageRank" for argument relevance. In: Proceedings of the 15th Conference of the European Chapter of the Association for Computational Linguistics, pp. 1117–1127. Association for Computational Linguistics, Stroudsburg (2017)

76. Easwara Moorthy, A., Vu, K.-P.L.: Privacy concerns for use of voice activated personal assistant in the public space. Int. J. Hum. Comput. Interact. 31, 307–335 (2015)

77. Lau, J., Zimmerman, B., Schaub, F.: Alexa, are you listening? Proc. ACM Hum.-Comput. Interact. 2, 1–31 (2018)

78. Hadian, M., Altuwaiyan, T., Liang, X., Li, W.: Privacy-preserving voice-based search over mHealth data. Smart Health. 12, 24–34 (2018)

Evaluation of Speech Input Recognition Rate of AR-Based Drawing Application on Operation Monitor for Communication Support During Endoscopic Surgery

Takuto Yajima[1](✉), Takeru Kobayashi[1], Kentaro Kotani[1], Satoshi Suzuki[1], Takafumi Asao[1], Kazutaka Obama[2], Atsuhiko Sumii[2], and Tatsuto Nishigori[2]

[1] Department of Mechanical Engineering, Kansai University, Suita, Japan
{k605214,k749499,kotani,ssuzuki,asao}@kansai-u.ac.jp
[2] Department of Surgery, Kyoto University, Kyoto, Japan
{kobama,asmii,nsgr}@kuhp.kyoto-u.ac.jp

Abstract. In endoscopic surgery, the surgeon and the assistant use both hands to proceed with the surgical operation. Therefore, the excision site cannot be shown by hand from the image inside the body displayed on the endoscopic monitor. Since there is a lack of communication between the surgeon and the assistant, it is necessary to have a system that indicates the excision point and prevents discrepancies between the surgeon and the assistant. Therefore, we developed a communication system that conveys the excision site from the in-vivo image on the endoscope monitor by operating the head movement and speech input without releasing the hand from the surgical instrument. There was a problem in using speech input in a noisy environment, such as an operation site. In order to make the system generate as few errors as possible, it was necessary to use words with high recognition performance and few unintentional behaviors by mistakenly recognized voice commands. In this experiment, the performance of recognition in the operating room environment and the possibility of unintentional operation were evaluated for each syllable number of words. As a result, the high recognition rate was possible with commands of 3 to 7 syllables, and commands with four or fewer syllables may induce unintentional system behavior. Consequently, we proposed to use the words of 5–7 syllables, which were highly recognized and have few wrong recognitions for voice commands.

Keywords: Head mounted display · Speech recognition · Endoscopic surgery · Usability

1 Introduction

With the advance of medical technology in recent years, endoscopic surgery has appeared characterizing with its minimal invasiveness, such as not making large incisions in and less pain after surgery compared with conventional laparotomy. Demand for endoscopic

© Springer Nature Switzerland AG 2020
C. Stephanidis et al. (Eds.): HCII 2020, LNCS 12424, pp. 321–331, 2020.
https://doi.org/10.1007/978-3-030-60117-1_24

surgery is rapidly increasing and the application of this surgical technique is expected to increase in the future [1, 2].

In typical endoscopic surgery procedure, the surgeon and assistant facing each other, require them to use both hands to expand the surgical field of view for the operations such as resection [3]. Therefore, in endoscopic surgery, it is not possible to indicate the resected part directly from the image of the body cavity displayed on the monitor. Nevertheless, it is necessary to convey information about the procedure orally. There is no doubt that this difficulty in communication between the surgeon and the assistant is a factor that may cause potential medical errors.

To solve these problems, we developed the AR-based head drawing system for medical operation (ARHD), where we use an optical see-through head-mounted display (HMD) as a communication support system for endoscopic surgery. The ARHD allows head motion and voice input to generate drawings holographically overlapped with monitors. Thus the operators can perform hands-free communication with assistants, and they do not have to move their hands away from the surgical tool during communication. In the previous paper [4], we reported the usability of the system's input method, especially evaluating whether the system can satisfy the drawing quality during the real operation.

Given the practical use of ARHD, improving the accuracy of the speech recognition function, which is one of the input methods, has become a major issue. There is an environment with various noises at the operating site, such as machine driving sounds and conversation, irrelevant to surgeon-assistant communication. Such noise may cause incorrect operation due to false speech recognition of the system. Moreover, surgery may be prolonged if ARHD does not readily recognize the command and take appropriate actions. Prolonged surgery means that not only the surgeon, assistants, anesthesiologists, and other staff involved in the operation, but also the burden on the patient itself increases [5, 6].

The objective of this study is to select the voice command to use for ARHD operation to optimize the voice recognition of the drawing application in the operating room environment to lead to the safer use of ARHD. In this study, we applied the method of Kanno et al. [7], where they conducted experiments on speech recognition in a noisy environment to propose an improved method with high noise immunity. They express various noise conditions by the S/N ratio in a speech recognition experiment under a noisy environment and calculate the command recognition rate at different S/N ratios. Nakagawa et al. [8] concluded that word length was the main factor affecting recognition accuracy. Therefore, we decided to select the number of syllables of words with high noise resistance and confirm to apply the words with that number of syllables in voice commands.

2 Drawing Application

Endoscopic surgery is a surgery performed while watching the in-vivo image on an endoscopic monitor [1]. Unlike general surgery, several 5-10 mm holes are made in the patient's abdomen, and surgical instruments such as an endoscope and forceps are inserted to perform surgery, as illustrated in Fig. 1.

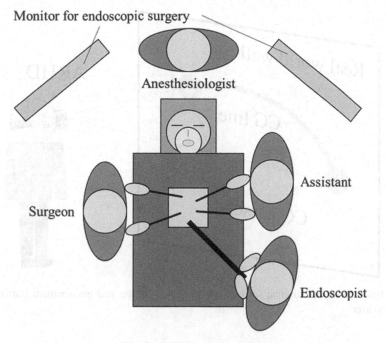

Fig. 1. Endoscopic surgery.

Since the system developed in this research was operated by head movement and voice input, operators (surgeons and assistants) wearing ARHD were able to operate hands-free. Therefore, operators do not have to take their hands off the surgical instrument while using the system. When the surgeon draws a line to convey instructions to the assistant, the system starts to draw the line by recognizing the command that is the signal to start drawing by voice input, and the line is drawn according to the movement of the surgeon's head. Also, ARHD was designed to finish drawing lines, delete drawn lines, and input commands corresponding to line thickness and color of the drawings by voice. Using this system, it becomes possible for operators to freely communicate the excision site from the in-vivo image on the endoscopic monitor.

In this study, Microsoft HoloLens was adopted as the ARHD platform. ARHD continuously detected spatial information with a camera, an acceleration sensor, and a gyro sensor. By recognizing the voice command by the operator with the microphone, the free line by CG was displayed on the transmissive display, and by overlaying on the actual object, the system was designed so that ARHD wearer can see the drawing lines overlapping with the monitor. (See Fig. 2).

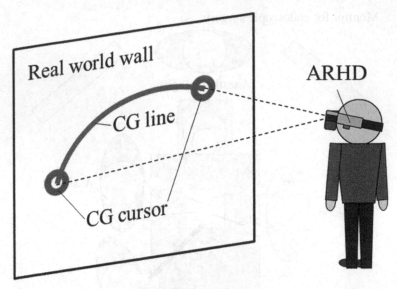

Fig. 2. Information for surgical instructions projected on the real environment drawn by the ARHD wearer.

Figure 3 shows the software configuration for driving ARHD. "HoloLens Camera" sets the viewpoint of the ARHD wearer. "Input Manager" analyzes camera and microphone information and manages basic operations such as gestures and voice recognition. In addition, a function called "Line Manager" was created and added to "Input Manager." By adding "Line Manager," the CG line can be drawn or deleted from the coordinates of the CG cursor displayed on the transparent display, and the line thickness and color can be changed. Also, operations such as line drawing and deletion are performed using voice recognition, and voice commands to perform each operation can be set. "Spatial Mapping" analyzes camera and sensor information and digitally grasps the geometric information of the real space such as walls and desks. By equipping this function, it became possible to detect the coordinates in the real space. "Cursor" displays the CG cursor in the center of the transmissive display.

With this system, operators with ARHD are hands-free and can precisely communicate by drawing a line, where CG information is shared between ARHD wearers.

There was a problem using speech input in a noisy environment, such as the surgery room we are targeting. Even though the surgeon tried to transmit the command to the system by voice, the system did not correctly recognize it due to the noisy condition. The problem of false recognition by the system prolonged the surgery. Consequently, the burden on the staff and patients involved in the surgery has increased [5, 6]. Also, if the system mistakenly recognized the command as intended, drawings may be generated at the part not to be cut, or the line at the region to be cut may be erased, leading to a potential medical error. Therefore, it is necessary to make a system where miscommunication due to the noisy environment does not frequently occur.

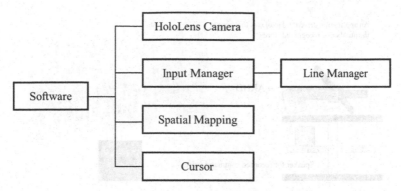

Fig. 3. Software configuration for driving ARHD.

Based on the above, the purpose of this study was to investigate the relationship between voice commands length and the correct recognition rate to optimize speech recognition in the operating room environment.

Through an empirical study of speech recognition in a noisy environment, Kanno et al. [7] evaluated the performance improvement under various noise conditions (SN ratio). Also, Nakagawa et al. [8] showed that recognition accuracy was affected by the length of the word. Therefore, we decided to optimize the number of syllables of words with high recognition performance and use the commands of that number of syllables for voice commands. In the experiment, the recognition performance in the operating room environment and the possibility of false recognition were evaluated for each syllable included in the command.

3 Experiment

3.1 Experimental Setup

Figure 4 shows the configuration of the experimental device. The experimental devices prepared were the ARHD, a device that fixed the ARHD, a speaker that played the voice of the participant, a speaker that played the surgical environment sound, and a sound level meter. The distance between the ARHD and the speaker that outputs sound was 5 cm, and the distance between the table on which the ARHD was placed and the speaker that outputs the operating environment sound was 30 cm. The distance between the ARHD and the speaker that plays the audio was chosen to simulate the distance between the ARHD and the surgeon's mouth when wearing the ARHD, as in the actual operating environment during surgery. We also developed an application for ARHD that counted the number of correct and incorrect words that were recognized. This application has a mechanism that counted the number of words when recognizing words to be spoken, and it counted as a misrecognized word if the word was different from the words spoken.

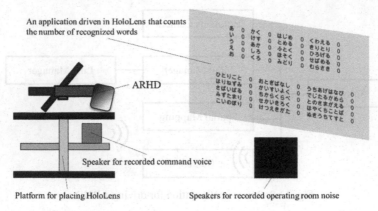

An application driven in HoloLens that counts the number of recognized words

ARHD

Speaker for recorded command voice

Platform for placing HoloLens   Speakers for recorded operating room noise

Fig. 4. Experimental apparatus for the evaluation experiment.

3.2 Experimental Procedure

The experimental procedure is shown as follows.

1. Participants uttered 40 trials each of 1 to 7 syllable words, that is, 5 words per syllable, consisting of 35 words, and the uttered speech was recorded.
2. The sound pressure of both the recorded voice and the sound recorded in the actual operating room environment was measured by a sound level meter installed immediately next to the microphone position provided in ARHD. For the recorded speech, the length of each of the 35 words was measured, and the average value was calculated for each syllable condition. Surgical environmental sounds were measured in seven different sizes.
3. The S/N ratio was calculated as the acoustic difference between the recorded participant's voice and the operating environment sound.
4. Using an application that counts the number of words from the uttered sound source, the number of recognized words and the number of misrecognized words were counted in an environment in which the voice of the participant and the operating environment sound were simultaneously transmitted from the speakers.
5. The correct recognition rate [%], the false recognition rate [%], and the number of cases that the ARHD mistakenly recognized as other command were obtained. Correct recognition rate was calculated by using Eq. (1), and false recognition rate was calculated by using Eq. (2).

$$Correct\ recognition\ rate = \frac{Number\ of\ successfully\ recognized\ commands}{Total\ number\ of\ commands\ uttered} \times 100$$

(1)

$$False\ recognition\ rate = \frac{Number\ of\ falsely\ recognized\ commands}{Number\ of\ successfully\ recognized\ commands} \times 100$$

(2)

6. Experimental procedures 4 and 5 were performed for a total of seven trials by changing the loudness of the environmental sound during surgery.

3.3 Experimental Conditions

Table 1 shows the experimental conditions. Six male university students (participant A to F) were engaged as experimental participants. In this experiment, we decided not to ask participants to wear ARHD and speak, but to record the participants' voices in advance and play the recorded voices from the speakers for evaluation. The reason for using recorded voice was to assure the internal validity. When a participant makes voice commands aloud with wearing ARHD, the volume of the voice changes by each trial. It is not possible to accurately measure the volume of only voice in an environment where surgical environment sounds (such as operator's conversations and machine sounds) were apparent. In this case, an appropriate SN ratio cannot be obtained.

Table 1. Experimental conditions.

Participants	A~F: 6 university students
Number of length of syllables to be pronounced	7 (1 to 7 syllables)
Number of different words tested for each level of word length	5 different words
Number of trials to be pronounced	40 trials
Number of loudness of surgical environment sound	7 levels

4 Results

Figure 5 shows the relationship between the average SN ratio of Participants A to F and the correct recognition rate. Figure 6 shows the relationship between the average number of syllables and the number of false recognitions of participants A to F. Figure 7 shows the relationship between the average SN ratio and the false recognition rate is shown. According to Fig. 5, the correct recognition rate for words with two or fewer syllables was lower than that for words with three or more syllables. The highest recognition rate was found for words with four syllables. Also, as shown in Fig. 6, many incorrect recognitions were observed in words with four or fewer syllables, and few incorrect recognitions have occurred in words with five or more syllables. As shown in Fig. 7, the false recognition did not seem to depend on the level of the operating environment sound. It was found that the false recognition rate of the command presented in one syllable was higher than any of the commands given in other numbers of syllables.

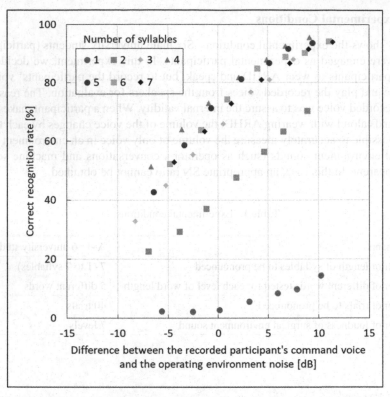

Fig. 5. Relationship between the average SN ratio and the correct recognition rate across participants.

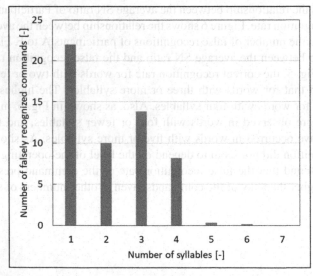

Fig. 6. Relationship between the average number of syllables and the number of cases that ARHD made false recognition.

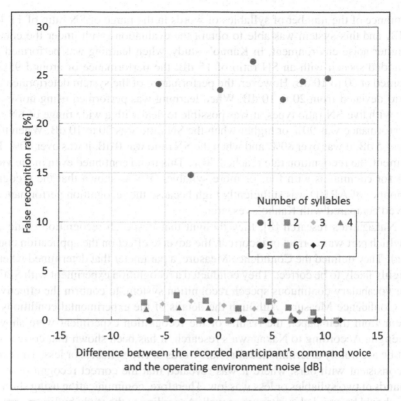

Fig. 7. Relationship between the average SN ratio and the false recognition rate.

5 Discussion

In this experiment, the performance of recognition in the operating room environment and the possibility of incorrect recognition were evaluated for each syllable number of words. As a result, ARHD did not show the appropriate recognition rate when using a few syllable words such as 1 and 2 syllables as voice commands since the recognition rate of 1–2 syllable words was lower than that of 3–7 syllables. It was also found that ARHD was erroneously operated at an average rate of 20% when a word of one syllable was given. Furthermore, the results showed that words with 5–7 syllables were rarely recognized as wrong commands. These results highlighted that it was considered adequate to select a word of 5–7 syllables as a voice command, which has a high recognition rate and causes almost no incorrect recognition.

Kanno's research [7] evaluated the performance improvement under the noise condition different from the learning condition when using the noise-added speech Hidden Malkov Model (HMM), assuming a sudden change of the noise condition in the unstable high noise environment. As the noise-added speech HMM, the case where the base SN ratio was 15 dB and the case where five types of SN ratio (25, 20, 15, 10, 5 dB) were tested. They conducted experiments by learning using two types of noise-added speech. Also, the SN ratio was set to 30 to 0 dB for verification. We compared the recognition performance of the number of syllables of words in the range of SN ratio of 11.4 to − 8.28 dB, and this system was able to obtain the evaluation result under the condition of a higher noise environment. In Kanno's study, when learning was performed using noise-added speech with an SN ratio of 15 dB, the performance of around 95% was maintained at 20 to 10 dB. However, the performance of the system deteriorated as the SN ratio deviated from 20 to 10 dB. When learning was performed using noise-added speech with five SN ratio types, it was possible to deal with a wide range of SN ratios, and performance was 90% or higher when the SN ratio was 30 to 10 dB. When the SN ratio was 5 dB, it was over 80%, and when the SN ratio was 0 dB, it was over 40%. In our experiment, the recognition rate reached 70%. This trend continued even in the vicinity of 0db for commands with four or more syllables. It was shown that the recognition performance of ARHD was sufficiently high because the recognition performance was improved compared with Kanno's research.

In Nakagawa's research [8], they thought that if speech recognition could determine which part was correct or incorrect, the adverse effect on the application could be reduced. They defined the Confidence Measure, a parameter that determined whether it was highly likely to be correct. They conducted a recognition experiment with SPOJUS, a large vocabulary continuous speech recognition system, to confirm the effectiveness of the Confidence Measure. Although the details of the experimental conditions were not clear from their paper, the results of the recognition experiment were shown by word length. According to Nakagawa's research, it has been shown that correct words cannot be accurately discriminated for short words of two syllables or less. Their results were consistent with ours, where it was revealed that the correct recognition rate for commands of two syllables or less was low. Therefore, communication using short commands should be avoided in our case as well. According to the study by Iijima et al. [11], they investigated the noise in the operating room environment, the intraoperative noise in the extra-cerebral OP room was 57.8 dB and that in the ophthalmic OP room was 56.3 dB. According to the results of Shiraishi [12], which measured the sound pressure level of conversational speech, the noise level of the A-weighted sound pressure level of the speech reaching the ears was 69 dB. Based on their results of intraoperative noise measurement in the OP room and sound pressure level measurement of the sound reaching the ear, the SN ratio when using the system was higher than 10 dB. Our experiment showed that 10 dB of the S/N ratio provided a 90% recognition rate or higher. Hence, it was expected that this system would be relatively effective even in an environment where the actual operating room environment becomes worse than that demonstrated by Kanno et al. [7]. Apparently, inappropriate speech recognition during surgery may generate a damaging influence on the surgery. The recognition rate does not reach 100% even in the best environment of the system developed in this research. Therefore, if the system behaves unpredictably during the operation, which is not intended by the operator, and the result is severe, the improvement of the appropriate user interface is one of the promising future issues.

6 Conclusion

We have developed an AR-based drawing application that can be operated only by head movement and speech input, as an endoscopic surgery support system. In this study, three main conclusions were drawn through the experiments for selecting appropriate command length using the ARHD. First of all, the result revealed that commands consisted of 3–7 syllables can be recognized at a considerably high level, and commands with four or fewer syllables may demonstrate the inaccurate recognition. Second, the risk of unintended behavior was most significant when the command was one syllable; thus the use of such commands should be avoided. Unexpected behavior also occurred when the 2–4 syllable commands were used, however, it was found that the use of the 2–4 syllable command did not pose a big problem because the number of unexpected behavior was small concerning the total number of recognized words. Finally, we concluded using words of 5–7 syllables to communicate voice commands using ARHD, which have a high recognition rate, and little unintended behavior.

References

1. Jinno, M.: Development for multi-degrees of freedom forceps with motor drive for assisting laparoscopic surgery. Inst. Syst. Control Inf. Eng. **57**(1), 14–18 (2013)
2. Yamashita, M., et al.: A new objective assessment of the suture ligature method for laparoscopic intestinal anastomosis. J. Jpn. Soc. Comput. Aided Surg. **17**(1), 15–22 (2015)
3. Kobayashi, E., Masamune, K., Suzuki, M., Dohi, T., Hashimoto, D.: Laparoscopic navigator. BME **11**(8), 40–45 (1997)
4. Kobayashi, T., et al.: Performance evaluation of head motion input used for AR-based communication supporting system during endoscopic surgery. In: Yamamoto, S., Mori, H. (eds.) HCII 2019. LNCS, vol. 11570, pp. 164–173. Springer, Cham (2019). https://doi.org/10.1007/978-3-030-22649-7_14
5. Gomi, Y., Morita, Y., Terada, T., Azuma, T., Tsukamoto, M.: A consideration of using head mounted display on endoscopic surgery. Trans. Hyman Interface Soc. **10**(4), 75–81 (2008)
6. Hoshiba, T., Sasaki, H., Hirabuki, S., Asamoto, A., Yabuki, Y.: Effect of operating time on surgical injury in laparoscopically assisted vaginal hysterectomy. Jpn. J. Gynecol. Obstet. Endosc. **17**(2), 67–69 (2001)
7. Kanno, S., Funada, T.: Improved noise robustness of word HMMs based on weighted variance expansion for noisy speech recognition. Syst. Comput. Jpn. **87**(5), 1052–1061 (2004)
8. Nakagawa, S., Horibe, Y.: Confidence measures for speech recognition by using likelihood of acoustic model and language model. IPSJ Trans. **2001**(55), 87–92 (2001)
9. Questionnaire for laparoscopic surgery: results for #14. J. Jpn. Soc. Endosc. Surg. **23**(6) (2018)
10. Kanbara, M.: Augmented reality: foundation 1: introduction to augmented reality. IPSJ Mag. **51**(4), 367–372 (2010)
11. Iijima, S., Furuya, Y., Yamazaki, Y., Haga, C., Ando, K.: Assessment of hospital environments by environmental measurement practice. Yamanashi Nurs. J. **7**(1), 45–52 (2008)
12. Shiraishi, K., Kanda, Y.: Measurements of the equivalent continuous sound pressure level and equivalent A — weighted continuous sound pressure level during conversational Japanese speech. Audiol. Jpn. **53**(3), 199–207 (2010)
13. Okahisa, K.: Investigation on improvement of surgery environment by introducing MR technology. Master's thesis, Kansai University (2018)
14. Accot, J., Zhai, S.: Performance evaluation of input devices in trajectory-based tasks: an application of the steering law. In: CHI 1999, pp. 15–20 (1999)
15. Shimono, H., Yamanaka, S., Miyashita, H.: Evaluation of the user performance in steering tasks using tilt controlling. IPSJ SIG Tech. Rep. **172**(7), 1–6 (2017)
16. Naito, S., Kitamura, Y., Kishino, F.: A study on the steering law in a 2D spatially-coupled style. IEICE Trans. **87**(9), 1834–1841 (2004)

TracKenzan: Digital Flower Arrangement Using Trackpad and Stylus Pen

Anna Yokokubo[1,2]([⊠]) [ID], Yuji Kato[3] [ID], and Itiro Siio[1] [ID]

[1] Ochanomizu University, Bunkyo-ku, Tokyo 112-8610, Japan
{anna.yokokubo,siio}@is.ocha.ac.jp
[2] Aoyama Gakuin University, Sagamihara-shi, Kanagawa 252-5258, Japan
[3] Nagoya, Japan

Abstract. We propose "TracKenzan," a training system for *Ikebana* (Japanese flower arrangement) in a 3D computer graphics space using a trackpad and a stylus pen. *Ikebana* includes a *Kenzan*, a flat metal base with hundreds of upward-pointing pins to hold flowers and branches in place. In the proposed system, a trackpad represents the *Kenzan*, and a stylus pen equipped with a 3D tracker resembles each flower stem. The users build the flower arrangement by selecting virtual flowers with adjustable length, whose position and orientation correspond to those of the pen, and then place the flowers by pressing the desired position on the trackpad. By using the trackpad and pen resembling the *Kenzan* and flower, respectively, TracKenzan provides an intuitive and straightforward interface for users to practice *Ikebana*. We present the system implementation and evaluation tests conducted by 11 beginner and 7 experienced users, as well as one *Ikebana* teacher. They verified the system usability and capabilities as a learning tool for *Ikebana*.

Keywords: *Ikebana* · Flower arrangement · Tangible device

1 Introduction

Ikebana is a traditional Japanese art in which flowers and plants are arranged in a vase for appreciation. *Ikebana* consists of a *Kenzan* often placed at the bottom of a vase to hold in place materials such as flowers, branches, and leaves, as illustrated in Fig. 1. The *Kenzan* is a metal object consisting of hundreds of upward-pointing pins set on a flat weight. Artists usually hold the *Kenzan* with their non-dominant hand and the flower arrangement materials with their dominant hand for placement on the pins, which secure the edges of the materials. This Japanese art form is enjoyed worldwide and being increasingly used for decoration.

Intense efforts are being devoted to the preservation of the traditional *Ikebana* skills with the support of technologies such as virtual reality (VR) [1] and 3D

Y. Kato—Indipendent Author.

C. Stephanidis et al. (Eds.): HCII 2020, LNCS 12424, pp. 332–343, 2020.
https://doi.org/10.1007/978-3-030-60117-1_25

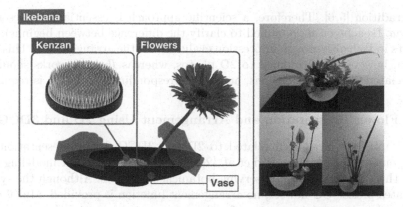

Fig. 1. In *Ikebana*, flowers and other materials are pierced on a *Kenzan* to form decorative arrangements.

computer graphics (CG) simulation [2,3]. Perfecting *Ikebana* demands practicing the combinations of flowers and layouts repeatedly to develop a sense of beauty for the arrangements [4–6]. Available learning tools using VR and CG simulation are usually effective, because learners can use as many flowers and layouts as they want without having to spend money on the materials. Likewise, digital practice enables learners to restore materials, such as a flower stem that has been trimmed too short by mistake for using a longer stem in the arrangement [7]. However, the user experience should be carefully designed when developing VR and CG-based learning tools, because the difference between the experience in the virtual and real world may hinder learning.

In this paper, we present the implementation of "TracKenzan," a training system for *Ikebana* in a 3DCG space using a trackpad and a stylus pen. The user manipulates the trackpad and stylus pen that represent a virtual *Ikebana* and flower stem, respectively. The similarity of these devices to their corresponding shapes enables a continuous user experience between manipulation in the real world and the CG interface.

2   Related Work

TracKenzan is related to 2D and 3DCG flower presentation and arrangement for research, training, and education, building computer peripherals, providing tactile feedback, and handling 3DCG virtual objects.

2.1   Ikebana Education and Evaluation

Ikebana has been a popular practice over generations mainly as enrichment lessons not only in Japan but also in many regions worldwide. However, details of the teachings differ among instructors because *Ikebana* skills are conveyed by oral tradition [5,6]. Therefore, a scientific approach is essential for preserving *Ikebana*. Ikenobo et al. [8] aimed to clarify the difference between beginners and experts in Ikebana through impression evaluation of the arrangements. This evaluation, however, was confined to 2D photos, whereas *Ikebana* works should be appreciated in three dimensions, and the corresponding evaluation is required.

2.2 Flower Presentation and Arrangement Using 2D and 3DCG

Several projects have been related to 2D and 3DCG flower presentation and arrangement. For instance, Ijiri et al. [2,3] proposed a system for modeling flowers in three dimensions by preserving botanical structures. Although the system generates precise CG flowers, no arrangement function is provided. Mukai et al. [1] introduced a training system for flower arrangement using haptic devices. The system aims to reproduce realistic haptic feedback when a user inserts a flower stem into a *Kenzan*. However, flower placement over a 2D *Kenzan* surface is not supported. Yokokubo et al. [9] proposed a system that recommends flower arrangements using pictures of actual flowers and related materials prepared by a user. The system arranges these materials on a 2D picture, but no 3D arrangement function is available. The *Ikebana* VR experience[1] is an application for *Ikebana* offering basic experiences of 3D flower arrangements using two motion controllers (i.e., Microsoft motion controller[2] and Nintendo Wii controller[3]), which controllers held on both hands by the user. Similarly, the system we propose provides a full 3D flower arrangement embedded into a 3DCG world but features two dedicated control devices, namely, a trackpad and a stylus pen, for the intuitive manipulation of the *Kenzan* and a flower stem, respectively.

2.3 Manipulation of 3DCG Objects

We use devices that resemble the *Kenzan* and flower stem for their accurate representation as virtual 3D objects to be manipulated. Similar interaction methods are common in consumer videogaming consoles. For example, controllers such as that of the Nintendo Wii have accelerometers and gyroscopes to detect and track user motion in games such as tennis simulators, where the controller resembles a racket. Likewise, handheld 3D trackers such as Microsoft motion controllers are used in VR and augmented reality environments to represent the user's hands. These devices can be also utilized to represent parts of virtual objects such as the grips of virtual weapons or door handles of vehicles. Wu et al. [10] proposed a stylus pen equipped with optical markers. As the accurate 3D positioning of the device can be detected at high frame rates, it has been used to control a handwriting pen in a virtual world. Hinckley et al. [11] proposed a modeling method for 3D shapes using a two-handed interface. Likewise, de Araùjo et al.

---

[1] BBmedia Inc., *Ikebana* VR experience (2018), http://ikebana-vr.jp/.

[2] Microsoft Co., Motion controllers (2018), https://docs.microsoft.com/en-us/windows/mixed-reality/motion-controllers/.

[3] Nintendo Co., Wii U gamepad (2012), https://www.nintendo.com/wiiu/features/.

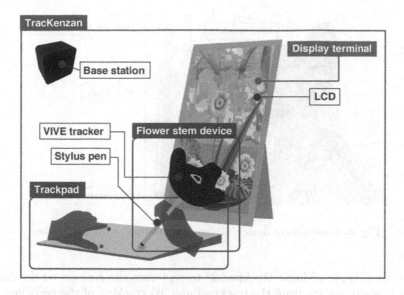

Fig. 2. Overview of TracKenzan.

[12], Brandl et al. [13], and Wu et al. [10] have proposed two-handed interfaces by combining stylus pens and touch devices. These physical devices are mainly intended for use in VR and augmented reality environments. Similarly, we used an off-the-shelf trackpad to represent a virtual *Kenzan* as it provides suitable functions such as precise touch detection, multitouch gestures, pressure sensing, and tactile feedback in a low-cost interface.

3 TracKenzan

TracKenzan is the 3DCG-based *Ikebana* training system illustrated in Fig. 2. The user manipulates the trackpad and the stylus pen equipped with a VR tracker at its end (Fig. 3). The trackpad represents the *Kenzan* placed in a CG vase, and the stylus pen represents a flower arrangement material in the CG world displayed on an LCD. The motion of the stylus pen with the VR tracker, hereinafter referred to as the flower stem device, determines the position and orientation of the flower arrangement material for placement.

3.1 Implementation

We implemented TracKenzan on a MacBook Pro (Apple Inc., Cupertino, CA, USA) running macOS 10.13.5 and the Unity environment. To enable a flexible arrangement of the computer display (e.g., switching between portrait and landscape view), an external LCD (ASUS MB 169C+, 15.6-inch full HD LCD; AsusTek Computer Inc., Taipei, Taiwan) was connected to the computer.

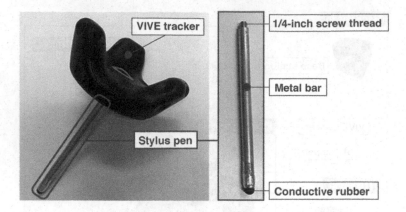

Fig. 3. Flower stem device: stylus pen equipped with VR tracker.

We used Apple's Magic Trackpad 2[4] to represent the *Kenzan* on the display. The XY position data from the trackpad and 3D tracking of the pen allows the user to place the CG flower materials more precisely. In addition, the built-in pressure sensor and vibration actuator of the trackpad enable tactile feedback to the user when a CG flower arrangement material is inserted into the CG *Kenzan*. By using the trackpad, the user can easily select the position for the material placement. We designed this setup aiming to improve the effectiveness of learning *Ikebana*.

The flower stem device consists of a metal rod and a conductive rubber composing the stylus, and a VIVE tracker[5], as shown in Fig. 3. We installed one base station of the VIVE tracker above the user to detect the position and orientation of the device. The detected data are expressed as movement of the currently selected CG flower arrangement material shown on the display. When the user holds and moves the rod, the CG material changes its position and orientation accordingly, improving the user experience and making the system more realistic. The flower stem device functions as a stylus pen on the trackpad, and hence touching or pressing the device on the trackpad surface sets the desired position for the material through the conductive rubber tip.

3.2 Operation

After completing the initial calibration, the user can perform *Ikebana* activities such as selecting, cutting, restoring, inserting, and extracting flower arrangement materials. As the precise position of the conductive rubber tip of the flower stem device is detected when it touches or presses the trackpad, the tracker position is calibrated on-the-fly while the user performs *Ikebana* tasks.

---

[4] Magic Trackpad 2, https://www.apple.com/search/Magic-Trackpad-2-Silver?tab=accessories.

[5] HTC Co., VIVE tracker (2018), https://www.vive.com/us/vive-tracker/.

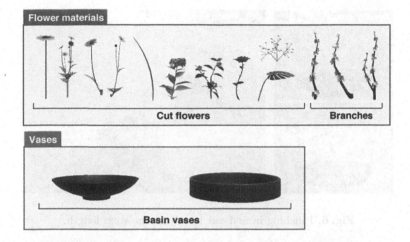

Fig. 4. Flower arrangement materials and vases available in TracKenzan.

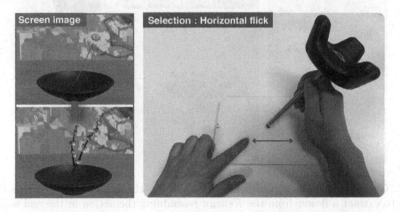

Fig. 5. Horizontal flicking to select flower arrangement materials.

Selection. Figure 4 shows the flower arrangement materials (i.e., flowers and branches) and vases available in TracKenzan. Users can switch materials by one-finger left or right flicking the trackpad (Fig. 5) and select the type of vase by three-finger flicking. The selections appear on the 3DCG world for manipulation of the materials using the flower stem device, whose motion determines the position and orientation of the selected material.

Cut and Restore. Two-finger pinching-in on the trackpad allows the user to cut and shorten the stem of the CG flower, as shown in Fig. 6. Cutting a stem is a basic *Ikebana* step to considerably modify the flower arrangement layout. However, in real practice, cutting is a very difficult step because it is irreversible. In contrast, the proposed digital system allows to increase the size of the stem by two-finger pinching-out on the trackpad, thus reversing a previous cutting action.

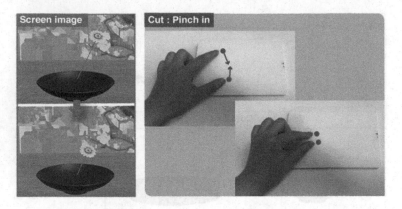

Fig. 6. Pinching in and out to adjust the stem length.

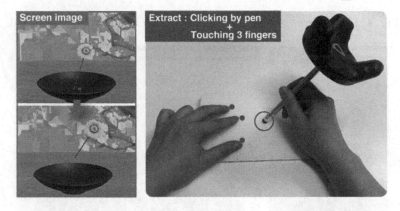

Fig. 7. Clicking with the stylus pen while pressing the trackpad with three fingers allows to extract a flower from the *Kenzan* resembling the action in the real world.

Insert and Extract. When the user presses the tip of the flower stem device on the trackpad surface, the corresponding CG flower material is inserted into the pressed trackpad position on the CG *Kenzan* within the vase. TracKenzan retrieves a trackpad vibration in response to the insertion for the user to obtain haptic feedback. After insertion, the position and orientation of the flower arrangement material become fixed regardless of the motion of the flower stem device. If desired, the user can extract a previously placed material to try different layouts. To regain control of a previously inserted material, the user should press at the position of the target flower using the flower stem device while pressing with three fingers the trackpad, as shown in Fig. 7. This action detaches the material from the CG *Kenzan* and makes it controllable by the flower stem device again. The three-finger press on the trackpad mimics the real-world action of holding the *Kenzan* to carefully remove a flower. Note that this action represents another advantage of using the proposed training system, because a stem is easily damaged by the *Kenzan* pins during real-world *Ikebana* practice, impeding the repeated manipulation of materials.

4 Usability Evaluation

To evaluate the usability and user experience of the proposed TracKenzan, we conducted experiments with the participation of beginners and experienced learners, and an *Ikebana* teacher.

The experiment was conducted at our laboratory with the beginner participants, and at an *Ikebana* school with the teacher and experienced participants. Twenty subjects participated in the study, from which 11 were beginners (4 males and 7 females), 8 were experienced learners (1 male and 7 females), and the *Ikebana* teacher was male. The beginners' age was 26.7 ± 9.9 years, and the teacher and experienced leaners' age was 41.1 ± 10.3 years.

An experimenter set up the TracKenzan system (trackpad, flower stem device, LCD, computer, and base station) on a table. The experimenter explained each participant the use of TracKenzan for approximately 3 min. Then, each participant started to create *Ikebana* works, as shown in Fig. 8. After completion, the participants verified their CG-generated works using a 360° view and completed a questionnaire about the TracKenzan usability. The experiment lasted approximately 10 min per participant, including the 3-min instruction.

The system usability scale (SUS) [14] was included in the questionnaire to evaluate the system. The SUS is a Likert-based evaluation to express the degree of agreement (from 1—strongly disagree to 5—strongly agree) of the participants with ten questions, five evaluating positive aspects, and the other five evaluating negative aspects of the system:

(1) I think that I would like to use TracKenzan frequently.
(2) I found TracKenzan unnecessarily complex.
(3) I thought TracKenzan was easy to use.
(4) I think that I would need the support of a technical person to be able to use TracKenzan.
(5) I found the various functions in TracKenzan were well integrated.
(6) I thought there was too much inconsistency in TracKenzan.
(7) I would imagine that most people would learn to use TracKenzan very quickly.
(8) I found TracKenzan very cumbersome to use.
(9) I felt very confident using TracKenzan.
(10) I needed to learn a lot of things before I could get going with TracKenzan.

4.1 Results and Consideration

We calculated SUS scores from the evaluations of the participants and mapped them to values from 0 to 100. The average score for beginners was 74.8, varying

Fig. 8. Subject using TracKenzan.

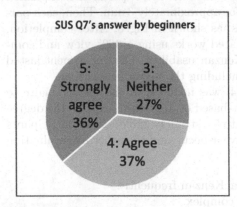

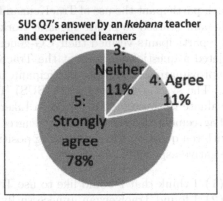

Fig. 9. Comparison of SUS Q7's answer between beginners and an *Ikebana* teacher and experienced learners.

between 52.5 and 90.0, and that for the *Ikebana* teacher and experienced learners was 75.2, varying between 50.0 and 92.5.

Beginners and experts answered similarly except for question 7. Figure 9 shows scores given by beginners (left) and by the *Ikebana* teacher and experienced learners (right). The percentage of beginners who answered "Strongly Agree" (score 5) and "Agree" (score 4) was 36%, whereas none of them answered "Strongly Disagree" (score 1) and "Disagree" (score 2). By examining the $\chi 2$ value to check for bias in the answers, we found no significant differences between the five scores ($\chi 2 = 7.63$, df $= 4$, ns). On the other hand, the percentage of beginners who answered "Strongly Agree" and "Agree" was 76%, and the percentage of those who answered "Neither" (score 3) and "Agree" (score 4) was 11%. By examining $\chi 2$ value to check for bias in the answers, we found signifi-

Fig. 10. *Ikebana* works produced by subjects using TracKenzan.

cant differences between the five scores ($p < 0.01$) ($\chi 2 = 19.33$, df $= 4$, ns). We consider the reason for the difference in scores for question 7, "I would imagine that most people would learn to use TracKenzan very quickly", as follows: the *Ikebana* teacher and experiences learners could create favorite *Ikebana* works by Trackenzan because they had expected completion image of an Ikebana work, on the other hand, beginner could not because they didn't have completion image.

All the participants highly agreed with scores of 4 or 5 to question 7 related to the learning speed for using TracKenzan. As free-form comments, we collected answers such as "I think TracKenzan can be operated intuitively," and "TracKenzan operation was very simple and allowed to mimic a real *Ikebana*" from nine participants. Many subjects also mentioned that the experience with TracKenzan was similar to that of working on an actual *Ikebana*.

Some of the *Ikebana* works produced by the participants using TracKenzan are shown in Fig. 10. Comparing the works of beginners to those of the teacher and experienced learners, it is clear that the latter use a smaller number of flower arrangement materials and group them more tightly on a small area of the *Kenzan*. From the experiments and results, we expect that people can easily train to achieve excellent *Ikebana* works as those produced by the teacher without having to pay for flower arrangement materials using TracKenzan.

5   Conclusion

We propose TracKenzan, a digital training system for creating *Ikebana* flower arrangements in a 3DCG space using a trackpad and a stylus pen. The trackpad resembles the *Kenzan* and the stylus pen resembles the flower stem on a CG environment. The similarity of their shapes to the actual objects provides a user experience close to that of working on an actual *Ikebana* for effective learning. We evaluated the usability of TracKenzan through user experiments. The SUS scores and comments given by the subjects suggest that the proposed system is useful and effective for *Ikebana* training. In future developments, we intend to improve the training system for every type of user based on the feedback received in this study.

References

1. Mukai, N., Takara, S., Kosugi, M.: A training system for the Japanese art of flower arrangement. In: 18th World IMACS/MODSIM Congress, pp. 1671–1677. The Modelling and Simulation Society of Australia and New Zealand Inc. and the International Association for Mathematics and Computers in Simulation (2009)
2. Ijiri, T., Owada, S., Igarashi, T.: Seamless integration of initial sketching and subsequent detail editing in flower modeling. Comput. Graph. Forum **25**, 617–624 (2006)
3. Ijiri, T., Yoshizawa, S., Yokota, H., Igarashi, T.: Flower modeling via X-ray computed tomography. ACM Trans. Graph. **33**(4), 48:1–48:10 (2014)
4. Ikenobo, Y., Kida, Y., Kuwahara, N., Goto, A., Kimura, A.: A study of the effect of the shape, the color, and the texture of ikebana on a brain activity. In: Duffy, V.G. (ed.) DHM 2013. LNCS, vol. 8026, pp. 59–65. Springer, Heidelberg (2013). https://doi.org/10.1007/978-3-642-39182-8_7
5. Ikenobo, Y., Kuwahara, N., Kida, N., Takai, Y., Goto, A.: The classification tendency and common denomination of the points paid attention in Ikebana instruction. In: Duffy, V.G. (ed.) DHM 2014. LNCS, vol. 8529, pp. 263–272. Springer, Cham (2014). https://doi.org/10.1007/978-3-319-07725-3_26

6. Ikenobo, Y., Mochizuki, Y., Kuwahara, A.: Usefulness of Ikebana a nursing care environment. In: Duffy, V.G. (ed.) DHM 2015. LNCS, vol. 9185, pp. 441–447. Springer, Cham (2015). https://doi.org/10.1007/978-3-319-21070-4_44
7. Goto, A., Sugiyama, N., Ikenobo, Y., Yamaguchi, N., Hamada, H.: Analysis of cutting operation with flower scissors in Ikebana. In: Karwowski, W., Trzcielinski, S., Mrugalska, B., Di Nicolantonio, M., Rossi, E. (eds.) AHFE 2018. AISC, vol. 793, pp. 378–385. Springer, Cham (2019). https://doi.org/10.1007/978-3-319-94196-7_35
8. Ikenobo, Y., Takai, Y., Goto, A., Kuwahara, N.: Difference between inexperienced persons and experts of ikebana through impression evaluation. Trans. Jpn. Soc. Kansei Eng. **13**(1), 307–314 (2014)
9. Yokokubo, A., Sääskilahti, K., Kangaskorte, R., Luimula, M., Siio, I.: CADo: a supporting system for flower arrangement. In: AVI 2012, pp. 42–45. ACM (2012)
10. Wu, P., et al.: DodecaPen: accurate 6DoF tracking of a passive stylus. In: UIST 2017, pp. 365–374. ACM (2017)
11. Hinckley, K., et al.: Pen + Touch = New Tools. In: UIST 2010, pp. 27–36. ACM (2010)
12. De Araùjo, B., Casiez, G., Jorge, J.: Mockup builder: direct 3D modeling on and above the surface in a continuous interaction space. In: GI 2012, pp. 173–180. Canadian Information Processing Society (2012)
13. Brandl, P., Forlines, C., Wigdor, D., Haller, M., Shen, C.: Combining and measuring the benefits of bimanual pen and direct-touch interaction on horizontal interfaces. In: AVI 2008, pp. 154–161. ACM (2008)
14. Brooke, J.: SUS: a quick and dirty usability scale. In: Usability Evaluation in Industry, p. 189 (1996)

Mapping Between Mind Cybernetics and Aesthetic Structure in Real-Time EEG Art

Minli Zhang[1](✉), Yiyuan Huang[2](✉), Salah Uddin Ahmed[3],
and Mohammad Shidujaman[4]

[1] Communication University of China, No. 1 Dingfuzhuang East Street, Beijing, China
minliz@yeah.net
[2] Beijing Institute of Graphic Communication, No. 1 (band -2) Xinghua Street,
Daxing District, Beijing, China
huangyiyuan122@hotmail.com
[3] University of South-Eastern Norway, Kongsberg, Norway
Salah.Ahmed@usn.no
[4] Tsinghua University, Haidian District, Beijing, China
shangt15@mails.tsinghua.edu.cn

Abstract. The popularity of brain computer interface leads many art researchers to explore the diversity of mind cybernetic methods and expression forms in EEG art. However, few focuses on the characteristics of cybernetic-aesthetic structure: whether there are paradigms that relates different EEG control modes to different aesthetic characteristics. Therefore, in this article, we make an artistic exploration of the recent EEG artworks and based on various cybernetic control, propose a cybernetic-aesthetics mapping structure that characterizes them. From the cybernetic classification, we find that various mind controls such as active control, explicit passive control, and implicit passive control can be targeted to various aesthetics which we have identified respectively as homogenous aesthetics, relational aesthetics, and subconscious aesthetics.

Keywords: EEG art · Active control · Explicit passive control · Implicit passive control · Homogenous aesthetics · Relational aesthetics · Subconscious aesthetics

1 Introduction

Electroencephalogram (EEG) is a subfield of Brain-Computer Interface (BCI). Typically, BCI devices fall into three categories: invasive, partially invasive, and non-invasive [1]. The invasive system, such as internal neuron recording, requires surgery to implant microelectrode arrays in the brain, which limits their use outside the experimental environment. The partially invasive system also needs to place electrodes inside the skull (under the dura mater and above the cortex). The electrodes are located outside the brain, such as Electrocorticography (ECoG). Compared to the invasive and partially invasive systems, the non-invasive system is completely safe. The electrodes are placed directly

---

M. Zhang and Y. Huang—These authors contributed equally to this study.

on the scalp. Brain signals are measured outside the human body without surgery. In summary, the invasive and partially invasive systems are relatively dangerous but have a high signal-to-noise ratio. They are appropriate for some specific medical fields. On the contrary, the non-invasive system does not have a high signal-to-noise ratio, but it is safe and suitable for general employment. EEG is an application of the non-invasive system. At the same time, EEG is more portable and commercialized at a relatively low cost than Functional Magnetic Resonance Imaging (fMRI) which is also a non-invasive system, but generally used in the medical scene. fMRI is large, expensive and not portable (see Fig. 1). As a result, EEG has opened up a more realistic and innovative field for artists than other BCI technologies. In this article, by EEG Art we mean the artworks that use EEG as the primary medium to conceptualize, create and experience the art expressions.

Through the low-cost commercial EEG system and computer interface, the artist insights into human thought process and explores the relationship between thinking and art. By facilitating and providing technical support, EEG realizes the possibility of poetic and aesthetic quantification in real-time interactive creation.

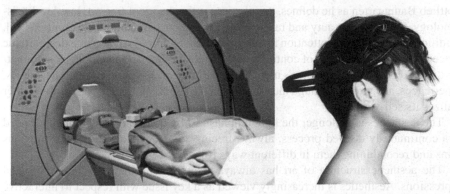

Fig. 1. Functional Magnetic Resonance Imaging (fMRI) and Portable Electroencephalogram devices (Emotiv EPOC)

In 1934, two prominent physiologists from Cambridge's Physiological Laboratory, Edgar Douglas Adrian and Brian Matthews, mapped alpha waves into audio signals [2]. It was the beginning of the creative exploration of brain activity, advancing beyond the science lab to the world of contemporary art. Then, after Alvin Lucier first revealed the artistic potential of EEG in his work *Music for Solo Performer* [3], the brain became the focus of artistic creation.

"… The artist is in a sense a neuroscientist, exploring the brain's potential and abilities, although using different tools… How this creation evokes aesthetic experience can only be fully understood in neurological terms [4]." It is because this potential of thought proved that the standards of aesthetics are never eternal. The position of aesthetics is a result of projection rather than reflection. It is complex and dynamic rather than straightforward and static. Human cognition is finally transformed into perception and emotion.

In this paper, we focus on the thought process of a viewer or art participant in building the perceived aesthetics while experiencing an EEG art and find a relation between the thought process and the aesthetics. The rest of the paper is organized as follow: in Sect. 2, we present the background by briefly addressing the concepts of aesthetics, cybernetics and EEG art. We also define aesthetics and role of cybernetics in EEG art. In Sect. 3, based on the role of cybernetic control and perceived aesthetics, we define three major types of mapping between control and aesthetics in EEG art. In Sect. 4, we elaborate and present the type of mappings along with real life artwork examples. Section 5 concludes the article and presents our opinion about the implications of our findings to the artist and researcher community.

2   Background: Aesthetics, Cybernetics and EEG Art

2.1   General Aesthetics

The discussion of beauty and emotion began with the German philosopher Alexander Gottlieb Baumgarten as he defines, "aesthetics, as the theory of free art, low-level epistemology, thinking of beauty and rationality, is the science of emotional cognition" [5]. Traditional aesthetics pay attention to the appearance of things. At the same time, artistic conception under the theory of control creates interactions sparking emotions, eliminating the gap between the audience's mind and environment, and providing new aesthetics, experiences, and views. Through interaction and the access of thought, aesthetics further realizes its self-worth.

The aesthetics is no longer the light emphasized by tradition. It is gradually treated as a continuously derived process, always freeing some elements from their previous veins and recombining them in different ways [6].

The aesthetic structure of art has always changed with the associated tools and expressions. Aesthetics is increasingly viewed as a key issue with respect to interactive technology [7]. Aesthetic logic in EEG Art interaction changes people's appreciation style, mode of thinking, formation and standard from cross-disciplinary perspective. Unlike scientists, EEG artists create metaphors that bring together hypotheses, conjectures, intuitions, perceptions, and thinking, rather than exploring the neural structure and mechanisms of the brain. This trend presents the aesthetic concept of changing from "material situation" to "spiritual situation". Art should be the product of free consciousness, "freedom" is the new aesthetic value of interactive art, including EEG art [8].

2.2   Cybernetic Aesthetics of Digital Art

In 1977, Herbert W. Franke began to explore the relationship between cybernetics and aesthetics in digital (computer) art [9]. Based on the perspective of cybernetics, he focused on the information in the digital image. His research was based on human short-term memory: the maximum rate at which the human brain consciously receives discrete information is about 16 bits per second. Therefore, in a short memory cycle (10 s), the brain can only locate 160 bits of information. In light of this principle, the author discussed the creation method of digital image and the audience's emotional feedback.

Afterward, with the development of computer technology, the discussion of cybernetics and aesthetics became more detailed. In 2002, Claudia Giannetti systematically reviewed the evolution of cybernetics and aesthetics based on information development. Automation and simulation influenced the art and aesthetics from early rational aesthetics to information aesthetics after the emergence of computers. These influences are separately positive, negative, logical, and psychological. Although there were many arguments among different schools, they seemed to ignore more or less the connection of communication and art. Therefore, Claudia put forward a paradox: if the aesthetic problem is simplified into pure rationality and digital evaluation of works (information as a quantifiable factor), people will not recognize the cognitive theoretical value of artwork and the aesthetic experience. Therefore, there must be a different understanding of communication, which can be applied to the field of aesthetics. To approach the theme of aesthetics, we must first unify the relationship between "communication" and "art", which is a study of existence and aesthetics [10]. Claudia's opinion broke the limitation of information aesthetics in computers and expanded the communication between cybernetics and aesthetics in interactive digital art.

After 2010, with the development and popularization of physiological sensing and interactive technology, digital art has developed as an interdisciplinary integration. The diversity of interactivity and technology gives art expression and cybernetic form unprecedented freedom.

2.3 Real-Time Interactivity and EEG

The stronger the intervention of scientific knowledge, the more the realization of aesthetics depends on technical support. In real-time interactive art, the technology support for "freedom" needs to be guaranteed by "time". Fortunately, one of the main advantages of EEG is the high timing resolution. This resolution is about 0.001 s, which is higher than other non-invasive brain-computer interface devices (functional magnetic resonance imaging and near-infrared spectrum instrument is 1 s). This advantage establishes the potential of EEG Art for real-time interaction. Today, real-time EEG creation is undergoing a considerable renaissance accompanied by the popularity of commercial EEG technologies such as dry electrodes and wireless systems.

Traditionally, EEG is an electro biological measurement technique for research and medical purposes. Because the electric field measured by EEG is weak, the medical EEG device usually uses conductive gel applied to the scalp to amplifying signals captured from electrodes. At the same time, for increasing the accuracy, medical EEG uses a large number of electrodes (up to 256) typically. Those limitations make the EEG very complicated and expensive but provide better spatial resolution. However, the emergence of commercial EEG technology significantly reduced the number of electrodes (from 1 to 14), and no need conductive gel. This improvement not only made the equipment lighter but also reduced the cost. At the same time, commercial EEG is generally equipped with a ready-to-use platform for PC or mobile terminal. Through the platform, the user can analyze in real-time mental states (attention, mediation, engagement, and so on).

Tanaka said, with the introduction of digital signal processing technology in the 1980s, artistic interest slotted from biofeedback to biological control [11]. EEG as a biological control is considered relatively implicit compared to traditional interactive feedback techniques. Most of the traditional interactive control is based on mechanical operation and motion detection. Based on the participant's movements and behaviors, the artworks realize a kind of explicit macro communication. However, EEG control directly uses electrodes to capture the activity of neurons and takes thinking as a controller. EEG artwork is a new kind of transmission that cannot be observed through body behavior but the mind.

2.4 Aesthetics and Cybernetics of Real-Time EEG Art

With the development of digital art based on physiology and interactive technology, the relationship between cybernetics and aesthetics has expanded from the information communication between computer and artwork to the relationship between physiological psychology, computer, sensors, and artistic value. This evolution is manifested in the spatiality and subjectivity between life (participant) and installation (artwork). Here, we need to introduce two representative research works by Fishkin and Wadeson et al.

Fishkin's classification of the perceptive interface based on the level of self-containment. Specifically, he classifies them according to the distance between input and output control [12]. Wadeson et al. offered different views on creative control, discussing four categories for participants: passive, selective, direct, and collaborative [13]. In the classification models of Fishkin and Wadeson et al., we can summarize the following characteristics of EEG art from the perspective of Cybernetics. The spatial relationship between existences, i.e., participants and artwork, determines the behavioral characteristics of aesthetic construction.

Real-time EEG art, as a combination of physiology, computing and interactive art, is one of the most representative forms. It possesses the characteristics explained by Fishkin and Wadeson et al., but not limited to the aesthetic framework based on computer and traditional behavior interaction. In real-time EEG art, we need to clarify the novelty of communication subjects with brain and thinking and build an aesthetic structure concerning cerebral control and digital art installation.

This is for the reason that EEG art has some cybernetic characters that other interactive art forms do not have. Different ways of controlling create differences in expressions, which we can define as a question of expressiveness. Artists working on EEG need to face up to the relationship between this new type of control and new aesthetics.

3   Towards a Cybernetic-Aesthetics Structure

In order to identify the relation between the cybernetics and aesthetics in EEG art-works, we selected a list of EEG artworks realized in the recent years from 2015-2019 which represent the latest and typical creative trends. A good number of artworks were selected from the book *Brain Art* [14] which contains descriptions of many representative art-works in the chapter Brain-Computer Interfaces in Art: A State of the examples listed in Art and Taxonomy; some were taken from other sources, and, in addition, some new artworks selected from the years 2018 and 2019.

EEG art is a generation of interactive art. It presents the evolution of life science and digital art. Therefore, the theories of Fishkin and Wadeson et al. in Sect. 2.4 need to be first explained to classifier the general background of interactive art evolution, and make clear the characteristics of spatiality and subjectivity. In Sect. 2.4, Fishkin divided the distance between input and output control into Distant, Environmental, Nearby, and Full. "Distant" means remote interaction. Input and output are located in two spaces, respectively, and interact through remote control. "Environmental" means output surround input. Both of them keep a certain distance but located in the same perceptible space. "Nearby" means input and output are combined. The distance between them is minimal. "Full" means input itself is output. Based on distance, art establishes conscious (selective and direct) and subconscious (passive) interaction between control and elements. Their spatial relationship determines whether the work is expressed in a limited space (nearby, full), or in a wide space (distant or collaborative).

Section 2.4 pointed out Wadeson et al. defined four categories for participants: passive, selective, direct, and collaborative. Passive refers to that the control system can automatically capture EEG signals and change artistic elements without conscious interactive commands delivered by the participant. Selective refers to the conscious mind or emotion changes by the participant, while artistic elements transform expression forms according to the participant's brain signals. Direct means the participant can choose items provided by application and output directly. Collaborative refers to collaborative control with multi-participation. Therefore, the realization of aesthetics is closely related to the communication between subject and object. The subjective (participant) consciousness determines two different aesthetic structures—conscious or subconscious.

Otherwise, In the book **Brain Art**, Mirjana Prpa and Philippe Pasquier presented a comprehensive overview of EEG Art in the recent years. The authors systematically classified EEG artworks into input, output, expression, and user participation (active/passive). They have listed 61 representative EEG artworks from 1965 to 2018 in the article. This article provided a basic classification framework of cerebral cybernetics. This framework provided us the basic foundation to construct the mapping between cybernetics and aesthetic structure.

Actually, the cybernetic-aesthetic relationship of real-time EEG art is a further development of the general relationship of interactivity. In 2003, French artistic professor Edmond Couchot defined interactivity as exogenous and endogenous [15]. Exogenous interactivity means the interaction between participant and computer; the endogenous means the autonomous interaction between computer algorithms. In EEG art, the exogenous is still based on participant and computer, but a bridge between them: consciousness. However, the endogenous no longer refers to the interaction between algorithms. The focus is on the communication between neurons. In a sense, the aesthetic structure of passive control is to realize aesthetic communication by deconstructing the brain and based on the subconscious independently.

Combined with the above cybernetic theories and classification methods, we decided to expand the part of the user engagement presented by Mirjana Prpa and Philippe Pasquier in [12], and based on the theories of Fishkin and Wadeson et al. We focus only on real-time interactive works. In this paper, we analyzed a series of EEG artworks with their cybernetic modes and their artistic expressions in recent years. We found an apparent corresponding relationship between the initiative of consciousness and aesthetic structure. The high conscious initiative establishes a beauty of empathy; the middle initiative expresses the beauty according to the characteristics of relational aesthetics; The low initiative shows the beauty of freedom in the subconscious universe. Therefore, we design three kinds of aesthetics. The first is called homogeneous aesthetics. It refers to creating a kind of empathy effect through the identity of subject and object in thinking and cognition. Generally, the subject refers to the participant and the object refers to the artistic element. The second is relational aesthetics. It refers to the construction of a behavioral or cognitive relationship between the subject and the object. Through the development of the relationship, artist explores the change of thinking and find the beauty in the relationship. The third is subconscious aesthetics. It means that when the subject is in a particular mental state (meditation, hypnosis, sleep), a kind of beauty created by the liberalization of subconscious thinking is expressed through the object.

Prpa and Pasquier divide user engagement into active and passive categories. Similarly, the aesthetic structure or the mapping between cybernetics and aesthetics follows the cerebral cybernetics: they can be also divided as active and passive. For example, the active cerebral control based on user consciousness can make the artistic elements move with their thinking rhythm. This synchronism produces a kind of homogenous aesthetic expression based on empathy. The passive cerebral control based on user instinct can express a kind of freethinking activity during the communication or in the state of unconsciousness. This cybernetic model elaborates on relational and subconscious aesthetics. However, when we use neural structure and cerebral function to research the information reception mechanism, the passive cerebral control needs to be divided into two additional categories: i) explicit and ii) implicit thinking. These two cybernetic categories match the structure of relational and subconscious aesthetics.

Therefore, we divide the cybernetic mode of real-time EEG art into three categories: Active Control, Explicit Passive Control, and Implicit Passive Control. Active control refers to the modification of artistic elements by the command emit from the participant's mind through the EEG headset under conscious condition. Explicit passive control refers to that the participant does not actively give orders to the EEG when they are conscious. His thinking focuses on other tasks. The EEG controls the artistic elements by monitoring the thinking generated by the participant in a passive situation. Implicit passive control means that the participant loses consciousness, and EEG controls artistic elements by monitoring his subconscious brain activities. Finally, we find that the classification model of active thinking control, explicit passive thinking control, and implicit passive thinking control can be matched to the aesthetic structure of homogenous aesthetics, relational aesthetics, and subconscious aesthetics.

In the later section, we explain our cybernetic-aesthetics structure in context of some real-life artwork example bringing out different characteristics of the structure for better understanding and comprehension.

4 The Cybernetic–Aesthetics Structure in Real Life EEG Artworks

4.1 Active Control and Homogenous Aesthetics

Active control presents itself as an injection of a particular thought into the artwork. At the same time, the work must ensure reasonable feedback. This control mode builds synchronization between the human brain and elements through real-time interaction between thinking and feedback. This synchronization creates an empathy effect between mind and artistic expression.

The concept of "empathy" was originally proposed by the German aesthetician Robert Vischer in his doctoral thesis *On the Optical Sense of Form: A Contribution to Aesthetics* (1873), which changed the name of "the symbolic role of aesthetics" to "empathy". The occurrence of aesthetic feelings lies in the realization of sympathies: the emotional resonance between the subject and the object [16]. "New interactive art, through its expression of symbols and significations, touches the audience's heart, causes association, perception, and emotion. Thought the aesthetic experience, the art creates sensory illusions, mapping emotions to the art by interaction, giving the art new ideas and significations. Finally, the echo is established [17]".

From the neural mechanism, in the book *In te mi specchio - Per una scienza dell'empatia*, Gnoli and Rizzolatti pointed out that the cerebral cortex has a special neuron called mirror neuron. It is the basis of the "empathy" mechanism. Mirror neurons let humans through imitation to learn, that is, to replace themselves (others) with others (themselves) to interpret behaviors: through imitation to achieve emotional resonance. That is empathy [18]. The empathy not only lets the human being establish the "emotional" connection, but also constructs the foundation of the human culture to be inherited and progressed. In *The Theory of Moral Sentiment*, Adam Smith describes an acrobat who swings precariously on a wire and moves cautiously. The audience below, as he swings, unconsciously mimics his movements [19]. The synchronicity of this movement is a common altogether. Similarly, this explains why children learn life skills by imitating their parents and form affection in the process.

Therefore, abstracting this synchronization into the symbol, we find that the synchronicity of cerebral behavior and artistic expression is in common with all the EEG artworks using active control mode. Excellent works achieve harmony between subjective thinking and expected feedback, realizing the empathy effect.

In work *You are The Ocean* [20] (see Fig. 2), participants bring an EEG headset to control the state of an ocean scene by focusing or relaxing. When the user concentrates, the sea clouds and the wind, the waves roll, showing a violent landscape. If the user relaxes, the sea is showing a calm and peaceful state of clear. Here, the user's concentration sits into a state of tightness, while the picture matches his state in real-time to present a tense atmosphere. The relaxed mood corresponds to a calming picture. This kind of psychological state and aesthetic expression realize a homogenous tone. Through cognitive imitation, the empathy effect is established.

The aesthetics of active control is embodied in the resonance of emotion and mind realized under the establishment of the perceptible effect. In this state, the mirror neurons in our brains are involved in the entire aesthetic process.

Fig. 2. *You are The Ocean* created by Samanci, O. and Caniglia, G. [20]

Cerebral synchronicity is not a simple behavior. We need to focus on whether the feedback of the artistic elements is consistent with the user's cognition, expectation, and social experience: it is psychological synchronization. Good artwork is not a reproduction of a phenomenon. It should be free, surreal, and embodied as a pure utopian imagination realized by vision, audition, olfaction, touch. Art must awaken the user's emotional resonance, enhance the sense of experience.

Self-conscience/Physical Memory [21] (see Fig. 3) is a brain-controlled robotic sculpture in the University of Houston's Noninvasive Brain Machine Interface Laboratory. Motorized and illuminated acrylic ceiling tiles shift the architecture of the space itself in response to EEG data. The height of the panels is driven by alpha power suppression in the central cortical areas. The tiles' color transforms with alpha power changes in the occipital and frontal lobes. Alpha power in central area channels is used to drive the height of the acrylic tiles. The higher the relative alpha power in a channel, the closer the tiles get to the ceiling. This kind of cybernetic design allows participants to inject "energy" into the elements by increasing their attention and resist the gravity to let tiles fly. Thin suspension cables are imperceptible to the visual system of participants. Therefore, the matching between the flying visual effect and the cybernetic expectation is achieved in aesthetics. This homogeneity enables participants to feel that they have the ability to control physic objects. The empathy effect is thus produced.

Another example is Oliver Gingrich's brainwave installation The *Crack* [22] (see Fig. 4). The artist invites the audience to wear an EEG header and require him to create cracks by focusing on the concrete structure in the video. The act of concentration requires intense energy of thought, which is embodied by the artist as the power to pierce the concrete object. Through visual expression, cement as a hard object has a strong visual and emotional impact. The crack of the concrete structure establishes a homology between the audience's thinking and unbiased feedback. Finally, the audience can feel the beauty conveyed by "power" and the power of their spirit.

EEG Art directly establishes the dynamic relationship between thinking and artistic expression through EEG, which is the most significant difference from traditional art. Therefore, its aesthetics is based on this synchronous control and biochemical output of a

Fig. 3. *Self-conscience/Physical Memory* created by Todd, E., Cruz-Garza, J. G., Moreau, A., et al. [21]

Fig. 4. The *Crack* created by Gingrich, O. [22]

kind of universal beauty. Using active control, we need to pay attention to the relationship between the way of thinking and the signification of the work. Artistic expressions are treated as a bridge that determines the degree of matching between thinking and concept.

Finally, the establishment of an aesthetic structure under active control requires attention to two aspects:

- Whether the conception can harmoniously product a suitable, artistic expressive element?
- Whether the elements of art can stir up an emotion that matches the mind and make the audience feel the meaning of work?

4.2   Explicit Passive Control and Relational Aesthetics

Explicit passive control refers to the emotional relationship shifted by the mind through behaviors, which is developed in a conscious context. With the environment, or with other participants, produced brain waves are used to influence artistic expressions. In this form of control, the brain no longer consciously gives orders but focuses on the emotional experience aroused by behaviors. This difference means integration of behavior and plastic art (art forms that involve modeling or molding, such as sculpture and ceramics, or art involving the representation of solid objects with three-dimensional effects. Less often the term may be used broadly for all the visual arts), in which relational aesthetics plays a decisive role.

"Relational Aesthetics" was invented in 1995 by a French critic and curator Nicolas Bourriaud, "a theory that focuses on the relationships produced and caused between people in the artworks." It is one of the basic aesthetic structures of performance art. The creative interest of art arises in the interaction between the audience and the work when the integration of oneself into art and personal consciousness changes. New images, relationships, thinking and experiences, bring discoveries or surprising feedback. The experience process of the emotion and inscrutability becomes the key to the aesthetics [23].

For example, in the artwork *NUE* [24] (see Fig. 5), Lisa Park wears a dress made of 150 meters of cloth. She performs a process of separation from the dress symbolizes metamorphosis of silkworm and its struggle during the transformation into a moth. At the same time, her EEG data is transmitted to the 4Dsound system to make the sound around the whole space expressing her impulse to pursue freedom and transformation. *NUE* is an example of a struggle between behavior and the environment, stimulating emotional impulses through the process of metamorphosis. This behavior-based relational aesthetic is finally transmitted to the audience through EEG waves into sound, allowing the audience to explore the relationship between behavior and thought.

Fig. 5. *NUE* created by Lisa, P. [24]

"SAY_SUPERSTRINGS" [25] (see Fig. 6) uses the digital image to visualize the changes of brain waves during the performance of musicians in real-time. This kind of colorful effect can perfectly integrate with the rhythm and mood of the music, which is a new way to create a stage effect. In this creation, the musician's behavior is immersed in the performance. His thoughts and emotions are synchronized with music, which is reflected in the changes of brain waves. Those changes are instinctive. Finally, EEG artist gives this kind of modification to the visual image, so that the audience can enjoy the beauty of musician's thinking space while hearing.

Fig. 6. *"SAY_SUPERSTRINGS"* created by Ouchhh Studio [25]

For the explicit passive control up to two people, it is more about exploring the aesthetics of interpersonal relationship. In the work *Brainstorming: Empathy* [26] (see Fig. 7), the two participants were carrying an octopus-shaped EEG casque consisting of 350 LEDs. Both of them constantly change their own and the other's mental state through nonverbal communication. Each participant was able to see their mental state and the synchronicity of their thoughts through the LED lights on other's casque. At the same time, the music in the environment changes according to the mood of both parties. The active cerebral commands do not reflect the EEG control mode, but passive control through changes in thinking during communication with each other.

In explicit passive control, EEG waves pursue a natural growth in the process of behavioral interaction, accompanied by the deepening of emotional communication (reflected in a proper rhythm), like the melody of music. Through the artist's creation, this rhythmic brain wave can be expressed through visual or auditory, even other sensory forms.

The artistic elements using explicit passive control can be divided into three categories depending on the interactive scenario:

The first type of element is designed for the participants, such as sound, lighting, image transition. The aim is to help participants understanding changes in thinking through some modifications in the environment, which promotes emotional communication in behavior.

Fig. 7. *Brainstorming: Empathy* created by Victoria, V. [26]

Still [27] (see Fig. 8) is a famous work that integrates different forms of expression. The artist creates a quiet audio-visual environment with a desk lamp, some swaying leaves, shaking ink. The artist places a book on the desk. When the participant starts reading, their attention level is subconsciously improved, the desk lamp turns on, and the movement of leaves and ink gradually calms down, so that the environment is related to the participant's mood and task. Participant focused on "reading". Based on this behavioral relationship, the brain instinctively raises attention, which is a passive brain behavior. It then adjusts the environment that helps participant read and enter the book's world.

Fig. 8. *Still* created by Liu, W. [27]

The second type is designed for the audience, such as external data visualization. Here, the participants' communication is not disturbed by artistic elements. They completely immerse in the process of behavior. Audiences experience their emotions inherent in this communication through the artistic expression generated by their brain waves. This experience is a human cognitive exploration process.

In *EEG KISS* [28] (see Fig. 9), for example, couples are asked to wear EEG headset on stage and perform a kiss. EEG measures the brain signals of two participants during kissing and projects the waveforms on the floor in real-time, surrounding them, expressing the changes of their thought and emotion. Throughout the process, participants focused on kissing behavior, and most of them closed their eyes and immersed themselves without observing the visual effects created by their brainwaves. The audiences experience the ideological relationships of people immersed in kissing through visual effects.

Fig. 9. *EEG KISS* created by Lancel, K., Maat, H., and Brazier, F. 2017

The third is felt by both audiences and participants, such as the background music in the *EEG KISS*.

The most significant difference with active control is that in explicit passive control, the brain always focuses on the experience of communicating behavior rather than on control. Changes in brain waves are subconscious behaviors triggered by this communication. This aesthetic is reflected not only in the expression of plastic arts but also in the aesthetic of emotional and mental state in communication behavior

4.3   Implicit Passive Control and Subconscious Aesthetics

Implicit passive control is entirely intuitive and implicit. This process of mind control is usually a passive control under subliminal consciousness or hypnotic states, such as sleep and meditation.

Unlike explicit passive control, implicit passive control involves mostly individuals and directs the brain into a hypnotic or meditative state before art is created. The inductive methods can be verbal guidance or non-verbal communication.

For example, in work *The Phrontesterion* [29], the artist uses stroboscopic flash to bring the participant with eyes closed into a meditation state. However, in *The Octave of Visible Light: A Meditation Nightclub* [30], the artist firstly guides the participant to meditate state by verbal suggestions.

When the brain enters a specific state, art manifests itself in two ways:

First is that the brain, in a fully immersive state, creates artistic expression by detecting changes in brain waves by EEG. This artistic expression cannot be observed by the area of consciousness of the brain. It is subconscious.

For example, in *The Phrontesterion* (see Fig. 10), when the brain is wholly hypnotized, with the continuous the pulsating light, various pictures emerge in the participant's mind. At the same time, brain waves in the forehead are obtained. The signals are converted into projections and sounds in the environment in real-time. Here, the artistic effect created mainly serves the audiences. They explore the beauty in the deep thinking of the participant from the artistic expressions. The consciousness of the participant's brain is not aware of the visual effects.

Fig. 10. The *Phrontesterion (PandoraStar)* created by Haill, L. [29]

Another example is the interactive installation *Paradoxical Bubble* [31] (see Fig. 11). Artist Virgile Novarina sleeps in public with electrodes that capture her brain's activity during sleeping. Sleeper's brain activity controls the movement of bubbles in a video. Through this kind of control, the audience can observe the aesthetic effect of concrete subconscious thinking. Besides, it is interesting that the artist also provides the audience with an EEG headset. They can wear this EEG and control the movement of bubbles on another screen. By comparing the images in the two screens, the audience can see the difference of aesthetic performance between implicit passive control and active control, as well as the different experience brought to themselves.

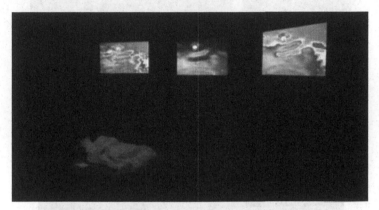

Fig. 11. *Paradoxical Bubble* created by Breidi, W. [31].

If the participants are experienced meditators, will the subconscious aesthetic expression under implicit passive control be more abundant? In the work *Mind Murmur* [32] (see Fig. 12), the artist invites experienced meditators as participants, who can enter into meditation without any guidance. During meditation, they enter several meditative stages at different depths. With sound and image, the audience can see different aesthetic rhythms hidden in different subconscious levels. This work is a bridge between the deep subconscious and the real world through audio-visual communication.

Second is that art created by the brain in a hypnotic or meditative state can rework on the brain again. For example, in *The Octave of Visible Light: A Meditation Nightclub* (see Fig. 13), after guided in a meditative state, participant's EEG signals control the change of environmental lighting color and sound. In turn, as the participant opens his eyes, the changing sound and light further induce his brain to deepen the meditation state. At this time, the artistic expressions must follow psychological suggestion principles. The purpose is to help the participant's consciousness immerse into a particular state and form a virtuous circle, ensuring subconscious aesthetic expression.

The aesthetics of implicit passive control is manifested in the liberalization of deep consciousness and the realization of subconscious cognitive beauty. Aesthetics is fundamentally the transmission of emotions. The most primary impulses and emotions are buried in the limbic system of the human brain. Thus, the aesthetics expressed through subconscious control from deep cognition is more instinctive, primitive. Without the

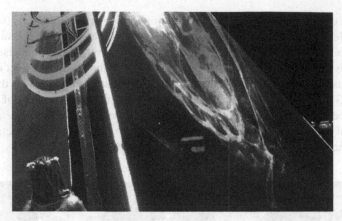

Fig. 12. *Mind Murmur* created by Fisher, D. et al. [32]

Fig. 13. *The Octave of Visible Light: A Meditation Nightclub* created by Lia, C. [30]. Photo credit: Samuel Cox

logical operation of the prefrontal cortex, the realization of aesthetic structure manifest as a free sensory propagation, similar to a dream.

Therefore, the artistic creation of implicit passive control needs to focus on the subconscious structure of the brain in the psychological suggestion and the re-stimulation stage. The artist needs to understand the methods to stimulate the most primitive, instinctive emotions and impulse in the subconscious space. Here, the artist should grasp the principle of psychotherapy, subliminal stimulation and psychological suggestion to support the establishment of aesthetic structure.

5 Conclusion

Through case studies, this paper takes the brain as the research object and looks for the aesthetic structure relationship under the cerebral control classification. Through research, we find that when thinking is classified based on cybernetics into active control, explicit passive control and implicit passive control, it can match three different aesthetic structures: homogenous aesthetics, relational aesthetics, and subconscious aesthetics. The three aesthetic characteristics are different. When we choose a cybernetic method, we must consider its proper aesthetic structure.

For the artist, clarifying aesthetic structure can help grasp the relationship between beauty and signification, so that the selected art form and elements conform better to the existence of mind and appearance. For the participant, the elements and interaction scenario conducted by appropriate cybernetic mechanism ensure a habitual cognitive behavior (emotional rather than logical). The aesthetic expression of work is natural and permanent. The structure contains a mechanism of guidance and symbol of form, and the form contains rationality and fluency of aesthetic realization.

According to the mapping of cybernetics and aesthetics, we hope this article can provide references for EEG art researchers and artists, return EEG art to its aesthetic originality. This field is currently dominated by cybernetic popularity. This return can help artists to achieve different expressions with appropriate control methods, allowing the emotion and concept of the artwork to be effectively disseminated to the audiences.

EEG art is an extensive and interdisciplinary domain. Although this paper mainly discusses and analyzes aesthetics and cybernetics in real-time EEG art, for our future research, we will also pay attention to the non-real time EEG artworks and their applications in the medical field and neuroscience. Therefore, we plan to study the aesthetics and cybernetics of non-real time EEG art in independent art creation, integrating and enhancing our current research results. If possible, we will further research the application and characteristics of EEG art as an auxiliary item in other interdisciplinary fields.

We hope that this study serves as a knock on the door to inspire artists' conception. It is also hoped that other researchers can take our points of view and realize much more mature EEG art aesthetic structures and theories.

References

1. Nicolas-Alonso, L.F., Gomez-Gil, J.: Brain computer interfaces, a review. Sensors 12(2), 1211–1279 (2012)
2. Adrian, E.D., Matthews, B.H.C.: The Berger rhythm: potential changes from the occipital lobes in man. Brain 57(4), 355–385 (1934)
3. Lucier, A.: Statement on: Music for Solo Performer. Biofeedback and the arts, results of early experiments, pp. 60–61 (1976)
4. Shimamura, A.P., Palmer, S.E.: Aesthetic Science: Connecting Minds, Brains, and Experience. Oxford University Press, Oxford (2012)
5. Liu, C.G.: Aesthetic: from the primitive cognitive function to the real existence. Jianghuai Tribune 6(5), 105–109 (2003)
6. Chen, C.K.: Emotional aesthetics and scientific aesthetics. Philos. Res. 7, 36–40 (1983)
7. Ahmed, S.U., Al Mahmud, A., Bergaust, K.: Aesthetics in human-computer interaction: views and reviews. In: Jacko, J.A. (ed.) HCI 2009. LNCS, vol. 5610, pp. 559–568. Springer, Heidelberg (2009). https://doi.org/10.1007/978-3-642-02574-7_63
8. Wang, R.Y.: Study on autonomous aesthetics of digital arts. J. Art Des. 1, 1–20 (2010)
9. Frank, H.W.: A cybernetic approach to aesthetics. Leonardo 10(3), 203–206 (1977)

10. Giannetti, C.: Estetica Digital: Sintopia del Arte, la Ciencia y la Tecnologia, pp. 53–63. L'Angelot, Barcelona (2002)
11. Tanaka, A.: Sensor-based musical instruments and interactive. In: Roger, D. (ed.) Oxford Handbook of Computer Music, pp. 233–257. Oxford University Press, Oxford (2009)
12. Fishkin, K.P.: A taxonomy for and analysis of tangible interfaces. Pers. Ubiquit. Comput. 8(5), 347–358 (2004)
13. Wadeson, A., Nijholt, A., Nam, C.S.: Artistic brain-computer interfaces: state-of-the-art control mechanisms. Brain-Comput. Interfaces 2(2–3), 70–75 (2015)
14. Prpa, M., Pasquier, P.: Brain-computer interfaces in contemporary art: a state of the art and taxonomy. In: Nijholt, A. (ed.) Brain Art. LNCS, pp. 65–115. Springer, Cham (2019). https://doi.org/10.1007/978-3-030-14323-7_3
15. Couchot, E.: A Tecnologia Na Arte Da Fotografia À Realidade Virtual. UFRGS Publisher, Porto Alegre (2003)
16. Sun, L.L.: Vischer's theory of empathy. Sci. Technol. Inf. (Acad. Res.) 30, 493&495 (2007)
17. Li, G.W.: The core function of empathy in art creation. J. Yuxi Normal Univ. 24(11), 30–36 (2008)
18. Gnoli, A., Rizzolatti, G.: In te mi specchio - Per una scienza dell'empatia. Rizzoli, Milan (2016)
19. Smith, A.: The Theory of Moral Sentiments (1759)
20. Samanci, O., Caniglia, G.: You are the ocean: interactive installation. In: Proceedings of the 2019 on Creativity and Cognition, pp. 414–421. ACM, San Diego (2019)
21. Todd, E., Cruz-Garza, J.G., Moreau, A., Templeton, J., Contreras-Vidal, J.L.: *Self-conscience/physical memory*: an immersive, kinetic art installation driven by real-time and archival EEG signals. In: Nijholt, A. (ed.) Brain Art, pp. 309–323. Springer, Cham (2019). https://doi.org/10.1007/978-3-030-14323-7_11
22. Gingrich, O.: The Crack (2019). https://olivergingrich.com/2019/07/02/the-crack-brainwave-installation-oliver-gingrich-2019/. Accessed 21 Jan 2020
23. Bourriaud, N.: Relational Aesthetics. Les Presses du Réel, Dijon (1998)
24. Lisa, P.: NUE (2015). https://www.thelisapark.com/. Accessed 21 Jan 2020
25. Ouchhh Studio: SAY_SUPERSTRINGS (2018). http://cargocollective.com/hellyeee/say_superstrings. Accessed 21 Jan 2020
26. Victoria, V.: Brainstorming: Empathy, October 2016. http://victoriavesna.com/brainstorming/. Accessed 21 Jan 2020
27. Liu, W.: Still (2017). https://www.liuwastudio.com/still. Accessed 21 Jan 2020
28. Lancel, K., Maat, H., Brazier, F.: EEG KISS: shared multi-modal, multi brain computer interface experience, in public space. In: Nijholt, A. (ed.) Brain Art, pp. 207–228. Springer, Cham (2019). https://doi.org/10.1007/978-3-030-14323-7_7
29. Haill, L.: The Phrontesterion (PandoraStar.) (2016). https://lucianahaill.wordpress.com/the-phrontesterion/. Accessed 21 Jan 2020
30. Lia, C.: The Octave of Visible Light: A Meditation Nightclub (2015). https://www.liachavez.com/the-octave-of-visible-light-a-meditation-nightclub/. Accessed 21 Jan 2020
31. Breidi, W.: Paradoxical Bubble (2019). https://virnova.wixsite.com/bulle-paradoxale/vierge-c16ae/. Accessed 21 Jan 2020
32. Fisher, D., et al.: Mind Murmur (2018). http://dinafisher.net/mind-murmur/about/mind-murmur.php/. Accessed 21 Jan 2020

User Experience Analysis for Visual Expression Aiming at Creating Experience Value According to Time Spans

Cairen Zhuoma[1(✉)], Keiko Kasamatsu[1], and Takeo Ainoya[2]

[1] Tokyo Metropolitan University, Tokyo, Japan
zoma1027@hotmail.com
[2] serBOTinQ, Tokyo Metropolitan University, Tokyo, Japan

Abstract. According to the popularity of O2O E-commerce model, which is used in digital marketing to describe systems enticing consumers within a digital environment to make purchases of goods or services from physical businesses, it shows us that online purchase becomes to the main way for customers in this days. However, the touch point from customers to the final goal becomes to a vital point. Based on the Human Centered Design (HCD), throughout the product promotion process, the customer is the starting point to promote the customer's purchase behavior through various marketing methods, but the ultimate goal is to achieve the long-term stable relationship between the product and customer.

By the online purchase, visual expression is considered as the most effective channel for customers to gain the information of the production. In this paper, I will summarize the brand image characteristics of existing dark chocolate brands to explore the relationship between the user's impression of the brand and the actual desire to buy the product. Mainly focus on the importance of vision in five senses, taking the color used in the packaging of the existing brand as the starting point, the analysis focuses on the relationship between different colors and different tastes, and the user's impression of the product.

Keywords: User experience · Time spans · Visual expression · Color · Taste

1 Introduction

1.1 Digital Marketing Selling

In order to different from other familiar products while making a product, designers will create a special concept. With online sales becoming increasingly mainstream, consumer behavior can be said to be even more efficient. As a result, promotion method is playing a vital role in online sales. Among them, it is considered that for a product be seen through online sales at the first time, the customer can judge only by the visual information, such as advertisements, packages, words and so on to understand the image and concept of the product itself. And, as the O2O (Online to Offline) is introduced into the marketing, it indicating the two-way flow between the online and the physical world, especially

© Springer Nature Switzerland AG 2020
C. Stephanidis et al. (Eds.): HCII 2020, LNCS 12424, pp. 363–373, 2020.
https://doi.org/10.1007/978-3-030-60117-1_27

retail and e-commerce, but also between brand marketing and shopper or point-of-sale marketing efforts to influence purchase decisions. Shopping with O2O, the customer's five senses can be further utilized by both methods of online and offline, and also provide the brand a unique experience which can become a selling point. Especially However, during this time, whether the concept was communicating to customers properly or not turn into an important issue for both company and customer. How to convey concepts that can be distinguished from similar products to customers, how to understand customer needs, and how to correctly communicate through mediation are considered to be significant in the design process. Since

Since the development of the Impressionists, color has become an increasingly sensitive visual form, and is increasingly attracting attention to artists and the public in artistic creation. I think the use of color in food packaging design is, to some extent, directly related to the impact of the product on consumers. Of the components that make up a food package, color is the one that can evoke the fastest response from customers. The "7-second rule" is known in the US marketing industry. A survey by the Center for Popular Color Research in the United States shows that there is a "7-second rule" when choosing products: In the face of a wide range of goods, people can determine whether they are interested in these goods or not in only 7 s. In this short and critical 7 s, the role of color accounts for 67%, which has become an important factor that determines people's likes and dislikes to goods. The US marketing industry also summarized the "7-second law", that is, consumers will decide whether they want to buy goods within 7 s. The first impression of a product on consumers may trigger consumer interest in the product, and hope to have a better understanding of the product in terms of functions, quality and other aspects. If a company not to think highly of visual design of a product, it will lose not only a focus, but also a business opportunity. In this short 7 s, the determining factor of color is 67%, which is the theoretical basis for the emergence of "color marketing" in the 1980s. In other words, the consumer decides in a matter of seven seconds whether he is interested in this product before various products. In that short seven seconds, the color effect reached 67%.

What's more, due to the popularity of online shopping, the sense of touch, taste, and smell in the five senses turn into ineffective during online shopping, so the role of visual information is more prominent and especially color plays a key role.

1.2 User Experience and Experience Value

As a way to communicate products and customers, promotion is playing the role to make customers willing to pay attention to the products and make purchases. Based on basic requirements to customers such as quality, price, materials of the product, it is necessary to analyze from the entire experience of the customer, and extract the elements which is matching the brand image that the company wants to express, and show it in the promotion completely in the end. Since different sorts of customers have different impressions on products, in this essay, I attempt to defend the view that observing customers and potential customers separately and provide several types of promotions is the key issue.

According to the user experience (UX), people can have indirect experience before their first encounter through expectations formed from existing experience of advertisements, demonstrations, others' opinions etc. Similarly, indirect experience extends after usage, for example, through reflection on previous usage, or through changes in people's appraisals of use. There are four parts in time spans, getting information before first encounter (anticipated UX), a specific change of feeling during interaction (momentary UX), appraisal of a specific usage episode (episodic UX), and views on a system as a whole, after having used it for a while (cumulative UX) (see **Error! Reference source not found.**). A major advantage of UX is that it can reflect the entire experience and feelings of a customer to a product or service. Qualitative methods offer an effective way of approaching customers' attitude toward products or services and show the value of experience which is also the benefit to create a new way for designing (Figs. 1 and 2).

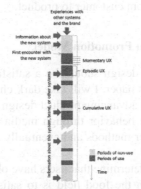

Fig. 1. UX over time with periods of use which is divided into Anticipated UX, Momentary UX, Episodic UX, Cumulative UX and non-use. (Roto et al. 2011, p. 8)

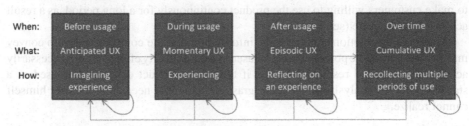

Fig. 2. Time spans of user experience, the terms to describe the kind of user experience related to the spans, and the internal process taking place in the different time spans. (Roto et al. 2011, p. 8)

From the perspective of UX, it combines episodic and cumulative experiences with products to maintain long retention with existing customers, providing even more meaningful experience value also unforgettable. It also emphasizes anticipated and momentary experiences to alert potential customers to the product. Finally, show the customer a complete experience in a visual representation with purchasing online also offline. Instead of using simple text and product appearance for visual expression, we aim to express the experience from the user's point of view in the four stages of the user experience.

These findings provide the following insights for future research: I will find out the key issue of designing concept of products or services which is also able to be used on promotion. According to the human centered design process (ISO 9241-230), after specifying the requirement of both customers and potential customers, producing design solutions, and evaluating the design against requirements, the effect of UX analysis will be figured out.

While in this research, I will focus on the impact of color on user perception during the product promotion stage which is corresponding to the anticipated UX in user experience's time spans. In order to maintain a long-term stable relationship with customers, through the design of the anticipated UX in the user experience, grasp the user's true feelings in the momentary UX, and use the result to realize the uniqueness of the episodic UX, and complete the cycle from customer to product.

1.3 Human Centered Design Promotion Model

The final goal to the product design should be a satisfactory user experience rather than purchase behavior. In this paper, I will take dark chocolate as an example. In the existing market, the process of advancing product design around the customers usually completes the user's purchase behavior through media advertising, market research, store sales promotion and other methods and eventually achieve to final goal which is eating chocolate enjoyable.

What is more, in order to determine that users have obtained a better product experience, the most basic need in the food field is to satisfy taste. In this process, the information conversion from vision to taste in the five senses is realized. Considering the visual information accepts the impact on the tasting experience and feeds back to the user according to the user experience, it is used in promotional marketing methods to make customers willing to use the product continuously for a long period, as a result achieve a stable cycle (see Fig. 3).

Marketing promotion simply by the information that the company wants to convey may not truly grasp the potential needs of users, so the publicity effect may not necessarily achieve the expected results. However, if the user's product experience is used as a starting point for analysis, it can better grasp the potential needs that the user himself cannot realize.

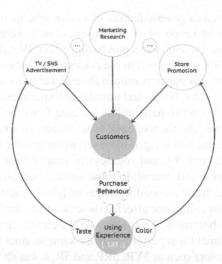

Fig. 3. Human Centered Design Promotion Model. Based on Human Centered Design, Customers obtain product information from various publicity channels in the market to achieve purchase behavior, but the ultimate purpose of product sales should not be to stop the purchase behavior but to focus on the customer's experience of using the product. It is determined by investigating the characteristics of the product. An essential element of the experience that can be used for product promotion.

2   Motivation

On every field of the designing, human centered design theory is necessary. The Human Centered Design Promotion Model, if applied widely, offers benefits and being able to grasp users' potential needs and spanning immediate product improvements. The motivation was to better understand user cognition and provide the proper marketing promotion approach point through my study. Attracting users to pay attention to the characteristics of the product, rather than completing a single purchase, it is more essential to focus on experiencing the product and to realize the value of user experience.

3   Previous Studies

So far, there are not so many studies analyzed for visual expression aiming at creating experience value by the time spans. Hence, I enumerate several typical studies about figuring out the relationship between color as visual information and taste as user experience.

According to Utsunomiya Tsunaki, Takeuchi Hiroshi, Niina Gen, Noshita Ryo, when we sale new items in e-commerce websites, customers have a problem that lacking of customer data: access logs, buying history, etc. Therefore, methods such as collaborative filtering, might not work in these cases. In this study, Tsunaki et al. (2019) worked on item data clustering among fashion e-commerce websites, and analogized which item cluster has a resemblance to the new item. From there, we inquest and apply the promotion method: valid to the item cluster in the past, and discuss the results in the new case.

Takeshi et al. (2010), as a general feature of a color scheme used for a food product package, a color in consideration of an attractiveness or a color reminiscent of a raw material of the food is used to enhance a purchasing effect. We speculated that the other reason for choosing a color scheme was to use colors to remind buyers of the taste image of the product. Therefore, this paper examined the effect of hue on the taste image of five basic tastes (sweet, sour, salty, bitter, and umami) in Experiment 1. To 30 participants, 15 chromatic colors and 5 achromatic colors selected from the Munsell color system were presented one by one, and the five basic taste images were rated on a 7-point scale. It became clear that sweetness is imaged from yellow such as 5YR, bitterness is imaged from gray such as N1.5 and N3, and sourness is imaged from 5Y. The color image had little effect on saltiness and umami. In Experiment 2, we focused on sweetness and bitterness, and examined the effects of differences in lightness and saturation (color tone) within a single hue on the colors that affected these two taste images. For the colors that affected sweetness and bitterness, 15 colors with different tones in a single hue were presented, and an experiment was performed in the same manner as in Experiment 1. As a result, for chromatic colors such as 5YR, 5RP, and 5R, it was shown that increasing the brightness increases the sweet taste image, and decreasing the brightness increases the bitter taste image. For grays such as 5G and 5BG, the overall taste image of bitterness was evoked, and the effect of sweetness was small. However, only in the combination of high lightness/medium saturation colors, the sweetness increased and the bitterness decreased. The results of this study suggest the possibility of controlling the increase and decrease of the taste image by changing the color tone, as well as the relationship between the hue and the taste image. With these results, the color becomes a taste image close to the actual taste of the food in the package, and information that serves as a criterion for making a purchase decision that meets the needs of the customer and leads to an increase in purchase motivation is expected.

Woods and Spence (2016) examined the basic taste recalled from monochromatic and color schemes, and clarified the relationship between color and the image of basic taste. The purpose of this study was to carry out a retest of this study. The color stimuli used were a total of 64 stimuli in 56 colors, each of which was combined with eight monochromatic stimuli of green, yellow, red, pink, blue, white, black, and purple. Chiaki (2018) is to allow the experimenter to evoke taste memory through visual information which is by observing the color, and judging the degree of the experimenter's affirmation of the result according to the speed of the reaction time. For the color stimuli presented in the center of the iPad screen, the participants selected the most appropriate taste from "sweet", "sour", "sour", and "bitter", and evaluated their confidence in the selection on a five-point scale. Sixty university students with normal color vision participated in the experiment. As a result, a similar tendency was observed in the study of Woods and Spence (2016) and this study. Black and bitterness, yellow and sourness, and pink and sweetness were found to be common to both monochromatic and color stimuli, and it was clarified that each taste was easily recalled from color. In these three tastes, it was clarified that presentation with a single color increased the consistency with the taste. On the other hand, in salty taste it was clarified that the consistency with taste can be increased by presenting two colors from white, red and blue, which are easy to recall.

However, I think that when analyzing the relationship between color visual information and taste, based on the Human Centered Design Promotion Model which is built between customers and products, instead of evoking users' taste memory with seeing color information, users should actually reverse the color survey through actual taste experience, which means it can get closer to the potential needs of users more accurately at the anticipated UX.

4 Preliminary Investigation

In the preliminary investigation, I mainly pick the anticipated UX in the user experience time spans to catch the proper touchpoint from customers to the product. Since I collected about 70 sorts of chocolate from the whole world. Extracting the main colors on the chocolate packaging, and the coordinate axis is established according to different tastes. The horizontal axis is the RGB color bar and the vertical axis is the chocolate taste. According to the distribution rule of the product in the coordinate axis, find out the colors that can be used to represent different flavors of chocolate packaging. Summarize the use of different color on distinct product taste to customers in existing brands.

4.1 About Dark Chocolate

Chocolate as a wide range of products, chocolate with different flavors has very unique characteristics, so I insist dark chocolate is in line with this research background. It's known that the different of proportion of cocoa is the standard to measure the type of chocolate. According to the national standard GB/T 19343, it can be divided into dark chocolate (Dark Chocolate or pure chocolate)-total cocoa solids ≥30%; milk chocolate (Milk Chocolate)-total cocoa solids ≥25% and total milk solids ≥12%; White Chocolate-Cocoa butter ≥20% and total milk solids ≥14%. Dark chocolate, with its notable deep brown color, is the second most popular type of chocolate. It is sometimes referred to as black or semisweet chocolate and is noticeably less sweet than milk chocolate. In recent years, dark chocolate has surged in popularity thanks to a number of articles being published about the health benefits.

According to the FDA definition, dark chocolate must contain at least 15% chocolate liquor but usually contains closer to about 50%. Most high-quality, dark chocolate does not contain added dairy and can be a great vegan-friendly chocolate. The lack of dairy and less sugar gives dark chocolate firmer texture than milk chocolate or white chocolate. This is why a well-tempered piece of dark chocolate will have a nice snap when broken in half.

The flavor profile of dark chocolate can vary widely based on the cocoa content of the chocolate. Dark chocolate's widely-acclaimed health benefits make it a favorite snack among health-conscious consumers.

4.2 Investigation Content

This paper will list the various chocolate brands and types around the world but mainly focus on dark chocolate and observe the different color applications through the proportion of cocoa ingredients.

Among them, the selection of color is not simply to select the color with the most area in the package, but to extract the color used to represent the taste in the package. Here is an example of the Japanese brand Royce's chocolate bar. In the packaging of this product, this series chocolate bar is mostly covered by creamy white color, therefore it is necessary to use different color to red represents milk taste, dark red represents almond bitter taste, yellow represents white taste, green represents almond milk taste, cyan-blue represents creamy milk taste, blue represents cacaonibs 70% dark chocolate taste, purple represents rum & raisin taste and black represents dark chocolate taste (Fig. 4).

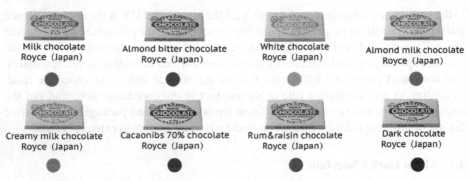

Milk chocolate   Almond bitter chocolate   White chocolate   Almond milk chocolate
Royce (Japan)   Royce (Japan)   Royce (Japan)   Royce (Japan)

Creamy milk chocolate   Cacaonibs 70% chocolate   Rum&raisin chocolate   Dark chocolate
Royce (Japan)   Royce (Japan)   Royce (Japan)   Royce (Japan)

Fig. 4. Color using of Japan chocolate brand packaging

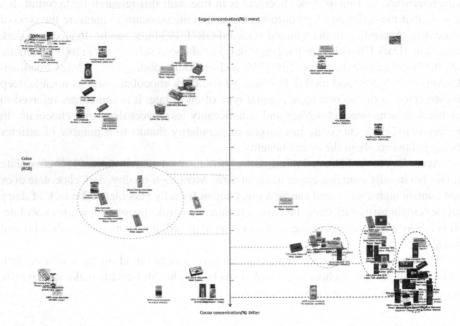

Fig. 5. Coordinates of chocolate taste and packaging color using.

The horizontal axis is RGB color bars, and the vertical axis is chocolate taste. The negative part of vertical axis represents dark chocolate with sort of bitter taste, and the positive part of vertical axis represents ordinary chocolate, taste chocolate and white chocolate with relatively sweet taste. We pick chocolates brand several countries in the world, which are Italy, Japan, Switzerland, Germany, Belgium, America, China, Spain, England, France, Poland, Russia. Extracting the representative colors used in various chocolate packages and position them in coordinates. Observing the distribution of each chocolate in the overall coordinate axis, we can recognize some rules (Fig. 5).

1. According original chocolate making country, we can find that the chocolate produced in Japan prefers to use various colors to reflect the characteristics of different flavors. In contrast, traditional chocolate producing countries still tend to use natural colors like white, brown and dark brown in chocolate ingredients as promotional materials.
2. Combining the relationship between taste and color, we can see that the color used in the relatively sweet flavor chocolate packaging is concentrated in the warm color area like white to yellow, and the opposite, the bitterer chocolate packaging uses cold colors more often like green, blue, purple and black.
3. Creamy white [R251, G238, B181] is frequently used in white chocolate;
   Red [R:202 G:58 B:28] is used in milk chocolate;
   Dark blue [R:28 G:68 B:139] is used in cocoa ingredients around 70% chocolate;
   Purple [R:135 G:62 B:147] is used in cocoa ingredients around 80% chocolate;
   Black [R:0 G:0 B:0] is used in cocoa ingredients around 100% chocolate (Fig. 6).

Types of chocolate	Color from package
White chocolate	R:251 G:238 B:181
Milk chocolate	R:202 G:58 B:28
≈70% dark chocolate	R:28 G:68 B:139
≈80% dark chocolate	R:135 G:62 B:147
≈100% dark chocolate	R:0 G:0 B:0

Fig. 6. Summary of color using in packaging according to different taste chocolates.

5 Conclusion

In general, in the existing chocolate brands, the packaging design of dark chocolate is focused on cold colors with dark brilliances and high color saturation. In other words, the chocolate market now will use cold colors to express the type of bitter chocolate.

Specifically, different levels of cocoa proportion will bring different tastes, which can be summarized creamy white is frequently used in white chocolate; red is used in milk chocolate; dark blue is used in cocoa ingredients around 70% chocolate; purple is used in cocoa ingredients around 80% chocolate in existing brands.

6   Future Tasks

In order to be able to better understand user needs, the focus should be on the user experience when using the product. So as to convey the brand image to customers, the existing brands match the color of their chocolate products brand, and stimulate users' purchasing desire in the end. For consumers who is about to buying products for the first time, whether they can establish a long-term stable relationship with consumers or not depends more on whether the product taste is consistent with the consumer. Under the premise that the product has not been experienced in person, the use of color in packaging can properly arouse the user's correct taste and need to conduct research on the premise of taste experience.

So, in the next step, I will implement an experience-based interview experiment to allow customers by stimulating the senses of visual and taste, and contact the color analysis results through a real experience of the product.

- First, investigate the experimenter's familiarity and preference about dark chocolate, and ask about personal experiences surrounding dark chocolate. These questions are aiming to further analyze the user's momentary UX and episodic UX.
- Second, a brand of chocolate products with different flavors will be taken as an example. Take a bite of chocolate at the first, and choose the color that can be correctly matched on the color card through the taste of the chocolate which can show the momentary UX. At the same time, record the response time of the experimenter from being asked question to the color selection. According to the result, we are able to judge the experimenter's affirmation on the result.
- Then, show the product packaging to the experimenter, and let the experimenter observe the use of color on the package and ask whether the use of color on the existing package meets personal expectations.
- Record all the data during the experiment, analyze from the customer's perspective, and judge whether it is consistent between the packaging design circulating in the existing market with the customers' experience and judgement.

In future research, it is also very important that different user types have different feelings about the product. Because of its unique taste, dark chocolate is not very popular which also means it has certain limitations on the user level. In recent years, the health benefits of dark chocolate have been widely known, and the customer has gradually expanded. Therefore, compared with users who are accustomed to the unique taste of dark chocolate, how to get the attention of potential users is also a worthy part of product promotion. The experimenter is not limited to users who regularly eat dark chocolate, but the feelings of users who do not regularly eat dark chocolate deserve more attention. The taste of the product itself must be a key factor in the success of the product. But whether the taste characteristics of the product can be correctly transmitted to consumers through visual information is also can't be ignored.

As the result, this will be the main content of my future research.

References

Mayum, H.: Life style and representative culture: 2. Visual images of mass production foods: simulacra foods. In: Proceedings of the Annual Conference of JSSD, vol. 48, no. 0, pp. 188–189 (2001)

Shigeno, S.: Effects of visual information on the identification of foods. In: The Proceedings of the Annual Convention of the Japanese Psychological Association, vol. 74, no. 0, p. 3EV032 (2010)

Takeshi, K., Ken, M., Katori, A.: Effects of taste image by three attributes of color. Des. Res. **54**, 107–112 (2010)

Roto, V., Law, E., Vermeeren, A., Hoonhout, J.: User Experience White Paper (2011)

Woods, A.T., Spence, C.: Using single colors and color pairs to communicate basic tastes. i-Perception **7**(4), 1–15 (2016)

Chiaki, O.: A study of single colors and color pairs to communicate basic tastes. J. Color Sci. Assoc. Jpn. **42**(3+), 93 (2018)

Tsunaki, U., Hiroshi, T., Gen, N., Ryo, N.: Proposal of new item promotion among fashion e-commerce websites, using item clustering. In: Abstracts of Annual Conference of Japan Society for Management Information, vol. 201906, no. 0, pp. 169–172 (2019)

AI in HCI

AI in HCI

Arny: A Study of a Co-creative Interaction Model Focused on Emotion Feedback

Sarah Abdellahi(✉), Mary Lou Maher, Safat Siddiqui, Jeba Rezwana, and Ali Almadan

University of North Carolina Charlotte, Charlotte, NC 28213, USA
{sabdella,m.maher,ssiddiq6,Jrezwana,aalmadan}@uncc.edu

Abstract. This paper presents an AI-based co-creative system in which the interaction model focuses on emotional feedback, that is, the decisions about the creative contribution from the AI agent is based on the emotion detected in the human co-creator. In human-human collaboration, gestures, verbal communications, and emotional responses are among the general communication strategies used to shape the interactions between the collaborators and negotiate the contributions. Emotional feedback allows human collaborators to passively communicate their experience and their perception of the process without distracting the flow of the task. In human-human co-creative collaboration, participants interact and contribute to the task based on their perception of the collaboration over time. In designing human-AI co-creative collaboration, we address two challenges: (1) perceiving the user's cognitive state to determine the dynamics of collaboration, such as whether the system should lead, follow, or wait, and (2) deciding what the agent should contribute to the artifact. This paper presents a model of an AI agent that addresses these challenges and the results of our study of participants that interact with the co-creative agent.

Keywords: Affect · Facial expression · Co-creative · Artificial intelligence

1 Introduction

Human-computer co-creativity involves both humans and computers collaborating on a shared creative product as partners. Emotion detection can enhance user engagement in a creative collaboration with an AI partner. Emotions align with different human cognitive states and allow humans to reflect and communicate with their collaborative partners in order to calibrate the collaboration dynamics and their behavior [1–3]. In a computational setting, facial expressions of emotions are an ideal candidate for feedback since they are passive, meaning that the user does not need to explicitly click or say anything. Unlike other negotiation methods such as voting buttons and verbal feedback, the passive characteristic of emotional feedback allows negotiation to happen without distracting the flow of the creative process. Moreover, passive emotional feedback does not require the user to learn or get used to any new method of communicating the feedback as required by methods such as verbal feedback. While there are many current studies

© Springer Nature Switzerland AG 2020
C. Stephanidis et al. (Eds.): HCII 2020, LNCS 12424, pp. 377–396, 2020.
https://doi.org/10.1007/978-3-030-60117-1_28

focused on emotion detection and interpretation of human facial expressions [4–6], these studies rarely focus on deploying their results in the design of novel interaction systems. Consequently, the current designs of co-creative systems lack a negotiation mechanism that is possible through emotional feedback in human collaboration.

Arny is a co-creative system designed to investigate the idea of adopting emotion as a feedback mechanism that effectively informs the co-creative agent on how it should behave to increase creative engagement and fluid interaction. In this paper, we describe an interaction model, Arny, as shown in Fig. 1, that deploys emotion as a feedback mechanism to modulate the interaction dynamics and behavior of a co-creative agent to enhance the user's engagement and satisfaction with the co-creative process in a collaborative drawing context. We present the iterative design of Arny and the considerations in developing the interaction models into a co-creative drawing system.

We report on our case studies of users' interactions with Arny in the context of an interior design task that allowed us to explore the possibilities and challenges of such an interaction approach. The results of our case studies of participants' interaction with Arny show possible interpretations of emotion factors such as valence and engagement while designing an emotion-focused interaction model for a co-creative system.

2 Background

Considering the critical role of emotion in human interactions, we seek to make human centered computational systems more spontaneous by incorporating human-like interactions, by including emotions in the dynamic. In natural human collaboration "Emotional expressions are crucial to development and regulation of interpersonal relationships" [1]. Studies have shown individuals with facial paralysis experience great levels of difficulty developing and maintaining even casual relationships as they are incapable of expressing emotions effectively. This inspires the consideration of affect in systems design [1].

Currently, in different contexts of system design, it is the system that is expected to understand the users and provide a low barrier method of interaction. This human-computer interaction philosophy of system design focuses on consideration of the user's characteristics and reactions [7]. The philosophy has been adopted to the level that Hudlica [7] states: "In some communities we no longer even speak of users and machines as separate entities, but rather of collaborative systems. ... The synergy of technological and methodological progress on one hand, and changing user expectations on the other, are contributing to redefining of the requirements for what constitutes effective and desirable in HCI".

When it comes to collaborative systems, however, consideration of affect is much more than user requirements. In a co-creative system when the user and the system contribute to a shared task, consideration of affect has a significant influence on the interaction between the participants and consequently the main sensemaking flows of the collaboration. Emotions elicited by stimuli events trigger responses in the participants and allow them to adapt to the collaboration [2, 3].

There is relatively little research about interaction models in the growing field of computational co-creativity, which is reflected in a lack of focus on interaction design in existing co-creative systems. In recent years, researchers designed many co-creative systems that are very intriguing and creative, yet sometimes users fail to maintain their interest and engagement while collaborating with the system due to the quality of interaction and collaboration from the AI. Most of the co-creative systems use voting buttons or direct manipulation from the user for communicating user preference to the AI. However, rating AI contributions or feedback buttons merely achieve the co-regulation needed between the participants for mutual engagement in collaboration. Gutwin and Greenburg [8] reported consequential feedback as a major element of collaboration mechanics, which includes facial expression, gaze and embodied communication. Collaborators pick up important information that is unintentionally "given off" by partners and this is considered as consequential communication.

Jaques et al. [9] show that making an AI agent aware of implicit social feedback from humans in the form of facial expression can allow for faster learning of actions that complement the user contribution and goal. They argued that an autonomous generative AI agent should be able to recognize facial expressions and optimize for actions that appear to please humans as measured through these signals. Thus, unlike previous approaches to learning from human preferences [11, 12], explicit supervision from humans is not required for the model to learn. Facial expression from participants was collected to produce sketch drawings by the generative system. They used a Latent Constraints GAN (LC-GAN) to learn from the facial feedback of a small group of viewers, and then showed in an independent evaluation with 76 users that the model produced sketches that lead to significantly more positive facial expressions. Thus, they established that implicit social feedback in the form of facial expression can improve the output of a deep learning AI model.

Kellas and Trees [13] refer to two distinct sense-making processes in an open-ended improvisational interaction, such as collaborative drawing or having a conversation: 1) functional sense-making that determines the content generated for a particular turn, e.g. choosing to draw a house or pattern, or choosing which words to say, and 2) interactional sense-making that structures and maintains how the interaction is unfolding through time i.e. the interaction dynamics, such as turn-taking, turn length, and the overall rhythm of interaction. Participatory sense-making occurs when there is a mutual co-regulation of these two sense-making processes between multiple participants, i.e. both participants are adapting their responses to each other and working to maintain an engaging interaction dynamic that supports the mutual exchange [14, 15].

In human collaboration, collaborators naturally co-regulate their sense-making processes through awareness of their collaborator's judgment of their contribution at each point of time. This awareness allows the collaboration path to intuitively shape itself. Awareness of collaborator's emotions during a collaboration allows the participants to validate their actions from their collaborator's point of view and use this awareness to proceed with the participatory sensemaking [16]. The meaning structures built by the interactional sense-making process guide the interaction forward by suggesting what can be added next given the history of the interaction. Also, interaction patterns are developed that circumscribe the type and amount of content to be generated at a given time. For example, when getting to know each other, people often employ a question and answer interaction pattern that suggests when each person should ask another question to keep the interaction moving. The same concept of having a pattern can be true for collaborative drawing – interaction dynamic patterns emerge such as call and response, mimicry, mutual building, antagonism, and transformation.

Once an interaction pattern is established through awareness of affect and context, cognitive resources can be turned from interactional sense-making to functional sense-making, and the participant can focus solely on generating a response to their partner in line with the latest interaction pattern being employed rather than generating a new contribution from scratch. This process can repeat during the collaboration which can direct the participant to choose to re-engage in interactional sensemaking to come up with a new way of interacting and establish a new interaction pattern [3].

3   Arny

Arny is an emotion aware co-creative drawing system designed to explore co-creative interaction focused on emotion feedback. Arny follows a human-AI collaboration model that considers not only the collaborators' contribution to the task, but also a method of interaction to communicate perceptions and expectations similar to what is followed in human-human collaboration. For this purpose, we decided to utilize affect and affect communication through facial expression as a channel of interaction between the user and the AI system. The current design of Arny is a result of two design iterations and evaluations that we describe in this paper.

3.1   Role and Detection of Affect

In order to design an affective system, some fundamental aspects have to be decided. The first and foremost decision to be made is what is the role of affect in the system design. Reference to affect in human system interactions can encompass various interpretations. Consideration of affect in system design can refer to recognizing user affect, adapting to a user's affective state, generating affective states within an agent or a combination of these options [7]. The interpretation addressed by Arny is recognizing the user's affect and adapting to the user's emotional state.

While typical co-creative AI systems only focus on the functional sense-making in order to collaborate with their human colleagues, as shown in Fig. 1(top), Arny follows a model similar to Fig. 1(bottom) to incorporate the partner's emotion in the system design and include the interactional sensemaking component to its sensemaking cycle.

Since the role of affect in the design of Arny is to investigate the user's emotional state and adapt to it, one fundamental aspect to investigate in Arny's design is affect recognition. User affect can be measured through a variety of biological and psychological methods including heart rate, facial expression, body gestures, diagnostic tasks, and self-report [17, 18]. These methods have advantages and disadvantages in terms of accuracy, ubiquity, and intuitiveness. The emotion recognition method in Arny uses the facial expression method of emotion recognition as it provides a sufficient level of accuracy for the purpose of this research. Moreover, using this method, emotions can be measured in real-time and without distracting the user or interrupting the user-system interactions. For its current iterations, Arny uses the user's emotional state reported to it by Affectiva - a facial expression emotion detection tool [19].

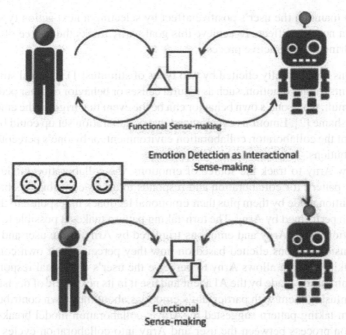

Fig. 1. Functional sense making in collaboration (top) and Arny's model of interaction (bottom)

Affectiva is a real-time facial expression recognition toolkit currently available as an add-on to the iMotion biometrics evaluation package [20]. Affectiva captures the participant's facial expressions using a basic webcam. To code the captured expressions, Affectiva uses the "Facial Action Coding System (FACS)" which is the most widely used model of coding facial behaviors [21]. Affectiva can code different factors of facial expressions such as valence value and engagement level based on a large data set of facial expressions previously coded manually by FACS experts for training purposes [21].

3.2 Interaction Model

Due to lack of research [22, 23] on interaction between a human and a co-creative AI agent based on emotion detection, we started with a simple interaction model influenced by our conjecture and our observations of human creative collaborations for Arny. A pilot study using this model then guided us to a revised version of an interaction model for a co-creative collaboration context.

Arny's interaction model includes two basic components, a collaboration model and a set of collaboration rules. The collaboration model provides the basic structure of the collaboration in addition to an overview of the feedback types used by Arny. The collaboration rules state how Arny responds to each specific feedback type.

Collaboration Model. Arny's collaboration model is structured to allow Arny to track the source of different emotions expressed by the user. The goal of Arny's collaboration model is to maintain the user's positive affect by selecting a next action type that does not trigger a negative affect. To achieve this goal, Arny tracks the source of a triggered emotion during the interactive process.

Emotions are generally elicited by two types of stimulus: 1) External stimuli, when outside events trigger emotion, such as natural causes or behavior of other people, and 2) internal stimuli, when one's own behavior can be the event that triggers the emotion, such as pride or shame [2]. Emotions experienced in a collaboration set up could be triggered by actions of the collaborator, collaboration environment, or by one's perception of their own contributions.

To allow Arny to track the source of emotions, the collaboration model follows a turn-taking pattern for collaboration and responds to user's contributions based on the last contribution made by them plus their emotional feedback in response to the previous contribution performed by Arny. The turn-taking pattern makes it possible to only focus on expectations from Arny and emotions triggered by Arny in the user and ignore the user's intrinsic emotions elicited based on how they perceive their own contributions. The turn-taking pattern allows Arny to perceive the user's emotional response to each specific contribution made by the AI agent and use it in its next cycle of decision making without confusing them with participant's emotions about their own contributions.

The turn-taking pattern suggested by Arny's collaboration model breaks down the collaboration process between the user and Arny into collaboration cycles. Each collaboration cycle includes a user's turn and an Arny's turn. On each user turn, the user contributes one drawing object to the shared drawing space. To contribute this drawing object, the participant can choose to converge to what was drawn in the previous turn or diverge from the previous drawing. A converging action in this definition refers to a contribution with the intention to follow the same mental model as the collaborator. Diverging actions, on the contrary, refer to the contribution of a new element that has the potential to cause a conflict between the AI and the user's mental models [24]. In the context of collaborative drawing, a converging contribution can be a contribution with visual or conceptual similarity to the collaborator's actions, while cognitive divergence refers to a distance in terms of visual similarity, conceptual similarity or both. Arny's turn happens right after the user's turn in each cycle. On each of Arny's turns, it contributes nothing or one drawing object to the shared drawing space. This drawing object is selected to converge to what was drawn in the previous turn of drawing or to diverge from the previous drawing. The decision on when to converge, diverge, or pass is made according to the collaboration rules and based on the user's emotion in the current cycle on user's turn and the user's drawing input from the previous cycle. Figure 2 illustrates the collaboration model followed by Arny V1.

Collaboration Rules. The collaboration rules in Arny's model of interaction are based on emotion interpretation and describe decision making. These rules describe how Arny selects its next contribution based on a memory of the collaborator's emotional feedback over the past turn(s) and the user's latest contribution to the task in the current cycle. Arny evaluates how satisfied the user is with the recent flow of interaction and decides when to converge to or diverge from the user's contributions.

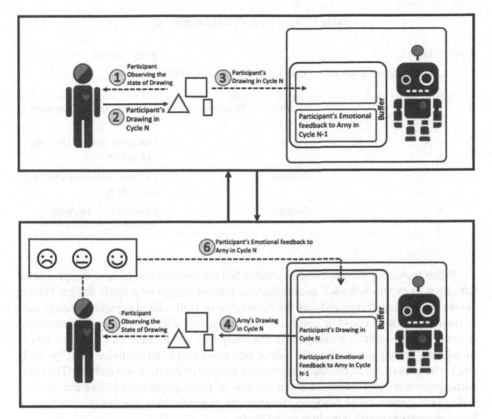

Fig. 2. Arny V1's collaboration cycle: user's turn (top) and Arny's turn (bottom)

3.3 Arny Version 1

Arny Version 1 (Arny V1) is the first iteration of Arny with an interaction model focused on the valence value of the user's emotional feedback. Figure 2 presents a schema of the collaboration model for this version of Arny. The collaboration rules followed by Arny V1 are presented in Table 1. The rules state that Arny will converge when the user had a positive response to the previous contribution, diverge when the user had a neutral response, and pass when the user had a negative response. This version of Arny was tested using the Wizard of OZ approach discussed in the next section.

4   Pilot Study

We performed a pilot study in order to better understand the user's interactions and expectations when collaborating with Arny V1. For this pilot study a Wizard of Oz prototype was designed to interact with the user's based on Arny's interaction model. The results from this study were then used to create Arny V2 which was evaluated in a follow up study.

Table 1. Arny version1 collaboration rules

Cycle	Input		Arny's action
	User's drawing in cycle	User's valence value in cycle N-1	
1	1	No Previous Reference	Converge to User Drawing in Cycle 1
N	N	Positive	Converge to User Drawing in Cycle N
		Neutral	Diverge from User Drawing in Cycle N
		Negative	Pass with No Drawing Action

When recruiting participants, we established the requirement to have design-related education or experience such as architecture, interior design or graphic design. Having design related experience reduces the occurrence of skill related negative feelings such as frustration which could be confused with the type of affect this study was exploring. Another requirement to participate in the study was not to have face cover or lots of facial hair. Participants with facial hair or face cover had to be excluded from the study due to the limitations of the facial expression method of emotion recognition. The study participants were not informed about the role of facial expression before the drawing tasks. This decision was made to eliminate the potential bias that being conscious of facial expression could introduce to the study.

4.1 Study Design

We performed a Wizard of Oz study in which the users collaborating with Arny were given the impression that there is an AI collaboration with them on Ziteboard, a simple online drawing platform. However, there were actually two members of our research team sitting in a different room and interacting with the participant in accordance to the Arny V1 interaction model and based on the Affectiva's report of participant's emotion which was captured by a webcam on the participant's computer. Our wizard team consisted of an Emotion Interpreter Wizard and a Drawing Wizard. The Emotion Interpreter Wizard was in charge of observing the real-time emotional feedback of the participant on the Affectiva platform and priming the Drawing Wizard when to take converge, diverge or pass actions. The Drawing Wizard was in charge of contributing to the interior design task according to the primes given by the Emotion interpreter Wizard and the last object contributed by the participant. The drawing wizard had a list of objects to choose from for each contribution. In time for a converging action, the Drawing wizard contributed by drawing an object from the list which was contextually similar to the user input. For diverging actions, on the other hand, the wizard drew a relevant object to the task with less contextual similarity to the input. The study setup followed for the pilot study is presented in Fig. 3.

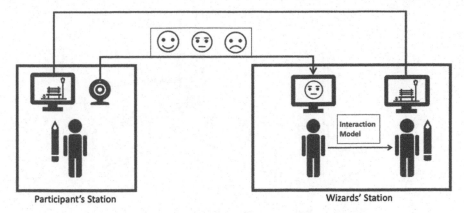

Fig. 3. Pilot study setup for testing of Arny V1

The participants were provided with a consent form. The consent form explained what the participant should expect and the estimated time to complete the study. In addition, the interior design task description was provided to the participants.

Participants in this study collaborated with Arny on an interior design task. For this task the participant is presented with the initial office layout shown in Fig. 4 in the Ziteboard online platform which is shared with the wizards sitting in the other room. For this design task, Arny collaborates with the users and contributes to the shared interior design challenge with consideration of their emotional feedback and their last drawing contribution as previously described in Arny V1 section. The main purpose of using an interior design instead of an open-ended task for our investigation was the simplicity of a constrained creative collaboration around an interior design task. The presence of restrictions was especially important since we are utilizing a Wizard of Oz method where a wizard has to engage with the participant actions without a significant delay. The collaborative task and the participant emotional feedback was screen recorded during the study for later analysis. The emotion factors other than the valence value (engagement, anger, etc.) were recorded during the pilot for the purpose of analysis but not used for the collaborative task.

When the task was over, the participant performed a semi-structured retrospective review of the process and answered some interview questions about their experience interacting with Arny. For this retrospective review and interview, participants saw a fast forward video of the collaboration and answered these questions about each cycle of the collaboration during the task:

- How did you feel about what Arny did on this turn?
- Do you think Arny was converging to or diverging from your idea? Did that have an influence on how you felt about it?
- How do you think what Arny did here influenced your engagement?
- How did what Arny did here influenced your next drawing?

The interview was audio recorded for the purpose of analysis.

Fig. 4. Initial office layout the participant starts with in pilot and follow-up studies

4.2 Results

The pilot study included six graduate student participants, three males and three females all with self-reported higher than medium drawing skills. The collaborative design task between Arny and each of these participants included 10 actions from Arny and 10 actions from each participant (total of 60 contributions by participants). We performed a thematic analysis of the interviews and the retrospective data. We also triangulated the responses to the interview and retrospective phase with the Affectiva report of emotions to evaluate the emotion detection accuracy. We identified three different themes:

Influence of Arny's Actions on the Participant's Engagement and Inspiration.
Based on the participants' responses, Arny's contributions had a positive impact on their engagement at a total of 24 turns out of the 60 Arny turns throughout the study. Participants reported only 3 cases when Arny's contribution (converge or diverge) had a negative influence on them staying engaged with the task. During the interviews, most participants described the influence of Arny's actions on their engagement in relation to how they were inspired by Arny. Also, in several cases, participants described a long-term influence of Arny's actions on them staying engaged with the process. Such long-term influences were cases when the participant already had an idea for their next contribution, but an inspiration by Arny encouraged them to think ahead about a future contribution.

Also, some participants reported negative emotions triggered by Arny's pass actions. They described these cases as times they were hoping for an inspiration from Arny but the system failed them by passing. Comparing these self-reports with the existing emotion data from the users we realized that we could have prevented these conditions if the participant engagement was used by Arny as a factor to predict the user expectation.

Participant's Perception of Arny's Actions. An interesting pattern in the retrospective protocols was the participant's interpretation of Arny's intention behind each contribution. Although the wizard's drawing actions were all performed based on Arny's model of interaction, participants had a human-like interpretation of these actions. Participants personified Arny as a collaborator who was: 1) understanding or not-understanding them 2) being considerate of their ideas and built on them, and 3) inspiring them and surprising them by bringing new ideas to the design. This was especially interesting when participants interpreted Arny's action in relation to its capability to understand their stance about the collaboration: "Arny understood that I didn't like what it did", "It was giving me space to develop my idea," "I liked that it cared about what I did," and "This was kinda freaky...I was thinking of drawing a circle here and then system did literary what I was planning to draw...so that was great." These types of statements about users' perception of Arny's actions suggest that the interaction model used for collaboration was successful in interactional sensemaking of the process and creating a human-like interaction dynamics pattern between the user and Arny.

Stoic vs Expressive Faces Affect Reports. Although Arny's interaction model was able to successfully maintain positive feelings between the participant and the system for most of the collaboration process, we noted several cases of affect intensity difference between the Affectiva reports and participants' self-reports. This observation and some follow up investigation of the literature [5] guided us to consider the impact of demographic factors such as ethnicity and personality type for our future studies and research. For future generations of Arny, we suggest development of a calibration feature that adjusts the affect reports based on a pre-test and demographic information.

4.3 Design Implications for Arny Version 2

Arny version 2 (Arny V2) is a modified design based on the results of the pilot study. Similar to Arny V1, the interaction model in Arny V2 follows a turn taking strategy. This new interaction model selects the next contribution from the AI agent based on three inputs: 1) a memory of the collaborator's valence in the previous contribution cycle that allows Arny to perceive the user's value judgment of that last contribution, 2) the user's engagement level in the beginning of the current cycle that allows Arny to predict user's expectation from Arny in the current cycle, and 3) the user's latest contribution to the task in the current cycle. In other words, the first input allows Arny to evaluate how satisfied the user is with the previous interaction pattern the agent followed. The second input on the other hand, allows Arny to know if the user expects Arny's assistance for discovery of new ideas or if they can continue without a major contribution from Arny. This change was based on participants' references to their expectations of help from Arny as a trigger for parts of their emotions. Finally, the user's drawing contribution is the third input, that is, the functional sensemaking around the artifact. Figure 5 is an illustration of Arny V2 collaboration model.

The collaboration rules for Arny V2 are shown in Table 2. In conditions where the user's emotion is positive and the engagement level does not reflect a desire for creative ideations from Arny, a converging action is more likely to maintain the positive feeling about the collaboration. In the case when the positive valence is followed by low engagement from the participant, there is a risk of boredom or distraction from the task and so a diverging action is presented by Arny.

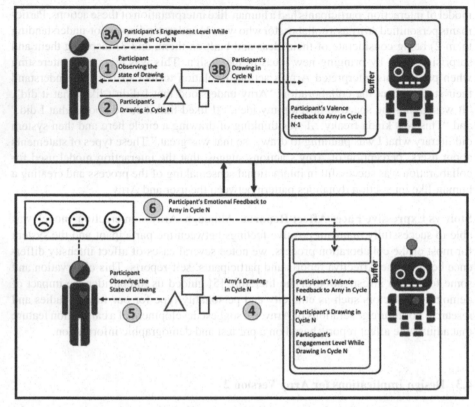

Fig. 5. Arny V2's collaboration cycle-user turn (top) and Arny turn (bottom)

5 Follow-Up Study

We performed a follow-up case study to explore the impact of the modifications in Arny V2 on the user. Unlike the previous study, the follow-up study included an AI system that can select a converging or diverging sketch based on the user's most recent sketch contribution to the design. In this study we had a control condition with no emotion detection in the interaction rules and a treatment condition with emotion detection.

5.1 System Development

Arny V2 is a combination of Affectiva emotion recognition platform as the emotion recognition component that captures user's emotional state during the collaboration, and an AI model for selecting sketches to contribute to the current design. The user experience is an interior design task designed on Microsoft PowerPoint to collect the user's contribution and present Arny's contribution in response to the user. We used TeamViewer [25] software and two human Wizards to facilitate the communication between the three main system components.

Table 2. Arny V2 collaboration rules

Cycle	Input			Arny's action
	User's drawing from cycle	User's engagement level in the beginning of cycle N	User's valence value in cycle N-1	
1	1	Not Referred to for First Cycle	No Previous Reference	Converge to User Drawing in Cycle 1
N	N	Medium to High	Positive	Converge to User Drawing in Cycle N
			Neutral	Converge to User Drawing in Cycle N
			Negative	Pass with No Drawing Action
		Low	Positive	Diverge from User Drawing in Cycle N
			Neutral	Diverge from User Drawing in Cycle N
			Negative	Diverge from User Drawing in Cycle N

Interior Design Interface. We used an interface created in Microsoft PowerPoint as the drawing environment for Arny V2 system design. We chose Microsoft PowerPoint over developing a new interface or using more complex online drawing platforms because PowerPoint drawing has a very simple and well-known interface. Using a familiar interface reduces the emotional feedback potentially triggered due to the frustrations caused by learning a new system.

The participant was asked to label their contribution on each cycle to reduce potential error that using a sketch recognition software can introduce to the study. Figure 6 is an illustration of the PowerPoint user experience for the study. This interface includes a text area in which the participant tells Arny what s/he drew in each turn and an interior background to which the participant draws or moves and places each new object drawn by Arny.

Emotion Detection Component. Arny-V2 uses the user's valence and engagement values reported to it in real time by Affectiva software. Affectiva calculates these values from the video of the user captured through a webcam on the user's computer.

AI Model. The AI component of Arny determines Arny's contribution to the collaboration based on the users' drawing contributions and Wizard's prime of the action type. As previously mentioned in Arny's interaction model, the collaboration between Arny and the user is shaped in the form of interaction cycles. Each cycle starts with a contribution from the user followed by a converging or diverging contribution, or pass action by

Arny that is decided on based on tracking the user's previous valence and engagement levels. On each cycle, the AI component is primed on the type of action to be taken and translates this action to a sketch to be contributed in response to the user's last action. To do so, Arny selects from a database of sketches relevant to interior design.

The data set of sketches includes 102 labels and corresponding sketches partly generated by a researcher of this study and partly from the human sketch dataset [10]. When participants draw a sketch, Arny takes the label of the sketch and uses a word embedding model [26] to prepare a list of converging and diverging labels from the 102 objects. Word2vec model is trained on a Wikipedia dataset and represents objects as vectors and puts similar objects together in the vector space. Cosine similarity scores capture the angle between two vectors. If cosine similarity is 0, the angle between the two vectors is 90°, which means the vectors are not similar. Conversely, when the cosine similarity is 1, the angle between two vectors is 0°, which means two vectors are pointing in the same direction, thus similar to each other. We use the Gensim Python library [27] to calculate the cosine similarity score of two labels and consider the score as the indicator of divergence and convergence level. Two labels diverge from one another when their cosine similarity score is less, and converge to one another when their cosine similarity is more. Arny calculates the cosine similarity scores between the label of participant's sketch and the labels of 102 objects and presents a ranked list of the top 10 labels with higher similarity scores to the study wizards.

Wizards in the study ensure that Arny selects the appropriate labels for generating sketches in the collaboration. We have noticed that sometimes cosine similarity scores in the word2vec model does not reflect the relevance of the collaborative environment. The reason could be that the model is trained on the Wikipedia dataset, but our study focuses on the interior design environment. We also explored the word embedding model trained on google news dataset. After investigating different combinations of cosine similarity score ranges and the models, we identified that the label list of top 10 high cosine similarity scores in the word embedding model trained on Wikipedia maintains the relevance and does not diverge too much that compromises the context of the collaboration. Arny selects the top 3 of that ten labels list as converging labels and bottom 3 of the list as the diverging labels. Table 3 shows Arny's calibration table for 'laptop' and 'picture' where Arny identifies that 'computer', 'cell phone', and 'iPod' labels are converging to 'laptop', whereas 'headphones', 'calculator', 'binoculars' labels are diverging from 'laptop'. Wizards consider both participants' emotional response and the calibration table generated from decision making AI to facilitate Arny's next action type: diverge, converge, or pass.

Wizard. The Wizards' role in Arny V2 is to facilitate the communication between the system components and the object selection by the AI model. Our wizard team consists of an Emotion Interpreter Wizard and a Drawing Wizard. The Emotion Interpreter Wizard observes the real-time emotional feedback of the participant on the Affectiva platform and directs the Drawing Wizard when to converge, diverge or pass. The Drawing Wizard is in charge of contributing to the interior design task according to the input from the Emotion Interpreter Wizard and the last object contributed by the participant. This wizard passes the label a participant assigned to their last contribution to the AI model and

Table 3. Arny's calibration table for convergence and divergence

Label of user's sketch	List of top 10 high cosine similarity scores									
	Converging labels						Diverging labels			
	Computer	Cellphone	iPod	Keyboard	Phone	Printer	Camera	Headphones	Calculator	Binoculars
Laptop	Computer	Cellphone	iPod	Keyboard	Phone	Printer	Camera	Headphones	Calculator	Binoculars
Picture	Camera	Poster	Painting	tv	Book	Window	Face	Tape	Computer	Table

receives a list of 10 relevant sketches in response. When converging, the Drawing Wizard chooses the most relevant sketch from the top 3 objects in this list and copies the selected sketch from the drawing dataset to the interior design interface. In the case of diverging action, the drawing wizard chooses the most diverging sketch from the last 3 items in the list of top 10 sketches and copies the selected sketch to the interior design interface.

5.2 Recruitment

We recruited participants based on drawing skill level and demographics, considering facial expressiveness, race, ethnicity and educational background. Due to the restrictions in the emotion detection software, we recruited candidates that did not have facial hair and considered themselves to be facially expressive Caucasian Americans. Our reason for choosing Caucasian Americans was based on facial expression research performed on this demography [5].

5.3 Lab Setting and Study Design

The software used in this study was Microsoft PowerPoint, TeamViewer, Skype, Affectiva, and the AI Model. The hardware used was the Tobii eye tracking device, a touch screen, and a stylus pen. The participants were provided with a consent form. The consent form explained what the participant should expect and the estimated time to complete the study. In addition, the interior design tasks descriptions were provided to the participant and the study interface was explained to the participants.

The participant is presented with the initial office layout shown in Fig. 4, which is shared with the wizards through TeamViewer along with Affectiva readings. The participant sits alone in one room and the two Wizards work from a second room. The participant can communicate with the Wizard via a microphone. The Wizards pass the input from the participant to the AI Model and back.

The study had two counterbalanced conditions with the same layout and slightly different task instructions. In the control condition the participant is asked to design an office for a female professor and in the treatment condition the participant is asked to design an office for a female startup manager. The treatment condition took into consideration the emotional feedback from the participant to decide on convergence and divergence. The decision on when to converge or diverge was random in the control condition. To provide the participants with images that converge or diverge with their ideas, the wizards used the trained word embedding model to choose the sketches in both conditions.

Debrief. A retrospective interview process similar to the pilot study was followed to collect additional information about the participant's experience in each cycle of both control and treatment conditions. The retrospective interview was audio recorded for the purpose of analysis.

Fig. 6. Images from the design of an office interior space: with emotional feedback (top), without emotional feedback (bottom)

5.4 Results

We analyzed the data collected from the follow up study which included three audio recordings of the interviews, the final drawings and facial expression data collected from Affectiva (engagement level and valence). The results showed significant differences between the two conditions in terms of user preference and engagement.

Control Condition. Users rated the control condition as least preferred. Most of the participants reported that Arny was contributing random objects to the office scene, which were irrelevant and inappropriate. For example, Participant 2 was disappointed when he saw Arny was drawing a dog in the office room. Some participants were so disappointed by the objects produced by the system that eagerness for achieving a good designed office room disappeared. Participants also mentioned the lack of influence and inspiration from Arny. To describe the negative feelings participants used phrases such as "I didn't like it" or "it was annoying" and then described an unmet expectation. Then unmet expectations in case of converging actions were described by a lack of creativity in Arny, not understanding what the participant wanted, contributing to an idea the participant was already done with, or leaving the participant helpless.

> "As I said before, I didn't have much ideas here. I was waiting for some ideas. (the system passed) It was annoying."

Mostly the results showed negative emotions in this condition. There were few positive emotions captured but the interview data demonstrated that it resulted from the complementary and related contributions from Arny. For some participants, negative emotion led to interesting results. Participants 2 and 3 had initial negative emotions resulted from random inappropriate contributions of Arny.

Treatment Condition. Based on a likert scale rating, the three participants indicated they preferred the collaboration with Arny V2 to the control condition. In addition, facial expression data demonstrated high user engagement and positive valence compared to the control condition.

Arny is Co-operative. The participants referred to Arny as a co-operative partner. Results suggested that Arny drew related objects to complement the objects drawn by the participants. They also said Arny influenced their contributions positively. Participants added that they felt associated with Arny in terms of their contributions. Arny created a story with them and communicated with the participants through its contributions. For example, in a case when the system converged to the participant's drawing of a window with drawing a frame, the participant stated:

> "I think it was interesting that the system basically did what I did. I just felt that it was interesting that it took something that I drew and did something else with it, that it responded accordingly."

Arny Helps in Design Ideation with Varied Ideas. Facial expression data showed high engagement and positive valence even when Arny contributed a divergent idea. One of the participants implied that Arny's varying and divergent ideas helped them when they ran out of ideas. Even if the system sometimes produced diverging ideas, they felt they were still on the same task. Participants described some diverging action that they liked by statements such as:

> "The system was diverging…Sometimes I didn't have much idea on what to draw, but the system encouraged me to draw some next things. Here the system added a monitor and I could keep continuing by adding a keyboard and a mouse"

6 Conclusions

This paper presents an interaction model for AI-based co-creative design that includes emotion detection in the collaboration rules. Two versions of the interaction model are presented: Arny V1 uses the detection of positive, negative, and neutral emotion in the rules for selecting a convergent or divergent sketch to contribute to the design or to pass on the AI contribution. Arny V2 uses emotion and engagement detection in the rules governing the AI contribution. A pilot study using Arny V1 shows that users are generally happy with collaborating with an AI partner and they experienced a mostly positive emotional experience. The pilot study also shows that emotion expression is not similar in all participants [5] and it is required to create user expression categories, calibrate the emotion reading mechanisms and combine them with other approaches such as eye-tracking to achieve a more comprehensive model of interaction based on emotional feedback. Our follow-up study, including engagement detection as well as emotion detection, had 2 conditions: a control condition in which the AI partner contributed sketches randomly, and a treatment condition in which the AI partner contributed based on the interaction rules of Arny V2. The participants were more satisfied in the treatment condition and expressed in the debriefing that they felt that the AI partner was responsive to their needs and expectations as a creative collaborator. Future studies are planned to fully implement the AI component of the system and to perform more user studies.

References

1. Ekman, P.: Basic emotions. Handb. Cogn. Emotion **98**(45–60), 16 (1999)
2. Scherer, K.R.: What are emotions? and how can they be measured? Soc. Sci. Inf. **44**(4), 695–729 (2005)
3. Sawyer, R.K.: Group Creativity: Music, Theater, Collaboration. Psychology Press (2014)
4. Ekman, P., Keltner, D.: Universal facial expressions of emotion. In: Segerstrale, U., Molnar, P. (eds.) Nonverbal Communication: Where Nature Meets Culture, pp. 27–46 (1997)
5. Jack, R.E., Garrod, O.G., Yu, H., Caldara, R., Schyns, P.G.: Facial expressions of emotion are not culturally universal. Proc. Natl. Acad. Sci. **109**(19), 7241–7244 (2012)
6. Guo, K., Calver, L., Soornack, Y., Bourke, P.: Valence-dependent disruption in processing of facial expressions of emotion in early visual cortex—a transcranial magnetic stimulation study. J. Cognitive Neurosci. **32**, 1–12 (2020)
7. Hudlicka, E.: To feel or not to feel: the role of affect in human–computer interaction. Int. J. Hum Comput. Stud. **59**(1–2), 1–32 (2003)
8. Gutwin, C., Greenberg, S., Roseman, M.: Workspace awareness in real-time distributed group-ware: Framework, widgets, and evaluation. In: *Sasse, M.A., Cunningham, R.J., Winder, R.L. (eds.)* People and Computers XI, pp. 281–298. Springer, London (1996). https://doi.org/10.1007/978-1-4471-3588-3_18
9. Jaques, N., Engel, J., Ha, D., Bertsch, F., Picard, R., Eck, D.: Learning via social awareness: improving sketch representations with facial feedback (2018)
10. Eitz, M., Hays, J., Alexa, M.: How do humans sketch objects? ACM Trans. Graph. (TOG) **31**(4), 1–10 (2012)
11. Christiano, P.F., Leike, J., Brown, T., Martic, M., Legg, S., Amodei, D.: Deep reinforcement learning from human preferences. In: Advances in Neural Information Processing Systems, pp. 4299–4307 (2017)
12. Knox, W.B., Stone, P.: Interactively shaping agents via human reinforcement: the TAMER framework. In: Proceedings of the Fifth International Conference on Knowledge Capture, pp. 9–16 (2009)
13. Kellas, J.K., Trees, A.R.: Rating interactional sense-making in the process of joint storytelling. The sourcebook of nonverbal measures: Going beyond words, p. 281 (2005)
14. De Jaegher, H., Di Paolo, E.: Participatory sense-making. Phenomenol. Cognitive Sci. **6**(4), 485–507 (2007)

15. DiPaola, S., McCaig, G.: Using artificial intelligence techniques to emulate the creativity of a portrait painter. In: Electronic Visualisation and the Arts, pp. 158–165 (2016)
16. Eligio, U.X., Ainsworth, S.E., Crook, C.K.: Emotion understanding and performance during computer-supported collaboration. Comput. Hum. Behav. **28**(6), 2046–2054 (2012)
17. Picard, R.W., Daily, S.B.: Evaluating affective interactions: alternatives to asking what users feel. In: CHI Workshop on Evaluating Affective Interfaces: Innovative Approaches 10(1056808.1057115), pp. 2119–2122 (2005)
18. Kapoor, A., Picard, R.W.: A real-time head nod and shake detector. In: Proceedings of the 2001 Workshop on Perceptive User Interfaces, pp. 1–5 (2001)
19. Affectiva Homepage. https://www.affectiva.com/. Accessed 11 June 2020
20. iMotions Homepage. https://imotions.com/. Accessed 11 June 2020
21. McDuff, D., Mahmoud, A., Mavadati, M., Amr, M., Turcot, J., Kaliouby, R.E.: AFFDEX SDK: a cross-platform real-time multi-face expression recognition toolkit. In Proceedings of the 2016 CHI Conference Extended Abstracts on Human Factors in Computing Systems, pp. 3723–3726 (2016)
22. Bown, O.: Empirically grounding the evaluation of creative systems: incorporating interaction design. In: Proceedings of the Fifth International Conference on Computational Creativity, pp. 112–119 (2014)
23. Bown, O.: Player responses to a live algorithm: conceptualising computational creativity without recourse to human comparisons? In: International Conference on Computational Creativity, pp. 126–133 (2015)
24. Fuller, D., Magerko, B.: Shared mental models in improvisational performance. In: Proceedings of the Intelligent Narrative Technologies III Workshop, p. 15 (2010)
25. Teamviewer Homepage. https://www.teamviewer.com/en-us/. Accessed 11 June 2020
26. Mikolov, T., Chen, K., Corrado, G, Dean, J.: Efficient estimation of word representations in vector space. arXiv preprint arXiv:1301.3781 (2013)
27. Rehurek, R., Sojka, P.: Software framework for topic modelling with large corpora. In: Proceedings of the LREC 2010 Workshop on New Challenges for NLP Frameworks. Citeseer (2010)
28. Ziteboard Homepage. https://www.ziteboard.com/. Accessed 14 June 2020

Towards Intelligent Technology in Art Therapy Contexts

Woud AlSadoun, Nujood Alwahaibi(✉), and Lean Altwayan

Human-Computer Interaction (HCI) Design Lab, Riyadh, Saudi Arabia
{walsadoun,Nujood,AltwayanL}@acm.org

Abstract. With the passing of time artificial intelligence (AI) is becoming essential to many fields, in this study we introduce a new methodological consideration of integrating AI with art therapy for people with complex communication needs such as autism spectrum disorders (ASD). Art therapy was first introduced to the medical world in 1993, developing over these two decades it has shown to be aligned with HCI research conducted in the Arab region. We will be studying the socio-cultural environment aspects of end users to develop a device suitable for their case with the help of local art therapists, designers, and developers to create an art therapy zone in a non-clinical context. We introduced a hybrid approach that combines Psychology and AI to build a smart art therapy system that autonomously communicates instructions and information to users independently from human guidance. The system was introduced to adopt computer vision technologies with AI to recognize a user's emotions and update the interactive content based on the target user's needs. Our findings have implications for the design of systems that involve AI in art therapy and chart a direction for future work that may upend or augment key aspects of technology-mediated communication theory.

Keywords: Human-centered computing · Accessibility · a11y · HCI · Art therapy · Artificial intelligence

1 Introduction

The expanding body of research for the therapeutic effectiveness of art therapy suggests potential for technology-mediated approaches [1, 2]. HCI research in the past two decades has highlighted the promising contribution of technology in enhancing the experience for art therapy sessions and the need for tools to spur consideration of social and cultural factors in accessible design [3, 4].

Art therapy was first acknowledged by Alyami [5] through educational courses that spanned academic institutions, art programs, and medical rehabilitation centers. Recently, art therapy in Saudi Arabia has notecable health and education benefits [5–7]; yet, adopting artificial intelligence (AI) with this field is considered a new approach.

Adrian Hill is a British artist who was known for creating the term 'art therapy'. He believed that in order for art therapy to work, the mind must fully engage while drawing [8]. However, as a result of the study conducted in this paper, it was confirmed by a

© Springer Nature Switzerland AG 2020
C. Stephanidis et al. (Eds.): HCII 2020, LNCS 12424, pp. 397–405, 2020.
https://doi.org/10.1007/978-3-030-60117-1_29

local art therapist that communication and therapy engagement is a challenge for some people, such as for people with autism spectrum disorders (ASD). People with ASD have a bigger challenge when it comes to starting the art therapy session, in the sense that they need to get used to a new environment (the clinic or new therapists).

To address this issue we used both sides of psychology and AI to build-up a methodological consideration that will help the end user to have a successful session. It introduces an AI-based system with an embedded agent that can recognize the user's emotions based on a set of features such as their facial features, their use of drawing tools and their health condition; subsequently, the agent interacts with the users based on the detected emotions. The proposed approach takes into consideration increasing the user engagement and satisfaction by focusing on the social and cultural factors when designing the system.

Ultimately, this paper explores the relationship between art therapy and technology to improve the end users' experience by proposing an intelligent system that connects the user, therapist, and developers. The proposed system will facilitate deploying comfortable, creative, and therapeutic zones for people with communication difficulties (e.g. autism spectrum disorder, learning disabilities, developmental disabilities).

The remainder of this paper is organized as follows: Sect. 2 describes related work to art therapy in Saudi Arabia and intelligent therapeutic systems. Section 3 discusses the proposed methodology and materials as how the proposed system will be built to adopt AI into art therapy. The paper is concluded in Sect. 4, and future work is discussed to improve this study.

2   Related Work

2.1   Art Therapy in Saudi Arabia

Art therapy is a relatively new concept in Saudi Arabia that was introduced two decades ago, and has received little to no attention due to the conservative cultural view towards art as a profession, in addition to the fact that Islamic cultural norms may not appear to align with the creative arts [9].

In [6], the study attempts to introduce the concept of art therapy in Saudi elementary school art education through the use of selected art therapy techniques, which include expressive painting, expressive collages and visual journals. The author showed that by incorporating art therapy processes into Saudi classrooms, elementary art teachers can help their students to develop their creative expression and better understand their inner feelings.

In [5], the study focused on using art therapy as a means of rehabilitation for physically injured patients in Saudi Arabia. The paper highlighted the process of incorporating the concept of art therapy as a medical profession in King Fahad Medical City, where four case studies were conducted on patients with different ages, genders and medical conditions, all of which achieved encouraging results. The authors explained that physical injuries are often followed by anxiety, depression, anger and withdrawal, which are discussed and treated in the art therapy sessions and used in co-treatment sessions with therapists at the hospital. In all four case studies, the patients found comfort in the practice of art therapy, and in some cases where patients have lost muscle control in their hands, art therapy has made significant improvements in their rehabilitation process due to the skills they learned during their sessions. Through the patients' experiences in art therapy, many patients in [5] have found making art to be personally enriching, even though art may have had little importance in their lives prior to their hospitalization. This shows that the practice of art therapy can change the way art and its role are perceived by patients and their caregivers in Saudi Arabia?

2.2 Art Therapy for Improving Communication

Problems in communication can occur for several reasons whether they are psychological by nature or as a result of mental trauma. Many patients have resorted to art therapy to help alleviate the communication barriers set in front of them, since it gives them room to freely express themselves.

The study in [10] shows that art therapy can be especially effective for children with ASD, since it can improve the patient's imagination and abstract thinking skills, while providing a less stressful, sensory regulated environment. The paper suggests that employing art therapy during recreation and leisure activities can help children with ASD mitigate their symptoms and develop socially appropriate skills. Additionally, art therapy can help persons with ASD tackle serious issues they face with anxiety, depression and frustration due to their symptoms in an organized yet comfortable environment.

In [11], the case study followed a six year old boy with ASD and the progress he had made in art therapy sessions during a 7-month period. Children with ASD struggle to relate with objects and people around them, which can contribute to social and communication issues including language development. Because of this, many children with ASD struggle to draw objects in their daily lives, which makes it more difficult for them to communicate their experiences. However, utilizing the techniques in art therapy can introduce children with ASD to a nonverbal way of communication, allowing them to relate to the world around them and increase their self-awareness. The study also demonstrated how art therapy has helped children improve their language development, maintain better eye contact and even improve their verbal communication skills. This study further highlighted how art therapy can be an important activity-based intervention for encouraging the growth of children with ASD.

2.3 Intelligent Therapeutic Systems

Due to the expansion of AI technologies, practices such as therapy can now be implemented using advanced algorithms such as neural networks. In [12], the authors employed an assisted therapeutic system using a facial expression-based emotion recognition, the method interprets the emotions of the child while interacting with the robot in order to have a better understanding of what the child is trying to communicate. This study implemented a Convolutional Neural Network (CNN)-Support Vector Regression (SVR) model based on reinforcement learning (RL) to detect a user's emotion and sent the results to the child's therapist in real time to validate the results.

In [13], the authors introduced an approach for engaging adults with dementia in creative occupations using AI assistive technology. The art platform can actively engage the client in an art activity by using AI-powered technology to monitor a client's level of engagement. Moreover, authors introduced a customizable art platform such that an art therapist can choose themes and tools that they feel reflect their client's needs and preferences.

A personalized framework was introduced in [14], the authors demonstrated the technical feasibility of using deep learning to formulate a personalized machine learning (ML) framework for automatic perception of the children's affective states and engagement during robot-assisted autism therapy. The framework was personalized to each child using their contextual information (demographics and behavioral assessment scores) and individual characteristics. The framework was evaluated on a set of features that include video recordings of facial expressions and body movements, audio recordings, and autonomic physiology (e.g. heart rate (HR), electrodermal activity (EDA), body temperature) of 35 children with autism from different cultures.

3   Proposed Methods and Materials

In this section we introduce a new system consideration of integrating artificial intelligence (AI) with art therapy. The workflow of the proposed system is shown in Fig. 1. The system is composed of three main components: a digital art program designed specifically for people with complex communication needs; an AI component that adjusts the interactive content based on recognizing users' emotion using a set of features such as facial features, mental health condition, and the used drawing tools (e.g. use of color, stroke, brush); and finally an embodied agent that responds to users independently of any expert human guidance. This process can provide insightful treatment and guide for each individual.

At first, the system will show instructions and guide the user while drawing. The content will be updated continuously based on the user's detected emotion using the AI component. The instructions will be communicated to the user through the embodied agent. Moreover, the collected data (used drawing tools, facial features) along with the detected emotion of the user will be sent to the therapist for assessment.

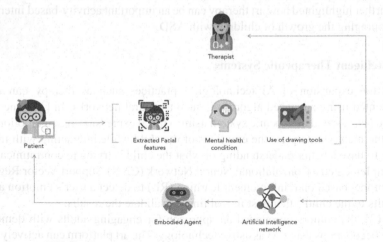

Fig. 1. Proposed approach workflow and conceptual design

People with impaired communication skills have different needs and preferences, and it is important to consider building a personalized framework when developing a system for them to avoid sensory overload and overstimulation situations and to increase the engagement level of the user. Thus, a single solution isn't effective when developing a product for people with impaired communication skills, the system needs to be customized for individual needs [15].

In order to develop a successful personalized framework, an active participation of individuals is needed during the design process. In addition, instructions and interactive content must be adjusted based on the user needs.

Many studies have developed personalized frameworks by implementing advanced algorithms. Li et al. in [12] employed a personalized assisted therapeutic system using CNN-SVR model based on reinforcement learning, the system adjusts the content by predicting children's emotion using their facial expressions, then, the therapist performs assessments. Another study [16] developed an audio-based emotion prediction for children with ASD, the system allows the robotic to assess the engagement level of the child and modify its responses based on the predicted emotion. These studies have introduced intelligent personalized systems. However, depending on one feature for predicting emotions can lead to one-sidedness of emotional judgment.

In the proposed system, we consider the AI component to have three important features to personalize the framework for each user:

(i) **Mental health condition:** including the mental health condition (e.g. depression, anxiety, etc.) of the target users and their needs can increase the ability of creating an accurate personalized framework.

(ii) **Use of drawing tools:** non-representational visual art has a lot of benefits in art therapy. Preimage elements of art, such as line, form, and color have a great potential to affect perceptions and behaviors [17].

(iii) **Facial features:** the process of extracting face component features like eyes, nose, mouth, etc. from human face image; can play an important rule for the initialization of processing techniques like facial expression recognition. The model needs to understand the facial expressions of the user who it is interacting with and be able to recognize their emotions in order to achieve an accurate communication between the embodied agent and user [18].

Before feeding the model with the proposed features, pre-processing and analysis techniques should be implied to the collected data (drawing tools used, facial features, mental health condition) to extract various behavioral features of the user. After that, the model will perform an estimation of the user's emotion based on the extracted features.

3.1 Digital Art Program

In this component, the user interface of the proposed system consists of canvas, drawing toolbox (e.g. paint brush, shapes, labels, etc.) and embodied agent. When designing an interface for people with complex communication needs, it is crucial to consider the socio-cultural environment aspects by addressing the social factors and follow certain guidelines and principles that have been established.

Designing a user interface that takes into consideration people's culture can make users feel more comfortable when interacting with the system. In this study, we emphasize the importance of the relationship between culture and usability by introducing the culturability factor. Barber W. and Badre A. [19] introduced the term "Culturability" which can be defined as merging culture and usability in an interface. In this study, we introduce the culturability factor by incorporating cultural characteristics into the design to help increase user engagement [20]. Designers should explore the variety of cultural factors that can impact the user interface design such as colors, pictures and language, which are crucial elements to be considered while designing a user interface.

Besides culture, it is important to focus on other factors that can affect users engagement such as their needs. The UK Department of Health [21] have created a set of guidelines when preparing documents for people with learning difficulties, the relevant principles are mentioned in Table 1. These guidelines can be the key requirements when building a user interface suitable for people with complex communication needs.

Table 1. Design principles for people with learning difficulties

Element	Principle
Words and pictures	Each idea needs both words and pictures Pictures and words go next to each other
Pictures	Pictures must be easy to understand Pictures can be drawings, photographs or other images Pictures should be as big as possible
Words	Words must be easy to understand If you use difficult words, say what they mean using easy words Words must be written clearly – a font like Arial is good Words must be big – a font size of at least 14 point is good
Length	Each sentence must be short as possible – more than 15 words is harder to read

3.2 Embodied Agent

Face-to-face interaction can be one of the effective methods for communicating information to users, as it allows health providers to use verbal and non-verbal behavior. Moreover, during face-to-face interaction, much of what we communicate is conveyed nonverbally through cues such as facial expressions and posture [22]. However, for individuals with impaired communication skills it could be uncomfortable for them when someone continuously looks at their faces, and being in this kind of situation can contribute towards increased anxiety and discomfort to that individual, which might affect the impact of the treatment. Therefore, we propose using a virtual embodied agent, where we hypothesis that the level of complexity presented can be controlled [23].

AI-supported virtually embodied psychotherapeutic devices are currently developing at a rapid speed [24], virtual embodied agents can assist therapists when dealing with people with impaired communication skills by engaging them in interactive activities, the capacity to customize the virtual agent and providing content to users based on their needs is a huge advantage.

In the proposed system, the embodied agent component will be build while focusing on the interaction style proposed by (Prizant et al. 2003) [25], "An optimal style is one that provides enough structure to support a child's attentional focus, situational understanding, emotional regulation, and positive emotional experience, but that also fosters initiation, spontaneity, flexibility and self-determination". Additionally, the agent should focus on performing two major skills; joint attention and symbolic use, these skills can be implemented by interacting verbally using simple language and interacting nonverbally through gaze and gestures [25, 26].

In the proposed approach, the embodied agent plays the role of an art therapy assistant by providing detailed directions for users to follow as they work while still encouraging abstract and imaginative thinking. The system can adjust the interactive content and act upon the information it perceived. The agent is fed so that it selects the corresponding content or guidance based on the classified emotion of the user.

4   Conclusion and Future Work

In this paper, an AI-based art therapy system is proposed to be used by users' who are suffering from impaired communication skills. Design of technology-mediated art therapy should address functional and social factors simultaneously. The information and recommendations presented in this paper may not be directly applicable to all users that HCI practitioners work with, though may provide HCI practitioners with foundational socio-cultural considerations when working with Arabic speaking populations.

In the future we aim to build a prototype of the robot and present it to local art therapists to analyse their feedback before the product reaches the end users. Then we will implement this method into the real world by fabricating the art therapy robot and having it as an available product to end users in Saudi Arabia. By that we would analyse end users feedback to make the system more beneficial and suitable to their case. Meanwhile seeing how this product will impact the idea of art therapy and AI technology locally.

Acknowledgement. We thank the Saudi Authority for Intellectual Property (SAIP) and the Saudi Health Council's National Lab for Emerging Health Technologies for hosting and mentoring this work. We also thank the Humanistic Co-Design Initiative and the Human-Computer Interaction (HCI) Lab for supporting this work. This work is part of the authors' project that is carried out under the CoCreate Fellowship for Humanistic Co-Design of Access Technologies.

References

1. Regev, D., Cohen-Yatziv, L.: Effectiveness of art therapy with adult clients in 2018—what progress has been made? Front. Psychol. **9**, 1531 (2019)
2. Alders, A., Beck, L., Allen, P.B., Mosinski, B.B.: Technology in art therapy: ethical challenges. Art Therapy **28**(4), 165–170 (2011)

3. Orr, P.: Technology use in art therapy practice: 2004 and 2011 comparison. Arts Psychother. **39**(4), 234–238 (2012)
4. Peterson, B.C.: The media adoption stage model of technology for art therapy. Art Therapy **27**(1), 26–31 (2010)
5. Alyami, A.: The integration of art therapy into physical rehabilitation in a Saudi hospital. Arts Psychother. **36**(5), 282–288 (209)
6. Alkhenaini, N.: Fostering creativity in elementary school art education in Saudi Arabia through the use of selected art therapy techniques. Doctoral dissertation. The University of the Arts (2013)
7. Alrazain, B.: Developing and evaluating an arts therapies programme for children with Attention Deficit Hyperactivity Disorder (ADHD) in primary schools in the Kingdom of Saudi Arabia (KSA). Doctoral dissertation. Queen Margaret University, Edinburgh (2016)
8. Edwards, D.: Art Therapy Creative Therapies in Practice Series, 2nd edn. SAGE, Thousand Oaks (2013)
9. Awais, Y.: Revolution calling: rehabilitative art therapy in Saudi Arabia. Int. J. Therapy Rehabil. **18**(11), 600–601 (2011)
10. Martin, N.: Art therapy and autism: overview and recommendations. Art Therapy J. Am. Art Therapy Assoc. **26**(4), 187–190 (2009)
11. Emery, M.: Art therapy as an intervention for autism. Art Therapy J. Am. Art Therapy Assoc. **21**(3), 143–147 (2004)
12. Li, M., Li, X., Xie, L., Liu, J., Wang, F., Wang, Z.: Assisted therapeutic system based on reinforcement learning for children with autism. Comput. Assist. Surg. **24**, 1–11 (2019)
13. Leuty, V., Boger, J., Young, L., Hoey, J., Mihailidis, A.: Engaging older adults with dementia in creative occupations using artificially intelligent assistive technology. Assist. Technol. Off. J. RESNA **25**(2), 72–79 (2013)
14. Rudovic, O., Lee, J., Dai, M., Schuller, B.W., Picard, R.W.: Personalized machine learning for robot perception of affect and engagement in autism therapy. Sci. Robot. **3**(19), 2–5 (2018)
15. Ali, M., Razavi, Z., Mamun, A., Langevin, R., Rawassizadeh, R., Schubert, L., Hoque, E.: A Virtual Conversational Agent for Teens with Autism: Experimental Results and Design Lessons, pp. 2–6 (2018)
16. Kim, J.C., Azzi, P., Jeon, M., Howard, A.M., Park, C.H.: Audio-based emotion estimation for interactive robotic therapy for children with autism spectrum disorder. In: 14th International Conference on Ubiquitous Robots and Ambient Intelligence (URAI), Jeju, pp. 39–44 (2017)
17. Withrow, R.: The use of color in art therapy. J. Humanist. Couns. Educ. Dev. **43**(1), 33–40 (2004)
18. Melinte, D.O., Vladareanu, L.: Facial expressions recognition for human-robot interaction using deep convolutional neural networks with rectified adam optimizer. Sensors (Basel) **20**(8), 2393 (2020)
19. Barber, W., Badre, A.: Culturability: the merging of culture and usability. In: 4th Conference on Human Factors and the Web (1998)
20. Almakky, H., Sahandi, R., Taylor, J.: The effect of culture on user interface design of social media - a case study on preferences of Saudi Arabians on the Arabic user interface of Facebook. World Acad. Sci. Eng. Technol. Int. J. Humanit. Soc. Sci. **2**, 107–111 (2015)
21. Basic guidelines for people who commission Easy Read information, Department of Health. https://www.easy-read-online.co.uk/media/10612/comm%20basic%20guidelines%20for%20people%20who%20commission%20easy%20read%20info.pdf. Accessed 01 June 2020
22. Lavelle, M., Healey, P., McCabe, R.: Nonverbal behaviour during face-to-face social interaction in schizophrenia: a review. J. Nerv. Ment. Dis. **202**(1), 47–54 (2014). https://journals.lww.com/jonmd/Abstract/2014/01000/Nonverbal_Behavior_During_Face_to_face_Social.10.aspx

23. Milne, M., Luerssen, M., Lewis, T., Leibbrandt, R., Powers, D.: Development of a virtual agent based social tutor for children with autism spectrum disorders, pp. 1–9 (2010)
24. Fiske, A., Henningsen, P., Buyx, A.: Your robot therapist will see you now: ethical implications of embodied artificial intelligence in psychiatry, psychology, and psychotherapy. Preprint (2018)
25. Prizant, B., Wetherby, A., Rubin, E., Laurent, A.: The SCERTS model: a transactional, family-centered approach to enhancing communication and socioemotional abilities of children with autism spectrum disorder. Infants Young Child. 16(4), 296–316 (2003)
26. Bernardini, S., Porayska-Pomsta, K., Sampath, H.: Designing an intelligent virtual agent for social communication in autism, pp. 9–15 (2013)

Explainable Classification of EEG Data for an Active Touch Task Using Shapley Values

Haneen Alsuradi[1]([⊠]) [iD], Wanjoo Park[2][iD], and Mohamad Eid[2][iD]

[1] New York University, Tandon School of Engineering, New York, NY 11201, USA
haneen@nyu.edu
[2] Engineering Division, New York University Abu Dhabi, Saadiyat Island,
Abu Dhabi 129188, United Arab Emirates
{wanjoo,mohamad.eid}@nyu.edu

Abstract. Machine learning has been used in the last decade to solve many problems in the haptics field. In particular, EEG data that is recorded during haptic interactions was used to train machine learning (ML) models to answer questions that are of interest to the neurohaptics community. However, the behavior of machine learning models in taking out their decisions is treated as black box hindering the interpretability of these decisions. In this paper, we used Shapley values, a concept from game theory, to explain the behavior of a tree-based classifier model in classifying electroencephalography data that was collected during an interaction with a surface haptic device under two conditions: with and without tactile feedback. We trained a tree-based ML model to classify data based on the presence or absence of tactile feedback. Using Shapley values, we identified the features (across and within channels) that contribute the most to the classification decision. Results showed channel AF3 and neural activity after 700 ms from the onset contributed the most in recognizing tactile feedback in the interaction. This study demonstrates the use of explainable machine learning in the field of Neurohaptics.

Keywords: Neurohaptics · Haptics · Explainable machine learning · EEG

1 Introduction

There is a growing interest within the haptics community to involve human brain assessment techniques as new tools to understand the human haptic experience. Methods such as electroencephalography (EEG) and functional magnetic resonance imaging (fMRI) are well-established and can record signals from the brain during haptic interactions [15]. Conventionally, self-reporting is used to assess the human haptic experience. However, brain assessment methods have many advantages that can complement self-reporting in many ways. Participants

© Springer Nature Switzerland AG 2020
C. Stephanidis et al. (Eds.): HCII 2020, LNCS 12424, pp. 406–416, 2020.
https://doi.org/10.1007/978-3-030-60117-1_30

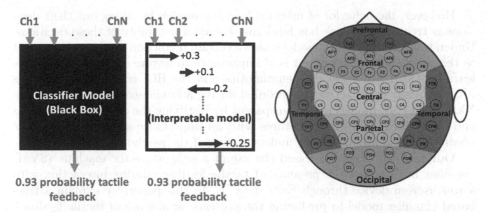

Fig. 1. Left: An interpretable model is capable of giving each of the features a credit in the final prediction probability. Right: Spatial map of EEG channels.

going under self-reporting are prone to difficulty in expressing themselves [14]. In addition, reporting is usually done once the experiment is over which means the response is not recorded during the time of interaction. As human memory is susceptible to forgetting or distortion, late reporting can be inaccurate [11]. Brain assessment methods emerged as quantitative and objective complementary measures to overcome the mentioned limitations of self-reporting. fMRI has a high spatial resolution; however, its temporal resolution is in the order of a few seconds which is much slower than a typical neural process [10], [6]. Moreover, fMRI imposes technical challenges in incorporating electronics within its vicinity due to the extremely high magnetic field. On the other hand, EEG is a more affordable apparatus that measures the brain's electrical activity with a high temporal resolution, making it particularly suitable for understanding the temporal aspect of the neural processes. Additionally, electronic devices which might be part of the haptic interaction are easily accommodated in EEG-based experiments.

In the past few years, EEG data was not only used to unveil information about the neural processes during a haptic interaction, but also was used to train machine learning (ML) models to answer questions that are of interest to the neurohaptics community. For example, ML models were employed to classify objects with different physical and geometrical properties through grasping tasks or tactile exploration using EEG data [3,9]. ML models were also used in affective haptics field, for example to recognize affective haptic stimuli conveyed by different fabrics or determine the degree of pleasure level during an interpersonal interaction using EEG data [7,16].

However, the behavior of machine learning models in taking out their decisions is treated as a black box hindering the interpretability of these decisions. Understanding why an ML model makes a certain prediction can be as important as the prediction itself. Thus, it is of importance to involve explainable machine learning (XML) to serve the neurohaptics and the HCI community that uses ML to classify brain activation recorded during a human-computer interaction. XML makes ML models more transparent by justifying the classifier predictions and accrediting each of the features with an importance score in making the prediction, thus improving our understanding of the psychophysics of the task.

Our previous work showcased the use of a support vector machine (SVM) classifier in detecting the presence of tactile feedback during interaction with a touchscreen device through EEG data [1]. In this paper, we explain a tree-based classifier model in predicting the presence or absence of tactile feedback using Shapley values [17]. Figure 1 (left) illustrates the idea behind this work; an explanation is given by crediting each of the channels/features with a contribution score in predicting the probability of the presence or absence of the tactile feedback.

2   Experimental Study

2.1   Experiment Design

In this study, we utilize the EEG data from our previous work [15]. The experiment consisted of an active touch task in which participants were asked to slide their index finger across guitar strings displayed on a Tanvas touchscreen device from predefined start to end locations. The screen is capable of providing friction-based tactile feedback which is turned on and off thus having two types of stimulation modes; one mode is activated per trial. The order of stimulation was randomized while considering the "counterbalancing" paradigm. That is to say, participants are divided in half such that one half performs the two conditions in one order and the other half performs the conditions in the reverse order. Visual (shaken strings) and auditory feedback (guitar sound), however, were always provided. Neural activation was recorded during the haptic interaction using a 64-channel EEG system; electrode locations are shown in Fig. 1 right. Participants were trained such that the interaction time with the touchscreen device in one trial would take around 1000ms. A number of 96 trials per condition (with or without tactile feedback) were conducted for each participant. Twenty-six participants were recruited for this study. The study was carried out with an approved protocol by New York University Abu Dhabi Institutional Review Board (IRB: #073-2017).

2.2   EEG Data Processing

EEG signals were first down-sampled from 2500 Hz to 1250 Hz and band pass filtered (0.1–55 Hz). After discarding eye-movement and muscle artifacts using the artifact subspace reconstruction, EEG data was epoched and divided into two categories depending on the presence or absence of the tactile feedback. Power spectral densities (PSD) of the frequency bands (theta, alpha, beta and gamma) were then calculated. A thorough analysis of the differences in PSD between the two stimulation modes was carried out in our previous work [15]; it was found that beta band power was significantly higher during the presence of tactile feedback on multiple locations including the ipsilateral-parietal, contralateral-parietal, middle-parietal and middle-frontal regions.

3 Proposed Method

Two ML classifiers were created; classifier 1 takes its inputs from the 64 EEG channels in order to predict the presence or absence of the tactile feedback. Shapley values were used to evaluate the most influential channel in the prediction process. Once identified, classifier 2 is trained using the EEG data solely from the identified channel. Shapley values are again employed to identify the timestamp/time-period during which the neural activation of the identified channel is most influential in the prediction process. For both models, we trained an XGBoost model which is a tree-based classifier. Below, the proposed method will be explained in detail.

3.1 Feature Extraction

For classifier 1, since the data is high-dimensional (from 64 channels), a data reduction/feature selection method is needed. After extracting the beta band PSD for every channel, we examined the grand average plots (mean over trials and subjects) of the channels across the scalp. Figure 2 shows an example grand average PSDs from channels F1 and POz from the middle frontal cortex and middle parietal cortex, respectively. It can be noticed that the peak amplitude and latency combined can be a representative feature for each channel. The use of peak as a feature is commonly used in PSD analysis [8] as well as ERP analysis [5]. We thus defined a feature for each channel by multiplying its peak amplitude value with its corresponding latency; we call it *peak-factor*. Due to the small number of observations (i.e. participants) we used a time-shifting data augmentation scheme in order to populate the training data, and hence improve the accuracy of the model. In the time-shifting scheme, each PSD signal (i.e.: each trial) was shifted in time 50 ms forward and backward. Thus, the size of the training data has tripled in size and hence the accuracy of the classifier has improved.

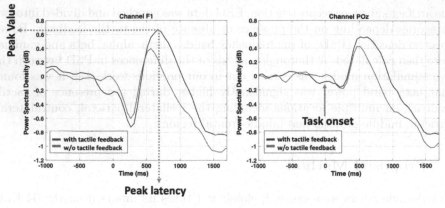

Peak Factor = Peak Value * Peak latency

Fig. 2. Grand average PSD plots from two channels in beta band, F1 (frontal area) and POz (occipital area) showing the distinctive features between the two stimulation modes.

3.2 Classifier

As mentioned earlier, two ML classifiers were trained. Classifier 1 was trained on the features extracted above, namely the *peak-factors* from the 64 channels. Once Shapley values are extracted for each of the 64 channels, the highest Shapley value corresponds to the most influential channel in the prediction decision. Classifier 2 on the other hand was trained feeding the full waveform of the beta-band PSDs of the most influential channel (instead of the feeding the *peak-factor* of the waveform) of all subjects under the two stimulation modes. Shapley values identified the timestamp/duration at which the neural activity of the channel was most influential in differentiating between the two haptic modes. For both classifiers, an extreme gradient boosting (XGBoost) model was trained to predict the class of the stimulation mode. XGBoost is an optimized decision-tree ensemble ML algorithm that has been widely accepted and recognized in the last few years [2]. A single decision-tree model suffers from high variance, which means the model tends to overfit to the training data [4]. An ensemble-of-trees model on the other hand, such as random forest, is based on growing trees randomly to reduce the variance. For further optimization, additive training (boosting) method can be used in growing trees such that each tree tries to resolve the deficiencies of the previous tree. XGBoost classifier implements the boosting technique with improved performance and accuracy [2]. Data was randomly split into 80% training and 20% testing and XGBoost model was trained and tested accordingly with 84% prediction accuracy for both of the classifiers.

3.3 Shapley Values

Shapley values, a concept from game theory, is a credit attribution method for a player in a game. Shapley values were first used in machine learning as part of a unified framework (named SHAP) for interpreting predictions such that the game is replaced by the model and the player is replaced by the features of the model. SHAP is used in ML to explain the contribution of each feature in the prediction of the model [13]. SHAP has been successfully used in ML models in the medical domain [12]. In this work, we use SHAP as a tool to explain a tree-based model in the neurohaptics field. SHAP is a local feature attribution method which means that SHAP accredits each feature with a contribution score given a single sample/trial input data. In other words, SHAP is designed to explain a prediction $f(x)$ based on a single input vector x. A global insight, however, can be extracted once all the local explanations are found. To calculate the Shapley value of a feature i, sets of all the possible combinations of the n features are created, excluding the ith feature. The model f is evaluated with $(f(S \bigcup \{i\}))$ and without $f(S)$ feature i and the difference in the prediction for the input data x is calculated. The input data (x) will contain $(S+1)$ features when fed to $(f(S \bigcup \{i\}))$ model while (S) features in the $f(S)$ model. The difference in the prediction is the marginal contribution of the feature i in prediction. This process is repeated for all the other formed features combinations. Thus, Shapley value for a specific feature i is calculated by finding the average of the marginal contribution across all possible permutation of features' combinations. The equation below is used to calculate the Shapley value for feature i under the model function f:

$$\varphi_{i(f)} = \sum_{S \subseteq N/\{i\}} \frac{|S|!(n - |S| - 1)!}{n!}(f_{S \bigcup \{i\}}(x_{S \bigcup i}) - f_S(x_S)) \tag{1}$$

where N is the set of all features, S is a subset of the features without feature i, n is the number of all features, $|S|$ is the cardinality of S (which is simply the number of elements in S for a finite set) and f is the function of the classifier model. Note that the second term in the bracket calculates the marginal contribution of feature i by considering a feature set with and without feature i and subtracting their predictions. The term before the bracket represents the number of all the possible ways of forming combinations per S divided by the total number of possible permutations.

4 Results and Discussion

As mentioned before, Shapley values are effective in revealing the impact of an input feature on an individual prediction; this is called local explanation. Combining many local explanations can lead to a global insight into the model's behavior [12].

4.1   Channel Level Explanation

To understand which of the EEG channels are the most influential for the XGBoost classifier 1 during prediction, we plot the Shapley values of each feature (channel's *peak-factor*) for all the trials in a beeswarm plot as shown in Fig. 3 (right). The channels are ordered with respect to importance (i.e. AF3 is the most important). Each dot represents a specific channel's *peak-factor* for a single trial (instance) in the training data. The color of the dot corresponds to the *peak-factor* value. High *peak-factor* values are colored in red while lower *peak-factor* values are colored in blue. The horizontal location of the dot on the other hand corresponds to the Shapley value of the feature; it explains whether the effect of that feature is associated with a positive or negative contribution to the prediction probability of the presence or absence of tactile feedback. From this plot, it can be observed that lower *peak-factor* values in AF3 channel, for example, will contribute negatively to the prediction probability of having tactile feedback. Another observation is that sometimes, a low AF3 *peak-factor* can greatly reduce the prediction probability of having tactile feedback, much more than a high *peak-factor* would increase the prediction probability of having tactile feedback. The global feature importance on the other hand is shown in Fig. 3 (left). For each channel, the mean absolute value of the Shapley values is plotted. Middle frontal electrodes rank the top in implying the presence/absence of tactile feedback. Another way to explore a single trial prediction explanation is through what is called the force plot shown in Fig. 4. The figure shows two different examples of trials, one with high probability of the presence of tactile feedback and one with low probability of the presence of tactile feedback. In each force plot, each of the channels contribution in pushing the prediction probability from the base value (0.5) is illustrated in magnitude and direction (i.e.: an indication of channels' correlation to presence/absence of tactile

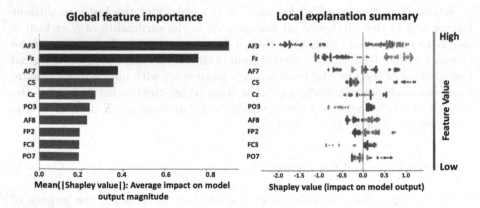

Fig. 3. Left: Global feature importance indicates that the channels in the middle frontal cortex, namely (AF3, Fz and AF7) contribute the most in the model's prediction. Right: Beeswarm plot showing the impact of each channel's *peak-factor* on the prediction probability. Each dot represents a sample. (Color figure online)

feedback). Note that only 5 of the channels' contributions are shown in the force plot for illustration purposes. From a neural perspective, beta activity at the middle frontal cortex is associated with an increased cognitive processing [5]. This is a possible indication that tactile feedback results in a more immersive interaction as it resembles reality [15].

A Trial having a High Probability of Tactile Feedback Presence

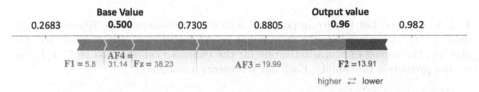

A Trial having a Low Probability of Tactile Feedback Presence

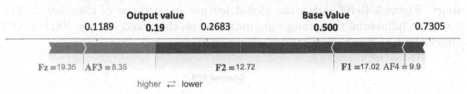

Fig. 4. Two different trials showing how the *peak-factor* of the shown channels contribute positively (red) and negatively (blue) in the prediction process. (Color figure online)

4.2 Activity Within-Channel Explanation

Since it is found that AF3 channel is the most influential channel in classifier 1, we would like to obtain further explainability and find the most impactful timestamp at which the neural activity of AF3 is important. As mentioned earlier, classifier 2 was trained using the full waveform of the beta-band PSDs of the most influential channel instead of the feeding the *peak-factor* of the waveform. Each value in the waveform at each timestamp is considered as a feature. The local explanation summary plot shown in Fig. 5 (right). The figure shows that neural activity after 700 ms from the onset of the task contribute the most in the prediction probability in a descending order with time. It can also be observed that the feature at 718 ms produces a strong force to pull up or down the prediction probability depending on the feature value (no sample points have a zero Shapley value). Additionally, long tails along the x-axis in the same figure (such as at feature 819 ms), indicate that for some individuals, this feature is extremely important in impacting the prediction probability. Note that due to EEG data digitization, a specific timestamp is not important per se, instead, a group of consecutive timestamps indicate that this period of time

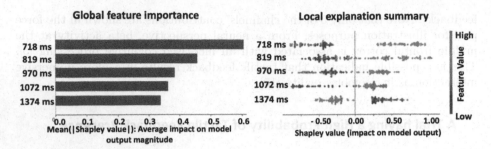

Fig. 5. Left: Global feature importance indicate timestamps after 700 ms from the onset of the task contribute the most in the model's prediction. Right: Beeswarm plot showing the impact of neural activation (at the indicated timestamps) of AF3 channel on the prediction probability. Each dot represents a sample.

(after the onset of the stimulus) is important in distinguishing the two classes apart. Figure 5 (left) shows the global feature importance of classifier 2. The five most influential timestamps are indicated on the grand average PSD of AF3 under the two stimulation modes, shown in Fig. 6.

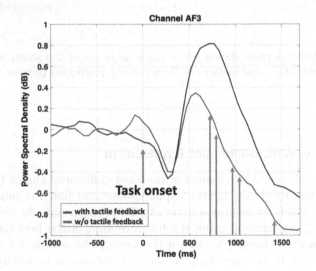

Fig. 6. Grand average PSD plots from AF3 channel with marked important features.

5   Conclusion

In this paper, we demonstrated the use of a game theoretic concept, Shapley value, in explaining the behavior of a tree-based classifier (XGBoost). The classifier was trained on EEG data to predict the presence or absence of tactile feedback during interaction with a touchscreen device. We found that the channel

AF3 located in the middle frontal cortex contributes the most in the decision making of the classifier. We could also demonstrate explanations of a specific sample prediction and the contribution of each channel in making the prediction. We further showed that Shapley values provided an interpretation of the classifier behavior by finding the most influential timestamps at which the neural activity is important towards classification. Neural activity after 700 ms from the onset contributed the most. These results are consistent with those found exploratively in previous studies [15]. Therefore, we believe that EEG channels and time periods that contribute the most in classifications found through Shapley values will assist researchers in exploring meaningful features in experiments in neurohaptics and HCI.

Acknowledgement. This research was funded by NYU Abu Dhabi PhD Fellowship Program.

References

1. Alsuradi, H., Pawar, C., Park, W., Eid, M.: Detection of tactile feedback on touchscreen devices using EEG data. In: 2020 IEEE Haptics Symposium (HAPTICS). IEEE (2020)
2. Chen, T., Guestrin, C.: XGBoost: a scalable tree boosting system. In: Proceedings of the 22nd ACM SIGKDD International Conference on Knowledge Discovery and Data Mining, pp. 785–794 (2016)
3. Cisotto, G., Guglielmi, A.V., Badia, L., Zanella, A.: Classification of grasping tasks based on EEG-EMG coherence. In: 2018 IEEE 20th International Conference on e-Health Networking, Applications and Services (Healthcom), pp. 1–6. IEEE (2018)
4. Dietterich, T.G., Kong, E.B.: Machine learning bias, statistical bias, and statistical variance of decision tree algorithms. Technical report, Department of Computer Science, Oregon State University (1995)
5. Egner, T., Gruzelier, J.H.: EEG biofeedback of low beta band components: frequency-specific effects on variables of attention and event-related brain potentials. Clin. Neurophysiol. **115**(1), 131–139 (2004)
6. Glover, G.H.: Overview of functional magnetic resonance imaging. Neurosurg. Clin. **22**(2), 133–139 (2011)
7. Greco, A., Nardelli, M., Bianchi, M., Valenza, G., Scilingo, E.P.: Recognition of affective haptic stimuli conveyed by different fabrics sing EEG-based sparse SVM. In: 2017 IEEE 3rd International Forum on Research and Technologies for Society and Industry (RTSI), pp. 1–5. IEEE (2017)
8. Grummett, T.S., et al.: Constitutive spectral EEG peaks in the gamma range: suppressed by sleep, reduced by mental activity and resistant to sensory stimulation. Front. Hum. Neurosci. **8**, 927 (2014)
9. Khasnobish, A., Konar, A., Tibarewala, D.N., Bhattacharyya, S., Janarthanan, R.: Object shape recognition from EEG signals during tactile and visual exploration. In: Maji, P., Ghosh, A., Murty, M.N., Ghosh, K., Pal, S.K. (eds.) PReMI 2013. LNCS, vol. 8251, pp. 459–464. Springer, Heidelberg (2013). https://doi.org/10.1007/978-3-642-45062-4_63
10. Kim, S.G., Richter, W., Uğurbil, K.: Limitations of temporal resolution in functional MRI. Magn. Reson. Med. **37**(4), 631–636 (1997)

11. Loftus, E.F., Pickrell, J.E.: The formation of false memories. Psychiatric Ann. **25**(12), 720–725 (1995)
12. Lundberg, S.M., et al.: From local explanations to global understanding with explainable AI for trees. Nat. Mach. Intell. **2**(1), 2522–5839 (2020)
13. Lundberg, S.M., Lee, S.I.: A unified approach to interpreting model predictions. In: Advances in Neural Information Processing Systems, pp. 4765–4774 (2017)
14. Morin, C.: Neuromarketing: the new science of consumer behavior. Society **48**(2), 131–135 (2011). https://doi.org/10.1007/s12115-010-9408-1
15. Park, W., Jamil, M.H., Eid, M.: Neural activations associated with friction stimulation on touch-screen devices. Front. Neurorobot. **13**, 27 (2019)
16. Saha, A., Konar, A., Bhattacharya, B.S., Nagar, A.K.: EEG classification to determine the degree of pleasure levels in touch-perception of human subjects. In: 2015 International Joint Conference on Neural Networks (IJCNN), pp. 1–8. IEEE (2015)
17. Shapley, L.S.: A value for n-person games. In: Contributions to the Theory of Games, vol. 2, no. 28, pp. 307–317 (1953)

SANDFOX Project Optimizing the Relationship Between the User Interface and Artificial Intelligence to Improve Energy Management in Smart Buildings

Christophe Bortolaso[1], Stéphanie Combettes[2], Marie-Pierre Gleizes[2],
Berangere Lartigue[3], Mathieu Raynal[4(✉)], and Stéphanie Rey[1]

[1] Berger-Levrault, Toulouse, France
{christophe.bortolaso,stephanie.rey}@berger-levrault.com
[2] SMAC team, IRIT lab, University of Toulouse, Toulouse, France
{stephanie.combettes,marie-pierre.gleizes}@irit.fr
[3] LMDC, University of Toulouse, Toulouse, France
berangere.lartigue@univ-tlse3.fr
[4] ELIPSE Team, IRIT Lab, University of Toulouse, Toulouse, France
mathieu.raynal@irit.fr

Abstract. This paper deals with energy efficiency in buildings in order to mitigate the climate change. Buildings are the highest source of energy consumption worldwide. However, a large part of this energy is wasted, mainly due to poor buildings management. Therefore, being accurately informed about consumptions and detecting anomalies are essential steps to overcome this problem.

Currently, some software exist to typically record, store, archive, and visualize big data such as the ones of a building, a campus, or a city. Yet, they do not provide Artificial Intelligence (AI) able to automatically analyze the streaming data to detect anomalies and send alerts, as well as adapted reports to the different stakeholders.

The system designed in the SANDFOX project has for objective to fill this gap. To improve the energy management, an innovative system should aim at visualizing the streaming data, editing reports, and detecting anomalies, for different stakeholders, such as policy makers, energy managers, researchers, technical staff or end-users of these buildings.

The paper presents the User-Centred Design approach that was used to collect the required needs from different stakeholders. The developed AI system is called SANDMAN (semi-Supervised ANomaly Detection with Multi-AgeNt systems). It processes data in a time constrained manner to detect anomalies as early as possible. SANDMAN is based on the paradigm of self-adaptive multi-agent systems.

The results show the robustness of the AI regarding the detection of noisy data, of different types of anomalies, and the scaling.

Keywords: Dashboard · Anomaly detection · Energy management · Smart buildings

© Springer Nature Switzerland AG 2020
C. Stephanidis et al. (Eds.): HCII 2020, LNCS 12424, pp. 417–433, 2020.
https://doi.org/10.1007/978-3-030-60117-1_31

1   Introduction

This paper deals with energy efficiency in buildings in order to mitigate climate change. Buildings are the highest source of energy consumption worldwide [7]. However, a large part of this energy is wasted [18], mainly due to poor buildings management [2,12]. Therefore, being accurately informed about consumption and detecting anomalies are essential steps to overcome this problem.

Currently, some software exist to typically record, store, archive, and visualize big data such as those of a building, a campus, or even a city. They provide simple reports on the data. They are well suited to provide data visualization dashboards on any device (tablets, phones, and computers). Yet, they do not provide Artificial Intelligence (AI) able to automatically analyze the data flow to detect anomalies and send alerts, as well as reports adapted to the different stakeholders.

To improve energy management, a single system should aim at visualizing the streaming data and detecting anomalies for those interested either in buildings and networks maintenance, or in energy management. Such users may be policy makers, energy managers, researchers, technical staff or end-users of these buildings and networks. Depending on their function, they need to visualize on an innovative dashboard different kinds of data and their dynamics, as well as dysfunction alerts.

The system designed in the SANDFOX project aims to fill this gap. The SANDFOX project involves the French company Berger-Levrault and the University of Toulouse III - Paul Sabatier, through a multidisciplinary team composed of ergonomists, energy specialists and computer scientists specialised in Human-Computer Interaction (HCI) and AI.

Our contribution can be summarized as follows: the development of a semi-supervised generic AI system able to detect anomalies in streaming data from smart buildings, coupled with an interactive dashboard adapted to different stakeholders.

Section 2 presents the SANDFOX project. Section 3 presents the user-centred interface. Section 4 is dedicated to SANDMAN (semi-Supervised ANomaly Detection with Multi-AgeNt systems), a generic and novel approach for automatic anomaly detection and features some experiments conducted with SANDMAN. Lastly, we will expose a conclusion and list some perspectives for the future of SANDFOX.

2   The SANDFOX Project

The main objective of SANDFOX project is to design and develop a dashboard dedicated to the energy management of buildings. SANDFOX allows to visualize energy consumption in different ways, and in order to improve the energy management, it is associated to the SANDMAN system. The SANDMAN system detects different types of anomalies in streaming data from buildings.

The SANDFOX dashboard targets different stakeholders, such as policy makers, energy managers, researchers, technical staff or end-users of these buildings and networks. Indeed, depending on their function, users need to visualize different kinds of data and their dynamics, as well as dysfunction alerts:

1. For example, the technical staff in charge of the maintenance of buildings and fluids (gaz, water) networks need all the relevant data issued by thousands of sensors.
2. Due to the huge quantity of data, an AI system is necessary to help them in detecting anomalies that could deteriorate the energy management;
3. HCI is also required to easily visualize the relevant data: (1) An energy manager would not need that level of data but the consumption over time for different buildings in order to propose solutions to mitigate the energy demand; (2) Policy makers would need global reports on the energy consumption; (3) Researchers may need detailed data on Heating Ventilation Air-Conditioning (HVAC) systems, specific sensors, over time, in order to conduct some research projects;
4. Depending on the stakeholders, the details level for the visualization is also different: it can be a room, a building, or a campus. SANDFOX is therefore multi-scale.

The interactive dashboard is the core of the SANDFOX project to allow the visualization and the analysis of such massive and complex data. The scientific contribution of SANDFOX is the interaction between the user-centered interface and the AI that supports each other.

The data processed by SANDFOX come from the buildings and fluids distribution networks of the University of Toulouse - Paul Sabatier campus. They are provided by the SGE, the organisation in charge of the energy and fluid consumptions to the University. The SGE manages about 6000 sensors measuring at least one value per hour. In addition, SANDFOX uses the data issued from sensors (temperature, illuminance, CO_2, humidity, occupancy, etc.) deployed on the campus by the scientific project neOCampus[1]. With the massive growth of the Internet of Things, the number of sensors in existing and new buildings sharply increased due to their low cost and their benefit in the buildings management. Sensors can be easily added in buildings or replaced by others. Consequently, the management of these sensors in situ, as well as the data they generate make building managers face a complex system.

An accurate control of the data is required for an optimal management of the energy on the campus. To do so, within the SANDFOX project, a tool to automatically detect anomalies in streaming data, SANDMAN (semi-Supervised ANomaly Detection with Multi-AgeNt systems), is coupled to the innovative HCI. SANDMAN is an important asset for buildings managers because it processes data in constrained time to detect anomalies as soon as possible and allows them to quickly solve problems in situ. Because the huge dataset, the research space of the anomalies is also substantial and cannot be done manually. SANDMAN learns to detect anomalies in a semi-supervised way thanks to the feedback of an expert of the domain. SANDMAN is based on a life-long learning self-adaptive multi-agent system.

---

[1] www.neocampus.org.

3   Interactive Dashboard

3.1   User-Centred Design

In order to take into account the needs of different users to guide the design of the SANDFOX dashboard, we have implemented a User-Centred Design method with the different stakeholders.

This method was first described in a book edited by Norman and Draper in 1985. It states: "User-Centred Design places the user at the centre of the design process, from the initial analysis of user needs to testing and evaluation" [1]. In 1999, an international standard ISO 13407 was introduced to formalise the "human operator-centred design process for interactive systems". This standard was then revised by ISO 9241-210 in 2010. It specifies the criteria for the implementation of the user-centred design process: the prior understanding of the users, their tasks and their environment; the active involvement of users throughout the product development; the iteration between the different steps of the design process; the constitution of a multidisciplinary design team; the appropriate distribution of functions between users (habits, personalities, skills) and technology (performance, functionalities). The iterative design cycle is composed of four main stages: 1) understanding the activity and needs, 2) idea generation and design, 3) system prototyping, and 4) evaluation of the solutions with the users [13].

We used a User-Centred Design approach to better take into account the needs, skills and behaviours of the different users. First of all, we identified all the people who might use the interactive dashboard to visualise energy data. In addition to the current users who regularly analyse these data, we also considered the people who could benefit from them if data were presented in a more user-friendly manner than the large tables of values.

We then categorised them according to the use they would make of this dashboard: energy manager, SGE (building and network maintenance), DGS (policy maker), energy researcher and campus user. We then conducted interviews with one user from each type of profile who is currently using the data from the university's meters, allowing us to better understand their work and needs. These meetings allowed to explain their tasks, the tools they currently use, the problems they encounter, and their needs in order to better use this data.

The different tasks extracted from these interviews were translated into requirements and usage scenarios for a future SANDFOX dashboard. An example scenario is presented below:

Flavie wishes to compare the electricity consumption of buildings U3 and U4 over the last winter period. After selecting the type of data and the buildings by switching to a map display, she adjusts the dates to have only the data between December 1, 2017 and February 28, 2018. The cumulative consumption over these 3 months shows that building U3 consumed 14% more than building U4. In order to understand this difference, she chooses to display the consumption graphs of both buildings. This view shows that over-consumption occurs mainly during the Christmas holiday period. Flavie decides to refine the time scale and to display the graphs only for the period from December 15 to January 8. Finally, she displays the graph for each electricity sensor in the U4 building to try to understand where this over-consumption comes from. After analysing the anomaly, Flavie wants to add an alert on building U4. She configures the notification settings, as this is the first alert she adds to the application. She chooses to be notified on the application and by email. She adds a threshold of 1500 kw/h on building U4. This alert is added to the alerts list available in the alerts tab.

Based on these scenarios and requirements, several iterative brainstorming and low-fidelity prototyping steps allowed us to come up with the solution presented in next section.

3.2 Visualisation, Selection and Comparison of Data

All users need to view the energy data by manipulating different criteria: the type of energy (electricity, water, calories, ...), location (building, floor, room, ...) and the period of time.

A majority of users use this dashboard to control the energy consumption of buildings for different fluids. To make this task easier, users need tools to filter data by type, location and time period. The fluid is selected using the list displayed on the left of the dashboard (cf. Fig. 1, on the left). Once the fluid has been selected, the buildings are coloured on the map according to their daily consumption. Each colour (green, orange, red) corresponds to a value interval (the legend for each fluid is displayed on the left bottom corner of the map). In order to be able to compare the buildings with each other, the energy consumption is normalised with respect to the surface of the buildings.

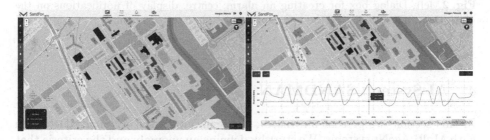

Fig. 1. On the left, the electricity is selected. The interactive map is displayed with the coloured buildings according to their consumption; On the right, buildings 1R1 and U4 are selected. Their electricity consumption is displayed on the timeline

By clicking on a building, the building is selected. Its energy consumption is displayed by timeline under the interactive map (cf. Fig. 1, on the right). By default, the timeline displays the data for the last 30 days. The user can increase or decrease this period of time by using the selector under the timeline. The user can also display a specific value of the timeline by hovering over it with the mouse pointer.

Users regularly compare several buildings. This comparison is possible on the dashboard by clicking on each desired building. The energy data for each building appears as a curve on the timeline. The names of the different selected buildings are displayed above the timeline in a rectangle of the same colour as the data curve for this building.

3.3 Alarms Management and Notifications System

Users can define limits for energy values that buildings should not exceed. They can define three minimum and maximum values for the same alarm (cf. Fig. 2, on the left). This helps to determine the severity of the problem. If one of the limits is exceeded, the user is then informed of the anomaly on the map: a dot appears on the concerned building. This dot displays the type of energy, the number of anomalies and is coloured according to the severity of the anomaly (see Fig. 2, center). The user can click on it if he wishes to have more information on the problem. He can also go to the notifications page where he will have the list of all the anomalies, with the detail of the values (cf. Fig. 2, on the right).

Fig. 2. left, Dialog box for creating an alarm; centre, display of notifications on the Map; right, interface listing the information of each detected anomaly

4 AI System: SANDMAN

In this section, we present SANDMAN, the semi-Supervised ANomaly Detection with Multi-AgeNt systems. We start by defining an anomaly and the criteria that an anomaly detection system should solve. We continue by a literature review on the relevant work. The core of the algorithm is then presented as well as some experiments showing the validity of the algorithm.

4.1   Definition of an Anomaly

In their review on anomaly detection, Chandola et al. [4] define an anomaly as *"an unexpected or undesirable behaviour in a system"* and they point out three kinds of anomalies:

- **point:** the measure is outside an acceptable range for the sensor,
- **contextual:** the measure is inside an acceptable range for the sensor but anomalous in some contexts (example: high heating consumption during summer),
- **collective:** a collection of measures is anomalous with respect to the entire data set although the individual measures may not be anomalous in themselves.

4.2   Criteria for a Smart Building Anomaly Detection System

A smart building equipped with sensors generates a large amount of available data that must be analysed to improve energy management. Thus, the design of anomaly detection systems has to take into account the following characteristics:

- constrained-time detection,
- detection of several types of anomalies,
- use of raw and heterogeneous data,
- scaling,
- genericity.

4.3   Relevant Work on Anomalies Detection

This section presents the state of the art of anomaly detection in smart buildings. The methods presented below have been analysed under the prism of the criteria defined above, necessary for an anomaly detection system. In this context, the methods and techniques featured in the literature are classified into the following categories:

Physical Models. This category gathers methods that require prior modelling of physical laws, such as building modelling, or heat exchanges between the inside and outside of a building. Physical models rely on an expert's knowledge and on specifying the type of tracked anomaly. It quickly becomes impractical regarding scalability.

Unsupervised Classification and Statistics. These methods are generally based on statistical studies using different techniques (ARIMA (Auto-Regressive Integrated Moving Average) method, ARMA (Auto-Regressive Moving Average) method, PCA (Principal Component Analysis), wavelets, etc.). Unsupervised classification methods have no access to expert feedback and are then ill suited for anomaly detection when considering that anomalies are undesired events from a human perspective rather than rare events.

Neural Networks. Neural networks are an important family of methods of non-statistical classifiers [21]. Nevertheless, they are rarely used for anomaly detection in smart buildings. Even though neural network can detect anomalies in real-time, a large set of labelled data is required to train the neural network before it can detect anomalies. This reliance on training data is problematic as labelling data is a fastidious task. Also, even with a large enough training set, it is still possible that some kinds of anomalies will not show up. Indeed, anomalies not present during the learning phase (so not learned), will not be detected during the detection phase.

Data Mining. Data mining methods extract knowledge from large amounts of data. Unlike most other method families, these methods can usually extract collective or contextual anomalies in addition to point anomalies. Data mining methods require special attention during data pre-processing and a human is required to help in the selection of the most relevant inputs to allow scalability.

Multi-agent Systems and Decentralised Systems. Our SANDMAN model uses a multi-agent system. It is worth noting that multi-agent systems have been widely used in the management of the operations of HVAC systems in buildings [10], but not for anomaly detection in this sector. Yet, Forestiero [9] and Seng Ng et al. [16] proposed two generic anomaly detection systems based on Multi-Agent Systems (MAS) that could be adapted to the building sector.

Table 1 presents a summary of the methods described above. In view of the adequacy of the methods presented to the criteria requested for anomaly detection, we can see that none of them exactly meets our needs.

Many studies focus only on building subsystems, such as heating or electrical energy consumption at different locations in the building. These studies fulfil their objectives but their ability to treat all the systems in a building in a generic way has not been shown.

To date, little research has been conducted to use heterogeneous sensors without knowledge of their data types.

In addition, all the studies use data pre-processing requiring human expertise, either by handpicking the data or by providing labelled data-sets to learn the relevant data.

In summary, this literature review on anomaly detection in buildings shows that none method is able to satisfy all the criteria. This gap convinced us to propose a semi-supervised method using multi-agent systems. The method is presented below.

4.4   Relation Between the AI and the Expert

The management of data issued from the buildings and fluids distribution networks (heating, water, electricity, etc.) at the scale of a campus is complex. Failures, dysfunctions, alarms, etc., are usual. Detecting them as soon as possible is critical to avoid waste of energy or fluids. The help of an AI is necessary to face the complexity due to the quantity of data to be processed and to the correlations between data to detect.

Table 1. Synthesis of anomaly detection methods in smart buildings in the literature

	Scaling	Real time	Raw data	Heterogeneous data	Genericity
Physical models:					
Turner [20]	−	+	−	+	−
Sklavounos [17]	−	−	−	+	−
Unsupervised classification:					
Yan [24]	−	+	−	+	−
Chou [6]	−	+	−	−	−
Ploennigs [15]	+	−	−	+	−
Chen [5]	+	−	−	+	−
Li [11]	+	−	−	+	−
Neural networks:					
Wu [22]	−	+	−	+	−
Zhu [26]	−	−	−	+	−
Data mining:					
Capozzoli [3]	+	+	−	−	−
Xue [23]	−	−	−	+	−
Pena [14]	−	+	−	+	−
Fan [8]	+	−	−	+	+
Yu [25]	+	−	−	+	−
Multi-Agent Systems:					
Forestiero [9]	+	N/A	N/A	−	+
Seng Ng [16]	+	+	N/A	N/A	+

We developed SANDMAN, to detect anomalies in raw and heterogeneous data sets. SANDMAN learns all along its functioning. To do so, an expert of the field, in our case an expert in buildings management, supervises the classifications (normal or anomaly) proposed by SANDMAN by confirming or dis-confirming them. The feedback from the expert to SANDMAN allows the system to learn from its mistakes and therefore increases its efficiency with time.

The feedback is given through an interface that has to take into account the huge quantity of data. It has to be designed so it is ergonomic: easy to use, easy feedback, and simple and evolving display.

The relation between the AI and the expert is two-way: the expert needs the AI to process the quantity of data and allows him to visualise more easily the points of interest. The AI needs the expert to improve its functioning while taking into account streaming data.

4.5   Presentation of the SANDMAN Operating Steps

SANDMAN works with unprocessed (raw) time-stamped data from all types of (heterogeneous) sensors.

We have defined two concepts of situation: (1) A *situation* is *the set of measured values of all sensors over 24* h; and (2) a *current situation* is the last (current) situation encountered. These situations are stored in a situation history.

Each sensor is associated with a profile learnt in real time by SANDMAN. A profile consists of 24 stored measured values (one for each hour of the day). A profile value is a value computed from all the previous nominal measured values (of this sensor), at the same hour of the day. This value becomes the value expected of the sensor for this hour. Thus a *profile* is *a set of expected data updated by* SANDMAN *throughout the system life.*

Detecting and Classifying Anomalies. To detect an anomaly, SANDMAN uses the profile of the sensors and the current situation. To this aim, it computes the disparity of a sensor. The disparity is the sum (in absolute value) of all the differences between the sensor profile and the measured values of this sensor for the current situation (Eq. 1).

$$Disparity_s^t = \sum_{t_i=t}^{t-23} \left| realValue_s^{t_i} - nominalValue_s^{t_i} \right| \tag{1}$$

with s: sensor s; t: time t of the current situation; $realValue_s^{t_i}$: real value of sensor s at time t_i; $nominalValue_s^{t_i}$: nominal value of sensor s at time t_i.

The period under consideration is a sliding 24-h window. From the current time-stamp (for ex. 13:00), the 24 previous hour are considered (from 14:00 the previous day to 13:00 the current hour). Then, SANDMAN computes the *Degree of Anomaly (DA)* of the current situation. The DA is the weighted sum of the measured values of all the sensors (the value of the current situation) (Eq. 2).

$$DA(Situation^t) = \sum_{s=1}^{S} Disparity_s^t * Weight_s \tag{2}$$

with $Situation^t$: Situation at time t; S: number of sensors; $Disparity_s^t$: Disparity of the sensor s at time t; $Weight_s$: Weight of the sensor s.

Thanks to the Degree of Anomaly, SANDMAN is able to classify the current situation, i.e. labels it as "normal" or "anomalous" by algorithm 1. The threshold is a static number chosen arbitrarily (1000 for SANDMAN). The calculation of each weight adjusts to the threshold whatever its value. SANDMAN classifies the

Algorithm 1. Algorithm of classification or anomalies detection

```
1: for each new current situation do
2:    if DA < Threshold then
3:        SANDMAN returns : "the situation is normal"
4:    else
5:        SANDMAN returns : "the situation is anomalous"
6:    end if
7: end for
```

situation (on the correct side of the threshold) according to the value of this weight. Note that the DA also depends of the threshold value.

To correctly detect anomalies, each $Weights_i$ associated with one of the sensors must therefore be correctly evaluated. Each sensor has only one associated weight used to calculate the degree of anomaly for all situations in the situation history. This weight is recalculated at each resolution cycle to take into account the situation changes.

To each resolution cycle, once the current situations classified, SANDMAN gives this classification (normal or anomalous) to the expert. The expert (possibly later after this detection) checks the classification and validates (allowed) or invalidates (compulsory) it. This feedback is sent to SANDMAN.

Analysing Expert's Feedback. Once SANDMAN has classified a situation (as normal or anomalous) and has an expert's feedback on this situation, the following resolution cycle enables SANDMAN to analyse whether or not it has to learn. The following are the various cases SANDMAN must analyse:

1. For a situation classified as "anomalous" by both SANDMAN and the expert,
   - SANDMAN does nothing
2. For a situation classified as "anomalous" by SANDMAN and "normal" by the expert, SANDMAN
   - updates the sensor profiles
   - creates and adds this "normal" situation to the situation history
   - self-adapts the weights of the sensors
3. For a situation classified as "normal" by SANDMAN and "anomalous" by the expert, SANDMAN
   - creates and adds a new "anomalous" situation to the situation history
   - self-adapts the weights of the sensors
4. For a situation classified as "normal" by both SANDMAN and the expert,
   - SANDMAN updates the sensor profiles.

Learning the Profiles. SANDMAN updates the sensor profile only if the situation is normal for both SANDMAN and the expert. Indeed, sensor values of an anomalous situation are neither reliable nor expected. Each sensor profile changes the value corresponding to the time of the analysed situation.

Updating the History of Situations. During this operation all the situations in the history must be correctly and evenly classified. A situation is correctly classified if its degree of anomaly (DA) enables to deduce the correct classification of this situation. In order to have a balanced classification of situations, the DA of the "normal" situation closest to (and below) the threshold and the DA of the anomalous situation also closest to (and above) the threshold are, in absolute value, at the same distance from the given threshold. An normal situation must be below the threshold whereas a anomalous situation must be above the threshold. To have a balanced classification of the situations, the weight of the sensors self-adapt.

Self-Adapting Weights. Each weight is represented by a weight agent. The goal of the multi-agent weight system is that each weight agent finds its value by cooperating with the others. During a resolution cycle, all situations require weight adjustments and the weight agents self-adapt and then, each situation calculates its new degree of anomaly using the updated weights. From a weight agent point of view, a weight agent decides whether or not it has to update its weight (independently and simultaneously from the other weight agents) once it has received messages from the situations. Agents cooperation guarantees that at least one weight agent updates its weight and that the global state is better. Once the update cycle of the weight agents is over, the system checks that each situation is well-classified by calculating t. Indeed, the best way to reduce the rate of wrong classification and thus to have a robust system, is to keep the two situations closest to the threshold (recorded in the history) as far away from the threshold as possible.

4.6   Validation of SANDMAN

In order to check the validity of the anomaly detection system SANDMAN, we have conducted several experiments.

The data used to conduct the experiments were generated using the TSimulus time series generator [19]. These time series include a signed value per hour for each sensor. Each sensor has its own range of values. The values for each sensor are cyclical, with or without noise over a 24-h period, meaning that the value of a sensor at 3 pm is the same every day, with the exception of noise. These simulated data have been then modified by a human expert to introduce several anomalies of each of the three types.

SANDMAN processes the data in constrained-time and the expert gives his opinion a posteriori in an asynchronous way.

All the experiments were carried out on a 4-core processor with a frequency of 2.6 GHz. The data sets used in the following experiments feature one value for each sensor every hour over one month, for a total of 744 h. The number of sensors depends on the experiment. Three separate data files are used to show the ability of SANDMAN to: i) detect point anomalies and mitigate noise, ii) detect collective and contextual anomalies, iii) scale.

The experiments have been conducted over one or two months and the results are presented as the number of:

- TN: True Negative, TP: True Positive,
- FN: False Negative, FP: False Positive,
- t/sit: calculation time for processed situation in ms.

Point Anomalies and Noise Mitigation. Point anomalies are the type of anomaly most often detected in the literature, as both univariate and multivariate approaches can detect them.

In this experiment, we study the efficiency of SANDMAN in detecting point anomalies in noisy data with different levels of noise. The data file contains 20 sensors, i.e. 20 x 744 = 14880 data. 58 point anomalies were added manually by an expert. Three experiments have been conducted, with the noiseless data, 1%-level data and 5%-level data.

Table 2 shows the results of the experiments over a one-month period. 40 over the 58 anomalies have been correctly detected and 18 have been detected as False Negative for a low level of noise in the data. A higher noise level (5%) leads to a higher False Positive rate.

Table 2. Results of point anomalies detection with noisy data

Noise level	TP	TN	FN	FP
No noise	40	686	18	0
1%	40	686	18	0
5%	58	679	0	31

Collective and Contextual Anomalies. In this experiment, we want to study the ability of SANDMAN in detecting the three types of anomalies: point, contextual and collective anomalies.

The data file contains the values of 20 sensors over one month, and the results are presented after one and two months to show the improvement due to the learning. The 3 types of anomalies have been manually added in the data file. The data have 1% of noise.

Table 3 shows the general results for our experiment. It features 14 anomalies of all kinds.

Table 4 shows the results of the detection of each type of anomalies in detail: the numbers of each type of anomaly, as well as the anomalies detected after the first month and then after the second month. SANDMAN created and added to the history the situations corresponding to the misclassified situations during the first month, to classify them without error during the second month, regardless of the type of anomaly.

Table 3. General results of anomaly detection with different kinds of anomalies

	Month 1				Month 2			
nb	TP	TN	FN	FP	TP	TN	FN	FP
Anomalies 14	4	730	10	0	14	730	0	0

Table 4. Detailed results of anomaly detection per type of anomaly

		Month 1		Month 2	
	nb	TP	FN	TP	FN
Point anomalies	6	2	4	6	0
Collective anomalies	5	1	4	5	0
Contextual anomalies	3	1	2	3	0
Total	14	4	10	14	0

Scaling. The scaling criterion for checking the efficiency of SANDMAN was done in detecting anomalies when the number of sensors increases. To do so, a large number of sensors is used to measure their effect on the computing time. A data set of 20 sensors is duplicated to obtain up to 800 sensors. The data used are the same as the initial data file with 58 anomalies and 1% noise. Table 5 shows the calculation time per situation as a function of the number of sensors. The calculation time of month 2 is always shorter than the calculation time of month 1 because the learning of the weights is only carried out in month 1. We also note that the resolution time is proportional to the number of sensors used and that the time difference between the two months is constant. This is due to the fact that most of the execution time comes from reading the raw data from a database, which has a fixed cost per sensor.

Table 5. Results of scaling

Number of sensors	Month 1 t/sit (ms)	Month 2 t/sit (ms)
20	2.7	1.7
40	4.8	3.5
100	22	20
200	48	45
400	102	100
800	185	180

5 Conclusion

In the context of growing streaming data in the management of buildings, it is necessary to have tools that help the stakeholders in their various tasks. The SANDFOX project proposes an innovative dashboard that easily provides to the stakeholders the information they need.

Among the different interests of the stakeholders is the detection of the anomalies that can be found in the streaming data, that possibly leads to an energy waste in buildings. We therefore propose to automatically detect anomalies that are undesirable rather than statistical outliers. In addition to point anomalies, collective and contextual anomalies can be detected with our model. The literature review shows that the detection of collective and contextual anomalies is not treated properly. Moreover almost all of the methods in anomaly detection require data pre-processing. Consequently, few methods can lead to a generic anomaly detection system able to operate with all buildings sub-systems.

We develop SANDMAN, a semi-supervised constrained-time anomaly detection system which uses raw data as input and classifies anomalies by learning from expert feedback. Experiments have shown that SANDMAN is able to detect several types of anomalies in a generic manner, and scales well with a large number of sensors. The feedback required from the expert is kept to a minimum as they are given at their convenience. In practice, this operating way is close to the reality of the tasks of a building manager, who has to check on the good operations of a building based on the sensors' raw data. In future works, SANDMAN shall be able to learn several sets of nominal profiles for the sensors, to account for the different behaviours of the users of the buildings.

In order to make easier the data management, an interactive dashboard has been developed. Thanks to a User Centered Design approach, we collect the required needs from different stakeholders. The user can then select the buildings for which he wants more details. Data for these buildings is presented using a timeline. The user can select several buildings at the same time and select the periods of interest. The user can also create alerts by defining, for a type of energy, the minimum and maximum values. As soon as these values are exceeded, the dashboard notifies the user of this anomaly with a visual feedback on the user interface.

The next step of the project will be to connect the dashboard to the SANDMAN system. The SANDMAN system will replace the user interface of alarm definition (the user will no longer have to set alarms manually as SANDMAN is able to detect and notify anomalies). The notification system will remain unchanged. A dialog box will be added to allow the expert user to validate or not the anomalies proposed by SANDMAN.

Finally, we will deploy SANDFOX dashboard towards real end-users in the context of the university campus to get feedback on all the aspects of the dashboard.

References

1. Beaudouin-Lafon, M., Mackay, W.E.: Prototyping tools and techniques. In: Human-Computer Interaction, pp. 137–160. CRC Press (2009)
2. Brady, L., Abdellatif, M.: Assessment of energy consumption in existing buildings. Energy Build. **149**, 142–150 (2017)
3. Capozzoli, A., Lauro, F., Khan, I.: Fault detection analysis using data mining techniques for a cluster of smart office buildings. Expert Syst. Appl. **42**(9), 4324–4338 (2015)
4. Chandola, V., Banerjee, A., Kumar, V.: Anomaly detection: a survey. ACM Comput. Surv. **41**(3), 1–58 (2009)
5. Chen, B., Sinn, M., Ploennigs, J., Schumann, A.: Statistical anomaly detection in mean and variation of energy consumption. In: 2014 22nd International Conference on Pattern Recognition, pp. 3570–3575 (2014)
6. Chou, J.S., Telaga, A.S.: Real-time detection of anomalous power consumption. Renew. Sustain. Energy Rev. **33**, 400–411 (2014)
7. https://ec.europa.eu/energy/en/topics/energy-efficiency/energy-performance-of-buildings . Accessed 17 Mar 2020
8. Fan, C., Xiao, F., Madsen, H., Wang, D.: Temporal knowledge discovery in big BAS data for building energy management. Energy Build. **109**, 75–89 (2015)
9. Forestiero, A.: Self-organizing anomaly detection in data streams. Inf. Sci. **373**, 321–336 (2016)
10. Labeodan, T., Aduda, K., Boxem, G., Zeiler, W.: On the application of multi-agent systems in buildings for improved building operations, performance and smart grid interaction - a survey. Renew. Sustain. Energy Rev. **50**, 1405–1414 (2015)
11. Li, S., Wen, J.: A model-based fault detection and diagnostic methodology based on PCA method and wavelet transform. Energy Build. **68**, 63–71 (2014)
12. Lin, M., Afshari, A., Azar, E.: A data-driven analysis of building energy use with emphasis on operation and maintenance: a case study from the uae. J. Clean. Prod. **192**, 169–178 (2018)
13. Mackay, W.E.: Educating multi-disciplinary design teams. Proc. of Tales of the Disappearing Computer, pp. 105–118 (2003)
14. Peña, M., Biscarri, F., Guerrero, J.I., Monedero, I., León, C.: Rule-based system to detect energy efficiency anomalies in smart buildings, a data mining approach. Expert Syst. Appl. **56**, 242–255 (2016)
15. Ploennigs, J., Chen, B., Schumann, A., Brady, N.: Exploiting generalized additive models for diagnosing abnormal energy use in buildings. In: Proceedings of the 5th ACM Workshop on Embedded Systems For Energy-Efficient Buildings - BuildSys 2013, pp. 1–8 (2013)
16. Seng Ng, Y., Srinivasan, R.: Multi-agent based collaborative fault detection and identification in chemical processes. Eng. Appl. Artif. Intell. **23**(6), 934–949 (2010)
17. Sklavounos, D., Zervas, E., Tsakiridis, O., Stonham, J.: A subspace identification method for detecting abnormal behavior in HVAC systems. J. Energy **2015**, 1–12 (2015)
18. https://www.iea.org/reports/the-critical-role-of-buildings. Accessed 17 Mar 2020
19. https://tsimulus.readthedocs.io/en/latest/. Accessed 18 Dec 2019
20. Turner, W.J., Staino, A., Basu, B.: Residential HVAC fault detection using a system identification approach. Energy Build. **151**, 1–17 (2017)
21. Venkatasubramanian, V., Rengaswamy, R., Kavuri, S.N., Yin, K.: A review of process fault detection and diagnosis: Part III: process history based methods. Comput. Chem. Eng. **27**(3), 327–346 (2003)

22. Wu, J., Zeng, W., Yan, F.: Hierarchical temporal memory method for time-series-based anomaly detection. Neurocomputing **273**, 535–546 (2018)
23. Xue, P., et al.: Fault detection and operation optimization in district heating substations based on data mining techniques. Appl. Energy **205**, 926–940 (2017)
24. Yan, K., Ji, Z., Shen, W.: Online fault detection methods for chillers combining extended kalman filter and recursive one-class SVM. Neurocomputing **228**(2016), 205–212 (2017)
25. Yu, Z.J., Haghighat, F., Fung, B.C., Zhou, L.: A novel methodology for knowledge discovery through mining associations between building operational data. Energy Build. **47**, 430–440 (2012)
26. Zhu, Y., Jin, X., Du, Z.: Fault diagnosis for sensors in air handling unit based on neural network pre-processed by wavelet and fractal. Energy Build. **44**, 7–16 (2012)

Safety Analytics for AI Systems

Yang Cai[✉]

Carnegie Mellon University, 4720 Forbes Avenue, Pittsburgh, PA 15213, USA
ycai@cmu.edu

Abstract. Growing AI technologies are a threat to safety and security in systems due to its obscurity and uncertainty. This study introduces a prevailing Deep Learning model, Convolutional Neural Network (CNN) and it's deep weaknesses through a simple case study of the CNN model based on Keras for handwriting recognition. It reveals that CNN algorithms don't adapt well to changes. Adding new cases to the training data may improve accuracy, but not to the same level as before. Synthetic training data may improve the accuracy *superficially* because of the similarity of data distributions between generated data and original data. Prevailing ML models such as Generative Adversarial Networks (GAN) have their limitations such as similarity-addiction and modality collapse. They could be toxic to safety engineering without domain expertise.

The study proposed four test strategies: 1) AI systems should be tested by the third parties, not the developers; 2) test datasets should be categorically different from training datasets; the test data should not be a part of the training data; the test data should be collected from independent sources to increase the "diversity" of data modality; 3) avoid fake data, or simulated data; and 4) don't collect the data that are conveniently available, but actively collect disastrous event data, unexpected, or the worst scenarios that may destroy the model. The study also introduces a multidimensional checklist for AI safety analysis, including sensors, data and environments, default and recovery mode, system architectures, and human-system interaction.

Keywords: AI · Safety · CNN · GAN · Deep Learning · Hand-writing recognition · Pattern recognition · Autonomous vehicle systems · Autonomy

1 Introduction

As autonomous systems heavily involve Artificial Intelligence (AI) algorithms such as machine learning, computer vision, and pattern recognition, it is increasingly difficult to detect and analyze the safety of the AI systems because the algorithms act like black boxes with significant uncertainty. Prevailing measurements such as classification accuracy, detection rate, false alarm rate, and false positive rate, are not enough to assess the overall system safety issues and potential risk areas that result from the implementation of AI in safety critical functions of systems. The term "Artificial Intelligence" has been widely used these days as the state-of-the-art technology. But it is vaguely defined. In order to assess the safety of AI-intensive systems, we ought to learn more about AI systems. For

© Springer Nature Switzerland AG 2020
C. Stephanidis et al. (Eds.): HCII 2020, LNCS 12424, pp. 434–448, 2020.
https://doi.org/10.1007/978-3-030-60117-1_32

example, "What is AI?", "What qualifies a system to become AI-based system?", "What can AI systems do?" "What are the limitations of AI systems?" "Is AI Deep Learning?" "Where are the resources to learn or try AI?" Artificial Intelligence was first proposed by four visionary scientists John McCarthy, Marvin L. Minsky, Nathaniel Rochester, and Claude E. Shannon in their seminal proposal for the Dartmouth Summer Research Project on Artificial Intelligence on August 31, 1955 [1]. It was the earliest and the most precise definition of AI: "The attempt will be made to find how to make machines use language, form abstractions and concepts, solve kinds of problems now reserved for humans, and improve themselves." For decades, AI has evolved from research labs to industrials. Some areas that were envisioned by the AI pioneers have made significant progress such as general problem solving, automatic computers, natural language processing, neural networks, theory of the size of a calculation, and randomness. Some areas in the Dartmouth proposal are still to be explored, for example, self-improvement that a machine can learn from its experiences and improve performance over time, abstractions that a machine can form abstractions from sensory and other data, and creativity where statistical "randomness must be guided by intuition to be efficient. In other words, the educated guess or the hunch include controlled randomness in otherwise orderly thinking."

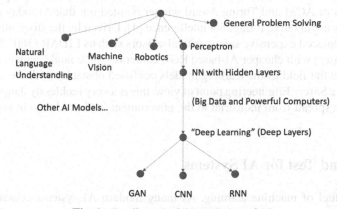

Fig. 1. Family tree of the evolution of AI

Several areas such as machine vision and autonomous vehicle systems have grown rapidly as robots are developed for mobile field applications. Pattern recognition has become a strong force of AI: it started with simple Perceptron and then more powerful but not computational efficient neural nets with hidden layers. It was not so popular until "Big Data" and more powerful computers became available in industry. Amazon, Google, Facebook and many data-centric companies started to mine the massive data for profit. The open sources of multiple layer hidden neural networks, such as TensorFlow and Keras, etc. enable the public to access the tools that were only available in research labs. Currently, many people refer to AI as Machine Learning (ML) and ML is often narrowed down to "Deep Learning," which is typically referred to Convolutional Neural Network (CNN) and its off-springs. Figure 1 illustrates a rough family tree of the evolution of AI. A typical Convolutional Neural Network (CNN) contains four operations: convolution, pooling, non- linearization, and classification. It is actually a combination of a few algorithms that have been used in signal processing and pattern recognition [2, 3]. The goal of the four operations is to extract the representative features and compress the data. Convolution is a feature filter operation. It can contain multiple filters to extract multiple features.

Although Deep Learning-related AI algorithms have been popular in many applications, they have many serious weaknesses: First of all, they need a lot of data. The supervised learning models need data labeling, typically by humans. The learning models are data-driven. It is easy to overfit the data. They are "Black Boxes" that are not explainable to human users. They are not adaptive to changes over time. Furthermore, they are not adaptive to different types of problems. Many Deep Learning models are computationally expensive, which yields a huge carbon footprint. Many Deep Learning in data service industries such as Amazon, Google and Facebook, can tolerate errors up to 40% and still can be profitable commercially, for example, shopping cart product recommendation, Facebook friend suggestions, and Google image search based on similarities. Unfortunately, this kind of error tolerance is not acceptable to safety-critical systems such as autonomous vehicles and weapons. Currently, there are no AI safety certificates like UL or TÜV for hardware. And there is no guideline for evaluating AI Safety. Experts started to look into the intrinsic nature of Deep Learning. Dr. Judea Pearl, Fellow of ACM and Turing Award winner pointed out that AI today and tomorrow is mostly about curve fitting, not intelligence [4]. Driven by the stock market, many companies replaced expensive safety-critical sensors such as LIDAR (360° 3D obstacle detection sensor) with cheaper AI-based RGB cameras. Some fatal accidents have been reported from the field as the learning models confused obstacles with the background pixels. From a Safety Engineering point of view, this is a very recklessly dangerous trend that has been spread from industrial to the government, and academy. In short, AI is a threat.

2 Data and Test for AI Systems

Data is the fuel of machine learning. As many modern AI systems contain machine learning with massive datasets, we need to look into data verification and validation first. Machine learning models need massive amounts of training testing data. Ideally, if we collect enough training data, then we might get good test results. Unfortunately, many machine learning models can survive in a laboratory environment, but fail in the real-world, because there are many exceptional cases. For example, autonomous cars are trained to drive on the highway and streets, not on forest fire and smoke-filled roads. An autonomous car trained in the US may not be able to drive safely in the UK or Japan because of different traffic rules and rights-of-way (Fig. 2).

Collecting training data and labeling each object in the data are very expensive. There are some open source resources for labeling images [5, 6], audio clips [7], and videos [8]. Deep Learning fans often claim that as the data size and model size increase, the accuracy of the model will increase and surpass the traditional feature-based models. The more data and bigger models, the better. Figure 3 is a frequently used diagram from typical Deep Learning lectures [9] and the reality – overfitting the model with fake

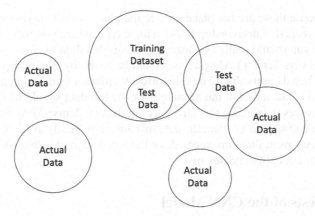

Fig. 2. Illustration of the connection between machine learning and the real-world

data. Instead of improving the accuracy, the performance degenerated after a certain point, due to *modality collapse*. The model confuses by itself because it gradually lost distinguishable features along the way.

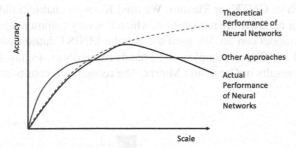

Fig. 3. The myth of Deep Learning (dashed line) and the reality (red line) (Color figure online)

There are four common "sins" in Deep Learning practice: first, the developers of the model are also the testers of the model. Second, the training data overlaps with test data. Third, generate more data by fake it. According to the Deep Learning Cheat Sheet, if the developers don't have enough data, the author suggested "...*fake it, till you make it.* An often-ignored method of improving accuracy is creating new data from what you already have. Take for example photos; often engineers will create more images by rotating and randomly shifting existing images. Such transformations reduce overfitting of the training set" [10]. Finally, the most hidden sin in Deep Learning is collecting the wrong data.

During WWII, the US Air Force engineers tracked bullet holes on Allied planes that encountered Nazi anti-aircraft fire. At first, the military wanted to reinforce those areas, because that's where the ground crews observed the most damage on the returning planes. Until the mathematician Abraham Wald pointed out that this was the damage on the planes that made it home, and the Allies should armor the areas there are no dots at all, because those are the places where the planes won't survive when hit. This phenomenon is called "Survivorship Bias," a logic error where you focus on things that survived when you should really be looking at things that didn't [11].

The take-always here: 1) AI systems should be tested by the third parties, not the developers. 2) Test datasets should be categorically different from training datasets. The test data should not be a part of the training data; the test data should be collected from independent sources to increase the "diversity" of data modality; 3) Avoid fake data, or simulated data; and 4) Don't collect the data that are conveniently available, but actively collect disastrous event data, unexpected, or the worst scenarios that may destroy the model. In short, test extreme cases first.

3   Crash Tests of the CNN Model

In the car industry, safety engineers often use the "Small Overlap Frontal Crashworthiness" protocol to evaluate the impact of the car [12]. The goal is to cause the maximal impact to the dummy driver with minimal test cost. We can adopt the same strategy to test AI systems. Here is a simple case study to reveal the vulnerability of Deep Learning algorithms. We selected Keras [13], an open source of a high-level neural network API, written in Python and capable of running on top of popular Deep Learning algorithms such as TensorFlow, CNTK, or Theano. We used Keras to enable rapid prototyping of the test model for handwriting recognition, which is a very common demo to show how good a learning model can do. We used the popular MNIST dataset with 60,000 training samples and 10,000 test samples of 10 handwriting digits. Figure 4 shows the test samples and the results in Confusion Matrix. The recognition results are very good, all above 99.63%.

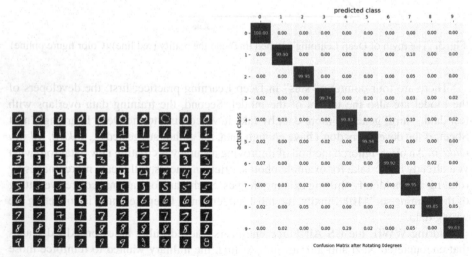

Fig. 4. The handwriting MNIST dataset input with 60,000 training samples and 10,000 test samples (left) and the test results for all 10 digits (right)

Then we simulated a sensory error, for example, the camera tilted at an angle. To be extreme, we rotated all 10,000 test samples between 0 to 360 ° as input test data. The accuracy drops drastically. See Fig. 5. The lowest accuracy is 2.29% for the number "9." In contrast, the number "0" was relatively immune from the damage and kept an accuracy of 97%. We also discovered that the accuracy is sensitive to the rotation angles, for example, the accuracy of number "3" and "8" changes as the rotation angle changes. See Fig. 6.

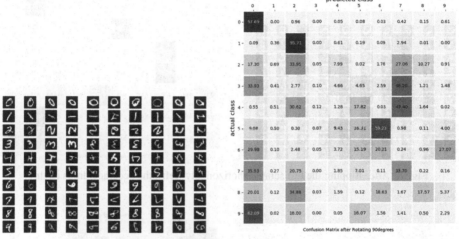

Fig. 5. Rotating 10,000 MNIST test samples in a 90-degree angle as new input test data (left), the accuracy drops significantly after the rotation (right)

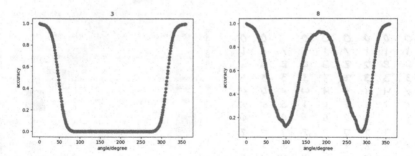

Fig. 6. The accuracy of number "3" (left) and "8" (right) rotated at 0–360°

In addition, we tested other extreme distortion cases, including horizontally flipping the character and inverting the pixel color (black-to-white and white-to-black). See Fig. 7 and 8. These cases are designed to simulate the reflection of the images and saturated imaging sensors under bright sunlight. We found that the accuracy of most numbers drops significantly except the number "0", after horizontally flipped the image samples, where "2", "3", "5", and "6" are worse. We also found that the accuracy of each number recognition drops significantly and rather evenly after inverting the color of each test sample image.

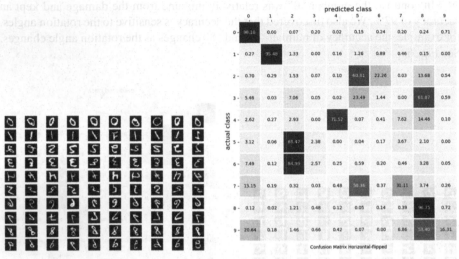

Fig. 7. After flipping the test samples horizontally (left), the accuracy drops (right)

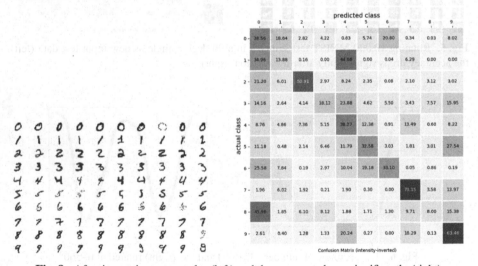

Fig. 8. After invert the test samples (left) and the accuracy drops significantly (right)

We may argue that the CNN model can be improved if we add more samples from those special cases. Therefore, we added rotated training samples. This time, we used the generator of Keras which is one of the most popular machine learning API to generate 44,941 randomly-rotated data. With the generated data and the original MNIST training set, we got a new training set. After training with rotated samples at 90 °, the accuracy improved but not the same highest values as before. The accuracy of "6" for example, drops to 74%. See Fig. 9.

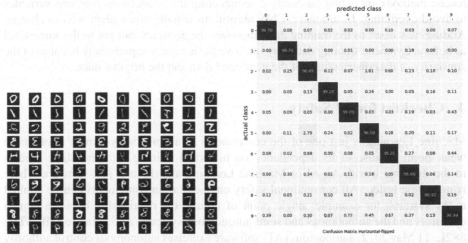

Fig. 9. Add randomly flipped training samples from Keras (left) and tested with *horizontally* flipped samples. The accuracy significantly improved but not as high as the previous ones.

We used the generator of Keras to generate 45,033 randomly-flipped data. With the generated data and the original MNIST training set, we got another new training set. After adding randomly flipped training samples from Keras (left), we tested with the horizontally flipped samples. The accuracy significantly improved but was not as high as the previous ones for example "2" and "9".

CNN is vulnerable to test data that are not *similar* to the training data. The similarity can be represented as probability distribution functions. From our handwriting testing cases, we found that the model performs poorly when the probability distribution functions of input data is significantly different from that of training data. Adding the data from extreme cases to the training dataset certainly would improve the performance. However, the recognition accuracy won't be as high as before when adding the new training data of the extreme cases.

There are several popular generative models for improving the robustness of machine learning. For example, Generative Adversarial Networks (GAN), which contains a data generator and a pattern discriminator [14]. The similarity between the generated data and the raw data is evaluated by the discriminator. See Fig. 14. Unfortunately, the assumption of a GAN is that the synthetic data should have the similar probability distribution functions as the raw data. In the real-world, this assumption is often not true. For example, natural disasters or the next flood may not have the same distribution as previous ones. In some cases, it could be totally different from previous ones. While GANs have been successful in generating "look-alike" synthetic dataset, such as Deep Fake artifacts of faces, voices, and writings similar to celebrities, they are not designed for generating disastrous scenarios, or the worst scenarios because of the intrinsic limitation of the similarity assumption. Furthermore, GANs also have "modality collapse" problems when the distinguished features or patterns gradually disappear over time. There are a few rescue methods, including randomly disconnecting the connections between variables to avoid overfitting. In summary, CNN algorithms usually don't adapt well to change. Adding new cases to the training data improves the accuracy, but not to the same level as before. Synthetic training data may improve the accuracy superficially because of the similarity of data distributions of the generated data and the original data.

4   Checklist for AI Safety

Machine Learning is just one of the components of a function system. It is often the weak point because of its dependency on historical training data and static models in the dynamic world. An AI or Machine Learning algorithm is just software. There is no magic inside. All conventional safety engineering measurements can be applied to AI systems, for example, single point of failure, the relationship between human operators and the autonomous and semi-autonomous systems. According to MIL-STD-882E, 11 May 2012, autonomous (AT) software exercises autonomous control authority over potentially safety-significant hardware systems, subsystems, or components without the possibility of predetermined safe detection and intervention by a control entity to preclude the occurrence of a mishap or hazard [15]. Semi-Autonomous (SAT) software, on the other hand, allows time for predetermined safe detection and human intervention by independent safety mechanisms to mitigate the mishap or hazard. Taking autonomous driving vehicles and drones for example, the basic concepts about machine learning and the cybernetic model of an autonomous system are illustrated in Fig. 10.

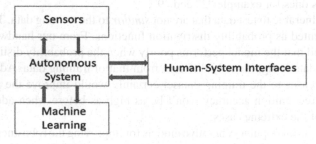

Fig. 10. A model of autonomous driving system

Here is a preliminary checklist to assess the safety of AI systems.

4.1   Sensors

Sensors are the most critical parts of systems in terms of safety and intelligence. In a modern autonomous system, complexity lies in three spaces: perception, control, and communication. The dimensions of a perception space depend on the types of sensors used. The dimensions of a control space depend on the degrees of freedom of actuators or stepper-motors. The dimensions of a communication space depend on the types of channels. *Sensors collect real-time data about the environment.* A machine learning system without effective sensors is like a blind person drives a car. For safety analysis, we want to know how many vital sensors in the system? Are the vital sensors redundant? Does the machine learning model take live sensory data?

4.2 Data Collection

As many AI systems contain a significant amount of data, we must examine the methodology for assessing the safety issues around the training datasets and testing datasets, including data labeling, representativeness, distributions, major assumptions, test team selection, test location selection, test sample selection, etc. Test datasets should be categorically different from training datasets. The test data should not be a part of the training data; the test data should be collected from independent sources to increase the "diversity" of data modality; 3) Avoid fake data, or simulated data (more details in the section of Generative Adversarial Networks); and 4) Don't collect the data that are conveniently available, but actively collect disastrous event data, unexpected, or the worst scenarios that may destroy the model. In short, test extreme cases first.

4.3 Default Design

Default Design usually begins with assumptions about the environment that the system encounters. Almost all autonomous mobile robots have a default mode. Using default mode can reduce complexity in control logic design. Perhaps the most important factor in default design is safety, which can be a baseline for default operation. Defaults contain static and dynamic conditions. Taking static defaults for example, the default position for a power switch should be the "off" position rather than the "on" position. The default position for a transmission gear in a vehicle should be the "parking" position instead of the "driving" position. Dynamic defaults should consider the worst-case scenarios. For instance, when a computer's accelerometer senses fast movement, it should shut down the power and activate the safety mode by default to protect the data. In the case of autonomous driving vehicles, any obstacle in front of the vehicle should be viewed as a hazard – a brick wall, a tree, a cow, or a shopping cart. The default action should be to activate the brakes of the vehicle.

Here is a drone crash case study. Small Commercial drones are designed for outdoor open space flight. That's the default design. When the DJI drone was operated in a woody area under trees, it violated the default operational conditions. It actually led to multiple crashes in an Alps archeology site. Many drones have the auto-pilot mode that overrides human control when the battery level is below a threshold. They would automatically return to a home landing without human intervention. It works well in an open space, but dangerous in the forest. There is a controllability factor here, where humans should always have controllability of the AI-device. There are observability issues in controlling a drone from line-of-sight, or FMV, because of lacking depth information. It would cause a crash when the drone flies around an obstacle. So multiple sensory fusion is needed. In August, 2018, at the archeology site near Paspardo, Alps, Italy, the drone ran out of battery and started auto-homing. The operator lost control of the drone. The drone encountered tree trunks and the automatic collision avoidance AI kicked in by flying upwards and hit the tree eventually flying into the rock. See Fig. 11.

Fig. 11. The COTS drones are designed to fly in an open space by *default*, not in a forest.

In many cases, the goal of default design is based on the mission of the system. Simple and unique default operations are most desirable. Default operation is not foolproof. Sometimes, default operations may cause traffic jams or even deadlocks. For example, insects use pheromones to lay trails back to their nests. Sometimes, a group of ants will lose the pheromone trail and end up circling back on themselves. Other ants then follow, and soon the entire group is going around in endless circles. This is an example of the so-called "ant-mill" behavior pattern. When an ant gets lost, it will randomly wander until it hits a trail marked with pheromones. A mouse does the same. Assume a mouse is placed at the start stem of a T-maze and given two trials with a brief inter-trial interval. First, the mouse would enter one arm and then the alternate arm with significant frequency multiple times. In fact, this pattern occurs in tests with many different animals. It is called *spontaneous alternation behavior* (SAB) [16]. SAB can be traced back to the microscopic mutation of genes. Spontaneous alternation of a fraction of genes helps to create diversity in offspring, and prevents genetic bottlenecking or deadlocks. *Spontaneous alternation* of paths for an autonomous robot, a search engine, or a problem-solving algorithm can help to explore new areas and avoid deadlock situations. Let us take the cleaning robot Roomba for example, its default mode enables the robot to move along one side of an obstacle. This may lead to a deadlock in the robot's path. It could potentially move in a repeating loop without exploring new areas. In order to avoid the possibility of a deadlock, whenever the robot collides into an obstacle, it could decide whether it is a frontal collision or a sideways collision, depending on the location of the collision sensor. If it were a frontal collision, the robot would turn at a random angle, which is a spontaneous alternation of its path, similar to SAB. If it were a sideways collision, then the robot would continue to move along one side of the obstacle until hitting a wall.

Collisions can be found in many modern electronic systems in various fields, from autonomous driving vehicles to data communication protocols. There is a variation of the SAB strategy for collision recovery. When a collision occurs, the system spontaneously switches to different sensors or channels, or the system waits for random intervals and reconnects. Let us take autonomous driving vehicles for example, in which several collision detection sensors are used for safety measures. When the sensory signals show obstacles within a dangerous range, the vehicle stops. The third competition of the DARPA Grand Challenge, also known as the "Urban Challenge," took place at the site of the now defunct George Air Force Base in Victorville, California [17]. The course consisted of a 96 km urban area, which was to be completed in less than 6 h. The autonomous vehicles were required to obey all traffic regulations while also negotiating with other traffic and obstacles. During the course of the race, one vehicle was ahead of another vehicle by a short distance as they were approaching an intersection. The second vehicle perceived two "obstacles": the static dust cloud behind the first vehicle, and a third vehicle waiting at the T-intersection. These two static obstacles created a deadlock for the second vehicle because it had no way to go forward, and had to stop. Luckily, the vehicle was programmed with a spontaneous alternation behavior that enabled it to wait at random intervals and restart the system to move forward. After a few SAB trials, the second vehicle finally got back in the race after the dust cloud settled down. The third vehicle was able to cross the intersection after the road was clear.

4.4 Observability and Controllability

There are two principles for control systems: *observability* and *controllability*. In order to be able to do whatever we want with the given dynamic system under control input, the system must be *controllable*. Furthermore, in order to see what is going on inside the system under observation, the system must be *observable*. The system's controllability is defined as an ability to transfer the initial state to any desired state in a finite amount of time. The system's observability is a dual problem of controllability. It is defined as the ability for us to learn everything about the dynamic behavior of the variables by using the information from the measurements of the input and output.

4.5 Complexity

To build an autonomous system, we must deal with many variables, many of which are unfortunately hidden. Such variables will not emerge until full-scale operation, perhaps even years later. The third architectural element is *complexity*. There are an enormous number of measurements of complexity in different fields, ranging from fractal dimensions to computational time. The emerging Network Science models potentially provide a new way to measure complexity in broader ecological environments for autonomous systems using a network or graph model, similar to food webs or cell interaction networks, which are far more complicated than current artificial systems. Empirically, we can use the number of variables, or nodes in a network, to describe the size of the problem.

The complexity of a network can be roughly estimated by the number of nodes n and edges m. However, not every node plays an equal role in the network. A few nodes have many edges but others have very few or none. The inequality of the connectivity can be measured by the *degree* of a node in a network to describe the number of edges connected to it. Assume the degree of the node i is given by k_i. For an undirected network of n nodes, the degree can be written in terms of the adjacency matrix [18]:

$$k_i = \sum_{j=1}^{n} A_{ij}$$

In a modern autonomous system, complexity lies in three spaces: perception, control, and communication. The dimensions of a perception space depend on the types of sensors used. The dimensions of a control space depend on the degrees of freedom of actuators or stepper-motors. The dimensions of a communication space depend on types of channels. Rapidly growing wireless telecommunication technologies bring potential opportunities to autonomous systems that were impossible before. The expansion of communication space has led to the further development of perception and control.

Today, there are many automated software validation tools for checking logic problems in large integrated circuits or control systems. A State Machine is a common method for checking control logic and production rules. A Petri net is useful for modeling concurrency in multi-tasking control software. However, its scalability is problematic. Simulation methods are a more flexible option, but it is expensive to develop a realistic model. Analytical tools will not detect "hidden" variables in real-world operation. For a large-scale system such as a city, a simulation model is necessary. For example, the US DOT sponsored a project for testing on-going V2V technologies with over 3,000 vehicles in a virtual city with streets, intersection, and freeways.

Simplicity is key to autonomous system design. Simplicity can be realized by isolation, reducing the degree of freedom, and synchronization. The train design simplifies the control and sensing systems [8]. It reduces a two-dimensional problem into a one-dimensional one. Field tests from the United States, Sweden, Japan, and Germany have shown that a semi-autonomous convoy can save a significant amounts of fuel. Semi-autonomous trucks can travel like a robotic convoy. If the lead truck has an active driver, the following trucks can be operated by passive automatic vehicle following systems and cooperative adaptive cruise control until there is a need to get out of the formation. The speed and distance between trucks can be pre programmed for the fleet.

4.6 Human-System Interaction

For interacting with autonomous systems, we must consider control strategy, complexity, and co-evolution. Control strategies are high-level human-system interaction modes which determine who is in control of the operation. When does the machine take control? When must the human override? Complexity is a major problem in autonomous systems. How does one simplify the design of such systems? The introduction of autonomous systems should have an enormous impact on our driving, working, living behaviors, and on public policy overall. In many cases, autonomous systems are needed to override human operations in emergency situations. For example, stopping a car on a slippery road or within a short distance of an obstacle. Pumping the brake is a common practice to allow the wheels to unlock so that the vehicle can stop quickly. However, in an emergency situation, human instinct causes drivers to continuously press the break hard, which locks the wheels and causes the vehicle to skid with less friction. To prevent wheels from locking up and to provide the shortest stopping distance on slippery surfaces, anti-lock brakes (ABS) were invented to automatically pump the brake pedal whenever the driver presses the brake pedal, taking control of braking safely. On the other hand, in many extreme situations, humans have to override machines to take over the task, when the machine fails to respond. For example, the DJI drone has an auto homing function when its battery falls below 20%. That autonomous function works well in an open space. However, when the drone flies in a woody area, it would encounter obstacles where the two autonomous algorithms confuse each other: auto homing versus auto obstacle avoidance.

5 Conclusions

The simple case study of the CNN model based on Keras for handwriting recognition reveals that CNN algorithms don't adapt well to changes. Adding new cases to the training data may improve accuracy, but not to the same level as before. Synthetic training data may improve the accuracy *superficially* because of the similarity of data distributions between generated data and original data. Prevailing ML models such as Generative Adversarial Networks (GAN) have their limitations such as similarity-addiction and modality collapse. They could be toxic to safety engineering without domain expertise. The study proposed four test strategies: 1) AI systems should be tested by the third parties, not the developers; 2) test datasets should be categorically different from training datasets; the test data should not be a part of the training data; the test data should be collected from independent sources to increase the "diversity" of data modality; 3) avoid fake data, or simulated data; and 4) don't collect the data that are conveniently available, but actively collect disastrous event data, unexpected, or the worst scenarios that may destroy the model. The study also introduces a multidimensional checklist for AI safety analysis, including sensors (interactions between a system and its environment), data and environments (sources and test cases), default and recovery mode (conditions, assumptions, and *spontaneous alternation behavior* SAB), system architecture (observability, controllability and complexity), human-system interaction (human override, machine override, and overlay).

For future work, we need more intelligent AI for AI-safety design. The Generative Adversarial Network (GAN) models are not adversarial enough because of the similarity between the synthetic data and the raw data. We need a better AI model to maximize the risk of the scenarios and minimize the computational cost. One potential alternative is an Evolutionary Algorithm that considers mutation and crossover operations with the goal of fitness.

Acknowledgement. The study is sponsored by ONR Summer Faculty Research Program in 2019. The author is grateful to Dr. Rani A. Kady for his discussions and Mr. Weizhe Sun for the experiments with the CNN model.

References

1. Wikipedia. https://en.wikipedia.org/wiki/Dartmouth_workshop
2. https://ujjwalkarn.me/2016/08/11/intuitive-explanation-convnets/
3. https://engmrk.com/convolutional-neural-network-3/
4. Marko, K.: AI today and tomorrow is mostly about curve fitting, not intelligence, Diginomia, 3 June 2018
5. https://diginomica.com/ai-curve-fitting-not-intelligence
6. https://labelbox.com/
7. https://github.com/Labelbox/Labelbox
8. http://www.fon.hum.uva.nl/praat/
9. http://www.anvil-software.org/
10. https://towardsdatascience.com/deep-learning-performance-cheat-sheet-21374b9c4
11. https://towardsdatascience.com/deep-learning-performance-cheat-sheet-21374b9c4f45
12. https://en.wikipedia.org/wiki/Survivorship_bias
13. https://www.iihs.org/media/ec54a7ea-1a1d-4fb2-8fc3-b2e018db2082/Ztykhw/Ratings/Protocols/current/small_overlap_test_protocol.pdf
14. https://keras.io/
15. https://en.wikipedia.org/wiki/Generative_adversarial_network
16. https://docs.google.com/viewer?a=v&pid=sites&srcid=ZGVmYXVsdGRvbWFpbnxqd25hc2l0ZXxneDoyZTQ2MGViZjkyZDQ5NDRl
17. Cai, Y.: Instinctive Computing. Springer, London (2016). https://doi.org/10.1007/978-1-4471-7278-9
18. DARPA Grand Challenge. (2016) https://en.wikipedia.org/wiki/DARPA_Grand_Challenge
19. Newman, M.E.J.: Networks: An Instruction. Oxford University Press, Oxford (2010)

Human-Centered Explainable AI: Towards a Reflective Sociotechnical Approach

Upol Ehsan[✉] and Mark O. Riedl

Georgia Institute of Technology, Atlanta, GA 30308, USA
ehsanu@gatech.edu, riedl@cc.gatech.edu

Abstract. Explanations—a form of post-hoc interpretability—play an instrumental role in making systems accessible as AI continues to proliferate complex and sensitive sociotechnical systems. In this paper, we introduce Human-centered Explainable AI (HCXAI) as an approach that puts the human at the center of technology design. It develops a holistic understanding of *"who" the human is* by considering the interplay of values, interpersonal dynamics, and the socially situated nature of AI systems. In particular, we advocate for a *reflective sociotechnical* approach. We illustrate HCXAI through a case study of an explanation system for non-technical end-users that shows how technical advancements and the understanding of human factors co-evolve. Building on the case study, we lay out open research questions pertaining to further refining our understanding of "who" the human is and extending beyond 1-to-1 human-computer interactions. Finally, we propose that a *reflective* HCXAI paradigm—mediated through the perspective of Critical Technical Practice and supplemented with strategies from HCI, such as value-sensitive design and participatory design—not only helps us understand our intellectual blind spots, but it can also open up new design and research spaces.

Keywords: Explainable AI · Rationale generation · User perception · Interpretability · Artificial intelligence · Machine learning · Critical technical practice · Sociotechnical · Human-centered computing

1 Introduction

From healthcare to finances, human resources to immigration services, many powerful yet "black-boxed" Artificial Intelligence (AI) systems have been deployed in consequential settings. This ubiquitous deployment creates an acute need to make AI systems understandable and explainable [5,7,8,12,25]. *Explainable* AI (XAI) refers to artificial intelligence and machine learning techniques that can provide human-understandable justification for their output behavior. Much of the previous and current work on explainable AI has focused on *interpretability*, which we view as a property of machine-learned models that dictates

© Springer Nature Switzerland AG 2020
C. Stephanidis et al. (Eds.): HCII 2020, LNCS 12424, pp. 449–466, 2020.
https://doi.org/10.1007/978-3-030-60117-1_33

the degree to which a human user—AI expert or non-expert user—can come to conclusions about the performance of the model given specific inputs. *Explanation generation*, on the other hand, can be described as a form of post-hoc interpretability [30, 32, 34, 41]. An important distinction between interpretability and explanation generation is that explanation does not necessarily elucidate precisely how a model works but aims to provide useful information for practitioners and users in an accessible manner.

While the letters "HCI" might not appear in "XAI", explainability in AI is as much of a Human-Computer Interaction (HCI) problem as it is an AI problem, if not more. Yet, the human side of the equation is often lost in the technical discourse of XAI. Implicit in Explainable AI is the question: "explainable to whom?" In fact, the challenges of designing and evaluating "black-boxed" AI systems depends crucially on *"who"* the human in the loop is. Understanding the *"who"* is crucial because it governs what the explanation requirements for a given problem. It also scopes *how* the data is collected, *what* data can be collected, and the most effective way of describing the *why* behind an action. For instance: with self-driving cars, the engineer may have different requirements of explainability than the rider in that car. As we move from AI to XAI and recenter our focus on the human—through Human-centered XAI (HCXAI)—the need to refine our understanding of the *"who"* increases. As the domain of HCXAI evolves, so must our epistemological stances and methodological approaches. Consequential technological systems, from law enforcement to healthcare, are almost always embedded in a rich tapestry of social relationships. If we ignore the socially situated nature of our technical systems, we will only get a partial and unsatisfying picture of the *"who"*.

In this paper, we focus on unpacking *"who"* the human is in Human-centered Explainable AI and advocate for a sociotechnical approach. We argue that, in order to holistically understand the socially situated nature of XAI systems, we need to incorporate both social and technical elements. This sociotechnical approach can help us critically reflect or contemplate on implicit or unconscious values embedded in computing practices so that we can understand our epistemological blind spots. Such contemplation—or reflection—can bring unconscious or implicit values and practices to conscious awareness, making them actionable. As a result, we can design and evaluate technology in a way that is sensitive to the values of both designers and stakeholders.

We begin by using a case study in Sect. 2, to delineate how the two strands of HCXAI—technological development and the understanding of human factors— evolve together. The case study focuses on both the technological development and the human factors of how non-expert users perceive different styles of automatically-generated rationales from an AI agent [19, 20]. In Sect. 3, using the insights from the study, we share future research directions that demand a sociotechnical lens of study. Finally, in Sect. 4, we introduce the notion of a *Reflective* HCXAI paradigm and outline how it facilitates the sociotechnical stance. We overview related concepts, share strategies, and contextualize them by using scenarios. We conclude by delineating the challenges of a reflective approach and presenting a call-to-action to the research community.

2   Case Study: Rationale Generation

The case study is based on our approach of post-hoc explanation generation called *rationale generation*, a process of producing a natural language rationale for agent behavior as if a human had performed the behavior and verbalized their inner monologue (for details, please refer to our papers [19,20]). The main goal for this section is to highlight the meta-narrative of our HCXAI journey; in particular, how the two processes—technological development in XAI and understanding of human-factors—co-evolve. Specifically, we will see how our understanding of human factors improve over time.

As an analogy while we go through the two phases of the case study, consider a low-resolution picture, say 16×16 pixels, that gets updated to a higher resolution photo, say 256×256 pixels, of the same subject matter. Not only does better technology (in our analogy, a better camera) afford a higher resolution image, but the high-resolution image also captures details previously undetectable, which, when detected broadens our perspective and facilitates new areas of interest. For instance, we might want to zoom in on a particular part of the picture that requires a different sensor. Had we not been able to broaden our perspective and incorporate things previously undetectable, we would not have realized the technical needs for a future sensor. As we can see, the two things—the camera technology and our perspective of the subject matter—build on each other and co-evolve. For the rest of the section, we will provide a brief overview of *rationale generation*, especially its technical and philosophical underpinnings. Finally, we will share key takeaways from the two phases of the case study. For fine-grained empirical details, please refer to [19,20].

With this narrative of co-evolution in mind, let us look at the philosophical and technical intuitions behind rationale generation. The philosophical intuition behind rationale generation is that humans can engage in effective communication by verbalizing plausible motivations for their actions, even when the verbalized reasoning does not have a consciously-accessible neural correlate of the decision-making process [9,10,22]. Whereas an explanation can be in any communication modality, we view *rationales* as natural language explanations. Natural language is arguably the most accessible modality of explanation. However, since rationales are natural language explanations, there is a level of abstraction between the words that are generated and the inner workings of an intelligent system. This motivates a range of research questions pertaining to how the choice of words for the generated rationale affect human factors such as *confidence* in the agent's decision, *understandability, human-likeness, explanatory power, tolerance to failure*, and perceived *intelligence*.

From a technical perspective, *rationale generation* is treated as the problem of translating the internal state and action representations into natural language using computational methods. It is fast, sacrificing an accurate view of the agent's decision-making process for a real-time response, making it appropriate for real-time human-agent collaboration [20]. In our case study, we use a deep neural network trained on human explanations—specifically a neural machine translation approach [31]—to explain the decisions of an AI agent that plays the

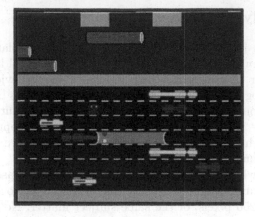

Fig. 1. A screenshot of the game *Frogger*. The green frog *Frogger*, seen in the middle of the image, wins if it can successfully reach the goal (yellow landing spots) at the top of the screen. (Color figure online)

game of *Frogger*. In the game, *Frogger* (the frog, controlled by the player) has to avoid traffic and hop on logs to cross the river in order to reach its goal at the top of the screen, shown in Fig. 1. *Frogger* can be thought of as a gamified abstraction of a sequential decision-making task, requiring the player to think ahead in order to choose a good action. Furthermore, sequential tasks are typically overlooked in explainable AI research. We trained a reinforcement learning algorithm to play the game, not because it was difficult for the AI to play but because reinforcement learning algorithms are non-intuitive to non-experts, even though the game is simple enough for people to learn and apply their own intuitions.

Having contextualized the approach, we will break the case study into two main phases. For ease of comparison in the co-evolution, we will cover the same topics for both phases—namely, data collection and corpus creation, neural translation model configuration, and evaluation. Table 3, at the end of this section, summarizes each aspect and provides a side-by-side comparison of the two phases.

2.1   Phase 1: Technological Feasibility and Baseline Plausibility

In the first stage of the project [19], our goal was an existence proof—to show that we could generate satisfactory rationales, treating the problem of explanation generation as a translation problem. At this stage, the picture of the human or end-user was not well-defined by construction because we did not even have the technology to probe and understand them.

Data Collection and Corpus Creation. There is no readily-available dataset for the task of learning to generate explanations. Thus, we had to create one. We developed a methodology to remotely collect live "think-aloud" data from players as they played through a game of *Frogger* (our sequential environment). To get a corpus of coordinated game states, actions, and explanations, we built a modified version of *Frogger* in which players simultaneously play the game and explain each of their actions.

In the first phase, 12 participants provided a total of 225 action-rationale pairs of gameplay. To create a training corpus appropriate for the neural network, we used these action-rationale annotations to construct a grammar for procedurally-generating synthetic sentences, grounded in natural language. This grammar used a set of rules based on in-game behavior of the *Frogger* agent to generate rationales that resemble the crowd-sourced data previously gathered. This entails that our corpus for Phase 1 was semi-synthetic in that it contained both natural and synthetic action-rationale pairs.

Neural Model Configuration. We use a 2-layered encoder-decoder recurrent neural network (RNN) [4,31] with attention to teach our network to generate relevant natural language explanations for any given action (for details, see [19]). These kinds of networks are commonly used for machine translation tasks (translating from one natural language to another), but their ability to understand sequential dependencies between the input and the output make them suitable for explanation generation in sequential domains as well.

Empirically, we found that a limited, 7×7, window for observation around a reinforcement learning agent using tabular Q-learning [39] leads to effective gameplay. We gave the rationale generator the same 7×7 observation window that the agent needs to learn to play. We refer to this configuration of the rationale generator as the *focused-view* generator.

Evaluation. For this phase, the evaluation was part procedural- and part human-based. For the procedural evaluation, we used BLEU [33] scores–a metric often used in machine translation tasks–with a 0.7 accuracy cutoff. Since the grammar contained rules that govern when certain rationales are generated, it allowed us to compare automatically-generated rationales against a ground truth. We found that our approach significantly outperformed both rationales generated by a random model and a majority classifier for environments with different obstacle densities [19].

With the accuracy of the rationales established via procedural evaluation, we needed to see if these rationales were satisfactory from a human-centered perspective. On the human evaluation side, we used a mixed-methods approach where 53 participants watched videos of 3 AI agents explaining their actions in different styles. After watching the videos, participants ranked their satisfaction with the rationales given by each of the three agents and justified their choice in their own words. We found that our system produced rationales with the highest level of user-satisfaction. Qualitative analysis also revealed important components of "satisfaction" such as *explanatory power* that were important for participants' confidence in the agent, the rationale's perceived relatability (or humanlike-ness), and understandability.

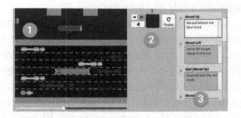

Fig. 2. The rationale collection process. (1) Game pauses after each action. (2) Automated speech recognition transcribes the rationale. (3) Participants can view and edit the transcribed rationales.

Fig. 3. The rationale review process where players can step-through each of their action-rationale pairs and edit if necessary. (1) Players can watch an action-replay while editing rationales. (2) Buttons control the flow of the step-through process. (3) Rationale for the current action gets highlighted for review.

To summarize, the goal of this first phase was an existence proof of the technical feasibility of generating rationales. We learned that our neural machine translation approach produced accurate rationales and that humans found them satisfactory. Not only did this phase inspire us to build on the technical side, but the understanding of the human factors also helped us design better human-based evaluations for the next phase.

2.2 Phase 2: Technological Evolution and Human-Centered Plausibility

Phase 2 [20] is about taking the training wheels off and making the XAI system more human-centered. Everything builds on our learnings from Phase 1. Here, you will see how the data collection and corpus is human-centered and non-synthetic, how our network produces two styles of rationales, and how our evaluation was entirely human-based.

Data Collection and Corpus Creation. We expanded the data collection paradigm introduced in phase 1. For phase 2, we built another modified version of *Frogger* that facilitates a human-centered approach and generates a corpus that is entirely natural-language–based (no synthetic-grammar–generated sentences). We split the data collection into three phases: (1) a guided tutorial, (2) rationale collection, and (3) transcribed explanation review. The guided tutorial ensured that users are familiar with the interface and its use before they began providing explanations. For rationale collection, participants engaged in a turn-taking experience where they observed an action and then explained it while the game is paused (Fig. 2). While thinking out loud, an automatic speech recognition

Table 1. Examples of different rationales generated for the same game action.

Action	Focused-view	Complete-view
Right	I had cars to the left and in front of me so I needed to move to the right to avoid them	I moved right to be more centered. This way I have more time to react if a car comes from either side
Up	The path in front of me was clear so it was safe for me to move forward	I moved forward making sure that the truck won't hit me so I can move forward one spot
Left	I move to the left so I can jump onto the next log	I moved to the left because it looks like the logs and top or not going to reach me in time, and I'm going to jump off if the law goes to the right of the screen

library [1] transcribed the utterances, substantially reducing participant burden and making the flow more natural than having to type down their utterances. Upon game play completion, the players reviewed all action-explanation pairs in a global context by replaying each action (Fig. 3). We deployed our data collection pipeline on Turk Prime (a wrapper over Amazon Mechanical Turk) and collected over 2000 unconstrained action-rationale pairs from 60 participants.

Neural Model Configuration. We use the same encoder-decoder RNN as in phase 1, but this time, we varied the input configurations with the intention of producing varying styles of rationales to experiment with different strategies for rationale generation. Last time, we deployed just one configuration, the *focused-view* configuration. This focused-view configuration accurately reflects what the agent is considering, leading to concise rationales due to the limitation of data the agent had available for rationale generation. To contrast this, we formulated a second *complete-view* configuration that gives the rationale generator the ability to use all information on the screen. We speculated that this configuration would produce more detailed, holistic rationales and use state information that the algorithm is not considering. See Table 1 for example rationales generated by our system. However, it remains to be seen if these configurations produce perceptibly different rationales to users who do not have any idea of the inner workings of the neural network. We evaluated the alignment between the upstream algorithmic decisions and downstream user effects using the user studies described below.

Evaluation. For phase 2, the evaluation of the XAI system was entirely qualitative, human-based analysis. We conducted two user studies: the first establishes that, when compared against baselines, both network configurations produce plausible outputs; the second establishes if the outputs are indeed perceptibly different to "naïve" users who are unaware of the neural architecture and explores

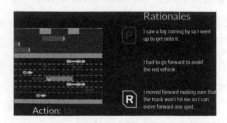

Fig. 4. User study screenshot depicting the action and the rationales: *P = Random (lower baseline), Q = Exemplary (higher baseline), R = Our model (Candidate)*

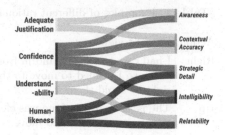

Fig. 5. Emergent relationship between the dimensions (left) and components (right) of user perceptions and preference

contextual user preferences. In both user studies, participants watched videos where the agent is taking a series of actions and "thinking out loud" in different styles (see Fig. 4 for implementation details).

The first user study established the viability of generated rationales, situating user perception along the dimensions of *confidence, human-likeness, adequate justification,* and *understandability.* We adapted these constructs from our findings in phase 1, technology acceptance models (e.g., UTAUT) [14,38], and related research in HCI [6,13,29]. Analyzing the qualitative data, we found emergent components that speak to each dimension; see [20] for details of the analysis. For *confidence,* participants found that contextual accuracy, awareness, and strategic detail are important in order to have faith in the agent's ability to do its task. Whether the generated rationales appear to be made by a human (*human-likeness*) depended on their intelligibility, relatability, and strategic detail. In terms of *explanatory power* (adequate justification), participants prefer rationales with high levels of contextual accuracy and awareness. For the rationales to convey the agent's motivations and foster *understandability,* they need high levels of contextual accuracy and relatability (see Fig. 5 for a mapping and Table 2 for definitions of these components).

In the second user study, we found that there is alignment between the intended differences in features of the generated rationales and the perceived differences by users. Without any knowledge beyond what is shown on the video, they described the difference in the styles of the rationales in a way that was consistent with the intended differences between them. This finding is an important secondary validation of how upstream algorithmic changes in neural network configuration lead to the desired user effects downstream.

The second user study also explores user preferences between the focused-view and complete-view rationales along three dimensions: *confidence* in the autonomous agent, communication of *failure* and *unexpected behavior.* We found that, context permitting, participants preferred detailed rationales so that they can form a stable mental model of the agent's behavior.

Table 2. Descriptions for the emergent *components* underlying the human-factor *dimensions* of the generated rationales (See [20] for further details).

Component	Description
Contextual Accuracy	Accurately describes pertinent events in the context of the environment
Intelligibility	Typically error-free and is coherent in terms of both grammar and sentence structure
Awareness	Depicts and adequate understanding of the rules of the environment
Relatability	Expresses the justification of the action in a relatable manner and style
Strategic Detail	Exhibits strategic thinking, foresight, and planning

2.3 Summary

As we wrap up our case study overview, we want to underscore how technology development and understanding of human factors co-evolve together. In the following section, we will see how the foundation laid by the case study generates new areas of research, enabling a *"turn to the sociotechnical"* for the HCXAI paradigm.

3 What's Next: Turn to the Sociotechnical

At first glance, it may appear that a case-study using *Frogger* is not representative of a real-world XAI system. However, therein lies a deeper point—considering issues of fairness, accountability, and transparency of sociotechnical systems, it is risky to directly test out these systems in mission-critical domains without a formative and substantive understanding of the human factors around XAI systems. By conducting the case study in a controlled setting as a first step, we obtain a formative understanding of the technical and human sides, which can then be utilized to better implement such systems in the wild. Subsequent empirical and theoretical work can then build on any transferable insights from this work.

Building on our insights, we will outline two areas of investigation and share preliminary challenges and opportunities: (1) Perception differences due to users' backgrounds, and (2) Social signals and explanations. These areas are by no means exhaustive; rather, these are ones that have come to light from our case study. It's important to note here that, without the formative insights from multiple phases of our case study, the depth and richness of the research areas would not have been obvious. That is, while we considered multiple end-users (developers, non AI-experts, etc.), the case study's findings highlighted further non-obvious striations in the technical and social aspects of human perceptions of XAI.

Table 3. Side-by-side comparison of each phase in the case study

	Phase 1	Phase 2
Data Collection	225 action-rationale annotations from 12 people	Over 2000 action-rationale annotations from 60 people
Corpus	Semi-synthetic grammar on top of natural language	Fully unconstrained natural language; no grammar
Neural Network Configuration	Only one setup: focused-view, a 7 × 7 window around the agent	Two configurations: focused-view and complete-view designed to produce concise vs. detailed rationales
Evaluation	Part procedural; part human-based evaluation along one dimension – satisfaction of explanation	Full human-based evaluation with metrics defining plausibility against baselines using two studies
Key Lessons	The technique works to produce accurate rationales that are satisfactory to humans. User study insights help unpack what it means to be "satisfactory", which enables the next generation of systems in Phase 2.	Both configurations produce plausible rationales that are perceptibly different to end-users. User studies further reveal underlying components of user perceptions and preferences, refining our understanding of "who" the human is

3.1 Perception Differences Due to Users' Backgrounds

How do people of different professional and epistemic backgrounds perceive the same XAI system? Do their backgrounds impact their perception? These questions came from the observation that explanations, by definition, are context-sensitive. The *who* governs *how* the *why* is most effectively conveyed. Moreover, qualitative data analysis in our case study also hinted that people's professional and educational backgrounds impact their perception of explanations. The differences in perception were salient namely in the dimensions of *confidence* and *understandability*. These differences were particularly remarkable for people who were familiar with the technical side of computing compared to ones who were not. This observation sparked the question: what might be the different explainability needs for end-users with different backgrounds? How might we go about teasing this apart?

From a methodological standpoint, we can run user studies similar to that in our case studies to get a formative understanding of how backgrounds impact perception and preferences of XAI systems. For instance, we can provide the same explanation to two related yet different groups (e.g., engineers vs. lay-riders of self-driving cars) and investigate if and how their backgrounds impact perception and preferences.

3.2   Social Signals and Explanations

What roles might social signals, especially in a team-based collaborative setting, play in HCXAI? How might we embed social transparency into our systems in order to facilitate user actions? This research interest stems from the observation that we seldom find consequential AI systems in isolated settings where only one human interacts with the machine. Rather, most systems are socially situated in organizational settings involving teams of people engaging in collaborative decision-making. How will our design evolve as we move beyond the 1-1 human-computer interaction paradigm? When we talk about a paradigm beyond the 1-1 human-computer interaction, we are referring to situations where the collaborative decision-making and relationships of multiple individuals in an organization or a team are mediated through technology. The scenario is complex now because we have two types of relationships to consider: the type that is between the machine and the humans as well as the interdependent accountability amongst different kinds of stakeholders.

Let us consider the following scenario: In an IT setting, Cloud Solutions architects often need to make purchasing decisions around Virtual Machine (VM) instances that help the organization run online, mission-critical services on the cloud. There are real costs of "wrong-sizing" the VM instance—if you underestimate, the company's system might become overloaded and crash; if you overestimate, the company wastes valuable monetary resources. Moreover, there are teams of people who are secondary and tertiary stakeholders of the VM instances. Suppose an AI system recommends certain parameters for the VM instances to a single Solutions architect who is accountable to and responsible for the other stakeholders. The AI system also provides "technical" explanations by contextualizing the recommendation with past usage data analytics. Given the interpersonal and professional accountability risks, is technical explainability enough to give the engineer the confidence to accept the AI's recommendation? Or does the explanation need to incorporate the embedded, interconnected nature of stakeholders such as the use of social signals? Social signals here can be thought of as digital footprints that provide context of the team's perspective on the collaborative decision-making; for instance, stakeholders can give a "+1" or an upvote on the recommendation.

From a methodological perspective, we can design between-subject user studies where we measure the perceptions of collaborative decision-making. One group would only get technical explanations while the other group gets both social and technical signals. We can simulate the aforementioned scenario and measure how confident each group is in their decisions to act on the right-sizing recommendations.

3.3   Summary: Socially Situated XAI Systems

In considering these research directions, we should appreciate the value of controlled user studies in generating formative insights. However, if we ignore the socially situated nature of our technical systems, we will only get a partial, unsatisfying picture of the *"who"*. Therefore, enhancing the current paradigm with sociotechnical approaches is a necessary step. This is because consequential technological systems are almost always embedded in a rich tapestry of social relationships. Take, for example, the aforementioned scenario with right-sizing VM instances. Our on-going work has shown that the organizational culture and its perception of AI-systems strongly impacts people's confidence to act on machine-driven recommendations, no matter how technically explainable they are. Any organizational environment carries its own socio-political assumptions and biases that influence technology use [37]. Understanding the rich social factors surrounding the technical system may be as equally important to the adoption of explanation technologies as the technology itself. Designing for the sociotechnical dynamics will require us to understand the rich, contextual, human experience where meaning-making is constructed at the point of interaction between the human and the machine. But how might we go about it? We will need to think of ways to critically reflect on methodological and conceptual challenges. In the following section, we lay out some strategies to handle these conceptual blocks.

4 Human-Centered XAI, Critical Technical Practice, and the Sociotechnical Lens

The prior section highlights the socially situated nature of XAI systems that demand a sociotechnical approach of analysis. With each hypothesis and technical advancement, the resolution of *"who" the human is* improved. As the metaphorical picture of the user became clearer, other people and objects in the background have also come into perspective. The newfound perspective demands the ability to incorporate all parties into the picture. It also informs the technological development needs of the next generation of refinement in our understanding of the *"who"*. As the domain of HCXAI evolves, so must our epistemological stances and methodological approaches. Currently, there is not a singular path to construct the sociotechnical lens and nor should there be given the complexity and richness of human connections. However, we have a rich foundation of prior work both in AI and HCI that will help us get there. In developing the sociotechnical lens of HCXAI, we are particularly inspired by prior work from Sengers et al. [36], Dourish et al. [16,17], and Friedman et al. [24].

In particular, we believe that viewing HCXAI through the perspective of a Critical Technical Practice (CTP) will foster the grounds for a *reflective* HCXAI. CTP [2,3] encourages us to question the core assumptions and metaphors of a field of practice, critically *reflect* on them to overcome impasses, and generate new questions and hypotheses. By *reflection*, we refer to *"critical* reflection [that] brings unconscious aspects of experience to conscious awareness, thereby making them available for conscious choice" [36].

Our perspective on reflection is grounded in critical theory [21,28] and inspired by Sengers et al.'s notion of Reflective Design [36]. We recognize that the lens through which we look at and reason about the world is shaped by our conscious and, more importantly, unconscious values and assumptions. These values, in turn, become embedded into the lens of our technological practices and design. By bringing the unconscious experience to our conscious awareness, critical reflection not only allows us to look *through* the lens, but also *at* it. A reflective HCXAI creates the necessary intellectual space to make progress through conceptual and technical impasses while the metamorphosis of the field takes place. Given that the story of XAI has just begun, it would be premature to attempt a full treatise of human-centered XAI. However, we can begin with two key properties of a reflective HCXAI: (1) a domain that is *critically reflective* of (implicit) assumptions and practices of the field, and (2) one that is *value-sensitive* to both users and designers.

In the rest of this section, we will provide relevant background about CTP, how it allows HCXAI to be reflective, why it is useful, and complimentary strategies from related fields that can help us build the sociotechnical lens. We will also contextualize the theoretical proposal with a scenario and share the affordances in explainability we gain by viewing HCXAI as a Critical Technical Practice. We conclude the section with challenges of a reflective HCXAI.

4.1   Reflective HCXAI Using a Critical Technical Practice Lens

The notion of Critical Technical Practice was pioneered by AI researcher Phil Agre in his 1997 book, *Computation and Human Experience* [3]. CTP encourages us to question the core assumptions and metaphors of a field and critically reflect on them in order to overcome impasses in that field. In short, there are four main components of the perspective: (i) identify the core metaphors and assumptions of the field, (ii) notice what aspects become marginalized when working within those assumptions, (iii) bring the marginalized aspects to the center of attention, and (iv) develop technology and practices to embody the previously-marginalized components as alternative technology. Using the CTP perspective, Agre critiqued the dominant narrative in AI at the time, namely abstract models of cognition, and brought situated embodiment central to AI's perspective on intelligence. By challenging the core metaphor, they successfully opened a space for AI that led to advancements in the new "situated action" paradigm [37].

In our case, we can use the CTP perspective to reflect on and question some of the dominant metaphors in Explainable AI. This reflection can expand our design space by helping us identify aspects that have been marginalized or overlooked. For instance, one of the dominant narratives in XAI makes it appear as though interpretability and explainability are model-centered problems, which is where a lot of current attention is rightfully invested. However, our experiences while broadening the lens of XAI has led us to reflect on explainability, leading to an important question: where does the *"ability"* in explain-ability lie? Is it a property of the model or of the human interpreting it, or is it a combination of the two? What if we switch the *"ability"* in interpretability or explainability to the human? Or perhaps there is a middle ground where meaning is co-creatively manifested at the point of action between the machine and the human? By enabling critical reflections on core assumptions and impulses in the field, the CTP perspective can be the lighthouse that guides us as we embark on a reflective HCXAI journey and navigate through the design space.

There are three main affordances of the CTP approach in HCXAI. First, the perspective allows traversal of the marginalized insights —in this case the human-centered side of XAI—to come to the center, which can open new design areas previously undetected or under-explored. Second, the critical reflection mindset can enable designers to think of new ways to understand human factors. It can also empower users with new interaction capabilities that promote their voices in technologies, which, in turn, can improve our understanding of *"who" the human is* in HCXAI. Take, for instance, our understanding of user trust. To foster trust, a common impulse is to aim for the "positive" direction and nudge the human to find the machine's explanation plausible and to accept it. As our case study shows, this is certainly a viable route. However, should that be the only route? That is, should this impulse for user-agreeableness be the only way to understand this human factor of trust? In certain contexts, like fake news detection, might we be better off by designing to evoke reasonable skepticism and critical reflection in the user? Since no model is perfect at all times, we cannot expect generated explanations to always be correct. Thus, creating the space for users to voice their skepticism or disagreement not only empowers new forms of interaction, but also allows the user to become sensitive to the limitations of AI systems. Expanding the ways we reason about fostering trust can create a design perspective that is not only reflective but is also pragmatic. Third, critical reflection can help us defamiliarize and decolonize our thinking from the dominant narratives, helping us to not only look *"through"* but also *"at"* the sociotechnical lens of analysis.

4.2   Strategies to Operationalize Critical Technical Practice in HCXAI

To operationalize the CTP perspective, we can incorporate rich strategies from other methodological traditions rooted in HCI, critical studies, and philosophy such as participatory design [11,18], value-sensitive design [23,24], reflection-in-action [15,35,40], and ludic design [26,27]. Reflective HCXAI does not take a normative stance to privilege one design tradition over the other, nor does it replace one with the other; rather, it incorporates and integrates insights and methods from related disciplines. For our current scope, we will briefly elaborate on two approaches—*participatory design* (PD) and *value-sensitive design* (VSD).

Participatory Design challenges the power dynamics between the designer and user and aims to support democratic values at every stage of the design process. Not only does it advocate for changing the system but also challenges the practices of design and building, which might help bring the marginalized perspectives to the forefront. This fits in nicely with one of the key properties of a reflective HCXAI: the ability to critically reflect on core assumptions and politics of both the designer and the user.

Value-Sensitive Design is "a theoretically grounded approach to the design of technology that seeks to account for human values in a principled and comprehensive manner throughout the design process" [24]. Using *Envisioning cards* [23], researchers can engage in exercises with stakeholders to understand stakeholder values, tensions, and political realities of system design. A sociotechnical approach by construction, it incorporates a mixture of conceptual, empirical, and technical investigations stemming from moral philosophy, social-sciences, and HCI. We can use it to investigate the links between the technological practices and values of the stakeholders involved. VSD aligns well with the other key property of reflective HCXAI: being value-sensitive to both designers and users.

With the theoretical and conceptual blocks in mind, let us look at a scenario that might help us contextualize the role of the CTP perspective, VSD, and PD in a reflective HCXAI paradigm. This scenario is partially-inspired by our on-going work with teams of radiologists. In a large medical hospital in the US, teams of radiologists use an AI-mediated task list that automatically prioritizes the order in which radiologists go through cases (or studies) during their shifts. While a prioritization task might seem trivial at first glance, this one has real consequences—failure to appropriately prioritize has consequences ranging from a missed report deadline to ignoring an emergency trauma patient.

The CTP perspective encourages us to look at the dominant narrative and think of marginalized perspectives to expand our design space. Here, we should critically reflect on the role of explanations in this system. In such a consequential system, fostering user trust is a core goal. Considering that the AI model might fail, is trust best established by creating explanations that always nudge users to accept the AI system's task prioritization? Or might we design with the goal of user reflection instead of user acceptance? Reflection can be in the form of reasonable skepticism. In fact, skepticism and trust go hand in hand; skepticism is part of that critical reflective process that helps us question our core assumptions. Even if we could build such a system, how might we *evaluate* explanations that foster reflection instead of acceptance? What type of prioritization tasks should privilege acceptance vs. reflection?

The answers to these questions are not apparent without a sociotechnical approach and constructive engagement with the communities in question. Having identified some of the marginalized aspects and critically reflecting on them using the CTP perspective, we can use the aforementioned strategies, such as participatory design (PD) and value-sensitive design (VSD), to operationalize the reflective HCXAI perspective. For instance, we can use the PD approach to ensure the power dynamics between designers and users are democratic in nature. Moreover, we can reflexively recognize the politics of the design practice and reflect on how we build any interventions. We can also incorporate VSD elicitation exercises using the Envisioning Cards to uncover value tensions and political realities in the hospital systems. For instance, what, if any, are tensions between the values of the administration, the insurance industry, and the radiologists? What values do the different stakeholders feel the XAI system should embody and how do these values play off of each other in terms of alignment or tensions?

4.3   Challenges of a Reflective HCXAI Paradigm

With the affordances of a reflective HCXAI in mind, we observe two current challenges where we need a concerted community effort. First, sociotechnical work requires constructive engagement with partner communities of practice. Our end-users live in communities of practices that have their own norms (e.g., radiologists within the community of medical practice). As outsiders, we cannot expect to gain an embedded understanding of the "who" without constructively engaging with partner communities (e.g., radiologists) on their own terms and timelines. This means we need to be sensitive to their values as well as norms to foster sustainable community relationships. Not only are these endeavors resource and time intensive, which could impact publication cycles, but they also require stakeholder buy-in at multiple levels across organizations.

Second, sociotechnical work in a reflective HCXAI paradigm would require active translational work from a diverse set of practitioners and researchers. This entails that, compared to T-shaped researchers who have intellectual depth in one area, we need more Π-shaped ones who have depth in two (or more) areas and thus the ability to bridge the domains.

5   Conclusions

As the field of XAI evolves, we recognize the socially situated nature of consequential AI systems and re-center our focus on the human. We introduce Human-centered Explainable AI (HCXAI) as an approach that puts the human at the center of technology design and develops a holistic understanding of *"who"* the human is. It considers the interplay of values, interpersonal dynamics, and socially situated nature of AI systems. In particular, we advocate for a reflective sociotechnical approach that incorporates both social and technical elements in our design space. Using our case study that pioneered the notion of *rationale generation*, we show how technical advancements and the understanding of human factors co-evolve together. We outline open research questions that build on our case study and highlight the need for a reflective sociotechnical approach. Going farther, we propose that a reflective HCXAI paradigm—using the perspective of Critical Technical Practice and strategies such as participatory design and value-sensitive design—will not only help us question the dominant metaphors in XAI, but they can also open up new research and design spaces.

Acknowledgements. Sincerest thanks to all past and present teammates of the Human-centered XAI group at the Entertainment Intelligence Lab whose hard work made the case study possible—Brent Harrison, Pradyumna Tambwekar, Larry Chan, Chenhann Gan, and Jiahong Sun. Special thanks to Dr. Judy Gichoya for her informed perspectives on the medical scenarios. We'd also like to thank Ishtiaque Ahmed, Malte Jung, Samir Passi, and Phoebe Sengers for conversations throughout the years that have constructively added to the notion of a 'Reflective HCXAI'. We are indebted to Rachel Urban and Lara J. Martin for their amazing proofreading assistance. We are grateful to reviewers for their useful comments and critique. This material is based upon work supported by the National Science Foundation under Grant No. 1928586.

References

1. Streamproc/Mediastreamrecorder, August 2017. https://github.com/streamproc/MediaStreamRecorder
2. Agre, P.: Toward a critical technical practice: lessons learned in trying to reform AI. In: Bowker. G., Star, S., Turner, W., Gasser, L. (eds.) Social Science, Technical Systems and Cooperative Work: Beyond the Great Divide, Erlbaum (1997)
3. Agre, P., Agre, P.E.: Computation and Human Experience. Cambridge University Press, New York (1997)
4. Bahdanau, D., Cho, K., Bengio, Y.: Neural machine translation by jointly learning to align and translate. arXiv preprint arXiv:1409.0473 (2014)
5. Barocas, S., Selbst, A.D.: Big data's disparate impact. Cal. L. Rev. **104**, 671 (2016)
6. Beer, J.M., Prakash, A., Mitzner, T.L., Rogers, W.A.: Understanding robot acceptance. Technical report, Georgia Institute of Technology (2011)
7. Berk, R.: Criminal Justice Forecasts of Risk: A Machine Learning Approach. Springer, New York (2012). https://doi.org/10.1007/978-1-4614-3085-8
8. Bermingham, A., Smeaton, A.: On using twitter to monitor political sentiment and predict election results. In: Proceedings of the Workshop on Sentiment Analysis where AI meets Psychology (SAAIP 2011), pp. 2–10 (2011)
9. Block, N.: Two neural correlates of consciousness. Trends Cogn. Sci. **9**(2), 46–52 (2005)
10. Block, N.: Consciousness, accessibility, and the mesh between psychology and neuroscience. Behav. Brain Sci. **30**(5–6), 481–499 (2007)
11. Bødker, S.: Through the interface-a human activity approach to user interface design. DAIMI Report Series (224) (1991)
12. Chen, H., Chiang, R.H., Storey, V.C.: Business intelligence and analytics: from big data to big impact. MIS Q., 1165–1188 (2012)
13. Chernova, S., Veloso, M.M.: A confidence-based approach to multi-robot learning from demonstration. In: AAAI Spring Symposium: Agents that Learn from Human Teachers, pp. 20–27 (2009)
14. Davis, F.D.: Perceived usefulness, perceived ease of use, and user acceptance of information technology. MIS Q., 319–340 (1989)
15. Djajadiningrat, J.P., Gaver, W.W., Fres, J.: Interaction relabelling and extreme characters: methods for exploring aesthetic interactions. In: Proceedings of the 3rd Conference on Designing Interactive Systems: Processes, Practices, Methods, and Techniques, pp. 66–71 (2000)
16. Dourish, P.: Where the Action Is: the Foundations of Embodied Interaction. MIT Press, Cambridge (2004)
17. Dourish, P., Finlay, J., Sengers, P., Wright, P.: Reflective HCI: towards a critical technical practice. In: CHI 2004 Extended Abstracts on Human Factors in Computing Systems, pp. 1727–1728 (2004)
18. Ehn, P.: Scandinavian design-on skill and participation. In: Adler, P., Winograd, T. (eds.) Usability-Turning Technologies into Tools (1992)
19. Ehsan, U., Harrison, B., Chan, L., O. Riedl, M.: Rationalization: a neural machine translation approach to generating natural language explanations. In: Proceedings of the AAAI Conference on Artificial Intelligence, Ethics, and Society, February 2018
20. Ehsan, U., Tambwekar, P., Chan, L., Harrison, B., Riedl, M.: Automated rationale generation: a technique for explainable AI and its effects on human perceptions. In: Proceedings of the International Conference on Intelligence User Interfaces, March 2019

21. Feenberg, A.: Critical theory of technology (1991)
22. Fodor, J.A.: The Elm and the Expert: Mentalese and Its Semantics. MIT Press, Cambridge (1994)
23. Friedman, B., Hendry, D.: The envisioning cards: a toolkit for catalyzing humanistic and technical imaginations. In: Proceedings of the SIGCHI Conference on Human Factors in Computing Systems, pp. 1145–1148 (2012)
24. Friedman, B., Kahn, P.H., Borning, A., Huldtgren, A.: Value sensitive design and information systems. In: Doorn, N., Schuurbiers, D., van de Poel, I., Gorman, M.E. (eds.) Early engagement and new technologies: Opening up the laboratory. PET, vol. 16, pp. 55–95. Springer, Dordrecht (2013). https://doi.org/10.1007/978-94-007-7844-3_4
25. Galindo, J., Tamayo, P.: Credit risk assessment using statistical and machine learning: basic methodology and risk modeling applications. Comput. Econ. **15**(1–2), 107–143 (2000)
26. Gaver, B., Martin, H.: Alternatives: exploring information appliances through conceptual design proposals. In: Proceedings of the SIGCHI conference on Human Factors in Computing Systems, pp. 209–216 (2000)
27. Gaver, W.W., et al.: The drift table: designing for ludic engagement. In: CHI 2004 Extended Abstracts on Human Factors in Computing Systems, pp. 885–900 (2004)
28. Held, D.: Introduction to Critical Theory: Horkheimer to Habermas, vol. 261. University of California Press (1980)
29. Kaniarasu, P., Steinfeld, A., Desai, M., Yanco, H.: Robot confidence and trust alignment. In: 2013 8th ACM/IEEE International Conference on Human-Robot Interaction (HRI), pp. 155–156. IEEE (2013)
30. Lipton, Z.C.: The Mythos of Model Interpretability. ArXiv e-prints, June 2016
31. Luong, M.T., Pham, H., Manning, C.D.: Effective approaches to attention-based neural machine translation. arXiv preprint arXiv:1508.04025 (2015)
32. Miller, T.: Explanation in artificial intelligence: insights from the social sciences. arXiv preprint arXiv:1706.07269 (2017)
33. Papineni, K., Roukos, S., Ward, T., Zhu, W.J.: Bleu: a method for automatic evaluation of machine translation. In: Proceedings of the 40th Annual Meeting on Association for Computational Linguistics, pp. 311–318. Association for Computational Linguistics (2002)
34. Ribeiro, M.T., Singh, S., Guestrin, C.: Why should i trust you?: Explaining the predictions of any classifier. In: Proceedings of the 22nd ACM SIGKDD International Conference on Knowledge Discovery and Data Mining, pp. 1135–1144. ACM (2016)
35. Schön, D.A.: The Reflective Practitioner: How Professionals Think in Action. Routledge (2017)
36. Sengers, P., Boehner, K., David, S., Kaye, J.: Reflective design. In: Proceedings of the 4th Decennial Conference on Critical Computing: Between Sense and Sensibility, pp. 49–58 (2005)
37. Suchman, L., Suchman, L.A.: Human-Machine Reconfigurations: Plans and Situated Actions. Cambridge University Press, Cambridge (2007)
38. Venkatesh, V., Morris, M.G., Davis, G.B., Davis, F.D.: User acceptance of information technology: toward a unified view. MIS Q., 425–478 (2003)
39. Watkins, C., Dayan, P.: Q-learning. Mach. Learn. **8**(3–4), 279–292 (1992)
40. Wright, P., McCarthy, J.: Technology as Experience. MIT Press, Cambridge (2004)
41. Yosinski, J., Clune, J., Nguyen, A., Fuchs, T., Lipson, H.: Understanding neural networks through deep visualization. arXiv preprint arXiv:1506.06579 (2015)

The Power of Augmented Reality and Artificial Intelligence During the Covid-19 Outbreak

Chutisant Kerdvibulvech[1]([✉]) and Liming (Luke) Chen[2]

[1] Graduate School of Communication Arts and Management Innovation,
National Institute of Development Administration, 118 SeriThai Road, Klong-Chan, Bangkapi,
Bangkok 10240, Thailand
chutisant.ker@nida.ac.th
[2] School of Computing, Ulster University, Shore Road,
Newtownabbey, Co. Antrim, BT37 0QB, UK
chen@ulster.ac.uk

Abstract. The Covid-19 outbreak, the disease elicited by the Severe Acute Respiratory Syndrome Coronavirus-2 (SARS-CoV-2), poses many significant challenges to scientific communities around the world, including computer scientific communities. At the same time, the rise of computer science fueled by advanced in connectivity of social media and smartphones throughout the world, the fields of augmented reality (AR) and artificial intelligence (AI) have recently grown very rapidly. Augmented reality is an emerging field of a physical scene where the things that reside in the physical world are mixed by virtual world, while artificial intelligence is a popular field for the machine simulation of human intelligence that is programmed to see, think and understand like humans. This paper presents the current development of augmented reality and artificial intelligence during the Covid-19 outbreak. First, we highlight a summary of recent tools using augmented reality to tackle the Covid-19 crisis. For instance, augmented reality-based thermal imaging glasses for detecting virus symptoms and methods of augmented reality on educational tasks that help people overcome the isolation for online learning effectively are reviewed. Second, we discuss an overview of recent tools using artificial intelligence to smartly fight against the Covid-19 pandemic. Our discussion include the artificial intelligence methods to approximate and prepare people for prevention the virus, a method for forecasting of the Covid-19 outbreak using non-linear regressive network (NAR) to predict the size, lengths and ending time of the virus, and susceptible-exposed-infectious-removed (SEIR) model for estimating the outbreak trend of the deadly virus. Finally, we suggest benefits and promising future integrations between augmented reality and artificial intelligence to tackle the research problems after the Covid-19 crisis.

Keywords: Augmented reality · Artificial intelligence · Data-driven · Covid-19 ·
Coronavirus · Non-linear regressive network ·
Susceptible-exposed-infectious-removed

© Springer Nature Switzerland AG 2020
C. Stephanidis et al. (Eds.): HCII 2020, LNCS 12424, pp. 467–476, 2020.
https://doi.org/10.1007/978-3-030-60117-1_34

1   Introduction

In recent years, the rise of big data and data-driven economy fueled by advanced in connectivity of social media and smartphones throughout the world, the fields of augmented reality and artificial intelligence have grown very rapidly. Augmented reality is a field of a physical-world environment where the objects that reside in the physical world are mixed by virtual world. Artificial intelligence is a field for the machine simulation of human intelligence that is programmed to see, think and understand like humans. In fact, these two technologies are sometimes distinct, but they can be utilized together to build interactive experiences uniquely. However, ever since the initial report of the Covid-19 outbreak at the capital city of China's Hubei province in the end of year 2019, the virus has affected billions of people from 215 nations and territories with seven million cases and over 400,000 deaths as June 2020. With the critically evolving outbreak, in this paper, we present the current development of augmented reality and artificial intelligence during the Covid-19 outbreak. Note that 'Co' represents Corona, 'vi' is virus, and 'd' stands for disease, while '19' represents briefly the year of discovery, which is 2019, but this paper will generally use the term 'virus' stands for the Covid-19 for convenience's sake. The paper is divided into two main sections as follows. To begin with, the first section introduces an overview of recent tools using augmented reality to tackle the virus crisis. Next, the second section explores recent tools using artificial intelligence to fight against the Covid-19 outbreak. Ultimately, we conclude and give a suggestion for future direction.

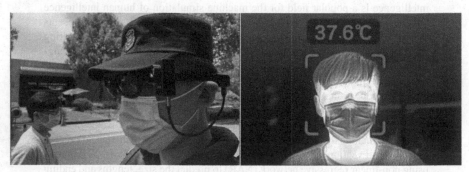

Fig. 1. An example when a security guard wearing the Glass T1 Thermal glasses during the Covid-19 outbreak [1, 2].

2   Augmented Reality to Tackle the Covid-19

In this section, we discuss a summary of recent tools using augmented reality to tackle the Covid-19 outbreak. For instance, we explore a pair of augmented reality-based thermal imaging glasses, called the Glass T1 Thermal glasses, for detecting possibly virus symptoms which is achieved by artificial intelligence start-up called Rokid [1]. The glasses are equipped with a camera and an infrared sensor by integrating thermal infrared sensor into augmented reality and artificial intelligence features, so that it can help people to see others' temperatures on the move in real-time. In fact, the concept of the glasses was started in 2018 and financed by Singapore's Temasek, Switzerland's Credit Suisse and other investors. Then, it has been upgraded into the Glass T1 Thermal glasses for taking multiple temperature readings concurrently in different colors, such as green (non-alert) and orange (alert), for use at the airports, the industrial parks, and the malls to tackle the Covid-19 outbreak in 2020. If the measured temperature is higher than the threshold they set, the readout will be shown on the glasses in an orange color together with a sound for alerting [2]. In the case of sound alerting, we can ask them to go to see the doctor, suggest them to work from home, or give them a facial mask. The Glass T1 Thermal glasses are composed of a Qualcomm CPU, an infrared sensor, 12-megapixel camera with augmented reality features for voice controls and video recordings automatically. In this way, it can identify the temperatures of about 200 people from as far as three meters within several minutes. Figure 1 shows an example when a security guard using the Glass T1 Thermal glasses during the Covid-19 outbreak. Similarly, SenseTime [3] also built a thermal imaging system and installed in railway stations, community centers, and schools in China for tackling the Covid-19 outbreak by spotting people with high temperatures. According to Pratik Jakhar's [4], the SenseTime's system can successfully identify masked faces (i.e., wearing facial masks) and make-up faces with a quick and high accuracy using artificial intelligence's facial recognition technology. Specifically, the system can recognize people in 0.3 s with 99% accuracy even if they are wearing glasses and facial masks. This is essential because many countries in Asia, such as China and Thailand, have made the use of facial masks mandatory in some specific places in public such as the malls, the airports, and the railway stations during the Covid-19 outbreak. Therefore, by using a mask algorithm, it can help to flag people who are not wearing a facial mask automatically when they enter some specific buildings for access control. Figure 2 shows the SenseTime's system for recognizing whether people are wearing facial masks in railway stations. A blue color shows people who are wearing facial masks, while a red color displays people who are not wearing facial masks. Also as presented by Maghdid et al. [5], there is a similar research, though they do not exactly use augmented reality technology, for diagnose the virus using artificial intelligence enhanced smartphone with embedded sensors.

In addition, Tely360 built a pair of augmented reality-based smart glasses, called the Ambulance Third Eye module [6], utilized with the Vuzix Blade for telehealth in Thailand during the Covid-19 outbreak to increase patient care productivity and efficiency. The system helps the doctors to communicate what is going on with their patients in the other places immediately. Therefore, it can reduce risks to healthcare personnel staffs to stay near the Covid-19 patients in the Ramathibodi Hospital in Bangkok, Thailand. Note that the number of confirmed active Covid-19 cases in Thailand in the early of June has dipped below 100 because the number of recovering from the disease approximately continues to outstrip the number of new infections recorded almost every day. In fact, many confirmed cases are returnees from overseas.

Furthermore, since it is essential for schools and universities to have visual communication and interactive experiences rather than over voice during the virus outbreak, we

Fig. 2. The SenseTime's system can help to flag people who are not wearing facial masks automatically for building access control using artificial intelligence's facial recognition [3].

review several methods of augmented reality on educational tasks suggested by Papagiannis [7] that help people overcome the isolation for online learning effectively, such as evaluating the skills of learners remotely and interactively [8]. During the Covid-19 quarantine period, Papagiannis suggests that augmented reality can perform three things well: visualization, annotation and storytelling. First, visualization in augmented reality can allow people to integrate a graphical object into a physical world. A good example of visualization during the Covid-19 crisis is utilizing Microsoft HoloLens and the HoloAnatomy augmented reality software [9] at Case Western Reserve University for helping 185 medical students from different locations in United States. and Canada to learn from homes. As shown in Fig. 3, it facilitates medical students to learn and visualize the three-dimensional human anatomy remotely. Second, annotation in augmented reality can guide people and give explanations of everything that's happening around us. A useful example of annotation is Project Tokyo, as proposed recently by Grayson et al. [10] from Microsoft, that aims to help people with disability using augmented reality (HoloLens) and artificial intelligence. The system can help blind people to artificially see by detecting the location of people in the user's environment. Then, it can recognize faces dynamically and relay the essential guidance to them via audio information. Similarly, for using augmented reality to help disabled people is a system of visual and touch communications, as presented in [11]. Third, augmented reality in storytelling can help expressing more unique experiences in both public and private places. A recent example of storytelling in augmented reality is RYOT's work, described in [12] in 2020, by building an augmented reality experience for exploring Oscars dresses from the past fifty years of Academy Awards fashion—the 1970s through the 2010s. In this work, it allows us to put ourselves in the dresses. Therefore, by using augmented reality, it can allow people to interact with the iconic Oscars dresses in a new way.

Fig. 3. An anatomy professor from Case Western Reserve University using augmented reality to teach a HoloAnatomy class during the Covid-19 outbreak [9].

3   Artificial Intelligence to Flight the Covid-19

This section highlights an overview of recent tools using artificial intelligence to smartly fight against the Covid-19 crisis. For example, a susceptible-exposed-infectious-removed (SEIR) model is utilized in [13], as presented by Yang et al., using population migration data approximately on 23 January 2020 and renewed Covid-19 epidemiological data to estimate the epidemics trend of the virus under public health interventions in China. They also use the past SARS (Severe Acute Respiratory Syndrome) data in 2003 to train the artificial intelligence algorithm for predicting the virus epidemic sizes and peaks. According to their study, they suggest that the implementation of control measures on 23 January 2020 should be essential in reducing the virus epidemic size. The suggestion has later been proved to be true. In addition, an artificial intelligence-based research of Bullock et al. [14] is discussed for using datasets to cope with the virus for three main applications: clinical application, molecular application and societal application. First, according to a clinical application, artificial intelligence, specifically deep learning, can help diagnosis using medical imaging data, such as patterns, computed tomography scans, and electromagnetic radiation images. Then it can track the evolution of disease severity, so that predictions on patient outcomes can be achieved using electronic health records. Also, in [15] as reviewed by Shi et al., they explain about the integration of artificial intelligence with computed tomography scans and electromagnetic radiation images, both of which are used by the doctors during this virus crisis for depicting the progress of radiology and medical imaging. Second, according to a molecular application, the virus structure of SARSCoV-2-related proteins can be forecasted by artificial intelligence, and therefore it can possibly help for the discovery and development of medicines and vaccines. Third, according to a societal application, empirical modelling for epidemiological research can be predicted by artificial intelligence. Some examples include predicting the number virus cases given various public policy choices, identifying differences and similarities in the evolution of the pandemic between countries and continents, and verifying the spread and scale of the fake news and hate speech during the virus outbreak. More recently in May 2020, Luengo-Oroz et al. [16] also gives a useful overview of artificial intelligence global partnership to help the response of the virus outbreak for code and model sharing, adapting tools to specific contexts, and partnership between countries.

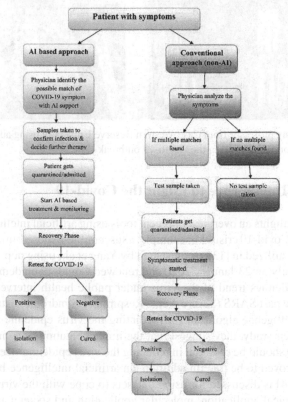

Fig. 4. Overview of artificial intelligence (left in green color) and non-artificial intelligence (right in blue color and red color) based-applications, as presented by Vaishya et al. [17], that support doctors and medical teams to recognize the virus symptoms (Color figure online)

In addition, Vaishya et al. [17] use the artificial intelligence methods to approximate and prepare people for prevention the virus. In fact, it is very crucial and important to slow down the number of new virus cases. This is because one of the reasons why the number of deaths in some countries is so high is that they do not enough medical workers, beds and quarantine facilities to help the patients properly. Figure 4 gives an overview of artificial intelligence and non-artificial intelligence applications that support doctors and medical teams to recognize the virus symptoms, so that they can do both the treatment of the infected patient and the control of virus prevention more effectively. They review seven main applications of artificial intelligence for dealing with the virus outbreak. The seven applications are early diagnosis of the disease, controlling the treatment, testing and tracing of each patient, projection of infected cases and deaths, discovery of medicines and vaccines, decreasing and lightening the load of healthcare people, and prevention of the virus. Furthermore similarly, Naudé [18] gives an early review of six areas where artificial intelligence contributes to deal with the Covid-19 crisis, including quickly warnings, tracing and forecast, strategic data dashboards, diagnosis and prognosis, treatments, and physical control. However, they suggest that artificial intelligence still do not fruitfully impact against the virus outbreak because of both a lack of data and, at the same time, too much data [19]. For this reason, it is suggested that a good balance between information privacy and protection, tools for public health, and precise human-artificial intelligence interaction critically is essential.

Moreover, a real-time method for forecasting of the Covid-19 outbreak using artificial intelligence is presented by Ghazaly et al. [20]. By using non-linear regressive network (NAR), they predict the size, lengths and ending time of this new virus through nine countries, i.e. USA, Brazil, Russian Federation, Spain, Italy, Iran, France, Saudi Arabia, and Egypt. According to the https://www.worldometers.info/coronavirus/ on 6 May 2020, it is important to note that USA, Brazil, Russian Federation, and Spain are the most confirmed coronavirus cases in the world, i.e., 1,902,031 cases, 584,562 cases, 441,108 cases, and 287,406 cases, respectively. In their study, they use the data which is received from the reports of the World Health Organization (WHO), including the virus's infected cases and mortality to analyze and predict the outbreak during the period from 23 March 2020 to 30 July 2020. Figure 5 depicts the map of nine selected countries (above) for prediction and the forecasting results (below) for the cases mean absolute percentage error (MAPE) and the deaths mean absolute percentage error using non-linear regressive network for nine selected countries. The vertical axis represents the cases and the deaths in percentage (error and accuracy). The blue line indicates cases forecast accuracy, while the red line shows deaths forecast accuracy. According to their study for global prediction, training error in the non-linear regressive network is 2.65 percent in cases forecast and 3.22 percent in mortality forecast, respectively. In addition, more recently, Kumar et al. [21] give a useful survey about some modern technologies, focusing on artificial intelligence, machine learning, and data science, that are used to deal with the virus outbreak. One of the examples mentioned is to use artificial intelligence technology for tracking illness of Covid-19 patients with place and time. Nevertheless, they suggest that there are still limitations and constrains for applying the technology for fighting the virus outbreak and pandemic.

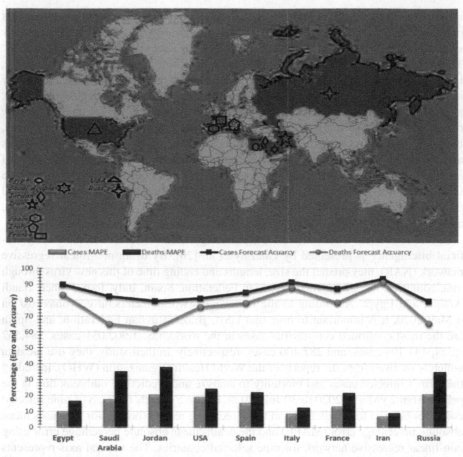

Fig. 5. Forecasting power for the cases mean absolute percentage error and the deaths mean absolute percentage error using non-linear regressive network between 30 March 2020 and 30 July 2020 are proposed by Ghazaly et al. [20].

4   Conclusion and Suggestion

This paper has presented the current development of augmented reality and artificial intelligence during the Covid-19 crisis. We first discuss an overview of recent tools using augmented reality to tackle the virus outbreak. After that, we give an overview of recent tools using artificial intelligence technology, including deep learning, to fight against the Covid-19 crisis. We recognize well that dealing with the Covid-19 outbreak is critically difficult worldwide because we must tackle in so many aspects, such as medical aspect, economical aspect, and social aspect. In fact, when the globe is fundamentally interconnected, even though a majority of countries in the world may start to success-fully contain the virus, we are not truly safe if there are a few countries that still cannot contain it. That is why we suggest applying latest technologies to cope with the outbreak quickly. Augmented reality and artificial intelligence can be good examples to help the virus outbreak in this case. But both technologies require data that are enough, valid, and truthful. Therefore, we believe that the future direction should be cooperation and partnership among countries in term of data exchange management for training artificial intelligence algorithms and building augmented reality-based applications. In other words, when artificial intelligence algorithms are trained with enough data qualitatively and qualitatively, it is possible to create augmented reality-based applications robustly and accurately using computer vision. By applying these technologies, it could help us advance the ways we deal with the virus crisis more smartly, effectively and efficiently.

Acknowledgments. This research presented herein was partially supported by a research grant from the Research Center, NIDA (National Institute of Development Administration).

References

1. Reuters, T.: Chinese startup Rokid sees opportunity with COVID-fighting smart glasses (2020). https://www.reuters.com/article/us-health-coronavirus-china-detection-gl/chinese-startup-rokid-sees-opportunity-with-covid-fighting-smart-glasses-idUSKBN22D4TQ. Accessed 5 May 2020
2. Inavate Virtual Events, "Chinese startup develops Covid-19 detecting thermal glasses" (2020). https://www.inavateonthenet.net/news/article/chinese-startup-develops-covid-19-detecting-thermal-glasses. Accessed 5 May 2020
3. Li, J.: China's facial-recognition giant says it can crack masked faces during the coronavirus (2020). https://qz.com/1803737/chinas-facial-recognition-tech-can-crack-masked-faces-amid-coronavirus/. Accessed 10 May 2020
4. Jakhar, P.: Coronavirus: China's tech fights back. BBC World (2020). https://www.bbc.com/news/technology-51717164. Accessed 10 May 2020
5. Maghdid, K.Z., Ghafoor, A.S., Sadiq, K., Curran, K.R.: A novel AI-enabled framework to diagnose coronavirus COVID 19 using smartphone embedded sensors. In: Design Study, pp. 1–5 (2020)
6. Tely360, "Vuzix Blade Smart Glasses Now Used for COVID-19 Patient Care in Thailand via Tely360's Ambulance 3rd Eye" (2020). https://ir.vuzix.com/press-releases/detail/1764. Accessed 11 May 2020
7. Papagiannis, H.: 3 ways Augmented Reality can have a positive impact on society, COVID-19. World Economic Forum (2020). https://www.weforum.org/agenda/2020/04/augmented-reality-covid-19-positive-use/. Accessed 1 May 2020
8. Kerdvibulvech, C.: Markerless vision-based tracking for interactive augmented reality game. Int. J. Interact. Worlds Issue Serious Games Interact. Worlds **2010**, article ID 751615, p. 14 (2010)
9. Scott, M.: HoloAnatomy goes remote, learning goes on during pandemic. Case Western Reserve University (2020). https://thedaily.case.edu/holoanatomy-goes-remote-learning-goes-on-during-pandemic/. Accessed 12 May 2020
10. Grayson, M., Thieme, A., Marques, R., Massiceti, D.: A dynamic AI system for extending the capabilities of blind people. In: Morrison, C.C. (ed.) CHI 2020 Extended Abstracts (2020)
11. Kerdvibulvech, C.: A novel integrated system of visual communication and touch technology for people with disabilities. In: Gervasi, O., et al. (eds.) ICCSA 2016. LNCS, vol. 9787, pp. 509–518. Springer, Cham (2016). https://doi.org/10.1007/978-3-319-42108-7_39

12. Walker, N.S., Tschorn, A., Harper, M.: See iconic Oscar dresses and then put yourself in them. Los Angeles Times (2020). https://www.latimes.com/lifestyle/story/2020–02-07/oscar-oscars-dresses-celebrities-3d-ar-augmented-reality. Accessed 12 May 2020
13. Yang, Z., et al.: Modified SEIR and AI prediction of the epidemics trend of COVID-19 in China under public health interventions. J. Thoracic Dis. **12**(3), 165 (2020)
14. Bullock, J., Luccioni, A., Pham, K.H., Lam, C.S.N., Luengo-Oroz, M.: Mapping the Landscape of Artificial Intelligence Applications against COVID-19 (2020)
15. Shi, F., et al.: Review of artificial intelligence techniques in imaging data acquisition, segmentation and diagnosis for COVID-19. IEEE Rev. Biomed. Eng. (2020)
16. Luengo-Oroz, M., et al.: Artificial intelligence cooperation to support the global response to COVID-19. Nat. Mach. Intell. **2**, 295–297 (2020)
17. Vaishya, R., Javaid, M., Khan, I.H., Haleem, A.: Artificial Intelligence (AI) applications for COVID-19 pandemic. Diab. Metab. Syndr. Clin. Res. Rev. **14**(4), 337–339 (2020)
18. Naudé, W.: Artificial Intelligence against COVID-19: an early review. IZA Discussion Paper no. 13110 (2020)
19. Naudé, W.: Artificial intelligence vs COVID-19: limitations, constraints and pitfalls. AI Soc. **35**(3), 761–765 (2020). https://doi.org/10.1007/s00146-020-00978-0
20. Ghazaly, N.M., Abdel-Fattah, M.A., Ahmed, A.E.: Novel coronavirus forecasting model using nonlinear autoregressive artificial neural network. J. Adv. Sci. 29(5), pp. 1831–1849 (2020)
21. Kumar, A., Gupta, P.K., Srivastava, A.: A review of modern technologies for tackling COVID-19 pandemic. Diab. Metab. Syndr. Clin. Res. Rev. **14**(4), 569–573 (2020)

V-Dream: Immersive Exploration of Generative Design Solution Space

Mohammad Keshavarzi[1]([⊠]), Ardavan Bidgoli[2], and Hans Kellner[3]

[1] University of California, Berkeley, USA
mkeshavarzi@berkeley.edu
[2] Carnegie Mellon University, Pittsburgh, USA
abidgoli@andrew.cmu.edu
[3] Autodesk Research, San Francisco, USA
hans.kellner@autodesk.com

Abstract. Generative Design workflows have introduced alternative paradigms in the domain of computational design, allowing designers to generate large pools of valid solutions by defining a set of goals and constraints. However, analyzing and narrowing down the generated solution space, which usually consists of various high-dimensional properties, has been a major challenge in current generative workflows. By taking advantage of the interactive unbounded spatial exploration, and the visual immersion offered in virtual reality platforms, we propose V-Dream, a virtual reality generative analysis framework for exploring large-scale solution spaces. V-Dream proposes a hybrid search workflow in which a spatial stochastic search approach is combined with a recommender system allowing users to pick desired candidates and eliminate the undesired ones iteratively. In each cycle, V-Dream reorganizes the remaining options in clusters based on the defined features. Moreover, our framework allows users to inspect design solutions and evaluate their performance metrics in various hierarchical levels, assisting them in narrowing down the solution space through iterative cycles of search/select/re-clustering of the solutions in an immersive fashion. Finally, we present a prototype of our proposed framework, illustrating how users can navigate and narrow down desired solutions from a pool of over 16000 monitor stands generated by Autodesk's Dreamcatcher software.

Keywords: Virtual reality · Generative design · Design solution exploration · Immersive data visualization · Machine learning · Optioneering

1 Introduction

Advances in design automation and cloud-based computing has facilitated the rapid shift of computer-aided design paradigms towards generative workflows [34,43]. Unlike traditional CAD-based processes, where a single design solution was modeled using a set of computational tools, in generative design workflows,

© Springer Nature Switzerland AG 2020
C. Stephanidis et al. (Eds.): HCII 2020, LNCS 12424, pp. 477–494, 2020.
https://doi.org/10.1007/978-3-030-60117-1_35

Fig. 1. V-Dream allows generative designers to search, inspect, and re-organize the solution space within Virtual Reality.

designers specify high-level goals and constraints and, the system automatically generates large sets of solutions all corresponding to the defined design criteria. In addition to geometrical attributes, generative design systems can be integrated with performance evaluators [38,43] and simulation engines [14] to quantitatively assess and optimize the generated solution landscape. With the availability of high-performance computing and cloud services, this process can be parallelized, allowing faster generation, improving the performance evaluation, and generating larger solution landscapes [4]. Users of such systems are then responsible to choose between plausible design candidates, which is often considered a complex task [45,46]. These users should inspect the high-dimensional properties of each solution as well as assessing their aesthetic qualities (Fig. 1).

There are two general approaches recognizable among the current generative design workflows: (i) Convergence generative design and (ii) divergence generative design [33]. In convergence generative design, the search mechanism is implemented in a way to converge the solution space into a single solution or a set of limited solutions. However, depending on the level of clarity and accuracy of the goals, constraints, and the fitness function, the optimization process may dismiss many potentially acceptable solutions, which could have been otherwise chosen by the designer. Also, automated optimization methods do not leverage human expertise and can only find solutions that are optimal with regard to an invariably defined problem space [42]. On the other hand, in divergent generative design, the whole solution space is generated, then the designers utilize sorting, clustering, and filtering tools to manually navigate and explore the

Search   Select   Re-Cluster

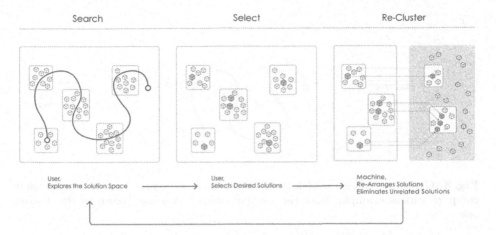

User,   User,   Machine,
Explores the Solution Space   Selects Desired Solutions   Re-Arranges Solutions
                                                              Eliminates Unrelated Solutions

Fig. 2. General workflow of the V-Dream framework: Performing exploratory search, labeling initial preferences of viable design solutions, re-clustering, and re-organizing the solution space based on user selection using a recommender system.

solution space. Rather than looking at a limited set of solutions, designers have the chance to continually re-define their goals and constraints, allowing a more comprehensive control over the generative process. As divergent generative workflows often produce large numbers of solutions, organizing the solution space to effectively explore the data is considered a critical step in design explorations.

The re-emergence of virtual reality (VR) technology as the next-generation human-computer interfaces has allowed various disciplines to explore how spatial interactions with virtual objects can benefit their field. VR can potentially elevate the sense of immersion and spatial awareness for users, providing designers the opportunity to interact with virtual objects in higher degrees of senses. Studies suggest that immersive environments enhance spatial understanding when compared to 2D or non-immersive 3D representations [39,41]. Moreover, VR has been broadly used in various decision-making processes, from design tasks [9] to data analysis workflows [10]. Immersive content generated within virtual experience can support collaboration and allow users to visualize various mediums of data to assist real-world decision-making.

In this paper, we introduce V-Dream, a virtual reality generative design exploration framework for analyzing large-scale solution spaces. Using V-Dream, users can navigate, organize, and cluster a solution space to locate or narrow down potential ideal design solutions from the generated outcomes. We use a hybrid approach of a user-centered stochastic search and a system-based recommender system to guide the user towards its desirable group of solutions. We believe the framework introduced in this paper can facilitate the integration of generative design workflows into next-generation spatial computing platforms. The exploration of large-scale data and the ability to intuitively perform spatial navigation tasks while analyzing design instances can be a promising step for the future generative design systems (Fig. 3).

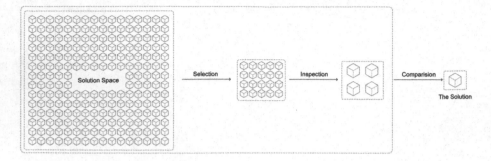

Fig. 3. Generative design workflows allow designers to explore, select, inspect, and compare various examples from the solution space and narrow down to the desired one.

2 Background

Dataset Exploration. There is a rich body of literature allocated to the general task of multi-variate dataset exploration [15,19,28] for various applications. Such approaches have integrated filtering and recommender systems with data visualization methods to allows user to explore and search within a possible solution space. Interaction with large datasets has also been widely investigated and reviewed in user interface literature. Koyama et al. [29] present a unique approach to encoding the parameter space of an attribute directly on a slider widget, providing interactivity with the data bounds. The work of Kim et al. [27] explores mapping multi-dimensional data onto a two-dimensional scatter plots. They address this by letting users drag examples to the extreme ends of the scatter plot to define how each axis should behave. We also incorporate a similar approach for bounding solutions spaces by allowing users to select desired data points, which would later reorganize the spatial visualization of the solution landscape.

Generative Design Exploration. Studies on how to interpret generative design solutions, and to provide the user with appropriate workflows to modify and interact with the generated solution space has been a topic of interest among various researchers [20,35,42]. Chaszar et al. [11] explored methods and tools for multivariate interactive data visualization of the generated designs and simulation results. They aimed at enabling designers to focus not only on high-performing results but also examine suboptimal ones. Mueller and Ochsendorf [36] proposed a computational design exploration approach that extends the existing interactive evolutionary algorithms to integrate the designers' preferences. They addressed this goal by allowing designers to set the evolutionary parameters, namely mutation rate, generation size, and parent selection. More recently, Bidgoli and Veloso [8] explored how generative systems could potentially learn both aspects of the problem definition and the design space through processing a database of existing solutions without the supervision of the designer.

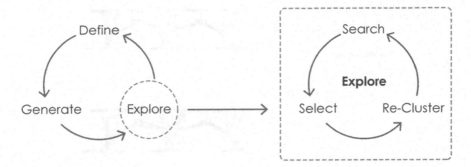

Fig. 4. V-Dream allows designers to engage with an External Generation Loop, which iteratively defines, generates, and explores design solutions (left), while also interacting with an Internal Exploration Loop to filter, cluster, and re-organize the generated solution space (right).

We use a similar approach in our clusterization steps while narrowing down the solution space based on users' previous selections of desired candidates.

Geometrical Interaction in VR. Designing and modeling 3D geometry within VR interfaces provides the opportunity for designers to spatially interact with virtual models in real-life scale. Examples of such applications are Gravity Sketch VR [16], Project Sugarhill [5], and vSpline [3], which allow designers to implement conventional CAD modeling procedures within an immersive environment. Immersive painting and sculpting have also been widely explored in commercial applications such as Google Tilt Brush and Oculus Medium. Abbasi-Asl et al. [1] explored non-physical input modules by using a Brain-Computer Interface in VR for virtual spatial sculpturing. Innes et al. [23] showed that designers tend to use significantly fewer actions in VR to achieve a similar result than working on a monitor. Hsu et al.[21] developed a VR system that allows multiple design stakeholders to discuss about an architectural model in VR and modify the geometry during discussion using mid-air sketching as well as on-surface sketching in the virtual environment. Other examples of collaborative evaluation and modeling for architectural and design applications within VR can be seen in the work of [17,26,30].

Performance Evaluation in VR. During the evaluation process, the user analyzes each solution concerning two distinct factors: 1) the aesthetic characteristics, 2) the simulated performance metrics. While the first factor is subjective and qualitative, the latter is quantitative and objective, which requires the user to utilize various methods to comprehend and assess effectively. In this regard, studies on immersive analytics [10,13] have explored how VR platforms can be used to support scientific data visualization, analytical reasoning, and decision-making. For example, for building performance evaluation, Nytsch-Geusen et al. developed VR visualizations using bi-directional data exchange

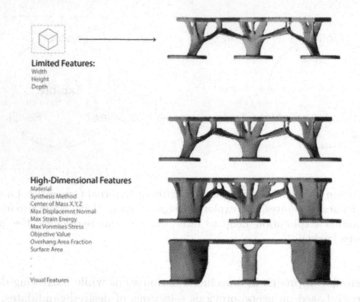

Fig. 5. Limited feature analysis vs high-dimensional feature analysis.

between energy simulation tools and the Unity game engine [37]. The work of Rysanek et al. introduces a workflow for managing building information and performance data in VR with equirectangular image labeling methods [40]. Immersive interfaces have also been applied for structural investigations, finite element method simulations [18], and CFD visualizations [7,32] and urban simulations [12,44]. Keshavarzi et al. demonstrated how interactive qualitative daylighting renderings can be overlaid with qualitative simulations within VR [25]. We take advantage of such overlaying methods in our, where various performance metrics are visualized within the surrounding space of the target object (Fig. 5).

3   The V-Dream Framework

3.1   Design Goals

The development of V-Dream is directed by two primary design goals. First, we aim to capture an iterative generative design workflow in which the designer can define, generate, and explore the design solution in multiple cycles. Each generative design cycle would allow the user to re-define the new cycle with adjusted goals and constraints. Second, we intend to provide a high dimensional exploration phase in which both qualitative and quantitative properties of individual solutions can be assessed. We elaborate more on each design goal below.

Iterative Generative Design Workflow. Specifying the right design goals and constraints is a critical task in generative workflows. Failure to define a set of correct and effective design criteria would result in limited or inappropriate solution spaces, where ideal candidates may be excluded, and therefore, not evaluated by the user or the optimization module. However, depending on the complexity of the design and the expertise of the user, correctly defining such properties may not happen in the early stages of design explorations. In such cases, users tend to redefine the objective functions to calibrate the solver to generate better solutions spaces. Therefore, we aim to design the generative design workflow in V-Dream as an iterative process, where generation, evaluation, and exploration are performed in a potentially cyclical workflow. Moreover, as generating each iteration of the solution space often requires heavy computation and time resources, minimizing the number of iterations using effective evaluation methods and recommender systems have also been explored during our development of V-Dream. In this regard, we aim to develop the exploration process as another internal cyclical workflow, where users can navigate, evaluate, and re-organize the generated solution space in each redefined generation. Figure 4 illustrates the external generation loop and internal exploration loop of our proposed framework.

Highlight Qualitative and Quantitative Properties. During the conceptual design phase, designers must consider a wide range of performance-oriented goals. These include quantitative and measurable goals, such as structural efficiency, cost, and embodied energy, as well as qualitative goals that cannot be expressed numerically, such as aesthetics, constructability, and contextual appropriateness. The designer's early-stage responsibilities include balancing these requirements to attain a satisfying initial design concept. There is a wide range of tools and methods to support designers' decision-making during this phase when it comes to processing quantitative data. In contrast, designers have limited options while handling qualitative data and subjective measures. We aim to propose a means to address both aspects in the proposed framework.

3.2   Workflow

In V-Dream, the search is an interactive process between the user and the algorithms in an immersive VR environment. The user relies on its subjective measures to initiate and direct the search process while the algorithm supports the process through a series of recommendations and reorganization of the solution space. Thus, a hybrid workflow that both relies on a stochastic approach and recommender system will be achieved which enhances the user's experience in searching within the solution space. The user starts from an exploratory search through the solution space, which is already clustered based on their visual and quantitative properties. Next, the user marks a limited number of solutions as the starting seeds. Then, the backend algorithm re-clusters and re-organizes the solution space based on the user's selection and eliminates irrelevant instances (Fig. 2). In the next sub-sections, we discuss the elements and steps of this workflow in more detail.

3.3 Solution Clustering

Divergent generative workflows often produce significantly large pool of solutions. Accordingly, organizing the solution space to ensure a practical data exploration is a critical prerequisite for the design explorations phase. Therefore, we propose to utilize high-dimensional data clusterization methods, which have been widely explored in various data exploration applications. This approach facilitates organizing the solution space based on performance features that can be simulated or extracted as quantitative values. However, as discussed in the previous sections, qualitative aspects of each solution, such as aesthetics and form, also play an essential role in design decision-making. Such qualities commonly correspond to geometrical features of the solution space, and therefore clustering techniques integrated into the system should also reflect geometrical properties of the data.

We therefore propose to use shape clustering methods introduced by Huang et al. [22], which allows representative subsets to be extracted and optimized using a set of point-to-point correspondences between each of the representative shapes and the entire collection. Such an approach would allow users to explore the geometrical dimension of the solution spaces by initially evaluating cluster representatives of the generated solutions to maintain a general comprehension of the aesthetic properties of the corresponding subsets. If the user intends to explore similar solutions, the corresponding subset would expand and new clusters and representative shapes would be calculated and visualized within the bounds of the selected subset. This approach can iteratively execute until the user narrows down its geometrical search with the solution space.

To implement the clusterization exploration in VR space, as shown in Fig. 6, we render the initial clustered results as a large room-scale map, above the user's height. The clusterization criteria are defined by the user and can be a combination of multiple performance factors or general geometrical properties, which organize the generated solution based on shape similarity. Each solution is rendered as a bright point, contributing to what is seen as a sky full of stars. Cluster representatives are positioned bellow corresponding subsets within the user's HMD height range and are visualized using the Visualization Tables described in the following section.

3.4 Visualization Tables

To allow the user to perform quantitative analyses of the generated solutions, V-Dream places each 3D model on a *Visualization Table*. As shown in Fig. 7, Visualization Tables plot a spider diagram on the top side of the surface, while generating radial graphs on the perimeter. Such property would allow the user to compare various quantitative factors while inspecting the aesthetic and visual quality of the object itself, which is placed on top of the table. A Visualization tables can be rotated in it's place allowing the user to assess the generated object the data visualization without needing to move around the table virtually.

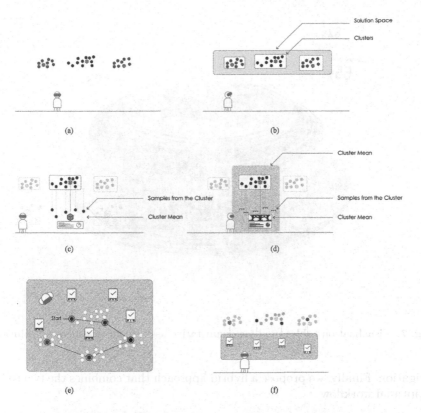

Fig. 6. Six stages of our proposed hybrid search approach: a) initial solution gener-ation and clusterization b) brief inspection of the solution space and clusters, c & d) approaching a cluster and observing the mean member on the Visualization table while the other samples in the cluster are visible as 3d objects e) exploring the space and adding various samples to its list of desired options, f) triggering the re-clustering process to let the backend engine reorganize the clusters based on the user preferences.

3.5 Navigation Strategy

The clustering algorithm maps the high-dimensional solution space into a 3-dimensional space. This allows clusters to be represented as a cloud of solutions in an immersive environment, where similar solutions are distributed in close proximity of each other to form a cluster. Meanwhile, larger distances between clusters imply the significant variance between them. Users can navigate and explore the solution space, visit clusters, and inspect each instance separately. However, the sheer size of the solution space renders it impossible to visit and inspect each instance independently. Finding a feasible yet inclusive method to efficiently navigate the solution space is a critical task that needed to be addressed. We discuss two different approaches for solution space navigation: 1) navigation based on stochastic approach, and 2) recommender system assisted

Fig. 7. Visualization tables used for quantitative assessment of generated solutions.

navigation. Finally, we propose a hybrid approach that combines the two to form an optimal workflow.

Stochastic Navigation. In stochastic navigation, the user starts from an arbitrary point in the solution space and navigates through it, inspecting one solution at a time. The organization of solutions in clusters based on their visual similarity allows the user to move from one cluster to its neighbors and gradually find the desired solution. During our initial user interviews, we found that this approach is popular among designers and users that are willing to explore and examine a wider range of options while developing a comprehensive mental map of solution space. This mental map provides these users with a sense of orientation and location for further navigation of solution space (Figs. 8 and 9).

Recommender System Navigation. In contrast with the stochastic approach, navigation based on a recommender system aims to utilize recommender algorithms to help the user efficiently narrowing down the solution space. In this approach, the algorithm provides the user with the first round of seeds, representing the most populated clusters of the solutions space to select from. After the first round, the algorithm searches for clusters with similar properties to the ones that the user has already selected from. The algorithm also eliminates non-relevant clusters from the pool. It then recommends the user with another round of seeds. This iteration continues until the user is satisfied with one or a limited selection of options from the solution space.

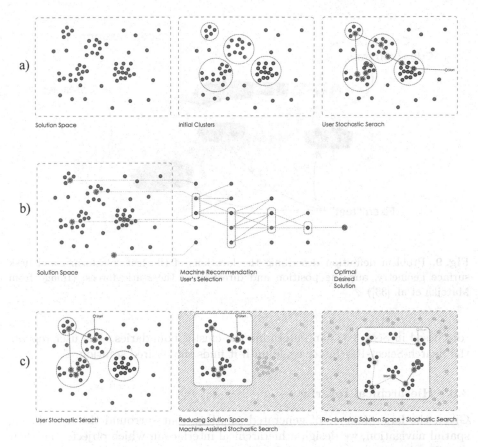

Fig. 8. Abstract illustration of the search process a) stochastic search b) recommender system c) hybrid approach.

Hybrid Navigation. While both approaches have their owns pros and cons, a comprehensive and optimal search approach might be a hybrid of these two. We propose a hybrid approach that starts with a stochastic search, followed by a recommender algorithm. This approach potentially helps the user to develop a mental image of solution space while collecting the first round of seeds. Furthermore, the user can activate the recommender algorithm to 1) eliminate unrelated solutions, 2) find new seeds from the most relevant ones to the current seeds, and 3) re-cluster the rest of the solutions space based on the fresh seeds. In this approach, users determine their desired features to measure the similarities between the instances of solution space. These features can be visual characteristics, performance data, or any high-dimensional metadata that comes from generative design backend. Machine learning methods can be used to extract visual features, while analytical methods can be used for quantitative and qualitative ones. Using dimension reduction methods (i.e., T-SNE [31], PCA [24]) features can be mapped on a 3D space while various clustering methods

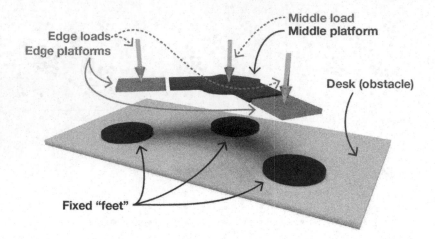

Fig. 9. Problem definition describing the locations of the feet, platforms, and desk surface geometry, and the position and direction of the static forces. (Image from Matejka et al. [33])

(discussed in Sect. 3.3) can determine the cluster boundaries. The user repeats the Search-Select-Re-cluster cycle until it finds the desired solution.

3.6   Hierarchical Interface

Given the large number of generated solutions that surround the user during spatial navigation, we design a hierarchical interface in which objects and their visualization tables are rendered with different levels of details in relation to their distance with the user. Clusters are initially represented by a single solution located on the Visualization table and surrounded by other solutions of the cluster rendered as bright points. Once the user navigates towards the cluster, the minimized solution points would expand to individual Visualization tables holding their corresponding objects. As the user navigates closer to each table, additional metrics and detailed values of the quantitative data would be visible, allowing detailed evaluation of the generated solutions. Such a hierarchical approach would allow the user to explore large datasets in various visualization scales, providing a chance to spatially organize the generated solutions for its stochastic assessment. Figure 10 illustrates three levels of the hierarchical process explained above within our developed prototype.

3.7   Re-Clustering

After the user selects a number of desired solutions, the re-clustering of the solution spaces using the recommender system is executed based on the aesthetic properties of the selected solutions. With such an approach, we integrate qualitative factors of the generated solutions with the generative design cycle, providing an additional design goal of the generative design definition. After each search/select/re-cluster cycle, users are more likely to view desirable solutions in their surrounding navigation space, which align with selections they had made in the previous cycles. In other words, the re-organization of the generated clusters would allow users to thoughtfully navigate the generated solution space, and decide whether an additional re-definition of the whole design space is necessary.

4 Prototype

To demonstrate V-Dream in action, we developed a Virtual Reality prototype to explore a pre-generated solution space generated using Autodesk Dreamcatcher [4]. Dreamcatcher is an internally developed experimental generative design plat-form for engineering design problems where multiple shapes and topology opti-mization algorithms are employed to synthesize model geometries that optimally satisfy defined criteria [2,6]. V-Dream is built on Autodesk's Stingray game engine. To provide custom modifications by potential users, we developed the framework on Stingray's Visual Programming Language (VPL) tool while pro-gramming the main functionalities using Lua, Stingray's primary programming API language. It is important to note that the Autodesk's Stingray software was discontinued after the initial development of this prototype. We evaluate our developed system by interviewing six user participants who are involved in Generative Design software design and development at Autodesk Research. We use an HTC Vive Pro for the VR experience.

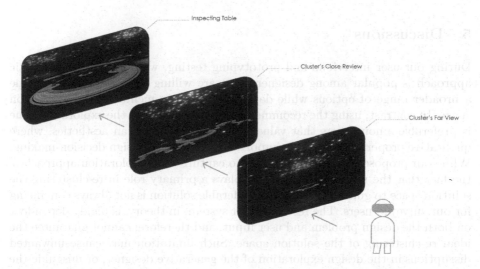

Fig. 10. Hierarchical visualization process: the three resolution stages for solution exploration and assessment.

4.1   Dataset

The design exploration dataset we used was initially introduced by [33], formulating a design problem that was (i) easy to understand without any specialized domain knowledge, (ii) could be used by a broad range of people, and (iii) was a problem that could be satisfied by a wide variety of designs options. The design task corresponding to the dataset generation was to create a 3D printed monitor stand and to raise the 80 mm off the surface of a desk. The geometry consists of three disks at the bottom, which represent where the monitor stand will contact the desk, and three flat sections 80 mm above the desk, which trace the shape of the monitor's base. The static weight of the monitor is defined 8.3 kg, so the stand should be able to support a load of at least 200 N, and the ability to support heavier loads is desirable as well.

The weight of the monitor is modeled as two independent forces: a middle load on the middle platform and an outer load distributed evenly to the two outside platforms. In addition to the geometry of the design, the following properties are calculated: Center of Mass (x, y, z), Weight, Overhang Percentage, Surface Area, Area/Volume Ratio, as well as properties related to the performance under the load conditions: Maximum Displacement, Max. Strain, Total Strain, Max. Vonmises, and Objective Value (for the simulation). Four parameters in the problem definition and solver configuration are varied in this dataset as follows: the middle load, the outer load, voxel size, and volume minimization. Combining these factors leads to 16,800 total designs. The generated solutions contain the 3D geometry of each design, a metadata file describing all the input parameters used, and properties calculated for each design.

5   Discussions

During our user interviews and prototyping testing, we observe the stochastic approach is popular among designers that are willing to explore and examine a broader range of options while developing a larger mental image of solution space. In contrast, using the recommender system to reduce the exploration time is preferable among users that value performance more than aesthetics, where qualitative properties play a less important role in their design decision-making. While our proposed framework intends to capture both exploration approaches, the fact that the recommender system plays a primary role in re-clustering the solution space to guide the user to its preferable solution is not always convincing for our surveyed users. The recommender system, in theory, is highly dependent on both the design problem and user input, and therefore, cannot guarantee the ideal re-clustering of the solution space. Such limitation may cause unwanted disruptions in the design exploration of the generative designer, or misguide the user towards non-desirable results.

In some instances, we found participants to navigate through the solution space and update their selection seed with new choices. Same as a shopping experience, we observed them delete the previous selections seed and replace them with new design options. This emphasized the need for a thorough exploration of generated solutions, in which some better solutions can be found once correct navigation is found. Furthermore, as expected, we observed users to simply walk by (virtually navigate) from some cluster representatives in which they found not as much attractive, or not as desirable than previously selected solutions, and in contrast, stopped and surveyed clusters in which they expected to find desirable solutions.

While V-Dream primarily targets generative design workflows, we believe the proposed framework can be a promising module for other search applications that require large-scale data exploration in future spatial computing interfaces. Applications such as immersive shopping where users intend to explore different product types and categories while assessing and analyzing the pros and cons of each individual product can be seen as an example of such integration. Social media platforms can also be integrated with hybrid exploration mechanisms proposed in this study, allowing thorough navigation between user-profiles and generated content in a targeted fashion.

6   Conclusion and Future Work

In this paper, we introduce an immersive exploration framework for analyzing large-scale generative design solution spaces. By targeting divergent generative design workflows, we propose a user-centric stochastic navigation approach coupled with a system-based recommender system to guide the user towards its desirable set of solutions. V-Dream allows users to assess quantitative and qualitative properties of generated solutions by organizing, clustering, and navigating the generated solution space. We believe the framework proposed in this paper can enhance design search and exploration by utilizing the spatial benefits of next-generation spatial computing platforms. Targeted exploration of large scale data integrated with machine-guided workflows introduced in our proposed framework can be a promising step for future generative design systems.

Our work, of course, comes with limitations. First, our developed prototype currently does not allow generative design goals and constraints to be defined directly in the virtual reality interface. Generative design solutions are generated and transferred from Dreamcatcher in an offline manner. Maintaining a bi-directional data-workflow between other generative design software (Fusion 360, Revit, Dreamcatcher) can be considered future work of our approach. Furthermore, running comprehensive user studies to evaluate how generative design users interact and design with our proposed workflow is a necessary next step. In addition, given the discontinuity of Autodesk's Stingray engine in which our prototype was developed, we hope to transfer our prototype to another platform (Unity or Unreal) in order to share our codebase with the community.

References

1. Abbasi-Asl, R., Keshavarzi, M., Chan, D.Y.: Brain-computer interface in virtual reality. In: 2019 9th International IEEE/EMBS Conference on Neural Engineering (NER), pp. 1220–1224. IEEE (2019)
2. Allaire, G., Jouve, F., Toader, A.M.: Structural optimization using sensitivity analysis and a level-set method. J. Comput. Phys. **194**(1), 363–393 (2004)
3. Arnowitz, E., Morse, C., Greenberg, D.P.: vspline: Physical design and the perception of scale in virtual reality (2017)
4. Autodesk: Project Dreamcatcher—Autodesk Research. https://autodeskresearch.com/projects/dreamcatcher
5. Autodesk: Project Sugarhill—Autodesk. https://blogs.autodesk.com/design-studio/2020/06/02/project-sugarhill-technical-preview-6/
6. Bendsoe, M.P., Sigmund, O.: Topology Optimization: Theory, Methods, and Applications. Springer, Heidelberg (2013). https://doi.org/10.1007/978-3-662-05086-6
7. Berger, M., Cristie, V.: CFD post-processing in unity3D. Procedia Computer Science **51**, 2913–2922 (2015)
8. Bidgoli, A., Veloso, P.: Deepcloud. The application of a data-driven, generative model in design. In: Recalibration: On imprecision and infidelity, Proceedings of the Association of Computer Aided Design in Architecture Conference, pp. 176–185 (2019)
9. Caldas, L., Keshavarzi, M.: Design immersion and virtual presence. Technol.—Arch.+ Des. **3**(2), 249–251 (2019)
10. Chandler, T., et al.: Immersive analytics. In: 2015 Big Data Visual Analytics (BDVA), pp. 1–8. IEEE (2015)
11. Chaszar, A., Von Buelow, P., Turrin, M.: Multivariate interactive visualization of data in generative design. In: Symposium on Simulation for Architecture and Urban Design, SimAUD, London (2016)
12. Cristie, V., Berger, M., Bus, P., Kumar, A., Klein, B.: Cityheat: visualizing cellular automata-based traffic heat in unity3D. In: SIGGRAPH Asia 2015 Visualization in High Performance Computing, p. 6. ACM (2015)
13. Donalek, C., et al.: Immersive and collaborative data visualization using virtual reality platforms. In: 2014 IEEE International Conference on Big Data (Big Data), pp. 609–614. IEEE (2014)
14. Echenagucia, T.M., Capozzoli, A., Cascone, Y., Sassone, M.: The early design stage of a building envelope: multi-objective search through heating, cooling and lighting energy performance analysis. Appl. Energy **154**, 577–591 (2015)
15. Evans, M., Jacobs, P., Stuart-Moore, J.: Interface design for browsing faceted metadata. In: Proceedings of the 6th ACM/IEEE-CS Joint Conference on Digital Libraries (JCDL'06), pp. 349–349. IEEE (2006)
16. Gravity Sketch: Gravity Sketch VR. https://www.gravitysketch.com/
17. Greenwald, S.W., Corning, W., Maes, P.: Multi-user framework for collaboration and co-creation in virtual reality. In: 12th International Conference on Computer Supported Collaborative Learning (2017)
18. Hambli, R., Chamekh, A., Bel, H., Salah, H.: Real-time deformation of structure using finite element and neural networks in virtual reality applications. Finite Elem. Anal. Des. **42**, 985–991 (2006). https://doi.org/10.1016/j.finel.2006.03.008, www.elsevier.com/locate/finel
19. Hearst, M.A.: UIs for faceted navigation: recent advances and remaining open problems. In: HCIR 2008: Proceedings of the Second Workshop on Human-Computer Interaction and Information Retrieval, pp. 13–17 (2008)

20. Herdy, M.: Evolution strategies with subjective selection. In: Voigt, H.-M., Ebeling, W., Rechenberg, I., Schwefel, H.-P. (eds.) PPSN 1996. LNCS, vol. 1141, pp. 22–31. Springer, Heidelberg (1996). https://doi.org/10.1007/3-540-61723-X_966

21. Hsu, T.W., et al.: Design and initial evaluation of a VR based immersive and interactive architectural design discussion system. In: 2020 IEEE Conference on Virtual Reality and 3D User Interfaces (VR), pp. 363–371. IEEE (2020)

22. Huang, Q.X., Zhang, G.X., Gao, L., Hu, S.M., Butscher, A., Guibas, L.: An optimization approach for extracting and encoding consistent maps in a shape collection. ACM Trans. Graph. (TOG) $31(6)$, 167 (2012)

23. Innes, D., Moleta, T., Schnabel, M.: Virtual inhabitation and creation: a comparative study of interactive 1: 1 modelling as a design method. In: Conference: DADA 2017 International Conference on Digital Architecture:"Digital Culture" (2017)

24. Jolliffe, I.T.: Principal components in regression analysis. In: Principal component analysis, pp. 129–155. Springer, Heidelberg (1986). https://doi.org/10.1007/978-1-4757-1904-8_8

25. Keshavarzi, M., Caldas, L., Santos, L.: Radvr: a 6 DoF virtual reality daylighting analysis tool (2019). arXiv preprint arXiv:1907.01652

26. Keshavarzi, M., Wu, M., Chin, M.N., Chin, R.N., Yang, A.Y.: Affordance analysis of virtual and augmented reality mediated communication (2019). arXiv preprint arXiv:1904.04723

27. Kim, H., Choo, J., Park, H., Endert, A.: InterAxis: steering scatterplot axes via observation-level interaction. IEEE Trans. Visual. Comput. Graph. $22(1)$, 131–140 (2016). https://doi.org/10.1109/tvcg.2015.2467615

28. Koren, J., Zhang, Y., Liu, X.: Personalized interactive faceted search. In: Proceedings of the 17th International Conference on World Wide Web, pp. 477–486 (2008)

29. Koyama, Y., Sakamoto, D., Igarashi, T.: Crowd-powered parameter analysis for visual design exploration. In: Proceedings of the 27th annual ACM symposium on User Interface Software and Technology, pp. 65–74. ACM (2014)

30. Kunert, A., Weissker, T., Froehlich, B., Kulik, A.: Multi-window 3D interaction for collaborative virtual reality. IEEE Trans. Visual. Comput. Graph. (2019)

31. Maaten, L.V.D., Hinton, G.: Visualizing data using t-sne. J. Mach. Learn. Res. 9(Nov), 2579–2605 (2008)

32. Malkawi, A.M., Srinivasan, R.S.: A new paradigm for human-building interaction: the use of CFD and augmented reality. Autom. Constr. $14(1)$, 71–84 (2005)

33. Matejka, J., Glueck, M., Bradner, E., Hashemi, A., Grossman, T., Fitzmaurice, G.: Dream lens: exploration and visualization of large-scale generative design datasets. In: Proceedings of the 2018 CHI Conference on Human Factors in Computing Systems, p. 369. ACM (2018)

34. McCormack, J., Dorin, A., Innocent, T., et al.: Generative design: a paradigm for design research. In: Proceedings of Futureground, Design Research Society, Melbourne (2004)

35. Meignan, D., Knust, S., Frayret, J.M., Pesant, G., Gaud, N.: A review and taxonomy of interactive optimization methods in operations research. ACM Trans. Interact. Intell. Syst. (TiiS) $5(3)$, 17 (2015)

36. Mueller, C.T., Ochsendorf, J.A.: Combining structural performance and designer preferences in evolutionary design space exploration. Autom. Constr. 52, 70–82 (2015)

37. Nytsch-Geusen, C., Ayubi, T., Möckel, J., Rädler, J., Thorade, M.: Buildingsystems vr - a new approach for immersive and interactive building energy simulation (2016)

38. Oxman, R.: Performance-based design: current practices and research issues. Int. J. Arch. Comput. **6**(1), 1–17 (2008)
39. Paes, D., Arantes, E., Irizarry, J.: Immersive environment for improving the understanding of architectural 3D models: comparing user spatial perception between immersive and traditional virtual reality systems. Autom. Constr. **84**, 292–303 (2017)
40. Rysanek, A., Miller, C., Schlueter, A.: A workflow for managing building information and performance data using virtual reality: an alternative to BIM for existing buildings? (2017)
41. Schnabel, M.A., Kvan, T.: Spatial understanding in immersive virtual environments. Int. J. Arch. Comput. **1**(4), 435–448 (2003)
42. Scott, S.D., Lesh, N., Klau, G.W.: Investigating human-computer optimization. In: Proceedings of the SIGCHI Conference on Human Factors in Computing Systems, pp. 155–162. ACM (2002)
43. Shea, K., Aish, R., Gourtovaia, M.: Towards integrated performance-driven generative design tools. Autom. Constr. **14**(2), 253–264 (2005)
44. Sobral, T., Galvão, T., Borges, J.: Visualization of urban mobility data from intelligent transportation systems. Sensors **19**(2), 332 (2019)
45. Turrin, M., Von Buelow, P., Stouffs, R.: Design explorations of performance driven geometry in architectural design using parametric modeling and genetic algorithms. Adv. Eng. Inf. **25**(4), 656–675 (2011)
46. Von Buelow, P.: Paragen: performative exploration of generative systems. J. Int. Assoc. Shell Spat. Struct. **53**(4), 271–284 (2012)

Usability in Mixed Initiative Systems

Sachin Kumarswamy[✉]

Signify Research, 5656AE Eindhoven, The Netherlands
skumarswamy13@gmail.com

Abstract. As computation becomes ubiquitous, our environments are enriched
with new possibilities for communication and interaction. These possibilities
involve various systems to aid the user in completing his tasks and one such system
is Mixed-initiative system. Any system that interacts with humans can leverage the
usability criteria. However, most of the existing work related to mixed-initiative
systems discusses the effectiveness of the system instead of overall usability. In
this paper, we first discuss the mixed initiative systems and then we consider the
usability of mixed-initiative systems. This involves learnability, efficiency, error,
memorability, and satisfaction, which are regarded as five facets of usability. This
examination can be used as a guideline while designing a mixed-initiative system
to improve overall usability of the system.

Keywords: Mixed initiatives · Mixed-initiative systems · Usability · User
experience · Joint cognition

1 Introduction

With the advent of Internet of Things (IoT) and Ubiquitous computing [1] the computation lies everywhere. The field of human-computer interaction confronts challenges of supporting complex tasks by mediating networked interactions and managing the ever-increasing availability of digital information [2]. There are discussions on integrating the field of HCI and Intelligent systems to make the intelligent systems more usable [3]. The focus and effort of this school of thinkers is to develop systems that senses user's activity and takes autonomous decisions to help with user's task [4–7]. Since there is direct partnership between the users and system, the usability and user experience play an important role [8]. The discussion on the principles of mixed initiatives [9] identifies key problems with the agents in the interfaces such as guessing goals and needs of users. Nielsen [10] defines usability using the five facets: learnability, memorability, efficiency, error, and satisfaction. However, no critical view is currently available in the context of mixed-initiative systems.

2 Background

2.1 Mixed-Initiative Systems

"Autonomous agents" are used to implement a complementary style of interaction in the field of Artificial Intelligence [11]. This style of interaction is known as indirect management [12]. Instead of user starting the task, the user can be involved in a cooperative process. Here, both humans and computer initiate, monitor events, and perform tasks [13]. There are attempts to model users' performance while completing a task. This is referred as Model Human Processor [14]. Such cognitive modeling methods are one way to evaluate usability of a product. Extending this, in Artificial Intelligence systems (AI), we try to model human cognition to create a machine or set of instructions which learns and performs human tasks. On the other hand, owing to the contributions to HCI field, we design and develop computer interfaces that aids the human users to complete tasks that require intelligence. Mixed-initiative systems can be considered as missing link between these two fields [15].

Mixed-initiative approach promises to improve human-computer interaction by allowing computers to behave more like associates. In such setting, agents can work with users to develop a shared understanding of goals and contribute to problem-solving in the most appropriate and collaborative way [9]. Collaboration means working together as a group. Taking initiative means the ability to direct the group's behavior. A mixed-initiative system is one that allows the participants to contribute separately to help with group's overall success [16]. A true collaborative behavior requires an agent to have several capabilities such as reasoning, communication, planning, execution, and learning [16]. This partnership depends on distribution of cognition thus, joint cognitive systems as an intellectual partnership. The partnership here is not the computer technologies that aid in cognitive processing and support intellectual performance to enrich individuals' minds [17]. Instead, the two systems (human and computer) work together by sensing each other to finish the task. Before discussing how usability and user experience in mixed initiatives plays a role, it is imperative to the paradigm of usability and user experience.

2.2 Usability and User Experience in the System

Usability and User-experience are concepts that are co-dependent. There are multiple debates on this topic [18]. ISO FDIS 9241-210 defines user experience as "A person's perceptions and responses that result from the use and/or anticipated use of a product, system or service"

Further, ISO FDIS 9241-R defines usability as "Extent to which a system, product or service can be used by specified users to achieve specified goals with effectiveness, efficiency and satisfaction in a specified context of use"

The ISO's definition of user experience concentrates on the perceived usability and can be loosely associated with "satisfaction" in definition of usability. Satisfaction as a concept comprises of Likability, Pleasure, Comfort and Trust [19]. Further, Nielsen [10] describes the usability comprising of five facets namely Learnability, Efficiency, Memorability, Errors and Satisfaction. He characterizes the satisfaction as user experience. Please note that user experience is not just about satisfaction with the product, but also their attitude, and more complex hedonic aspects [20]. Gaver and Martin [21] stressed on the importance and role of non-instrumental needs such as intimacy, surprise, diversion, and involvement of user to be addressed by technology. UX also involves beyond-instrumental components, emotion and, affect and the experiential, which is referred to as the facets of UX [20]. However, this article mainly focuses on the five facets of usability and regards the satisfaction as user experience component.

The above discussion leads to the research question "How to define guidelines for improving usability of the mixed-initiative systems by considering the facets of usability such as learnability, efficiency, memorability, errors, and satisfaction?"

3 Discussion

In the previous section, we identified some of the existing work related to mixed-initiative systems. Now, we will discuss each of five facets of usability as applied to the mixed-initiative systems.

3.1 Error

Anderson [22] mentions that, complex cognition arises from interaction of procedural and declarative knowledge. Production rules are the units of procedural knowledge; chunks are the units of declarative knowledge. Anderson [22] further mentions "The individual units are created by simple encodings of objects in the environment (chunks) or the various transformations in the environment (production rules)"

A mixed-initiative system which aids human task collaboratively is a complex system. Further, success in complex systems is achieved through work performed by joint task completion [23]. Increasing task complexity with system complexity means more opportunities for malfunctions. This not only means more opportunities for humans to make mistakes but also means more cases where actions have unexpected and adverse consequences [23]. Such a situation springs several strong implications, such as, does the user really have authority to override, or the user's only practical choice is to accept or reject the system's output? [24]. Simply defining errors as "incorrect or wrong user action" does not take the varying impact of different errors into account. Since there is a degree of uncertainty involved because of multiple cognitive systems, the user might be unable to discover the error. This might lead to faulty work product, which might be in some cases unrecoverable. In gist, to identify and flag an error in mixed initiative systems, the system should anticipate the error and help in preventing users from committing the error with sufficient options to override. It is also important that users are aware of implications of overriding an error. Such implementation may contribute to reduced cognitive fatigue of the users [25] (Fig. 1).

3.2 Learnability

In a case study about the evaluation of spoken dialogue agents, the subjects had difficult time learning to use a mixed-initiative system [26]. In this study, the mean recognition score (performance of the speech recognizer), tended to be worse. Asynchronous nature of the system could be an important reason. Since different agents might take the initiative at different times, it should be more predictable by taking turns [15]. Mixed-initiative systems are dependent upon the user's action to learn about them. Agents learn novel ways of performing tasks and help in solving problems. This can occur by learning through observation or by command or control from the users. Finally, agents respond and solve new problems that arise while performing the task, which often involves progressive

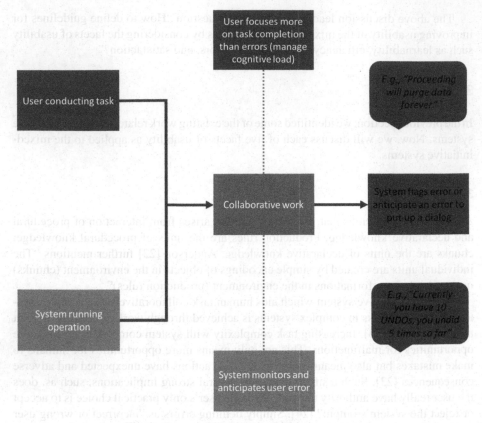

Fig. 1. Error usability in mixed initiative systems

learning. This complex behavior involves at times asserting the user with seemingly odd and unanticipated questions and such behavior can contribute in increasing the learning curve.

Also, affordances play significant role in discoverability, which has direct effect on learning [27]. The system can present the environment where some actions appear (visually, aurally, etc.) to be easier or more direct than others [28]. The agents should continue to learn by observing [9] with minimal intervention, therefore enabling less-steep learning curve (Fig. 2).

3.3 Efficiency

Learnability has direct impact on the efficiency. When the agent efficiently handles the task by reducing the complexity for the user, learnability is improved. Further, joint activity embodies a more efficient form of mixed-initiative interaction [15]. Identifying appropriate metaphors that promote efficient grounding by providing an optimum way for users and the agent to communicate about the intended or continuous contribution to a solution for a problem or a task can benefit the overall efficiency [29]. The essence of

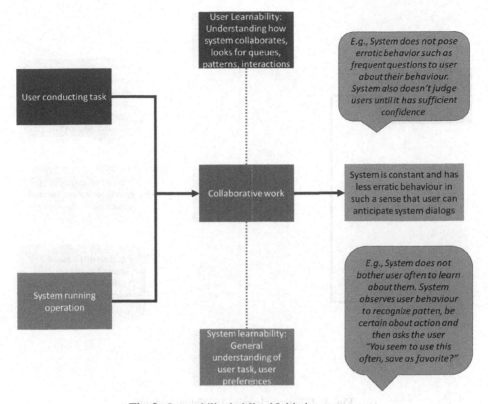

Fig. 2. Learnability in Mixed Initiative systems

mixed initiative is built upon to avoid or reduce the direct manipulation through which efficiencies can be gained with automated reasoning. This further reinforces the point that efficiency can be attributed to the measure of time for task completion [30], which can be improved with mixed-initiative systems.

An appropriate degree of control can improve the efficiency. By providing efficient means to the user, by which they can terminate the automated services can further increase the value of the agents in the mixed initiative system [9] (Fig. 3).

3.4 Memorability

Effective joint cognitive system design mainly requires a problem driven approach rather than technology driven approach [24]. According to Nielsen [10], memorability greatly depends on the type of usage. Usage can be intermittent or regular, but the system should be memorable for the user to complete the task with ease. While the learnability, specifically discoverability operationalizes usability for first time usage of the application, memorability concerns the repeated use (intermittent or regular). For example, if the user uses the tool for the first time, the usability majorly depends on the discoverability (learnability). However, when user visits the same website again, usability depends on

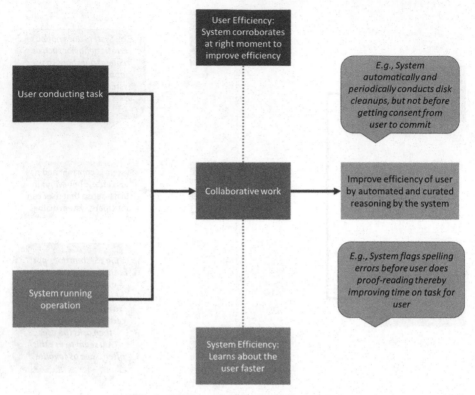

Fig. 3. Efficiency in mixed initiative systems

recognition and recall [31]. The design of mixed-initiative systems should be in such a way that upholds the working memory of interactions [9]. By doing so, it can allow the users to make efficient natural references to the objects, which is a part of shared short-term experiences. This shared experience can reduce number of actions user needs to perform, therefore, fewer things to remember (Fig. 4).

3.5 Satisfaction

Attitude towards a system concerns the acceptable levels of human cost such as tiredness and effort, and users need enough satisfaction to continue using the system [32]. Subjective satisfaction depends on various factors, in essence, points to the pleasing nature of the application [10]. One of the ways of achieving satisfaction in mixed-initiative systems is by providing automated services that offer genuine value over the solutions that are attainable with direct manipulation of the system. For example, while using MS Word, the document editor automatically highlights spelling error there by enabling the users to pay attention, thereby reducing effort and tiredness of proofreading the article.

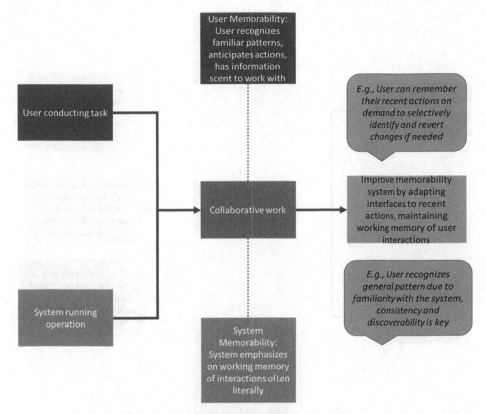

Fig. 4. Memorability in mixed initiative systems

This effective integration [9] helps to establish trust, which in turn augments the perceived satisfaction [19]. Further, mixed initiative system should intuitively anticipate user's actions to make decisions on its own. This will introduce simplicity to the system, upholding satisfaction [33] (Fig. 5).

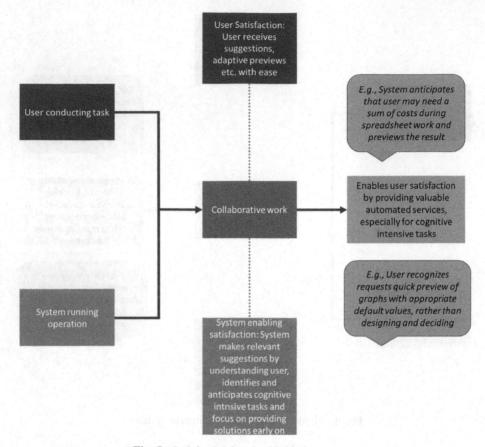

Fig. 5. Satisfaction in mixed initiative systems

4   Conclusion and Future Work

This examination can be used as a guideline while designing and developing a mixed-initiative system to improve the usability and UX of a mixed-system. Mixed initiatives have become part of our daily routine ranging from simpler applications such as document editors to a more complex systems such as Mobile Robotic systems with bidirectional computational trust [34]. Mekler and Hornbæk [35] mention that UX is not only a hedonic aspect but Eudaimonic. Hedonism in UX refers to relaxation, enjoyment, pleasure, and fun aspects while eudaimonia in UX is often associated with user's beliefs, personal goals, bringing best self, developing a skill, learn, or gain insight into something [35].

Future work can explore more complex aspects of UX in mixed initiative systems and can involve empirical studies to establish stronger guidelines on usability and UX in mixed-initiative systems.

Acknowledgments. I would like to thank Dr. Paul Parsons, my instructor who has inspired me to write this paper. Most of the concepts that have been leveraged in the paper were introduced in class. I would also like to acknowledge the efforts of Department of CGT at Purdue for introducing this interesting course.

References

1. Weiser, M.: Hot topics-ubiquitous computing. Computer **26**, 71–72 (1993)
2. Hollan, J., Hutchins, E., Kirsh, D.: Distributed cognition. ACM Trans. Comput. Hum. Inter. (TOCHI) **7**, 174–196 (2000)
3. Grudin, J.: AI and HCI: two fields divided by a common focus. AI Mag. **30**, 48 (2009)
4. Heckerman, D., Horvitz, E.: Inferring informational goals from free-text queries: a Bayesian approach. In: Proceedings of the Fourteenth Conference on Uncertainty in Artificial Intelligence, pp. 230–237 (1998)
5. Horvitz, E., Barry, M.: Display of information for time-critical decision making. In: Proceedings of the Eleventh Conference on Uncertainty in Artificial Intelligence. http://dl.acm.org/citation.cfm?id=2074191
6. Horvitz, E., Breese, J., Heckerman, D., Hovel, D., Rommelse, K.: The lumière project: Bayesian user modeling for inferring the goals and needs of software users. In: Proceedings of the Fourteenth Conference on Uncertainty in Artificial Intelligence, pp. 256–265 (1998)
7. Lieberman, H.: Letizia: an agent that assists web browsing. In: Proceedings of the 14th International Joint Conference on Artificial Intelligence, vol. 1, pp. 924–929 (1995)
8. Kraft, C.: User Experience Innovation. Springer, Dordrecht (2012)
9. Horvitz, E.: Principles of mixed-initiative user interfaces. In: Proceedings of the SIGCHI Conference on Human Factors in Computing Systems the CHI is the Limit - CHI 1999 (1999)
10. Nielsen, J.: Usability Engineering. Morgan Kaufmann, Amsterdam (2010)
11. Omicini, A., Ricci, A., Viroli, M.: Artifacts in the A&A meta-model for multi-agent systems. Auton. Agent. Multi-Agent Syst. **17**, 432–456 (2008)
12. Laurel, B.: The Art of Human-Computer Interface Design. Addison-Wesley, Boston (2007)
13. Maes, P.: Agents that reduce work and information overload. Commun. ACM **37**, 30–40 (1994)
14. Card, S.: The model human processor: a model for making engineering calculations of human performance. Proc. Hum. Factors Soc. Ann. Meet. **25**, 301–305 (1981)
15. Allen, J., Guinn, C., Horvtz, E.: Mixed-initiative interaction. IEEE Intell. Syst. **14**, 14–23 (1999)
16. Ferguson, G., Allen, J.: Mixed-initiative systems for collaborative problem solving. AI Mag. **28**, 23 (2007)
17. Salomon, G., Perkins, D., Globerson, T.: Partners in cognition: extending human intelligence with intelligent technologies. Educ. Res. **20**, 2–9 (1991)
18. Law, E., Roto, V., Hassenzahl, M., Vermeeren, A., Kort, J.: Understanding, scoping and defining user experience. In: Proceedings of the 27th International Conference on Human Factors in Computing Systems - CHI 2009 (2009)
19. Bevan, N.: Extending quality in use to provide a framework for usability measurement. In: Kurosu, M. (ed.) HCD 2009. LNCS, vol. 5619, pp. 13–22. Springer, Heidelberg (2009). https://doi.org/10.1007/978-3-642-02806-9_2
20. Hassenzahl, M., Tractinsky, N.: User experience - a research agenda. Behav. Inf. Technol. **25**, 91–97 (2006)

21. Gaver, B., Martin, H.: Alternatives. In: Proceedings of the SIGCHI Conference on Human Factors in Computing Systems - CHI 2000 (2000)
22. Anderson, J.: ACT: a simple theory of complex cognition. Am. Psychol. **51**, 355–365 (1996)
23. Woods, D., Hollnagel, E.: Joint cognitive systems. CRC, Taylor & Francis, Boca Raton, Fla (2006)
24. Woods, D.: Cognitive technologies: the design of joint human-machine cognitive systems. AI Mag. **6**, 86 (1985)
25. Robertson, I., Kortum, P.: The effect of cognitive fatigue on subjective usability scores. Proc. Hum. Factors Ergon. Soc. Ann. Meet. **61**, 1461–1465 (2017)
26. Walker, M., Litman, D., Kamm, C., Abella, A.: Evaluating spoken dialogue agents with PARADISE: two case studies. Comput. Speech Lang. **12**, 317–347 (1998)
27. Norman, D.: THE WAY I SEE IT Signifiers, not affordances. Interactions **15**, 18 (2008)
28. Pegram, D.A., St. Amant, R., Riedl, M.: An Approach to Visual Interaction in Mixed-Initiative Planning. American Association for Artificial Intelligence (1999)
29. Horvitz, E.: Uncertainty, action, and interaction: in pursuit of mixed-initiative computing. In: Intelligent Systems (1999)
30. Frøkjær, E., Hertzum, M., Hornbæk, K.: Measuring usability. In: Proceedings of the SIGCHI Conference on Human Factors in Computing Systems - CHI 2000 (2000)
31. Borkin, M., et al.: Beyond memorability: visualization recognition and recall. IEEE Trans. Visual Comput. Graph. **22**, 519–528 (2016)
32. Benyon, D., Murray, D.: Adaptive systems: from intelligent tutoring to autonomous agents. Knowl.-Based Syst. **6**, 197–219 (1993)
33. Norman, D., Nielsen, J.: The definition of user experience (UX). https://www.nngroup.com/articles/definition-user-experience/
34. Saeidi, H., Wagner, J., Wang, Y.: A mixed-initiative haptic teleoperation strategy for mobile robotic systems based on bidirectional computational trust analysis. IEEE Trans. Rob. **33**, 1500–1507 (2017)
35. Mekler, E., Hornbæk, K.: Momentary pleasure or lasting meaning? In: Proceedings of the 2016 CHI Conference on Human Factors in Computing Systems (2016)

Human Versus Machine and Human-Machine Teaming on Masked Language Modeling Tasks

Ming Qian[1(✉)] and Davis Qian[2]

[1] Pathfinders Translation and Interpretation Research, 513 Elan Hall Rd, Cary, USA
qianmi@pathfinders-transinterp.com
[2] School of Information Science, University of North Carolina, Chapel Hill, USA
davisq@live.unc.edu

Abstract. The objective of AI-based masked language modeling (MLM) is to mask one or more words in a sentence and have the Natural Language Processing (NLP) model identify the masked words given the other words (representing context) in a sentence. In this study, using real examples collected from an online translation study group, we identify multiple human strategies to perform masked language modeling tasks: looking up definitions; comparing/contrasting; relying on common sense and knowledge; relying on statistical properties of past experiences; building an augmented context (using a list of keywords); and using it on a web search engine. In terms of human versus machine performance, the MLM algorithm's performance is equal to the level of an average human expert, but it still cannot compete with the best human performance. The human experts' strengths are the awareness of global knowledge, deep understanding of concepts, events, public opinion, etc. The human experts' usual weaknesses, on the other hand, are the lack of domain knowledge and human biases. The machine's strength is its comprehensive and encompassing coverage gleaned by learning from a large corpus, so that it can sometimes fill human experts' knowledge gaps and correct human bias. But the machine could suffer from lack of true understanding and machine bias due to misleading statistical patterns. One common trait shared by human experts and the MLM algorithm is that they both can make decisions based on statistical observations. Therefore, it stands to reason that a human and machine can form a team to achieve better overall performance. In most cases, humans are not aware of their knowledge limitation or bias, so AI algorithm should take a proactive role in making suggestions, not a reactive role to be activated when human feels the need. In addition, it would be beneficial if the AI algorithm lists definition and sample usages of the word they suggest because humans need to be educated. The important skills demonstrated by human experts seem to be their ability to manipulate context for sensitivity analyses and/or the ability to gauge context-word interactions to understand the context. To improve human-machine teaming, it would be beneficial to incorporate human creativity into interface and interaction designs—humans can quickly input different context manipulation and word-context combinations, and the machine can provide quick feedback based on its extensive knowledge based from a large corpus. This teaming arrangement helps facilitate the joining of forces between human creativity and machine intelligence.

© Springer Nature Switzerland AG 2020
C. Stephanidis et al. (Eds.): HCII 2020, LNCS 12424, pp. 505–516, 2020.
https://doi.org/10.1007/978-3-030-60117-1_37

Keywords: Human-machine teaming · Human-machine interaction · Artificial intelligence · Masked language model · Language modeling · Human creation · Machine intelligence · Human-Machine collaboration · Natural Language Processing

1 Introduction

1.1 Masked Language Modeling

The objective of masked language modeling (MLM) is to mask one or more words in a sentence and have the Natural Language Processing (NLP) model identify those masked words given the other words (representing context) in a sentence [1]. By training the model with this objective, it can learn certain statistical properties of word sequences embedded in a training corpus. BERT is the first large transformer architecture to be trained using this masked language modeling task [2].

1.2 Human Versus Machine on Masked Language Modeling Task

As MLM tools (e.g. [3]) become widely available, it becomes possible to compare human performance and preferences with machine performance on predicting masked words in a sentence. The benefits of such comparisons are to identify human considerations (which are centered around using various strategies for achieving understanding, gathering evidence to support alternative understandings, and making the final selection) versus an AI algorithm's decisions based on statistical properties. By gaining insights on the pros and cons, we aim to find novel methods to improve human-machine teaming (HMT).

One group of professionals who are highly skilled in masked language modeling tasks are professional translators. For professional translators, word selection is of utmost importance. That is why professional translators are usually native speakers of the language they translate into for both idiomatic reasons and for the sake of precision and accuracy [4].

In this study, we used "word selection" examples, which are very similar to masked language modeling tasks, from an online translation study group to represent human performance and the masked language modeling online demo tool provided by the Allen Institute for AI (Ai2) to represent the machine performance.

1.3 Human-Machine Symbiosis and Human-Human Collaboration

Human-machine symbiosis [5] has been identified as one of the primary challenges of HCI research. The ideal vision of human-machine symbiosis is one where humans are coupled to machines in a harmonious way. To achieve this, related technology needs to exhibit characteristics typically associated with human behavior and intelligence [5].

In this study, we identify human strategies to perform masked language modeling task and define potential Human-Machine Interface (HCI) and Human-Machine Teaming (HMT) models that leverage the AI-based algorithm to augment human capability.

2   Methodologies

2.1   Translators' Study Group

Human translators practice in order to gain competency in understanding the source language and generating appropriate target language based on that understanding. One way for translators to improve their skills is to have a group dialog in which they: (1) explain/discuss their understanding of the source text and context; (2) explain/discuss their target language choices; (3) have a dialog/argument about differing opinions, with the goal of building a consensus. The treasure trove of information encoded in these explanations, discussions, and dialogs can be of great use for defining potential Human-machine interfaces and interactions.

We used a data set collected from an online translation study group. The group was composed of 32 members, of which 11 were American Translator Association (ATA) certificated translators (specializing in English to Chinese, or Chinese to English language pairs), and 9 members who either held graduate degrees in translation, had multiple years of experience working for well-respected translation companies, or had had experience translating published books. The goal of this study group was to improve translation skills and help the participants prepare for ATA certification exams. The format of the group study was as follows: every member translated an assigned piece, then all versions produced were put into a shared document where everybody could comment on the other members' results and a back and forth dialog could ensue from multiple comments on the same piece.

Ten examples, associated with extensive discussion, were selected in order to illustrate a variety of human strategies for making decisions on "masked" word selection.

2.2   Research Questions

We try to answer the following research questions (RQ) in this study:

(1)   RQ1: What are the typical human strategies to solve MLM task?
(2)   RQ2: By comparing the words chosen by human experts versus the words chosen by NLP/AI tool, what are the pros and cons of human decisions and machine decisions?
(3)   RQ3: How to design a human-machine teaming model, so a human and an AI algorithm can work together to augment the overall performance on the task?

3   Analysis Results and Discussions

3.1   Human Versus Machine on Masked Language Modeling Task

For the masked word in example 1, a direct translation from the original Chinese text is "capital market". But the translator who came back with this solution felt that this word was too abstract: obviously the money would come from some business entity or individual. Therefore, another translator suggested venture capital/capitalist because that would reflect a subset of the market and refer more specifically to an entity or person. Then a suggestion was made to use the word "investor" because it could refer

Table 1. Example 1: financial term

Sentence with masked word	Human decisions	Machine predictions
The startup invented cutting edge technologies and attracted a lot of money from [MASK]	capital market venture capital investor capitalist	23.6% investors 5.0% industry 4.6% China 3.8% entrepreneurs 3.6% abroad

to an organization (e.g. a VC company) or an individual, and the word had been used frequently in similar context. Therefore, a consensus was reached between multiple translators that the word "investor" was a good choice.

This also happened to be the top choice chosen by the AI tool.

In this example, the humans and machine both reached the same conclusion. The result was a tie. Human, like the transformer-based AI algorithm, can make decisions based on statistical properties (Table 1).

Table 2. Example 2: sci-fi

Sentence with masked word	Human decisions	Machine predictions
Perhaps you will never receive this letter, which I stored in the [MASK] of a bank and asked the bank to send to you on the 200th year after my death	safe safe box	55.5% vault 6.4% safe 5.2% basement 3.8% trunk 3.1% drawer

The context for example 2 was that a famous sci-fi writer wrote letter to his daughter who was just born and saved the letter in the bank so that the letter would be opened by his daughter 200 years later—under the assumption that some scientific breakthrough will happen to make humans live much longer. While the human experts settle on the word "safe box", the AI algorithm's top choice is "vault".

A bank vault is essentially a room that has been reinforced with steel and other protective devices, while a safe box could be free-standing and lightly protected. Therefore, for a letter waiting to be opened 200 years later, the machine makes a better choice than human experts (Table 2).

In example 3, human experts focused on the perspective of traveling and there were some discussions regarding the fact that Mr. Barclay was not just a tourist and that it should be emphasized that he was a "enthusiast" because he aimed to travel all around the world. With the relatively recent emergence of China's middle class, traveling around world has been regarded as a cool activity and travelers who visited many places around the world are envied.

The AI algorithm, on the other hand, focused on Mr. Barclay's expertise as a photographer.

Table 3. Example 3: traveling photographer

Sentence with masked word	Human decisions	Machine Predictions
The biggest wish of Luke Barclay, a 33-year-old British [MASK], was to travel to every corner of the world and to capture every fascinating scenery with his camera	tourist travel enthusiast	56.1% photographer 10.2% filmmaker 3.9% artist 2.9% journalist 2.3% cinematographer

In this example, the humans and machine reached complementary conclusions: the humans focused on the traveling and the machine focused on the craft. The result was a tie (Table 3).

Table 4. Example 4: sci-fi

Sentence with masked word	Human decisions	Machine predictions
I do not know how your generation did it - perhaps you edited the human genes and turned off the switch for aging and death, or perhaps your memory can be digitized, uploaded and downloaded, and the body has become merely the [MASK] of consciousness, something that can be replaced once worn out...	carrier vessel	14.6% object 6.5% product 4.7% result 2.9% center 2.4% shell

In example 4, we go back to the same sci-fi letter described in example 2. The author speculated possible ways humans could live longer—for example the body being able to be separated from consciousness. The human experts chose the words "carrier" or "vessel"—viewing the body as a kind of vehicle to carry the consciousness.

The AI algorithm chose the phrase "object of consciousness" which is a concept defined in Sartre's philosophical masterpiece "Being and Nothingness" [6], where he defines two types of reality which lie beyond our conscious experience: the being of the *object of consciousness* and that of consciousness itself. This philosophical term fits with the context very well.

In this example, the AI algorithm filled a knowledge gap of human experts and pointed to a concept that was both highly relevant to the context and unknown by human experts (Table 4).

In example 5, the AI algorithm chose relatively neutral words while the human experts rely on their cultural knowledge—Shanghai to China is the equivalent of New York to the US or Paris to Europe—to use stronger words.

Human selections are better than the choices made by the AI algorithm in this example (Table 5).

Example 6 comes from the piece of writing on the city of Shanghai's household registration policy. Shanghai was famous for its emerging industry and commercial development at the beginning of the 20th century. The masked text obviously refers to

Table 5. Example 5: city policy

Sentence with masked word	Human decisions	Machine predictions
The problem is that it is already questionable if a city, in the 21st century, has to use its Household Registration as a lure for talents. It is all the more bizarre when such a policy comes out of Shanghai, which [MASK] itself as the most modern metropolis of China	proclaim pride	22.2% sees 10.9% bills 10.4% describes 7.6% regards 4.7% views

Table 6. Example 6: city policy

Sentence with masked word	Human decisions	Machine predictions
Shanghai will not only embarrass itself in the eyes of developed countries, but also let down its own [MASK1] who first opened the port of Shanghai as a gateway to the world. Among those early [MASK2] of industry and commerce, how many came here for Shanghai's Household Registration? Did they even have a Shanghai Household Registration?	creators pioneers tycoons champions industrialists entrepreneurs	Mask 1 Predictions: 19.7% people 19.5% citizens 7.6% leaders 5.2% founders 3.5% merchants Mask 2 Predictions: 22.8% pioneers 12.6% leaders 6.5% giants 9% founders 2.7% men

the first-generation businessmen and industry tycoons who laid the foundation for this modern city.

Even though the AI algorithm chose some words that are the same as the human experts' choices, overall, given their understanding of the history of the city, human experts seem to come up with better choices in this example (Table 6).

Table 7. Example 7: AI commercialization

Sentence with masked word	Human decisions	Machine predictions
While we are pleasantly surprised by the initiatives taken by Tencent's Medical AI Lab, we must also recognize the multiple barriers that need to be crossed before medical AI can be successfully [MASK]. The first barrier is a technological one… The second barrier has to do with standards…	make… a reality commercialization put into practice	27.3% applied 20.4% used 16.8% implemented 9.0% deployed 2.9% developed

In example 7, the masked word refers to the commercialization of AI technology in the lab and transitioning them successfully into a sustainable product on the market. The human experts reached a consensus on the word "commercialization" after gaining some understanding of the context.

The AI algorithm was able to provide some sufficient answers like some human experts initially proposed. But, without the understanding built upon global context, the AI algorithm was unable to produce a solution as good as the human experts' consensus (Table 7).

Table 8. Example 8: western deception

Sentence with masked word	Human decisions	Machine predictions
The root cause of this terrible economic structure goes back to the collapse of the Soviet Union. Russia became a textbook example of how Western deception led to disastrous consequences Back in the 1990s, western [MASK] such as democracy and universal values still seemed enticing enough for Russia to buy into the promises of western powers - chiefly Britain and the US - and embark on an audacious experiment of all-out westernization	propaganda fanfare	37.7% values 23.4% concepts 12.6% ideals 7.5% ideas 4.2% principles

In example 8, the context is that the author believed that the Soviet Union was cheated by Western deception and chose to start with the experiment of all-out westernization. The human experts weighted their choices between the word "propaganda" and "fanfare" to emphasize the deception and empty promises.

The AI algorithm was able to provide some relevant words. But, without the understanding built upon the global context, the AI algorithm was unable to produce a solution as good as the human experts' consensus (Table 8).

Table 9. Example 9: industry revolution

Sentence with masked word	Human decisions	Machine predictions
The fifth scientific and industrial revolution will be a cross-integration of the scientific revolution, technological revolution, and industrial revolution. It will be a compounding technological and industrial revolution in a [MASK] manner, which would be significantly different from the previous four scientific and industrial revolutions	Complete comprehensive thorough all-encompassing full sense	8.0% unified 7.3% complex 6.7% new 6.5% similar 4.5% unique

In example 9, the masked word should reflect that the fifth revolution is a cross-integrated one. The human experts' solutions are reasonable.

On the other hand, the AI algorithm's top word "unified" provides a better answer than all the human experts because it reflects a cross-integration across science, technology and industry, indicating a unified phenomenon across all domains (Table 9).

Table 10. Example 10: international development project

Sentence with masked word	Human decisions	Machine predictions
The "One Belt, One Road" initiative has been an international sensation ever since its introduction in 2013. Projects based on the initiative have been [MASK] all over the world, attracting both domestic and foreign partners	Distributed Spread	14.5% launched 5.2% implemented 3.2% successful 2.8% undertaken 2.5% shown

In example 10, the human experts were impacted by the direct translation of the Chinese source text which indicated that those projects were widely distributed. Since human experts were aware of this global context, nearly all of them chose the word "distribute" or "spread".

The AI algorithm's top choice is the word "launched" which is a reasonable solution given the limited context it observed. The result was a tie (Table 10).

3.2 Discussion on Human Strategies

Several typical human strategies were identified based on the human experts' discussion content:

(1) Gaining understanding by looking up definitions and real usage examples from dictionaries, Wikipedia, and other linguistics sources. In example 1, one expert looked up the definition of "venture capital"—a form of private equity that investors provide to startup companies that have long-term growth potential but huge risks—and argued that this fits the context very well.

(2) Gaining understanding by comparing/contrasting alternative word choices using examples of candidate words in the specific application context. In the example 4, a human expert commented that "I had thought about using "carrier", but then I thought the carrier, a lot of times, could be associated with a virus, therefore I think maybe vessel is a better word.

(3) Relying on common sense and human knowledge. In example 1, the word "investor" is often used in the context of startup finance; in example 2, the bank has safe box; in example 8, the word to describe empty promise and deception is "propaganda".

(4) Relying on statistical properties based on past experiences (e.g. seeing this word used in this context very often). This is very similar to transformer-based AI algorithm.

(5) "Building an augmented context"—adding additional text based on understanding (making implicit context explicit) and using the augmented text to find the right word. Usually a human expert relies on a web search engine to find related text. The availability of MLM provides human experts one more useful tool for that purpose.

Discussion on Human Versus Machine. To compare the MLM algorithm's performance with human choices, we realize that there are two types of human performance: one where several human experts make their own independent decisions and some decisions are good and the others may not be so good, so we have to evaluate the average human performance. And one where the human experts discuss and analyze results to find the best solution that the collective group can achieve (an optimized human performance).

We found that in 8 out of 10 examples (with the exception of example 5 and 8), the MLM algorithm performs better than or equivalent to an average human expert. In addition, in 5 out of the 10 examples (example 1, 2, 3, 4, and 9), the MLM algorithm performed better than or equivalent to the optimized human performance.

Therefore, it is fair to say that the MLM algorithm's performance is equal to the level of an average human expert, but it still cannot compete with the best human performance.

Based on our analyses in Sect. 3.1, the human experts' strengths are the awareness of global knowledge (e.g. in examples 5 and 6, the awareness of the city's history which was not even discussed in the essay), deep understanding of public opinion (e.g. biased public opinion towards western deception in example 8) and business concepts (e.g. commercialization in example 7). The human experts' weaknesses, on the other hand, are the lack of domain knowledge (e.g. vault versus safe-box in example 2 and philosophy concept in example 4), and human biases towards per-existing cultural stereotypes (e.g. choosing the word tourist in example 3).

The machine's strength is its comprehensive and encompassing coverage by learning from a large corpus, so that sometimes it can fill human experts' knowledge gap and correct human bias. At the same time, the machine's usual weaknesses are lack of true understanding and machine biases due to misleading statistical patterns.

One common trait shared by human experts and the MLM algorithm is that they both can make decisions based on statistical observations. In example 1, the human expert reached the same conclusion as the MLM algorithm because the word "investor" was frequently used in this context.

3.3 Discussion on Human-Machine Teaming

The AI algorithm's main strength is to complement human experts on domain knowledge and human biases. In some cases, human experts are aware of their ignorance or bias, but in most cases, they are not aware of their knowledge limitation or bias (see examples 1, 2, 3, 4, and 9 in which the AI algorithm provided much better solutions while none of the human experts were aware of the possibilities suggested by the machine). Therefore, the AI algorithm should take a more proactive role in making suggestions, not a reactive role to be activated when a human feels the need. In addition, it would be beneficial if the AI algorithm lists definition and sample usages of the word it suggests (e.g. the philosophy concept "object of consciousness" listed in example 4) because they need to be educated.

The important skills demonstrated by human experts seem to be their ability to manipulate context for sensitivity analyses (evaluating multiple examples and comparing the "distances" between the contexts featured in the examples and the specific context under study) and/or the ability to gauge context-word interactions to understand the context (evaluating the impacts of inserting different words into the specific context, and comparing/contrasting their impacts). To improve human-machine teaming, it would be beneficial to incorporate human creativity into interface and interaction designs—humans can quickly input different context manipulation and word-context combinations, and the machine can provide quick feedback based on its extensive knowledge based from a large corpus. It is a process in which human and machine not only complement but also stimulate each other. This teaming arrangement helps facilitate the joining of forces between human creativity and machine intelligence.

Since the AI algorithm relies on the context to find the right solution, richer context can impose further constraints and implications for the algorithm. With the human in the loop, the human experts can use the following tactics to re-configure the context: (1) include additional highly relevant context (e.g. sentences before and after the sentence for the MLM task); (2) remove less relevant context; (3) adding customized context solely for the purpose of building a contextualized environment for the algorithm even though the customized context might not need to be kept for the final draft. For example, in examples 5 and 6, a human expert who is more familiar with the city history can add a context-building sentence such as "The most famous characters during the heyday of old Shanghai were successful businessmen and knowledgeable intellectuals who set the foundation for the modern city". And in example 8, a context-building sentence such as "the majority of Russia citizens felt cheated by western promise" can be added. The added

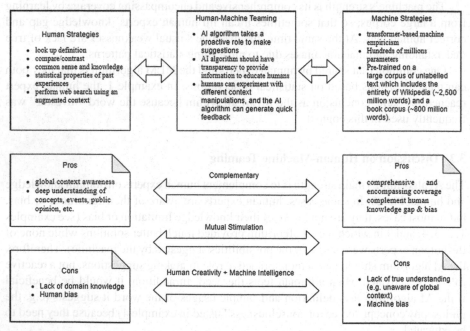

Fig. 1. Human and machine (AI algorithm) team can be designed to complement each other, stimulate each other, so that human creativity can be combined with machine intelligence to achieve overall superior performance.

context-building sentences re-shape the overall context under the guidance of human knowledge, leading to better prediction on masked words. The machine suggestions based on the enriched context can then be feedbacked to the human for reference (Fig. 1).

4   Conclusion

Human-machine symbiosis has been identified as one of the primary challenges of HCI research. The ideal vision of human-machine symbiosis is one where humans are coupled to machines in a harmonious way.

In this study, using real examples collected from an online translation study group, we identify multiple human strategies to perform a masked language modeling task: looking up definitions; comparing/contrasting; relying on common sense and past knowledge; relying on statistical properties of past experiences; building an augmented context and using it on a web search engine.

In terms of human versus machine performance, the MLM algorithm's performance is equal to the level of an average human expert, but it still cannot compete with the best human performance. The human experts' strengths are their awareness of global knowledge, deep understanding of concepts, events and public opinion. The human experts' weaknesses, on the other hand, are their lack of domain knowledge and human biases. The machine's strength is its comprehensive and encompassing coverage by learning from a large corpus, so that it can sometimes fill human experts' knowledge gap and correct human bias. One common trait shared by human experts and the MLM algorithm is that they both can make decisions based on statistical observations.

Human and machine can form a team to achieve better overall performance. In most cases, humans are not aware of their knowledge limitation or bias, so the AI algorithm should take a more proactive role to make suggestions, not a reactive role to be activated when a human feels the need. In addition, it will be beneficial if the AI algorithm lists definition and sample usages of the word they suggest because humans need to be educated. The important skills demonstrated by human experts seem to be their ability to manipulate context for sensitivity analyses and/or their ability to gauge context-word interactions to understand the context. To improve human-machine teaming, it would be beneficial to incorporate human creativity into interface and interaction designs—humans should be able to quickly input different context manipulation and word-context combinations, and the machine can provide quick feedback based on its extensive knowledge based from a large corpus. This teaming arrangement helps facilitate the joining of forces between human creativity and machine intelligence.

References

1. Wang, C., Li, M., L., Smola, A.J.: Language Models with Transformers (2019). https://arxiv.org/pdf/1904.09408.pdf
2. Devlin, J., Chang, M.W., Lee, K., Toutanova, K.: BERT: Pre-training of Deep Bidirectional Transformers for Language Understanding (2018). https://arxiv.org/abs/1810.04805
3. Masked language modeling demo, AllenNLP, Allen Institute for AI. https://demo.allennlp.org/
4. Virginie Ségard, Professional Translators: an Endangered Species (2009). http://www.cttic.org/Opinions/VSegard0910_EN.pdf

5. Stephanidis, C.C., et al.: Seven HCI Grand Challenges. Int. J. HCI **35**(14), 1229–1269 (2019). https://doi.org/10.1080/10447318.2019.1619259
6. Sartre, J.P.: Being and Nothingness: An Essay on Phenomenological Ontology. Editions Gallimard, Paris (1943)

Using Artificial Intelligence to Predict Academic Performance

Arsénio Reis$^{(\boxtimes)}$ ⓘ, Tânia Rocha ⓘ, Paulo Martins ⓘ, and João Barroso ⓘ

INESC TEC, University of Trás-os-Montes and Alto Douro, Vila Real, Portugal
{ars,trocha,pmartins,jbarroso}@utad.pt

Abstract. The academic performance of a higher education student can be affected by several factors and in most cases Higher Education Institutions (HEI) have programs to intervene, prevent failure or students dropping out. These include student tutoring, mentoring, recovery classes, summer school, etc. Being able to identify the borderline cases is extremely important for planning and intervening in time. This position paper reports on an ongoing project, being developed at the University of Trás-os-Montes e Alto Douro (UTAD), which uses the students' data and artificial intelligence algorithms to create models and predict the performance of students and classes. The main objective of the IA.EDU project is to research the usage of data, artificial intelligence and data science to create artificial intelligence solutions, including models and applications, to provide predictive information that can contribute to the increase in students' academic success and a reduction in the dropout rate, by making it possible to act proactively with the students at risk, course directors and course designers.

Keywords: Artificial intelligence · Data science · Higher education · Prediction and inference · Academic performance

1 State of the Art

The problem of student failure and students dropping out have always been a major concern for educators and educational institutions. In higher education, some very distinct approaches have been adopted, addressing different aspects of the problem. Two major fields for action are establishing a close contact with the most fragile students and addressing the design of the graduation curriculum. The close contact with the most susceptible students, most frequently takes the form of personalized tutoring, which is a very time- and resource-demanding solution, as it requires tutoring time provided by a properly qualified professor. The redesigning of the graduation curriculum might be another solution, in cases where an educational offer deficit is identified. In both cases, a major factor for success is the correct identification of the problem as early as possible. In fact, the most desirable solution would be to predict the problem from the available data.

To be able to accurately predict students' success or whether they will dropout might be considered a holy grail, although with the current research on the application of

© Springer Nature Switzerland AG 2020
C. Stephanidis et al. (Eds.): HCII 2020, LNCS 12424, pp. 517–526, 2020.
https://doi.org/10.1007/978-3-030-60117-1_38

artificial intelligence and data science, combined with the existence of large amounts of data, is becoming a more attainable endeavor.

Academic success and dropout rates have been a research theme for some time. Kin Fun et al. addressed the problem of students dropping out of engineering schools and their academic performance prediction [1]. They concluded that most of the publications on performance prediction and data mining were exclusively targeted at e-learning and tutoring, without any specific work targeted at performance predictors based on a student's academic record. Good examples of this approach are Nghe et al. [3], who use decision trees and Baysian Network algorithms to predict a student's third-year GPA score by using the student's second year record, as well as Azmi et al. [2] who use similar techniques to predict and classify students in various categories of academic performance. Both cases lack the identification of relevant predictors of success. Kin Fun et al. developed a methodology to collect and prepare data for further analysis and used Principal Component Analysis (PCA) [4] to identify the important features that have larger impacts on the dataset. Thus, they identify the features with the largest impact on student performance or grade.

In a similar context as the one for this project's proposal, Plagge [6] researched the use of Artificial Neural Networks (ANNs) to predict first year students' retention rates at Columbus State University's Information Technology department. He used a large dataset ranging from 2005 to 2011 and concluded that the overall accuracy was high when including the first and second semesters worth of data and dropped significantly when using only one semester of data. He achieved an overall prediction accuracy of 75% by researching more complex learning algorithms and better training strategies with different network designs. The machine learning techniques seem promising [7–9] and have also been used by Wongkhamdi et al. in [10]. To further explore the machine learning technique for student retention management, Dele [9] conducted a comparative analysis using five years of institutional data along with several datamining techniques and developed analytical models to predict and to explain the reasons behind freshmen students' attrition. He used the popular data mining methodology Cross Industry Standard Process for Data Mining (CRISP-DM) as a systematic and structured way of conducting data mining studies and assure accurate and reliable results. The study compared four classification methods (neural networks, decision trees, support vector machines and logistic regression), together with three ensemble techniques (bagging, busting and information fusion). His conclusion confirmed other studies and found machine learning methods to be superior to statistical methods for being less constrained by assumptions and providing better prediction results [13–17]. In the broader sense, Dele also concludes that the datamining techniques performed better as ensembles and the sensitivity analysis of the models revealed that the educational and financial variables were the most relevant predictors. These conclusions are in line with other authors from the social sciences fields, e.g., Astin and Tinto [11, 12], who declare that interactions with colleagues, faculty and staff are important factors for success. Tinto [12] considers that the most important factors in students dropping out include academic difficulty, adjustment problems, lack of clear academic and career goals, uncertainty, lack of commitment, poor integration within the college community, incongruence, and isolation. Therefore, better soft skills and better student integration can have a great impact on academic success, especially on the transition year following high school.

Using a different approach, Márquez-Vera et al. [5] used genetic programming to predict student failure at school, considering the high dimensional and imbalanced data. Their work used real data of about 670 high school students from Zacatecas, Mexico, and proposed a genetic programming algorithm and different data mining approaches to solve the problems of imbalanced and high dimensionality data. They selected the best attributes to resolve the problem of high dimensionality and evaluated a genetic programming model versus different white box techniques to obtain both more comprehensible and accurate classification rules. Their work is particularly interesting as they have carried out several experiments using real data from high school students and applied different classification approaches to predict the academic status or final student performance at the end of the course. They have shown that some approaches, e.g., selecting the best attributes, cost-sensitive classification, and data balancing can be very useful to improve the overall accuracy.

2 The AI.EDU (EDU.IA) Project

2.1 Inception

The AI.EDU project concept came as way to address academic failure and dropout rates, by increasing the information to students and academic staff, so that students and staff can act as early as possible.

The University of Trás-os-Montes and Alto Douro (UTAD) has always invested a great deal of effort to have properly suited information systems that address the problems of academic management [18–20]. UTAD owns detailed data of the last 15 years regarding students, courses, teaching, and research, and academic failure and student dropout rates are very important factors for the academic community (students, teachers and institutions). These factors motivated the development of a project using the last 15 years of data from UTAD and making usage of advanced techniques of artificial intelligence and data science to create models, algorithms and software prototypes able to infer and predict critical points in the academic performance and development of the academic record of students.

The main objective is to research the usage of data, artificial intelligence and data science to create artificial intelligence solutions, including models and applications, to provide predictive information that can contribute to the increase in students' academic success and a reduction of the dropout rates, by allowing for the university to act proactively with the students at risk, course directors and course designers.

The project proposal includes two components, which are listed below:

- The research and assessment of the most suitable artificial intelligence approaches to adopt (neural networks, Baysian networks, genetic algorithms, support vector machines, etc.); the development of a full functioning prototype of an informatics system, composed of the following: a normalized and anonymized database (AI.Edu.Store), with all the information imported and consolidated from the several institutional data sources; a nuclear module of artificial intelligence (AI.Edu.Core) to provide software services with the predictive artificial intelligence and data analysis models; a set of applications prototypes to demonstrate and assess the use of the algorithms and methods, researched and implemented in the AI.Edu.Core module, in the context of virtual assistance to students, course directors and course designers.

● The creation of an artificial intelligence platform to predict academic performance will enable the university to plan and act preventively before the failure or dropping out occurs. The creation of models and algorithms will identify and use patterns from the previous years' data, to be identified and used by students and academic decision makers, who will be able to act.

2.2 The Methods

The methods will address the data, the AI and DS algorithms and methods, and the user software prototypes.

The Data. Regarding the data, a central date storage will be created, where all the existing data will be collected, consolidated and anonymized. This storage will be a software module (AI.Edu.Datastore) in the form a relational database. The datastore will have two distinct data sets, one for model training and another one for testing, validation and accuracy measurement.

The AI and DS Algorithms and Methods. The AI and DS algorithms and methods will include the most commonly used ones in other prediction scenarios and the most researched in the literature. Some of the literature review identifies artificial neural networks and machine learning as superior to statistical prediction for academic performance prediction, but we will research both, as most of the literature refers to isolated and limited cases. The research will be based on machine learning, using anomaly detection, decision trees and association rules approaches. Regarding the models, the artificial neural networks (ANNs) and the Bayesian networks will be considered as the two most promising models, but Support vector machines (SVM) and Genetic algorithms will also be considered.

The learning algorithm will be of the supervised and semi-supervised learning, for which we will have two distinct data sets to be able to train and test independently. In terms of software components, we will develop a core module (AI.Edu.Core) with the software implementation of the AI and DS prediction features.

User Software Prototypes. The software prototypes will be developed as mobile applications that will use the software features of AI.Edu.Core to provide contextual predictive information to students, course directors and course designers.

2.3 System Architecture

The system architecture is presented in Fig. 1 and includes the following other main elements: the data sources (databases, files and user directory); the main data repository AI.Edu.Store, with all the consolidated and anonymized data; the AI.Edu.Core software component implementing the AI and DS algorithms and methods, provided to the applications as software services; and the three application prototypes targeted at individual students – the AI.Edu.VirtualTutor, the AI.Edu.Director, targeted at course directors, and the AI.Edu.Architect, targeted for Course designers.

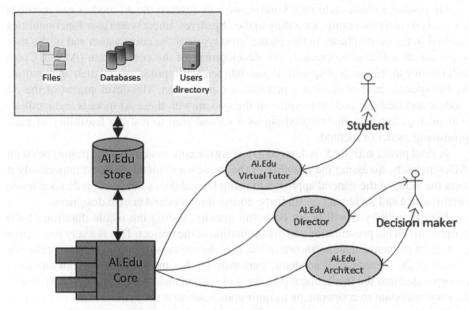

Fig. 1. System architecture and elements.

2.4 Project Plan

Artificial Intelligence (AI) and Data Science (DS) are well established research fields that in last years have gathered attention due to their applications in several areas of people and organizations' daily lives. This is particularly true regarding the system's features related to suggestion and prediction, e.g., shopping suggestion, route predictions, etc. This recent success is greatly dependent on the combination of algorithms and methods with large enough amounts of data.

In this project we will research the combination of the UTAD's 15 years of student data and the most promising AI and DS methods, with the main objective of predicting students' academic performance, by using that information to enhance the decisions of the individual students, the course directors and the course designers. The ultimate goal is to have fewer students failing or dropping out.

To develop the project, we intent to carry out 6 activities, grouped in three phases. The first phase constitutes of two initial short activities, to assess and characterize the problem, the objectives and the impact of the proposed solutions, as well as to make an inventory of data and its quality and quantity. Although these activities have been already partially executed to create this project proposal, it will be necessary to undertake a deeper approach at the start of the project as the results will be the basis for the project development. At the end of this first phase, there should a clear perspective of which users (students, course coordinator and course designer) functionalities need to be researched and developed for the system's core and final prototypes, as well as exactly which data can we used to develop and train the AI models.

On a second phase, activities 3 and 4, we will develop the AI models and methods for analysis and processing, according to the objectives, impacts and user functionalities defined in the initial phase. In this phase, prototypes of the core system and of the user applications will also be created. The development of the core system (AI.Edu.Core) will include the research of several AI and data science approaches and their applications in this specific case of academic performance prediction. The development of the AI models and methods and prototyping of the system with these AI models and methods will go together with the prototyping as a second step to test the feasibility of each promising model or method.

A final phase, activity 5, is devoted to testing the core system and the prototypes with different users, assessing the usability of the models and methods. Most importantly it tests the value of the general approach to using IA and data science to predict academic performance and its impact on students, course directors and course designers.

Finally, activity 6 will be an on-going activity, lasting the whole duration of the project, involving presentation and dissemination of the project. This is a very innovative project in the sense that, as shown in the literature review, there is plenty of research regarding the prediction of academic performance, but the solutions are not currently incorporated into the institutional processes of student and course' management. It will be very important to cooperate on a continuous basis with the general academia and the AI research community in order to understand how to best take the step of going from theoretical solutions to practical and useful solutions.

The project plan is organized in seven activities as follows.

Activity 1 - Assessment and characterization of the problem, the objectives and the impact of the proposed solutions

In this activity, the initial project configuration will be developed, establishing the domain in which the project will be developed, as well as the process to manage uncertainty and risk at the earliest stage, which is very important due to the innovative research and application objectives.

Objectives
- To establish the problem domain and a resolution proposal.

Tasks
- To create a user's group on the areas of software, student tutoring and course management;
- To coordinate the project actions with the UTAD's Ethic Committee and Data Protection Officer, in order to ensure legal and ethical compliance.

Results
- A project advisory user's group;
- The positive opinion of the Ethic Committee and Data Protection Officer.

Activity 2 –Data inventory and preparation. UTAD owns a large quantity of data (over 15 years), regarding students and their academic performance in the courses, which will be used to create and train the AI models and algorithms. In this activity the datastore in which the data will be collected, consolidated and anonymized will be created.

Objectives
- To identify and diagnose the data sources, including files, databases, and users' directories;
- To assess the available data, the formats and quality, and the methods for normalization, consolidation and anonymization;
- To build the database corresponding to the AI.Edu.Store element.

Tasks
- Assessment and audit of the data quality and quantity;
- Design and implementation of the relational database, represented by the element IA.Edu.Store in the system's architecture.

Results
- A list of the data sources and their formats;
- A report regarding the data quantity and quality;
- A relational database containing all the academic data, teaching and research, comprising the last 15 years.

Activity 3 – Development of the models and methods for analysis and processing. In this activity, several artificial intelligence (IA) and Data Science (DS) approaches and models will be researched and tested, including the following: machine learning; the anomaly detection, decision trees and association rules approaches; and the models using artificial neural networks (ANNs), Bayesian networks, Support vector machines (SVM), and Genetic algorithms. The learning algorithm will be of the supervised and semi-supervised learning, for which we will have two distinct data sets to be able to train and test independently.

Objectives
- To identify and research the AI and DS techniques models and algorithms to use and that best suit the prediction requirements for the users' applications.

Tasks
- To design and train the predictive models of academic performance, using distinct approaches and techniques;
- To evaluate the predictions and select the most accurate ones to implement in the AI.Edu.Core element.

Results
- Selection of the best models and AI approaches;
- The implementation of the AI.Edu.Core element.

Activity 4 – Prototyping of the systems with the AI models and methods. In this activity the full functional prototypes of the prediction platform (the AI.Edu.Core element) and the user applications will be developed. The most innovative aspect of this project is the AI.Edu.Core element, which is an inference and prediction software engine, containing models and algorithms modeling academic trajectories and the critical points, trained with the data from the AI.Edu.Store element. This prediction platform will provide software prediction services to the user applications. The full functional prototypes of the user applications to be developed in this task are the Virtual Tutor for students and the Director and Architect for academic decision makers.

Objectives
- To develop full functional prototypes of the prediction platform (the AI.Edu.Core element) and the user applications.

Tasks
- To develop the full functional prototype of the prediction platform (the AI.Edu.Core);
- To develop the full functional prototype of the Virtual Tutor user application;
- To develop the full functional prototype of the Director user application;
- To develop the full functional prototype of the Architect user application.

Results
- The software developed according to the Tasks.

Activity 5 – Prototype testing. In this activity tests will be conducted to evaluate the prototypes. There will be different types of tests, carried out by different types of users, to assess the overall impact of the system, usability, efficiency, efficacy, and user satisfaction. It will also be presented to a group of researchers, specialists in the field artificial intelligence, to discuss the quality and accuracy of the predictions and prediction techniques.

The tests will be carried during the development cycles, so it may be possible to integrate the results into the following cycle.

Objectives
- To test the prototypes of the prediction platform and the user applications by different types of users and by artificial intelligence specialists.

Tasks
- Tests of the application prototypes with final users;
- Presentation and tests of the system with AI specialists.

Results
- Reports of the tests and Scientific papers.

Activity 6 – Systems deployment. This activity is a production deployment activity in which the successful models and applications will be deployed to the end users.

Activity 7 – Presentation of results and dissemination. Because this is a very special research project due to its innovative approach of applying AI in the context of assessing the performance of students and organizations, we will disseminate the concept and objectives of the project from the beginning, in order to include the different types of users and have their input in the different project phases.

We will use the science and research dissemination channels, e.g., conferences, journals, symposiums, books, etc. to present and discuss the project results with peers. We will also work with students to include the project theme in their own academic activities, e.g., Msc or Phd work and thesis. In addition, we will disseminate the project to other stakeholders, e.g., other institutions, academic management events, etc.

Objectives
- To include the different academic stakeholders, whose opinion is important for the different phases of the project;
- To disseminate the project results in the scientific community;
- To include the project in the research agenda of Msc and Phd students.

Results
- Publication in scientific journals and conferences;
- Inclusion of the project's work on Msc or Phd thesis;
- Publication of news in general communication media.

3   Conclusion

The project is in its initial stages and in the next year we expect to gain greater knowledge of how to use data science and AI to effectively address the problems related to academic performance, as well as to create a tool that goes beyond the scientific validation and impacts on the real world of academic management. The results of the project should be transferable to other academic scenarios where they might even be more relevant, e.g., secondary education, etc.

Acknowledgements. This work was supported by Project "SAMA EDU.IA", operation number: POCI-05-5762-FSE-000199, financed by the Program COMPETE 2020, Portugal 2020.

References

1. Li, K.F., Rusk, D., Song, F.: Predicting student academic performance. In 2013 Seventh International Conference on Complex, Intelligent, and Software Intensive Systems, (pp. 27–33). IEEE
2. Azmi, M., Paris, I.: Academic performance prediction based on voting technique. In: IEEE International Conference on Communication Software and Networks, pp. 24–27 (2011)
3. Nghe, N.T., Janecek, P., Haddawy, P.: A comparative analysis of techniques for predicting academic performance. In: 37th ASEE/IEEE Frontiers in Education Conference, pp. T2G 7–12 (2007)
4. Jackson, J.E.: A User's Guide to Principal Components. Wiley (2003)

5. Márquez-Vera, C., Cano, A., Romero, C., et al.: Appl. Intell. **38**, 315 (2013). https://doi.org/10.1007/s10489-012-0374-8
6. Plagge, M.: Using artificial neural networks to predict first-year traditional students second year retention rates. In: Proceedings of the 51st ACM Southeast Conference, p. 17. ACM, April 2013
7. Barker, K. et al.: Learning from student data. In: Proceedings of the 2004 IEEE Systems and Information Engineering Design Symposium, pp. 79–86 (2004)
8. Bogard, M., et al.: A comparison of empirical models for predicting student retention. White Paper. Office of Institutional Research, Western Kentucky University (2011)
9. Delen, D.: A comparative analysis of machine learning techniques for student retention management. Decis. Support Syst. **49**(4), 498–506 (2010)
10. Wongkhamdi, T., Seresangtakul, P.: A comparison of classical discriminant analysis and artificial neural networks in predicting student graduation outcomes. In: Proceedings of the Second International Conference on Knowledge and Smart Technologies (Chonburi, 2010), pp. 29–34 (2010)
11. Astin, A.W.: What matters in college: four critical years revisited. Liberal Educ. **4**, 4 (1993)
12. Tinto, V.: Leaving College: Rethinking the Causes and Cures of Student Attrition, p. 5801. University of Chicago Press, Ellis Avenue (1987)
13. Delen, D., Walker, G., Kadam, A.: Predicting breast cancer survivability: a comparison of three data mining methods. Artif. Intell. Med. **34**(2), 113–127 (2004)
14. Delen, D., Sharda, R., Kumar, P.: Movie forecast guru: a web-based DSS for Hollywood managers. Decis. Support Syst. **43**(4), 1151–1170 (2007)
15. Kiang, M.Y.: A comparative assessment of classification algorithms. Decis. Support Syst. **35**, 441–454 (2003)
16. Li, X., Nsofor, G.C., Song, L.: A comparative analysis of predictive data mining techniques. Int. J. Rapid Manuf. **1**(2), 150–172 (2009)
17. Sharda, R., Delen, D.: Predicting box-office success of motion pictures with neural networks. Expert Syst. Appl. **30**(2), 243–254 (2006)
18. Reis, A., Martins, P., Borges, J., Sousa, A., Rocha, T., Barroso, J.: Supporting accessibility in higher education information systems: a 2016 update. In: Antona, M., Stephanidis, C. (eds.) UAHCI 2017. LNCS, vol. 10277, pp. 227–237. Springer, Cham (2017). https://doi.org/10.1007/978-3-319-58706-6_19
19. Borges, J., Justino, E., Gonçalves, P., Barroso, J., Reis, A.: Scholarship management at the University of Trás-os-Montes and Alto Douro: an update to the current ecosystem. In: Rocha, Á., Correia, A.M., Adeli, H., Reis, L.P., Costanzo, S. (eds.) WorldCIST 2017. AISC, vol. 569, pp. 790–796. Springer, Cham (2017). https://doi.org/10.1007/978-3-319-56535-4_77
20. Reis, A., Martins, M., Martins, P., Sousa, J., Barroso, J.: Telepresence robots in the classroom: the state-of-the-art and a proposal for a telepresence service for higher education. In: Tsitouridou, M., A. Diniz, J., Mikropoulos, Tassos A. (eds.) TECH-EDU 2018. CCIS, vol. 993, pp. 539–550. Springer, Cham (2019). https://doi.org/10.1007/978-3-030-20954-4_41

Why Did the Robot Cross the Road?

A User Study of Explanation in Human-Robot Interaction

Zachary Taschdjian[1,2(✉)]

[1] Georgia Institute of Technology, Atlanta, GA 30332, USA
ztaschdjian@gatech.edu
[2] H2O.ai, Mountain View, CA 94043, USA

Abstract. This work documents a pilot user study evaluating the effectiveness of contrastive, causal and example explanations in supporting human understanding of AI in a hypothetical commonplace human-robot interaction (HRI) scenario. In doing so, this work situates "explainable AI" (XAI) in the context of the social sciences and suggests that HRI explanations are improved when informed by the social sciences.

Keywords: Explainable AI · Human-robot interaction · HCI

1 Introduction

The relevance of AI in our society is self-evident. With relevance comes ubiquity and with ubiquity come magnified consequences. Couple this with the fact that AI/ML is generally poorly understood by the public and there's a strong possibility of accidental misuse/misinterpretation. Consider the following example. A physicians AI-enabled tool tells her that a patient with pneumonia AND asthma is LESS likely to die than a similar, non-asthmatic patient. This seems counter-intuitive; the presence of asthma suggests a stronger likelihood of a negative outcome. But as Caruana et al. found, this is not the case. Asthmatic patients with pneumonia are admitted directly to the intensive care unit and receive aggressive treatment, thus explaining the counter-intuitive finding (Caruana et al. 2015). In this case, a more accurate neural net was rejected in favor of a less accurate rule-based model because physicians could understand how the rule-based model worked. Without explainability this finding could easily be dismissed as model error likely leading to the AI tool not being adopted in mission critical environments like hospitals.[1] We contend that this is fundamentally a problem of education and knowledge acquisition. Blackbox algorithms are not architected with these needs in mind.

Current AI systems are often approached from a technical perspective leading to engineering-centric explanations created by and for AI experts. Despite XAI's popularity, it's extremely easy to get wrong (Kozyrkov 2018). While explainability, interpretability and causation are relatively new to AI, they are not new concepts. Explanation and

---

[1] The terms "explainable" and "interpretable" are used interchangeably despite their slightly differing meanings.

© Springer Nature Switzerland AG 2020
C. Stephanidis et al. (Eds.): HCII 2020, LNCS 12424, pp. 527–537, 2020.
https://doi.org/10.1007/978-3-030-60117-1_39

causation can be traced back to Aristotle and have been instrumental in philosophy in the intervening millennia. The unmet need for XAI is easily documented for example through DoD and NSF funding opportunities (Gunning 2019), the popular press (Kuang 2017) and in philosophy (Miller 2018), computer science (Kim 2015), cognitive psychology (Moreno and Mayer 2007) and doubtless others.[2] There is also evidence that the problem of AI model opacity (the inverse of XAI) has real social impacts for example in loan origination, pre-trial sentencing, fake news/propaganda and healthcare (as noted above). Could an interdisciplinary approach drawing from these areas lead to more understandable, ethical and effective AI? This study is premised on the answer being "yes".

The study presented here is an attempt to engage these disciplines in the XAI dialogue beyond the theoretical. This work draws on Miller's summary of explanations. Miller relates three types of explanation; contrastive (i.e. "A and not B"), causal (i.e. "A caused B; without A, B would not occur") and examples (i.e. "A is like B, C, D") (Miller 2018). Study 2 presented here compares these three types of explanations using three modes of explanation; narrative text, iconographic images and data charts. The contribution of this work is to evaluate the hypothesis that one of these combinations will provide a "better" explanation than others. A possible implication of this is that one or more of these combinations better fits the users mental model given the context of the human-robot interaction in the test.

The remainder of this paper will first outline related prior work in the contributing disciplines and preparatory work. It will then describe the user study. Finally, it will discuss the study and present findings and opportunities for improvement and future work in this area.

1.1 Related Work

As noted above, XAI is inherently interdisciplinary. While there's overlap between the disciplines, related work can be organized by discipline for clarity and structure. This is not a comprehensive list of related work but represents the breadth of issues, questions and history of the contributing disciplines.

1.2 Prior Work in Philosophy

Much of the work in philosophy falls into philosophy of mind, formal epistemology and causation but it can be traced back as far as Aristotle's four causes of action (i.e. ways of answering "why" questions) (Reece 2019). David Hume also did significant work in causation and epistemology some 2000 years later. He believed that just because two events seem to be conjoined there's no evidence that one causes another. In short, that no amount of data ever justifies belief. This leads Hume to dismiss all inductive inference, leading to his famous skepticism that we can ever truly know anything. Others have built on Hume's approach in more pragmatic ways. Popper, for example, suggests an approach built on refutation of theories (Parusniková 2019) More recently, researchers

---

[2] Each of these references is an example. This is not intended to be a comprehensive list.

have looked at ways of axiomatizing epistemology in the context of AI systems (Vasconcelos et al. 2018), causal discovery algorithms (Malinsky et al. 2017) and structural equation modeling approaches (Halpern 2005), among others. It's important to note that causation is not the same as explanation although they are related.

1.3 Prior Work in Computer Science

Computer science has had an obvious fascination with XAI. Explanation was at the heart of Seymour Papert's Learning and Epistemology group at the MIT Media Lab for example (Papert 1988). Some early interest in XAI came out of work in machine translation systems and later expert systems. 4 XAI has had a renaissance in the last ~5 years. This takes many directions ranging from arguments for inherently interpretable models (Rudin 2019) to a more pragmatic understanding of explainability (Paez 2019) to using XAI for model debugging (Winikoff 2017). There has also been some relevant work in HCI. Grudin for example draws a clear connection between AI and HCI as early as 2009 (Grudin 2009) and more recently Google (among others) has produced guidelines for HCI practitioners working with AI (Google n.d.). Springer, et al. take on model explainability and black box algorithms directly demonstrating that users put unfounded trust in systems perceived to be "intelligent" (Springer et al. 2017).

1.4 Prior Work in Cognitive Psychology

Cognitive psychology has perhaps the most direct relevance to the educational aspects of XAI. A great deal of research has gone into theories of knowledge acquisition and construction. One of the most transformational was Piaget's application of Maria Montessori's work to develop the concept of "constructivism". This empirical approach to pragmatic knowledge acquisition (and accommodation) has had deep impact not just on developmental psychology but on a range of other disciplines. Li et al., operationalized constructivism in the context of predictive analytics (Li et al. 2017). While Piaget's work was foundational, Gopnick has contributed of more recent work building on Piaget's ideas including a useful survey of post-Piaget developments (Gopnick 1996). Another relevant concept from the cognitive psych field is mental models; the idea that humans represent knowledge as mental representations such as scripts. Mental models are relevant to the ed tech agenda because their construction and transference are core to understanding in AI. Johnson-Laird did much of the formative work in this area (Johnson-Laird 2010). Jonnassen (among others) also made important contributions around mental models in the context of computer supported collaborative learning (Jonnassen 1995).

2 Methodology

2.1 Preparatory Work with Data Scientists

Preparatory work included a series of between-subjects, think-aloud interviews with professional data scientists and developers. Interviews were conducted with developers and data scientists who are colleagues of the author at H2O.ai. The goal of this work was to identify industry best-practices, or at least a rough heuristic of the mental model(s) professional data scientists employ when interpreting and explaining AI predictions.

Additionally, the study evaluated whether the tool/user interface frames or constrains explanation selection. An affirmation that tool selection and interface constrain and/or frame explanation selection would imply that the user's mental model of the problem is similarly framed and/or constrained by the tool which has relevance for both designers and trainers of such systems. This is somewhat akin to bias caused by leading questions; the explanation type (as implemented in a user interface) frames the users approach to the problem. This is captured by the adage that when the only tool one has is a hammer, every problem starts looking like a nail. It seems likely that confirming that tooling effects explanation interpretability should generalize, at least to other kinds of analytical use cases. To be clear, confirming this hypothesis is outside the scope of this work.

2.2 Assumptions

This study assumes that the choice of AI tool constrains the kinds of explanations that are selected. For example, if the tool uses static (i.e. non-interactive) charts, then it could be expected that explanations using contrastive/counterfactual "what-if" scenarios would not be possible since they would require re-scoring the model (often a cumbersome and time-consuming operation on large data sets). More concretely, in a use case asking why the model denied a loan to a particular person, the user might cite a model feature called "missed payments" and draw the conclusion that this person had a high number. The professional data scientists involved in this preparatory work noted that more analysis would be required to conclude that the high number in variable "missed payments" *caused* the model to classify this person as a risk or *caused* it to deny the loan. In other words that a lurking variable was equally likely to cause this phenomenon and/or that by Simpsons Paradox, this phenomenon might disappear or reverse on deeper analysis. However, the underlying assumption was confirmed (at least qualitatively) by the participants.

2.3 Methods

This study was a blind, semi-random, between-subjects study of 120 participants using a Google form administered in 3 cohorts via Amazon Mechanical Turk (AMT). Participants were compensated $0.45 for completing the ~5-min survey question. Participants could only complete one study one time to avoid priming bias. The only qualifications to participate were English fluency and the ability to access AMT (i.e. have an account and a computer/network capable of connecting). English fluency was somewhat problematic as AMT workers opted-in and not all of their levels of fluency appeared equal. The study was conducted in three phases, each phase corresponding to a row in Table 1 (contrastive, causal and example). The test scenario was designed to be easily understood by a non-technical audience. Clearly, this scenario doesn't generalize to more complicated use cases or use cases requiring subject matter expertise. The test scenario was the following:

*"Pretend you have a robot that folds your clothes. The robot has accidentally folded a shirt which is inside out, presumably because it couldn't see the tag. Below are three ways the robot can explain the mistake. Please pick the **best** explanation."*

Participants were then shown the answer choices in Table 1 corresponding to their cohort. The cohorts were the explanatory modes listed in column 1 of Table 1. Users could select explanations based on text, images or chart/visualizations. For each cohort, the selected explanation type (i.e. contrastive, causal and example) was shown using each of the three delivery modes shown in Table 1. Text explanations used narrative written text to explain the robots mistake. Icons used simple, iconographic images to illustrate the explanation. Charts used simple data visualizations as an explanatory device. Answers were presented in the same order between cohorts for consistency.

A survey asking the following questions was also included. Question 1 used a freeform text field and question 2 used a 5-point Likert scale;

1) *Why did you select the answer you did?*
2) *On a scale of 1 to 5 (1 is worst, 5 is best) how well did the answer you selected explain the robots mistake?*

Asking about scale was intended to elicit how confident participants were in their answers. For example, someone might select an answer believing it was the best choice among a number of poor choices, in which case they could rate it accordingly (i.e. it answered the question but badly).

Table 1. The matrix of answer selections shown to each participant.

2.4 Analysis

The raw answer selections (i.e. answer frequency) for each cohort were analyzed using Python in a Jupyter notebook. Analysis was done following the industry standard sequence for exploratory data analysis of ingestion, cleaning, visualization and analysis. A Chi square was used to analyze correlation.

The question *"why did you select this answer?"* was analyzed separately using NLP techniques for thematic analysis. Tokenization and lemmatization were done using NLTK (wordnet and porter). Unsupervised topic modeling was done with Gensim. Results were displayed based on saliency (relevance metric = 1) and intertopic distance of the principal components using multidimensional scaling. The most salient words were visualized in a word cloud (Table 4).

2.5 Results

120 individuals participated; 40 for each explanation cohort. It's hard to draw statistically valid conclusions with such a small sample size, but **participants showed a clear preference for text explanations, especially contrastive explanations** as shown in Table 2 and Fig. 1.

Table 2. Results by selection frequency.

Explanation	Mode	Frequency scale
Contrastive	Charts	4
	Images	12
	Text	25
Causal	Charts	13
	Images	11
	Text	16
Example	Charts	9
	Images	11
	Text	21

Visualizing the results of study 2 showed a clear preference for contrastive, text-based explanations. Explanations using charts had the lowest explanatory power. Participants had a high degree of certainty in their answer selections based on the Likert scale question "how well does your selected answer explain the error?" graphed by frequency. Likert scale; 1 lowest, 5 highest. Almost 50 chose 5 and almost 60 chose 4, the first and second highest levels of confidence, respectively (see Fig. 2).

For the NLP analysis of the freeform text field ("why did you choose this answer?"), the top 3 words in the word count were "understand" (19 times), "robot" (16 times) and "explains" (10 times) (see Fig. 3). However, this demonstrates the obvious fact that there's little useful context in this finding (Tables 3 and 5).

Table 3. Frequency of participants response to the question "how well does your selected answer explain

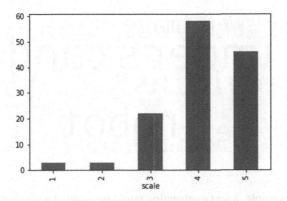

Table 4. Chart of results by selection frequency.

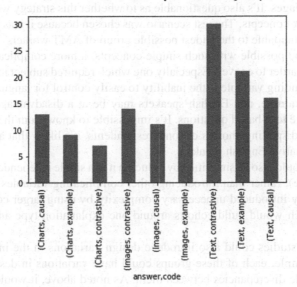

be difficult. For example, a text explanation could be worded in many ways, a chart could use lines, bars, scatter or other plotting approaches.

Similarly, more content could be conveyed in a more complicated chart, or conveyed in many images. It's also questionable as to whether this strategy would generalise to a wide sample of people. The test scenario was chosen because it was perceived to be more understandable to the widest possible group of AMT workers. While matching locations might be possible with each single concern, a more complicated linked concern would be harder to convey. Especially, one where explained sufficiently demanding content. Additionally, the inability to easily control for language proficiency of AMT workers. While English speakers may be on a disadvantage to our target English usage about locations. It's impossible to know within the study whether this issue might influence the results. Additionally, we did not test the accuracy of them, were not particularly validated.

This study could also gain much more with a wider set of conditions, extend the explanation types. This examination only considered one scenario and a single type of explanation, the delivery mode. The study individual experiments could exist by comparing larger cohorts. Perhaps a better approach, would examine both set and more complex explanation type and one delivery mode.

Subsequent studies could also combine or contrast portions of the images, text and charts. For example, each of these groups could exist in variations in design within the report. For while the exercises between. As noted above, I would also be more exhaustive, and be tied with a wider variety of use cases, and varying levels of complexity. However, this examine if the results generalise beyond the simplest use cases. Often sufficient frequency and limiting higher quality data could probably be obtained.

3 Discussion

3.1 Limitations of the Study

As mentioned above, it's difficult to draw statistically valid conclusions from such a small sample. Additionally, there are a number of confounding factors which are difficult to control for. For example, achieving perfect parity between the modes of representation is likely impossible. There are many possible ways to articulate a concept using images, charts and text. Having a perfect mapping between them for the same concept would

Table 5. Word cloud of top 30 terms in the freeform text field. Larger size indicates higher frequency.

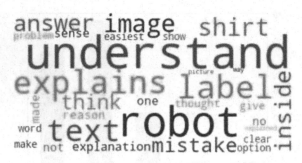

be difficult. For example, a text explanation could be worded a number of ways, a chart could use lines, bars, scatter or other plotting approaches.

Similarly, more complex scenarios might not map neatly to informational charts or iconographic images. It's also questionable as to whether this strategy would generalize to more complex concepts. The test scenario was chosen because it was perceived to be the most understandable to the widest possible group of AMT workers. While comprehension might be possible with such simple concepts, a more complicated robot error state would be harder to convey. Especially one which required subject matter expertise. Another confounding variable is the inability to easily control for language proficiency in AMT. For example, non-English speakers may be at a disadvantage in answering English language text-based questions. It's impossible to know from the data but given the grammar and spelling choices of some respondents, it's likely that at least a few of them were not native English speakers.

This study could also be simplified by reducing it to a single independent variable (i.e. explanation type), rather than introducing other complicating variables in the delivery mode. The study introduced unnecessary complexity by using larger cohorts. Perhaps a better approach would build cohorts around one explanation type and one delivery mode.

Subsequent studies could also introduce design variations in the images, text and charts. For example, each of these groups could have variations in design/wording to control for subtle discrepancies between them. As noted above, it would also be interesting to run the test with a wider variety of use cases with varying levels of complexity. This would help determine if the results generalize beyond the simplest use cases. Given sufficient time and funding, higher quality data could probably be achieved without using AMT.

3.2   Free-Form Responses

The NLP analysis of the freeform text is also somewhat problematic. The structure of the question elicited trivialities like "It was the most clear" or "It makes the most sense". Asking users to articulate why they chose one answer over another is likely unrealistic, especially in an AMT study. AMT workers are generally incentivized to complete a task as quickly as possible and don't appear especially vested in the quality of their responses. It was extremely difficult to control for participants who randomly wrote in whatever triviality they came up with.

However, this does point to a possibly deeper observation; that participants are actually unaware (rather than unable to articulate) why they selected one answer over another and hence they resorted to trivialities. That is, the participants are asked to ascribe causes to the robot's behavior based on its internal "mental state". Perhaps in the absence of obvious causal agents, participants frame the robots response using their own unconscious causal scripts as if they were in the robot's situation. This supposition is related to the concept of "unconscious bias" and the idea that our own internal mental states are unavailable to our reflective, conscious mind. This remains outside the scope of this work, but if true, compensating for this phenomenon would require further research in areas such as pre-attentive processing.

4 Future Work

This work was intended to evaluate a simple, universal human-robot interaction. Future work might address more complex use cases and use cases requiring subject matter expertise on the part of the human interlocutor. This could involve scenarios designed to discover the limits of visual explanations. For example, would the explanation types generalize to human-robot teaming scenarios like emergency response or on the battlefield? These types of scenarios would introduce many complicating variables such as comprehending robot state under time constraints.

Another promising scenario involves introducing interactivity in the human-robot interaction. Much of the work cited in Sect. 1.4 draws on the concept of "constructionism" in which users construct explanations via interaction with their environment. Introducing interactivity to the explanation scenarios evaluated in this paper would likely elicit a very different set of responses. For example, allowing users to frame foils in contrastive explanations such as "why did you take action A and not action B?"

Humans use a variety of imperfect methods to communicate explanations to each other including text, images and data among others. Perhaps future work will invent new methods of explanation and ways to illustrate causation based on the strengths of machines. Specialized professional domains like scientific data visualization and AutoML applications have broken interesting ground in these areas recently. Currently, the main limitation appears to be the technical feasibility of implementing a robot-operating system (or ML algorithm more generally) capable of articulating its internal states in any human-understandable format.

5 Conclusions

This research contributes a preliminary analysis of contrastive, causal and example-based explanations in a hypothetical but potentially common-place human-robot interaction. These explanation methods are evaluated using text, chart/data visualization and simple images. This research is valuable because understanding how humans learn, explain, interpret and develop mental models relating to AI behaviors is crucial to safe, effective and ethical human-AI interaction.

References

Ackermann, E.: Piaget's Constructivism, Papert's Constructionism: What's the difference?, vol. 5 (2001)

Caruana, R., Lou, Y., Gehrke, J., Koch, P., Sturm, M., Elhadad, N.: Intelligible models for healthcare: predicting pneumonia risk and hospital (2015)

30-day readmission. In: Proceedings of the 21st ACM SIGKDD International Conference on Knowledge Discovery and Data Mining – KDD 2015, pp. 1721–1730. https://doi.org/10.1145/2783258.2788613

Chapman, A., Hadfield, M., Chapman, C.: Qualitative research in healthcare: an introduction to grounded theory using thematic analysis. J. R. Coll. Physicians Edinb. **45**(3), 201–205 (2015). https://doi.org/10.4997/JRCPE.2015.305

Gopnik, A.: The post-piaget era. Psychol. Sci. **7**(4), 221–225 (1996). https://doi.org/10.1111/j.1467-9280.1996.tb00363.x

Grudin, J.: AI and HCI: two fields divided by a common focus. AI Mag. **30**(4), 48 (2009). https://doi.org/10.1609/aimag.v30i4.2271

Gunning, D.: DARPA's explainable artificial intelligence (XAI) program. In: Proceedings of the 24th International Conference on Intelligent User Interfaces (IUI 2019), ii. Association for Computing Machinery, New York (2019). https://doi.org/10.1145/3301275.3308446

Halpern, J.Y.: Causes and explanations: a structural-model approach. Part I: causes. Br. J. Philos. Sci. **56**(4), 843–887 (2005). https://doi.org/10.1093/bjps/axi147

Johnson-Laird, P.N.: Mental models and human reasoning. Proc. Natl. Acad. Sci. **107**(43), 18243 (2010). https://doi.org/10.1073/pnas.1012933107

Jonassen, D.: Operationalizing mental models: strategies for assessing mental models to support meaningful learning and design supportive learning environments. In: The First International Conference on Computer Support for Collaborative Learning (CSCL 1995), pp. 182–186. L. Erlbaum Associates Inc., Mahwah (1995). https://doi.org/10.3115/222020.222166

Kim, B.: Interactive and Interpretable Machine Learning Models for Human Machine Collaboration. MIT, Cambridge (2015)

Kozyrkov, C.: Explainable AI won't deliver. Here's why (2018). https://hackernoon.com/explainable-ai-wont-deliver-here-swhy-6738f54216be. Accessed 11 Oct 2019

Joyner, D.A.: Intelligent Evaluation and Feedback in Support of a Credit-Bearing (2018)

Penstein Rosé, C., et al. (eds.): AIED 2018. LNCS (LNAI), vol. 10948. Springer, Cham (2018). https://doi.org/10.1007/978-3-319-93846-2. MOOC

Kuang, C.: Can AI be taught to explain itself? The New York Times, 21 November 2017. https://www.nytimes.com/2017/11/21/magazine/can-aibe-taught-to-explain-itself.html

Li, X., Huan, J.: Constructivism learning: a learning paradigm for transparent predictive analytics. In: Proceedings of the 23rd ACM SIGKDD International Conference on Knowledge Discovery and Data Mining – KDD 2017, pp. 285–294 (2017). https://doi.org/10.1145/3097983.3097994

Malinsky, D., Danks, D.: Causal discovery algorithms: a practical guide. Philos. Compass **13**(1), e12470 (2018). https://doi.org/10.1111/phc3.12470

Miller, T.: Explanation in artificial intelligence: insights from the social sciences. arXiv:1706.07269 [Cs] (2018). http://arxiv.org/abs/1706.07269

Moreno, R., Mayer, R.: Interactive multimodal learning environments: special issue on interactive learning environments: contemporary issues and trends. Educ. Psychol. Rev. **19**(3), 309–326 (2007). https://doi.org/10.1007/s10648-007-9047-2

Páez, A.: The pragmatic turn in explainable artificial intelligence (XAI). Minds Mach. **29**(3), 441–459 (2019). https://doi.org/10.1007/s11023-019-09502-w

Papert, S.: One AI or many? Daedalus **117**(1), 1–14 (1988). www.jstor.org/stable/20025136. Accessed 19 Feb 2020

Parusniková, Z.: Popper and hume: two great skeptics. In: Sassower, R., Laor, N. (eds.) The Impact of Critical Rationalism. Palgrave Macmillan, Cham (2019)

People + AI Research: Google Design (n.d.). https://design.google/library/ai/

Reece, B.C.: Aristotle's four causes of action. Australas. J. Philos. **97**(2), 213–227 (2019). https://doi.org/10.1080/00048402.2018.1482932

Rudin, C.: Stop explaining black box machine learning models for high stakes decisions and use interpretable models instead. arXiv:1811.10154 [Cs, Stat], September 2019. arXiv.org. http://arxiv.org/abs/1811.10154

Springer, A., Hollis, V., Whittaker, S.: Dice in the black box: user experiences with an inscrutable algorithm. In: AAAI Spring Symposium - Technical Report, SS-17-01-, pp. 427–430 (2017)

Vasconcelos, M., Cardonha, C., Gonçalves, B.: Modeling epistemological principles for bias mitigation in ai systems: an illustration in hiring decisions. In: Proceedings of the 2018 AAAI/ACM Conference on AI, Ethics, and Society – AIES 2018, pp. 323–329 (2018). https://doi.org/10.1145/3278721.3278751

Winikoff, M.: Debugging agent programs with why? Questions. In: Proceedings of the 16th Conference on Autonomous Agents and Multi-Agent Systems (AAMAS 2017). International Foundation for Autonomous Agents and Multiagent Systems, Richland, SC, pp. 251–259 (2017)

Author Index